Mastering
English Literature

Palgrave Master Series

Accounting
Accounting Skills
Advanced English Language
Advanced Pure Mathematics
Arabic
Basic Management
Biology
British Politics
Business Communication
Business Environment
C Programming
C++ Programming
Chemistry
COBOL Programming
Communication
Computing
Counselling Skills
Counselling Theory
Customer Relations
Database Design
Delphi Programming
Desktop Publishing
e-Business
Economic and Social History
Economics
Electrical Engineering
Electronics
Employee Development
English Grammar
English Language
English Literature
Fashion Buying and Merchandising
  Management
Fashion Marketing
Fashion Styling
Financial Management
Geography
Global Information Systems
Globalization of Business

Human Resource Management
International Trade
Internet
Java
Language of Literature
Management Skills
Marketing Management
Mathematics
Microsoft Office
Microsoft Windows, Novell
  NetWare and UNIX
Modern British History
Modern European History
Modern German History
Modern United States History
Modern World History
The Novels of Jane Austen
Organisational Behaviour
Pascal and Delphi Programming
Personal Finance
Philosophy
Physics
Poetry
Practical Criticism
Psychology
Public Relations
Shakespeare
Social Welfare
Sociology
Statistics
Strategic Management
Systems Analysis and Design
Team Leadership
Theology
Twentieth-Century Russian History
Visual Basic
World Religions

www.palgravemasterseries.com

Palgrave Master Series
Series Standing Order ISBN 0–333–69343–4
(outside North America only)

You can receive future titles in this series as they are published by placing a standing order. Please contact your bookseller or, in case of difficulty, write to us at the address below with your name and address, the title of the series and the ISBN quoted above.

Customer Services Department, Macmillan Distribution Ltd
Houndmills, Basingstoke, Hampshire RG21 6XS, England

Mastering
English Literature

Third Edition

Richard Gill

© Richard Gill 1985, 1995, 2006

All rights reserved. No reproduction, copy or transmission of
this publication may be made without written permission.

No paragraph of this publication may be reproduced, copied or
transmitted save with written permission or in accordance with
the provisions of the Copyright, Designs and Patents Act 1988,
or under the terms of any licence permitting limited copying
issued by the Copyright Licensing Agency, 90 Tottenham Court
Road, London W1T 4LP.

Any person who does any unauthorized act in relation to this
publication may be liable to criminal prosecution and civil
claims for damages.

The author has asserted his right to be identified as the author
of this work in accordance with the Copyright, Designs and
Patents Act 1988.

First edition 1985
Second edition 1995
Third edition 2006

Published by
PALGRAVE MACMILLAN
Houndmills, Basingstoke, Hampshire RG21 6XS and
175 Fifth Avenue, New York, N.Y. 10010
Companies and representatives throughout the world

PALGRAVE MACMILLAN is the global academic imprint of the Palgrave
Macmillan division of St. Martin's Press, LLC and of Palgrave Macmillan Ltd.
Macmillan® is a registered trademark in the United States, United Kingdom
and other countries. Palgrave is a registered trademark in the European
Union and other countries.

ISBN-13: 978-14039-4488-7
ISBN-10: 1-4039-4488-1

This book is printed on paper suitable for recycling and
made from fully managed and sustained forest sources.

A catalogue record for this book is available from the British Library.

A catalog record for this book is available from the Library of Congress.

10   9   8   7   6   5   4   3   2   1
15   14   13   12   11   10   09   08   07   06

Printed and bound in Great Britain by
CPI Antony Rowe, Chippenham, Wiltshire

■ⱱ Contents

▇ ⌄ Acknowledgements

The author and publishers wish to thank the following for permission to use copyright material:

Carcanet Press Ltd for material from Ivor Gurney, 'Song' and 'Crickley Hill' from *Collected Poems* by Ivor Gurney, ed. P. J. Kavanagh (2004); Curtis Brown Group Ltd on behalf of Eric Robinson for material from John Clare, 'The Mores' from *The Oxford Authors: John Clare*, ed. Eric Robinson and David Powell, Oxford University Press (1984). Copyright © Eric Robinson 1984; James & James (Publishers) Ltd on behalf of the Estate of James MacGibbon and New Directions Publishing Corporation for material from Stevie Smith, 'I Remember' from *Collected Poems of Stevie Smith*. Copyright © 1972 by Stevie Smith; Peter Newbolt for material from Henry Newbolt, 'Vitai Lampada'; The Orion Publishing Group Ltd for material from William Langland, *The Vision of Piers Plowman*, ed. A. V. C. Schmidt, J. M. Dent (1978); Oxford University Press for material from Gerard Manley Hopkins, 'God's Grandeur' from *Poems of Gerard Manley Hopkins*, ed. W. H. Gardner and N. H. Mackenzie (1970); PFD on behalf of the estate of the author for material from Hilaire Belloc, 'Lord Luck' from *Cautionary Verse* by Hilaire Belloc, Red Fox; The Society of Authors as the literary representative of the estate of the author and Henry Holt & Company, LLC for material from A. E. Housman, 'Bredon Hill' from 'A Shropshire Lad' from *The Collected Poems of A. E. Housman*. Copyright © 1939, 1940, 1965 by Henry Holt & Company, copyright © 1967, 1968 by Robert E. Symons and 'Tell me not here' from 'Last Poems' from *The Collected Poems of A. E. Housman*. Copyright © 1922 by Henry Holt & Company, copyright © 1950 by Barclays Bank Ltd; A. P. Watt Ltd on behalf of Michael B. Yeats for material from W. B. Yeats, 'In Memory of Major Robert Gregory', and with Scribner, an imprint of Simon & Schuster Adult Publishing Group, for W. B. Yeats, 'Blood and the Moon' from *The Collected Works of W. B. Yeats, Vol. I: The Poems*, ed. Richard J. Finneran. Copyright © 1933 by The Macmillan Company, copyright renewed © 1961 by Bertha Georgie Yeats.

Every effort has been made to trace the copyright-holders but if any have been inadvertently overlooked the publishers will be pleased to make the necessary arrangement at the first opportunity.

Many people have helped me with this book by way of conversation and contributions to lessons. In particular, I would like to thank Jane Clarkson and John Florance, both of whom will recognize how much of their thinking I have used.

I am aware of my debts to the following: Pip Batty, Tania Benedictus, the late Raymond Brett, Alan Caine, Fiona Chamberlain, Danielle Cluer, Philip Collins, Stephen Cranham, Caroline Freeman, Miriam Gill, Naomi Gill, Laura Gould, Susan Gregory, Catherine Groves, David Hopkins, Craig Johnstone, A. R. Jones, the late Monica Jones, Margaret Jull Costa, Roger Knight, T. McAlindon, Kate McCauley Alex Marshall, Tony Moore, Nick Montague, Azreen Mussa, John Prince, Sally Nelson, Pat Phillipps, Neil Roberts, David Roe, Ian Robinson, Olivia Schelts, Marion Shaw, Ben Sherriff, John Spanos, Dawn Stephenson, Robin Stevenson, the late Eric Swift, Jan Todd, Joan Ward and Hayley White.

I dedicate this book to all my pupils, both past and present; they have helped me in the life-long quest of understanding and enjoying literature.

Introduction

It's likely that you are reading this book because you are studying English Literature, that you are attending lessons or lectures, and that you will be sitting examinations. This book is designed to meet the chief demands of A-level examinations and the first year of university. It can also be used as a 'refresher' for teachers, providing as it does a map of the issues and the kind of thinking that literary study involves.

The first three parts reflect the requirements of the A-level syllabus. Students are required to study prose fiction (which usually means novels), drama and poetry. In addition, they must study at least one work by Shakespeare and ensure that pre-twentieth-century literature is covered. Study in the first year at university makes similar demands.

This book presents ways to think about what you are studying. The important features of literary texts are presented, and the issues and problems they raise are discussed. Many of the examples are chosen from the texts that appear regularly on syllabuses. This allows some questions associated with particular texts (and particular authors) to be explored, which will help in the study of those texts, but even if you are unfamiliar with them, the discussions may enable you to see how literary thinking works.

Frequently, examination questions require a student to discuss a text in relation to the genre or type of literature to which it is regarded as belonging. Questions often ask to what extent a text can be said to be, say, tragic or comic or satiric. To answer such questions, you need to know what people mean (and have meant) by the major genres. Genre is a matter of writing and reading. Authors know when they are writing according to the conventions of a particular genre; they are aware of the elements and ground rules that make a genre what it is. To know the rules also means that they can experiment by extending, amending and even, at some points, departing from them. Similarly, readers who are told that a particular work is, say, a comedy, need to know what features are commonly associated with that particular genre. Traditionally, there are five genres – Tragedy, Comedy, Epic, Lyric and Satire. To these I have added three that exert strong influences on literature – Romance, Gothic and Pastoral.

Knowing what makes a tragedy, say, is an aspect of the literary tradition in which authors write. Literature is never news from nowhere. Writers inherit ideas about what literature is like and how it might be written. But the literary traditions of genre are not the only things with which an author works. Authors – and hence the books they write – always have a context. Books are always written by people who live in particular places at particular times.

Context is now recognized as a major aspect of literary study. At A-level, for example, students are required to know about the historical circumstances in which works were written. There are examination papers with titles such as 'Texts in Time' or 'Texts in Context'. The basic idea of context is that the times in which a work is written influence that work: in addition to the literary traditions of genre, works are shaped by popular ideas, by barely recognized assumptions, by the books an author reads, and by prevailing religious and political beliefs. Furthermore, the way families are organized, the way the young are treated and how wealth is distributed open up plot possibilities. Moreover, these are present in the language of the texts. The historical or contextual study of literature involves finding past times in the words of a text.

Contexts are not just made by this or that assumption or belief. A context forms a whole world. Each historical period (and that includes today) is a kind of web or network of assumptions, attitudes, beliefs and ideas. Together, these form what scholars have variously called a background, a culture, a milieu, a world picture or world view, and a Zeitgeist (the spirit of the age). Contextual study often identifies the feel, flavour or texture of the times in which the work was written. This is why, where possible, I have supplied the date of the works discussed. This is either the date of writing or publication (including first performances). In some cases, it isn't known when a work was written. In the case of Geoffrey Chaucer's *The Canterbury Tales* I have chosen c.1390, and for Thomas Wyatt, John Donne and George Herbert have given the dates of publication, even though they are posthumous. For William Shakespeare, the date is a probable one of composition.

To look at the context of a work is a way of interpreting it. People have always thought about the nature of interpretation. In the Bible, for example, Joseph claimed that it was God who interpreted dreams. Today, the business of interpretation is built into examinations. A familiar form of question is one that asks the candidate to debate two very different interpretations of a work. An aspect of this interest in interpretation is the popularity since the 1970s of literary theory. Many university English degrees start with a course on theories such as Feminism, Marxism and Structuralism. What usually emerges from such courses is the point that how a work is looked at tends to determine what is found in it. Part Six of this volume – Interpretation – examines several of these approaches to literature and raises questions about how helpful they are.

Interpretation is a way of finding out what a book is about. Many examination questions ask students to discuss a book's subject matter. The most frequently used word for what a book is about is *theme*. Hence, in Part Seven of this volume, some of the major interests of English literature are considered. Broadly speaking, literature has been about everything (one of the delights of studying it is that there is a lot on the table) – the doings and thoughts of people, the world of animals, the realms of nature and of God. One of the reasons we read literature is that it brings before us ourselves and the world about us. Some people complain that studying books blunts the freshness and delight they bring to what matters in human life. If this is so, it is a great pity. Speaking personally, I can only say that studying it makes a book more alive, and therefore it matters more to me as a result.

When we study we do at least two things. First, *we think*. This is what this book is designed to help you to do, by raising the issues that are frequently encountered in literary study. For example, it explores the different ways in which stories can be told. Once we see that certain things in a book matter (for instance, what an author chooses to tell us about the minds of the characters), we have to ponder what effects this has, how it shapes our responses, and what it contributes to the meaning of the work. Most of the time we have to do this for ourselves. A book such as this can point us in the right direction, but we still have to walk the path ourselves.

The second thing we do is *to work* – we read, make notes, write essays and sit examinations. As you are likely to be doing, or preparing to do, these things throughout your course, the rest of this Introduction will be taken up with suggestions as to how you might go about studying.

Hints on reading

You should read frequently. And it may seem obvious, but it needs saying: you have to read *all* the book. Because you don't know the book, you can't know what is important in it until you have read all of it. Re-reading novels helps you to see the movement of the plot and the development of the characters. The frequent reading of poetry helps you to recognize the style, the tone, the attitudes and the thinking of the poet. It is also helpful, particularly in the case of poetry, to vary the pace of reading. The slow reading of passages can alert you to the ways in which meaning is established, tone created and the movement of the writer's mind made evident. Finally, you will need to find out the circumstances in which you can read with appropriate concentration on the text.

Reading with understanding

Study is attentive reading. Ask youself:

Do I understand what I am reading?

The following questions may help:

- Am I following what is happening?
- Why are the characters behaving in these particular ways?
- Am I aware of the mood of the scenes?
- Can I see how the plot is moving?
- In what ways is this work similar to others? (This is important in the study of collections of poetry.)
- Can I visualize what is happening? (Applicable to drama and novels.)
- How are the words inviting me to respond, and am I responding in that way?

Making notes

Pencilled notes in the margins of a book can be used to explain a passage, draw attention to the development of a theme, single out the recurrence of an image and mark decisive moments in plot development.

You will also need to make longer notes, either in an exercise book or on separate sheets of paper. You may want to keep longer notes on the following topics:

- Your responses to a work. These can be very helpful, particularly as these responses may change as you read on.
- The problems that books raise. You will also find it helpful to mention the different ways in which these problems may be tackled, and the stages of each argument.
- Contextual material. You might, for example, make notes about ideas that were popular at the time, contemporary events, the organization of society and books written in the same period.
- Plot summaries. If this helps you to see the plot as a whole, then the notes are useful. But, of course, the more you get to know a book, the less useful such summaries will be.

It is unlikely that you will be told to take notes in class, and even more unlikely that notes will be dictated. Taking notes is something you will have to learn to do for yourself. You should remember that this is a very useful way of learning, chiefly because you have to judge what is important.

Some 'dos and don'ts' of note-making

- Notes should be brief.
- Develop a consistent code of abbreviations, such 'K' for John Keats.
- Distinguish the different kinds of notes you take, perhaps by adding headings.
- Don't lump notes together; leave a line between each one.
- Don't mix notes. It is better to have separate sheets on different issues.

As you study

Always remember that:

> What happens in the classes and lectures is a necessary but not sufficient condition of successful study. What matters is what you do in your own time.

In a lesson or lecture you listen and talk. Listening helps us to see what might be important. If a passage provokes lots of questions, it may be that this is because it is of particular importance. Talking about literature is more difficult than you might imagine. Talk arises out of understanding and requires the talker to find an appropriate way of framing ideas. This is a way of saying that talk is thought.

Preparation and follow-up

There are, however, things that can be done both before and after the lesson or lecture. Beforehand, you can remind yourself of what has already been said about the book. It is also wise to look through the passages that are going to be discussed and try to identify anything that looks important or that you find difficult.

After a lesson or lecture, it is a good idea to look through what has been discussed and explore the ideas further. This may involve putting ideas in your own words. Also, keep your notes in order; they can easily get out of hand. And while you are sorting out your notes, look at the earlier ones. We are likely to forget what we have noted down unless we review it regularly.

Making up your mind

We make up our minds as we study, as we write essays and as we prepare for examinations. It takes time, and much of it happens without consciously realizing that we are doing it.

We can, however, deliberately think things through. The following are tips as to how this might be done:

- You need to recognize that books present problems, and that there are issues each of them has raised for generations of readers and playgoers. For example, is Hamlet consistently mad?
- One way of coming to see that a work presents problems is to note down the ideas of teachers and lecturers. It may be that you don't fully see the importance of the point being made, but if you make a note you may see its significance later.
- It is as well to realize that issues raised are not matters that are likely to be settled; what matters is that we understand why they are debated.
- One way of consciously thinking through a problem is to see how it looks from a number of different perspectives. Part Six of this book may help in this.
- When you are thinking about a way of understanding a problem, try to think through the consequences. This might help you to see why a particular aspect of a book is problematic. Even if thinking through the consequences does not help you come to a satisfactory conclusion, it might help you to discount some views. There is often greater certainty about what we don't know than what we do.

Essays

Writing essays helps us to think about the issues raised by literary works. As has already been indicated, you are not required to 'solve' problems but rather to show that you can think through them. This is why essays are often in the form of 'How far do you agree that…' or 'To what extent do you think that…'. Saying how far you agree with a particular view involves framing arguments about how the book works. These arguments will be based on the features of the book that have emerged during study, and the ideas you have got about what the work means and how it makes its meanings. Here is a possible way of going about writing an essay:

- As an essay is usually an answer to a question, you need to understand exactly what the question is about. Questions should be answered in the terms in which they are put. It is a good idea to spend some time deciding what the issue of the question is.
- Once you have identified what the question is requiring you to do, you need to frame arguments that will address it. Some arguments will probably occur to you. You may find others by looking through the book, bearing in mind the question you are trying to answer. Looking through the text will also provide you with material you can use to support what you are saying.
- You need to plan your essay so it is clear to you (and to the reader!) why you are moving from one point to another. Sometimes this is made easier once you have decided what your conclusion is going to be. Good essays are sometimes written 'backwards'.
- Write a first draft. This should include the main arguments and the support from the text. It is wise to discuss the language of some of the quotations. Once it is written, it is a good idea to leave the essay for a couple of days. When you return to it, you are often aware of imprecise statements, woolly arguments and awkward transitions from one argument to another.
- Once you are satisfied that you have written what you think, you can then add the opening and concluding sentences. You can't start and finish an essay until you know what it is about. Remember to run the spell-check – and be careful about names!

A point about time: use all the days you are given. Some days will be spent in thinking, some in making notes, some in organizing and some in writing. In short: if you are given a week, use a week.

Coursework and long essays

Coursework and long essays are a welcome feature of study. You have time to think and time to get things right. They are an opportunity to exercise considerable control over the process of assessment. Much of what has been written in the section above also applies to coursework. In addition, the following points may be made:

- If you are allowed to choose your own topic and frame your own question, make use of the opportunity. You are likely to write better about topics that interest you.
- Because you usually have a long time to complete the work, make use of it. However, it is a good idea to get something down on paper early. You should also be prepared to change your mind, both about the content and the way

you present the argument. If conditions permit, make use of your teacher or tutor. They can help you to recognize issues, see other ways of tackling them, frame clearer arguments and organize your work.

- Coursework is generally marked against assessment objectives. Make sure you have met these. Try to fulfil the objectives that will award you with a top grade.
- Coursework is a chance to explore, so don't be afraid of trying out unusual ideas. Sometimes it helps to make it clear that the ideas you are advancing are speculations.

Revision

The following suggestions may help with revision:

- The best revision is done throughout the year as you study. For each subject, set aside time to look through what you have done. Start with recent work and relate it to earlier work. If you do this, you will find that when the examination date approaches you know the books and have an understanding of their important features.
- Any revision should be active. It is better to recall ideas or quotations actively than merely to read your notes (this applies to any form of learning). Similarly, it is wise to do some writing as part of revision. Timed essays are obviously helpful, and so are sketching outlines to answers and putting the main arguments down on paper.
- Making revision notes can be helpful. Indeed, the process of making notes – of selecting what is important and devoting separate sheets to the different issues – can be as helpful as reading through the notes you have made.
- Look through past questions to identify the kinds of issues examiners require students to think about, and the terms in which they frame the questions. Remember that questions often require you to discuss four or five major points.
- If you want to learn quotations, go for short ones. The business of selecting which ones to learn can help you to think about what matters in a book.
- Seek help from your teachers or tutors. They can often help you to see the major issues. Also, go to revision classes. If nothing else, they are a relief from working on your own!

Examinations

Much of what has been said above applies to examinations. Given that marking is becoming more systematic (even mechanistic), you will need to know what the assessment objectives are for each paper. You will also need to know what kinds of questions you will be facing. For example, an extract question is different from an essay question. You will need to know your books, and need to know what you think about them. But always remember: it is the question on the paper you must answer, and *not* one that you would like to write about. It is therefore vital (and you should spend some minutes on this) that you understand what you are being asked to do. There are three things to remember about how to organize your time in the examination room:

- Decide at the outset which questions you are going to answer. This gets rid of the tension of uncertainty at once, and you may find that as you are writing one answer, your mind is thinking through the questions you have yet to do.
- Essays need to be planned. As you are sorting out your arguments and the order in which you are going to set them down, remember to keep in mind the terms of the question. An answer is only an answer if it meets the demands of the question.
- Make sure you time yourself. It is better to leave an essay unfinished than write two long ones and one very short one. If you time yourself sensibly, you will be able to check through your answers.

Part One   The novel

▮ ⌄ ▮ Stories

1.1 Popularity

A best-seller

Harry Potter is news: shops open at midnight on publication day; there are special covers for adults who don't like being seen reading children's books; there are books explaining the 'meaning' of Harry's deeds, and the films are 'big box-office'. And people talk about them.

The *Harry Potter* phenomenon tells us three things:

- We are still a nation of readers.
- We discuss what we read.
- Stories allure us.

The popularity of novels

People still read, and they read novels.

> **The novel is the literary form in which many of us encounter stories.**

Novels are abundantly available; they can be bought in both bookshops and supermarkets. They are news. Each year, the winner of the Booker prize is discussed on radio and television. Novels are even peak-time popular entertainment, as when the final of *The Nation's Favourite Read* was broadcast on a Saturday night. Radio and television regard the serialization of a 'classic' as high-class entertainment. People still recall the BBC adaption of Jane Austen's *Pride and Prejudice* in 1995, and in 2005 the novel was made into a film starring Keira Knightley.

Talking about novels

We enjoy discussing what we have read; we want to understand what a book is about, and why it did or did not engage our interest. For example, people have debated whether the Harry Potter novels are original. The school story, they point out, is not new. Ever since Thomas Hughes wrote *Tom Brown's Schooldays* (published in 1857), we have been accustomed to the genre (type or kind) of the school story. Jennings and Mallory Towers are part of many people's childhoods.

We have also (again, often as children) read stories of ghosts and goblins, dragons and demons. C. S. Lewis used those figures in the Narnia books, and Alan Garner often used a plot in which, as in C. S. Lewis, an ordinary present becomes entwined with a mythical realm. In that sense, J. K. Rowling is not original; she draws on the genres of the school tale and the folk story. In keeping with the school story, Harry has a friend – Ron Weasley – and an enemy – Draco Malfoy. What *is* original, however, is her combination of the two genres: *Harry Potter* is a school story about wizards. Consequently, she invents (and does so entertainingly) a series of wizard equivalents to the conventions of the school tale. Hence the game of Quidditch and the entertaining idea of a corridor that leads to somewhere different on a Friday (*Harry Potter and the Philosopher's Stone*, 1997).

Summary

We are a nation that reads, and we discuss what we read. When we talk about novels we are drawn into a debate about originality and genre.

1.2   Human identity

We sometimes ask what it is that makes human beings what they are. There are many answers to this big question, one of which is:

We are story-tellers.

If we are asked about what has happened to us today, we reply in terms of little narratives. These narratives have settings, dialogue, are delivered from a particular viewpoint and have a form: introduction, climax and close. Stories allure us, because we see our lives as stories. We do this in two ways.

Stories in our lives

Thomas Hardy called Chapter 8 of *Far from the Madding Crowd* (1874) 'The Malthouse – The Chat – News'. He shows how

Story-telling establishes our identities.

Gabriel Oak, a man with ambitions, has lost his flock of sheep because of an accident and has been forced to seek employment on a farm in Weatherbury. He goes as a stranger to the Malthouse, where he is welcomed by the little group of rustics (country dwellers). The rustics have gathered to tell stories, one of which is about a bashful man, much given to blushing, called Joseph Poorgrass. Jan Coggan, in spite of a protest from Joseph himself, tells a story about how Joseph 'lost his way as he was coming home-along Yalbury Wood':

'– And so 'a lost himself quite,' continued Mr. Coggan, with an impassive face, implying that a true narrative, like time and tide, must run its course and would respect no man. 'And as he was coming along in the middle of the night, much afeared, and not able to find his way out of the trees nohow, 'a cried out, "Man-a-lost, man-a-lost!" A owl in a tree happened to be crying "Whoo-whoo-whoo!" as owls do, you know, shepherd' (Gabriel nodded), 'and Joseph, all in a tremble, said, "Joseph Poorgrass, of Weatherbury, sir!"'

This wonderfully comic yet affectionate tale shows how this little community works. People are given identities through the stories people tell about them. In turn, these stories define the community.

Stories also give our lives meanings.

Our lives in our stories

Beyond individual and communal narratives there are larger, over-arching stories, that give meaning and a context to our lives.

> We tell national stories about how our nation came into being and received its character.

This is one purpose of Epics (see Chapter 22). In *The Aeneid* (written between 29BC and 19BC), Virgil told of the foundation of Rome by relating how Aeneas fled from the destruction of Troy. The impulse to define the nature, and therefore the significance, of a nation appears in later works. Nathaniel Hawthorne's story of New England, *The Scarlet Letter* (1850), explores the identity of America by presenting the early days of its Puritan settlers.

Bigger than national stories are the stories religions tell. These are stories that people live by.

> Religious stories give a picture of our history and how we stand in relation to God, so they form our ideas strongly of who we are and how we should live.

The Bible presents stories ranging from the beginning of the world to the end of time. It has given Western literature plots, characters and themes that still arouse us (see Chapter 29, Sections 29.2–29.5).

Summary

We are story-tellers. The tales we tell establish our individual identities, the identity of our nation and, in religious stories, a sense of our place in the world.

1.3 Thinking about stories

Most television programmes are stories. Some have distinct beginnings, middles and ends, while others (the soap operas) might continue indefinitely. Even the news might be said to be a set of tales. Journalists often talk about 'news stories'.

Those who enjoy novels find a number of things in them – interesting characters, convincing atmospheres and a picture of what human life is like. These emerge in and through stories.

Fiction

The word 'fiction' has been in the language since the late Middle Ages. It has acquired a number of meanings. Here are two definitions from The *Shorter Oxford English Dictionary*:

Fictitious composition. Now usually prose novels and stories collectively, or the composition of such works.

Feigning, deceit, dissimulation, pretence.

These definitions date from 1599 and 1609, respectively. From very early on, therefore, 'fiction' was a slippery word. For much of its history, it has hovered between a technical literary meaning and a negative moral one.

Fictions and lies

The fact that the word denotes both a literary work and a lie indicates that people have long held ambivalent views about art. In Ancient Greece, Plato conducted a moral debate about the status of art. He wanted to banish poets from his ideal Republic. His reason is strictly philosophical. Because what we see is a shadow of what is real, art is less real because it is a shadow of a shadow.

This debate has left its mark on our language. Take the word 'design'. We use it to discuss the organization of a work of art, but when applied to human actions, it indicates something morally questionable. In *Pride and Prejudice* (1813), Mr Wickham, intent on seducing Darcy's sister, travelled to where she was staying 'undoubtedly by design' (Chapter 35).

The ambiguity of the word points to one of the puzzles of literature. We know that literary works are made up and yet we treat them as real. The characters are invented and yet we take a moral and emotional interest in their lives. This is the mystery of art – what is made up matters to us.

Written and read

We sometimes assume that works of art (of which novels are an example) are windows on the world, unmediated slices of life. But

Fiction is art. Art means whatever has been made.

Other words used for the making of art are: created, fashioned or produced. There are many terms for the process of making art: constructed, crafted, designed, edited, moulded, selected, shaped and trimmed. And someone did the making. Novels have been *written*.

A novel is how it is because someone made it that way.

When we ask whether someone has read, say, Jane Austen, we are recognizing that a novel has been written – put together in a particular way – by a writer.

It follows from this that the characters of any novel are as they are because the author has made them that way. All too often, students write about characters as if they can be met at the bus stop. Characters only exist in the pages of a book.

Readers have a part to play in knowing and understanding characters. A novel is written by an author and read by a reader. We could not know any character in a book unless we read what the author had written. There are therefore three elements in the understanding of a novel:

- The characters and events of the book.
- The author who made the book in a particular way.
- The reader who responds.

To put it altogether:

The reader reads the words that the author has written.

Writing about novels

At this point, a hint about how to write about novels is necessary. Teachers often sit down to mark well-organized and fluently written essays that could be about the boy next door rather than a character in a book, but those essays don't get highly rewarded. Poor essays rarely mention the author or the reader.

So, when you write, make sure that you show how events and characters are what they are because of the way they have been made by the author and read by the reader.

For example, if you are writing about the opening chapters of *Jane Eyre* (1847), you might say that Charlotte Brontë leads the reader to sympathize with Jane by showing how her relatives treat her badly.

The elements of novels

Because novels are varied, precise definitions are very difficult. (In any case, what would we *do* with a definition?) We can, however, point to the following elements:

- It is a composition, usually in prose, concerned with the acts and speech of imagined characters.
- A story is told; there is a teller of the tale.
- It is a story in which the events are related to the reader in a particular order and for a particular reason.
- The events are imagined as taking place in specific places.
- The characters and events form a fictional world, which may be close to or remote from our everyday world.

- The totality of characters and events adds up to something. We can find meanings in the work.

   Consider these points in relation to Jan Coggan's tale about Joseph Poorgrass lost in Yalbury Wood, discussed above:

- It is a tale of characters, action and conversation, although the conversation is with an owl!
- The story is told by Jan Coggan and told with the purpose of showing what kind of a person Joseph Poorgrass is.
- The order of events is selected to show why Joseph was lost: he had been working late and had been drinking.
- The story takes place in a wood, which, as in so many tales, is a place where travellers lose their way.
- The story creates a world of rustic labour in which people travel to relatively distant places for a day's work.
- The story is about timidity and an innocence that perhaps is only possible in the countryside.

Literary study

When we talk about how an author prompts a reader to respond to and think about what he or she has written, and when we see how an author has made a work, we are doing what is traditionally called Literary Criticism. Mastering a novel (or mastering any literature) starts when we see that it is something that has been made. Once we see that we can think about how the making has been done, and then ponder what the effects of this making are. It seems obvious to a lot of readers that a good place to start this thinking is with the characters.

Summary

Fictions are stories that have been made up. There is always a writer and reader, or teller and hearer. The events of the story occur in particular places and together they form a special world. Moreover, this world adds up to something – it has a meaning.

■ ▼ 2 Characters

2.1 Responding to characters

Teachers and examiners sometimes talk about characters as if they don't matter very much. They sometimes advise students to attend to other aspects of a novel – its structure or imagery – with the implication that concern for characters is a low-level response.

But this runs in the face of generations of critics and readers, who have found that

Characters cannot be ignored.

Characters show how creative a writer is. One of the reasons that Charles Dickens is valued is that, in any one of his novels, there are sufficient characters for three or four works by a lesser novelist.

Engaged by characters

As readers, we find we are drawn into the lives of characters: we listen to them, observe their actions, try to understand their thinking, feel for their plights, judge their motives, recoil from their attitudes, appreciate their wit, and wonder at their insights.

This is one of the mysteries of art. We know that characters only exist in books and yet we respond to them as we do to people whom we know. Like many of the people we meet in everyday life, we are engaged by – drawn to and interested in – the characters we meet in books. Readers follow characters with fascination and concern, often regarding them as real, and imagining, as the 'Janeites' do with Jane Austen's characters, a world separate from the novel, in which the characters carry on living. We can't understand the popularity of sequels – books that continue the story of a novel's central characters – apart from a concern for the characters. If it is argued that characters don't matter very much, then our response to novels is incomprehensible. Any discontent we have with novels is often related to characters. This is particularly so with novels in which we are invited to approve (or disapprove) of some of the characters. A notorious case is D. H. Lawrence's *Sons and Lovers* (1913), a novel about a young man, Paul Morel, who is torn between devotion to his mother and the feelings he has for Miriam Leivers. The novel is written so that we are sure to find Paul Morel sympathetic and recoil from Miriam. But many readers don't respond in this way.

Summary

Characters cannot be ignored. Readers are drawn into their lives. Writers expect us to approve or disapprove of their characters.

2.2 Characters, readers and authors

Knowledge

It is a fact of reading that we sometimes feel far more for fictional people than real ones whom we don't know particularly well. People weep more over books than over stories of accidents that they read in the newspapers. The reason for this is probably that we know a lot about fictional characters. The more we know, the more likely we are to be concerned. Reading books is a matter of knowledge. Reading, to use a philosophical term, is epistemic. Furthermore:

What we know about a character depends on what an author has told us or shown us in the words of the book.

Reading novels is a matter of gaining knowledge, and there is only one source of knowledge in the case of novels – words the author uses.

The way in which a character is put together will shape how we understand him or her.

Readers at work

But it is not quite as easy as that. Authors expect us to use our imaginations and infer things that are not directly given to us in the text. For example, in *Wuthering Heights* (1847) we might infer that because Heathcliff wins at cards, he has spent his time away as a professional gambler. Inferring must not be confused with imagining that characters are as we would like them to be. The only way to curb such unhelpful inventiveness is to attend to the words of the text.

Characters, characterization and persons

We need to distinguish between 'character' and 'characterization'.

Character is product; while characterization is process.

To think about characters involves thinking about how they are made.

'Characters' is the word we use when we are discussing how we understand books. But *within* a book a character is a person. Characters in books regard each other as persons. Fiction works through means of the fictional characters not behaving as if they were fictional. This might be why we are moved; we see that they matter to each other.

Summary

The only way we can get to know a character is through the author. Sometimes, the reader is expected to work on what the author has supplied. Characters are the figures in a book; characterization is the process that creates them. When we talk about a book we regard characters as figures that have been made. Within a book, however, characters regard each other as persons.

2.3 Language and the making of characters

Said and made

> All literary criticism is a consideration of the dual nature of literature: it says something and in doing so it makes something.

The difference between people we meet in the street and characters we meet in books is that the second group is 'constructed'. They would not exist but for the words that have made them.

But making – construction – is an activity practised in the everyday world. We make images of ideal men and women, we turn pop stars into what we call 'icons', and we bring up children with pictures of what adults are like. Those who study the media are aware of how people in public life are packaged and presented. Perhaps we enjoy fiction because it is a pure form of what happens in everyday life.

Language revealing character

The seventeenth-century poet and dramatist, Ben Jonson, made a collection of remarks about culture, behaviour and literature that he called *Explorata: or Discoveries* (published posthumously in 1640). One remark of his is that language reveals who we are:

> Language most shows a man: speak that I may see thee. It springs out of the most retired, and inmost parts of us, and is the image of the parent of it, the mind. No glass renders a man's form, or likeness, so true as his speech.

> (2515–19)

We are more clearly present in our speech than we are in our reflections in a mirror ('glass'). Language shows us most clearly; when we speak, others know who we are.

Novelists know this. Mr Casaubon, a scholarly clergyman in George Eliot's *Middlemarch* (1871), talks in this way (Chapter 42):

> 'Not immediately – no. In order to account for that wish I must mention – what it were otherwise needless to refer to – that my life, on all collateral accounts

insignificant, derives a possible importance from the incompleteness of labours which have extended through all its best years. In short, I have long had on hand a work which I would fain leave behind me in such a state, at least, that it might be committed to the press – by others.'

The language is the man. Mr Casaubon so piles up clauses that in the second sentence we have to wait some time to hear what it is that gives his life a possible importance. All that he says, as in a work of intricate scholarship, has to be qualified. In the last sentence, 'In short' leads not to an incisive conclusion but to yet another wordy meander. In Jonson's terms: he speaks, and we see him. Mr Casaubon is dry, over-correct and incapable of being either brief or exact.

The life of reason

We reason in words. In Chapter 13 of *Pride and Prejudice* (1813), Elizabeth Bennet is puzzled by Mr Collins' self-approving letter, in which he expresses regret that he will be the means of depriving the Bennet sisters of their family home. Elizabeth comments:

'And what can he mean by apologizing for being next in the entail? – We cannot suppose he would help it, if he could. – Can he be a sensible man, sir?'

Jane Austen gives Elizabeth the language of reasoning. She sees that a man cannot apologize for a state of affairs which he would not change, even if he were able. Her language is both logically probing and tentatively exploratory. Her dismantling of pretension encapsulates something of English common sense.

The language of value

Language embodies values.

> Authors can use language in such a way that the reader can see the words express values that should be honoured.

This is what it means when one says that vocabulary is 'moral'. 'Moral' does not have to mean rules about what is right and wrong; it is concerned with value, with what matters. Words such as 'reasonable' and 'friend' can be used to show that the user values rational thinking and the expression of friendship. And, of course, there is also a *negative* moral language. Words such as 'mean', 'narrow' or 'shallow' can denote qualities that we deplore.

Moral words are most telling when they are ones that are normally used in a non-evaluative way. This is the impressive feature of Joseph Conrad's short story, *The Secret Sharer* (1912). The plot concerns a young captain who hides a fugitive on his ship. When the captain first talks to the fugitive he discovers that his guest is a wanted man, who freely confesses: 'I've killed a man'. That would be sufficient for the captain to arrest the fugitive, but, instead, trust develops. They learn they were both at the Conway Naval School, and the captain begins to see life from the other man's point of view: 'I saw it all going on as though I were myself inside that other sleeping-suit.' The word 'saw' comes to mean a moral perception. 'Inside' has multiple layers of meaning: inside the suit, inside someone's mind, and sharing an outlook on life. The last point is important. The language of value discloses an understanding of life.

The moral ambiguity of fluency

We are suspicious of those who are too articulate. In particular,

> We are unhappy about characters who remain unruffled and smooth in speech despite the most trying of circumstances.

We expect people to show in their speech the moral and emotional difficulty of a situation. We feel they should have difficulty in controlling their emotions, and be hesitant about what and how much to say. Perhaps this is a characteristically English trait: emotional inarticulacy being seen as a virtue, and confident fluency a moral failing?

In the first chapter of Marian Halcombe's diary in Wilkie Collins' intricate and mysterious novel *The Woman in White* (1860), Laura Fairlie indicates unambiguously to Sir Percival Glyde, the man to whom she is engaged, that she no longer loves him, and that he would, therefore, be justified in seeking an end to their engagement. Collins alerts us to the moral delicacy of Laura by showing that this is a very difficult thing to say: 'She hesitated, in doubt as to the expression she should use next'. But Sir Percival shows neither hesitation nor doubt. Even when she plainly tells him she no longer has feelings for him, he is unabashed: 'You have said more than enough,' he answered, 'to make it the dearest object of my life to keep the engagement.'

We are suspicious at such assurance, and when we read of Sir Percival's tone and manner – 'he spoke with such warmth and feeling, with such passionate enthusiasm...' – we judge that his untroubled ease is morally dubious.

Declarations

Drama, and particularly Shakespeare, has had a strong influence on the language of the English novel. Shakespeare's influence can be found in the design of plots, the presentation of characters, and their actions. A Shakesperian feature is the self-revelation of a character in a long speech.

Shortly before his murder, Julius Caesar talks of how firm and resolute he is, comparing his consistency and integrity to the unmoving northern star. In Chapter 9 of Emily Brontë's *Wuthering Heights*, Cathy delivers a long speech to Nelly, the housekeeper, in which she compares her love for Linton, the man whom she will marry, and Heathcliff, the companion of her youth. The passion of her speech has the momentousness of seventeenth-century drama. This is a part of it:

> 'My love for Linton is like the foliage in the woods: time will change it, I'm well aware, as winter changes the trees. My love for Heathcliff resembles the eternal

rocks beneath: a source of little visible delight, but necessary. Nelly, I *am* Heathcliff.'

Her speech is hardly part of a dialogue; it is more like what has been called direct self-explanation (see Chapter 10, section 10.1). The author gives a character a speech in order to reveal what the character is like. So we know that Caesar is firm, and that Cathy has an almost mystical sense of sharing her identity with another.

The mannerisms of speech

Many of the most compelling and vivid characters in fiction achieve distinctiveness through verbal mannerisms.

In Dickens' *Oliver Twist* (1837), Fagin, the most memorable character, frequently addresses Oliver as 'My dear'. The reader soon sees that this is, in part, a strategy to persuade Oliver into a life of crime. By contrast, there is in F. Scott Fitzgerald's *The Great Gatsby* (1925), Gatsby's 'Old sport', an indication of his self-image as a man who has received an English education. The reader, however, might feel the pathos of a man whose embarrassing English is an attempt at elevated self-definition. Gatsby is an example of a character who creates his own public image. The reader sees that it is not easy to see who he really is.

Class and dialect

Often, in praise of a novelist, it is said that he or she has a good ear. What is often meant by this is that

The novelist picks up the class features of conversation with such accuracy that we see characters authentically exhibiting the marks of the social class to which they belong.

There is a class aspect to language. Certain words are used frequently in some classes and only rarely in others. K. C. Phillipps, in *Language and Class in Victorian England* (1984), points out that, in the nineteenth century, the term 'sweetheart' was almost completely confined to the working class. Class was evident in grammar. The word 'ain't' – short for 'is not' – was a speech mannerism of the upper classes. (Later in the twentieth century, 'ain't' came to be regarded as slang.)

A feature of working-class speech is its dependence on proverbial sayings, its resort to generalizations and its avoidance of abstract words. When, in Chapter 12 of Thomas Hardy's *Tess of the d'Urbervilles* (1891), Tess returns, pregnant, from working away from home, her mother sums up the situation: 'Well, we must make the best of it, I suppose. 'Tis nater, after all, and what do please God.' 'Making the best of it' is proverbial, and the appeal to 'nater' (nature) and what 'do please God' stand in for more abstract phrases such as 'necessity' or 'providence'.

Joan Durbeyfield here borders on dialect – the language of a particular region which often survives in a relatively complete state among the rural classes. In *Wuthering Heights*, Emily Brontë bravely introduces an important character,

Joseph, who speaks in a dialect so thick that many readers just skip what he says. (The clue is to read it aloud with a Yorkshire accent.) Joseph's dialect speeches give a strong sense of the local community (very carefully presented by Emily Brontë), and the difference in speech from the main characters enforces the idea that he has other ideas about the conduct of life from the strident characters such as the elder Cathy. He is also, for those who bother to work out what he is saying, an invaluable source of information about what happens – in particular, the death of Hindley.

Summary

Characters are created by the language they speak. Style of speech reveals character. There is considerable variety in speech. Characters reason. Their values emerge in their language. Sometimes readers are invited to mistrust those who are too fluent. Some characters make revelatory speeches, and others have distinctive verbal mannerisms. Dialect and class have a role in creating characters.

2.4   Dialogue

Everyday dialogue

The language of dialogue in novels has little in common with the fragmented and imprecise exchanges of everyday life. Everyday conversation is less formal in its grammar, and its structures are less complex. Its vocabulary is simplified; there are very few abstract terms. Our language is more colloquial and is more likely to include taboo terms (swearing, obscenities). We do, however, frequently use titles, such as 'Doctor'. We tend to use proverbial expressions, either couplings such as 'hale and hearty' or fixed expressions such as 'But at the end of the day…'. And some of the expressions are uninformative – when asked how we are, we might say 'Not bad'. This list does not include the contractions – 'shouldn't'ave', for example, and the 'ums' and 'ahs'.

> Dialogue in novels, by contrast, is conversation raised to the level of polished art.

This is why we so often envy the elegant intelligence of Jane Austen's heroines. In Chapter 56 of *Pride and Prejudice*, the over-bearing Lady Catherine, aunt of Mr Darcy, visits Elizabeth to extract from her a denial of the report that she is engaged to Darcy. Elizabeth is not, of course, though at this point in the novel such a prospect is not disagreeable. Lady Catherine says the report is 'a scandalous falsehood':

'If you believed it impossible to be true,' said
Elizabeth, colouring with astonishment and disdain,
'I wonder you took the trouble of coming so far. What
could your ladyship propose by it?'

'At once upon having such a report universally contradicted.'
'Your coming to Longbourn, to see me and my family,'
said Elizabeth, coolly, 'will be rather a confirmation of it;
if, indeed, such a report is in existence.'
'If! Do you then pretend to be ignorant of it? Has it not
been industriously circulated by yourselves? Do you not
know that such a report is spread abroad?'
'I never heard that it was.'
'And can you likewise declare, that there is no *foundation*
for it?'
'I do not pretend to possess equal frankness with your
ladyship. *You* may ask questions, which *I* shall not choose
to answer.'

Dialogue is at the heart of Jane Austen's work. It is the means by which the reader sees how the characters are engaging with each other, and through those engagements, character is revealed, and the substance – the themes and issues – of the book emerge. It is worthwhile thinking about this dialogue under several headings.

Dialogue and everyday speech

The dialogue quoted has little in common with everyday speech. The sentences are clearly and (in the case of Elizabeth) deftly organized. The vocabulary is high-level, though Jane Austen shows Elizabeth using Lady Catherine's title.

The presentation of speech

The passage is written in direct speech – we hear the actual words the two speakers use – and to assist us there are what some critics call 'tags' – those indicative statements such as 'said Elizabeth'. Sometimes these tags tell us how the words were delivered, as in 'said Elizabeth, coolly'.

The shaping of speech

There are elegant balances in the language, a feature rare, though not unknown, in everyday talk. Elizabeth's last sentence, with its telling contrast of 'you' and 'I' neatly represents the conflict between the two women.

The politics of conversation

'Politics' is here used in the sense of a struggle for power and advantage. Critics often talk about the control of discourse. In conversation, people persuade, pressurize and seek to out-manoeuvre. This is what we see here. Lady Catherine wants Elizabeth to bend to her will, but Elizabeth resists firmly. One form of resistance is Elizabeth's refusal to use Lady Catherine's vocabulary. Lady Catherine asks (though is it really a question?) whether the news of the engagement has 'been industriously circulated' by Elizabeth and her family. The standard meaning of 'industriously' was 'diligently', but it also had the meaning of working with a set purpose – that is, with design. As set out in section 1.3, 'design' is a morally dubious word, which can have suggestions of manipulation and deceit. Elizabeth resists the imputation by avoiding the word.

The revelation of character

The dialogue reveals characters. Lady Catherine's language is loose and betrays her lack of intelligence. How can one person 'universally' contradict a rumour? But Lady Catherine thinks so, probably because she is accustomed to her words being universally obeyed.

Dialogue and theme

The dialogue indicates the theme of the novel. One of Jane Austen's concerns is the future of her nation. Though conservative by temperament, she has suspicions about those who control her country. Is the future to be left in the hands of stupid snobs? England depends on alliances between the wealthy and the witty. The powerful Darcy needs the wit and charm – and the sheer, elegant intelligence – of an Elizabeth Bennet. Though Elizabeth is not engaged to Mr Darcy, she can relish the pleasure of that prospect by contemplating the report as if it were true.

Summary

Dialogue, unlike everyday conversation, employs high-level language and complex sentences. Authors sometimes tag conversations to indicate who is speaking and how the words are delivered. In dialogue there is a struggle for power (the politics of conversation) and a revelation of character and themes.

2.5   Last words

As novels are shaped works of art, special importance is attached to the way they close. Consequently, the last words of a character have special status.

Novelists often make last words the revelation of character and/or the disclosure of theme. Consider the last words of Kurtz in Conrad's *Heart of Darkness* (1902). Marlow, the narrator, has travelled up a river into the heart of Africa to meet the sophisticated Kurtz, who, rather than civilization, has brought (indicated by heads on poles), savagery. This is the moment of Kurtz's death (Chapter 3):

Did he live his life again in every detail of desire, temptation, and surrender during that supreme moment of complete knowledge? He cried in a whisper at some image, at some vision – he cried out twice, a cry that was no more than a breath –

'The horror! The horror!'

What we hear in the repeated phrase is the summation of his life, a life that has entered the heart of darkness and found something so overwhelmingly dreadful that he is almost inarticulate. 'The horror!' is not a description but an appalled recoil from the knowledge that he yielded to the temptation of an undefined desire. That is the heart of darkness.

Summary

Last words can reveal character and indicate theme.

2.6 Language about characters

Novelists, and through them narrators, create characters in two kinds of language: physical language, and mental and moral language.

Physical language

Physical or external language is concerned with whatever is open to the senses – whatever can be seen, heard, felt and so on.

> It is convention that when a character is first introduced, there is a detailed presentation of his or her appearance.

These presentations are not neutral. They consist of those things that the author has chosen to tell us, and the way in which they are told, may indicate to us their relative importance. Jane Austen, for example, chooses not to describe many physical details about a character's face. In the first sentence of *Emma* (1816), Emma Woodhouse is said to be 'handsome', but we are not told what it is that makes her so.

Later in the nineteenth century, readers expected very full character delineations. In *Far from the Madding Crowd* (1874), Thomas Hardy satisfies that expectation in his opening presentation of Gabriel Oak:

> When Farmer Oak smiled, the corners of his mouth spread till they were within an unimportant distance of his ears, his eyes were reduced to chinks, and diverging wrinkles appeared round them extending upon his countenance like the rays in a rudimentary sketch of the rising sun.

That is a complex sentence, all about a smile. It is closely observed, not only in the sense that there are many details but also because the reader is placed very near the imagined face; we see minute details – the 'chinks' and 'wrinkles'. The image at the end shows us how we should respond: Gabriel Oak's smile is warm, even radiant. The smile is the man.

Mental and moral language

> **Mental and moral language reveals what characters are like in themselves – how they think, what they value and, possibly, how the reader might value *them*.**

As in *Far from the Madding Crowd*, George Eliot's *Middlemarch* opens with the central character, Dorothea Brooke. The long passage weaves together the physical and mental language, dress and character – the outer with the inner –

> Miss Brooke had that kind of beauty which seems to be thrown into relief by poor dress. Her hand and wrist were so finely formed that she could wear sleeves not less bare of style than those in which the Blessed Virgin appeared to Italian painters…

The physical detail says much about the mind. Dorothea's plain dress suits her; its absence of self-conscious style implies she has the inner poise of the Blessed Virgin. The passage continues to give an insight into Dorothea's family:

> The pride of being ladies had something to do with it: the Brooke connections, though not exactly aristocratic, were unquestionably 'good': if you inquired backward for a generation or two, you would not find any yard-measuring or parcel-tying forefathers…

Here the language of history and the language of class (very much a matter of economics) are used to contextualize, and thereby characterize, Dorothea's pride in herself.

Still using Dorothea's plain dress as a key to her character, the narrator says that 'well-bred economy' would have sufficiently explained Dorothea's unassuming clothes 'quite apart from religious feeling; but in Miss Brooke's case, religion alone would have determined it…'. Dorothea, the narrator continues, cannot reconcile a preoccupation with clothes with weighty spiritual considerations. Having established that, the language becomes decidedly inward: 'she was enamoured of intensity and greatness, and rash in embracing whatever seemed to her to have those aspects…'. The turn of Dorothea's mind is given in the words 'enamoured', 'intensity' and 'rash'. She is the kind of character whose strong emotional commitments can make her heedless of consequences.

The power of character language

We should resist the assumption that inner language is better than outer language. The test case is Dickens. His characters can be vigorous and entertaining even though they consist almost entirely of external details. Here is Mr Bounderby from Chapter 4 of *Hard Times* (1854):

> He was a rich man; a banker, merchant, manufacturer and what not. A big, loud man, with a stare and a metallic laugh. A man made out of coarse material, which seemed to have stretched to make so much of him. A man with a great puffed head and forehead, swelled veins in his temples, and such a strained skin to his face that it seemed to hold his eyes open, and lift his eyebrows up.

There is no inner language in the passage, yet the writing is forceful and entertaining. Mr Bounderby is monstrously funny: a manufacturer in a manufacturing town, he is like a factory-made article. The coarse material of which he appears to be made is 'stretched' and 'strained'. Through the comedy, an important point emerges: as in the cases of the workers in his factory, the manufacturing has diminished Bounderby's humanity.

Summary

Language about character can be external or internal. We should not assume that one is better than the other.

2.7   Growing up

Assumptions about age are present in fiction. Mr Brownlow in *Oliver Twist* (1837) has learnt to judge and be charitable. But age does not automatically bestow such qualities: Mrs Bennet in *Pride and Prejudice* has never learnt tact, and Miss Havisham in *Great Expectations* (1860) has learnt no wisdom in her life of resentment.

From childhood to adulthood

> The passage from childhood to young adulthood, from a carefree to a burdened life, from ignorance to knowledge, has become the special preserve of the novel.

In and through the polarities of childhood innocence and adult experience, individual identities emerge.

The *Bildungsroman*

The *Bildungsroman* is the novel of formation – formation of character and identity. The German writer Goethe is usually credited with initiating the genre in *Wilhelm Meister* (1795). The *Bildungsroman* is therefore a romantic and post-romantic genre. Many romantic concerns – innocence and experience, childhood, the nature of subjective experience, the place of memory, the work of the imagination – are central to such writing. Given the subject matter, the *Bildungsroman* has several common features.

Places

To grow is to be aware, and an important part of a character's experience is awareness of place.

Great Expectations opens with Pip coming to consciousness of who he is when he looks at the graves of his parents and brothers in the churchyard on the marshes. He becomes aware of himself by way of his awareness of the place he is in. The evening in the churchyard is his 'first most vivid and broad impression of the identity of things'. He finds out for certain that 'this bleak place overgrown with nettles was the churchyard', that the graves were his dead family and that 'the dark flat wilderness beyond, intersected with dikes and mounds and gates, with scattered cattle feeding on it, was the marshes'. Dickens' writing sharply and indelibly delineates the scene. The nouns with their substantiating adjectives enact the moment when a character becomes aware of the concrete actuality of the world. This abrupt, unavoidable experience of the abrasive solidity of the world ends with the discovery of the self: 'and that the small bundle of shivers growing afraid of it all and beginning to cry was Pip'.

Authority figures

To be a child is to be weak, dependent and under the control of adults. In some cases the adults are parents. This is the case with Paul Morel in D. H. Lawrence's *Sons and Lovers*. The presentation of a marriage between two characters of widely divergent expectations is masterly. Deprived of the kind of companionship she sought in marriage, the mother turns to her children for consolation and inspiration. Hence the struggles in Paul's later life between being a son and a lover.

Sexual awakening

Before novelists described sexual encounters in detail, sexual attraction and sexual expression were coded. The first sight of the beloved is a traditional element in the code of sexual attraction. In *Great Expectations*, Pip sees Estella at the end of a corridor holding a light, which will guide him to Miss Havisham's room. Although he is a young man, Gabriel Oak's first sight of Bathsheba fulfils the same function. Sexual expression is intense in Charlotte Brontë's *Jane Eyre* (1847). Jane and Rochester are remarkably physical in their expression of affections. They squeeze each other's hands tightly. *Jane Eyre* is a novel that works with an intense awareness of the erotic impulse. In this it is interestingly different from *Wuthering Heights*. We are brought up to think of Emily Brontë's novel as one of the great romantic novels, but its heroine, the elder Catherine Earnshaw, is virtually without sexual feelings and is only fleetingly aware that she arouses them in others.

Choices

To be an adult is to face choices. The child becomes an adult when he or she is faced with dilemmas or temptations. Jane Eyre effectively grows up when she decides to seek a post outside Lowood School; Pip has most of his decisions made for him until he encounters his real benefactor.

When choices are related to love, there is the familiar plot element of whom to choose. Plots are frequently designed around two characters. The two characters are either the basis of the contrast novel, as in Jane Austen's *Sense and Sensibility* (1811), or form the romantic options of the central figure. In Dickens' *David Copperfield* (1849), the hero is attracted to two women.

Summary

The *Bildungsroman* – the novel of formation – concentrates on the growth of the young into adulthood, paying attention to how places become the sites of self-realization, the shaping influence of parents and other authority figures, how sexual awakening occurs, and how in making choices, identities are confirmed.

2.8   The contexts of characters

We are shaped by our contexts or situations. We are situated in life by material factors and by the assumptions of the society into which we are born. We are, to use the term broadly, people of cultures.

Gender

An aspect of the *Bildungsroman* is that characters arrive at an understanding of what it is to be a man or a woman. Novelists are sometimes very conscious of the extent to which male and female identity is a matter of adapting to the expectations of other people. We learn what it is to be a man or woman from those who have responsibility for us when we are young (see also Chapter 40, section 40.1).

Catherine Earnshaw in *Wuthering Heights* is particularly interesting, because her adoption of a female manner and outlook happens with symbolic suddenness. Heathcliff recounts to Nelly about how he and Cathy roamed the moors until they came to Thrushcross Grange, where they gaze through the window at the luxury of the Linton children's home life. They are detected, a dog is loosed, Cathy's foot is bitten, and she bleeds. She has to stay at the Grange for five weeks and is visited by her brother's wife, who starts the transformation by raising 'her self-respect with fine clothes and flattery'. When she returns (Chapter 7), she has become a young woman:

> instead of a wild, hatless little savage jumping into the house, and rushing to squeeze us all breathless, there lighted from a handsome black pony a very dignified person, with brown ringlets falling from the cover of a feathered beaver, and a long cloth habit, which she was obliged to hold up with both hands that she might sail in.

The transformation works in a number of ways. She dresses fashionably and behaves as a young lady. She has entered superior society and has acquired social ambitions. She has also entered womanhood. Symbolically, her change coincides with her bleeding. The wild, hatless Cathy is now Catherine in her beaver hat. Furthermore, we can work out from Cathy's diary that when they left to roam the moors, they took the dairymaid's cloak. That symbol of the childhood bond between Cathy and Heathcliff now gives way to the long habit, which, in a ladylike manner, she carefully holds up with both hands as she, again symbolically, sails into her new life. Clothes, it should be observed, are significant in nineteenth-century novels, no doubt because class was very evident in the way people dressed. But, as with Dorothea Brooke, choice of clothes also indicates character.

Culture and nationality

The nineteenth-century novel often dealt with the meeting of two cultures, usually the working class and the middle class. Elizabeth Gaskell's *North and South* (1855) is about a sometime clergyman who moves north to an industrial town to seek employment as a tutor. This allows the author to treat a number of cultural encounters: north meets south, poverty meets wealth, and managers encounter workers.

In the twentieth century, another cultural difference has emerged in the novel. This is the relationship between the British and those countries that once constituted the empire. The postcolonial novel can now be regarded as a separate genre. New countries, or old countries that have secured independence, seek to establish their own identities through re-discovering their histories and presenting themselves in their own terms.

One way of doing this is through rewriting English classics. In *Windward Heights* (1998), Maryse Conde creates a Caribbean version of Emily Brontë's *Wuthering Heights*. Another way is to find a setting that is representative of the new nation. Thus, in *Things Fall Apart* (1958), the Nigerian novelist, Chinuha Achebe, presents African village life rather than the more Western cities. The theme of cultures meeting (or, as is sometimes the theme, not meeting) is long established in the English novel. *Robinson Crusoe* (1719) can be read as a parable of colonialization, and there is a critical controversy about where *Mansfield Park* (1814) stands in the debate about slavery. Certainly, some of the wealth of the Bertrams' English estate derives from the colonial one, and almost certainly Jane Austen imagined that the Antiguan estate was worked by slaves. But where does Jane Austen stand? Fanny Price, the unobtrusive heroine, seeks to engage Sir Thomas in conversation, but she is disappointed to find him silent on the matter. Does Sir Thomas sense that Fanny is in favour of moves to further control the trade in slaves and therefore avoids the topic? E. M. Forster's *A Passage to India* (1924) explores the cultural differences between the British and the Indians, and seems to conclude that the differences are considerable. Recently, postcolonial criticism has further stressed differences, partly in an attempt to make English Literature shed some of its claims to speak universally (see Chapter 42, section 42.1).

Summary

Novels place characters in broad cultural contexts. Characters learn what it is to be male or female, and express this identity in matters such as clothing. Another context is the relationship between Britain and its former colonies.

2.9 Character range

Growth

It is sometimes said that the mark of a successful novel is that the characters change and grow. Some of the things we value in novels – the moment of awakening, facing up to temptations and making choices – rest on a character's capacity to change. Much of the pleasure of reading about Dorothea Brooke, Pip, Paul Morel and Elizabeth Bennet comes from seeing how they grow.

We must not forget one of the principles upon which this section is based. Characters have been made by authors. The capacity to change is, therefore, a function of how a character is created. Dickens makes Pip grow to see his faults – his snobbery, his neglect of Joe and his pursuit of a false idea of what it is to be a gentleman. But some characters don't grow. The comically self-absorbed Mr Wopsle, also from *Great Expectations*, consistently fancies himself as a performer: first, as the Parish Clerk and later as an actor.

Open and closed characters

There are a number of terms to describe the capacity of a character to change. In his still highly influential *Aspects of the Novel* (1927), E. M. Forster makes the distinction between flat and round characters. A flat character has few features, is often comical and comes near to being a caricature. Above all, flat characters do not change and are, therefore, enjoyably predictable. By contrast, a round character is complex, composed of a number of features, has a rich inner life and can adapt and change.

An alternative way of talking about characters is to call one sort closed and the other open. The usefulness of these terms is that they highlight the possibility of change. The closed character is impervious to change, but the open character is subject to external influences and can therefore respond, and in responding change and grow.

Mrs Bennet in *Pride and Prejudice* is a closed character. The entertainment she provides derives from her predictability, and though, unlike some closed characters, her language is not entirely restricted to catchphrases and repetition, we look forward to the inappropriate ways in which she behaves in a crisis. Furthermore, as with other closed characters, she is not central to the plot.

An open character, because he or she can adapt to new circumstances, is central to the plot trajectory. It is often said that George Eliot devised plots by making them develop from her characters. This is only possible with open characters. Dorothea grows to see beyond her youthful and blinkered idealism. All the central issues of the nineteenth-century novel – the making of moral choices, the struggle for a role in a changing society, the competing claims of love and duty, the tension between ambition and responsibility – need for their plot enactments characters who are open to change.

Critical terminology has its limitations. It's a mistake to think that characters always work according to the tidy schemes of critical distinctions. There are surprises: Alec d'Urberville in *Tess of the d'Urbervilles* behaves like a closed character but he changes, even though we don't see the change take place. Significantly, his change is presented visually: his clothes, manners and speech alter when he absorbs evangelical Christianity. And even if Hardy simplifies matters (is the change too complete?) at the end, when he has forsaken his faith, he behaves with more consideration to Tess than does the absent Angel.

Summary

Some characters are closed in that they are not capable of changing. Others are open in that they can respond anew to circumstances, and are therefore capable of change.

◼ ⩗ **3** Narration

3.1 A tale that is told

To insist on the made-up or fabricated nature of characters is to be aware, once again, that fiction is constructed. Even when a novel is written to give us the impression of everyday life, we have to remember that this impression is one that the *author* has sought to *create*. Perhaps we value art in part because, while it is something that has been made, it nevertheless gives us a clearer picture of the lives we lead and the world in which we lead them. Why and how it does this is one of the mysteries of art that no one has accounted for satisfactorily.

Tales and tellers

When there is a tale, there are two presences in addition to the story:

> **A tale implies a teller and a reader (or audience).**

Someone must relate the events, and someone else must listen.
   To study novels and short stories is to be aware that

> **The way a tale is told shapes *what* is told.**

Tales and knowledge

This touches on the issue of knowledge raised in section 2.2. Reading literature is epistemic – a matter of knowledge.

> **What a reader knows depends upon what he or she has been told and how the teller has told it.**

Take, for example, the case of the detective story. We know that someone has been murdered and we also know enough to make us suspect that a number of people might have done it, but the success of the story – its suspense and its mystery – depends on the author *not* telling us who the murderer is until very near the end.
   We might remember at this point that the words 'tell' and 'teller' have meanings in Economics. To 'tell' is to count (usually money), and a 'teller' is one who counts. Knowledge in stories is like this. In the same way that we only have the money that has been handed to us by the teller, so in literature we only know what the (story) teller has given us. But, as with all comparisons, we can only take this one so far.
   When we are given money we are passive receivers, but

> **Readers are not always passive; they think for themselves.**

In literature, we can only work with what we have been told, but we still have freedom as to *how* we think about it.

Summary

Tales, like any art, fascinate us because we know that though they have been devised, they give us a clear picture of our lives. Tales give readers knowledge. What is made of that knowledge depends, in part, upon the readers.

3.2   Narration, knowledge and characters

What readers can know

What readers know shapes how they react to and think about characters. What we know of characters will be shaped by what the author has decided to tell us; and what we have been told includes how characters respond to each other and the situations in which they find themselves. When a character reacts to other characters, readers can see in that reaction an indication as to what the character is like. In Nathaniel Hawthorne's *The Scarlet Letter* (1850), Hester Prynne has conceived a child that cannot be her husband's. For this, she is condemned to wear a scarlet letter, presumably 'A' for adulteress, though this is never specified in the novel. Hester complies with the sentence but elaborately embroiders the letter. She does not say why. Yet her embroidery (a distinctly female accomplishment) provokes us into thinking about what she is like and, possibly, what she thinks of those who have condemned her.

Human responses

Human responses – physical responses – reveal what we are thinking and feeling. The thoughts and feelings of people inside and outside of literature are generally not private. Most of the time we know what someone is thinking and feeling from the way he or she behaves. There are, of course, occasions when we don't know what's going on in someone's heart and mind. But a lot of the time, facial expressions and postures tell us. They are a kind of language. We can do this in literature as well as in life. Look at this passage from the end of the fifth chapter of *The Great Gatsby* (1925). Gatsby has met Daisy again. She is the girl he has never stopped loving. Nick narrates that, after initial awkwardness, they become absorbed with each other:

> They had forgotten me, but Daisy glanced up and held out her hand. Gatsby didn't know me at all. I looked once more at them and they looked back at me, remotely, possessed by intense life.

Nick knows that Gatsby has forgotten him and that both are 'possessed by intense life', because emotion is visible in what they do (see also Chapter 52, section 4).

Looking into minds

But there are passages in novels when the reader is told directly what a character is thinking. Such a communication is private, but only in the sense that it has not been made public. But it could be: what a character is thinking is thought in words, and words, to be words, must be public. The same goes for feelings: we can keep feelings to ourselves, but were we to express them, people would recognize what they were.

When we know what a character thinks and feels we are in a privileged position. There are two aspects to this privilege.

> First, we are privileged to know what the other characters don't know; and, second, we are privileged because we stand in a special relationship to the author.

The privilege of knowing what a character is thinking and feeling is crucially important for a reader, because

> Being aware of the intentions, opinions, resentments, and memories of a character will shape the way we read the novel.

What we make of a novel – its events, the behaviour of the characters, the outcome of the plot – will be shaped by what we, as readers, know of the inner lives of some or all of the characters.

Summary

Reading novels involves acquiring knowledge. We know what characters are like from how they behave. Sometimes an author tells us what a character is thinking and feeling. Our knowledge of characters shapes the way we read a novel.

3.3   The tellers of tales

Authors and narrators

All that we know of any story comes from the story itself. The story might have been other than the form in which we see it. Dickens, for example, rewrote the ending of *Great Expectations* (1860). To say of any story that the things in it are as they are is to recognize the controlling presence of the one who tells the tale.

We must make the following distinctions.

- There is a story-teller who is the author of the book, the one who puts the words down on paper.
- There is the figure within the book who presents him- or herself to the reader as the one who is telling the tale.

We may call the first the author and the second the narrator. For example: Jane Austen is the author of *Pride and Prejudice* (1813), and in that novel the events are related by a narrator, who is not named but who is the source of all we know.

Handling this distinction is a matter of knowing when to use one term and when the other. The following is a brief guide.

Author

In one sense, 'author' is the simple matter of the name that appears on the cover of the book. But the word has two more specific uses:

- It can be used when discussing the basic conception of the work, and the specific choice of its various elements. It is the author who created the plot, the characters and the settings.
- It can be used in a more detailed way to talk about the design of the book. So, when discussing the moment by moment unfolding of the action, it is appropriate to speak of the author deciding to put one event after another.

Narrator

We must remember that the narrator is a creation of the author. He or she is one of the basic elements of the tale. The term narrator can be used in the following ways.

- The narrator is encountered directly in a way that the author is not. Authors are known through their effects; narrators often announce themselves either as the author or as a named individual. When a narrator becomes a sharply defined individual, he or she may indicate the particular interest taken in the tale, and this might lead to judgements on the characters.
- A narrator can also be an anonymous figure who conceals him- or herself in the telling and yet knows what characters do and what goes on in their minds.
- Narrators, as often said in the nineteenth century, can be godlike; like God, they can be present everywhere and all-knowing. But, again like God, they are nowhere visible (see section 3.5).
- It is not always possible to distinguish between the author and the narrator. Sometimes, the figure within is a fictionalized version of the author – the author's particular presence and identity he or she has adopted for this work of fiction. As long as it is made clear that the narrator is the form through which the author is present in the text, the narrator can be referred to by the author's name.

Summary

When talking about how a tale is told, we should normally distinguish between the author who is responsible for the conception and design of the tale, and the narrator figure whom the author creates to conduct the moment-by-moment unfolding of the story.

3.4 The grammar of narration: first person

Narration is a matter of grammar, of the way we conjugate verbs.

A verb denotes an action or state of being that can be carried out in three ways or, as the traditional vocabulary has it, three *persons*: first, second and third. The conjugation of the verb 'to sing' in the present simple tense is:

First person:	I sing.
Second person:	You sing.
Third person:	He, she, it or one sings.

It is virtually impossible to sustain a narrative in the second person. Sword and sorcery game books are an exception, but they are really instructions rather than narrations. This leaves first and third: we either tell tales by saying 'I went to town on Thursday…' (first person) or 'She went to town on Thursday…' (third person).

Two types of first-person narrator

There are two kinds of first-person narrator: central figures (hero narrators) and observer figures (witness narrators). Pip in *Great Expectations* is an example of the first, and Nick Carraway in *The Great Gatsby* of the second.

Our view of life

First-person narration is close to how each of us experiences life: all is seen from a single and particular perspective.

> **First-person narrations allow us to recognize that what is seen and felt is what *we* might have seen and felt.**

First-person narration is particularly suited to the exploration of the mind.

In Ian MacEwan's *Enduring Love* (1997), we are implicitly invited to admit that we, like Joe, would have felt a growing terror at being stalked.

First-person narration and knowledge

In first-person narration, readers are only told what the narrator tells them. Thus,

> **All that we know about other characters, and all we know about incidents, comes from the narrator.**

(We can, of course, think for ourselves, but such thinking can only work with what we have been given.) Because we see things through the narrator, it is possible to know what the narrator thinks and feels: we know what the narrator's plans, hopes, reactions and judgements are. The pathos of *Great Expectations* stems from our knowing how much Pip desires Estella and, increasingly, how little hope he has of gaining her love.

But, like each of us, first-person narrators are confined:

First-person narrators cannot know other characters' minds.

The narrator (and, of course, the reader) can only discern what other characters are thinking and feeling by relying on external signs – what they say and do (see section 3.2). First-person narration introduces into fiction some of the uncertainties we experience in our daily lives. The excitement of Wilkie Collins' *The Woman in White* (1860) depends on each of the narrators, and in particular Marian, being unsure as to what the other characters are up to.

The position of the reader

Although the reader only knows what the narrator tells him or her, this does not mean that the reader can only sympathize and judge as the narrator does. Readers think for themselves; they retain a measure of independence. Sometimes the reader has to be alert to the differences between the author and the first-person narrator.

Authors sometimes invite the reader to judge things differently from narrators.

Mark Twain's *Huckleberry Finn* (1884) depends on the reader seeing what Huck sees but, at crucial moments, judging things differently. We can see what Huck is sometimes unaware of – the humanity and dignity of Jim, the runaway slave.

Security

There is a fundamental and obvious kind of security in first-person narration. Because the narrator narrates, he or she must have survived the events of the tale. Perhaps this is why fiction that is intended for or associated with children often adopts the retrospective first-person narrator – the narrator who looks back on his or her life. Robert Louis Stevenson's narrators in *Treasure Island* (1882) and *Kidnapped* (1886) both look back on the adventures of their young days.

Yet this security poses two problems. How does the novel end, and should the situation reached at the end be indicated in the narrative? To take one example: *Jane Eyre* (1847) ends with what Jane has wanted, but the perspective of the narration is not obviously the situation in which she finds herself at the novel's close.

Growth

First-person narration is particularly suited to tracing a character's growth.

Pip in *Great Expectations* learns and grows. The older Pip retrospectively exposes the moral shortcomings of his younger self. Moral exploration is at the heart of the novel's concerns, and the reader can follow through the inwardness of the process.

The growth of the self can also be seen as a process of self-making. *The Great Gatsby* shows Gatsby making himself, but, although it is a quieter element in the narrative, Nick, the witness narrator, is trying out versions of himself – the soldier adapting to civilian life, the young man who escorts the fashionable Jordan Baker, the man adjusting to city life, the writer dealing with an excessive romanticism, and the man who, for all the allurements of the East, realizes he is a Mid-Westerner.

Levels of awareness

First-person narration makes possible the exploitation of disparities of awareness between character and reader.

Because Huck is a morally impercipient narrator (he doesn't see the moral significance of what he is doing), his moral struggles require the narrator to see things differently. But 'differently' is not always quite the term we need. Twain often encourages us to make opposite judgements. There are two incidents in *Huckleberry Finn* when Huck could turn the runaway slave, Jim, in to the authorities. Huck, who has accepted the morality of a slave-owning society, thinks that this is what he *ought* to do. But though Huck has no moral doubts, he finds himself unable to do it. Guiltily, he feels that he will go to 'Hell' because he has saved Jim. (Significantly, these two passages are the only moments in the novel when the word 'Hell' is used.) The reader sees two things. The first is that Huck is right in what he does, and the second is that Huck cannot see this because his moral language is entirely corrupted by Southern prejudices.

Unreliability

First-person narration can explore the subtleties of uncertain judgement. The shifting feelings, the half-formed ideas, the competing pressures and the uncertain motives make readers see that

A first person narrator might not always be reliable.

Nick Carraway, the witness narrator of *The Great Gatsby*, doesn't quite know what to make of Gatsby. And because Nick is uncertain, the position of the reader is unstable. Should a reader be content with Nick's uncertainties or, in the absence of assurance in the narrator, exercise his or her judgement and judge Gatsby firmly?

No narrator can be wholly unreliable, because if that were the case, the reader would have no bearings whatsoever. The famous cases of unreliable narrators, such as Henry James' *The Turn of the Screw* (1898) and Ford Maddox Ford's *The Good Soldier* (1915), are only comprehensible because there are some things that the reader can rely on. For example, it may be that the governess in *The Turn of the Screw* invents the demonic possession of the children in her care, but there is no doubt that there were two servants, who, when alive, exercised influences over the boy and girl.

We often know that a narrator is unreliable because they declare it. Nick starts his narration by declaring unambiguously that Gatsby is the one exception to the world he was happy to leave behind in New York. Yet he then says Gatsby 'represented everything for which I have an unaffected scorn'. In *Wuthering Heights* (1847), Emily Brontë does something similar with Nelly Dean. She is our sole source (apart from the 'diary' Lockwood finds) as to what Catherine Earnshaw is like, but Nelly admits that she doesn't like Catherine.

It should be noted that moral uncertainty is easier for a reader to handle than factual unreliability. We are entitled to make our own judgements, but if we are unsure as to what has happened we have nowhere else to turn. The novel alone provides the facts.

Moral understanding

Novelists are sometimes described as moralists. This is a tricky term. A moralist lays bare the moral significances of human life; he or she ponders why things matter morally to us. A good case can be made that the novel is a more suitable form of moral understanding than, say, a philosophical treatise, because in a novel we see the situations that make human life a matter of moral significance.

The novel makes possible an understanding of human life by a close engagement with the particularities of human experience. These particularities can be given concrete force in the form of first-person narration.

For example, in *The Handmaid's Tale* (1985), Margaret Atwood's understanding of the place of women in our society is given force through a first-person narration that makes the reader pay attention to what certain experiences are like from a female point of view.

Summary

First-person narrators are usually of two kinds: the hero narrator and the witness narrator. First-person narrators offer a single perspective on the action. Retrospective first-person narrators offer the security of knowledge that the narrator survives, and the opportunity to explore moral growth. They can provoke different judgements from readers, and are difficult to cope with when unreliable. First-person narration is an appropriate way in which a novelist can fulfil the role of the moralist.

3.5   The grammar of narration: third person

Third-person narrators are not characters involved directly in the plot but in so far as they emphasize and comment they are distinctive figures. They are, to use a popular term, dramatized. A third-person narrator can be dramatized in a number of ways. He or she can comment on the action, can generalize about human experience, can pass judgement and can address the reader directly.

A narrator who enters the narrative by way of comments is often called an *intrusive narrator*. Jane Austen's narrator in *Mansfield Park* (1814) is particularly prominent at the end, when exacting judgements are passed on the major characters. Some third-person narrators are non-dramatized or covert, in that they do not intrude themselves upon the tale they are relating.

Telling and showing

Third-person narrators can tell and show.

> To tell is to speak directly; to show is to present action or dialogue through which a reader is able to see something about a character or an action.

Thus if we read 'John told lies', we are being *told*, but if there is an incident in which we can see that John is not telling the truth, then we are *shown* that he lies.

Readers sometimes prefer novels in which they are left to work things out for themselves rather than constantly being told what they see. Emily Brontë leaves the reader to make connections between separate incidents. It might be thought an improbability in *Wuthering Heights* that Cathy's body should remain almost perfect in the grave, but very near the beginning of the novel Lockwood says that the ground of the churchyard has the quality of preserving whatever is buried in it.

Telling and showing are in fact far more difficult to separate than the distinction implies. In order to be shown something, a narrator will tell the reader many things. And the act of telling depends in many cases on 'showings' that the narrator doesn't feel it is necessary to spell out. Perhaps the best thing to do is to reserve the use of these terms for very obvious passages, and refrain from building too much on the distinction. Dickens, for example, does use telling a lot, and there is little point in avoiding the term just because most telling also involves showing.

What narrators know

The act by which a narrator reveals what a character thinks is called *privileged access*. The narrator, and therefore the reader, enters the minds of characters. This knowledge is reliable.

> A first-person narrator can be deluded and lack self-knowledge, but a third-person narrator can enter a character's mind and report his or her undisclosed thoughts and feelings authoritatively.

If we are told that John wondered what to do, the reader doesn't disagree. We have to believe what the third-person narrators tell us.

Omniscient narrators

Some narrators are omniscient – all-knowing (see section 3.3).

> Like God, omniscient narrators look into the hearts and minds of all their creations.

George Eliot presents her readers with her characters' private thoughts and feelings. We know what each is thinking, and what each knows or doesn't know. It's like a play in which each character has disclosed his or her thoughts to us in soliloquy (see Chapter 8, section 8.4).

In Chapter 74 of *Middlemarch* (1871), Nicholas Bulstrode's past crimes have been exposed. Furthermore, his wife is aware of his 'bad past life', and 'she could not judge him leniently'. He is alone:

> He felt himself perishing slowly in unpitied misery. Perhaps he would never see his wife's face with affection in it again. And if he turned to God there seemed to be no answer but the pressure of retribution.
>
> It was eight o'clock in the evening before the door opened and his wife entered. He dared not look up at her. He sat with his eyes bent down, and as she went towards him she thought he looked smaller – he seemed so withered and shrunken. A movement of new compassion and old tenderness went through her like a great wave, and putting one hand on his which rested on the arm of the chair, and the other on his shoulder, she said, solemnly but kindly –
> 'Look up, Nicholas.'

The focus of the narration here moves from one mind to another. We know she thinks she cannot treat him leniently, so we can register the significance of the change that overcomes her when she, reading his feelings from his posture, sees him so apparently withered and shrunken. Through omniscient narration, her moment of perception coincides with his feelings of hopelessness, so the reader sees that Bulstrode is the recipient of a pity that his wife did not expect to feel. George Eliot is a moralist. She shows that we are often inclined to judge others severely, but when we sense what goes on in each human heart, we are full of pity. To understand all is to forgive all.

Single cases of privileged access

The most common form of privileged access is when the reader is only admitted to the mind of the central character. This is the closest that third-person narration comes to first person narration. The effect is that we feel close to those characters to whose minds we have access.

Jane Austen's narrators consistently have access to the minds of the heroines, so the reader can follow their hopes and anxieties with an informed sympathy. But neither heroine nor reader knows what is going on in the minds of the other characters. Thus, in matters of love, the reader can be as uncertain as the heroine. We can, for example, see Elizabeth Bennet's feelings changing towards Mr Darcy, but we do not know what he is feeling.

Pride and Prejudice is an interesting case of the author coping with the restrictions of single privileged access. At one moment (in Chapter 6), we are given a momentary glimpse into what Mr Darcy is thinking, and later, Jane Austen resorts to a letter to disclose his thoughts. Letters work like soliloquies;

they act as declarations of a character's thoughts. Interestingly, *Pride and Prejudice* includes more letters than the other Jane Austen novels.

Direct free style

Direct free style is the name sometimes adopted for those narratives in which a third-person narration shifts into the language of first person.

This is often a matter of vocabulary, as it is in Jane Austen's *Emma* (1816). *Emma* is a teasing narrative in which the reader has to see what Emma sees *and beyond* what she sees. The narration has Emma's commanding assurance; she is popular, intelligent and very certain in her judgements. Emma decides that Mr Elton, the vicar of the parish, will be a suitable husband for Harriet Smith, a pretty girl whom Emma has chosen to encourage. Mr Elton sends a charade (a riddle) to add to Harriet's collection. The reader, however, sees that Emma is probably his object, and that the charade (its subject is courtship) is meant for her. In Chapter 9, Mr Elton pays a visit:

> Later in the morning, and just as the girls were going to separate in preparation for the regular four o'clock dinner, the hero of this inimitable charade walked in again. Harriet turned away; but Emma could receive him with the usual smile, and her quick eye soon discerned in his the consciousness of having made a push – of having thrown a die; and she imagined he was come to see how it might turn up.

Emma is a kind of novelist in that she has a strong idea as to how the course of life should run, and she directs events in accordance with her (conventionally romantic) conceptions. She also appropriates the narrative. The word 'hero' is hers. He is playing the role Emma has designed for him.

If there are any rules of narrative, they are grammatical rather than stylistic. As noted above, first- and third-person narration are the only grammatical possibilities in narration, but there are no stylistic rules allowing or forbidding Jane Austen from using first-person vocabulary in a third-person narration. Nor are there rules saying that the two forms cannot be used in the same work. Readers new to William Golding's *The Spire* (1964) might be confused, because in one paragraph there are both third-person and first-person sentences. In a novel about aspiration and desire, it is fitting that third-person narration gives way to the blinkered obsessions of first-person.

Tense

Most tales, be they first- or third-person narrations, are told in the past tense. The world of fiction is a separate world, because in terms of time it is one that is finished. Occasionally, novelists (for example, Helen Dunmore and Penelope Lively) use the present tense. This has the effect of immediacy, but the depth of understanding that reflecting on the past makes possible is of necessity absent.

Summary

Third-person narrators both tell and show. In practice, the two ways of writing are dependent on each other. Third-person narrators disclose the inner lives of the characters. How they do this shapes the reader's response. Some narrators are omniscient in that they know all, whereas others choose to have privileged access only to the mind of a single character. It is rare for narrators not to use the past tense.

3.6   External narration

Novelists find privileged access very useful, but it is possible to narrate a story without it. Many folk tales work in this way, as do the stories in the Bible. What we know of the characters is either achieved through telling, or shown through action and dialogue. Perhaps because his plots are like ballads and folk tales, Hardy often avoids the use of privileged access. In some scenes, characters are revealed entirely, or almost entirely, through what they say and do. The narration is third-person, but the reader learns no more from the narrator than would a bystander observing the event. Hardy, in fact, is drawn to the idea of the casual observer. He often refers, in the manner of Wordsworth, to a traveller who has stopped and observed the scene.

At the start of *The Mayor of Casterbridge* (1886), Michael Henchard, a hay-trusser, gets drunk and sells his wife. By the second chapter he has sobered up, so goes into church to make a vow:

> Hence he reached the church without observation, and the door being only latched he entered. The hay-trusser deposited his basket by the font, went up the nave till he reached the altar-rails, and opening the gate entered the sacrarium, where he seemed to feel a sense of the strangeness for a moment; then he knelt upon the foot-pace.

We observe the event, which unfolds, action by action, like a story in the Bible. It has an undramatic solemnity, which arouses our feelings for Henchard. It is viewed externally. Even saying that he felt the strangeness of the place is something that an observer might see.

Summary

External narration is an ancient form of story-telling. It can be effective because we see characters (and can feel for them) as we see, and feel for, people in everyday life.

3.7   Readers and problems

The authority of the reader

Narrations, particularly first-person ones, can become problematic when we take into account the unpredictability of readers (see section 3.1). Readers are not passive and pliable.

> Readers have their own views and consequently respond to fiction in their own distinctive ways.

Readers always enjoy a degree of autonomy. They bring to any text their own attitudes, experiences and beliefs. When a reader sits down with a novel, he or she has the freedom to see, to make connections, to frame expectations and to pass judgements. There is no way that readers can be *made* to respond in a particular way. And readers change their minds: re-reading can alter judgements.

Readers have strongly differing views, particularly about characters. Jane Austen's chief character in *Mansfield Park* (1814), Fanny Price, arouses loving admiration from some readers and dismissive hostility from others. Yet, to repeat the point, reading is not merely subjective. Readers with no religious beliefs have admired John Bunyan's forceful vision of the Christian life in *The Pilgrim's Progress* (1678).

Naïve narrators

> Sometimes the very nature of the narrator requires the reader to think in terms different from those the narrator proposes.

In Mark Haddon's very successful *The Curious Incident of the Dog in the Night-time* (2003), the first-person narrator is a boy with Asperger's syndrome. This naïve, innocent and impercipient narrator neither sees nor judges as the reader does. For example, it is left to the reader to see that the narrator's father is a good man.

Disagreeing with narrators

Readers sometimes disagree with narrators. In the penultimate chapter of Jane Austen's *Northanger Abbey* (1818), the narrator tells the reader that Henry Tilney's affection for Catherine 'originated in nothing better than gratitude'. Readers might recoil against the narrator's superior tone, and they may also decide that, because Henry Tilney appeared to be fascinated by Catherine at their first meeting, the statement is questionable.

Multiple narrations

> When there are several narrators in one novel, the reader has to be sensitive to each voice, and alert to the different perspectives and judgements.

Mary Shelley's *Frankenstein* (1818) is a series of enclosed narratives, and enclosing all of them is Captain Walton's letters to his sister about a voyage into the polar regions. Within the letters is Walton's journal, the source of Victor Frankenstein's narrative of his ghastly experiment. And within Frankenstein's narrative is the story the Creature tells of his life. We make adjustments for each: Frankenstein and his Creature compete for our sympathy. We know how repelled Frankenstein is by what he has made, and we also know the pain and longing of the Creature he has made and abandoned.

Multiple narrations make the business of reading complex. In Jean Rhys's *The Wide Sargasso Sea* (1966) (a re-working of *Jane Eyre*), the narration is emotionally complex, because we are given two views of the relationship between Edward Rochester and Bertha Mason. The achievement of the narration is to give a voice to the one whom Charlotte Brontë (and subsequent readers) has silenced in the interests of the heroine, Jane Eyre.

In multiple narrations, we have to remember who knows what. In Wilkie Collins' *The Woman in White*, there is a chilling moment when, at the close of Marian Halcombe's diary, we learn that it has also been read by the man with whom she has been struggling – Count Fosco.

Epistolary novels

A traditional form of fiction that sometimes involves the complexities of multiple narration is the epistolary novel – the novel comprising a series of letters. Samuel Richardson adopted this mode in *Pamela* (1740–1) and *Clarissa* (1747–8). In the twentieth century, the epistolary mode was used by Thornton Wilder in *The Ides of March* (1948). This novel is about the assassination of Julius Caesar. Through the various letters, the reader sees the many human concerns involved in one momentous incident. The novel closes with a passage from the Roman historian Suetonius, which, unlike many of the letters, coldly recounts the killing.

Metafiction

In some recent novels, the act of narration has become the central business of the writing.

> **In metafiction, or the reflexive novel, the process of relating a tale – changes in viewpoint, shifts in tone and style – becomes the central business.**

In metafiction, narrators comment on their own writing. The most popular English work produced in this manner is John Fowles' *The French Lieutenant's Woman* (1969). He writes of how characters act independently of his wishes; he adjusts his style to imitate nineteenth-century novelists, and he provides two endings for the book. The novel becomes a kind of game played with the reader, who, in order to enjoy the work, must have a sense of the history and conventions of Victorian fiction. A term often used to describe such art is ludic, from the Latin 'to play'. Other novelists can join in the game. In Julian Barnes' *Flaubert's Parrot* (1984) there is a discussion by the first-person narrator of contemporary novelists who provide alternative endings.

Summary

Readers have a role in the act of narration. How readers respond is an inseparable element in the telling of a tale. In multiple narratives, readers need to be aware of what they know and how the viewpoint of the story shifts. The playful aspects of metafiction are one of its chief attractions.

3.8 Irony

Irony is found in poetry and drama, but it is treated here because it creates a number of effects in the relating of stories.

Irony is a matter of narration because it involves viewpoint and knowledge. It works in the following ways:

- Irony depends on viewpoint. Ironical effects occur when the reader is able to look at what is going on in the story with the awareness of the aims of the various characters and what has happened (or may very well happen).
- Irony is therefore dependent on knowledge, and consequently also on its opposite – ignorance. Irony can depend on the respective knowledge and ignorance of characters, but it must *always* depend on the knowledge of the reader.
- In irony, the reader sees more than some, or all, of the characters. The reader is percipient (able to see); the characters impercipient (unable to see).
- Being able to see more means that there is a gap between reader and character. Irony is the effect of this gap.
- Whenever there is an ironic effect, there is always a distance or discrepancy between reader and character. This means that irony is always *against* someone.
- The usual pattern of irony establishes a bond between reader and narrator/author. Even when, as occasionally happens, an irony works against the reader, a bond is established between reader and narrator/author when the reader realizes that an ironic gap has been opened up.

There are different kinds of irony, each of which is dependent on the nature of the gap between the percipient and the impercipient. We shall look at five of them. In each case, the point will be illustrated by references to Jane Austen's *Emma*.

Words and truth

Sometimes a character says something that the reader perceives as being untrue.

> **Irony is in the gap the reader sees between words and truth.**

Emma Woodhouse is a matchmaker who has decided that Mr Elton, the young vicar, is taking an interest in Harriet Smith, a pleasant but not very bright girl whom Emma is encouraging. When Harriet questions whether this can be so, Emma replies confidently: 'I cannot make a question, or listen to a question about that. It is a certainty' (Chapter 9). However, the words are not true: the reader can see that Mr Elton's interest is in Emma, so, ironically, Harriet was right to wonder whether it *was* in fact true.

Words and meaning

When a character is unaware of the real significance or implication of what he or she has said:

> **Irony occurs in the gap between what is said and the actual meaning of the words used.**

In his courtship of Emma (a courtship of which Emma is entirely unaware), Mr Elton gives Harriet a charade (a riddle), which is intended for Emma. Emma's judgement is: 'I never read one more to the purpose, certainly' (Chapter 9). Emma is right; there *is* purpose behind it, but not the one Emma supposes. The word 'read' is significant. Emma has *misread* the meaning of the words.

Intention and outcome

When a character intends one thing, but another happens:

> **The reader sees an ironic gap between intention and outcome.**

This discrepancy is often called *dramatic irony*.

When Mr Elton proposes to Emma (Chapter 15), she is shocked. This is not the outcome she had planned. The delight of the scene is that Mr Elton is also shocked to think that Emma had supposed he was interested in Harriet. The irony reveals the pride and snobbishness of both.

Appearance and reality

When a character interprets the world in one way, but the reader is led to see that this is wrong.

> **The reader is aware of an ironic gap between appearance and reality.**

Many of the numerous ironies in *Emma* stem from her interpreting the world incorrectly. Having been warned by her brother-in-law about the interest Mr Elton is taking in her, Emma reflects in Chapter 13 on how misled even the wisest can be:

> she walked on, amusing herself in the consideration of the blunders which often arise from a partial knowledge of circumstance, or the mistakes people of high pretensions to judgement are for ever falling into...

To her, Mr Elton appears to be interested in Harriet, yet although she knows we are all prone to 'blunders' (a central word in the novel) she cannot apply this insight to herself. Here, the irony exposes not only her need to see the world more clearly, but also her need for self-knowledge.

Double irony

There are moments when one irony undercuts another.

> Double irony occurs when the reader sees that a later irony has relativized an earlier one.

Because Emma's father, Mr Woodhouse, is preoccupied with his own health, he becomes the object of humour when he uses this as the sole means of judgement. Thus, when Frank Churchill – lively, gallant and slightly mysterious – visits his father, the people of Highbury all find him delightful – apart from Mr Woodhouse. When discussing the arrangements for the supper to be taken at the ball Frank is organizing, Mr Woodhouse opposes it 'on the score of health'. In Chapter 29, he discloses what he thinks of Frank:

> That young man (speaking lower) is very thoughtless. Do not tell his father, but that young man is not quite the thing. He has been opening the doors very often this evening, and keeping them open very inconsiderately.

This looks like irony against Mr Woodhouse, who can't see beyond his own very particular sense of comfort. But the plot reveals a double irony. Frank opens doors but, it is later revealed, he is not open with the people of Highbury. Irony opens up to the reader that Frank is indeed 'not quite the thing'.

Summary

Irony works through bonds of knowledge and awareness between narrator/author and reader. These bonds are occasioned by the opening of gaps between percipient reader and impercipient character.

▪ ✔ 4　Plot

4.1　Plots and stories

A plot is the sum total of a book's events, and it is, we must always remember, a literary construct.

> **A plot is the particular order in which an author has chosen to arrange the events of the tale.**

A plot is not, therefore, necessarily the same as the chronological order of events. This is the difference between a plot and a story.

> **A plot is the order of events in which they appear in a tale. A story is the chronological order in which those events would have happened.**

Plots and knowledge

Plots provide readers with knowledge. There are some things that a reader needs to know early in the tale, and other things that must be concealed until the plot requires their disclosure. Think of any plot you are familiar with and you'll see that, in very many cases, the order of events in the book is not a chronological one. In *Pride and Prejudice* (1813) we need to know that there is a tension between Mr Darcy and Mr Wickham before we learn of the events that, before the plot opened, led to their mutual hostility. In plots that depend on the discovery of secrets (and many plots do), there are some things it is necessary for the reader *not* to know. In *Jane Eyre* (1847), we must not know that Mr Rochester is married.

Summary

In order to understand how the events of a novel engage us, we need to distinguish between the chronological order (the story) and the actual order in which the reader is acquainted with the events (the plot).

4.2　Beginnings

Beginnings establish the terms of whatever fictional world the author has established. We need to know the basics: who, what, where?

What we encounter in the beginning of a novel is what can be called a *situation*. This is usually a world in which there is recognizable order. This is so even when the order is very different from ours – as in futuristic novels, say. The opening paragraphs of Philip Pullman's *Northern Lights* (1995) establishes that very particular fictional world in which each character carries around his or her own daemon.

The exposition

The beginning of a novel goes on to do more. There are certain things that a reader needs to know, all of which are expansions of 'who', 'what' and 'where'. It might take several chapters to do this. For example, it is not until Chapter 15 of *Pride and Prejudice* that it is established that the Bennet girls will not inherit their family home, that Bingley is interested in Jane, that Darcy and Elizabeth appear to be hostile, that Mr Collins is seeking a wife, and that there is tension between Darcy and Wickham.

> **The section of a plot in which the basic conditions for its development are set out is called the *exposition*.**

Very frequently, the exposition gives the reader knowledge of the past; in *Great Expectations* (1860), for example, Pip reveals why he lives with his sister.

Summary

Plots begin by establishing the conditions – the who, what and where – that will allow the reader to understand subsequent events. The section that supplies this knowledge is called the exposition.

4.3   Disjunction

Breaks, breaches, interruptions

For a plot to develop, there must be a disjunction – a break, breach, interruption, disturbance or rupture of the conditions established at the beginning. This disjunction makes possible the series of events that will constitute the plot. We can put the point briefly:

No disjunction, no plot.

An alteration in the fictional world gives the plot momentum. What starts the plot of *Jane Eyre* is her retaliation against John Reed. She has suffered his bullying, but when she retaliates the chain of events that brings her to Lowood School is initiated.

Disjunctions can come in many forms. They are sometimes prompted by a question, such as: who is the woman in white? Some kinds of disjunctions are frequently used. One is a disruptive dramatic action. In *Nicholas Nickleby* (1838), Nicholas finds Squeers' treatment of Smike intolerable, so beats him, with the result that he has to leave his job. Death very often changes the circumstances of the central character. In Angela Carter's *The Magic Toyshop* (1981) the death of Melanie's parents takes her from the country to London. A contemporary version of sudden death happens at the start of *Enduring Love* (1997), when the balloon accident interrupts Joe and Clarissa's picnic. This accident precipitates another disjunction. Joe, the first-person narrator, becomes the object of Jed Parry's desire.

Another disjunction is an unexpected meeting: Pip meets the convict in the opening pages of *Great Expectations* (1860), and in *The Great Gatsby* (1925), Nick sees a lonely figure standing by the water's edge. Sometimes, the meeting is by way of an unexpected arrival. In *Wuthering Heights* (1847), Mr Earnshaw goes to liverpool and comes back with a child – Heathcliff.

There can be several disjunctions in a plot, which means, of course, that they do not all have to occur at the beginning. Jane Eyre's disrupted wedding changes the direction of the novel about half way through.

Summary

The development of plots requires a disjunction in the fictional world, established at the beginning of a work.

4.4 Trajectory

Plots and aims

Purpose and causality usually determine plots. E. M. Forster said that to say that the King died and then the Queen died of grief is to establish a plot, because 'grief' supplied a causal connection between the two events. Novels are usually given direction and readers expectations because the central character has aims and desires. In Hardy's *Jude the Obscure* (1895), the hero wants education, and in Golding's *The Spire* (1964), Jocelyn, Dean of the Cathedral, wants to build a spire.

Plot movement

The movement of the plot can be called its *trajectory*.

'Trajectory' means the path of a moving object, so, as plots move in time, the term is appropriate to the events, the sequencing and the causes and effects of a fictional work.

'Trajectory' is a better term for plot movement than 'structure' because it does justice to the element of time, which is basic to all literature.

To say that plots move in time is not, of course, the end of the matter. There are different kinds of trajectories.

Parallels

Some plots work by parallels. The reader sees that the various plot elements are related. This usually involves juxtaposition and contrast. In *Tess of the d'Urbervilles* (1891), the heroine is courted and misused by two men, Angel and Alec. The phases of their influence are juxtaposed so that, when one leaves the scene, the other enters. They never meet. They are also contrasted. Angel, as his name suggests, is sensitive and idealistic, whereas Alec is sensual. Because they are paralleled, the reader is prompted to ask which of them treats her better.

Plots as journeys

A traditional and popular form of plot trajectory is the journey. Ancient literature such as *The Epic of Gilgamesh* (3rd millennium BC) is based on a journey searching for the secret of eternal life.

When prose fiction emerged in sixteenth-century Europe, an early form was the *picaresque*. The term is derived from 'picaro', which is Spanish for 'rogue'. Picaresque plots usually consisted of the adventures that befell a roguish servant on journeys with his master. The plot line was usually simple, and the overall purpose of the journey often vague. What mattered was what happened on the way. One thing that picaresque novels made possible was coincidence. Characters from earlier in the plot turn up, sometimes to help and sometimes to complicate matters. Miguel de Cervantes' *Don Quixote* (1605), though not exactly a picaresque novel, has many of these characteristics.

In England, Thomas Nashe's *The Unfortunate Traveller* (1594) is a very early example. Daniel Defoe's *Moll Flanders* (1722), is a first-person picaresque tale. The form allows Defoe to present a series of very vivid encounters, such as the scene in which Moll steals from a child. This event, like many in picaresque plots, is isolated from the others, and nothing actually comes of it.

The lively possibilities of picaresque can be seen in Henry Fielding's *Joseph Andrews* (1742). What makes this novel so engaging is the character of Parson Adams, a clergyman who, when in difficulties, resorts to using his fists. Mark Twain's *Huckleberry Finn* (1884) uses the form of the journey to explore both the relationship between Huck and the runaway slave, Jim, and also life in America, with its love of the showman.

The figure of the wanderer occurs as an individual motif in several novels. These novels are usually ones in which the settled community is a major feature, so wandering is seen as a sign of mental distraction. In Jane Austen's *Emma* (1816), Jane Fairfax is reported to wander by the river in her distress, and in George Eliot's *Adam Bede* (1859), Hetty wanders when she is close to mental collapse.

Summary

Because a plot moves in time, it is important to consider what drives it. Trajectory is a useful term for talking about the various ways in which plot movement occurs. Plot movement can be generated by parallels and journeys.

4.5 Features of plot movement

Looking backwards and forwards

Sometimes, in order to appreciate the significance of what is happening, we have to look backwards to previous events, and also look forward to what is going to happen. Two terms have been given to these kinds of reading: *analepsis* is looking backwards, and *prolepsis* is looking forward.

Looking backwards or forwards is something that *we* do.

The novel prompts us to do this when we realize that there is a connection between events. In fact, what we often do is to look forward *and* backwards at the same time. When we recall an earlier event that is relevant to a present one, we also look forward to the possible consequences.

William Golding's *The Spire* constantly requires us to be analeptic and proleptic. Near the beginning, Pangall, the man in charge of the maintenance of the Cathedral, complains to the Dean that the masons employed to build the spire continually make fun of him. Previous to this conversation, the Dean had remarked to himself that the workers digging the pit at the centre of the Cathedral looked like priests of some pagan religion. Later, when the foundations begin to shudder, there is a terrible riot. When the riot has died down, Pangall's broom is found, but he has disappeared. Later, the Dean realizes that he has been murdered and put into the foundations. The reader's mind might go back to the thought he had about pagan religion. The strong possibility is that Pangall has been sacrificed, placed in the earth to make the dangerous work a success.

Discoveries

Plots, particularly those in popular fiction, often turn on discoveries and revelations. In *Treasure Island* (1882), Jim Hawkins, hiding in the apple barrel, overhears Long John Silver's plot to take over the ship. In the *Poetics* (c. 335 BC), Aristotle defined one of the crucial moments in plot movement as *anagnorisis* – discovery or recognition. This is the moment when a character, usually the central one, becomes aware of what has been happening. Anagnorisis can occur with new knowledge (we must remember that plots are concerned with knowledge) or when what has been familiar takes on a new significance (see also Chapter 20, section 20.2). *The Spire* works with several moments of discovery.

The Dean has sensed something about the way in which the chief mason and Pangall's wife look at each other, but it is only when he overhears them in private conversation that he realizes they are lovers. Similarly, it is only later that he understands that Pangall's talk about being the last of his family means that Pangall is impotent.

Reversal

Aristotle also stressed that plots work through reversals. His term for this is *peripeteia*, or, as it is sometimes written, *peripety*. Sometimes at the moment of discovery, the plot turns round, often with ironic force (see Chapter 20, section 20.2). Moments of reversal can be complex. In Dickens' *Great Expectations*, the return of the convict occasions Pip's discovery that his benefactor is not, as he has led himself to believe, Miss Havisham, and that the beautiful Estella, Miss Havisham's adopted daughter, is not intended for him. He has always felt inferior to Estella, but later a plot discovery reveals that she is even more deeply implicated in the world of criminality than he is.

Summary

Plots are so devised that readers look backwards and forwards to other events. The movement of the plot usually involves a moment of discovery, and this often results in the reversal of the plot.

4.6 Plot incidents and materials

Thematic strands

Themes are inseparable from characters and plots. Characters' aims drive plots, and the events enact themes. For example, in *Pride and Prejudice*, Elizabeth Bennet has allowed herself to be blinkered by her pride, and in her pride has rejected Mr Darcy's proposal. It is not until she thinks about the letter she receives from him that she realizes: 'Till this moment, I never knew myself' (Chapter 36). This is her moment of discovery, and the moment that the plot is reversed. Rather than turning away from Darcy, she starts the long movement towards him. In this way, the movement of the plot enacts the theme of self-knowledge.

Parabolic moments

Sometimes a moment in the unfolding of the plot works with the force of a parable to illuminate the reader's understanding of characters and actions. There is a scene in *Tess of the d'Urbervilles* (1891), in which the sleepwalking

Angel carries Tess and lays her in a medieval coffin. As he does so he mutters that she is dead. The moment is parabolic in at least two ways. Because he has discovered what her past was like, she is dead to him. Also, it shows how he, misled by the idea he has formed of her, has sleepwalked into a marriage based on his own false image of her.

Re-using plots

Material for plots and individual scenes is often drawn from earlier works. This should not surprise us. Literature is built on conventions, so plot ideas are often repeated. For example, Bunyan's *The Pilgrim's Progress* (1678) stands behind *Jane Eyre*. The image of a solitary individual working out her own 'salvation' in a world that is often hostile and in which there is no permanent abode owes much to Bunyan's lonely and tempted pilgrim, who follows the straight and narrow highway to the Celestial City.

Novelists have gone to Shakespeare for entire plots and individual scenes. *The Great Gatsby*, for example, is plotted on *Romeo and Juliet* (1597). Once Gatsby has kissed Daisy, his life is a romantic pursuit. The image of him standing at the water's edge gesturing to the green light at the end of her dock is an image of a man living out the high romantic style of the courtly lover, spellbound, as was Romeo, by the beauty of his beloved. Its dependence on *Romeo and Juliet* reminds the reader that *The Great Gatsby* is chiefly a love story. In *The Mayor of Casterbridge* (1886), the scene in which Henchard consults Wide-O (Chapter 26), the man who can predict the weather, is modelled on Macbeth's resorting to the Witches in order to know what his future will be.

Summary

Plots enact themes. There are several literary sources of plot material, and these can be used in a number of ways to enforce the thematic significances of novels.

4.7 Endings

Neat conclusions

Plots move towards an ending or closure. Perhaps the difference between fiction and everyday living is that the former is capable of a neat conclusion. Readers experience the satisfaction of closure; they know what has happened and, in some cases, what will happen to the characters in the future. Narrators sometimes draw the reader's attention to the fact that the plot is being brought to a close. In the final chapter of *Northanger Abbey* (1818), the narrator observes that readers 'will see in the tell-tale compression of the pages before them, that we are all hastening together to perfect felicity'.

A conclusion is a feature of Victorian fiction. In Dickens' *Hard Times* (1854), for example, the last pages are taken up with what Louisa might imagine happening in the future, accompanied by the remarks of the narrator as to whether these things would come to pass.

The climax

The close of a novel often follows the climax, in which the plot reaches its fulfilment. Climaxes can be of many kinds and can occur in different places, though all of them, to be a climax, must lead to the close. Climaxes can be dramatic changes or changes of heart and mind. Two examples from Jane Austen bring this out. In *Northanger Abbey*, the climax is Catherine's ejection from the Abbey. This reversal – the welcome guest becomes the unwanted stranger – precipitates the quarrel between Henry and his father, and Henry's visit to Fullerton, where he proposes to Catherine. In *Emma*, however, the climax (Chapter 47) is internal. Emma reflects sadly on the mischief she has caused, and then 'It darted through her, with the speed of an arrow, that Mr. Knightley must marry no one but herself!' Cupid's arrow is a moment of clarity, an anagnorisis. Once Emma has seen this, the novel can move to its close.

Leaving can have about it a note of finality. It is a kind of death. Michael Henchard dies at the end of *The Mayor of Casterbridge*, but his leaving is the point at which the plot climaxes. *Frankenstein* (1818) climaxes with the exit of the Creature. His maker is dead, and there is nothing left for him. The Arctic wastes seem an appropriate close on his now meaningless life.

Forms of climax and closure

Death is, of course, a final exit. In *Wuthering Heights*, the moment that brings about the conditions for the close is the death of Heathcliff. He is found at the window at which the spectral Catherine knocked at the start of the novel. *The Great Gatsby* effectively comes to an end with the body of Gatsby in the swimming pool. His is a death by water in a novel that is dependent on T. S. Eliot's *The Waste Land* (1922), a post-First World War poem in which the fourth section is called *Death by Water*. Illness can be a climax, particularly when the sufferer recovers. The fever scene was popular in nineteenth-century fiction. Because of the gravity of the illness, certain social regulations are relaxed, and the sick room becomes a place of meeting and a space for honest speech. The recovery of Marianne in Jane Austen's *Sense and Sensibility* (1811) makes possible several of the happy arrangements that mark the close of the novel. For example, it allows Colonel Brandon to talk to Marianne about shared enthusiasms.

Traditionally, death leads to judgement, and so it is in many novels. The ends of novels often work as judgement on the characters and their actions. In *The Scarlet Letter*, the climax comes very close to the end. Dimmesdale's guilt is exposed, and in being exposed, he is freed from the guilt. His exposure and death echo the beginning of the novel, when Hester emerges from gaol into a life in which, by wearing the scarlet letter, she is marked out publicly as a sinner.

The Scarlet Letter opens and closes with references to the trial. The trial is a popular climax and close in English fiction, probably because it is the enactment of what readers feel should happen at the end of a novel – the judgement of the characters. It has also become a fitting close of plays, films and television serials. In both novel and film, the trial in *To Kill a Mockingbird* (1960) is crucial.

In *Adam Bede* (1859), the climax is a trial scene in which not only Hetty is judged but also Adam, who testifies on her behalf. It is the judgement of Adam because it tests his moral character. Because he is seen to be faithful to her, the reader sees that he is worthy of Dinah, the woman he eventually marries.

Denouement and resolution

Denouement is (originally) a French word, meaning 'untying'. When a plot has depended on the interweaving of multiple strands, the denouement unties the knots. With the denouement, we know who is who, how they stand in relation to one other, and why. Sometimes the tensions in a plot are reconciled; in particular, love and money. It is interesting to observe the degree to which Jane Austen's heroines are successful in both love and riches. In *Sense and Sensibility*, Elinor Dashwood will never be as rich as her sister, though Elinor marries the only man she has ever loved.

'Resolution' is the word we use for the feeling that things are settled, either by events or by a fulfilment of the themes. Sometimes, when we are wondering what a work is about, a consideration of how it closes helps us to see its thematic significance. At the close of *The Great Gatsby*, Nick, standing at the water's edge (the place where he first saw Gatsby) sees in his imagination America as it was when Dutch sailors first saw it: 'the last and greatest of all human dreams'. This dream of a new land, as promising and inviting as a woman's body – 'a fresh, green breast of the new world' – is linked in Nick's imagination with Gatsby's wonder and his high, romantic pursuit of Daisy. What Gatsby found in Daisy is what the early settlers found in America.

Summary

The end of a story follows from its climax. Ends can involve the death or the exit of central characters. Ends often pass judgement, and many of the issues and feelings are resolved. Themes are sometimes particularly evident at the close of a novel.

4.8 The short story

There is some sense in treating the short story under the general heading of plot, because what often characterizes it is the handling of plot movement.

Economy

The writer of short stories has to make every sentence count. This is why short stories often work with a symbolic force. Several meanings emerge within the economy of a few sentences. Short stories are not unlike poetry: multiple meanings are compressed into a few words. In Katherine Mansfield's 'The Life of Ma Parker' from *The Garden Party* (1922), an elderly cleaning lady arrives for work the day after her grandson's funeral. She looks through the kitchen window:

> Out of the smudgy little window you could see an immense expanse of sad-looking sky, and wherever there were clouds they looked very worn, old clouds, frayed at the edges, with holes in them, or dark stains like tea.

That sentence evokes the atmosphere of a dreary day *and* what Ma Parker is feeling – the sad sky reflects her immense sadness. It also indicates the narrow scope of her life (as if seen through a small window), her own old and frayed self and the dark stain can be read as the death of her grandson.

The basic elements of a short story are made more prominent by the brevity of the tale. Beginnings have to bring the reader into the business of the plot, set the tone, arouse expectations and anticipate the close. The disjunction often occurs at the very start. Daphne du Maurier's story 'The Birds' (1952) opens with a sudden change in the weather, a condition that impels the birds to attack people.

Narrative

In short stories, authors often choose a narrative mode that allows privileged access into the mind of a single character. James Thurber's 'The Secret Life of Walter Mitty' (1939) depends on the reader seeing how Walter, a reader of pulp fiction, escapes his unremarkable life by fantasizing. As he carries out his hum-drum tasks – shopping for dog biscuits and parking his car – his mind is casting him as the hero of a popular tale.

Themes and epiphanies

Narrative is inseparable from themes. The climax of the tale is often the moment when the significance of the action emerges. This is often in the form of an illumination that comes to one of the characters. The character sees something, perhaps for the first time. The word that James Joyce used for these moments of insight was 'epiphany'. This is a religious word meaning the manifesting of God's shining presence. Joyce used it to refer to any situation in which 'the penny drops', and we see something vividly and splendidly.

D. H. Lawrence spells out a moment of illumination at the close of 'Odour of Chrysanthemums' (written 1909). A miner is brought home dead, and his wife sees what she had never seen before – the wonder of his existence, the luminous truth that he was himself and nobody else. The moment is terrible yet strangely hopeful:

> She had denied him what he was – she saw it now. She had refused him as himself. And this had been her life, and his life. She was grateful to death, which had restored the truth. And she knew she was not dead.

The simple narrative style (all those 'ands' is reminiscent of the way the Bible tells stories) speaks plainly of life and death. Perhaps we should think of the dead Christ cradled in the arms of his mother – a death that brings life.

Katherine Mansfield's epiphanies are more numerous and more subtle than Lawrence's. Sometimes, as in 'Her First Ball' (*The Garden Party*), the epiphany belongs to the reader. We see that, in the overwhelming pleasure of the dance, Leila forgets the swift and troubling passage of time. Sometimes the epiphany is felt but cannot be articulated. In 'The Garden Party' Laura encounters death when she is shown into a room, where a young man who has died in an accident is laid out. She feels he is 'So remote, so peaceful.' It seems inexplicable to her that, amid the bustle of the party, a young man is lying dead in such peace. At the end she tries to express her emotions:

> 'Isn't life,' she stammered, 'isn't life' – But what life was she couldn't explain.

The epiphany is real yet inexpressible.

Types of short story

There are several different kinds of short story. Some of Katherine Mansfield's are 'mood pieces'. In 'Bank Holiday' (*The Garden Party*), for example, the scene is rendered with pinpoint clarity. Events hardly matter; its significance lies in the arresting images. In *The Bloody Chamber and other Stories* (1979), Angela Carter rewrites traditional fairy stories, either to realize a meaning latent in the tale or to give, usually by way of the close, an alternative meaning such as presenting the wolf not as savage but as the embodiment of a satisfying animality.

Although there are several very successful crime novelists – Colin Dexter, P. D. James, Donna Leon, Ruth Rendell – the short story is often the chosen form of detective fiction. There are four Sherlock Holmes novels, but by common consent the shorter fiction is a better form for showing the art of deduction. In a story such as 'Silver Blaze' (1895), the very economy of the genre allows Conan Doyle to puzzle the reader with many apparently unconnected details, until Holmes' eagle mind seizes on what is significant and assembles the various clues into a consistent narrative of crime and death. One of these clues is something that never happened – 'the curious incident of the dog in the night-time'.

The thriller works by creating a tense situation, in which the life of the main character is threatened. An early example is Wilkie Collins' 'A Terribly Strange Bed' (1852), a nightmarish tale in which the protagonist (the central figure), disabled by drugs, lies on a bed watching the tester (the top) descending on him.

In the ghost story, characterization does not matter quite so much as in some short fiction. What does matter is an event (usually near the close) that generates mystery. In *Ghost Stories of an Antiquary* (1931) by M. R. James, the climax is a dark epiphany, the emergence of something terrifying and inexplicable. It can be unnervingly nasty in a brilliantly unexpected way. This is the eerie climax of 'The Rose Garden':

> and she turned and stared at seeing what at first she took to be a Fifth of November mask peeping out among the bushes. She looked closer. It was not a mask. It was a face – large, smooth and pink.

The force of 'pink' shows that James makes ordinary words uncomfortable.

Summary

Short stories are of various kinds. Their economy often results in writing that works on several levels of meaning. The end often involves a moment of illumination, called an epiphany.

▼ 5   Settings

5.1   What readers remember

What often sticks in readers' memories are places, locations and settings. The opening of *Great Expectations* (1860), for example, has an impact of its own, in addition to the drama of young Pip meeting the convict (see Chapter 2, section 2.7).

Some books, including those set in public examinations, have setting as the main focus. For example, Flora Thompson's *Lark Rise to Candleford* (1954) is concerned chiefly with village community. Edmund Blunden's record of the First World War, *Undertones of War* (1928), has a central figure, the mild and slightly detached Blunden, but it is what he sees about him that forms the main interest of the book. He shows us pastoral landscapes despoiled by bombs, deserted villages, damaged buildings, graveyards churned up by shelling, and tall trees that with the addition of a ladder have becomes reconnaissance points.

The enjoyment of settings

Fiction sometimes strains our credulity. But if we find some events difficult to take seriously, we might still read with enjoyment because the settings engage us. Hardy is a good example of this. Sometimes, we cannot believe all those chance meetings, and many readers have refused to take so much ill-luck seriously. But we recall Hardy's landscapes.

Scenes can be enjoyed for their own sake. The imaginative presentation of the constituent details often delights readers. After Henchard's drunkenness at the opening of *The Mayor of Casterbridge* (1886), he looks at the landscape (Chapter 2) that, in the weariness of his journey, he had hardly noticed:

> he now beheld it as a new thing. It exhibited itself as the top of an open down, bounded on one extreme by a plantation, and approached by a winding road. At the bottom stood the village which lent its name to the upland and the annual fair that was held thereon. The spot stretched downward into valleys, and onward to other uplands, dotted with barrows, and trenched with the remains of prehistoric forts.

The passage is like English landscape painting. The eye takes in the wide sweep of down, bounded by the plantation and the winding road. And then, as in looking at a picture, smaller details become evident. This is a landscape with a long history of human habitation – the barrows where the dead are buried, and old forts 'trenched' into the landscape, a verb expressive of the tenacious purposefulness of human activity. The reader can hear in the writing a voice frequently sounded in Hardy. He is the local historian or topographer, the one who dwells on the details of a place and draws out the significances of the interplay between nature and humanity.

Hardy also links the landscape and the viewer. Henchard sees the landscape afresh, just as he must see his life anew. He has come along, and will now continue to travel on, 'a winding road'.

Summary

Settings are often the most memorable aspects of a novel. They are engaging and have links with characters.

5.2 The functions of settings

Setting and action

Jane Eyre receives two proposals: one from Rochester and the other from Rivers. The nature of the proposal and the proposer are evident in their respective settings. Rochester's warm and romantic nature is present in the dark night and the great over-arching tree beneath which they sit (Chapter 23), while Rivers' proposal is a summons to duty: he needs a wife for the mission field. The setting is a barren moor with a cold stream falling on hard rock (Chapter 34).

In *Far from the Madding Crowd* (1874), there is a scene charged with sexual danger in which Troy demonstrates sword practice to a mesmerized Bathsheba (Chapter 28). The place is enclosed – 'The pit was a saucer-shaped concave, naturally formed' – and the bottom is inviting – 'a thick flossy carpet of moss and grass intermingled, so yielding that the foot was half-buried within it'. It is a place formed for seduction – secret, apart, soft. The setting gives us the significance of the action that takes place in it. Bathsheba is won over by Troy even though she knows he is dangerously unreliable: 'Bathesheba's adventurous spirit was beginning to find some grains of relish in these highly novel proceedings'. Both setting and writing about Bathsheba's sense of adventure indicate the parallel between this scene in the hollow and a first sexual encounter.

Setting and mood

Scenes can also enact a character's mood. In *Tess of the d'Urbervilles* (1891), Tess's journey to the Vale of the Great Dairies (Chapter 6) opens in the spring:

> On a thyme-scented, bird-hatching morning in May, between two and three years after her return from Tantridge – silent, reconstructive years for Tess Durbeyfield – she left home for the second time.

The words have the spring of poetry. The anapaestic opening – 'Ŏn ă thý́me-sčentĕd, bírd-hatchĭng mórniňg ĭn Máy' – carries the reader on in hopeful expectation. That is Tess's mood. As the pulse of life stirs in her – a later passage speaks of 'The irresistible, universal, automatic tendency to find sweet pleasure somewhere' – Tess is buoyant. Hardy is not exactly saying that Tess's mood makes her see the landscape with a particular emotional colouring. It is more a case of the *reader* recognizing the appropriateness of the one to the other.

Setting and plot movement

Settings can be appropriate to the stages of plot movement. The opening pages of *The Adventures of Huckleberry Finn* (1884) show Huck confined either by the well-intentioned efforts of the Widow to civilize him, or the violence and neglect of his father. But when, with Jim, he launches out on the great river, the scope of the novel appropriately widens. Huck feels free, and there is, correspondingly, a zest and fluency in Twain's writing. The scenes evoking the majesty and solemnity of the river mark an important change in the direction of the novel.

Setting and the situation of characters

Novelists also use settings to indicate how characters are situated. When Tess is abandoned by Angel, she works in the fields at Flintcombe Ash, a place 'uncared for either by itself or its lord' (Chapter 43). Those words express the analogy between the landscape and the situation of Tess. Like the landscape, Tess is not being cared for by Angel – her lord.

The dreariness of her circumstances is shown in the landscape:

the whole field was in colour a desolate drab; it was a complexion without features, as if a face, from chin to brow, should be only an expanse of skin.

Both the field and Tess's life are drab. It is a world without love, a world with the eerily disturbing anonymity of a face consisting only of skin.

Dickens gives symbolic force to his settings. Towards the end of *Hard Times* (1854), Stephen Blackpool, Dickens' representative worker, falls into a disused mine – the Old Hell Shaft. In searching for him, Rachael and Sissy find 'the brink of a black ragged chasm hidden by the thick grass' (Chapter 34). The setting stands for his situation. Chasms divide. Industry has divided people and made some of them victims. The pit stands for the plight of those who, like the mine, have been exploited and abandoned.

Setting and the author's outlook

Settings can display an author's views and judgements. One of Hardy's pre-occupations is the place of figures in a landscape. Many of his landscapes, like paintings, include figures. This is how he presents the workers in the fields of Flintcombe Ash:

> The sky wore, in another colour, the same likeness; a white vacuity of countenance with the lineaments gone. So these two upper and nether visages confronted each other all day long, the white face looking down on the brown face, and the brown face looking up at the white face, without anything standing between them but the two girls crawling over the surface of the former like flies.

Hardy presents his understanding of the natural world and people's relationship to it. He was troubled by his understanding but he had to accept it. Nature is indifferent to us, as indifferent as the blank stares of the faces of earth and sky. We are like flies crawling over its surface, and in the scheme of things we have no more significance than flies (see Chapter 49, Section 49.2).

Opening and closing scenes can give a writer's view of things. The opening scene of Dickens' *Bleak House* (1852) conveys his criticism of of the legal system through the image of thick fog. The law fogs-in the nation. The jungle of Conrad's *Heart of Darkness* (1902) is a symbol of the darkness in us all – our weakness and our inclination to abandon all moral restraint. This emerges through successive passages on the density of the jungle, and is confirmed at the close when we see the brutality and callous indifference to life that Kurtz has brought.

Summary

Settings can bring out the significance of actions. They can match characters' moods and indicate a new stage in the movement of the plot. Settings also indicate the characters' situations and enact authors' outlooks.

▪ ⌄ 6 The Scope of the Novel

6.1 Fictional worlds

A fictional world is a made world. It is the work of an author. In making it, the author has done a number of things: chosen features, arranged the features in a particular order, heightened some of them and subdued others, included some things and omitted others. To reiterate the point:

A fictional world is a world that has been put together.

But we may want to ask: what has this world been made with? What are the things that have been included or omitted, and what is it that has been shaped and edited?

The answer to these questions comes in two stages. The first, and shortest, answer is that the fictional world is made of words. This is true, but we need to be more specific, which leads to our second answer.

Novels and the world

A novel is about the world. That is a very sweeping statement, so some qualifications are necessary. The world about us is the world of human interactions. The way we engage with each other, what we want from each other, and what we hope and fear for each other is the stuff of the novel. Novels are social; they are about people. Yet they are not about people in the way in which, say, a television documentary or an article in a magazine is about people. People in novels are people, but they are not the same as the ones we meet every day. They are fictional; they have been made up.

Making worlds

A fictional work is not a transcription of the world we know outside the book. It is not reportage. But we do recognize characters in books as being people, so there must be some links. One link is that both the fictional and the everyday worlds are, in some senses, made. Our ideas about the society in which we live consist of notions that have been formed.

Summary

A novel is a world made in words which has some links with the world we know outside literature.

6.2   Realism

Realism is the name we give to art that faithfully reproduces the world with which we are familiar. Often, when we encounter realism, we just accept that what is described is the sort of thing that happens in daily life.

Yet realism is a genre. It is a way of writing. Like any other sort of fiction (science fiction, for example) it has been put together. It is the work of an author. What, then, makes it appear real? The answer must be that

> There is an implicit agreement between author and reader
> that the book is to be read as though it were referring to an
> actual world with which the reader might be acquainted.

This is still the case when the novel is set in what is now the past. For example, Arthur Morrison wrote about late-nineteenth-century London. We no longer live in the late nineteenth century, but his novels can still be read as being about what life was like at that time. We still keep our agreement with the author. In fact, realism exists, as any other fictional world does – it is the product of careful selection, concentration and heightening. We take realism as being about the world we live in, or might live in. When we read it that way we supply and infer what is absent in the narrative. If a character goes on a train journey but there is no mention of purchasing a ticket we assume that this took place, not that the character is dishonest.

Realism does not attempt to be value free. It is not an objective view of how things are. In asking the reader to take the world within the novel as being real, the author is also showing what he or she thinks the world is like. This is what a closely related mode, naturalism, does.

Naturalism

Naturalism rests on a philosophical belief that the world is all there is and, consequently, should be understood as an entirely natural thing. There is no reference to God or spiritual reality. The naturalistic novel is French in origin (Emile Zola being its most famous writer), but English writers such George Gissing and George Moore are broadly naturalistic. Yet naturalistic novels invite the reader to regard what is presented as real. The fact that a specific view is taken of reality does not prevent the author from making this implicit invitation.

Summary

Realism is a special way of writing, so a realistic novel is not a direct transcription of life. Realism works through the reader accepting an implicit invitation to treat the book as being about a world that he or she might be familiar with outside the pages of the book.

6.3   Departing from realism

A moment's reflection shows us that, although television presents itself as an unmediated slice of life, it is no such thing. Even 'fly-on-the-wall' documentaries are edited. What we see depends on where the camera has been placed.

Fiction departs from our sense of everyday life in a number of ways. The elegant wit of Elizabeth Bennet is admirable rather than realistic. Dickens' novels, often thought of as exploring the realities of Victorian life, have what has been called a 'dream-like' intensity.

Time

Sometimes time is adjusted or displaced. When, for example, does *Tess of the d'Urbervilles* (1891) take place? It is a world in which new and old styles of farming exist side by side. It is a world of traditional folk customs *and* one in which young men read advanced books.

Sometimes the displacement of time is very radical. There are books in which characters have ideas that were not around at the time in which the novel is set. In Barry Unsworth's *Sacred Hunger* (1992), a late-eighteenth-century doctor is supposed to have worked out the principles of Darwinian natural selection.

A fictional world is sometimes separated from a non-fictional one by making a disturbing change in the familiar. *Nineteen Eighty-Four* (1949) starts with a clock striking thirteen.

Fantasy and magic realism

In the nineteenth century, authors began to write novels and short stories in which there was a blurring of the natural and the non-natural. Edgar Allan Poe's *Tales of Mystery and Imagination* (1845) launches the reader into a world in which, to take one example, Death can suddenly make an appearance at a dance ('The Masque of the Red Death'). The effect of this literature is that the reader doesn't know how things in the story are to be explained. It is not, for example, clear whether the tale is a kind of allegory of psychological realities or whether the book is dealing with a world in which causality is not always at work. Science fiction is an interesting variation on this idea. Is there a reason behind the strange goings on, or is the mode of science fiction merely a way of making fantastic worlds, as in, say, Douglas Adams' *The Hitchhiker's Guide to the Galaxy* (1979)?

Recently, the term '*magic realism*' has been coined for novels that suddenly depart from the familiar. There is something fascinating and bracing about a work which is apparently set in a recognizable world but in which the characters suddenly fly or, as in Gabriel Garcia Marquez' *One Hundred Years of Solitude* (1967), ascend into heaven. Magical realism is usually thought of as dating from the 1950s but, in England, the novels of T. F. Powys share something of the same spirit. In the most famous, *Mr Weston's Good Wine* (1928), God visits a village in the form of a man who sells wine that heals all human hurts. If there is a difference, it is that Powys gives us a world which, in a more than metaphorical sense, he holds to be true.

Mixed worlds

In Jane Austen's *Mansfield Park* (1814), the narration is a retrospective account of the important events in Fanny Price's childhood and young adulthood. The writing is selective, and the effect is of a recognizable social reality. But with the visit to Sotherton, a large country estate, the mode of writing changes. When some of the characters choose to wander off by themselves, they come to a gate barring the way to the wilderness – a wilder part of the garden. Two characters want to go beyond the gate, although it is locked and neither have the authority to go any further. The gate stands for the limits that morality sets upon behaviour. (And what might the wilderness stand for?) The desire to go beyond the gate can be read as an inclination to break moral codes.

We might use two terms to indicate the way the gate generates meanings. One is *allegory*, a story in which each feature stands in a one-to-one relationship with elements in a system of belief. The other is *metonymy*. Originally, metonymy meant the substitution of one name for another, but now it tends to be used for the process by which we link one thing with another. Modern fiction is often metonymic. Michael Frayn's *Spies* (2000) works by inviting the reader to see links between the different sorts of spying (several characters observe others) and enclosure (there are tunnels and fears of coffins).

Summary

Most fiction departs from what we think of as real. Characters talk with polished fluency, time is shifted, settings change surprisingly and fictional worlds are mixed.

6.4   The personal and the public

There is often a tension among English writers between the personal and the public. Some writers (and, of course, readers) tend to settle for what is personal; they write about moral growth, self-discovery and love. Yet even so, the public world – responsibility, social influence, class – is present.

Social and political readings

In order to see that novels engage with social and political issues, we have to widen the range of those terms. If we do, we can see the behaviour of individual characters in social and political terms.

> When we become aware of the attitudes and assumptions that colour a character's conduct, we are in touch with outlooks and values that shape social and political behaviour.

The nineteenth- and early-twentieth-century novel is political in that it addresses the beliefs that shape social change. We might ask what beliefs are evident in a novelist's presentation of society.

In *Mansfield Park*, for example, there is a sharp polarity (too sharp for some readers) between Fanny Price, who lives by received codes of conduct and values the traditions of the home she is privileged to enjoy, and the Crawfords, who hold lightly to received values in order to gratify personal whims and desires. In that polarity there is the political opposition between the politics of inherited responsibility and a newer politics of choice, enterprise, self-fulfilment and, surely in Jane Austen's view, indulgence.

Summary

Although personal issues are often focused on in novels, we should not forget that the social world is very often a major preoccupation of the English novel.

6.5 Social issues

Thematic locations

A writer's interest in the social world is often evident in locations. Locations can be read thematically. Dickens' subject might be said to be the life of London (see Chapter 51, section 50.3). There he found a sprawling and rapidly changing world that engaged his imagination. Significantly, several of his novels – for example, *Oliver Twist* (1837) and *Great Expectations* (1860) – start in the countryside and then move to London. Dickens was not the first author to do this. In the eighteenth century, Henry Fielding and Tobias Smollett take their characters to London. F. Scott Fitzgerald's New York is even more centrally thematic: in the second chapter of *The Great Gatsby* (1925), Nick travels into New York past the valley of ashes – the symbolic dumping ground of the city's material (and, by implication, human) waste.

Urban and rural

There is an ancient contrast between urban (town) and rural (country) life. This goes back to Latin literature. Interestingly, the assumptions about life in each area have not changed much: the town is exciting but dangerous, whereas country life is peaceful though limited. Today, most novels are urban. The countryside, as at the beginning of *Enduring Love* (1997), is there as a foil to the urban world in which many scenes are located.

The English novel has found the town stimulating. In the nineteenth century there was a tradition of the northern novel. Elizabeth Gaskell sets *Mary Barton* (1848) in the industrial north, and Charlotte Brontë also sets *Shirley* (1849) in an urban and industrialized society. Thomas Hardy is an interesting case of someone who tried the urban setting but realized that the world about which he could write with authority and imagination was the rural one. Yet it is clear that he is not writing for a rural readership. The careful evocations and explanations of rural life show that his intended reader is urban. Hardy might be said to have established the genre of the rural novel. Many of the writers in that tradition – Adrian Bell, Constance Holme, Eden Phillpotts – are not well known, but Mary Webb, who deals with the mining areas of rural Shropshire, is still read, and *Precious Bane* (1924) appears on A-level syllabuses, as does Stella Gibbons' parody of Mary Webb – *Cold Comfort Farm* (1932).

Understanding society

Novels present understandings of society. Elizabeth Gaskell shows that people in northern industrial towns are influenced by the kind of work they do and the economic system that sustains it. In Chapter 8 of *North and South* (1855), she presents the Hale family, who are from the south, adjusting to life in the aptly named Milton – the town of mills. Mr Hale looks for work as a private tutor, but education in Milton is shaped by the need to produce industrial workers. In Chapter 8 the narrator says that the boys he met

> were mostly of the age when many boys would be still at school, but, according to the prevalent, and apparently well-founded notions of Milton, to make a lad into a good tradesman he must be caught young, and acclimated to the life of the mill, or office, or warehouse.

The writing shifts from the narrator's (or Mr Hale's) voice to the viewpoint of the people of Milton, who want to 'make a lad into a good tradesman'. Their desire to make boys fit for the life in the mill, office or warehouse results from living in a society that is shaped economically by industry.

Novelists are not sociologists, but they share some of their material – and in some cases their outlook. When a novelist such as Elizabeth Gaskell shows the intimate links between money, work and values it would not be wrong to talk about her having a sociological imagination; that is, she presents characters as being formed by the circumstances of their social existence.

The condition of England

Sometimes novels that present the social realities that shape the nation's life are called 'condition of England' novels. These novels seek to show what the nation is like. Sometimes the issue is debated, as in the famous conversation in Benjamin Disraeli's *Sybil* (1845) when a discussion about the state of the nation leads to the declaration that England is two nations – the rich and the poor. Many of Dickens' novels, particularly the middle and later ones – *Bleak House* (1852), *Little Dorrit* (1855), *Great Expectations* (1860), *Our Mutual Friend* (1864) – can be said to explore what the nation is like now. Significantly, a word that is often used in Victorian novels is 'today'. In the late twentieth century, something of this spirit can be found in the novels of Kingsley Amis, Malcolm Bradbury and David Lodge. To take examples from each, Amis's *Lucky Jim* (1954), Bradbury's *The History Man* (1975) and Lodge's *Nice Work* (1988) are all set in universities. Amis explores the possibilities of the genre and in doing so reveals a merry irreverence about established institutions. Bradbury presents a fascinated critique (is Howard hero or villain?) of a particular kind of social thinking that, at one time, was popular in universities. Lodge's novel is explicitly a 'condition of England' novel, because he relates university thinking to the economic world that, through taxes, supports the work of the literary theorist who is the central character.

Summary

Though there is a tradition of the rural novel, many novelists engage with urban life, sometimes seeking to show how the social world forms the characters they present. This 'sociological' investigation leads to an interest in what the nation is like.

6.6　Money

Money is social. At the beginning of *North and South*, Margaret Hale is made to feel less important than her rich cousin through the elegance of the latter's clothes. Margaret is first asked to fetch some Indian shawls and then to act as 'a sort of block for the shawls', a block being a wooden model upon which garments were displayed. Margaret is turned round to display her cousin's wealth.

The uncertain treatment of wealth

Margaret acting as a 'block' encapsulates with vivid exactitude the social distinctions of wealth. Sometimes, however, Elizabeth Gaskell is less precise about the sources of wealth. What exactly goes on in the factories of Milton? The problems of an industrial society also puzzle her. She is interested in the disruption of production and the talk of strikes, though she can't imagine an economic solution. In Dickens there is an imaginative engagement with the basis of wealth – the factories in *Hard Times* (1854) and the dust-heaps in *Our Mutual*

Friend – but it looks as if it is the visual appeal of factories and mountains of muck rather than economic processes that interests him.

In novels it is often the fact of wealth that is important. Fitzgerald, like his narrator, seems both attracted and repelled by Gatsby's wealth. What that wealth does – the lavish parties – is very prominent in the novel, but we are never sure where it comes from. This is, in part, deliberate. The hints of the black market are there to qualify Gatsby's glamour. Yet if we look elsewhere, there is a silence about wealth. What exactly is the origin of Tom's money?

Money and plot movement

Wealth is a motive in human behaviour. We think of *Wuthering Heights* (1847) as a love story, but it might be described more accurately as a story in which disappointed love seeks wealth as a substitute. Heathcliff cannot have Cathy, so he seeks to possess all that belonged to the man who, as he sees it, took Cathy from him.

Money and morality

There is a moral tradition that teaches us that wealth is a snare. In George Eliot's parable-like novel, *Silas Marner* (1861), the central figure is consumed by wealth, until he is rescued from himself by the golden glow of a child's hair. This moral tradition is probably present in the suicide of Merdle in Dickens' *Little Dorrit*. In death, Merdle's (Chapter 61) compose is reduced to just 'a heavily-made man, with an obtuse head, and coarse, mean, common features'. Soon the truth spreads; Merdle made his wealth by 'Forgery and Robbery'. The physical coarsening is a revelation of his economic corruption. Perhaps Dickens recaptures something of the stuff of tragedy: wealth destroys because it is the material manifestation of self-destructive pride and ambition.

Money and conclusions

Money is a useful way of bringing a plot to its close. The good can be given the comforts and securities of wealth. Elizabeth Bennet marries a very rich man. Interestingly, Jane Eyre comes into money but that is before she marries the man she loves.

Summary

Wealth has many uses in literature. The visual manifestation of production and the lavish display of material goods is imaginatively engaging to many authors. In some novels there is also a more sober recognition that wealth corrupts. Wealth is also used as a reward at the close of a novel.

6.7 Debate

The need to talk

The need to talk, to debate, to exchange ideas is frequently presented as one of the essentials of society. Elinor Dashwood, in Jane Austen's *Sense and Sensibility* (1811), needs intelligent talk, and shows that in conversation a woman can be equal to men.

In later novels, the issues of the day are debated through conversations and narratorial summaries. There is talk of strikes, often passionate, in *North and South*. Several major issues, such as conflicts between masters and men and the fate of social outcasts, are dramatized in Margaret Hale's conversations.

Charity is a difficult issue. John Thornton, the factory owner, is pleased that the men want to organize their own canteen, and he refuses to offer money precisely because he doesn't want the enterprise to become a charity. Perhaps, given the emphasis on individual motivation in the English novel, it is inevitable that talk about these problems ends with solutions that are personal rather than economic. The narrator states in Chapter 50 that when men are brought 'face to face', they begin to recognize that 'we have all of us one human heart'. The quotation is from Wordsworth. Its liberal generosity – we have more that unites than divides us – is the conclusion that the debate in the novel comes to. The way out of industrial conflict is through a recognition of our common humanity.

Summary

The novel provides an opportunity, through conversation and the narrator's reflections, to debate the important issues of the day.

6.8 Education and codes of behaviour

Self-improvement

It is probably one of Elizabeth Gaskell's purposes to show that John Thornton can respond so generously to the painful problems of industrial life because he has sought education. Education in the nineteenth-century novel is a means of self-improvement. Education bestows status. This insight is fundamental to Dickens. Pip is sent to London to be educated. In *Our Mutual Friend*, Bradley Headstone is proud to be a schoolmaster. Furthermore, he encourages Charley Hexham to escape the confines of his upbringing through learning (see Chapter 39, Section 39.7).

Social models

In nineteenth-century novels, characters achieve social prestige by following codes of public behaviour. There is much emphasis on courtesy, consideration for others, and appropriate ways of talking as well as dress and bearing. Education helps a character to live up to these often quite demanding codes.

Novelists recognize the social pressures that oblige characters to live according to these codes, but they are also sceptical about them. The point about Mr Elton in *Emma* (1816) is that while his manners are appealing, he is self-seeking and (at least in Emma's eyes) a presumptuous man. The problem for Jane Austen's characters is discerning true gentility from (usually selfish) pretence. Mr Elton is too smooth. The manners mask rather than reveal his moral character.

Crime

Crime is sometimes called deviancy. The idea is that what is counted as criminal is a departure from accepted codes of behaviour. There is a pathos about Bradley Headstone. He is a man who has pursued social status by way of the teaching profession. He sees it as part of his vocation to rescue children from the constrictions of ignorance. The pathos is that this ardent self-improver is also a would-be murderer. Two opposites meet in him: education as a means of social improvement, and its dark opposite – crime. The juxtaposition of these two polarities is also present in *Hard Times* (1854): bad education turns Tom into a criminal.

Crime is often presented as a world apart. Pinkie, the central figure of Graham Greene's *Brighton Rock* (1938), is created deliberately as a figure apart from the common interests of people. In *Oliver Twist* the world of Bill Sikes and Nancy is physically separated from the rest of London.

Crime and resolution

Crime is useful as a plot resolution. In *Adam Bede* (1859) Hetty is tried and then dramatically rescued from the gallows. In Wilkie Collins' *The Moonstone* (1868), Sergeant Cuff brings clarity regarding the fate of one of the characters. His presence has led critics to call this the first detective novel. Like marriage, catching the criminal is a good ending. The arrest of Tess at Stonehenge gives a sense of finality to the close of *Tess of the d'Urbervilles*.

Summary

Education features in novels as a means of self-improvement. Social prestige also depends on following codes of behaviour. Novelists are sometimes sceptical of those characters who value such codes very highly. Crime matters in novels because it is often presented as the polar opposite of the social codes that characters attempt to live up to.

6.9   Domestic life

The family

The family is central to nineteenth-century fiction. *David Copperfield* (1849) closes with the happiness and security of a family around the fire. Some critics have suggested that Dickens' world exists between the poles of prison and the fireside.

The trajectory of many plots is towards domestic happiness. *Jane Eyre* (1847) closes with the heroine happy with her husband and baby. The close of *Pride and Prejudice* (1813) celebrates the life Elizabeth and Darcy enjoy at Pemberley. Happy domesticity is more desirable when the plot concerns the search for a family. Such plots often turn on the unexpected discovery of a relative or, as in *Oliver Twist*, the friend of a relative.

The presentation of family life touches on the presentation of marriage. It may well be that because there is more scope in a difficult marriage than a happy one, novelists tend to write of marital failures. There is a sober reflection from the narrator in Chapter 42 of *Pride and Prejudice* about the unsatisfactory picture that Elizabeth has formed of her parents' marriage:

> Had Elizabeth's opinion been all drawn from her own family, she could not have formed a very pleasing picture of conjugal felicity or domestic bliss.

Characters in fiction have to learn *not* to learn from their parents. In terms of the design of the novel, the unsuccessful marriage of her parents makes the Gardiners very important. In them, we have a family that works. Paul Morel in *Sons and Lovers* (1913) is drawn to the Leivers' farm because the family is not like his own.

Brothers and sisters

An important element in domestic life is the relationship between brothers and sisters. There is a very interesting passage in *Mansfield Park*, in which Jane Austen's narrator discourses on 'fraternal love'. In Chapter 24, William Price visits his sister. Their happiness consists of retracing, with 'the fondest recollection', the shared memories of trouble and joy. The narrator comments:

> An advantage this, a strengthener of love, in which even the conjugal tie is beneath the fraternal. Children of the same family, the same blood, with the same first associations and habits, have some means of enjoyment in their power, which no subsequent connections can supply.

The narrator is forthright. Not even marriage (the conjugal tie) can equal the strength of the bond between siblings. In a world in which we assume, following Freud, that a child's relationship to the parent of the other gender (daughter/fathers, sons/mothers) is crucial, this comes as a bracing shock. But perhaps there is sense in it. Do daughters see more of their fathers or their brothers?

Summary

Authors find the material for novels in the everyday circumstances of domestic life. This allows them to explore the institutions – family, marriage – that national life has traditionally relied on. It is also evident that strains in these institutions sometimes provide material for the novelist.

Part Two Drama

■ ☑ 7 Familiar Drama

7.1 Theatre-going

You may have been in more plays than you have seen, as there are usually opportunities to perform in school, and you may be doing, or have already studied, A-level Theatre Studies. If you've been in plays, you will have gained, even if you are not aware of it, potentially valuable insights into how drama works. This includes minor matters such as when characters are on stage. There is, for example, about half an hour in Act IV of *Hamlet*, a period when Hamlet himself is *not* on stage.

Television and film

Television and film provide our most familiar forms of drama. People remember dramatized novels on the television, and cinematic epics such as *Star Wars*.

Television sitcoms are often successful pieces of drama. *The Likely Lads*, *Some Mothers Do 'Ave 'Em*, *The Fall and Rise of Reginald Perrin*, *Fawlty Towers*, *Only Fools and Horses* and *The Office* are memorable precisely because they work as successful dramas: ingenious plots, interesting characters and scenes that establish the themes of the plot.

Sitcoms are like soap opera in that they draw on recognizable aspects of life. But their plots are different. The sitcom is tightly organized to produce a resolution, whereas the soap can be extended week after week with no concluding event.

Real life

Television drama usually has a feature that is not always characteristic of the kind of drama studied for examinations. To put it simply: much television drama is presented as real life. Soap opera works when the audience accepts that what they see is, for example, a typical back street in the north of England. The characters are such as we can imagine in our world because they want love, success and status, and encounter the problems we read about in the newspapers – bullying at school, marriage break-ups, 'coming out', abortion, mental illness and the celibate priest falling in love and so on.

However, sitcoms depart from our everyday world through the marvellous improbability of their events.

> Comedy is the art of locating extraordinary incidents in ordinary situations.

When a sitcom becomes very realistic, we have difficulty in accepting it. *The Royle Family* consists of a set of people who do nothing but sit around and talk, to the permanent accompaniment of the television. It is supposed to sound unscripted. It was praised by critics, who saw it as an interesting experiment, but some viewers found it too close to their everyday world to accept as entertainment.

Art

People who study television and film insist that what we are watching is something that has been constructed.

> Television and film have been been designed and are not, therefore, unmediated slices of life.

For all its fragmented and meandering conversations, The *Royle Family is* art – there is a script, a director, a designer and an experienced cast. The beginning of literary study is the realization that what looks real has been made. We are dealing with something that has been brought to us – mediated – and in being brought to us, it has been formed and shaped. Look at the credits of television programmes and films, and you will see that they have editors.

Television, films and drama

Though neither television nor films are very reliable guides to what happens on stage, thinking about them might enable us to see some of the distinctive features of the plays we study. When we are getting to know something, it's often very helpful to remind ourselves what it's *not* like.

Summary

The dramatic arts with which we are most familiar are television and film. Sometimes these work to convince us that what we are watching is real life. But we are not. As with all art, television and film have been made.

7.2   Drama and the dramatic

Excess

Consider how we use words relating to drama in everyday life. Disturbances are described as 'dramatic', and changes are 'dramatic turn-arounds'. Sweeping gestures are described as 'theatrical', and people who behave like that are said to be 'drama queens' or 'prima donnas' who want to 'hold the centre stage' or 'throw a scene'. In everyday life,

> **'Dramatic' refers to anything that is powerful, significant and memorable. Moreover, it is usually public; dramatic events are seen.**

The everyday use of words drawn from drama carries a further implication:

> **The dramatic tends to be excessive.**

When drama refers to itself it often draws attention to its excessive aspects. Playwrights and actors know that the emotional intensification required on stage can sometimes be taken to excess. In late medieval plays about the life of Christ (mystery plays), two figures provoked much amusement: Pontius Pilate and King Herod. Both of them were presented as villains who stormed wildly through their roles. When Hamlet gives instructions to the First Player, he warns against the performance that tears 'a passion to tatters', adding that such an actor 'out-Herods Herod' (*Hamlet* 3.2. 9.13, 1600).

The strange and the wonderful

Drama is about the dramatic. It starts from whatever is surprising and arresting. Hence, we are likely to find it dealing with the strange and wonderful.

Drama's world is not an everyday one. The plot of *Hamlet* (1600) turns on a disclosure made by a ghost; in *A Midsummer Night's Dream* (1594) we see the magic of fairies; witches appear in *Macbeth* (1606); in *The Winter's Tale* (1609) we hear, in awed and hushed tones, of a visit to the Oracle at Delphi (3.1), and Jupiter descends in *Cymbeline* (5.5) (1610). The theme of a man meeting a God appears in the plays of Peter Shaffer. In *The Royal Hunt of the Sun* (1964) there is an Inca King who claims divinity, and in *Equus* (1975) a young man meets the divinely mythical in the form of a horse god.

Human extremes

Drama is concerned with heightened actions, strange characters and language pushed to the limit. In John Ford's *'Tis Pity She's a Whore* (1633), Giovanni enters, holding the heart he has torn from his sister. In Ben Jonson's *Volpone* (1607), the central character's excessive greed is matched (or surpassed) by the rapacity of those who hope to benefit from his death.

The extreme and the everyday

In most of the drama you will see or study, neither the playwright nor the performers will be out to convince you that what you are viewing is an everyday occurrence. Even when plays have everyday settings, the action is far from 'everyday'. This is what happens in Harold Pinter's *The Birthday Party* (1958) and *The Homecoming* (1965). Sometimes an everyday setting acts as a foil to the action. J. B. Priestley's *An Inspector Calls* (1946) is about an affluent dinner party, but the Inspector who calls is no ordinary figure.

From the beginning, English drama was no ordinary thing. The mystery plays presented the greatest wonder of all – the drama of salvation. These plays of the fourteenth and fifteenth centuries deal with Old Testament stories such as Noah's flood and Abraham undertaking to sacrifice Isaac, his son. Plays based on the New Testamant include the harrowing of Hell, in which Christ crushes the Devil and rescues the imprisoned souls of Adam, Isaiah and Moses. Even in the most touchingly ordinary of the plays – *The Second Shepherd's Play* (fifteenth century) from the Wakefield Cycle – the mischief of Mak, who steals a lamb and hides it in a cradle, mimes the wonder that in Christ the Lamb of God was cradled in a manger.

Summary

Drama deals with whatever is extraordinary or excessive: actions, characters and language often engage with that which is strange and wonderful. Even when the setting is ordinary, the action is not.

7.3 Outlandish action: the sixteenth and seventeenth centuries

Given the miracles and wonders of the mystery plays, it is hardly surprising that the great age of English drama – the sixteenth and seventeenth centuries – produced plays that explore the extreme aspects of life. To adopt a phrase from Shakespeare's *King Lear* (1605), drama brings us to 'the extreme verge' (4.5. 26).

Vast schemes

What stirs the viewer of a Christopher Marlowe play is the way the vastness of its dramatic scope is expressed through visual splendour. In *Doctor Faustus* (1591), the audience sees Faustus conjuring up Mephastopheles and cutting his arm to sign a pact with the Devil; Lucifer and Beelzebub appear in a hellish epiphany; the Seven Deadly Sins cavort and caper with grotesque vitality, Alexander the Great and Helen of Troy are conjured up, and at the close Faustus is dragged off to Hell. In a good performance, the audience never forgets that this is a play about magic.

Language that fits the action

To enact this vast imaginative undertaking, Marlowe creates a rich, supple and evocative language. The adjective '*marlovian*' has been coined to indicate this aspiring, sweeping, high-sounding language. For example, when Faustus faces the actuality of his damnation (less than an hour away) his thoughts turn to God:

> O I'll leap up to my God! Who pulls me down?
> See, see where Christ's blood streams in the firmament!
>
> (sc. 13. 71–2)

Marlovian language stimulates the imagination, charms the ear and enacts the play's themes. The language comments ironically on Faustus's ambitions: though in his extremity he wants to leap up to God, his most ardent aspiration in the play has been to ascend to his own Heaven of knowledge and power. And the shape of the line – the rise of the voice to 'God' and the fall to 'down' – gives us the play's theme and plot. Furthermore, the very magnificence of the verse (we can hear it in the chiming of 'see, see' with 'streams') suggests that to Faustus leaping up to God is mere spectacle, yet another of the sights and wonders magic might contrive.

Horrible events

Even so, many people have found that there is something magnificent about Faustus. But in other plays there are actions so horrible that their presentation on stage is highly problematic. How does a theatre company present Marlowe's Edward II murdered in a grotesque parody of the homosexual act by having a red-hot spit thrust up his rectum?

Examples of the horrible abound in plays of this period. Indeed, it might be said that in the Jacobean period (the reign of James I that started in 1603) dramatists (perversely?) created ever more ghastly bits of theatrical business. In the darkness of a prison, John Webster's Duchess of Malfi is offered a hand in an apparent gesture of reconciliation. The stage direction reveals the truth: '*Gives her a dead man's hand.*' She kisses it and remarks: 'You are very cold' (4.1. 51).

Deception

Drama of this period (and many others) deals with deception. Ben Jonson builds his major comedies on characters who are so boldly imaginative that audiences find themselves admiring and perhaps even liking such villains. In *Volpone*, deception is an art. Mosca, Volpone's assistant, says of one of their most stupendously outrageous deceptions (a court scene in which the innocent are found guilty) that 'this is our masterpiece' (5.1. 13). Moreover, those whom they deceive unpleasantly show combined greed and gullibility. At times they are so gullible that the audience suspects wilful self-deception. Corvino sends his young and beautiful wife to sleep with Volpone because he thinks that Volpone will reward such a gift by making Corvino his heir. Of course, it has been announced that Volpone is impotent, but Corvino has seen that even the decrepit can fondle. When Corvino gives the apparently bed-ridden Volpone a pearl, Mosca remarks: 'See how he grasps it!' (1.5. 19). When his wife is properly reluctant to share

Volpone's bed, Corvino dismisses her pleas with words that revealingly show that he knows what might happen to her:

> What, is my gold
> The worse for touching?
>
> (3. 2. 40–1)

Emotional intensity

The plays of this period are about three hours long, so what is done on stage must be both brief and yet full. Hence, feelings are often intense. Significant feelings are expressed in a single speech. Faustus's restless spirit – his discontent with traditional learning, and his desire for power – is established in his opening speech, which in just over sixty lines compresses his whole intellectual history. Shakespeare's abundant imagery gives an economical and yet graphic expression of feelings and ideas. Think of *Macbeth* (1606), and what is conveyed in Macbeth's words about the blood on his hands:

> This my hand will rather
> The multitudinous seas incarnadine,
> Making the green one red.
>
> (2.2. 60–2)

The last line is virtually a repetition of the previous one. The polysyllabic and Latinate 'multitudinous seas' becomes the Anglo-Saxon, and monosyllabic, 'green one'. The meaning therefore is that his hand will make the green sea red, or, as some have argued, entirely red. And more than that; the phrase 'green one' can mean the innocent one. The passage, and so much of the play, concerns the corruption of innocence.

Summary

Sixteenth- and seventeenth-century drama deals in several kinds of extreme action. The canvas of a play can be vast (including Heaven and Hell), and deceptions (a popular theme) can be almost preposterously extreme. Because drama is brief, plays are emotionally intense.

7.4 Two desires: love and power

Drama of this period shows two major desires at work: love and power.

Passion

Othello (1604) is about the passion of jealous love. It shows that emotions frequently presented as elevating can also belittle and destroy. Othello is a man of rare nobility, natural authority, quiet dignity, easy fearlessness and an almost innocent trust and openness. In this most painful of all Shakespeare's plays, the audience is taken to the extreme when it sees this man cowering in the shadows to overhear what he has been deceived into imagining: a rough and dismissive account of Desdemona's doting on Cassio.

Other kinds of loving

Othello deals with the standard material of literature: romantic heterosexual attraction. But drama knows of other kinds of love. As indicated above, *Edward II* (1594) is concerned with homosexual love. Parted from his beloved Gaveston, the king dwells sadly on his loss:

> He's gone and for his absence thus I mourn.
> Did never sorrow go so near my heart
> As doth the want of my sweet Gaveston
>
> (1.4. 304–6)

This is deep feeling. The finality of 'gone' reminds us that poets of this period spoke of parting from a beloved as a kind of death, thus making it natural that Gaveston's absence should be something that he mourns. The note of mourning is again heard in the chiming 'sorrow go so' – the standard sounds of lamentation. And we should remember that 'sweet' had the meaning of free from corruption.

John Ford explores a social taboo: *'Tis Pity She's a Whore* is about incest. Giovanni is presented as the typical lovesick youth, the type we often laugh at in plays of this period. His sister, Annabella, is, to him, the unattainable object of his longing. He argues that

> Nearness in birth and blood, doth but persuade
> A nearer nearness in affection.
>
> (1.3. 109–10)

Ford might have written a play in which a clever young man with all the intellectual swagger of a university education seduces his sister with, as in the quotation, the high-sounding arguments of Philosophy. But Ford daringly refuses this option. When Giovanni first pleads with his sister, she replies:

> thou hast won
> The field, and never fought: what thou hast urged,
> My captive heart had long ago resolv'd.
>
> (1.3. 115–16)

It is a convention, particularly in poetry and drama, that love is spoken of as warfare. The imagery is appropriate because, as in Annabella's words, warfare has disturbing similarities with the sexual act. War is like the battle for a woman's body, and both victory and sexual possession turn on penetration. The image of woman as being like a prisoner longing for an attacker to set her free makes the link between war and sex uncomfortably graphic. Annabella willingly commits incest by imagining Giovanni penetrating her, so that her 'captive heart' might be freed (see also Chapter 54, section 54.3).

Appetite

The lust for power is an insatiable appetite. Marlowe's *Edward II* is a double tragedy: the king falls and is horribly murdered, and the one who plans his death, proud Mortimer as the play calls him, also falls, because his voracious appetite for power consumes him. Before the latter's fall he sums up his achievement in a self-approving soliloquy:

> The prince I rule, the queen do I command;
> And with a lowly conge to the ground
> The proudest lords salute me as I pass.
>
> (5.4. 48–50)

In his boasting – prince, queen and lords all deferring to him – we can see the satisfaction of one who has schemed and manipulated his way to power and, before he falls, will order the death of the king.

Killing the king

Perhaps the most extreme act Shakespeare could imagine is killing the king. We get drama of this period wrong unless we can feel our way into this terrible act. It seems to have haunted Shakespeare, who wrote about Richard II, Henry VI and Richard III, all of whom were killed.

The king is at the apex of society; he dispenses justice, and controls life and death. Monarchy is ancient; kings were attesting to this aspect of their sovereignty when they claimed descent from figures of myth and scripture. Many medieval monarchs claimed kinship with the kings that visited the infant Christ at Bethlehem. So the monarch's office was holy; when crowned, English monarchs are anointed with holy oil, just as were the kings of Israel. To kill the king is a fundamental violation of the sacred. It is indeed the stuff of myths – Oedipus kills King Laius, not realizing that he has killed his own father, and Agamemnon is killed on his return from the Trojan War.

Something of this mythic aura broods over *Hamlet*. In the first act, Hamlet hears that his father was murdered by the man who now wears the crown. In the third act, the players, at Hamlet's command, perform *The Murder of Gonzago*, a play that Hamlet says somewhat resembles the account of his father's death. At the close of the play, Hamlet orders 'Let the door be locked!' (5.2. 264) and then kills the king. There is something ritualistic about the death of this king: isolated behind the closed door, Hamlet purifies the nation by shedding the blood of the one who has defiled it.

Love and power together

In *Richard III* (1592) and *Macbeth*, Shakespeare created figures who exhibit the passions of love and the lust for power. Richard III plans to murder his brother, and then woos Anne Neville in the presence of the body of Henry VI, whom Richard has murdered. In the following scene, Clarence suffers a horribly funny death in a butt of Malmsey (imagine his legs wildly kicking in the air).

Like Richard, Macbeth is the ambitious man who murders his way to the throne; he is also the husband of a forceful woman. Lady Macbeth entices him to kill the king in language that blends murder and sexuality. Her taunts stimulate him to do what he desires. In a sort of lover's game, she goads him to action, by climaxing her speech on a significant word:

> From this time,
> Such I account thy love. Art thou afeard
> To be the same in thine own act and valour
> As thou art in desire?
>
> (1.7. 38–41)

'Desire' has a double force: its immediate meaning is the plan to murder Duncan, but also, like the word 'act', it has a sexual charge. The fusion of murder and sex is uncomfortably present in his final claim that he 'dare do all that may become a man' (1.7. 46). 'Do' works like 'act' and 'desire'. This is the extreme verge of human passions.

The image of the Tarquins

An image that haunts Shakespeare's imagination is drawn from his reading of Roman history. In Sir Roger North's translation of Plutarch's *Lives* (1579), he found the story of the Tarquins. The *Life of Brutus* (the source for *Julius Caesar*) opens with this sentence:

> Marcus Brutus came of that Junius Brutus for whom the ancient Romans made his statue of brass to be set up in the Capitol with the images of the kings, holding a naked sword in his hand, because he had valiantly put down the Tarquins from the kingdom of Rome.

The Tarquins were early, tyrannical kings of Rome. Their expulsion was momentous because it brought about the Roman republic, the final days of which are the subject of *Julius Caesar* (1599). Brutus, the central figure of that play, contemplates in soliloquy his ancestor's part in ridding Rome of a tyrant:

> My ancestors did from the streets of Rome
> The Tarquin drive when he was called a king.
>
> (2.1. 53–4)

Shakespeare creates the pride of a leading citizen, who can look back to 'My ancestors'. The syntax of the speech suspends the significant verb – 'drive' – and so makes the expulsion of one who was 'called a king' (not who *was* the king) the climax of this particular service rendered by his illustrious family.

The Tarquins haunt Shakespeare; there are nine direct references in the plays. One story concerns a nephew of the Tarquins who, on hearing a fellow soldier speaking eloquently of the beauty and virtue of his wife, Lucrece, becomes obsessed with her. He visits her on the pretext that he is a fellow warrior of her husband, and in the night he finds his way to her room. Lucrece prefers death to shame and so, in public, commits suicide the following day. She is familiar in literature as a representative of violated virtue and therefore a prototype of the wronged woman undone because of beauty or virtue. (Hardy's Tess is a Lucrece figure.)

Tarquin represents both desires: the political and the sexual tyrant. In *Cymbeline*, Iachimo, who has hidden in Imogen's room, compares himself to Tarquin:

> Our Tarquin thus
> Did softly press the rushes, ere he waken'd
> The chastity he wounded.
>
> (2.2. 12–14)

To press the rushes is to walk. Very possibly in Shakespeare's theatre there was a particular way of striding – stealthy, malevolent and lecherous – that the audience would recognize as Tarquinian.

Given the dual role of Tarquin, it is entirely appropriate, though disturbing, that Macbeth, once he has bent his will to the terrible deed of killing Duncan, should use the image of Tarquin:

> withered murder,
> Alarumed by his sentinel, the wolf,
> Whose howl's his watch, thus with his stealthy pace,
> With Tarquin's ravishing strides, towards his design
> Moves like a ghost.
>
> (2.2. 53–7)

As with Iachimo, Shakespeare makes the actor draw attention to the Tarquinian stride with the self-referential 'thus'. The audience will see the 'stealthy pace' and the 'ravishing stride' as Macbeth, like a ghost in the dead of night, moves 'towards his design'.

Shakespeare's preoccupation with this embodiment of the two lusts is present in an early work. *The Rape of Lucrece* (1594) is a long narrative poem in which Tarquin, driven by lust, heeds neither the warnings of his conscience nor the doors and gates through which he has to pass to fulfil his terrible purpose. In a poem of 1855 lines, nearly 200 are devoted to his leaving his bed, his stealthy walk and his arrival in her room.

Madness

The lust for power and the lust of sexual desire are passions which might be controlled. But when control has gone, madness follows.

In *The Duchess of Malfi* (1623), Ferdinand goes mad after ordering the torture and death of his sister. The Doctor reports that Ferdinand was seen at midnight 'with the leg of a man/Upon his shoulder', howling that he was a wolf except that 'a wolf's skin was hairy on the outside:/His on the inside (5.1. 13–18). In the terms of twentieth-century cinema, Ferdinand thinks he is a werewolf.

Webster's language renders mental states in uncomfortably physical terms –
hair on the inside!

Summary

**Two passions dominate drama: sexual desire and political power. Some-
times, the two unite. When control is lost, madness ensues.**

7.5   Provocation

Drama is public and communal. What is done on the public stage is seen and
heard by people who have gathered for the purpose of enjoying the theatrical
presentation and are united by their concentration on the action on stage. Certain
things follow from this.

A political experience

The first is that a performance constitutes the audience as a society. In the theatre, our primary sense of ourselves is as a group. This means that there is a sense
in which the theatre is political.

> **Our membership of the audience may lead us to think about our
> membership of society at large.**

'Politics' is derived from the Greek word 'polis', meaning 'city'. What we experience
in the theatre may therefore be a *microcosm* (a world in miniature) of the one to
which we all belong.

A mirror

The political dimension of the theatre is particularly evident when a society is
changing. The theatre can offer a mirror and an ideal. In effect, it says: this is what
we are like and what we might be. It was Verdi's operas that gave nineteenth-
century Italy an image of what the nation was going through and where it might
be going. 'The Chorus of the Hebrew Slaves' in *Nabucco* (1841) expresses the desire
to escape from oppression.

Questioning the audience

A consequence of drama being the vehicle for national aspirations is that playwrights question their audiences. Plays can provoke us into thinking about the
way we live. Because of the communal nature of drama, some playwrights (an
example is John Arden) are overtly left-wing.

Controversy

If the extreme nature of dramatic action and the communal nature of the the-atre are put together, what often results is controversy. Though the theatre is not uniquely the place of controversy in literature, its public and communal nature has often provoked hostile reactions. Howard Brenton's *The Romans in Britain* (1980) draws a parallel between the Roman invasion of Britain and the United Kingdom's military presence in Northern Ireland, a country which Irish nation-alists claim should be part of the Republic of Ireland. Those who saw the play claimed that whatever one thought about the political case, the drama of the Romans leaving the stage to be followed immediately by a modern army vehicle full of British soldiers graphically provoked audiences to explore the possible parallel.

Controversy in performance and profession

Theatre is a matter of tradition, so when an audience sees something done in an unexpected way, complaints are not unusual. There was a production of *Hamlet* in which the Prince got into a big trunk to deliver one of the soliloquies. *The Winter's Tale* has been produced by an all-male cast, and women have played Richard II and King Lear. Sarah Bernhardt famously played Hamlet. Unusual settings for familiar works sometimes occasion controversy, particularly in opera. Wagner's epic *Ring Cycle* (1851–74) – a saga of heroes and gods – was staged in a hydroelectric plant, and Britten's *Billy Budd* (1951), a tale of nineteenth-century sea life, was set on a nuclear submarine. Nudity used to be controversial, though today it is largely accepted.

Traditionally, the theatre has not been a respectable profession. Noel Coward's song 'Don't put your daughter on the stage, Mrs Worthington' sums up the unease that the theatre has often aroused. That song is about the moral danger (chiefly sexual promiscuity), but the theatre was also socially questionable. It was virtu-ally impossible for an actor to be considered a gentleman. Today, when actors are Sir this or Dame that, it is hard to think it was ever otherwise. In Shakespeare's day, actors might perform at Court, but there was an unbridgable gulf between player and audience.

And the plays themselves, although very popular, were not thought of as works of which an author could be proud. Ben Jonson caused a stir when his published *Works* (1616) included plays. Shakespeare published poetry in his lifetime, but his plays were not published together in a single book until 1623, seven years after his death.

Puritans thought there was something inherently immoral about theatrical representation, in particular the unnatural business of boys representing girls. When the Civil War ended with victory for the Parliamentary cause, the theatres were closed, and the accusations of immorality continued long after the the-atres were reopened after the return of Charles II in 1660. Women were allowed to perform, but for over 200 years actresses (and later ballet dancers) were com-monly held to be sexually loose. Perhaps it was in part his association with the theatre that made people reluctant to stand bail for Oscar Wilde. The person who eventually agreed to help Wilde was Stewart Headlam, an East End priest, who, as an ardent lover of ballet, had welcomed dancers to his church.

Political control

The theatre was politically dangerous, because it could satirize public figures. In the early days of theatre history, the government insisted on control. In Shakespeare's day, the Master of the Revels, originally the organizer of court entertainment, had from 1581 authority over public performances throughout the nation. He licensed plays, performers and publications, and could also censor them.

Staging drama could be dangerous. Ben Jonson was imprisoned in 1605 for *Eastwood Ho!*, a play that the authorities claimed mocked the Court of the Scottish James I. Another of its authors, John Marston, had to flee London to avoid arrest. In 1605, John Day's *The Isle of Gulls*, another mockery of James and his Scottish courtiers, landed the boy actors who performed it in gaol.

An Act of 1606 forbade blasphemous or profane language. Its target was oaths that invoked the name of God. This Act probably accounts for the number of oaths in plays that are sworn in the name of pagan deities such as Jove.

Shakespeare and Elizabeth I

Shakespeare's *Richard II* (1595) was involved in a notorious political event. The play deals with a monarch who indulges his favourites to such an extent that the leading nobles turn against him and support his usurping cousin, Henry Bolingbroke. In the deposition scene (4.1) Richard, like an actor, flamboyantly plays out the fall of a king doing the unthinkable – giving up the throne that has been given to him by God. He plays the role superbly, ensuring that though he has no power he is still the central figure of a great drama. The scene was politically sensitive. In the first published version in 1597, the deposition scene was omitted.

People must have been aware of the parallel between Richard and Elizabeth, however, because when, in 1601, the Earl of Essex, one of Elizabeth's favourites, mounted a rebellion, his supporters paid Shakespeare's company to perform *Richard II* the night before the uprising. It might have had disastrous consequences for Shakespeare, but no action was taken. In 1604, however, Samuel Daniel lost his position as the Master of an acting company, because his *Philotas* was regarded as being too close to the Essex rebellion.

Summary

The communal nature of the theatre gives plays (at least potentially) a political dimension. The subject matter is often concerned with the life of the nation. Throughout the history of drama in England, both plays and players have been controversial.

8 The Language of the Stage

8.1 Verse and prose: mixing language

People are sometimes puzzled that plays use verse as well as prose. Yet if we think about how drama presents whatever is excessive and extreme, a choice of language that is different from everyday speech is not surprising. Most drama is not realistic. Nor is the use of verse confined to the sixteenth and seventeenth centuries; throughout the eighteenth century there were verse tragedies, and in the nineteenth century poets such as John Keats and Alfred, Lord Tennyson wrote verse plays. In the twentieth century, there was a fashion for verse drama both before and after the Second World War, the most famous plays being T. S. Eliot's *Murder in the Cathedral* (1933) and *The Cocktail Party* (1950). *Murder in the Cathedral* is self-consciously stylized: the Tempters and Knights speak in a ritualized order, and the action is commented on by a Chorus, in the manner of Greek tragedy.

The conventions of dramatic language

> English drama, like much English art, is not a matter of playwrights closely observing fixed rules.

English drama is flexible; the writers enjoy the freedom of using both verse and prose according to how they judge the demands of the action. Nevertheless, certain conventions of usage are evident in their practice. These conventions are grounded in the nature of the two forms of language. What, then, do verse and prose offer a playwright?

Blank verse

Shakespeare and his contemporaries wrote what is now called *blank verse*. 'Blank' means that it doesn't rhyme. The blank verse line consists of ten syllables in which a 'beat' is created by the even ones bearing a heavier stress. This line is called an *iambic pentameter*. An 'iamb' is the name given when the second of two syllables is emphasized, and a 'pentameter' is a line of five stresses. Audiences don't usually listen out for the 'beat'. Consider, for example, these lines from *Twelfth Night* (1599), spoken by Viola to the Sea Captain, who has rescued her from a shipwreck:

> There is a fair behaviour in thee, captain,
> And though that nature with a beauteous wall
> Doth oft close in pollution, yet of thee
> I will believe thou hast a mind that suits
> With this thy fair and outward character.
>
> (1.2. 44–8)

When reading these lines, certain words (important ones?) will stand out because of the pattern of stresses, yet the lines don't sound as if they have been written to a metronome; that is, they don't rigidly observe a tick-tock pattern. What you will almost certainly find is that there is a variation between the stresses. In the last line, for example, 'fair' is stronger than the earlier 'this'.

Verse, therefore, is rhythmical, and the rhythm need not be distractingly obtrusive; audiences might hear a measured, even stately, movement in the lines and feel the gentle pressure of an emotional impulse. Rhythm helps to create and sustain pace. Iambic pentameters can be compared to walking – they are steady, controlled and purposeful. Because there is an underlying pattern, variation for dramatic purposes is possible. Quickening or slowing the pace, breaking up the rhythm, thickening or lightening textures, and emphasis on an emotionally charged word can vary the tone of what is being said. Verse can be light, playful and jesting as well as dignified, weighty and serious.

Diction

Verse also can use a heightened diction or vocabulary. Elevated words (those of a higher register) convey the importance of what is being said. In the opening scene of *1 Henry IV* (1596), the king speaks of Sir Walter Blunt's journey. Sir Walter is 'Stained with the variation of each soil/Betwixt that Holmeden and this seat of ours' (1.1. 64–5). The king is talking about Sir Walter's boots.

The uses of prose

Prose is very often direct and immediate, and as such is an appropriate medium for some dramatic purposes. Greeting, giving orders, delivering messages (though important ones are often written in verse), giving directions and even, as in *The Taming of the Shrew* (1595), the rapid wordplay of wooing, are frequently done in prose.

Prose, again unlike verse, doesn't draw attention to itself. As a result it is very useful for conveying 'information'. Shakespeare begins a number of plays in prose. Even some of the tragedies – *Hamlet* (1600), *Timon of Athens* (1604) and *Coriolanus* (1608) – begin this way.

The themes of a play can be established through an opening prose scene. *King Lear* (1605) opens with a prose dialogue between Kent, Gloucester and

Edmund, which establishes that the kingdom is to be divided, that there was controversy concerning which son-in-law would most benefit, and that Edmund is Gloucester's illegitimate son. As soon as Lear enters to divide the kingdom, the language appropriately changes to verse.

Summary

Drama uses both verse and prose. Verse impresses through its measured (and sometimes varied) rhythms and diction. Prose is direct and can be used to convey thematic material.

8.2   Verse and prose at work

Social distinctions

The rule of thumb (though there are plenty of significant exceptions) is that verse and prose depend on social rank: kings and queens, princes and princesses, lords and ladies, leading citizens and generals use verse, whereas servants, workmen, soldiers and members of the crowd speak in prose.

The opening of *Romeo and Juliet* (1594) shows the difference. The brawling servants of the Capulet and Montague households speak in prose, but order is restored by the Prince, who speaks authoritatively in high-sounding verse about 'the fire of your pernicious rage' and the 'purple fountains issuing from your veins' (1.1. 81–2).

The distinction between verse and prose can be political. *Coriolanus* opens with the starving mob, who blame Caius Martius for their misfortunes. They speak in a convincingly lively prose, which has its own grim (characteristically London?) humour: 'Let us revenge this with our pikes ere we become rakes...' (1.1. 21). When Menenius, a patrician (ruler), enters, the gulf between the powerless and the powerful is evident in his use of verse. He speaks with the quiet assurance and common sense that is typical of the speech of those who exercise authority:

> For the dearth,
> The gods, not the patricians, make it, and
> Your knees to them, not arms, must help.
> (1.1. 69–71)

Like the crowd, he plays on words, but rather than the obtrusive pun on 'rakes' (we compare thin people to rakes), he sets out in the neat juxtaposition of 'arms' and 'knees' two alternative courses of action. He exercises power through his words, because the juxtaposition effectively tells them what they should do.

Verse and prose don't always make a social distinction. The opening Chorus of *Doctor Faustus* (1591) tells us that Faustus is not of noble birth: 'his parents base of stock', yet Faustus, the central character of the play, speaks eloquent verse.

Kings and verse

The heightened diction of dramatic verse is especially suitable for Court scenes. The authority of a monarch and the duty owed by a subject are present in the language. In *Hamlet* (1600) Claudius refers to his queen as 'Th'imperial joint-ress of this warlike state' (1.2. 9). If his queen deserves the word 'imperial', then he, the king, is claiming the title of emperor. This is a shrewd move, because the court business includes a territorial dispute with Sweden, hence the balancing of 'imperial' with 'warlike'.

Because it is so clearly art, verse can bring out the ceremonial life of the court. *Richard II* (1595) has a stately and ritualistic solemnity, which evokes the majestic high art of the late fourteenth century. It has the intricacy of a tapestry or the symbolic brightness of an illuminated manuscript. This is Richard in the opening scene, summoning the two disputants to appear before him:

> Then call them to our presence. Face to face
> And frowning brow to brow, ourselves will hear
> The accuser and the accused freely speak.
> High-stomached are they both and full of ire;
> In rage, deaf as the sea, hasty as fire.
>
> (15–19)

Richard enjoys doubling his words – 'face to face', 'brow to brow', 'accuser and accused'. They are verbal elaborations that could be delivered with appropriately graceful gestures. Moreover, the doubling of the words might anticipate the ritualized positioning of the two men on the stage. His couplet is conclusive in two ways: the final line contains two comparisons, which are opposites among the four elements – sea and fire – and the rhyme neatly clinches the idea that 'ire' (anger) is like 'fire'.

Emotional emphasis

Variation occurs in the expression of powerful feelings. The upsurge of emotion is manifest in added emphasis and the quickening of a line's pace. In an emotionally complex scene in *Twelfth Night*, Viola says what she would do if she were to love Olivia as her master does. She imagines herself living outside Olivia's house in a willow cabin (the willow was an emblem of rejected love) and calling out to Olivia:

> Halloo your name to the reverberate hills,
> And make the babbling gossip of the air
> Cry out 'Olivia'
>
> (1.5. 261–3)

The first line is not regular. The voice is obliged to hurry eagerly over 'to the' so that proper weight is given to 'reverberate'. Both being words about sound, 'reverberate' and 'babbling' prepare us for the almost ecstatic 'cry' and the even more ardent 'Olivia'.

Verse and ideas

The discipline and flexibility of verse make it appropriate for the expression of ideas. Moreover, the movement of verse can convey, as in the case of Hamlet, the very process of thinking – the uncertainties, the hesitations, the moments of illumination and the excitement of pursuing an idea. Feeling and thinking are not unrelated. Hamlet thinks passionately; it is an emotional necessity. Take, for example, the most famous of his soliloquies – 'To be or not to be'. To be is to act and to live, not to be is to opt for suicide. In thinking through the consequences of choosing death, he twice formulates the familiar idea that to die is to sleep. This is the second time:

> To die, to sleep;
> To sleep, perchance to dream. Ay, there's the rub,
> For in that sleep of death what dreams may come
> When we have shuffled off this mortal coil
> Must give us pause.
>
> (3.1. 66–70)

By using infinitives – 'To die, to sleep' – he makes his problem one that we might all share. He repeats 'to sleep' (think how the actor would deliver that) and then frames the thought that to sleep is to dream. Then his mind is illuminated. Eagerly, and possibly with something of a fearful shudder, he recognizes the problem. Not even his colloquial 'there's the rub' can disguise the dread of 'what dreams may come' in the sleep of death. He settles the issue: such a thought must 'give us pause.'

Madness and prose

In Shakespeare, the mad speak in prose. Madness is, of course, one of those extreme states that drama, particularly that of the sixteenth and seventeenth centuries, seems to relish. The wildness, the flouting of social conventions, and the failure of the mind to control the tongue are enacted in the fragmentary scraps of memory and vituperation that befits prose. Ophelia quotes bawdy songs in her mad scene (*Hamlet*, 4.5. 47–64), and, in the sleepwalking scene, Lady Macbeth discloses the horrors of Duncan's murder.

The madmen in *The Duchess Malfi* (1623) speak in sentences, which sound rational until Webster, in a word or phrase, indicates derangement. The astrologer says: 'I cannot sleep, my pillow is stuffed with a litter of porcupines' (4.2. 76). The Duchess, and, more disturbingly, her torturer, Bosola, show their sanity by their use of verse.

Prose, verse and dramatic function

Prose does one thing and verse another. In *Julius Caesar* (1599), Casca is a blunt, direct fellow who gives a pithy account of how Caesar fell down in some sort of faint when he was offered a crown. He speaks with a conversational vigour, making comparisons with a graphic thrust:

> If the tag-rag people did not clap him and hiss him, according as he pleased and displeased them, as they use to do the players in the theatre, I am no true man.
>
> (1.2. 258–61)

Prose creates Casca's character as an unsophisticated man with a bluff and direct manner. His comparison (a simile rather than a metaphor) might remind us of a man telling a story in a pub. Also reminiscent of bar talk is claiming authority by way of a conversational filler – 'I am no true man'. But in the storm scene that follows, Casca speaks in verse:

> Are you not moved, when all the sway of earth
> Shakes like a thing unfirm? O Cicero,
> I have seen tempests when the scolding winds
> Have rived the knotty oaks...
>
> (1.3. 3–6)

This is carefully crafted verse, not the language of the man who talked about 'the tag-rag people'. Here, Casca follows through the poetic implications of the words; if the earth 'shakes', then it is 'unfirm'. And when he talks about the ferocious sound of the 'scolding winds', he adopts the more compressed (and more poetic?) form of the metaphor rather than his conversational similes.

Why the change? The answer is that Shakespeare has different dramatic needs. The only way he can create a storm is through language, so Casca, rather than his customary prose, is given the majestic rhythms and the lofty diction of verse.

Summary

Verse and prose can make social and political distinctions. Verse is spoken in the Courts of kings. Verse can capture changes in feelings and the processes of thinking. Prose is always used of madness. Sometimes the use of verse and prose depends upon the dramatic demands of the action.

8.3   Dramatic language

The distinctive feature

What is distinctive about the verse and prose that is used in drama? To answer that question, we must be clear about what we are studying. Drama is not just something read or heard; it is acted out before an audience. There must therefore be something about the language of drama that makes it different from non-dramatic poetry or prose. The difference might be put this way.

The language of drama is a language that is performable.

People who work in drama and who teach Theatre Studies often say that the text of a play is something that has to be acted out. The test of a dramatic text is its performability.

But what does it mean when we say that dramatic language is *performable*? The answer is:

> **The language of drama suggests movement. It is as if the words are saying: 'Play me, act me out'.**

Two comments are necessary:

- Many (probably most) of the words in a play are not ones that invite movement, yet if no words do so, the play will be undramatic.
- In most cases the words don't specify exactly what the movement should be. Performability doesn't mean one particular action only.

The actions of actors

Actors do a number of things; they point, beckon, challenge, accuse, ask questions, give orders, hand things over, indicate states of mind, pray, sit down, get up and so on. These require actions: hand gestures, waving the arms, turning or inclining the head, shrugging the shoulders, striking a posture and many others.

It would be wrong to think that playwrights have in mind a list of movements and they then provide the words that will invite the actors to perform them, still less perform them in a particular way. What follows, therefore, is not the definitive list of the sorts of things actors do with words, but rather examples of some of the different actions dramatic language makes possible.

Language and specific actions

The text of a play sometimes requires the players to do specific things. In *Twelfth Night*, Viola, disguised as Cesario, visits Olivia, who is veiled. Boldly, Viola asks: 'Good Madam, let me see your face.' Viola has a good reason; Olivia is the object of Orsino's love, and Viola has fallen in love with Orsino. Olivia, though a little shocked, agrees:

> we will draw the curtain, and show you the picture. Look you, sir, such a one I was this present: is't not well done?

(1.5. 222–3)

Olivia employs the image of a curtain hanging before a picture. The process of unveiling is very clearly indicated in the text. It is worth asking how 'is't not well done?' might be delivered.

Language and authority

In plays about kings, many of the gestures invited by the text will be orders and commands. Think about how an actor might deliver the following lines from a later scene in *Twelfth Night*. Duke Orsino is ordering Viola to visit Olivia again:

> Once more, Cesario,
> Get thee to yon same sovereign cruelty.
>
> (2.4. 78–9)

'Get thee to' is an order. But exactly how the order is to be delivered is up to the actor. And what of 'Once more'; does that phrase invite a gesture – perhaps a raised finger or the sweep of the hand. And how might he indicate the 'yon same sovereign cruelty'?

Language and indication

In the second scene of *Macbeth* (1606), Duncan, King of Scotland, asks: 'What bloody man is that?' (1.2. 1). The question indicates that Duncan points to a soldier covered in blood. Significantly, the soldier tells a tale of blood, the central figure of which is Macbeth, the character whom the play shows to be a man of blood.

Language and grouping

In Shakespeare, there are very few stage directions; all that performers (and students) have to go on is the text. There are, however, indications. These can show us the mood of a scene, and even sometimes the meaning of the play as a whole.

At the start of Act 2, Scene 1 of *The Winter's Tale* (1609), the heavily pregnant Hermione is reluctant to play with her lively son, Mamillius. Grouping is immediately suggested in the opening line: 'Take the boy to you: he so troubles me.' Hermione must be sitting apart from her ladies in waiting. One of the ladies invites Mamillius to join them:

> Come my gracious Lord,
> Shall I be your playfellow?

He talks to the ladies, indicating that he has probably joined them. Later, Hermione invites Mamillius to join her:

> Come, sir, now
> I am for you again: pray you, sit by us,
> And tell's a tale.

He says he will tell a tale of 'sprites and goblins'. Hermione indicates that he's not yet settled: 'Nay, come, sit down, then on.' His tale is to be a ghostly one; it is about a man who 'Dwelt by a churchyard'. In response to his reluctance to let the ladies hear, she again invites him to sit close by her: 'Come on then, and give't me in mine ear.' This innocent, playful intimacy – Hermione with her son and the Ladies at some distance – is disrupted by the obsessed Leontes, her husband. Believing her to be an adulteress, he bursts into the room with a horror surpassing anything that might have been aroused by listening to the tale of the man who dwelt by the churchyard. There are now three groups. He demands the boy – 'Away with him'. Hermione is now alone. Leontes directs everyone to gaze at her: 'Look on her, mark her well' (2.1. 1–67).

The changes in grouping mark a shift in power. Before Leontes entered, there was an easy interchange in positions, but now Hermione is alone and has, effectively, lost her status as queen. Leontes' condemnatory 'mark her well' gives us the theme of the play. It is by looking at Hermione (particularly in the last scene) that we see the renewal that is basic to the play.

Language and emotional states

A special kind of stage direction is when the emotional pitch of a speech is indicated. In *Much Ado About Nothing* (1598), Claudio has been deceived into believing that the girl whom he is to marry, Hero, has been unfaithful to him. Claudio denounces her at the wedding in words at once cruel and contrived, calling her 'most foul, most fair' (4.1. 102).

Many have been shocked. The balance of 'fair' and 'foul' strongly indicates that this is a speech he composed beforehand. If, however, we look at a speech (153–4) from Leonato later in the scene we see how Claudio delivered the speech:

> speaking of her foulness
> Washed it with tears?

Claudio wept while he spoke. This makes the words no less cruel, but it shows they express distress and regret as well as anger.

Language and theatricality

Sometimes dramatic language calls attention to the business of performance. This is particularly the case with those plays that have a Chorus figure (see Chapter 8, section 8.4). In Christopher Marlowe's *Doctor Faustus*, the Chorus begins and ends the play, and links episodes. At the end of the first speech (Prologue 28), the Chorus, having told the audience about the life of Faustus, indicates his presence on stage: 'And this the man that in his study sits.' 'This' might invite the actor either to point to the figure or pull open the curtain that hung in front of the inner stage.

Summary

Theatrical language is distinctive because it invites performance. Gestures, actions, use of props, grouping and emotional states are implicitly present in dramatic language.

8.4 Monologue

Monologue is a distinctive theatrical form of speech. It is usually an extended passage, sometimes addressed to others, but more often there is no one else on stage.

The Chorus

In Greek drama, the Chorus was a group; but in early English drama it was an individual. There are Chorus figures in Shakespeare – in, for example, *Romeo and Juliet* (1596) and *2 Henry IV* (1596). The Chorus has three functions: to outline the shape of the plot, to draw attention to the themes of the play, and to comment on the moral significance of the action. These functions are all present in Marlowe's *Doctor Faustus*.

The Chorus tells us what we are going to see, and what has not been presented on stage, such as Faustus answering questions about astronomy. The Chorus can also involve itself in exposition, as in telling us about incidents that happened before the play began.

The Chorus deploys a diction that sets out the themes of the action. The Prologue contains the following significant words: 'excelling', 'self-conceit', 'glutted' and 'surfeits'. The movement of the plot will show exactly how these words are important.

Setting out the themes is close to the third function: commenting on the play's moral significance. The last line of the play insists firmly that Faustus practised 'more than heavenly power permits'.

Sometimes a character in a play occasionally performs the role of the Chorus. Thersites in *Troilus and Cressida* (1601) comments on the action, as does the Common Man in Robert Bolt's *A Man for All Seasons* (1960).

Soliloquy

'Soliloquy' is a speech by a character, who is usually alone on the stage and who explores his or her thoughts, feelings and intentions. Soliloquies often start or finish a scene. A distinction may be made concerning the relationships with the audience and the self-presentations of the speaker.

Public soliloquies

In a public soliloquy, a character talks directly to the audience. Because characters speak of their plans in this way, public soliloquies are particularly fitted to villains. Iago outlines his plots quite openly, and with charming honesty Richard of Gloucester shares his wicked plans with us. Done well, this can be disturbing; we are taken into the villain's confidence and become accomplices.

The private soliloquy

In a private soliloquy, the audience overhears or listens in to a character's inner-most thoughts. Private soliloquies therefore distance the audience more than do public ones. Hamlet puts questions to himself:

> Am I a coward?
> Who calls me villain? Breaks my pate across?
> (2.2. 572–3)

Because Hamlet doesn't know what to make of his responses, he dramatizes himself as one who is accused of and abused for his cowardice.

Soliloquies and truth

It is a convention that characters in soliloquies speak the truth, so in most cases we can trust that a character is sincere. This convention can help us think through puzzles about plays. In *Henry V* (1599), the king is consistently presented as a man of strong religious beliefs. For example, he ascribes his victory at Agincourt to God alone. But Henry is so clever a politician that this show of religion might be no more than a front to impress his followers. One soliloquy decides the issue. Alone before the battle, Henry prays (4.1. 286–302). He has no listeners (except for He who hears and knows all), so there is no point in putting on an act. If Henry tells the truth here, then his other expressions of belief must be sincere.

The self who speaks

In soliloquies, characters identify themselves in three ways: they use the first person singular, the first person plural and their own names.

First person singular soliloquies – 'I' soliloquies – lay bare the workings of a character's heart and mind. When dramatists started to create characters with distinctive personal features, the soliloquy was one of the ways they chose to do this. Macbeth contemplating killing Duncan is a revelation of the cast of his mind – his careful weighing of consequences, his motives and his fears. There is also the pitch of his imagination – his pictorial imaginings of the Last Judgement (1.7. 1–28). The imagery in this and other speeches makes him distinctive. No other tragic hero has such a poetic imagination.

A soliloquy can also be representative. A character can speak for all of us. It is interesting that Hamlet, often regarded as one of Shakespeare's most distinctive characters, often uses the first person plural – the 'we' form. In the 'To be or not to be' soliloquy, he says that the dreams that might come 'When we have shuffled off this mortal coil/Must give us pause' (3.1. 68–70). He speaks then not as one person, but as all people.

When characters refer to themselves by their own names, the sentence, grammatically speaking, becomes third-person. It's as if the character is talking about someone else. In *Julius Caesar*, for example, all the major characters adopt this way of speaking, in dialogue as well as in soliloquy. Using one's name in this way gives the impression that one is sufficiently detached to be able to judge oneself properly. This creates two effects. The first is the impression that the character is attempting to achieve a clearer, more objective understanding of him- or herself. Faustus uses his own name throughout the play. At one point he gets his terrible situation clear:

> Now, Faustus, must
> Thou needs be damned, and canst thou not be saved
>
> (sc. 5. 1–2)

'Must' is very strong, and the rhythm singles out 'needs' for a particularly heavy stress. This is not the language of appetite he has used earlier in the play, but rather a cold assessment of his spiritual state.

The second effect is that the distance achieved by using one's name allows the speaker to express self-admiration. In the speech that opens the first scene, Faustus says this of his disappointment with Medicine: 'Yet art thou still but Faustus, and a man' (23). The illusion of objectivity allows him to see that he hasn't done anything worthy of his great talents. This second effect is, of course, psychologically complex. Faustus is so consumed by the contemplation of his own abilities that objectivity is an illusion.

The aside

In an aside, a character turns away from other characters and addresses the audience directly. The speech is usually brief, and the convention is that no one on stage hears it. It is distinctly theatrical and may remind us that the theatre is not a replica of everyday life.

The effect of an aside is to establish a bond between audience and character. We feel privileged. In the opening scene of *King Lear*, Lear demands that his three daughters declare how much they love him. Two speak in terms so glibly polished that we recoil from their insincerity, but the youngest, Cordelia, turns to us to express her plight:

> Then poor Cordelia –
> And yet not so, since I am sure my love's
> More ponderous than my tongue.
>
> (1.1. 76–8)

When she does answer, she is curt and perhaps unfeeling in her language, but because she has spoken so anxiously and openly to us, we believe her and feel for her.

A different effect is created when the audience knows why a character is puzzled. Comedy is often based on audiences knowing more than some, or even all, of the characters. We enjoy being in the know and find the confusion of characters amusing. In Oliver Goldsmith's *She Stoops to Conquer* (1773), Marlow and Hastings arrive at their intended destination – the home of Mr Hardcastle – but they have been deceived into believing that it is an inn. Mr Hardcastle treats them as welcome family guests, and their feelings that he is too familiar are expressed in asides. Hardcastle drinks to their better acquaintance, and Marlow observes to the audience:

> A very impudent fellow this. But he's a character, and I'll humour him a little. Sir, my services to you.

Because he has divulged his thoughts to us, we enjoy his gentlemanly attempts to humour this rather extraordinary 'character'.

Sometimes an aside can make our estimation of a character very teasing. Audiences find Shylock in *The Merchant of Venice* (1596) a very difficult character. He is the object of hostile prejudice yet he schemes against Antonio with sadistic glee. In his very first scene there is an aside, the effect of which is difficult to assess. Bassanio has been inquiring whether, if Antonio will guarantee the sum, Shylock is prepared to lend money. Bassanio is courteous to the extent of inviting Shylock to dine. Shylock's reply comes in an aside:

> Yes, to smell pork, to eat of the habitation which your prophet the Nazarite conjured the devil into

> (1.3. 31–2)

What might we feel? Should we say that it was insensitive of Bassanio not to realize the dietary differences between Christians and Jews, or is it that Shylock is imagining an unintended insult?

Summary

Monologue – solo speech – is a distinctly theatrical device. The Chorus can explain the plot, point out the theme and pass judgement. A public soliloquy can recruit the sympathies of an audience, while a private one offers insight into a character's mind. The aside can arouse sympathy and prompt humour.

8.5   Dialogue

Dialogue is the engagement in words of one character with another. One character speaks, and the other replies. The to and fro of dialogue constitutes the life of most plays. Drama happens in exchanges, interplay, making contact and the giving and receiving of views.

Declaration and response

A basic pattern of dialogue is declaration and response. One character says something to another, and the other character makes some sort of response.

There are many ways in which this happens. *Hamlet* (1600) opens with a formal challenge from one guard to another. The second scene of *Twelfth Night* starts with a question: 'What country, friends, is this?' (1.2. 1). An answer is given.

The contours of dialogue

The life of drama often consists in the contours – the ups and downs – of dialogue. This is the politics of a play – the mutual attempts to exercise power. One character questions, proposes or orders, and another answers, complies, resists or refuses.

In *Volpone* (1607), Mosca is trying to enable Volpone to sleep with Celia, the wife of the jealous Corvino. His plan is to say that Volpone, old and sick, can only be restored by having a young woman in his bed. Mosca assures him that a prostitute will not do:

MOSCA	... we may perchance
	Light on a quean may cheat us all.
CORVINO	'Tis true.
MOSCA	No, no; it must be one that hast no tricks, sir,
	Some simple thing, a creature made unto it;
	Some wench you may command. Ha' you no kinswoman?
	Godso – Think, think, think, think, think, think, sir.
	One o' the doctors offered, there, his daughter.
CORVINO	How!
MOSCA	Yes, Signor Lupo, the physician.
CORVINO	His daughter!
MOSCA	And a virgin, sir, Why, alas,
	He knows the state of's body, what it is;
	That nought can warm his blood, sir, but a fever;
	Nor any incantation raise his spirit;
	A long forgetfulness hath seized that part.
	Besides, sir, who shall know it? Some one or two –
CORVINO	I pray thee give me leave...

(2.6. 54–68)

Think about how the dialogue shifts. Corvino is at first resigned; he sadly acknowledges that a 'quean' (prostitute) will not do. But when he hears about the doctor offering his daughter, he is both shocked and interested. 'How!' can mean 'How can I do something similar?' When Mosca repeats the doctor's offer and explains that Volpone can do very little, the actor playing Corvino needs to show a growing preoccupation with an, as yet, unstated plan. What seems to persuade him to offer his wife is the practical point that very few people will know. His asking to be given leave indicates a pause. He might walk a few paces from Mosca in order to think through the scheme. Mosca has not been bullying but he has persuaded Corvino.

'Thou' and 'you'

In the sixteenth and seventeenth centuries, there was a distinction between addressing an individual as 'thou' and as 'you'. The distinction works in two closely related ways:

- 'Thou' was the form of address used for a social equal, whereas 'you' marks a distinction between superior and inferior.
- 'Thou' is intimate and 'you' is formal and more emotionally distant.

At the beginning of *Hamlet*, Claudius, the new king, clearly shows his gratitude to Polonius, his chief minister, by talking to Polonius's son, Laertes, in terms of easy familiarity: 'Take thy fair hour, Laertes, time be thine' (1.2. 62). But with Hamlet, his nephew, the king's manner of address is chilly: 'How is that the clouds still hang on you?' (1.2. 66). The delay of 'you' till the end of the line pointedly establishes Claudius' power.

Summary

The force of dialogue is present in the contours of thoughts and feeling as two characters engage in persuasion and resistance. Social status is present in the uses of 'thou' and 'you'.

8.6 Wordplay

In wordplay, each character exploits the ambiguities of the language the other has used.

In wordplay, language controls dialogue.

Characters 'play' with words; and they play to win by excelling in inventiveness and ingenuity.

Shakespearian wordplay can be problematic, because many of the double meanings are no longer part of our language. Students working with annotated editions have, however, the advantage of looking at the notes, so they can see how the dialogue works. Look, for example, at the wooing scene from *The Taming of the Shrew*. Petruchio's ploy is to say that, having heard of Katherina's virtues and beauty, he was 'moved' to woo her. She picks on that word.

KATHERINA	'Moved', in good time. Let him that moved you hither
	Remove you hence. I knew you at the first
	You were a movable.
PETRUCHIO	Why, what's a movable?
KATHERINA	A joined stool.
PETRUCHIO	Thou hast hit it. Come sit on me.
KATHERINA	Asses are made to bear, and so are you.

PETRUCHIO	Women are made to bear, and so are you.
KATHERINA	No such jade as you, if me you mean.

(2.1. 194–202)

Petruchio uses 'moved' to mean emotionally compelled, but Katherina recasts the word as 'movable' – a piece of furniture that can be moved about, and a person who often changes. His devotion, she implies, is neither fixed nor lasting. A 'joined stool' was a contemporary joke: a simple piece of furniture, which, by extension, came to mean an unimportant person easily ignored. Petruchio invites her to do what we do with stools – sit on him. She says that he will bear her weight as asses do, but he chooses to treat 'bear' as meaning bear the weight of a man and bear children. Katherina, still playing with the idea of Petruchio as an ass, says he is a jade – an animal too weak for sustained copulation.

Wordplay pleases when, as here, the paricipants are equally matched. Wordplay is also found in later drama. The dialogues of George Bernard Shaw and Tom Stoppard often depend on wordplay, and Oscar Wilde is at his most engaging when the dialogue becomes an end in itself. For one character in *The Importance of Being Earnest* (1895), the elegance of talk is a virtue. Asked whether she believes what Algernon has said, Cecily declares that she doesn't, yet adds: 'But it doesn't spoil the beauty of his saying it' (Act 3).

Summary

Wordplay is dialogue in which the associations of words become ends in themselves. It is enjoyable, particularly when the participants are equally matched.

8.7   Common speech and bawdy

Common speech

Playwrights can use common language forcefully and eloquently. J. M. Synge found in the peoples of western Ireland an everyday language that was like poetry. In *The Playboy of the Western World* (1907), the language is rhythmically supple and emotionally eloquent. In Act 1, Christy Mahon, a newly arrived stranger, talks to Pegeen in her father's shebeen (a rural public house):

I'm tired surely, walking wild eleven days, and waking fearful in the night.

The sentence is balanced; one clause includes 'walking' and the other the alliterating 'waking'. 'Wild' is unexpected; has his walking been wild, or the eleven days of his journey? The sentence has a beautiful shape; it rises up to 'eleven days' and then satisfyingly subsides to an appropriate close – 'in the night.'

In *Death of a Salesman* (1949), Arthur Miller uses everyday language to create the pathos of Willy Loman's increasing isolation. Willy is a salesman who believes in the self-images of his society: 'America is full of beautiful towns and fine, upstanding people' (Act 1). Sometimes his graphic depiction of his failures is like the patter of the comedian, who specializes in the humour of lucklessness. Of his broken consumer durables, he says: 'I'm always in a race with the junkyard' (Act 2). He depends on proverbial bits of wisdom, sometimes put in the form of 'A man …'. The pathos is at its most intense when Willy tries to express his yearnings for an ideal life in the reach-me-down language of American success. Success in life cannot be a matter of being 'rugged, well-liked, all-round' (Act 1).

Bawdy

Bawdy is the word for language about sexual matters. In Shakespeare's day, and later in the period of the Restoration, bawdy language was expected. It occurred in wordplay, jokes and double entendres.

Sometimes, bawdy is there to entertain. People have always found sex funny, so sometimes humour is an end in itself. In the delightful all-girl scene in *Much Ado About Nothing*, the bawdy jokes are just that. Beatrice complains she is 'stuffed' with a cold, and Margaret quickly responds with 'A maid, and stuffed' (3.4. 60). Such talk doesn't promote the plot, though it is consistent with character. Margaret has shown herself to be a sexually adventurous woman.

Bawdy can illuminate the situation of a character. When in *Twelfth Night* Malvolio looks at the letter which he, all too hastily, believes to be from Olivia, we see in his reaction that he is bent on bettering himself through an advantageous marriage. So intent is he on rising in society that he does not attend to what he is saying:

These be her very c's, her u's, and her t's, and thus makes she her great P's.

(2.5. 95–6)

It doesn't take much imagination to appreciate the rude jokes that Malvolio is 'unintentionally' making. Malvolio is imagining more than social status. And it is imagination: the rude meaning depends on letters – 'c' and 'p' – *not* in the address of the letter.

Summary

Ordinary language can express a character's plight. Bawdy provides diversion and can reveal character and situation.

8.8   Ideas and issues

Plays deal with ideas: Arthur Miller's *The Crucible* (1953) is about speaking the truth in a society dominated by the intimidating pressures of a ruling group, and Timberlake Wertenbaker's very popular *Our Country's Good* (1988) is about colonialism and the power of the arts to enrich people's lives.

Thematic words and images

Ideas and issues are expressed in words. In Shakespeare, the frequency of a word usually indicates thematic importance. *Twelfth Night* is about imagined (and possibly real) madness. So the word occurs frequently.

In the early twentieth century, Shakespeare scholars identified images as the bearers of a play's meaning. They argued that in each play there was an image cluster – images drawn from a particular area of life – that embodied the themes of the plays. Animal imagery in *King Lear* raises the issue of whether we are any more than animals.

Plots and themes

Playwrights tend to place thematically significant words in three places: the opening, the turning point and the close. The examples below are from Shakespeare's *Measure for Measure* (1604):

- *The opening*. There is a thematically rich line: 'Of government, the properties to unfold' (1.1. 3). The play is about governing the state and governing the self.
- *The turning point*. Shakespeare shows that government requires the law to exercise mercy. In pleading for her brother's life, Isabella says that none of the symbols of office 'Become them with half so good a grace/As mercy does' (2.2. 63–5).
- *The close*. At the close, the man who imposed justice on Vienna is now himself subject to the same justice that he meted out to others: 'Like doth quit like, and Measure still for Measure' (5.1 412).

Themes and action

As drama is something that is done in front of an audience.

> **The playwright must provide an action that will embody the themes of the play.**

It is not just that something must be said; it must be *performed*.

Measure for Measure deals with government, justice, mercy and measure. Once condemned, Angelo will not plead for himself, so Mariana, now effectively his wife, appeals to Isabella (the woman he has wronged and who thinks Angelo has had her brother executed), asking for mercy. She does more than ask, in fact – she kneels (5.1. 440). Kneeling enacts the theme of the play. We have no right to mercy. All we can do is ask, and what better form of asking is there than the humility of the bended knee?

Summary

The themes of a play are evident in its language; in particular, repeated words. Clusters of imagery also enact a play's themes. Themes are often most evident in the beginning, the turning point and the close of a plot. Sometimes the themes are present in a character's actions.

▼ 9 Action

9.1 Plot and actions

A plot is about what the characters are up to, what they want and what they do to achieve their goals. Actions embody what the play is about.

J. M. Synge's *The Playboy of the Western World* (1907) is about Irish people's love of heroes. When Christy Mahon arrives in a remote part of the country with the story that he has murdered his father, the people treat him as a hero, because he has done something awesome. In the second act, girls bring him gifts:

SARA	And asking your pardon, is it you's the man killed his father?
CHRISTY	I am, God help me!
SARA	Then my thousand welcomes to you, and I've run up with a brace of duck's eggs for your food today.

There's a revealingly comic charm in the delightful contrast between the attempt at august speech in a 'thousand welcomes' and the homely gift of duck eggs. This is an endearingly innocent society.

How plots begin

Because plays are short, the plot and its themes need to be established quickly. Arthur Miller's *Death of a Salesman* (1949) starts with the essential matter of the plot. Willy, the salesman, enters, and Linda, his wife, anxiously asks him whether he is all right. She also asks him whether he smashed the car. Willy is a man who is losing control; we see the beginnings of the death of a salesman.

Scene after scene

When a playwright places one scene after another, there may be an implicit invitation to think about what links them. Scenes look backwards (analepsis) and forwards (prolepsis); back by taking up material from the previous scenes, and forward by arousing our expectations (see Chapter 4, section 4.5).

Perhaps one of the most interesting linkages is one that introduces new characters. In *Twelfth Night* (1599) there is a hopeless love triangle: Viola loves Orsino, Orsino loves Olivia, and Olivia, deceived by Viola's disguise as a young man, falls in love with her. One scene ends with the pathos of Olivia contriving to make

Viola visit her again. If things remain as they are, the needs of the three characters are not going to be met. But immediately, Shakespeare introduces Sebastian, Viola's twin brother. Expectations are raised. The hopeless love triangle might become a happy case of two couples.

Sub-plots

Sometimes the main plot is supplemented by a subsidiary one – the *sub-plot*. Quite often the sub-plot echoes the themes of the main plot. In some plays (*King Lear*, 1605, is an example) the themes of the play are more evident in the sub-plot than the main one.

In *Doctor Faustus* (1591) there are two likeable low-life characters called Robin and Rafe. They steal one of Faustus's magic books and set out to enjoy themselves. In the middle part of the play, the Robin and Rafe scenes alternate with the Faustus scenes. In this way, Marlowe establishes links between the two sets of characters. In one scene, Faustus, when invisible, snatches a goblet from the pope, and in the next scene Robin and Rafe steal a goblet from a vintner (owner of an inn). The linkages raise a question: how different are Robin and Rafe from Faustus?

Summary

The themes of a play are enacted by the plot. Themes emerge at the start of a play and the sequence of scenes raises issues of meaning. Sub-plots embody themes by reflecting the main plot.

9.2   Expectation, pace, climax and close

Expectation

Plots raise expectations. They also prompt the question as to how the playwright will bring about what we have been led to expect. In comedies, expectation is inseparable from that word 'how'. How, for example, will Oscar Wilde, in *The Importance of Being Earnest* (1895) solve the problem of two young men, neither of whom are called Ernest, who wish to marry two girls, each of whom will only marry her admirer if he is called Ernest?

Expectation in tragic or troubling plays often works by foreboding. The audience knows what is going to happen, so the tension of such plays lies in witnessing the unavoidable. We know Willy Loman will die, and that Romeo and Juliet are 'star-crossed lovers' (Prologue 6).

Samuel Taylor Coleridge said that Shakespeare was the poet of expectation and not of surprise. Most of the time in Shakespeare we know what is going to happen. The two exceptions, *The Winter's Tale* (5.3) (1609) and *Cymbeline* (2.2) (1610), come from late in his career, when his art was becoming experimental. Synge gives his audience a surprise in the third and final act of *The Playboy of the Western World*, when the father, whom Christy claims to have killed, returns, often being portrayed in productions with a comical bandage round his head. Further surprises ensue: Christy attacks his father again, but when the people who had made him a hero see the actuality of violence they turn against him. And there's one final surprise: with the timing of farce, the father, battered and bleeding, appears once more – still alive.

Pace

To be successful on stage (not an easy thing to achieve), *Macbeth* (1606) needs to move swiftly to its first plot climax – the murder of Duncan. When the idea of becoming king is posed to Macbeth in the third scene, he anticipates murdering Duncan. From that point onwards, nearly all the action serves to hasten its fulfilment. Five scenes later (all but one of which is less than a hundred lines in length) Macbeth exits with the dagger in his hand.

Tension is created by variations of pace. In the fourth act of *Antony and Cleopatra* (1606), there are twelve short scenes amounting to a total of 280 lines. These include strange noises, preparations for battle, a desertion, a suicide, two battles and recriminations. Then in two scenes totalling 230 lines there is the final meeting of the lovers and the death of Antony. The slowing of the pace allows the audience to turn from the scurry of events to concentrate on how the hero dies.

Climax

Aristotle's two ideas about climax – recognition and reversal – were discussed briefly in Chapter 4, section 4.5. Here we need to add that there are a variety of recognitions and reversals in English drama.

In *Much Ado About Nothing* (1598), there is a double recognition, when both Beatrice and Benedick come to see that, in spite of their pretended hostility, they love each other. Recognition can occur in strange circumstances. In *Hamlet* (1600), the Prince, witnessing Ophelia's funeral and Laertes' excessive show of grief, realizes that he *did* love her. Some plays do not have a moment of recognition. Volpone is caught out, but because he is so aware of what he has been doing, no moment of recognition is required. The pathos of Willy Loman is that he never quite sees the real nature of his plight. And does King Lear ever see?

As in many plots, recognition often occurs when the fortunes of the protagonist are reversed. In *The Merchant of Venice* (1596), the reversal occurs when Shylock realizes that he cannot insist on the terms of the bond.

Close

Ends fulfil expectation and the emotional yearnings of characters and audiences. The marriage of the lovers in *A Midsummer Night's Dream* (1594), fulfils Puck's words that 'Jack shall have Jill' (3.3. 45).

Sometimes, the denouement – the untying of the plot strands – leaves no mysteries. There is sometimes a feeling that things have come to a satisfactory halt. It is hard, for example, to imagine anything further happening to the characters in *The Importance of Being Earnest* (1895). Other plays offer no satisfying finality. What will happen to Pegeen now she knows, in the final words of the play, 'I've lost the only Playboy of the Western World'? In Shakespeare, the extent to which we can imagine a world after the close of the play varies. We might wonder about the married life of Kate and Petruchio, but can anything be imagined after the close of *King Lear*?

Summary

Plots work by expectation and, occasionally, by surprise. Dramatic tension is created by the momentum of a plot and by variations in its pace. The climax of a play very often involves a recognition, which leads to a reversal. Sometimes the close makes us think about the future.

9.3   Ends and beginnings

In Shakespeare, ends mirror beginnings. *Othello* (1604) ends as it began, with the lovers together at night, and in spite of the fraught nature of the action, the symmetry of the form produces a satisfying close.

Sometimes, the end reverses the beginning. *Romeo and Juliet* (1594) starts with street brawls and ends with the once-hostile families united in grief for their dead children.

Unities

Aristotle said that a plot should have a single action, which takes a few hours. In Sophocles' *King Oedipus* (5th century BC), an issue was raised, the protagonist recognized it and fortunes were reversed in about two hours.

In the sixteenth and seventeenth centuries, and particularly in France, Aristotle's acute observations were elevated into rules. A play, it was said, *ought* to observe unity of action, unity of time and unity of place. Action, it was argued, should be completed in a day and there should be one location. Sub-plots were condemned. In French drama, events, as in Greek drama, happened off-stage and were reported.

Only in *The Tempest* (1610) does Shakespeare observe the unities. R. C. Sherriff's play about the First World War, *Journey's End* (1928), is a twentieth-century example.

But English art resists rigid rules, perhaps because Shakespeare did so. Certainly, most of the individual pieces of stage action discussed below would be impossible if English drama had observed the unities.

Summary

Plays establish a pleasing symmetry when the ends mirror the beginnings. This formal quality raises the issue of the unities of time, place and action. Most English plays do not observe the unities.

9.4 Role-playing

Drama might be understood as being a formalized version of something we do in our daily lives – playing roles. This is an insight to which the theatre keeps returning: what is done on stage is art's version of what we do in our daily lives. Jaques' speech in *As You Like It* (1599) is Shakespeare's most detailed exploration of the idea: 'All the world's a stage' (2.7. 139–66). Each age of our lives is like playing a part in a play: there are costumes, attitudes, manners and actions appropriate to each phase. What emerges from an examination of Shakespeare is that he conceived of the link between the theatre and life in two fundamental ways.

Roles and society

Shakespeare shows us that our place in society gives us certain roles to play. Fathers, for example, have to be protective of their children, and in the case of their daughters, they have to be firm yet understanding and seek their happiness, particularly in marriage.

The matter of what roles to adopt is the central business of the two *Henry IV* plays (1596 and 1597). The king is grieved that his son lives the life of the irresponsible young rather than that of the heir apparent. In fact, the prince is playing a third role – the shrewd politician who is keeping himself apart from the tainted regime of his usurping father. Once his father is dead, he adopts further roles: the new king eager for advice, the kind and protective brother and the reformed man who rejects his former wild companions.

Theatrical self-awareness

Characters are sometimes aware of the theatrical nature of their own behaviour. *Hamlet* is Shakespeare's most self-consciously theatrical play. The language of the stage is used throughout, and one of the climaxes is the performance of *The Murder of Gonzago*, the play within the play.

Hamlet draws attention in his first speech to theatrical playing: 'they are actions that a man might play' (1.2. 84). His point is that he is not playing at mourning. When he has received his commission from the Ghost, he tells his friends that he may 'put an antic disposition on' (1.5. 173). From this point, things become very difficult. We don't know when he is or is not acting out a role.

Summary

There is a link between the roles we play in everyday life and the roles characters play on stage. Furthermore, playwrights sometimes present characters as self-consciously playing theatrical roles. Learning to play a role can be the theme of a play.

9.5 Present and past

Jaques' speech closes with a picture of final senility, in which the one who has played many parts is now 'sans everything'. Immediately, however, one who is close to his final dissolution – the servant, Adam – is carried in and treated with care and kindness. The immediacy of the action following the bleak words is something that theatre does so well. The audience can see it all; it is there now on the stage before them.

Drama is supreme in the art of the immediate. But what of the past – those events that have preceded the opening and without which it is difficult to understand the action of the play? The standard way of representing material that cannot be presented directly is to introduce it in dialogue. *King Lear* opens with two conversations that supply what we need to know in order to understand the plot.

Twentieth-century treatments of the past

In twentieth-century drama, two factors have prompted playwrights to experiment with the presentation of the past.

The first is the cinema. The cinema evolved conventions such as captions and fuzzy fades to indicate that a particular sequence happened in the past. Through these 'flashbacks', theatre audiences came to accept that a performance can also move about in time. Tennessee Williams achieves this in *The Glass Menagerie* (1944) by having Tom as a narrator figure who announces that he can perform all sorts of tricks. Knowing that we are watching a 1930s story from a 1940s perspective turns a tiny domestic drama into a parable about America sleepwalking into the Second World War.

The second factor is Freud. His idea that emotional events in the past shape our present behaviour is now so deeply embedded in our thinking that we hardly ever question it (but see Chapter 41, section 41.4). On the stage, it was Arthur Miller who found ways of representing how the past shapes the present. Throughout *Death of a Salesman*, there is hostility between Willy and one of his sons, Biff. The climax of the play is the discovery by Biff that Willy has a mistress.

Miller presents this through his organization and use of the stage. Extensive stage directions at the start of the play establish that the walls of the house are transparent, and that when the scene shifts to the past, characters can walk through these walls. There is something Freudian about this. Walls stand for the mental discipline we impose on ourselves, but in the freedom of our memories we can escape these restrictions. There are other techniques – voices-off penetrating scenes like uncontrollable memories, and music that signifies the emotions of a recollected past. It owes a lot to the cinema, as, perhaps, flashbacks in the cinema owe something to the influence of Freud.

Summary

Playwrights have used the techniques of the cinema and Freud's theories to represent the past.

9.6 Transformation

Transformation is any marked change in a character or situation. Plays are often about such events as when Romeo ceases to love Rosaline once he meets Juliet. Transformation can be funny. Audiences laugh when Lucentio, in *The Taming of the Shrew* (1595), suddenly falls in love.

Transformation is one of the oldest subjects in literature. Ovid's *Metamorphoses* (after 2 AD) makes transformation the basis of the world in which we live. Before Ovid, Sophocles presented Oedipus undergoing a change in self-understanding when he learnt the truth about himself. Synge's *The Playboy of the Western World* is based on the Oedipus story. Oedipus was king until he discovered the truth – that he had killed his father and married his mother. On discovering this, he blinds himself and, at the close, leaves Thebes, once his city, as an abject beggar. Synge does not deal with the issue of the mother; instead, he shows that what to others would be a matter of shame – killing his father – can, when viewed by people who have the capacity for savage communal celebration, be the stuff of mythic heroism. What the audience sees is Christy, with apparent ease, taking on the roles his new society honours. He becomes a lover (Pegeen is charmed by his rhapsodic innocence) and, in the annual games, a sporting hero who wins the race on the sands. (The race is reported in the manner of the Greek theatre.) At the end of the play, he leaves with his father, and we are confident that he is now the authority figure, a situation that delights and puzzles the old man: 'Glory be to God! I am crazy again.'

The mythic element in transformation is found in one of Shakespeare's most spectacular pieces of staging. In the final scene of *The Winter's Tale*, the newly reconciled characters visit the statue of Leontes' dead wife, Hermione. Only it is not a statue: it is Hermione herself. Perhaps we continue to call this the statue scene, because Shakespeare awakes in us the idea of transformation such as he found in Ovid, probably his favourite poet. The force of the scene depends on our seeing it in terms of mythic transformation.

Summary

Transformation, one of the oldest literary subjects, can be effective on stage and thematically important.

9.7 Thematic actions

Drama is visible, immediate and economical. Working within those confines, a playwright must find actions that embody a play's themes.

Image and actuality

Playwrights sometimes introduce an image which later becomes an actuality. In John Webster's *The White Devil* (1612), there is talk of poison. In 2.1. 306, Flamineo says: 'he will poison with a kiss', and in 2.2. 37, Isabella kisses a poisoned picture and dies.

Emblematic actions

One of the themes of *King Lear* is moral blindness. Lear cannot see that his elder daughters are deceiving him. Kent urges him: 'See better, Lear' (1.1. 158). In the sub-plot, Gloucester is also blind to the intentions of Edmund. In an emblematic scene, Gloucester is bound to a chair and his eyes put out. Once blinded, Gloucester begins to see with a clarity that Lear probably never achieves.

Characteristic actions

King Lear is a play that polarizes starkly good and evil. Throughout the play, the evil characters bind their enemies, whilst the good ones lead or carry those who have suffered. After Gloucester has been blinded, his son leads him. The two contrasting actions embody the struggle in the play between good and evil.

Summary

Actions can embody themes by transforming an image into an event, by making some actions emblems of the play's themes, and by giving characters actions that sum up what they are like.

9.8   Community and nation

Because twentieth-century drama has been preoccupied with the anguish of individual characters, it has become difficult to create a sense of a wider community. In Samuel Becket's *Waiting for Godot* (1952), is there anything beyond the tree, the tramps, Pozzo, Lucky and the boy who brings messages?

Opera and musicals are better equipped to give us a sense of society, because here the Chorus can represent the thoughts and feelings of the people. In Benjamin Britten's *Peter Grimes* (1944), for example, the sense of a people dependent on the sea is brought out by the Chorus, who sing of the labour of fishing, the tides, and the children who play on the shore.

Shakespeare's way of handling this problem is to introduce the cowd. In two of his Roman plays – *Juilus Caesar* (1599) and *Coriolanus* (1608) – the action starts with a tense meeting between the crowd – the ordinary citizens of Rome – and representatives of the governing body. The people are moody, witty and volatile. In *Julius Caesar*, there is a lively dialogue between an angry Flavius, an official, and a perky cobbler, who, with the verbal dexterity that often marks intelligent people with a rudimentary education, spars successfully with puns.

Critics have asked whether Shakespeare is antagonistic to the common people. They certainly change their minds. But this could be the idea that good fortune in this world is unreliable, and that the one who is popular one day is vilified the next.

Society in twentieth-century drama

Arthur Miller successfully gives us a sense of society in *The Crucible* (1953). Perhaps the pressing political context of the play's composition – the committee inquiring into Communist influence in public life – made it more important that this be a play about a society oppressed by prejudice and fear.

Miller creates a distinctive community in three ways:

- There is a large cast. There are twenty main roles as well as the extras that can pack the courtroom.
- Characters refer to each other, so there is a sense of people who know each other's doings.
- Most importantly, Miller creates a common language. It is a stylized and selective version of seventeenth-century Puritan speech. There are biblical references, and characters address each other in the formalities of the period (married women are 'goody'). Grammar is distinctive: 'suspicion' can be used as a verb – 'you will suspicion such a woman' (Act 2); there is ellipsis (the omission of words): 'we ought rely' (Act 1), and third-person verbs that are, to us, non-standard – 'She have robbed you' (Act 4).

History

In his history plays, Shakespeare also creates the early stages of a nation. In the *Henry IV* plays we see many levels of society: the Court, lords, country gentry, drinkers in London taverns, and ostlers minding the horses. He moves from London to Northumberland, and from a forest in Yorkshire to a garden in Gloucestershire. One of the basic themes of the history plays is the nature of England.

Summary

It is difficult for drama to create a sense of society. Attempts to do this include the presentation of crowds, a large cast, characters referring to each other, and talking in a distinctive way. Showing different social classes helps to create a sense of the nation as a whole.

9.9 Props

Props are any items that the action of the play requires to be on stage. In *The Importance of Being Earnest* (1895), John Worthing hands round cucumber sandwiches, and in *Doctor Faustus*, the central character refers to books.

Few or many

There are three standard props in Shakespeare's plays: letters, weapons and blood. By contrast, Ben Jonson's plays are full of things. In *Volpone* there must be a considerable pile of gold, and Jonson is very specific about the gifts each character brings Voplone in the hope of being made his sole heir. *Bartholomew Fair* (1614) requires whole stall-fulls: Leatherhed says 'let's pack up all, and be gone' (3.6. 19).

Props and themes

The high number of props in Jonson has thematic significance. Jonson, as is often observed, is the playwright who reflects the thriving commercialism of the early seventeenth century, a commercialism manifest in the abundance of material objects. His plays abound in people who are trading, either in goods or lies. One of his central themes is the relationship between greed and deceit: the greed of the foolish makes them victims of the deceit of the clever. The object of greed is material possessions, so the presence on stage of props is a manifestation of the thematic drive of his plots.

In twentieth-century drama, props also have thematic significance. The set of *The Glass Menagerie* is dominated by the portrait of the father, who walked out on the family, and in the climax of John Arden's *Sergeant Musgrave's Dance* (1959), the Gatling gun and skeleton are twin symbols of what war does to people.

Summary

Props can bring out the themes of a play and can be important in crucial scenes.

9.10 Excessive action

Burlesque

Drama is often self-aware: actors know they are on the stage, and the audience knows that it is in the theatre. This self-awareness is the basis for the tradition of burlesque.

Burlesque is dramatic parody, action that deliberately mocks the higher and more serious conventions of theatre by subjecting it to exaggeration, distortion and inappropriate stylistic treatment. Few plays are entirely burlesques, but sometimes individual scenes have the function of burlesquing the loftier parts of a play. The low-life scenes in *Doctor Faustus* burlesque the serious ones. This burlesque makes a point: Robin and Rafe practise magic without selling their souls as Faustus does. In the *Henry IV* plays, Falstaff burlesques the high seriousness of both the Court and the business of war (see Chapter 54, section 54.2).

Farce

Farce is exaggerated, often manic, action in which characters are beaten or chased. Because the audience views the frantic activity externally, the action is amusing. When in *The Taming of the Shrew*, Petruchio beats his servant, we enjoy the cries and gesticulations rather than imagining how painful it must be.

Plays within plays

Plays within plays are popular in the theatre. They remind us that what we are watching is a theatrical event. They were frequent in sixteenth- and seventeenth-century drama. There are plays within plays in Kyd's *The Spanish Tragedy* (1592) and Shakespeare's *Hamlet*. The settings of these plays within plays show that both playwrights are representing the practice of performing short plays during banquets or public celebrations. These were called Interludes.

It is such an Interlude that Theseus in *A Midsummer Night's Dream* (1594) has commanded to celebrate his wedding. What the Mechanicals do (unintentionally) is to burlesque the conventions of a high-minded entertainment about love and fate. Acted in excessive language, with lumbering alliterations and emotional clichés, we recognize that Shakespeare is enjoying playing with theatrical conventions. To enjoy burlesque, the audience has to have a pretty good idea of the dramatic style that is being parodied.

Summary

To appreciate the humour of burlesque we have to recognize the dramatic form that is being parodied. Farce only works if we view the frantic actions externally.

9.11   Stage competition

We often assume that writers blend and balance the elements of their works. We feel this particularly in matters of sympathy and judgement. We like complex works in which all aspects of a moral dilemma are explored, so that if we are drawn to one set of characters we also recognize the virtues of others. In short, we like works which have checks and balances built into them.

A theatrical imagining

But does drama have to work like this? Are there not too many uncontrollable factors in any performance to allow for the careful presentation of all sides of a play's themes? So, imagine another possibility.

Shakespeare's company is about to give the first performance of *The Merchant of Venice*. Shakespeare recognizes the emotional struggle of the trial scene, so he speaks to those who play Portia and Shylock. He tells the former to persuade the audience that mercy is the highest of virtues. And he tells the actor playing Shylock to persuade the audience that he is a man who has suffered prejudice and the loss of his daughter, and that though his revenge might be terrible it is, humanly speaking, entirely understandable. Shakespeare hands over the scripts, leaving the two players to use all their resources of stage presence and delivery to convince the audience.

The result might be that the struggle between Portia and Shylock also becomes a struggle in performance. If members of the audience submit themselves to this struggle, there is the constant tension of wondering how their thoughts and feelings are going to be engaged, and whether they will be forced to realign their sympathies. If drama does work in this way, we are reminded that it is a dangerous art.

Summary

It may be that drama works by each player trying to recruit our sympathies for their respective characters.

▪ ▼ 10 Characters

10.1 Characters and language

Whenever an examination question asks you to say what a character is like, your answer must concentrate on the words the playwright has given the character to speak.

The starting point for any discussion of character must therefore be the particular ways in which a character speaks.

Verbal mannerisms

A character may have individual verbal mannerisms. The third scene of *The Merchant of Venice* (1596) opens halfway through a conversation between Shylock and Bassanio about a loan. Here are two of Shylock's lines: 'Three thousand ducats. Well.' 'For three months. Well.' Shylock's 'well' is a verbal mannerism. Perhaps it is virtually involuntary (a verbal tick), or it could be played as his weighing the consequences of the deal. As the scene unfolds, further mannerisms occur. He repeats words; the ominous 'bound' occurs in his next two sentences. His repetitions might be delivered with a nervous energy; his first lengthy speech begins: 'Ho, no, no, no, no!' As he is a foreigner in Venice, his language is not entirely standard: 'My meaning in saying he is a good man is to have you understand me that he is sufficient.' Within twenty lines, a character has emerged.

Pope on language and character

Alexander Pope, the eighteenth-century poet, said that even if all the names of Shakespeare's characters were lost, it would still be possible to work out who said what. His point was that Shakespeare gave each of his characters an individual way of speaking. It might not apply to all his minor characters (but there are two quite distinct murderers in the early – 1592 – *Richard III* – 1.4), but it is generally true. Consider Polonius, the chief minister of Denmark in *Hamlet* (1600), addressing the king and queen:

> My liege and madam, to expostulate
> What majesty should be, what duty is,
> Why day is day, night night, and time time,
> Were nothing but to waste night, day and time.

Therefore, since brevity is the soul of wit,
And tediousness the limbs and outward flourishes,

(2.2. 87–92)

Polonius is confused, repetitious and contradictory. He multiplies examples – day, night, time – but when he returns to those topics he muddles the order. He says he will be brief, but then elaborates the metaphor of brevity being the soul of wit by talking of 'limbs' and, rather vaguely, of 'outward flourishes'.

Poetry is rich and supple, but prose can also individualize characters. In Shaw's *Saint Joan* (1924), the heroine visits the Dauphin for the first time:

Gentle little Dauphin, I am sent to you to drive the English away from Orleans and France, and to crown you in the cathedral at Rheims, where all true kings of France are crowned.

(sc. 2)

Shaw's prose establishes that Joan is direct, kind and purposeful. She has a touching yet forceful simplicity. The word 'and' shows that driving the English from France and crowning the Dauphin are tasks so connected that one will lead to the other.

Characters on themselves

Characters talk about themselves. This is part of the theatricality of the theatre. Chorus figures often say things about themselves by way of explaining who they are and why they are doing what they are doing. Tom in *The Glass Menagerie* (1944) does this, when he steps out of his role as the discontented son.

Trial scenes allow characters to comment on themselves. A Shakesperian example is Hermione in *The Winter's Tale* (1609). John Webster makes Vittoria central to the trial in *The White Devil* (1612). The trial scene in *The Crucible* (1953) allows Miller to show John Proctor coming to an understanding of himself.

Characters sometimes talk about themselves in scenes of high emotion. In the scene discussed in Chapter 8, section 8.3, Hermione talks about her emotions, assuring her ladies in waiting that although she is not 'prone to weeping' she has an 'honourable grief' that 'burns' within 'worse than tears drown' (*The Winter's Tale*, 2.1. 107–17). Although it is not implausible that someone might talk like this, the best way to understand these dramatic self-disclosures is in L. L. Schucking's phrase 'direct self-explanantion'. What a character says is not psychology but a dramatic device that reveals character.

Characters talking about other characters

Characters talk about each other. In *King Lear* (1605) a Gentleman says of Cordelia that she

redeems nature from the general curse
Which twain have brought her to.

(4.5. 201–2)

That remark helps us to understand one of Cordelia's roles. She has a redemptive function, which rescues nature from the fall brought about by Adam and Eve.

The comments of some characters make us think. In *Julius Caesar* (1599), Caesar notes that Cassius has 'a lean and hungry look', and adds that 'He thinks too much' (1.2. 195–6). The remark might prompt us to ask whether he is right. Does Cassius think too much? Was it wise of him to involve Brutus in the plot?

Summary

Characters are created in language. Playwrights use verbal mannerisms and give some characters distinctive styles of speech. Sometimes we learn about characters from their comments on themselves and on each other.

10.2 Characters contrasted

Playwrights bring out what is distinctive in characters through juxtaposition. We see what they share, how they differ and what uniquely belongs to each. In examination questions, the various juxtapositions are usually summed up in a single term – contrast.

Leading characters contrasted

In *Richard II* (1595) the king and Bolinbroke are contrasted with the clarity of a medieval illumination: Richard is flamboyant, poetic, irresponsible and volatile; Bolinbroke is subdued, prosaic, taciturn and single-minded. Their characters are revealed in their contrasting responses in the deposition scene (4.1).

Thematic contrast

Sometimes contrast works thematically. This is so in *Richard II*. The play raises the issue of whether poetry and imagination has a place in the world of power politics. In *The Tempest* (1610), two sides of nature are embodied in the two natives of the Island: Ariel and Caliban. Ariel is fire and air, Caliban earth. Ariel, though not human, is sensitive to people, whereas for most of the play Caliban is hostile. A play can contrast qualities thematically and yet be rooted in a recognizably contemporary world. Sean O'Casey does this in his play about the Irish troubles, *Juno and the Paycock* (1925). Juno is sensible, determined and sensitive to the terrible times she's living through, whereas Jack, the Paycock of the title, struts, idles and drinks. They represent the dependable and the feckless or, in gender terms, the patient, suffering woman and the irresponsible man.

Summary

The juxtaposition of characters enables the audience to see what they share and what is distinctive about them.

10.3 Stock characters

Stock characters are traditional figures, whom audiences recognize and know how to respond to. Stock characters are not complex; usually they have three or four distinguishing features. Stock characters are more usually associated with comedy, because it is easier to fit such a character into a fast-moving plot. Moreover, the predictability of such characters provokes laughter. They don't work psychologically; we don't ponder their motives or think about what they might be feeling.

In English drama, we encounter the following stock figures:

- The bashful lover.
- The domineering wife.
- The henpecked husband.
- The lovesick young man.
- The bold girl who takes risks to get a husband.
- The stern father who forbids his daughter to marry the man of her choice.
- The clever servant who gets his dim-witted master out of trouble.
- The revenger who rights a wrong by murder.
- The malcontent who shuns and is shunned by society.
- The fop who follows fashion.
- The rake who leads a riotous life.
- The stupid person.
- The witty jester.
- The boasting soldier.
- The melancholy man who is never cheerful.
- The clever priest, whose plans put everything right.

You might like to look through the plays you are studying to see how many of the characters can be described as stock.

There are two closely related points to bear in mind when thinking about stock characters:

- It is not necessarily a lesser achievement to create a stock character. The challenge is to re-create a familiar figure so that he or she is fresh rather than just a repetition of previous stock characters. Frank Spencer of *Some Mothers Do 'Ave 'Em* is a re-creation of the stupid man.
- Complex characters can be developed from stock types. Juno, for example, might be close to the domineering wife, but her compassion and sensitivity make her much more than that.

Some of Shakespeare's central characters have links with stock types. But he does far more with them. Brabantio in *Othello* (1604) looks like the stern father opposing his daughter's wishes, but when we hear he has died of a broken heart we see he is more than a comical stock type. Falstaff, perhaps Shakespeare's greatest creation, has links with the boasting soldier and the rake.

Summary

Stock characters have few distinguishing characteristics. They are often funny and are suited to comic plots. They are not easy to create, and many more complex characters are re-creations of stock types.

10.4   Characters and functions

Symbolic characters

Some characters, particularly in the plays of Shakespeare's era, function symbolically or emblematically. Their qualities are often evident in their names. In Ben Jonson's *Volpone* (1607), Voltore's name means vulture; Corbaccio means raven and Corvino means crow. Volpone himself is sly and cunning like a fox. All are voraciously greedy. These characters have some distinguishing features beyond their symbolic ones, but the force of the drama depends on their emblematic function.

Characters as mouthpieces of dialogue

What chiefly matters in some plays is the life of the dialogue. Oscar Wilde's *The Importance of Being Earnest* (1895) is memorable for its dazzling exchanges, but with the notable exception of Lady Bracknell, what we remember is what is said rather than who has said it. And when we look up who said it, we don't usually think of the line as being expressive of the character. We enjoy Gwendolen saying 'I had no idea there were any flowers in the country' (Act 2), but we don't regard the remark as an insight into her character.

Character and plot function

Sometimes characters are created in order to perform functions required by the plot. Because they are created only to perform these tasks, it is often difficult to make complete sense of them as individuals. If they are consistent, their consistency is dramatic, not psychological.

In order to make the plot of *Measure for Measure* (1604) develop, Shakespeare requires the Duke to do a number of things. He delegates power to Angelo, leaves Vienna and then returns in disguise, prepares a young man for his execution, implements the bed-swap plot with the woman Angelo refused to marry, and returns to judge how Angelo has conducted himself. It's difficult to make the Duke psychologically consistent. If he knew about Angelo's past, why did he leave him in charge? If, however, we see that Shakespeare is an opportunist, the Duke makes *dramatic* sense. In a complex plot, someone in authority has to do certain things; those certain things constitute the functions of the Duke.

Summary

Some characters are created to perform certain tasks. A character can be symbolic, the mouthpiece of ideas and can say and do what the plot requires. We should not look for psychological consistency in such characters.

10.5   Characters and trust

The only way an audience can understand a play is by trusting what the characters say. Of course, some characters are out to deceive, but the playwright makes it clear either that a character is lying or is prone to lie.

What can be questioned

Within a play there are moments when the audience might question what is being said; for example, what one character says about another. Consider Macbeth's soliloquy in which he prepares to kill Duncan:

> Besides this Duncan
> Hath borne his faculties so meek, hath been
> So clear in his great office, that his virtues
> Will plead like angels, trumpet-tongued against
> The deep damnation of his taking off;
>
> (1.7. 16–20)

Killing the king will be so tumultuous that it will seem like the last judgement, with angels pleading in voices that sound like the trumpet that awakens the dead. And this is not just because Duncan is the king – crowned, anointed and ruling with the permission of God – but because he has been 'So clear in his great office'. Macbeth suggests that Duncan has a transparency of soul, through which his purity shines. But is this true? Duncan is genial, courteous, firm and generous – but is he, as Macbeth's words imply, a candidate for sainthood? Perhaps the disturbing truth is that it is Macbeth who creates the holiness of Duncan so that he can destroy it.

Summary

We usually trust what characters say, but we should be prepared to question what one character says of another.

▄▼ 11 Audience

11.1 Knowledge

Drama is immediate and communal. The audience, therefore, is a necessary constituent of drama, as the reader is to a novel, and the speaking voice to a poem.

> **The audience is the point of reception, the point at which the drama actually becomes the thing it is.**

Audiences acquire knowledge from what they hear (that is what 'audience' means) and see. To be an audience is to know something. All literature depends on knowing. The audience needs to know a character's history and (in most cases) plans in order to understand the play. Knowing is rarely simple. It exists on different levels. Hamlet tells his friends that he will behave as if he is mentally unbalanced. Therefore, his friends and the audience know that, but the rest of the characters don't. Hence Hamlet's behaviour puzzles Claudius, Polonius, Rosencrantz and Guildenstern.

Drama often arises out of disparities in knowledge; sometimes characters create disparities through the tricks and schemes they implement against each other. Knowledge is the currency of drama. We desire it, and possession gives us power. To know something about someone, who doesn't know that you know it, gives you an advantage.

In most plays, the audience knows all. One of the enjoyable aspects of watching a play is recognizing the multiple layers of awareness. Take Act 3, sc. 4 of *Twelfth Night* (1599). For his own pleasure, Sir Toby deceives both Viola and Sir Andrew into fighting a duel. He tells each that the other is an expert swordsman. Toby has the advantage of knowing that both think the other is deadly, and that neither in fact is. But the audience knows something that Toby doesn't. The audience knows that Viola is Viola – a young woman – and not the young gentleman, Cesario.

This example emphasizes two very important things:

- In the theatre the audience is more involved, more a participant or collaborator, in realizing the text than, say, the reader of a novel.
- What an audience knows firmly shapes its understanding and judgement of the characters and the action.

Summary

Plays work through the exploitation of disparities of knowledge. The audience is active in realizing the significance of what happens on stage. What the audience knows shapes its understanding and judgement.

11.2 Disguise

Disguise is a special form of role-playing. It is distinctly (and most of the time, exclusively) theatrical. In plays, characters frequently disguise themselves; but people hardly ever do so in everyday life.

The essential point about disguise is that a character conceals his or her identity. 'Guise' means a person's customary manner and external appearance. Disguise is the concealing or effacing of that manner and appearance. So disguise is not dressing up. You might go to a fancy dress party dressed up as a policeman, but the other guests know that it is *you*. Disguise might involve impersonation; that is, pretending to be someone else. But it need not. All that is required is that people don't recognize you as *you*.

The freedom of disguise

In drama, the audience has to accept that characters in disguise are not recognized. No one sees that the brilliant young lawyer in *The Merchant of Venice* (1596) is really Portia – not even her husband.

Disguise, therefore, creates freedom:

> **Characters in disguise can say and hear what otherwise they would not be able to.**

Before the Battle of Agincourt, Henry v, disguised as an ordinary soldier, hears what his soldiers truly think of him (they doubt he will keep his word) and he can say, in soldier-like prose, what he really feels:

> For, though I speak it to you, I think the king is but a man, as I am. The violet smells to him as it does to me; the element shows to him as it doth to me. All his senses have but human conditions.
>
> (4.1. 101–3)

Only disguise can give a king the freedom to say that his senses – his awareness of the world about him – are merely human. In a play about brotherhood, Henry shares in the brotherhood of those, who, protected by his disguise, can speak their minds.

Impersonation

Impersonation is taking on the identity of another person. In *The Taming of the Shrew* (1595), Tranio impersonates his master, Lucentio, so that Lucentio can disguise himself as a teacher and woo Bianca. But the impersonation of Lucentio by Tranio allows the audience to enjoy the convention of the dim-witted master being helped out of scrapes by a crafty (and bright) servant. Tranio does a splendid job as 'Lucentio', winning the bargaining for Bianca and becoming, very quickly, the man in whom her father confides.

Cross-dressing

We are sometimes surprised that cross-dressing is so prominent in the English theatre. Some people think it rather cheap and frivolous to have women dressing up as men.

Two things might be learnt from this hesitation.

- We have to accept that the theatre is a world in which strange and playful things can happen.
- Theatrical art mixes the frivolous and the profound. Beethoven's only opera, *Fidelio* (1804), is about the struggle for freedom, yet it involves the standard comic ploy of a woman dressing up as a man in order to be near her beloved.

Sometimes there are practical reasons why a playwright opts for cross-dressing. Women are vulnerable, so it is sensible for them to dress as men when they are in a strange place. In *As You Like It* (1599), Rosalind dresses as a man before entering the Forest of Arden.

But Shakespeare occasionally goes further. *Twelfth Night* probes the very interesting issue of whether a girl dressed as a boy begins to understand what it feels like to be male. Viola has to listen to Orsino's romantic (and very male?) yearnings. In order to persuade him that perhaps he might be wasting his time over Olivia, she has to speak in a masculine manner. In the intimate Act 2, sc. 4 – the emotional heart of the play – she adopts a mode of speech that takes melancholy pleasure in the passing of time and the fading of female beauty:

> And so they are. Alas that they are so:
> To die even when they to perfection grow.
> (39–40)

She expresses male melancholy nicely in the regretful rising and falling of the cadence on 'perfection'. Later, in order to lend authority to her words, she speaks as a man: 'We men may say more, swear more' (116). And in another scene she recognizes that she is both: 'As I am a man … As I am a woman' (2.2. 36, 38).

Summary

A disguised character has the freedom to say and hear what otherwise would be impossible. Impersonation can be used to explore theatrical conventions, and cross-dressing is useful in plot promotion and can raise issues of gender identity.

11.3   Deception

Misinformation

Virtually anything a disguised character says is likely to misinform. Because he is merely playing at being Lucentio, Tranio can invent fabulous wealth in order to win Bianca (*The Taming of the Shrew*). A case of deception without disguise occurs in *Julius Caesar* (1599). Cassius discloses in a soliloquy (1.2. 308–22) that he will encourage Brutus to think Caesar is a threat to Rome by throwing letters in his window that appear to come from citizens concerned about Caesar's growing influence.

Misinformation is a form of lying. Playing the role of the 'honest' man (direct, bluff, open), Iago lies to everyone. He even lies in his soliloquies – or, at least, he probably does. The difficulty with habitual liars in both art and life is that the more they lie, the more difficult it becomes for others to be sure of anything they say.

Misreading

Another form of deception practised by Iago is allowing a character to misread a situation. Desdemona does lose her handkerchief and, as intended, Cassio finds it. He asks Bianca to take out the decoration. All these things are true. But Iago so positions Othello, both physically and mentally, that Othello tells himself a story in which Desdemona is unfaithful to him.

Misleading role-play

In Ben Jonson's plays, deception often takes the theatrical form of misleading role-playing. Subtle and Face in *The Alchemist* (1612) announce that they have discovered how to turn ordinary metals into gold. Volpone plays the role of the sick man on the brink of death. On stage, we can see that this is deceitful. If at the opening of the play, Volpone were to jump zestfully from his bed to make his customary adorations to his god (gold), the point would be made that here is a man in perfect health.

Summary

Because the audience knows about characters, it can detect when one is deceiving another. Deception can take place through disguise, through misinformation, through leading a character to misread what is happening, and by playing a role.

11.4   Overlooking, overhearing

One character can gain advantage over another through overlooking and overhearing. This can be done by concealment or disguise. Volpone, for example, having made it known that he is dead, conceals himself and watches the responses of those who want to inherit his wealth.

In the theatre, the audience sees all: those who overlook and those who are overlooked. The experience is immediate and can be complex; we might both appreciate the comedy of their impercipience and feel for them in their exposure to prying eyes. What we feel will, of course, be dependent on how the scene is played. When Malvolio reads the letter which he is led to believe is from Olivia, the players might opt for the comedy of his absurdity – such fantasies, such hopes – or bring out the pathos of a man deceived by self-delusion.

Usually, the one who is overlooked is at a disadvantage. Thus Othello, overlooking a meeting between Iago and Cassio, thinks he is at an advantage. What he doesn't know is that Iago questions Cassio not, as Othello has been led to believe, about Desdemona but about Bianca, a prostitute whom Cassio finds tiresome. Othello hears Cassio's scornful laughter and assumes Cassio is talking of Desdemona.

Summary

The audience enjoys seeing one character overlooking another. Overlooking creates a disparity between the overlooker and the overlooked, though this can be reversed if the overlooker is misled into believing that what he/she sees is true.

11.5   Framed action

What physically happens on stage when characters overlook is close to another theatrical device – the framing of action.

A frame is created when one set of characters comments on the actions of others.

At the beginning of *Antony and Cleopatra* (1606), the comments of Demetrius and Philo create a frame. As Antony and Cleopatra enter, Philo establishes what, in public reputation, Antony has become:

> Look where they come.
> Take but good note, and you shall see in him
> The triple pillar of the world transformed
> Into a strumpet's fool. Behold and see.

(1.1. 10–13)

Philo's language invites distinctly theatrical gesturing. This is *deictic language* – words that depend on the circumstances in which they are uttered. 'Look,' he says; and 'Take but good note' and Demetrius 'shall see'. There is even something of the presenter or impresario in his final and decidedly triumphant 'Behold and see.' The thematic ambiguity of the play is present in that theatrical invitation to 'behold'. Antony has fallen away from his former splendour, but there is still glory in what we see.

Summary

A frame is a highly theatrical device that allows characters to comment on the action and on other characters. Both the framed scene itself and the comments made can embody the themes of the play.

11.6　Audiences and theatrical traditions

Audiences steeped in theatrical traditions know what plays are like and how other productions have handled the stage business of a particular work. Furthermore, playwrights know this. Playwrights don't write in a vacuum.

Theatrical history

Theatrical history can be relevant to an audience. For example, some plays are clearly dependent on each other. *Macbeth* (1606) has a lot in common with the earlier *Richard III* (1592); and *The Winter's Tale* (1609) can be compared illuminatingly with *Othello* (1604). In those plays, the same playwright thinks through how to present such things as murderous ambition and jealousy.

There are, however, cases in which one playwright works on the ideas of another. John Ford's *'Tis Pity She's a Whore* (1633) is disturbing because it has much in common with *Romeo and Juliet* (1594). It is difficult to escape the conclusion that Ford presumed that his audience saw the connection. Both plays make young love central, and both pairs of lovers – impetuous and ardent – choose death. Both include a Friar and a Nurse. There are also rival suitors. *Romeo and Juliet* is about a love forbidden because of the ancient rivalry of two

families, but Ford explores the bar to love that operates in virtually every society – incest.

Distance

In plays that depend on disparities of knowledge, the audience needs to keep
a check on what it knows, and what individual characters do and do not know.
We are amused, entertained and diverted by disparities of knowledge, but such
are the shifts in advantage that we rarely become involved in the emotional life –
the hopes and fears – of many of the characters. The kind of play described here
is one that falls within the genre of comedy. Comedy often promotes laughter,
but laughter is more difficult when we have very strong feelings of pity and
compassion for some of the characters.

It is in plays that we usually call tragedies that there is a close emotional bond
between the audience and the central figures. Through soliloquies and intimate
dialogues, the audience learns of the turmoils of a character's inner life. Fifteen
per cent of *Macbeth* consists of monologue. Perhaps we know him better than
any other of Shakespeare's tragic heroes; he shares his plans, his fears and his
regrets with us.

Summary

**Audiences who know theatre history can see links between plays. The
experience of watching a play is shaped by how we stand in relation to the
characters on stage. Comedy works when there is distance between
audience and characters; tragedy requires an audience to be closer.**

11.7 Laughter

We value a play and a production if it prompts us (appropriately) to laugh.

Detachment makes laughter possible. It's only when we are removed from
the actuality of experience that we find events amusing. The closer we are, the
more uncomfortable we can be.

Expectation

Expectation prompts laughter through fulfilment and denial. We say we found
something funny both because we anticipated it *and* because it was unex-
pected. Drama very frequently works by the arousal of expectation. In *She
Stoops to Conquer* (1773), we expect to be amused by the arrival of Hastings and
Marlow at what they think is an inn, but the audience knows is the home of
Mr Hardcastle. Equally, however, there is laughter when, in *The Playboy of the*

Western World (1907), Christy Mahon's father, whom Christy claims to have killed, enters. Laughter is further provoked when the old man can't recognize his son from the heroic descriptions the villagers give of him.

Like machines

Comedy, unlike tragedy, has traditionally been free from theorizing. Philosophers have not found much to say about it. But there is one theory about laughter that makes sense of the distance of the audience.

The French philosopher, Henri Bergson, said that we laugh when we see the human body presented as if it were a machine. The more a body is depleted of personality, the funnier scenes become. This makes sense of the traditional business of the banana skin. What we see is not a person, but a machine malfunctioning.

The particular kind of comedy that this theory fits is farce (see Chapter 9, section 9.10). Farce consists of chases and violence, but we laugh because what is represented to us is not a person but rather a set of flailing arms and legs. If farce works, we don't say 'Ow!' sympathetically when a character is punched. We laugh at the beating of servants in *The Comedy of Errors* (1594) and the chases of a Ben Travers farce.

Proportion

We all have a sense of proportion, a sense of what is to be expected. When that sense is flouted, we laugh. In *Twelfth Night*, Malvolio's yellow stockings, we must understand, are inappropriate, so his wearing them to accompany equally unexpected behaviour – smiling, for example – delights us by outraging our sense of proportion.

What a sense of proportion tells us about is the social context of drama, particularly comic drama. What we think is normal arises out of the kinds of lives we lead. Comedy disrupts that normality, and we respond by that potentially dangerous thing – laughter.

Limits

Because laughter can be dangerous, there is always going to be a problem with it, especially for those who have very definite ideas about the conduct of society. We can put the issue in the form of a question: are there some things we should not laugh at? When Lear sees the blinded Gloucester, he cries: 'Goneril with a white beard?' Goneril is the daughter whose actions have contributed to Lear's madness. What does the audience do? Is laughter in any way appropriate? The difficulty with laughter is that while it may not be proper, it happens. What we can learn from that is the anarchic potentiality of laughter.

Purpose

The relationship between comedy (and therefore laughter) and morality is very often strained. Ben Jonson says, in his Prologue to *Every Man in His Humour* (1601), that the purpose of comedy is to 'sport with human follies, not with crimes'. We laugh, in other words, at personal excesses and not at wickedness. We might in some plays, but not in all: audiences enjoy the zestful cheating practised by Volpone, and they have even laughed at the gullibility of Othello. In the case of Volpone we can enjoy his knowing evil and see it as being better than the equally corrupt fools he cheats but who don't know their own wickedness. But if we laugh at Othello, are we endorsing the unaccountable evil of Iago?

Summary

Both expectation and surprise prompt laughter. Laughter is provoked when we are invited to view people as mere machines. We laugh when our sense of proportion is outraged. Sometimes, we feel we ought not to laugh – but we do.

☑ 12 Watching and Studying

12.1 The theatre of the imagination

If you are studying a play for an English Literature examination, most of the time you will be looking at the words on the page. In Theatre Studies, other issues can be raised, but in English Literature, words are the object of study.

However, the text of a play cannot be read in the same way as a poem or a novel. It is a set of words intended for *performance*. Examiners sometimes complain that candidates don't do justice to what is *dramatic* about drama.

Performability

What, therefore, you have to do in study is to become the audience; that is, imagine the impact the words of the text might have in performance. In fact, it is not for just one performance. The test of a play is its performability, and performability means that it can be done in a number of ways.

In drama, interpretation means the possibility of different performances.

Some plays offer more possibilities than others; Shakespeare's texts are so rich, for example, that people continue to find new ways of presenting his plays. But on stage a scene can only be done in one way, therefore those putting on the play have to make choices, and to choose to perform a play in one particular way means excluding other ways. It is often said that plays should be seen, not studied. It is easy to see why people say this: the immediacy of the actors' physical presences is a distinctive and forceful experience. Yet reading a play has this advantage: you can allow yourself to think of the various ways in which a scene might be performed.

Imagining performances

Thinking through some of the theatrical possibilities of a play is acting it out in the theatre of the imagination. To imagine a performance is to become both a company of players and the audiences for whom they perform. A student can always ask:

- How might this be done?
- What effect might it have?

Summary

Performability is the distinctive feature of a play. When studying a play, it is possible to see that there are several different ways of performing it. To study a play successfully, the student has to act it out in the theatre of the imagination.

12.2 Types of stage

The stage is the most flexible medium in literature. In a single play, the stage (particularly in Shakespeare) can be the site of several levels of reality. The action can shift from recognizable, and sometimes uncomfortably raw, feelings to strange and even magical occurrences. The stage, unlike the 'flat' medium of television, can accommodate such shifts.

Yet some kinds of stage are more flexible than others. It is always profitable to ask: what kind of stage would be the most suitable?

The earliest plays you are likely to study are those by Shakespeare and his contemporaries. It is therefore wise to know about the kind of stage for which they wrote.

Shakespeare's stage

- The stage was a very large one which projected into the audience. There were two doors at the back and very probably an inner stage, screened off by a curtain. Above the inner stage was a balcony. The size of the stage was equivalent in size to a double tennis court; that is, larger than most modern stages.
- The stage was both neutral and flexible, in that it could be anywhere, and in a single play represent a number of different places. Moreover, it could be the location of strange and magical actions. In Shakespeare, the action can change from events that are drawn from the familiar world to the kinds of things that only occur in drama.
- Some of the audience stood around the stage; others sat in tiered seats, some of which would look down on the stage from a considerable height. Shakespeare's theatre probably held about 2,000 people.
- Because most people in the audience were near the players, the soliloquy was particularly effective; a player could address the audience directly or allow them to hear his innermost thoughts without having to boom out his words.
- Except when a character is already on stage (very rare), all scenes start with characters entering through the doors, and end with their exiting through them. Thus the movement of the plays remains fluid, and it makes possible significant entrances and exits, such as Perdita appearing as the Queen of the Revels in *The Winter's Tale* (1609) and Malvolio's angry exit in the last scene of *Twelfth Night* (1599).

- The hostility of opposing groups could be staged by having them enter through different doors. This would have happened at the beginning of *Romeo and Juliet* (1594).
- The inner stage could be used for eavesdropping scenes, as in *Othello* (1604), and for revelations (usually called discoveries), as in the prison scenes in *The Duchess of Malfi* (1623).
- The balcony could become castle walls, as in *Richard II* (1595). *Romeo and Juliet* has a famous balcony scene.
- The fact that plays were performed during the day, and that members of the audience could see each other, emphasizes the theatricality of the theatre. The audience always knew it was watching a play.

The proscenium arch

Later in the history of the theatre, the acting space was behind an arch (the *proscenium arch*) from which a curtain hung. The audience look, as it were, through the window of the arch into other people's lives. Such a stage is appropriate for those realistic plays of the nineteenth century – by Henrik Ibsen and Anton Chekhov, for example – and plays which deal with manners and morals. It would be misleading to call *The Importance of Being Earnest* (1895) a realistic play, but because it touches on the fashions of the time, a proscenium arch would be appropriate.

Summary

The performance of a play is shaped by the type of stage on which the play is performed.

12.3 Characters on stage

When studying a play, it is helpful to remember how many people are on stage, and to ask what effects are created as a result. *Waiting for Godot* (1952) has a cast of five characters. Something of its strange atmosphere – bleak yet not without affection and merriment – comes from the sight of so few on stage. If the stage were large, perhaps the bleakness would be increased. *Macbeth* (1606) is a play with a big cast, but for the most emotionally and thematically charged scenes all the audience sees are the Macbeths – two haunted creatures, a husband and wife who have brought terror upon Scotland. And think how so many comedies end with a stage full of people to show that those who who have been isolated from society are now restored to it.

Silent characters

In Act 2, sc. 1 of *The Winter's Tale*, Leontes bursts into his wife's room to take away his son, Mamillius. The father rants, but the son – bewildered, frightened and lost – says nothing. We never see him again. Harold Pinter's *The Caretaker* (1960) opens with a character who says nothing. He stands alone in a room, looks about him and exits. The audience wonders: Who is he? Where is he going? Will we see him again?

Summary

When we act out a play in the theatre of the imagination we should remember the number of people on stage at any time. We should also think of the effect of silent characters.

12.4   Design

Scenery

It is important to ask what kind of scenery would be appropriate to the themes and atmosphere of the play. In some cases the action makes it clear exactly what is required: *The Caretaker* needs two beds and a pile of junk, and *Waiting for Godot* needs a tree. In other plays, the action requires a particular kind of setting, though the designer (the one responsible for the scenery) has considerable freedom of execution. *She Stoops to Conquer* (1773) needs a rambling, old-fashioned set, but there are many ways of achieving this.

Scenery can help to distinguish particular places. *The Winter's Tale* (1609) moves from Sicilia – a place of suspicion, madness and death – to Bohemia, where Spring is welcomed with communal festivity. In *Antony and Cleopatra* (1606) there is a contrast between the severe world of Rome and the erotic opulence of Egypt. Both of these contrasts might be captured in the scenery.

Costume

Costume should help to create character, contribute to the atmosphere and, when possible, articulate the themes of the play. Hamlet, for example, opens the play in mourning – his 'customary suits of solemn black' (1.2. 78) – whilst all the other characters will be elegantly dressed to celebrate the new king's marriage. Hamlet's black indicates his character, creates an atmosphere of hostility between him and the Court, and indicates the presence of death.

Settings

Designers and producers can experiment. They can ask whether a play might be given a different social setting. For example, *Much Ado About Nothing* (1598) concerns soldiers returning from a war, but it doesn't have to be a sixteenth-century one. It might be set in, say, the Crimean war, the American Civil War or the First World War. Plays that deal with the politics of a nation, such as *Julius*

Caesar or *Henry v* (both 1599) are frequently given twentieth-century settings. It is worth asking what aspects of the play such settings bring out.

Lighting

Theatres had no artificial lighting for centuries. But as we now have lighting, we can ask how a scene might be lit. How, for example, should Shakespeare's night scenes in *A Midsummer Night's Dream* (1594) and *Othello* be lit? It's an important issue, because lighting creates atmosphere. *Twelfth Night* (1599) can be festive or melancholy, and lighting can help to establish either mood.

Smells

Smells can be the most evocative of all the senses – the longings of nostalgia and happy or sad memories can all be aroused by a fragrance. Thornton Wilder's *Our Town* (1938), a play of American family life, might be accompanied by the smells of cooking (apple pie perhaps), and John Whiting's *The Devils* (1961) has been performed with incense burning.

Summary

The work of the designer and producer should bring out a play's themes and atmosphere. Distinctive theatrical experiences can be created through scenery, costume, socially appropriate settings, atmospheric lighting and smells.

12.5   Actors and acting

Acting is the area where the freedom enjoyed by the student's imagination departs radically from the constraints of the theatre. In your imagination you can envisage who might play a particular part.

You might go to the theatre, and there on stage is a very familiar face from a soap or a sitcom. That can be the starting point for a game: think about the play you are studying and ask who would best play each of the characters. This is more than fantasy theatre, as it works through the recognition that actors bring something of their own personalities to the parts they play.

If you broaden this imaginative activity, you might ask, more generally, what *kind* of actor would best suit this or that role? You can make this question more detailed by thinking about particular scenes and particular speeches.

Age

In many plays, particularly those by Shakespeare, there are often no exact indications of a character's age. Deciding on the age of a character has consequences for interpretation. *Twelfth Night* (1599) is concerned with age and the passing of time. Sometimes Orsino and Olivia – the yearning lover and the mourning daughter and sister – are played as being older than the twins – Viola and Sebastian – they become involved with. To make them older lends a poignancy to the action. Are they aware that they should secure a beloved before it is too late? If it were done that way, the twins, because they are younger, might seem harder and more adventurous, more willing to taste the different aspects of the world of love. But play them all at about the same age, and Olivia would become someone trying out mourning because she has got youth and time for it. She quickly drops it when she meets, as she supposes, a suitable young man. And is Malvolio old or young? If he's played as middle-aged or older, his hopes of Olivia are pathetic and grotesque, but if he is young (and Puritanism was fashionable), then *Twelfth Night* (1599) becomes a play of social aspirations. If the yeoman of the wardrobe can marry the lady of the Strachy (2.5. 36–7), why then....

Size

The build of an actor can have a bearing on the responses of an audience. Here are some issues:

- What would be the effect if Lady Bracknell, the dominating figure of *The Importance of Being Earnest* (1895), were to be played by someone who was physically small?
- What effects would be achieved if there were considerable disparities in size between Othello and Iago?
- Falstaff is fat. What if he were also tall?

Voice

The voice is an actor's chief instrument. As voices differ in timbre and pitch, you may like to imagine the effects of different voices. A voice, of course, should be appropriate to a character, but there are many ways to be appropriate. Take the example of Hamlet. He is such a multifaceted character that different voices can realize different aspects of the text. If his voice has a boyish quality, then the scenes with his mother might bring out the difficulty he has with her remarriage. If the voice has a harsh, grating edge, then his savage treatment of Ophelia will be particularly uncomfortable. And what kind of voice (and style of speaking) would suit the soliloquies – rhapsodic, clipped, incisive, wondering, heavy...?

Summary

The physical qualities an actor brings to a role can shape the performance and, consequently, the interpretation of the play. We can imagine the effects of age, size and voice.

12.6   Centralizing women

Some theatrical art is either female-centred or frequently gives women a central role. Ballet is an example of the first, and opera of the second. There are plays in which a woman is the central character, such as Shaw's *Saint Joan* (1924). This play might also be said to explore the role of women in contemporary society as does, for a different time and society, Ibsen's *A Doll's House* (1879).

Women in Shakespeare

Shakespeare's comedies are usually female-centred. Viola in *Twelfth Night* and Rosalind in *As You Like It* (1599) are the motivating forces of the plots. They also outshine the men in their maturity, stability and common sense. But, particularly in his late plays, Shakespeare does something else. He places women so that they take on a thematic and representative role. They become icons. In the sheep-shearing festival in *The Winter's Tale* (1609), Perdita is hostess and a kind of festival queen. In a framing comment, Polixenes – 'Nothing she does or seems/But smacks of something greater than herself' (4.4. 157–8) – expresses the kind of awesome admiration we should feel. Such moments are a challenge to the director.

Summary

Plays make female characters central by creating roles which give a woman an iconic status.

12.7   Music, dance, songs, ghosts, fights

Music

Music, singing and dancing were elements in Greek drama. In Shakespeare, there were fanfares, and music for dances. There might have been musical accompaniments to the songs that pepper his plays.

Melodrama

In melodrama the cast delivered their lines to a musical score that was intended to orchestrate the emotions of the various exchanges. It was very popular in the nineteenth century, and some of the famous examples (for example, Leopold Lewis's *The Bells* (1871)) have a simple force that can still rouse an audience to feelings of pity and horror. We still use the term (often critically) as an adjective – melodramatic – to refer to any performance or work that is emotionally high-pitched and sensationalist in subject matter, action and tone. Although short-lived as a genre, melodrama has had a lasting effect on public entertainment. Film replaced the melodrama as public entertainment, and in the days of silent films, there was music provided by a pianist or, in larger cinemas, an orchestra. The film distributors sent the score along with the reels of film. When the 'talkies' replaced the 'silents', music was added to the sound track. When we watch a film without music, we realize how important music still is in the cinema.

Songs

Shakespeare's plays contain songs. Sometimes, as in *As You Like It* (1599), a song is hardly integrated with the action. Touchstone and two Pageboys enter and sing 'It was a Lover and his Lass'. Touchstone even comments that 'there was no great matter' in the song (5.3. 40). But Feste's songs in *Twelfth Night* contribute to the scenes in which they appear by making indirect comments on the characters and the action. When Feste sings 'Youth's a stuff will not endure' (2.3. 40) to the drunken Sir Toby and Sir Andrew, there is expressed the sad truth that their youth has all but gone. *Twelfth Night* is often praised for its creation of an atmosphere tinged with melancholy. The songs – in particular Feste's final one about the rain raining every day – have an important place in the creation of that feeling.

Dances

For one who just reads a play, the impact of dances is very difficult to imagine. If, however, you have seen dance, or danced yourself, the sheer physical presence of gesture, movement and pattern has an immediacy and strength, perhaps matched only by very loud music. When done well (not an easy achievement), the audience enjoy the physical thrill of seeing bodies moving rhythmically to music.

Dance on stage is ancient. W. B. Yeats, protesting against what he thought of as the passive suffering of Wilfred Owen's poetry, pointed out that in Greece the tragic Chorus danced. In Shakespeare's day, there is evidence that a play, whatever the tone or topic, concluded with a dance. There is a record of a German traveller (Thomas Plater) who saw in 1599 what in all likelihood was *Julius Caesar*, at the conclusion of which the actors danced, in spite of the fact that the play concludes with a funeral march. The play within a play in *A Midsummer Night's Dream* concludes with a bergamasque, a rustic dance. Theseus has declined to hear the Mechanicals deliver the Epilogue, perhaps because, in a world where dance was important, he knows that the dance will be well done. (Though it has to be said that most productions play it for laughs.)

Communal celebration

Dances connect us to a tradition of communal celebration. The English year was punctuated by days set aside for revelry, and these communal festivals included dancing – the Morris and the Maypole. No doubt some of the dances in Shakespeare's plays were akin to ones people would remember celebrating. C. L. Barber, in *Shakespeare's Festive Comedy* (1959) argues that the dances at the close of *A Midsummer Night's Dream* would follow a recognizably traditional pattern, with Oberon leading a processional dance – 'after me' (5.2. 25) – and Titania leading a round dance like those associated with Maypoles – 'hand in hand' (5.2. 29). The effect is to link the blessing of the fairies with those customs which the audience would recognize as rituals of communal celebration.

Dance and plots

Shakespeare uses dance to forward the plot and to conclude a play on an appropriate note. In *Much Ado About Nothing* (1598) there is a masked ball. This allows Shakespeare to create the deceptions that are the stuff of the play. It allows Beatrice to mock Benedick to his (masked) face, and the deceiving Don John, who is trying to stop the betrothal of Hero and Claudio, speaks to Claudio under the pretence that he thinks he is Benedick.

Dancing is thematically central to *Twelfth Night* (1599). Dance is the essence of celebration, and Sir Toby and Sir Andrew discuss how life might be conducted to dance steps. It is a jest, but perhaps it reveals something about Sir Toby's attitude to life. His 'very walk', he says, 'should be a jig' (1.3. 124). We might have reservations. Dancing is special – celebratory and festive – so it should be confined to holidays. Those who would turn all life into a holiday would destroy the rhythm of life.

Dances and the close of plays

Shakespeare often closes comedies with dances. To the Elizabethans, dancing was an expression of peace and harmony among people, and an image of order in the whole universe. To conclude a play with a dance is to show that all is well.

The dance is not confined to Shakespeare's stage. In *A Doll's House* (1879), Ibsen has Nora dance a tarantella (wild southern Italian steps danced to cure the bite of the tarantula spider). This expresses her yearning for freedom, a freedom she can only reach for in dance and, later, by leaving home – her doll's house.

John Arden made dance central to his anti-war play *Sergeant Musgrave's Dance* (1959). Pretending to be a recruiting party, some renegade soldiers force the people of a Durham town to look at the skeleton of one of their lads, who went to war. Musgrave, in defiance of a system that sends boys to die, dances his dance. The dance is very difficult to stage. It is an enactment of freedom from tyranny and a vision of a better world. And how do you do that? The point seems to be that the dance stands for drama, the theatre, and that Arden is trying to show how the theatre, a great communal experience, can change our lives. However, he also recognizes that this might be a failure. Musgrave dances his dance, but the people are indifferent.

Fights

Dances are harmonious; fights are discordant. In the theatre, there are different kinds of fights. The street fighting in *Romeo and Juliet* (1597) and the fights in which Mercutio and Tybalt are killed must be acted with the roughness and high tempers of the swaggering young men who participate.

A very different kind of fight is the one at the close of *King Lear* (1605) in which Edgar, who has always been outwitted by Edmund, kills Edmund in single combat. This is an emblematic struggle between good and evil, so the action might be ritualized, and perhaps Edgar's victory could be achieved with symbolic ease.

Sometimes fights have thematic significance. The duel at the end of Hamlet, conducted according to the rules of courtly fencing, sums up the games of attack and defence, advance and retreat, thrust and parry that Hamlet has played with the Court throughout the play. His verbal skirmishings with Polonius and the strategies and counter-strategies of his baiting of Claudius are given immediate expression in the clash of the rapiers.

Ghosts

Performers face two issues: how to present the ghost and how to bring out its significance.

In an inventory of theatrical props from Shakespeare's day, there is an entry: cloak of invisibility. This must have been a garment that indicated to the audience that the figure, visible to them, was invisible to the characters. Today, theatres can resort to technology – lights, music, sound effects, stage machinery. Alternatively, a ghost can be done without the glamour of technology. A particularly tall actor could play the part, or there could be variations in the pace and pitch of the voice. A ghostly presence might also be conveyed through stylized movements.

It can be a problem for staging if only one character, as in the banquet scene in *Macbeth* (1605), sees the Ghost. Whether the Ghost is presented or not has an effect on how the audience sees the play: if the Ghost is represented, Macbeth's guilt is made visible and objective; if absent, his guilt is seen exclusively in psychological terms.

Ghosts make a number of contributions to the themes of a play. It might seem odd that Shakespeare called his Roman play about the change from a republic to a monarchy, *Julius Caesar* (1599), when Caesar is assassinated in the third act. Yet Shakespeare's point is that the power of Caesar grows after his death. He becomes a revenging spirit, destroying the conspirators and effectively establishing his nephew, Octavius, as the ruler. His power is made theatrically present by his ghostly appearance in Brutus's tent before the decisive battle at the play's climax. In this scene, it is up to the actor playing Brutus to convey the terror of the Ghost 'That makst my blood cold and my hair to stare' (4.2. 313).

Shakespeare's fullest treatment of a ghost is in *Hamlet* (1600). It's a significant part. It is silent in the play's first scene, but in the long fifth scene, the Ghost reveals how Hamlet's father died and commissions Hamlet to revenge 'his foul and most unnatural murder' (1.5. 25). That command constitutes the plot of the play. But Shakespeare does two further things with the Ghost. First, he makes the Ghost couch his command in language so vituperative that the revenge is inevitably enmeshed in Hamlet's turbulent feelings about his mother and her new husband – his uncle, the king. The duty of revenge (if that's what it is) cannot be a simple affair. Shakespeare also relates the Ghost to a problem Hamlet feels acutely – the problem of what we can know. Later, it occurs to him that the Ghost may be a devil seeking to destroy him by poisoning his mind. Is the Ghost, in Hamlet's word, 'honest' (1.5. 142); that is, genuine? His uncertainty is an important aspect in that much debated topic – Hamlet's delay.

Theme and atmosphere

All these bits of stage activity contribute to two things: theme and atmosphere.

Productions usually add up to something; they attempt to say something about the play being presented, and in the theatre of your imagination you must do the same. Once you decide what you think is central, you have to ask how this might be conveyed on stage. And you can do this for different themes. Is it the relationship between a mother and her son that is crucial to *Hamlet*? Those who have thought so have staged the meeting between Hamlet and Gertrude, not just in her apartment but in her bedroom. *Hamlet* is also about the struggle for power, the misuse of love, the uncertainty of knowledge, the failure of friendship and the instability of the mind. How might these be presented?

If you think a possible production can bring out certain themes, you have almost certainly also decided on the atmosphere of the play. Atmosphere covers both place and people. Directors must ask: what sort of sets, what kinds of clothes and what kinds of relationships between the characters will create an appropriate atmosphere? And even if the general atmosphere is clearly indicated in the text, you still have the options of nuance. Should *The Importance of Being Earnest* be played with any degree of social satire or should it be a world quite separate from issues of class and status? Whichever choice is made, the atmosphere will be affected.

Summary

The sounds and sights of a production are engaging in themselves and can establish theme and atmosphere.

■Ⓜ **Part Three**   Poetry

▪ ☑ 13 Valuing, Performing, Hearing

13.1 Immediacy

Poetry is more popular than we think. There is a weekly radio programme devoted to poetry; *The Nation's Favourite Poems* (1996) can be found in most bookshops; and we have a Poet Laureate but not a Novelist Laureate. Public occasions require the dignity and discipline of verse.

Poetry is memorable; it lives in our heads and hearts, and some lines enter the common stock of sayings we value for their wisdom and consolation. There is a story about Philip Larkin being asked who wrote one of his own lines: 'What will survive of us is love.'

Directness and force

Poetry is immediate; through its sounds and rhythms it can speak to us directly and forcefully. Sometimes readers talk with admiration about how arresting or striking a poem or part of a poem is. This is particularly so in the case of the openings of poems. Certain poems seize the reader. Consider this opening of a sonnet by Sir Philip Sidney (1591):

> My true Love hath my heart, and I have his

Why does this quiet, yet forthright, declaration engage us? Perhaps it is something to do with the way the steady monosyllables express the reciprocity – the give and take – of love. The line is balanced around the crucial word 'heart', and before and after it there is a verb of possession – 'hath' and 'have'. It is not easy to say anything new about love; what we find appealing here is the simplicity and verbal deftness with which an old truth – that lovers own each other – is voiced.

Summary

The rhythms and sounds of poetry make it both immediate and memorable.

13.2   An ancient art

The earliest examples of literature are almost invariably poetic. Stories were told in verse. Homer, the author of the foundation Epics of Western Literature, *The Iliad* and *The Odyssey* (eighth century BC), was a poet.

Poetry has its roots in the ancient world of myth and magic. Spells, charms, fortune-telling and curses took poetic forms. In fact, we still talk about poetry in terms derived from magic; it 'charms' or 'haunts' us.

Poetry and religion

Liturgy (the words of a religious ritual) and hymns (songs of praise) are ancient. Liturgy is recited and hymns are sung. Originally, both were probably danced. The poetic roots of liturgy can still be appreciated in the way it draws on the multiple meanings of words. Consider, how the *Sursum corda* – 'lift up your hearts' – depends on the connotations of 'hearts'. Liturgies usually include the chanting of scriptures, a practice that brings out the rhythmical nature of their language.

The English hymn is rarely studied on Literature courses, though J. R. Watson, in *The English Hymn* (1997), has shown how rich hymnody is. Perhaps the most famous poem in English is a hymn: John Mason Neale's 'Good King Wenceslas' (1853). And some hymns are worth reading whatever religious sentiments a reader might or might not have. Isaac Watts and Charles Wesley are considerable poets. Nor should we forget that there is a tradition in English of translating the Hebrew psalms (see *The Psalms in English* (1996), edited by Donald Davie). One of the distinctive features of the psalm is the long line. Does this reflect a strong pressure to speak fully about what matters? This amplitude of thought and feeling may have been the reason why William Blake and Walt Whitman turned to the long line of the psalms (and the Hebrew prophets) for their oracular and stirring verse.

The Muse

A special link between poetry and religion is found in the honour that poets give to inspiration. Poets claim inspiration, and religious scriptures are said to be inspired. Poets and religious people are not talking about exactly the same thing, a point Milton is careful to make at the beginning of *Paradise Lost* (1667) in his invocation of the Holy Spirit as the source of his inspiration (see Chapter 22, section 22.6).

Talk about the Muse – the source of poetic inspiration – goes back to Ancient Greece. Greek mythology distinguished nine Muses – the daughters of Zeus and Mnemosyne (goddess of memory), each of which inspired one of the arts. They were: Calliope (epic poetry), Clio (history), Erato (lyric and love poetry), Euterpe (flute music), Melpomene (tragedy), Polyhymnia (hymns), Terpsichore (dance and song), Thalia (comedy) and Urania (astronomy). Later, the Muse was spoken about as the inspiration for any work (though usually a poetic one) and of anything that inspired a poet to write. In particular, sixteenth- and seventeenth-century poets spoke of their beloveds as muses.

It is a convention that poets call on the Muse. This is called the *Invocation*. At those times when the work of poets was held to be important (for example, the Romantic period – 1780–1830), the imagery of inspiration was a central feature of verse. This is how Wordsworth opened *The Prelude* (1805):

> Oh there is a blessing in this gentle breeze,
> That blows from the green fields and from the clouds
> And from the sky

The poet welcomes the breeze, finding in its gentleness a blessing. Exactly what kind of blessing is revealed later:

> For I, methought, while the sweet breath of heaven
> Was blowing on my body, felt within
> A corresponding mild creative breeze,
> A vital breeze which travelled gently on
> O'er things which it had made, and is become
> A tempest, a redundant energy,
> Vexing its own creation.

> (41–7)

The wind – unpredictable and uplifting to the human spirit – is an image of inspiration. The breeze within is the creative impulse, nurtured by the one without. It is gentle yet it gives life – 'vital' – and its overflowing energy – 'redundant' – will become the 'tempest' of the poetic imagination. The image of the wind as inspiration is ancient. Those who wish to explore its many significances should read M. H. Abrams' article 'The Correspondent Breeze: A Romantic Metaphor' in *English Romantic Poets*, edited by M. H. Abrams (1975).

Four things can be said about the place of inspiration in English poetry:

- *The language of external influence.* The experience of inspiration is of something that comes from beyond. It is a pressure that compels. The poet is open to the influence but is not the author of the inspiring impulse. Even the inward and subjective Wordsworth repeats the words 'from' and 'o'er'.
- *Religious imagery.* The imagery of inspiration is drawn from the Bible. In the first chapter of Genesis, the Spirit of God is present at the Creation, moving the face of the waters, and in the second chapter of the Acts of the Apostles the Holy Spirit comes 'like a mighty rushing wind'. Inspiration is the creative breath of God.
- *The language of breathing.* There are links in language between inspiration and breathing. In both medicine and writing breathing in is inspiration and breathing out is expression. Inspiration is the very life and breath of the writer.
- *The language of the Muse.* Nowadays we are inclined to feel that talk about inspiration is too elevated. It seems too much of a claim. But throughout the history of English poetry, the Muse has been the traditional way of talking about the prompting to write. In *Poets on Poets* (1990), a collection of poems about poets, David Hopkins remarks that 'poets believe that, when inspired by the Muse, they have the power to defy the normal laws of Nature and give

permanence and stability to phenomena that are normally hopelessly fitful and transient.'

Language about the Muse is present in twentieth-century poetry. In 'The Circus Animals' Desertion' (1939), Yeats says: 'I sought a theme and sought for it in vain'. The Muse is present by her absence. Philip Larkin, towards the end of his life, said regretfully that he had not given up poetry, but it had given him up.

Summary

Poetry is the most ancient of literary arts with links to magic and religion. Poets often talk of being inspired. The conventional language of inspiration is the Muse. The Muse, the very breath of poetic life, comes to a poet and is spoken of in language akin to religion.

13.3   Poets as artists

What distinguishes literary from non-literary language? Some have argued that art is emotive, whereas non-literary writing is concerned with argument. This won't do; there is argument in poetry.

It is more helpful to remember that the original meaning of the word 'poetry' is derived from the Greek verb 'poieo' – 'to make'. This idea has survived. In Scots the word for poet is 'makir' – maker, and W. H. Auden, in his 'Ode to the Medieval Poets' (in *Epistle to a Godson*, 1972) contrasts the full-blooded cheerfulness of Chaucer, Langland and Douglas with our morose, contemporary 'makers'.

All literature has been made. What we are often aware of in poetry is the formal evidence of making – line, rhyme, rhythm – and a consciousness in the poet that he or she is a maker.

Nature and art

Poetry is making, and making is art.

There is an ancient and important distinction between art – what we have made – and nature – what is already present in the world. The vocabulary of critics brings out the 'made' quality of art: poetry is like sculpture; it is moulded, fashioned and shaped.

Poets describe their art in several ways. It is 'measures' and 'numbers'. In the introductory poem to Blake's *Songs of Innocence* (1789), the poet is a piper. This is in keeping with the pastoral tradition, in which shepherds are poets who pipe songs to their flocks and shepherdesses (see Chapter 27). In one of his most memorable poems 'The Solitary Reaper' (1807), William Wordsworth presents himself as the traveller stopped in his journey by the song of a highland girl, working in a field. Implicitly, he recognizes her as another poet. He sings because she has sung.

Summary

Poetry is art. It has been made. Poets are very often aware of this and have a wide range of terms for talking about the making of poetry.

13.4 Reading and hearing

Talk of inspiration and singing make it clear that poetry is something that is read aloud.

Poetry, like drama, is a performance art.

Poems are usually the only works students hear complete, at least in a single lesson. There is a long tradition of reading aloud. *Beowulf* (tenth century), an Anglo-Saxon epic, was probably performed to the accompaniment of a harp.

Questions about reading

The issue of how poetry might be read is still with us. When we read in private, do we silently 'sound' the words? Do we read poetry more slowly, if only slightly more slowly, than we read prose? When we read aloud, to what extent are we consciously giving an interpretation of the poem? How different would a poem's meaning be if we radically altered volume, pace and pitch?

Tone and voice

Tone means the attitude heard in a voice. The attitude gives a particular emotional colouring to the subject matter. Tone is also a matter of outlook, attitude, understanding, stance, position and pose. Behind the idea of tone is the audible nature of poetry; we *hear* tone in pitch and pace, in timbre and intonation.

Poetry is a form of address, a way of speaking, something said and heard. *Voice*, as in everyday life, is something that is adopted by the speaker. It is therefore self-presentation, a matter of how the poet presents him-/herself. We usually mean two things when we speak of 'voice':

- Voice is a matter of the sound of the poet in a particular poem. For example, Thomas Hardy's voice is sometimes one of amused detachment, and sometimes wistful and reflective.
- Voice is a tonal attitude heard across the entire work of a poet. There are many distinctive voices in Robert Browning, but there is also a single voice – bold, direct, dauntless and aspiring – that is heard throughout.

In both cases, voice is very much 'made', be it close to ordinary speech or theatrical. W. B. Yeats wrote both in an 'ordinary', conversational voice and in a strident, public manner, as in 'Ben Bulben' (1939).

Hearing, overhearing and the public

Poetry is heard when the poet appeals to the listener, and overheard when the poet addresses another or muses privately.

We hear poetry on public occasions such as weddings or funerals. (W. H. Auden's 'Stop All the Clocks', written in 1937, became popular when it was read in the funeral sequence of *Four Weddings and a Funeral*.) Some poems are deliberately written for a public. Laurence Binyon's 'For the Fallen' (1914), used on Remembrance Day, speaks on behalf of the whole nation.

Summary

Whenever we read, we should think about how the poem might be spoken. The 'voice' of a poem refers either to a voice in a particular poem or a manner heard across a poet's work. We often think of poetry as intimate address, but a poem can be public – heard rather than overheard.

13.5 Persona

The self in a poem is called the *persona*. The word was originally used of the mask worn by Greek actors, and much later in psychology – to Carl Jung it meant a self we create as our public face.

Personas give poems the sense of a living presence.

Sometimes we distinguish between the persona in particular poems and the persona of the poet. For example, the three voices in Philip Larkin's 'Livings' are individuals he has invented, whereas the persona in 'High Windows' (1974) sounds like a version of himself.

Dramatic monologues

The most developed persona is found in the dramatic monologue, a nineteenth-century genre largely invented by Robert Browning and continued by T. S. Eliot, Carol Ann Duffy and U. A. Fanthorpe. In dramatic monologues the protagonist (the speaker) is presented in a specific situation. It has five important features:

- *The debt to prose fiction.* Victorian poets explored some of the same territory as the novel, by creating fictional characters in verse.
- *The influence of drama.* Dramatic monologues gave poets an opportunity to create the speaking voices of distinctive characters, such as are found in Shakespeare. They can be like plays in that often there is a silent character to whom the protagonist speaks.
- *Forbidden territories.* Dramatic monologues offered poets the opportunity to explore dangerous subjects. Browning's 'Porphyria's Lover' (1836) is about a man who, quite without guilt, strangles his beloved.

- *Contexts*. As in prose fiction, a dramatic monologue creates a context for the speaker. The reader learns of the situation of the speaker and the history that has created this particular circumstance.
- *Protagonist, poet and reader*. There is often the problem of how protagonist, poet and reader relate. This is frequently a sensitive matter. How do we balance sympathy and moral judgement? We talk carelessly about identifying with literary characters, but Browning's monologues often work because we are unable to do this.

Summary

A persona is a created self. Dramatic monologue requires a very clearly defined persona. Dramatic monologues are a poetic response to fiction and the theatre. It allows poets to explore dangerous areas of experience and to create a context for the poem's actions. It is not always clear how readers should judge the protagonists.

13.6 Fluency

We value some poetry for its fluency – the feeling that the words have poured spontaneously from the poet. William Wordsworth touches on this in his famous definition of poetry as 'the spontaneous overflow of powerful feelings'. However, Wordsworth's idea has been questioned. What about, for example, poets who work on poems for years? Here Yeats may help. In 'Adam's Curse' (1904), he says of poets that:

> A line will take us hours maybe;
> Yet if it does not seem a moment's thought,
> Our stitching and unstitching has been naught.

> (4–6)

The relaxed, conversational style is probably the result of the process it describes. It *sounds* fluent – a thought offered as part of easy conversation – yet achieving that relaxed lilt might have been the work of hours. What matters is the *impression* of lyrical ease.

Summary

Our valuation of poetic fluency is compatible with our knowledge that poetry is often the product of hard work.

◧ ⍙ 14 What Poets Make

14.1 Story-telling

Words would not be words if they did not have meanings. Without meanings, they would just be sounds and therefore would not be part of language. Words have meanings only when they play a part in language. One way in which words function in language is in the telling of stories. The eighth-century Greek poet, Homer, told tales of the Trojan War (*The Iliad*) and the wanderings of Odysseus (*The Odyssey*). In Latin, Virgil wrote in *The Aeneid* (written 29–19 BC) of how Aeneas escaped Troy, landed in Italy and founded Rome. English poets – George Chapman, John Dryden and Alexander Pope – have translated Homer and Virgil.

Chaucer's tales

Geoffrey Chaucer's gift is story-telling. Chaucer does four things in his stories. He works within a tradition, often extending its possibilities. He presents characters, who, like most characters in comedy, have aims and the ingenuity to achieve their ends. He draws us into the life of these characters (though some more than others) and he makes us think.

Take, for example, 'The Miller's Tale' (c. 1390). The tale stands in a contemporary tradition of stories (called *fabliaux*) about how the young deceive the old by seducing their wives. The tale works in the following ways.

Introducing the characters

Three characters are introduced in the first eighty lines: the aged carpenter; Nicholas, a refined and polished Oxford scholar interested in astrology who lodges in the carpenter's house; and in a long, deliciously inviting passage, the carpenter's eighteen-year-old wife. Little is said about the carpenter except that he is fiercely possessive and fears being cuckolded. We tend to view him distantly, a perspective helped by the narrator's knowing comment that the old should not marry the young. (He very learnedly quotes Cato to support the latter view.) The reader might think of lines from 'The Miller's Prologue' about finding 'Goddes foison' – the plenty, abundance and the riches of God's creation – and ask how much of 'Goddes foison' will the wife find in this marriage.

First moves

Nicholas makes an indecent move when the Carpenter is out at Oseney, the local Abbey. Chaucer's presentation of Nicholas's crude grope of the young wife is one of the pleasures of 'The Miller's Tale'. Nicholas is frequently called 'hende' – courteous, gentle and handy. The narrator also says that scholars are 'queynte' – clever and knowing. Chaucer does not rhyme at this point; he repeats 'queynte', which in the context has another meaning. The young wife is soon won over.

New character

Three characters ought to be enough for a tale of cuckolding, but, to the reader's surprise, a fourth character is introduced – Absolon, the parish clerk. There is a detailed presentation of this very particular young man: curly hair, red stockings, dancing, singing and (what looks like a gratuitous detail) a squeamish dislike of farting. Absolon sees the carpenter's wife and falls for her. He courts her as if she were a high-born lady, singing, in the manner of a troubadour, outside her window. The highly comical scene in which he first does this involves a conversation between the carpenter (now named as John) and his wife (named as Alison) as they lie in bed, listening to Absolon's high-pitched voice.

Absolon is consistently treated as a figure of fun. The reader realizes that, as he appears on the scene after Nicholas, he stands no chance.

The plan

Nicholas, confident he can outwit a carpenter, formulates his plan – when John is at Oseney again. Chaucer does not disclose to the reader what the plan is. Nicholas mysteriously stays in his room until the carpenter, after reflecting that too much study can turn the brain and that we should not inquire into 'Goddes pryvetee', breaks down the bedroom door. Chaucer now makes use of an earlier-mentioned detail. Nicholas, who claims he has been engaged in astrological study, tells John a preposterous tale, to be disclosed to no one, about a flood that will drown the world, and from which escape is only possible if the carpenter does all that Nicholas tells him. The carpenter, who has said that we should not inquire into 'Goddes pryvetee', listens attentively. All three of them are to sleep in tubs suspended from the roof to avoid the flood.

Sympathy

So far, the story does not encourage us to feel very much for John. But in the conversation he has with Nicholas, he says something that makes us regard him with more feeling. John is distraught: 'allas, myn Alison!'

When John tells Alison about the flood, she, with the advantage of knowing that Nicholas is scheming, urges him to make all the necessary preparations. When we remember that she intends to be unfaithful, we see the cruelty of her saying: 'I am thy trewe, verray wedded wyf'. Nothing in the situation requires her to make that dishonest declaration.

The plan in operation

John is tricked. In the night, Nicholas and Alison stealthily descend from their tubs. Their 'revel and the melodye' shows them enjoying 'Goddes foison'.

Climaxes

As Nicholas's plan has succeeded, the reader might expect the tale to be over. A tale of cuckolding the old requires one climax. And this is it. But Chaucer gives the reader four – one for each character.

The first is the return to the tale of Absolon. He comes to the window, hoping for a kiss. Alison sticks out her naked bottom, and upon kissing it Absolon is amazed to discover she has a beard. The second is when Absolon, after a lengthy conversation with the blacksmith, returns with a hot coulter (the pointed end of a plough). This time Nicholas sticks his bottom out of the window and farts in Absolon's face. (Apparently gratuitous details usually have a purpose in short stories.) The third is Absolon burning Nicholas's bottom. Nicholas yells 'water', and this precipitates the final climax. John, thinking the flood has come, cuts the rope, falls to the floor and breaks his arm. The neighbours laugh at him for believing that the world would end.

Judgements

Chaucer makes us think. The narrator rounds the tale off smartly with one line summaries of what each has suffered. But perhaps the tale works by prompting the reader to be less dismissive. The alluring Alison has been reduced to 'a thing al rough and long yherd'. And what of John? He is 'hold wood (mad) in al the toun'. What future has he? The story has a life beyond its close. And it might be said: crude stories rarely do this.

The issue of narrators

A traditional line about Chaucer is that, in subject matter and style, the tale reflects the character that tells it. Thus, the Knight writes of chivalrous lovers. Some narrators have verbal characteristics. The Prioress uses the word 'little' with (aggravating?) regularity.

According to this argument, 'The Miller's Tale' fits his character. In 'The General Prologue', the narrator says that the Miller's stories were 'moost of sin and harlotries' (mostly immoral and obscene).

Yet the argument is faulty. 'The Miller's Tale' is certainly crude, but if the reader is right to feel sympathy for the carpenter, can it simply be said to be obscene?

If that is right, then either the Miller is a more sophisticated man than we expected, or the tale is not exactly fitted to the teller. Consider also the fact that the Miller quotes from Cato. Are we to imagine the Miller reading Latin?

Perhaps it would be wiser to acknowledge that what we hear is not the personality of the teller but that of the tale. Chaucer's narratorial manner is opportunistic; if he wants to make a point or a joke, if he wants to include some learning or debate ideas (as he does, for example, in 'The Wife of Bath's Prologue') he does so. He is not constrained by the strict idea that the tale is a revelation of the teller.

Summary

Poets tell stories. Chaucer engages the reader by allowing us to follow the schemes of his characters, but when it comes to judgement, we are not always secure in what we should think. We should also be cautious about the theory that Chaucer's tales always fit the teller.

14.2 Ballads

Traditional ballads

In the eighteenth century, scholars began to take an interest in traditional fifteenth- and sixteenth-century North Country ballads. These ballads use epic material of high deeds, great battles and heroes (many of the Robin Hood stories originate in the fifteenth century). Their style is direct and unembroidered. Their stanza forms are usually simple – quatrains of short lines, rhyming ABCB. This is the opening of 'The Wife of Usher's Well':

> There lived a wife at Usher's Well
> And a wealthy wife was she;
> She had three stout and stalwart sons
> And sent them o'er the sea.

Ballads depend on conventional phrases enforced by overt alliteration – 'stout and stalwart' – and, in the shorter lines, formulaic additions: were it not for the point that she is wealthy, the second line would virtually repeat the first.

Ballads are of more than historic interest. They are lean, spare and have a strong narrative thrust. Though imagery and psychological probing are not prominent, they can be mysterious and not without pathos. 'Twa Corbies' is an eerily bleak tale of a dead knight lying in a ditch, abandoned by hawk, hound and lady, and two crows discourse on how they will pick his bones clean. (Dialogue is a ballad feature.) The textures of the words and their haunting sounds – thin and piercing like a North Country wind – create an appropriately pitiless tone. The poem closes with the wind blowing through his dry bones:

> O'er his white banes, when they are bare,
> The wind sall blaw for evermair.

The final rhyme on an open vowel, unstopped by a consonant, blends the rasping call of the crows with his only requiem – the moaning of the wind.

The literary ballad

The rediscovery of ballads led to a conscious imitation of the old tales – the literary ballad. There is a stylistic continuity; they often use the quatrain and conventional verbal formulas. A good example is Sir Walter Scott's 'Proud Maisie', a dialogue song from his novel *The Heart of Midlothian* (1818). It is sung by a deranged character on her deathbed. The ballad mounts to the climax of Maisie – proud, young and yearning for love – being welcomed to the grave by glow-worm and owl:

> The glow-worm o'er grave and stone
>   Shall light thee steady;
> The owl from the steeple sing
>   Welcome, proud lady.

As in the case of 'Twa Corbies', 'Proud Maisie' is effective because it plays with our expectations of appropriate ritual. 'Twa Corbies' is an anthem for doomed youth, and instead of a wedding bell, the owl welcomes Maisie to the grave. There is an added chill in those words, because Scott makes the owl speak with the formal grace of a courtier.

Romantic ballads

The ballad form is central to romantic poetry. John Keats' medieval tales 'Isabella' and 'The Eve of St Agnes' (both 1820) owe much of their drama to ballads, although neither uses the ballad form. William Wordsworth and Samuel Taylor Coleridge called their book of 1798 *Lyrical Ballads*. The first poem is the most experimental ballad in English: Coleridge's 'The Rime of the Ancyent Marinere'. This, with some thrilling variations, adopts both ballad form and features such as repetition, overt alliteration, dialogue and supernatural presences. Coleridge's style is also in the ballad tradition in another respect – the writing is terse. What he achieves, however, is something only rarely found in ballads – emotionally rousing and visually evocative imagery:

> All in a hot and copper sky
>   The bloody sun at noon,
> Right up above the mast did stand,
>   No bigger than the moon.
>   (107–10)

'Copper' makes the heat visible and tangible; we see its lurid colours and feel its metallic abrasiveness.

Though the poem is still recognizably in the ballad tradition, Coleridge makes it thematically rich. It is about the violation of nature, the spiritual pains of sin and guilt, the joy of atonement and absolution and, through the imagery of the moon and the wind, Coleridge explores inspiration and poetic composition.

Victorian stories

The nineteenth century might be called the age of narrative. The novel was the dominant literary form, pictures were often narrative in content, and in the sciences massive narratives were formed about the prehistoric world. (Most of our terms for prehistory, including 'dinosaur', were coined in the nineteenth century.)

Given that narrative was primary, it's not surprising that Victorian poets wrote stories in verse. Christina Rossetti's huge output contains many narrative poems. She is a very adroit teller of tales. In 'Maude Clare' (1858), the setting is medieval – a world of lords, ladies and, we may assume, politically necessary marriages. Thomas leaves the church with his bride, Nell, and is questioned by his mother and Maude Clare. Christina Rossetti's elusive narrative works by hints and teasing references to past events. The truncated narrative makes the reader guess, deduce and assume. The bride is 'like a village maid', and Maud Clare is 'like a queen', but we assume that Maude Clare is of lowly birth, for otherwise Lord Thomas, who gazes 'long on pale Maude Clare', would have married her. Again, we can only speculate about what went on 'That day we waded ankle-deep/For lilies in the beck'. And what is meant by Maude Clare's cryptic 'The lilies are budding now'?

Thomas Hardy is another poet who writes stories, some of which are consciously in the ballad tradition, while others oblige the reader to supply a narrative situation. His great love poems – 'After a Journey', 'The Voice' and 'Beyond the Last Lamp' (written in 1912/1913) – work by encouraging the reader to supply an unwritten tale of happy love that now pressures the poet to write of his lost beloved in her 'air blue gown' ('The Voice').

Summary

Ballads are spare and at their best haunting. Later writers made them elusive, thereby encouraging the reader to invent narratives to explain the tales related by the poets.

14.3 Worlds

Faery lands

We sometimes find the special world a poet makes – the buildings, flowers and trees, weather, geography and culture – the most memorable thing about a poem. Keats' 'Ode to a Nightingale' (1819) is about how poetry creates imaginary worlds (nightingales are often symbols of the imagination). The song of the immortal bird

> hath
> Charm'd magic casements, opening on the foam
> Of perilous seas, in faery lands forlorn.
>
> (68–70)

Keats' lines can be interpreted as being about saying and making. Windows ('casements') have been opened on to distant, imaginary worlds. The magical natures of these worlds are heard in the sound patterns of the verse. As if by poetic magic, the word 'forlorn' repeats in the same order the 'f' of 'faery' and the 'l' and 'n' of 'lands'. The repeated sequence of sounds is like a spell summoning up another world.

Literary worlds

Alfred, Lord Tennyson re-creates and extends the worlds of Classical literature (see Chapter 30). In 'Ulysses' (1842), he imagines Homer's hero having returned home but yearning for one more journey. He wants to escape from a landscape of 'barren crags' and seek

> that untravelled world, whose margin fades
> For ever and for ever when I move.
>
> (20–1)

This world is also a state of mind. The 'margin' that fades 'for ever and for ever' embodies his divided mind; he has an unappeased desire to roam, and yet the heavy tread of the verse, heard in the laborious repetition of 'for ever', evokes the weariness of his old age.

Tennyson also imagined worlds from Shakespeare. In *Measure for Measure* (1604), we hear of the abandoned Mariana in her moated grange. In 'Mariana' (1830), Tennyson renders that silent and rotting house with the intense observation of a medieval manuscript. Virtually nothing happens. It opens with a minutely observed picture of dereliction:

> With blackest moss the flower plots
> Were thickly crusted, one and all:
> The rusted nails fell from the knots
> That held the pear to the gable-wall.

The lines themselves are 'thickly crusted' with closely packed details, given in abruptly textured vowels and consonants. Nearly all the syllables in the third line are heavily stressed. Sometimes it seems that her isolation has made her see with an almost surreal penetration – 'Weeded and worn the ancient thatch' (7) and 'The blue fly sung in the pane' (63). Her sexual frustration might be embodied in lines about the poplar – 'The shadow of the poplar fell / Upon her bed' (55–6).

Dream worlds

Tennyson was strongly influenced by Keats. The lucid images and thickly textured details make Keats' medieval worlds remote and eerily dream-like. 'The Eve of St Agnes' (1820) contains a scene in which Madeline goes to her room, which is dominated by a huge stained-glass window:

> A casement high and triple-arch'd there was,
> All garlanded with carven imag'ries

Of fruits, and flowers, and bunches of knot-grass,
And diamonded of panes of quaint device,
Innumerable of stains and splendid dyes,
As are the tiger-moth's deep-damask'd wings;
And in the midst, 'mong thousand heraldries,
And twilight saints, and dim emblazonings,
A shielded scutcheon blush'd with blood of queens and kings.

(208–16)

There is a sense of action suspended and time stopped. In this single sentence, the main verb is the intransitive 'was'. Because 'was' cannot take an object, what follows is a series of elaborations of the subject rather than any actions that subject might perform. The stanza is indeed 'carven' with 'imag'ries' – fruits, panes, saints, wings, heraldries – none of which can, because of the grammar, do anything other than exist in a strange stillness.

Twentieth-century worlds

Re-creating worlds is a permanent feature of poetry. In some cases, specially created worlds become ways of thinking through intellectual problems. In his poems on Byzantium – the capital of the Eastern Roman Empire – W. B. Yeats fashioned a world that expressed the conflict between nature and art. Poets have long felt the tension between nature's pattern of birth, flourishing and decline, and art, which is fixed and unchanging. So, in the first verse of 'Sailing to Byzantium' (1928), Yeats sees that 'the young/In one another's arms' and the living, natural world 'neglect/Monuments of unageing intellect'. The imagery gives us the problem: nature – 'Whatever is begotten, born and dies' – is warm, but art that does not age is a 'monument' – cold, hard, austere and impersonal. In imagination, the poet sails to Byzantium, a world in which living is raised to the level of art. Once there, he refuses the forms of 'any natural thing' but takes instead that of the mechanical bird made by 'Grecian goldsmiths'. But Yeats has made his Byzantine world so that it continues to express the nature/art tension. In the final line, the bird he so admires sings of life and time – 'past, passing, or to come'.

New worlds

Very occasionally, a poet can create a world that is almost entirely new. This is what William Blake does in *Songs of Innocence* (1789). What makes this world distinctive is what *isn't* there. *Innocence* has significant absences. There are no questions that disturb, and all questions, as in 'The Lamb', are answered immediately. It is a world in which the lost are found, as in the two poems 'Little Boy Lost' and 'Little Boy Found'. And certain key words lose their negative connotations. To us the word 'naked' means bare and exposed, so there are associations of vulnerability. But look how Blake handles 'naked' in 'The Chimney Sweeper'. The sweep dreams that he and his mates are locked up in black coffins. An Angel with 'a bright key' frees them into an idyllic country, where they run, laughing, down a green plain: 'And wash in a river, and shine in the Sun'. The imagery is of release:

> Then naked and white, all their bags left behind,
> They rise upon clouds and sport in the wind.

The language of washing in the river, shining in the sun, being white and leaving their bags (containing their brushes) behind enables us to see that 'naked' is a positive, primal state of innocence, a state associated with strength, energy and joy. Blake, of course, has sources for this idea. What he does here is something he does in other *Innocence* poems: he gives the reader a picture of the world before the Fall of humankind, an original and primal state of innocence in which sin, evil and death are absent. He creates a new world by re-pristinating (making new) a word that has gathered many troubled associations.

Re-created worlds

Poets create worlds that are neither dreams nor ideals. Some poetic worlds are re-creations of how things are. Poets have always written about war, but in the twentieth century war changed, so poets had to find new ways of dealing with the subject. One who did this in the First World War was Wilfred Owen. He makes poems out of mud, gas, blood and the sounds of guns. But his poetic master was Keats, so he sometimes gives his actions and scenes a visionary intensity. In the first stanza of 'The Show' (1917), for example, he looks down from a 'vague height' to see

> a sad land, weak with sweats of dearth,
> Gray, cratered like the moon with hollow woe,
> And pitted with great pocks and scabs of plague.

It is as if in the ravaged wastes of no man's land he sees that nature herself is diseased. And in the sweats and pocks he sees the disease of a civilization that has so wasted the land. The word 'plague' introduces another element. It is one of the words that echo through the 'Book of Revelation' (the final book in the Bible), so the devastation of the First World War becomes apocalyptic (see also Chapter 54).

Familiar worlds

Some poets, particularly twentieth-century ones, establish a quotidian world – a recognizable one of everyday things. John Betjeman's poetry abounds in proper nouns – names of streets, towns, motor cars and manufactured goods. The poet gives 'the HP Sauce another shake' in 'Lake District'.

Philip Larkin has continued the Betjeman tradition. The pleasure of his poetry depends in part on our recognition that this is what such-and-such a scene is like. The recognition is an acknowledgement that the poet has selected those salient details that make a scene what it is. In 'Toads Revisited', for example, he writes of a public park and the kind of people we meet there. In 'Blurred playground noises' he captures that distant, indistinct buzz of children's voices that is an ever-present but hardly registered sound in any park.

Past and present

A special kind of poetic world is one in which a poet deliberately blends the past and the present. A contemporary example is Seamus Heaney's *North* (1975), which establishes links between the sectarian problems of Northern Ireland – punishment beatings, roadblocks, policemen with guns – and the bodies of men and women, exhumed virtually whole from Danish peat bogs, who have been punished by an ancient Northern society. In 'The Grauballe Man', 'Punishment' and 'Stange Fruit' he establishes the links between the two worlds, both intensely tribal and savage to enemies and traitors. In the ritualized violence of a Northern past, Heaney finds a way of coming to terms with the ambiguities and horrors of Ireland's contemporary troubles.

Summary

Both past and contemporary poets create various kinds of imaginative worlds; some drawn from literature and some from dreams. Poets also make new worlds or remake a familiar one. They present essential features of a familiar world and juxtapose past and present ones.

■ ⊻ 15   What Poets Think

15.1   Poets as thinkers

There is a famous poem by Archibald MacLeish called 'Ars Poetica' (the title of the Latin poet Horace's poem on the art of poetry) which ends with the statement that

> A poem should not mean
> But be.

MacLeish is being playful: to state that poems 'should not mean but be' is to state a meaning. Yet it was once popular to play down the extent to which poems say something. Poems, it was sometimes said, did not so much make statements as express what it is to make statements.

The trouble with this view is that many people read and value poetry precisely because it *does* say things. Poets think. Readers find encouragement in what poets think. And nor do they forget that the power of the poem comes from *how* it says what it says. They might say they don't find ideas expressed with such force and clarity elsewhere.

Taking poetry seriously

In the opening of *Paradise Lost* (1667), Milton, in accordance with the epic convention of announcing his theme, says that his aim is to 'justify the ways of God to men' (Book 1, 26). The syntax is ambiguous: is he justifying how God treats people, or is it human beings to whom God's ways are being justified? But syntactical ambiguity does not change the fact that here Milton is *saying something*. Either way, what we are going to read is an argument.

Dealing with big issues

In 1851, Matthew Arnold wrote 'Dover Beach', a poem about the loss of religious certainty. Listening to the retreating waves, the poet says

> I only hear
> Its melancholy, long, withdrawing roar,
> Retreating, to the breath
> Of the night-wind, down the vast edges drear
> And naked shingles of the world.

This offers the reader many of the satisfactions of poetry. The sad, sighing movement of the sea enacted in the plangent (heart-plucking) sounds of its 'long withdrawing roar' and the raw exposure of the word 'naked' juxtaposed with the cold, hard shingles are the kinds of things for which we value poetry. Yet the poignancy of the poetry is inseparable from its lament that faith is retreating. To say that is to think.

Poetry does not need to be explicitly 'philosophical' to deal with important matters. Robert Herrick's 'To the Daffodils' (1648) does not set out an argument, yet it is clearly about the passing of time and the transitoriness of life. A poem can be about those things that matter to us – love, change, time and death – without using philosophical vocabulary.

Religion

John Donne and George Herbert wrote about God. In some of their poems we see not so much theology as the struggle to align the human will with God's will. Donne's *Holy Sonnets* (1633), particularly in the violence of 'Batter my heart', and Herbert's 'The Collar' (1633) are poems about the soul's struggle to be obedient.

The engagement of the mind with the Ultimate continues with William Wordsworth. His 'Immortality Ode' (1807) is concerned with that sense of freshness and brightness that distinguishes experience when we are young, and how, with the passing years, it fades 'into the light of common day'. But Wordsworth does not leave us with a meditation on experience. He advances the idea that the brightness of our early days is a reflection of the home from which the soul has come:

> Not in entire forgetfulness,
> And not in utter nakedness,
> But trailing clouds of glory do we come
> From God, who is our home
>
> (62–5)

The imagery of clouds of glory and the assertion – 'we come/From God' work together to make this poem a statement of belief as well as the evocation of particular feelings.

We should add that the religious impulse of twentieth-century poetry is surprisingly strong. T. S. Eliot is consistently religious even when his subject matter is not. Religious yearning is there in the aching longing of Prufrock's song (1917), and 'The Waste Land' (1922) is religious in the way that it explores the emptiness of a world (without God).

Re-making thought

Though what we have called the 'big' issues have often taken a religious form, some poets re-formulate traditional ideas. Blake's starting point in 'A Poison

Tree' (*Songs of Experience*, 1794) is, as in his original title, Christian forbearance, but he departs radically from the Christian tradition to write about the deliberate and pleasurable nursing of resentment. The poem opens:

> I was angry with my friend:
> I told my wrath, my wrath did end.

The word 'end' ends the sentence. Its playful snappiness enacts the healthy process of expressing anger. But when he is angry with his enemy, there is no release of feeling. Instead, the anger grows. Blake's image of that growth is the anxious and furtive tending of a tree, not the Tree of Life, as in the Bible, but one which bears poisonous fruit. The middle stanzas express the secret pleasure of the one who with obsessive glee engages in his secret work. The enemy is attracted by the 'apple bright' and, in the darkness of night, ventures to steal it. The close of the poem exhibits the glib pride of the protagonist at what he has achieved:

> In the morning glad I see
> My foe outstretch'd beneath the tree.

'Glad' might work ironically for the reader, but there is no irony for the protagonist. He rejoices in what he has done. Today, we have what Blake did not have – the psychological language of repression – with which to express the danger of nursing unacted desires. Blake had to re-cast the imagery of the past to express his thought. And thought it is: he shows us that though the protagonist has killed the enemy, there is a return to health in the blithe freedom from hatred.

Summary

Readers value poets who think. Poets touch on ideas that are treated in philosophy. They write about the relationship between God and the soul, and sometimes re-cast the language of religion.

15.2 Experience and thought

Experience is often followed by reflection. English poets probably adopt this pattern because the English favour ideas that are rooted in experience. English thinking, to use the technical term, is *empirical*. The first two stanzas of Philip Larkin's 'Church Going' (1955) are empirical. The poet stops, as he always does, at a church and in an awkward and off-hand tone lists what he sees – flowers, font, organ – and encapsulates with a sensitive precision the atmosphere of its 'tense, musty, unignorable silence'. Then he turns to reflection by way of a question: what will we use churches for when we have abandoned them as places of worship? The rest of the poem ponders various answers to that question, culminating in the poet's insight that this is a serious house on serious earth.

General statements

General statements make assertions about a whole class of things. They are broad and wide-ranging, asserting that something is true for all individual cases. When they are successful, they have an arresting authority. We listen to the general statement, because it might give us a universal truth.

Philip Larkin closes his 'An Arundel Tomb' (1964) with what has become one of the most famous lines in modern poetry: 'What will survive of us is love.' Given that the poem is set in a cathedral, we might feel there is something sermonic about about the close. General statements might not always be as consolingly final as that. They can be hazards at a truth, attempts to tell us something. Though we often value poetry for being specific, we should not dismiss attempts to say something true of all situations.

Unfamiliar views

Poetry sometimes looks at things from an unfamiliar perspective. This has become something of a feminist strategy. Readers are asked: have we got things wrong by only looking at them from a male point of view?

A well-known modern example of the alternative perspective is U. A. Fanthorpe's wryly amusing 'Not My Best Side' (1978). It is a comical, though not unkind, subversion of a painting by Uccello of St George and the Dragon (which hangs in the National Gallery, London). The maiden, whom St George is rescuing, is more interested in the very manly dragon: 'Well, you could see all his equipment/At a glance'. As for St George, the maiden (who is not in distress) wonders what he was 'like underneath the hardware'. The workaday word 'hardware' is entertainingly subversive of male pride in machinery. A woman, the poem suggests, might not value a man in the way a man wants her to.

Titles

Sometimes titles indicate themes. U. A. Fanthorpe's *Safe as Houses* (1995) indicates that the poems deal with a family of themes: houses are metaphors for the spaces we make for ourselves, both real and imagined, and our feelings of safety and security. There are poems about the lavatory – 'The Room Where Everyone Goes', Tyndale in prison, the children of Nora (central figure in Ibsen's *A Doll's House*), and in 'Sirensong', the central poem of the collection, the poet thinks about how her house, apparently so secure, was shaken by the war. The collection implicitly asks: what can we depend on?

Thought and language

Two comments need to made about the language in which poets think.

The first is that there is a language for reasoning. In particular, there are words that scaffold an argument. Words such as 'if' or 'only' specify the condition, or starting point, for an argument; 'so' and 'then' and 'therefore' show consequences; and the scope of an argument is given in 'all', 'any' and 'some'. We can't argue without these words. The important point is that these words function in poems in pretty much the same way that they do in arguments outside poetry.

John Donne, often praised for his tough and forthright arguments, depends on scaffolding words. The concluding three stanzas of his snappy 'The Undertaking' (1633) form a single sentence, beginning with 'If'. There follows a set of conditions, at the conclusion of which (the opening of the final stanza) he comes to his point with a logical 'then'.

The second comment is that poets can think in images. Coleridge said that the imagination (the creator of images) is the agent of the reason (the faculty that forms concepts). If that is true, then images are related to concepts. The test of this is the way we talk about symbols. We say, for example, that the image of the garden can become a symbol of the ideal order in nature and human society (see Chapter 47, section 47.5). As soon as we say 'ideal order' we are dealing with concepts. Poets can therefore think in and through the images and symbols they deploy.

Summary

Poets think in a number of ways. Some reflect on experience, some advance general statements, and some poets – in particular, the feminists – take unfamiliar looks at common beliefs. Poets' thinking is sometimes evident in the titles of their books. Poets use the scaffolding words of arguments and think in symbols.

15.3 Selves

To write a poem is to create a voice, and to create a voice is to create a self.

> Whenever a poet writes as 'I', a self is created, a person who thinks, feels and responds to the world through the senses.

Discovering the self

Because we value individuality – the importance and value of subjective experience – it is something of a surprise to discover that interest in the self is relatively recent. It was what we now call the Romantic era (1780–1830) that made individuality and subjectivity a matter of central importance in literature. This period gave us the idea that what chiefly matters is not what things are like, but how we feel about them. A representative poem is Keats' 'In dear-nighted

December' (1817) in which the poet reflects that the feeling of no longer having feelings has never been the subject of poetry. The poem ends:

> The feel of not to feel it,
> When there is none to heal it,
> Nor numbed sense to steel it,
> Was never said in rhyme.

This poem is representative because it makes the matter of feeling central. The feel of 'not feeling' only matters because subjective experience is valued. Furthermore, the poem is concerned with art, with the impulse of the self to express itself in poetry. Though the feeling of not feeling hadn't previously been the subject of poetry, it has now – in this poem.

'Autobiography'

An indication of the Romantic interest in the life of the self is present in the fact that the word 'autobiography' was not coined until 1809. It was only when people became interested in the nature of a subject's experiences that the word was required. The word 'autobiography' covers more than subjective thoughts and feelings. It denotes the experiences of an individual life as seen from the perspective of the one who was their subject. A self has a history.

The great experimental poem about the growth of a self (and the creation of that self in verse) is William Wordsworth's *The Prelude*. The poem started as a two-book work of 1799, was re-cast in a four-book version, and then became, in 1805, a thirteen-book work. None of these were published; only after Wordsworth's death in 1850 did it appear in public in a massive fourteen-book form. The number of books is significant. An Epic was usually written in twelve books; the implication is that there is more to be said about the growth of a poet's mind than about high deeds, battles and the founding of nations.

The Prelude is a series of narratives. In the first book, for example, there are stories about taking eggs from birds' nests, stealing a boat and skating on a frozen lake. What connects the poem is the way everything feeds or stems from the poet himself.

Summary

The Romantic period made the expression and exploration of the self a crucial element in poetry. The emphasis is on subjectivity – what it feels like to have an experience.

15.4 Art

Whenever a poet is aware of another poet's works – either by echo or quotation – that poet is aware that poetry is an art. Poets have long recognized their dependence on each other, and shown that dependence through verbal parallels. There are echoes of Spenser in Milton and of Milton in Wordsworth.

Allusion

Allusion is a reference, often oblique, to another poet. T. S. Eliot's 'The Waste Land' (1922) alludes to, among others, Goldsmith, Marvell and Spenser. The effect is teasing. Do the allusions show up the drabness of the modern world, or do they show that a new kind of poetry is needed to cope with urban life?

Art about art

The term 'reflexive' is used of literature, which is about itself – literature about literature. This is one of the concerns in Tennyson's 'In Memoriam' (1850). Throughout the poem, the poet comments on the kind of verse he is writing. He wonders, for example, about whether he ought to restrain his outpouring of grief. The fifth poem opens: 'I sometimes hold it half a sin/To put in words the grief I feel'.

Earlier than Tennyson, Herbert considers the nature of art in 'Jordan' (1633). English poets have been drawn to what has been called 'the plain style' – a poetry of unadorned statement and deliberately prosaic rhythm. Herbert wants to praise God in simple language, so he opens with questions:

> Who says that fictions only and false hair
> Become a verse? Is there in truth no beauty?
> Is all good structure in a winding stair?

Verse, he is arguing, need not be elaborate. Stairs don't have to wind stylishly to be sound.

Summary

Poets have written about the process of writing poetry. This 'reflexive' poetry takes as its subject the art of poetry and the particular poem the poet is writing.

16 What Poets Do: Words and Meanings

16.1 Meaning and grammar

Meaning is created in and through the workings of language. There can be no *meanings* outside language. Even when poets (as they have done) stretch words, it is still *words* they are working with, and words are controlled by *rules*. The strongest control on meaning is *grammar*. Grammar is a series of rules and procedures, the operation of which determines the ways in which meanings are generated. We can therefore approach meaning in poetry (and in other literature) by way of parts of speech or word classes. What follows is not a detailed grammar but rather an exploration of the way in which some of the elements of grammar, particularly parts of speech or word classes, offer possibilities to the writer.

Summary

A knowledge of grammar can help us to understand how meaning is made.

16.2 Nouns

Nouns, as we are told when young, are naming words. A noun denotes things – objects or entities. 'Chair' and 'table' are nouns. So also are 'Charlotte' and 'Jennifer' – names that designate particular people. 'Curiosity', 'belief' and 'nonsense' are not things in the sense in that chairs and tables are but, in a sentence, they function as such. These examples give us three kinds of nouns: *common*, *proper* and *abstract*.

Common nouns

Common nouns, such as 'chair' and 'table', indicate the concreteness and physicality of the world. In grammar they are *primary*, because they are presupposed by other words such as *adjectives* and *verbs*.

The tradition that dominated English Philosophy for over 200 years was Empiricism. This means 'drawn from experience', and experience shows us that the world is full of things. Nouns can bring out the sheer materiality of the world – its density and solidity.

In *The Rape of the Lock* (1712), Alexander Pope gives a marvellous sense of the triviality of contemporary London in his presentation of Belinda's dressing table: 'Puffs, powders, patches, Bibles, billet-doux' (Canto 1, 138). Here, in common nouns, is the clutter of an empty life, the very profusion being indicative of what is crucially absent. Pope's nouns are things we might long for and, once possessed, give status. But Pope also judges: a life is empty which so easily juxtaposes Bibles with ephemeral billet-doux.

Proper nouns

Proper nouns are names such as 'Charlotte' and 'Jennifer'. Proper nouns don't just apply to people: 'city' is a common noun, but 'London' is a proper noun. Proper nouns are specific and particular. It's *this* girl and *that* city. Proper nouns work through association: what we know of a person or city is invoked in their names.

In sixteenth- and seventeenth-century poetry, there were representative beloveds such as Corinna, Julia or Laura. These proper nouns are representative because they allow the reader to think of any beloved by way of the proper noun.

A feature of poetry is that it is happy to name actual places, whereas novelists tend to invent names. There was a real Tabard Inn, where Chaucer's fictionalized pilgrims met, and there is a place in Norfolk called Bawdeswell, near where the Reeve lives. There is a tradition, going back to Sir John Denham's 'Cooper's Hill' (1642), of poems about specific places. Wordsworth inherits this tradition, so can write about his native Lake District, Cambridge and London.

Twentieth-century poetry is full of place names. The habit of writing about villages with curious names, such as Edward Thomas's incomparable poem, 'Adelstrop' (1915) links it wih his contemporaries, who introduced the evocative power of First World War place names into their poetry. These names have a significant place in our culture. Siegfried Sassoon, for example, writes about corpses round Bapaume, and soldiers slogging up to Arras with rifle and pack.

Abstract nouns

Curiosity, belief and nonsense are abstract nouns. They are ideas or notions. They are words we use in public when we think about important issues such as justice and peace. Wordsworth wrote 'Ode to Duty' (1807), an address to the 'Stern daughter of the voice of God!' It is sometimes said that abstract nouns don't have the concrete force of common nouns. This is not entirely true. Abstract nouns are closely related to allegory and symbolism, because allegoric and symbolic figures stand for qualities such as Faith or Hope. In William Blake's poetry, for example, there are great looming figures, as carefully drawn as the monuments in Westminster Abbey, which Blake copied as a young engraver. 'The Divine Image' opens with luminous abstractions:

> To Mercy, Pity, Peace, and Love
> All pray in their distress

By the second line, Blake is moving towards personifying these abstract nouns by giving them a physical precision. He goes on to say in the third stanza that

> Mercy has a human heart,
> Pity a human face.

The abstract nouns are the qualities of 'the human form divine'. Blake is working here with a feature of the English language, namely that an abstract noun can become the subject of a third-person verb. Grammar therefore opens up the possibility of talking about abstract nouns in the terms we use in talking about people.

Pronouns

Pronouns stand in place of nouns. The most common are 'he', 'she' and 'it'. Sometimes these can be used to sap the identities of people. Auden's 'The Unknown Citizen' (written 1939), a poem about the man who always conforms, is fittingly conducted in terms of the anonymizing pronoun, 'He'.

Summary

The common noun can give a concrete actuality to poetry. Proper nouns can arouse associations. The abstract noun expresses concepts and has a concrete aspect through its relation to allegory and symbolism.

16.3   Verbs

Moods

Verbs are words of *action* (doing words) or *being* ('is' is a verb). Verbs function in different ways, called *moods*. In the *indicative* or *declarative mood*, the verb points out or declares. Poetry that is either narrative or has a narrative element uses verbs in the indicative mood. Thomas Hardy opens 'Drummer Hodge' (1899) with 'They throw in Drummer Hodge'.

We use the *subjunctive mood* when we are thinking about possibilities. Its usual form is: 'If I were to…'. Andrew Marvell's 'To his Coy Mistress' (first published, 1681) opens appropriately in the subjunctive:

> Had we but world enough and time,
> This coyness Lady were no crime

The strategy of this would-be lover is to say what he might do *if* he had all time. The subjunctive is the mood for imagining.

The *interrogative* is the mood of questioning (hence, interrogation). William Blake realized the unsettling force of interrogatives. In the twenty-four lines of 'The Tyger', Blake asks fifteen (unanswerable) questions.

The *imperative* is the mood for orders. With imperious swagger, Donne in 'Song' orders a would-be lover to undertake strange and impossible tasks:

> Go, and catch a falling star,
> Get with child a mandrake root

As with drama, imperatives invite us to imagine or even act out accompanying gestures. We can imagine the sweep of the hand in 'go' and the clenched fist in 'get'.

Infinitives

Infinitives express the basic form of an action, as in 'to shout' or 'to sing'. The infinitive does not have a subject; that is to say, you can't put 'John' or 'Jane' or 'he' or 'she' in front of 'to sing'. This lack of a subject makes infinitives feel impersonal. At the end of Tennyson's 'Ulysses', the protagonist anticipates action: 'To strive, to seek, to find, and not to yield.' The infinitives attenuate the sense of the protagonist and thereby enforce the feeling, present throughout the poem, that he is old and tired.

Transitive and intransitive verbs

A *transitive verb* is one that takes an object. An object is anything, usually a noun, that can be governed by a transitive verb. An object can usually be identified by asking 'what?' or 'whom?' So, 'I hit' prompts the question: What do you hit? An *intransitive verb* can't take an object. For example, you can't ask 'what?' or 'whom?' of 'I go'. Transitive verbs give the impression of an active world, in which energy is purposefully expended. John Donne's 'The Undertaking' (1633) starts with confident boasting:

> I have done one greater thing
> Than all the worthies did,

'To do' is transitive. What the speaker has done is greater than anything done by the heroes of the ancient world (the worthies). The transitive verb expresses his proud achievement.

Most English verbs are transitive. Intransitive verbs can be effective when an action or state cannot pass its energies over to an object. The verb 'to be' is intransitive. In Sonnet 129, Shakespeare presents a picture of lust. Lust is potentially violent, but because the main verb is 'to be', the energy cannot be released. The poem opens:

> The expense of spirit in a waste of shame
> Is lust in action, and till action, lust
> Is perjured, murd'rous, bloody full of blame

Lust remains deceitful and violent 'till action', but as the main verb is the intransitive 'to be' there can be no action.

The participle

Participles have some of the features of verbs in that they can have a tense (past, present, etc.) and can govern an object. Past participles usually end in '–ed' and present ones in '–ing'. They can indicate continuous movement as in 'floating' or 'going'. They don't have the full force of verbs. For example, 'Going down the road' would not be recognized as a sentence.

Because it is weaker than a verb, it can also express aspiration rather than achievement. Hardy's poem 'The Oxen' (1915) is about the tradition that on Christmas Eve, the oxen kneel in honour of Christ's birth. The poet says he knows this is a 'fancy', but if someone on Christmas Eve invited him to go to see the kneeling oxen:

> I should go with him in the gloom,
> Hoping it might be so.

The participle 'hoping' is weaker than the full verb 'go'. He goes in hope, but without the assurance of what he will see.

Delayed verbs

Because the verb does the main 'work' of a sentence, the delay of the verb creates tension. In the opening of *Paradise Lost* (1667), Milton delays the main verb for six lines:

> Of man's first disobedience, and the fruit
> Of that forbidden tree, whose mortal taste
> Brought death into our world, and all our woe,
> With loss of Eden, till one greater man
> Restore us, and regain the blissful seat,
> Sing heavenly Muse

It is not until we reach 'Sing' that the sentence (and the poem) has a direction. The 'heavenly Muse' is to 'sing' of 'man's first disobedience'. This *suspensive syntax* (word order that delays a full statement of meaning) gives a grandeur to the song of the Muse.

The main verb

The main verb does the chief work of a sentence. Once the reader locates a main verb, it becomes clear where the sentence is going. Some poems, however, do not have a main verb. This is Blake's 'Ah! Sun-Flower' (1794):

> Ah, Sun-flower, weary of time,
> Who countest the steps of the Sun,
> Seeking after that sweet golden clime
> Where the traveller's journey is done:
>
> Where the Youth pined away with desire,
> And the pale Virgin shrouded in snow

> Arise from their graves and aspire
> Where my Sun-flower wishes to go.

The poem sounds weary. Each clause adds to the previous one, but nothing is said directly about what the Sun-flower does. In one line after another, we read of the place the Sun-flower is 'seeking', but without a main verb the 'seeking' is left without an action that will complete the movement.

Summary

The moods of verbs indicate action, open up possibilities, form questions and give orders. When verbs have no subjects (as in infinitives) the action itself becomes central. Whether a verb is transitive or intransitive shapes the direction of a poem. The participle, because it is not as strong as a verb, can express aspirations. The delayed verb creates tension by suspending meaning temporarily. Main verbs give poems directions.

16.4 Modifiers

Modifiers make nouns and verbs more specific. We shall at look at three: the *adjective*, the *adverb* and the *article*.

Adjectives

An *adjective modifies* (in traditional language, *qualifies*) a noun. 'Big', 'little', 'red' and 'green' are adjectives. They make nouns more specific. Look at this couplet from George Crabbe's *Peter Grimes* (1810) about the sea-coast:

> The sun-burnt tar that blisters on the planks,
> And bank-side stakes in their uneven ranks.
>
> (177–8)

The physical palpability of the scene is established by two adjectives – 'sunburnt' and 'bank-side'. They could be nouns, so work with a substantive force. 'Uneven' is arrestingly visual; it sharply focuses the weird sight of stakes projecting crazily at odd angles.

Some adjectives have become conventional. We speak of the 'blue sky'. But poets can use these conventional words successfully. This is Wordsworth writing in 'Tintern Abbey' (1798) about his sense of a presence felt in and through all things. He feels it in

> the round ocean, and the living air,
> And the blue sky
>
> (99–100)

Because it follows the unusual 'living', used as an adjective to qualify 'air', 'blue sky' feels like a fresh insight into the natural world. Wordsworth is trusting the reader to accept the truth that the sky *is* blue, even though both he and the reader know it's a conventional phrase. Perhaps also there is the sense that the adjectives are part of the noun. We don't see a sky that happens to be blue, but the 'blue sky'.

Sometimes the context moulds the connotations of the adjective. 'Green' is often used to indicate what is fresh and living, but in Blake's 'Nurse's Song' from *Songs of Experience* (1794) the protagonist says: 'My face turns green and pale'. 'Green' here means jealousy, the green-eyed monster.

Poets sometimes seek a new, and therefore unexpected, adjective. Larkin describes the sky as 'pewter' in 'Dublinesque' (1974). Pewter is an alloy of tin and lead. The adjective works by making the reader compare the sky with the colours of the heavy, dull and leaden tone of the metal. Perhaps it is a comparison that no poet has ever thought of making. Some poets are very adjectival. George Herbert's 'Virtue' (1633) depends on a series of adjectives that define and characterize the day. It opens: 'Sweet day, so cool, so calm, so bright'. One noun and three adjectives, which clarify and enrich the image of the day. In Gerard Manley Hopkins' 'Pied Beauty' (1877), there are four adjectives, all placed, as in Herbert, after the noun: 'All things counter, original, spare, strange'. Coming after the noun, the adjectives make the reader linger over each word, allowing each modifier to further refine the image.

Compound adjectives

'Bank-side' and 'sun-burnt' are compounds: two words linked together by a hyphen. It is an ancient form of writing, used by the Greeks and the Anglo-Saxons. Its effect is dependent on the fact that we can imagine the poet at work, linking, joining, blending and melding the words. As in the case of adjectives after a noun, compounds remind us that poetry is not ordinary language. Larkin uses compounds. In 'Here' (1964), a poem about Hull, he writes of 'grain-scattered streets'. As in Crabbe, this has the force of a noun. The compound adjective gives a closely textured feel to the narrow streets near the docks.

Adverbs

Adverbs modify verbs. In most cases, what was said about adjectives also applies to adverbs. They refine and can be effective when placed after the verb.

A particularly interesting effect is created when the adverb is appropriate to both the noun and the verb or participle. Keats' 'La Belle Dame sans Merci' (1820), a literary ballad, begins:

> O what can ail thee, knight-at-arms,
> Alone and palely loitering?

'Palely' modifies 'loitering'. The knight moves as if bereft of purpose. But we can easily imagine that he is also physically pale, so the adverb is appropriate to the noun 'knight-at-arms'.

Articles

The *definite article* is 'the' and the *indefinite* 'a' or 'an'. 'The' is used when there is one specific thing and 'a' when it could refer to any one thing of a kind. So, 'the Queen' is specific, whereas 'a queen' refers anyone who has that role.

The definite article can give a representative quality to a noun. This is often achieved by attaching the definite article to an object that the reader knows is one of many. For example, when Blake wrote 'London' (1794), he knew there were many chimney-sweeps. Yet he speaks of 'the Chimney-sweeper's cry'; 'the Chimney-sweeper' thereby becomes a figure who represents the plight of all sweeps. The same is true of the other two victims: 'the Soldier' and 'the youthful Harlot'. The definite article fixes them uncomfortably in our imaginations; their sufferings are the sufferings of many.

A feature of *Songs of Innocence* (1789) is that Blake frequently uses the indefinite article. For example, in the 'Introduction': 'On a cloud I saw a child'. The poem is quite without the intense gaze that the definite article brings to the victims of 'London'. The meaning, we feel, lies in scenes, sounds and visions rather than specific and symbolic figures.

Summary

Adjectives, adverbs and the article modify nouns and adverbs. Adjectives can enforce the substantial quality of the noun. The definite article can be both specific and representative.

16.5   Other parts of speech

In the discussion of literature, we tend to give consideration to the nouns, adjectives, verbs and adverbs, but we should not overlook the apparently less important ones: *prepositions, conjunctions* and *interjections*.

Prepositions

Prepositions – words such as 'in', 'on', 'up', 'down' – help to show where a sentence is going. English has many prepositions; they position nouns and give verbs direction. They are also used for subjective states – sensations, thoughts and feelings. Thoughts are said to be 'in' our heads. Wordsworth's prepositions denote both physical space and mental states. In the second book of *The Prelude* (1805), he and his friends row to the beach of a small island, where they leave the 'minstrel of our troop' with his flute:

> he blew his flute
> Alone upon the rock, oh, then the calm
> And dead still water lay upon my mind
> Even with a weight of pleasure

(175–8)

'Upon' works physically and mentally: the minstrel 'upon' the rock makes music, and the stillness of the water lay 'upon' the poet's mind. The power of the second 'upon' is strangely increased by being compared to something physical (and perhaps even sexual) – 'weight of pleasure'.

Conjunctions

Conjunctions join parts of sentences; they include 'because', 'but' and 'for'. 'And' is the most common. This apparently unpromising word has many uses. For example, there is a difference between 'I got married, and Mary got married' and 'Mary and I got married'. Again, it is Wordsworth, in many ways a very plain poet, who can use the conjunction with evocative power. This is a passage from the fifth book of *The Prelude* (389–413), in which a boy blows 'mimic hootings' to owls across a lake:

> And they would shout
> Across the water'y vale, and shout again,
> Responsive to his call, with quivering peals
> And long halloos, and screams, and echoes loud

'And' works in two different ways. It is narrative, though not exactly causal. The boy hoots, and the owls shout. The second use of 'and' is the familiar one of listing. The repeated word creates a sense of the overwhelming variety and volume of the tumultuous calls.

Interjections

The interjection is any word that breaks into a sentence either to dramatize what is being said or to express feelings. In everyday conversation, interjections can both establish or change the tone of what is being said. Gerard Manley Hopkins is the poet of the interjection. Sometimes, his religious meditations become so intense, that feeling breaks out. The feelings express intense observations or moments of insight. This is how 'God's Grandeur' (1877) ends:

> And for all this, nature is never spent;
>   There lives the dearest freshness deep down things;
> And though the last lights off the black west went
>   Oh, morning, at the brown brink eastward, springs –
> Because the Holy Ghost over the bent
>   World broods with warm breast and ah! bright wings.

The poet has faith in the inexhaustible freshness of nature. Even when black night has taken away the day, the poet spontaneously utters a cry of wonder – 'Oh' – at the springing of morning in the east. In the last line, there is a moment of spiritual illumination when he senses – 'ah!' – the bright wings of the Holy Ghost (pictured as a dove) brooding over Creation.

Negation

Negation – the reversal of meaning – is not a part of speech but rather a function of grammar. Negation is carried out either by using a negative prefix – 'sung' becomes 'unsung', and 'permanent' becomes 'impermanent' – or by negating the verb – 'I did this' becomes 'I did not do this'.

Wordsworth's poetry uses a number of negative prefixes. In the first book of *The Prelude* (1805), he leaves the city and in his relief says he has thrown off the 'burthen of my own unnatural self' (23) and that he now anticipates 'Long months of ease and undisturbed delight'. Both of these negations work by obliging the reader to think of the non-negated form of the word and then see the effects of negating it. So, in the case of 'unnatural', we see him restored to his real, his actual self; and in 'undisturbed' we see that whatever has troubled him has now been removed. The negated forms of the words create a positive state and, perhaps, a sense of what the human self was like before it was made unnatural by the disturbances of the city.

Double negatives

In Algebra and Logic, double negatives make positives, but not always in ordinary language. Wordsworth explores the double negative in a passage from Book 1 of *The Prelude*. Writing of the stirring within him of a 'mild creative breeze' (discussed in Chapter 13, section 13.2) he says:

> This a power
> That does not come unrecognized

Wordsworth follows common language rather than logic. If you are asked whether you are well, and you reply: 'I'm not unwell', we know that you are not feeling quite as well as you might. So in Wordsworth: the creative impulse is not fully recognized but he is not entirely unaware of it. Wordsworth's double negative is a way of exploring that undefined world of mental activity for which there is no exact language. The promptings, elusive intuitions, cloudy perceptions and partially grasped hints hover between the light of awareness and unconsciousness.

Summary

Poets can make creative use of prepositions, conjunctions, interjections and negations.

16.6 Words and their meanings

Meaning is a matter of usage.

The part a word plays in a sentence establishes its range of meaning.

Dictionaries don't decide word meanings; they merely record the meanings established by usage.

Denotations and connotations

There is a distinction between the plain, standard, overt meaning (the *denotation*) and the associative meaning (the *connotation*). A dictionary gives denotative meanings. Connotative meanings are arrived at when we think of how a word is filled out with associations and implications. Connotations, therefore, are different from denotations in that it is the reader who actively makes them part of the meaning of the text. For example, 'blood' is the red liquid that circulates in our veins and arteries (the denotative meaning) as well as the very stuff of life, an offering in sacrifice, the inheritance of our families, the passions that stir us and a sign of villainy and guilt (*some* of the connotations).

Most of the time we don't allow connotations to contribute to the meaning of a passage, but there are moments in literature when they do. Consider the second stanza of Blake's 'The Echoing Green' (1789):

> Old John, with white hair,
> Does laugh away care

By the end of the two lines, 'old' has the connotations of wise and serene rather than frail or senile. Because it is 'care' John laughs 'away', 'laugh away' is blithe and not dismissive or cynical.

Range of meanings

Poetry exploits the rich and varied meanings of words. Think about a range of colour words: white, black, green, blue, yellow and red. Poetry can realize the potential of these words. In 'The Retreat' (1646), Vaughan wrote of 'a white, celestial thought'. As 'celestial' means both the skies and the dwelling-place of God, the connotations of both – radiant white and unsurpassable purity – are both present in 'white'. The word 'yellow' can have very different connotations. In one of his beautiful free translations of Chinese poetry, Ezra Pound writes of a 'yellow stork' after a passage about 'magnolia' and 'gold', so the connotations of 'yellow' are rich and natural and living ('The River Song' from *Cathay* (1915)). However, in the second line of Sonnet 73 (1609), Shakespeare writes of bare trees on which 'yellow leaves' hang. Here 'yellow' has connotations of autumnal decay.

Value words

Value words convey and bestow a judgement on meaning, either positive or negative. 'Generous' is a positive value word, and 'spiteful' a negative one. In such words, meanings and judgements are inseparable.

Occasionally, a poet can so use language that an individual word functions as a value word. In Shakespeare's 'Sonnet 130' (1609), the poet playfully mocks his fellow lover-poets, because they offer unrealistic praise to their beloveds by writing as if each woman had all the conventional features of an ideal beauty. Not so Shakespeare's beloved: 'My mistress' eyes are nothing like the sun'. For twelve lines, the poet says what his beloved lacks: she isn't blonde, has neither red lips nor snow-white breasts, doesn't walk like a goddess and, enforced by it being a rhyming word, her breath 'reeks'. And then in the penultimate line he says: 'And yet by heaven I think my love as rare'. 'Rare' is the word that counters the rest of the poem. Here it means fine, splendid and wonderful (see also Chapter 53, section 53.2).

Diction

The words of a poem are collectively known as *diction*. They are words selected specially by the poet. There was a period (eighteenth century) when poetic diction meant a special language used just for poetry. Sometimes, this involved calling winds 'zephyrs', or using standard comparisons such as 'freshening' dew, 'trembling' leaves, 'passing' clouds and 'whispering' winds. Poetic diction was lofty (of a high register), specialized and complex in its organization. This is from James Thomson's *The Seasons* (1726):

> By wintry famine roused, from all the tract
> Of horrid mountains which the shining Alps,
> And wavy Appenines, and Pyrenees
> Branch out stupendous into distant lands,
> Cruel as death, and hungry as the grave!
> Burning for blood, bony, and gaunt, and grim!
> Assembling wolves in raging troops descend
> *(Winter*, 389–95)

It takes six lines for Thomson to introduce the main subject and verb – 'wolves … descend'. Before that, the mountains are 'horrid' (dreadful and rugged), 'stupendous' in extent and personified as 'cruel'. They form an appropriate setting for the 'raging' wolves.

The idea of a specialized language for poetry is no longer current. We now use 'diction' to refer to the words of a particular poet. One might, for example, comment on a poet's consistent use of monosyllabic words, of similes, of the consistent use of images of taste.

The abandonment of a special diction allows a poet to choose the unexpected word. Wordsworth was instrumental in the decline of poetic diction. In his *Home at Grasmere* (completed 1806) he writes about the setting of his cottage:

> have we not perpetual streams,
> Warm woods and sunny hills, and fresh green fields
> (126–7)

Who before Wordsworth said that woods were 'warm'? Yet Wordsworth does not abandon poetic diction entirely. The originality of the 'warm' depends upon the vestiges of poetic diction in the phrase 'fresh green fields'.

Complexity and ambiguity

In the middle decades of the twentieth century, poets and critics valued multiplicity of meaning: the ability of language to say several things at once. A word often used as a term of praise was '*complex*' – the existence of several meanings. The mutual life of a complex of meanings was often described as 'tension'. Dylan Thomas's villanelle about facing death opens 'Do not go gentle into that good night'. The tension arises out of the complexity of 'good'. In addition to the lightness of a conventional farewell – goodnight – the word raises the issue of whether or not death is good: is it the gateway to a greater life (in which case, it is good) or to oblivion. And there are complex feelings about oblivion. Philip Larkin recoiled with horror (see 'Aubade' in *Collected Poems*, 1988), whilst to A. E. Housman it was 'ensured release/Imperishable peace' ('Parta Quies', 1936).

Critics enjoy exploring the ways in which meanings strain against each other. When the strain is conceptual, the word '*paradox*' is appropriate, and when verbal, '*oxymoron*'. Donne relishes the paradoxical nature of religious language in 'Batter my heart' (1633), which ends with the strident assertion that he will never be chaste until God ravishes him. In Robert Browning's 'Bishop Blougram's Apology' (1855), there are playful oxymorons: 'The honest thief, the tender murderer' (396).

A more general word for the tensions of different meanings is *ambiguity*. In a famous book, William Empson defined seven types. We have learnt to value multiplicity of meaning, but because we also associate the word with confusion, 'ambiguity' might not be the best term. Other possible terms include: multivalency, multiple nuances, and variety of meaning.

Verbal play

There is often a playful – a *ludic* – element in art. Poets play with words because they enjoy the multiplicity of meanings – the overt denotations and the various connotations. There is a line in W. B. Yeats' 'An Irish Airman Foresees his Death' (1919) about 'balance': 'I balanced all, brought all to mind'. The word 'balanced' refers to his balancing of options, the steadying of his plane and the neat balancing of the line of poetry.

The playful element can be a matter of positioning. It might seem surprising that Wilfred Owen should be playful in the positioning of his words, but if we remember that his favourite poet was Keats (Keats invented words such as 'soothest') it is, perhaps, not surprising. In 'Spring Offensive' (written 1917), Owen exposes the word 'exposed' at the beginning of a line.

Poets can play with sounds and meanings. The pun sometimes works by combining a serious with an almost flippant meaning. In the first book of *Paradise Lost*, Milton puns on 'sole'. The denotative meaning of 'sole' is single or alone: 'ever to do ill our sole delight' (160). The use of the word allows a further meaning; it is not the only delight of the devils to do evil, but the delight of their 'souls'.

Multiple meanings

Imagery often creates multiplicity of meaning. Imagery is a very general word for any way in which language appeals to the senses. An image is more than a verbal picture, because there are images of touch and taste. The word applies both to descriptive and figurative language.

Symbols and emblems

A *symbol* is an object that stands for something else. Quite often, it is part of a system of belief. Hence, there are Christian symbols such as the cross or the lamb. Symbols work by creating a penumbra of meaning; the meanings of the symbol cannot therefore be precisely circumscribed. The cross, for example, stands for grief and joy, darkness and victory, justice and mercy, and love. Just think of the many things that the sun or the sea, a tree or roads stand for. Some symbols are unmistakable. Keats' urn in 'Ode on a Grecian Urn' (1820) stands for the ideal world of art. Far less obtrusive is Robert Frost's 'Mending Wall' (1914) in which the wall approaches being a symbol for the necessity of making distinctions. These examples make an important point: a symbol is always related to concepts (see Chapter 15, section 15.2).

Emblems are narrower than symbols. They originally referred to symbolic pictures, and so, by association, the emblem has come to mean the visual representation of a quality. They are usually more direct, concise and fixed in their meanings than are symbols. Emblems are also part of a culture, usually one that is accustomed to the visual presentation of ideas. In the seventeenth century, there were emblem books, in which a poem accompanied a picture. The most famous is *Emblems* by Francis Quarles (1635). The fourth poem is about how worldly riches can never compete with the riches of God. The illustration is a pair of balances. The tradition of picture and poem is continued in Blake's poems, which approach the hard-edged clarity of emblems. In 'The Sick Rose' (1794) Blake explores the tradition of the worm in the bud as an emblem of corruption.

Imagery: clarity and evocation

Some images are exact and clear; but in others, meanings merge and blur. The firmness of an image is often praised; we are being given something hard and concrete. This was the aim of the early-twentieth-century movement called Imagism. In Ezra Pound's memorable 'In a Station of the Metro' (1916), pale faces are compared to petals on a 'wet black bough'. But some images work by elusive suggestiveness. In the first stanza of Sir Thomas Wyatt's 'They flee from me' (1557), it is not clear to what he is comparing the women who once sought him but who now flee:

> I have seen them gentle, tame, and meek
> That now are wild and do not remember
> That sometime they put themselves in danger
> To take bread at my hand

In the imagery's flickering light, the creatures are sometimes birds and sometimes deer.

Experiment

Most symbols are traditional. If they were not they would not resonate as they do. But there are moments in poetry when a new symbol emerges. Blake's *Songs of Experience* (1794) are full of new symbols. Perhaps the most inventive is 'The Clod and the Pebble', in which the clod is pliable, passive and loving, and the pebble selfish, resilient and durable. 'The Tyger' with its combination of the imagery of God's Creation and industrial processes is bracingly inventive.

Critical language

Images are instances of figurative language – language that works by picturing. Sometimes we think of figurative language as a departure from an original literal language. This is a mistake. There is no evidence, historically or logically, that one kind comes before another. They usually go together. If we describe literal language as one that can be set down parallel to the objects it describes we are in fact using a figure of speech.

Simile

Simile has the verbal/grammatical form of an explicit comparison. We say that something is 'like' or 'as' something else. Similes are close to ordinary speech; every day we say that something is like this or that. One of the pleasures of similes in literature is that sense of the poet seeking and finding an apt comparison. Similes therefore recognize an actual world and do justice to the imaginative efforts we make to understand it through comparisons. Donne's 'The Ecstasy' (1633) opens with a simile:

> Where, like a pillow on a bed,
>   A pregnant bank swelled up, to rest
> The violet's reclining head,
>   Sat we too, one another's best.

The simile is appropriate, familiar and yet imaginatively unexpected. The associations are right – the bank like a pillow to rest the lover's heads.

Metaphor

The second line of the above stanza is a *metaphor*: 'A pregnant bank swelled up'. Unlike similes, metaphors have no comparative indicators such as 'like' or 'as'. Metaphors are semantic equivalents; they say that something *is* something else. A metaphor emerges in and through the meanings of the words. For example, the 'cat sat on the mat' is not a metaphor, but 'the mat sat on the cat' is. The metaphor is often present in an adjective, adverb or verb, as 'pregnant' (an adjective) and 'swelled' (a verb).

The metaphor is often valued for its economy and compression. Possibly because of this, it is often valued more than a simile. But there is no need to have preferences. They are different figures of speech, and work in different ways and provide different opportunities.

Conceit

The *conceit* is a comparison noted for its excess and extendability. Both are found in Donne's 'A Valediction: Forbidding Mourning' (1633), in which he compares the union in heart and mind of lovers with compasses or dividers:

> If they be two, they are two so
> As stiff twin compasses are two,
> Thy soul the fixed foot, makes no show
> To move, but doth, if th'other do.
> And though it in the centre sit,
> Yet when the other far doth roam,
> It leans, and hearkens after it,
> And grows erect, as that comes home.

The conceit works through shock. How, we ask, can compasses be like the union of lovers? This is where extendability comes in. We see the poet's mind at work hammering out the comparison, so we can see that it is oddly appropriate. This raises the problem of conceits: is it merely strange, or can it also be true?

Tenor and vehicle

I. A. Richards distinguished between the subject – the *tenor* – from the thing in terms of which it is spoken about – the *vehicle*. So in the 'pregnant bank', the tenor is the bank and pregnancy the vehicle. Sometimes, a vehicle becomes a tenor. In Shakespeare's 'Sonnet 18' (1609), the poet offers to compare the beloved 'to a summer's day' but finds the beloved so exceeds anything that can be said about a summer's day that the sonnet explores the discrepancy by talking about what is often wrong with a summer's day – too windy, too short, too hot and so on. What was the vehicle – a summer's day – is now the subject – the tenor – of the poem.

Summary

The figurative functions of language give poetry a richness of meaning and, as the term 'imagery' implies, an imaginative appeal. Symbolism depends on a tradition of usage, but new symbolic meanings can be created. Readers should recognize the different ways in which simile, metaphor and conceit work.

■ ⌄ 17   Poetic Shapes and Sounds

17.1   Line

In formal terms, the line is a basic feature of any poem. Unlike prose, poetry is written out in lines of a given length. Lines give poems shape.

Line endings

Grammar determines whether a poetic line is *end-stopped* or *run-on*. The end of an end-stopped line is co-terminus with a syntactic unit; it coincides with the end of a clause or sentence. Hence, punctuation marks close an end-stopped line. Look back through the lines quoted above and you will see, for example, that the first, third and fourth lines of 'The Ecstasy' are end-stopped.

A run-on line is one in which the line is not co-terminus with a grammatical unit, and therefore there is no punctuation mark. Sometimes this effect is called *enjambment*, and a run-on line is called an *enjambed line*.

The satisfaction of the end-stopped line is the coincidence of two sorts of organization. The sentence organizes meaning, and the line is an artistic arrangement, often dependent on rhythm and syllable count. There is no reason why the two should coincide, but when they do, we may feel the pleasure of neat correspondence. Run-on lines are pleasurable for another reason. There is the feeling that the intellectual and emotional thrust of the line impels the reader forward in order to complete thought and feeling. Consider the first stanza of William Wordsworth's 'The Solitary Reaper' (1807):

> Behold her, single in the field,
> Yon solitary Highland lass!
> Reaping and singing by herself;
> Stop here, or gently pass!
> Alone she cuts and binds the grain,
> And sings a melancholy strain;
> O Listen! For the vale profound
> Is overflowing with the sound.

The poet builds up the scene with a series of self-contained observations and injunctions to the reader. Each line adds to the picture. But when he comes to her song, his feelings, like her song, overflow in a run-on line.

Line length

Poets have written in long lines of twelve syllables (*hexameters*), but English is not suited to that measure. The hexameter is better used as a variation, as in the last line of the stanza Edmund Spenser used in *The Faerie Queene* (1590). Keats used the hexameter for the final line of his stanza in 'The Eve of St Agnes' (1820). (The hexameter is sometimes called an *alexandrine*, after a late medieval French poet.)

English poets have usually adopted either an eight-syllable or a ten-syllable line. This opting might reveal a distinction in subject matter and class. The eight-syllable line is found in the ballad tradition (see Chapter 14, section 14.3). The pithy, trimmed down, direct style finds the short line an appropriate form of expression. Another feature of the short line is that it is used for humorous and light verse. Hilaire Belloc's comical poems and most limericks use the short line. By contrast, the long line is suited to poems on serious, elevated topics. Wordsworth writes in a ten-syllable line, and John Milton uses it to present the drama of the Fall in *Paradise Lost* (1667).

Of course, the remarks about class and subject matter are generalizations. John Donne writes incisively in the short line of 'The Undertaking' (1633), and although the ballad, the poetry of the common people, uses a short line, there are ballads and popular poems in ten- and twelve-syllable lines.

Caesura

When reading a line of poetry, we are often obliged to pause. This is because there is a *caesura* – a break in the line (indicated by ||). The caesura dramatizes the emotional life of the poem; it checks the pace and allows the reader to recollect and ponder. It often marks a change in tone; the line might become more ardent, more wistful or more longing.

In the close of the first stanza of 'Thyrsis' (written 1862), Matthew Arnold mourns the death of his friend by addressing the countryside around Oxford, where they once walked:

> See, 'tis no foot of unfamiliar men
> To-night from Oxford up your pathway strays!
> Here came I often, often in old days –
> Thyrsis and I; we still had Thyrsis then.

Try to hear where the ceaesuras fall. For example, is there a break both before and after 'often', in which the poet regretfully remembers? The break in the last line marks a sharp change in tone. A heavy caesura marks the change from the companionship of the past to the desolation of the present, a desolation marked as final by the poignant irreversibility of time indicated in the final 'then'.

Caesuras often influence the close of a line, stanza or poem. Philip Larkin's poignant 'Home is so Sad' is full of objects that once embodied the hopes of those who set up home together. When the hopes have been disappointed, the objects remain. The poem closes with four of them:

> Look at the pictures and the cutlery.
> The music in the piano stool. || That vase.

The heavy caesura after 'stool' allows us to see how sadly expressive these things are of long-disappointed aspirations. Perhaps, also, the double stress in 'That vase' invites us to think about the finality of the failure.

The caesura, particularly when it enacts a change in tone, can be funny. Consider one line from Alexander Pope's 'The Dunciad' (1728) about a wild young man who toured Europe: 'Europe he saw, || and Europe saw him too' (Book Four, 294). The change in subject from the young man to Europe prompts the reader to amused imagining at his embarrassingly juvenile antics.

Summary

The fixed line is fundamental to poetry. Different effects and pleasures are created by whether the line is end-stopped or run-on. Traditionally, the length of the line has associations of subject matter and class. Caesuras mark the emotional movement of the poem.

17.2 Stanza form

Line comes before stanza, because a *stanza* is a grouping of lines. Because poetry is an obvious instance of the truth that literature combines content and form – these *words* in this *order* – then the particular way in which lines are grouped in a stanza will shape the meaning and feel of a poem. Keats' 'Odes' (1819–20) are often written in appropriately long stanzas, in which thoughts and sensations press upon the poet. The Odes on Indolence, the Nightingale and Melancholy all use a ten-line stanza, while the sensuously replete 'To Autumn' is in eleven-line stanzas. Given its subject matter – the uncertain and fleeting life of the soul – the 'Ode to Psyche' is written in irregular stanzas.

The couplet

The *couplet* is two consecutive rhyming lines. When the lines are written in *iambic pentameters* (lines of ten syllables with a heavier stress falling on the even syllables) they are called *heroic couplets*. The heroic couplet is a stanza form. Although poems written in heroic couplets are now written as a continuous passage, originally each couplet was printed with a gap between.

The couplet has a self-affirming quality. What is said in the first line is developed and concluded in the second. By the time the rhyming word is reached, the reader might feel that the point of the couplet has been established. The heroic couplet is therefore particularly suited to argument. This clinching effect of the couplet can be seen and heard in these lines from John Dryden's translation (1685) of the Roman poet, Lucretius:

> From sense of grief and pain we shall be free,
> We shall not feel, because we shall not be.
> ('Against the Fear of Death', 11–12)

The first (entirely monosyllabic) line states with uncomfortable boldness that in death we shall be free from 'grief' and 'pain'. The second line develops the argument. We 'shall not feel' is a consequence of the thinking of the first line, and, after the caesura, 'because' gives the reason. The rhyme clinches the argument: 'we shall be free' because 'we shall not be'.

Three-line stanzas

The *three-line stanza* – the *tercet* – is not a popular form. There are, however, some notable exceptions. Percy Bysshe Shelley used *terza rima* – an Italian form invented by Dante Alighieri in which the second line of the first tercet provides the rhyme word for the first and third lines of the next – in 'Ode to the West Wind' (1820). The movement of the rhyming words from stanza to stanza is appropriate to the restless hurrying of the wind. The villanelle is formed by alternating the last line of the first two tercets and then using the two lines in a final quatrain. The challenge is to find a new meaning for the repeated line. Dylan Thomas's 'Do not go gentle' (1951) is a twentieth-century example.

Hardy successfully used the tercet in his poem about the sinking of the *Titanic*, 'The Convergence of the Twain' (1914). Philip Larkin, who learnt much from Thomas Hardy, uses it in 'Talking in Bed' (1964) and 'The Explosion' (1974). In the first poem, the tercet is appropriate to the subject of finding it difficult to talk, and in the second the form helps to give a diagrammatic (even symbolic) spareness to the narrative.

Quatrains

A *quatrain* is a *four-line stanza*. It is popular, being used in ballads and lyrical verse. Handled well, the quatrain is economical; arguments, stages in stories or emotions can be framed neatly and held together harmoniously by various rhyme patterns.

In Robert Herrick's 'To the Virgins to make much of Time' (1648) the opening line tells the young to gather rose-buds, and each of the remaining three is a stage in justification of the argument:

> Gather ye rosebuds while ye may,
>   Old time is still a-flying:
> And this same flower that smiles today
>   Tomorrow will be dying.

The first line urges the virgins to gather the rosebuds and the next gives the reason for the urgency. The third line makes the point through the particular example of a single bloom, and the fourth indicates the consequences of time flying in an answering feminine rhyme (see page 191).

Sonnets

Sonnets have fourteen lines. They are distinguished by the way their rhymes divide them up. The *Petrarchan sonnet* has an eight-line section (*octave*) followed by a six-line one (*sestet*). The *Shakespearian* sonnet consists of four quatrains concluded by a couplet.

In the Petrarchan sonnet, the poet explores an idea or experience in the octave and then comes to a conclusion in the sestet. Sestets often begin: 'and', 'but', 'for', 'if', 'then' or 'thus'. The octave of Sir Philip Sidney's *Astrophel and Stella* – 'Loving in truth, and fain in verse my love to show' (1591) is about the poet's yearning desire to write in such a way that his beloved – 'she, dear she' – will see his pain and respond to him. He thus 'sought fit words' to represent his state by studying other poets' work. But, the sestet records, his writing was without 'invention' (originality) until he listened to his Muse: 'Fool,' said my Muse to me, 'look in they heart and write.'

The Shakesperian sonnet can present the stages of an argument or elaborate a single idea. In both cases the closing couplet is important either for confirming or, as in Sonnet 130 (see Chapter 16, section 16.6), countering the argument. Sonnet 2 works in three stages. In the first, the poet imagines the effects of time on his friend – 'When forty winters shall besiege thy brow' – and, in the second quatrain, asks how, at forty, the man will respond to the question about where his beauty is. In the third quatrain, the poet claims that a beautiful child will be a better representation of his beauty than his now ruined state. The couplet compresses the point that a child is like being made new when one is old.

Mechanical and organic form

Readers debate the value of formal regularity as opposed to experimentation. Samuel Taylor Coleridge coined the term '*mechanical form*' for strict adherence to a form, and '*organic form*' for the way some poets allow their thoughts and feelings to mould and alter the form. Coleridge favoured organic form, but there is no reason why readers should. Expressing thoughts and feelings in an established stanza form can arouse the admiration of readers, who appreciate the poet's deft control.

Free verse

The argument in favour of organic form leads to *free verse* or *vers libre*. Free verse is now very popular, perhaps in part because it gives a sense of freedom from form and, consequently, of sincerity. But the sense of freedom is an illusion. All verse has form; otherwise it would not be verse. So free verse cannot mean lines free from any of the disciplines of verse. Some poets (Thom Gunn in 'Touch' (1967), for example) write in *syllabics* – lines that have the same number of syllables but no regular metrical patterns. Other poets dispense with line-to-line regularity, making each line work in its own terms. What this means is that the lines are given shape by clusters of sounds (alliterations, assonances), repetitions and rhythmical units. So free verse is verse.

Walt Whitman, regarded as one of the founders of free verse, is unmistakably rhythmical. This is from *Leaves of Grass* (1855):

> Swiftly arose and spread around me the peace and joy and
>   knowledge that pass all the art and argument of the earth;

And I know that the hand of God is the elderhand of my own,
And I know that the spirit of God is the eldest brother of my own,
And that all men ever born are also my brothers ... and the women my
    sisters and lovers

(82–5)

In this passage about Whitman's ecstatic experience of union with the world, the first very long line is sustained by the alliterations on 'p' and the assonances on the 'ar' sound. The second and third lines repeat words at the beginning of lines (*anaphora*) and at the end (*epistrophe*). The lines are rhythmical. Think about the stresses in the last line: 'all men ever born'.

Summary

Stanza forms contribute to the thought and feeling of a poem. The various ways in which stanzas can be formed make possible different kinds of effects. Regularity and departures from a given form can both be valued. Free verse is not necessarily more sincere or more effective than verse that observes the discipline of forms.

17.3   Rhyme

Rhyme schemes

Rhyme schemes – the pattern of rhymes in a series of lines – give stanzas shape. There is a standard form of notation for rhymes. The first word in the rhyming position (at the end of a line) is called A and any word that rhymes with it is also designated as A. The next word in the rhyming position is B and so on. In the case of Donne's 'The Ecstasy' (see Chapter 16, section 16.6) the rhyme scheme is ABAB.

Interlaced and enclosed rhymes

ABAB is an example of *interlaced rhyme*. Most long stanzas use it. The effect is to make the poem press forward in anticipation of the next rhyme. Poems thus interlaced often close, as many sonnets do, with a rhyming couplet.

    Enclosed rhyme occurs when a couplet is contained in another rhyme. In Robert Browning's 'Meeting at Night' (1845), two rhymes enclose a couplet. This is the first stanza:

> The grey sea and the long black land;
> And the yellow half-moon large and low;
> And the startled little waves that leap
> In fiery ringlets from their sleep,
> As I gain the cove with pushing prow,
> And quench its speed i' the slushy sand.

This mysterious and erotic poem appropriately uses enclosing rhyme to enact the stealthy secrecy of the lover's arrival at night.

Rhymes and syllables

Robert Herrick's rhymes 'a-flying' and 'dying' were described in section 17.2 above as 'feminine'. This (rather odd) term refers to a disyllabic rhyme (two syllables) in which the stress falls on the first syllable. (This is sometimes called a '*feminine ending*'.) There is, therefore, a slight effect of the rhyme dying away. A masculine rhyme is a monosyllabic rhyme as in 'bed'/'head' in 'The Ecstasy'. Masculine rhymes can sound settled and determined, feminine rhymes fluid and musical. Because feminine are far rarer than masculine rhymes, they are surprising. This may be why they are often successful in comic poetry. The surprise of the rhyme matches the oddity that provokes amusement. In William Makepeace Thackeray's 'Sorrows of Werther' (1855), the subject Werther, a romantic young man created by the German playwright and poet Goethe, falls completely for Charlotte. The prosaic occasion of Werther first seeing his beloved is matched by the inappropriate dexterity of the feminine rhyme:

> Werther had a love for Charlotte,
> Such as words could never utter;
> Would you know how first he saw her?
> She was cutting bread and butter.

Resolution

Rhyme works both forwards and backwards. Forwards because in rhyme schemes we anticipate the coming rhyme, and backwards because we have to remember the previous word in order to hear the rhyme. This movement forwards and backwards of ear and mind creates a feeling of *resolution*, a sense of things being completed. Listen to the neat opening of T. S. Eliot's 'Burbank with a Baedeker: Bleistein with a cigar' (1920):

> Burbank crossed a little bridge
> Descending at a small hotel;
> Princess Volupine arrived,
> They were together, and he fell.

It is a little story: Burbank, associated with small hotels, meets and falls for the exotic Princess Volupine. 'Hotel' and 'fell' enact the fatal finality of the attraction. The tale is complete.

Harmony

Very close to resolution is the feeling of *harmony*. In Eliot a story is resolved, though we may anticipate that the relationship will not be harmonious.

In Stevie Smith's strangely moving 'I Remember' (1957), an old man lies in bed with his new bride:

> It was my bridal night I remember,
> An old man of seventy-three
> I lay with my young bride in my arms,
> A girl with tb
> It was wartime, and overhead
> The Germans were making a particularly heavy raid on Hampstead.
> What rendered the confusion worse, perversely
> Our bombers had chosen that moment to set out for Germany.
> Harry, do they ever collide?
> I do not think it has ever happened.
> Oh my bride, my bride.

There is some (probably) deliberately clumsy rhyming here – 'overhead'/ 'Hampsted' – but the final rhyme – the unlikely 'collide'/'bride' creates a heartfelt harmony among all the banal confusion.

Intensification through rhyme

A line can be intensified through internal rhyming. This occurs when the word at the end of the line rhymes with an earlier word in the same line. The last line of William Blake's 'The Garden of Love' (1794) is about what the priests do to the young man who sought love in the garden. They come at him with a terrible and relentless force: 'And binding with briars my joys and desires'. The internal rhyme increases the pace of the line, and there is a curious feeling that when the line stops the priests still carry on their work of binding. This may be because 'binding', being a participle, indicates a continuous action.

Rhyme and meaning

The chiming of rhymes draws attention to words. In Blake, the internal rhyme of 'briars' and 'desires' encapsulates the conflict in the poem between painful restrictions and natural yearnings.

In Geoffrey Chaucer's 'The Pardoner's Tale' (c. 1390), three reckless young men are up early, drinking:

> Were set hem in a taverne for to drinke;
> And as they sat, they herde a belle clinke
> Biforn a cors, was carried to his grave.
>
> (200–2)

The inescapable presence of death is focused in the rhyme 'drink'/'clinke'. It is the 'clinke' of the funeral bell and not of their ale mugs. Those ideas – indulgence and mortality – are central to the poem.

Comic poetry

Comic verse often depends on rhyme. Hilaire Belloc's 'Lord Lucky' (1939) is about an accident, whereby a man 'by a curious fluke/Became a most important Duke'. The incident that raised him to the peerage occurred when Mr Meyer, who had never used a gun, was out shooting with the previous duke:

> As he was scrambling through a brake,
> Discharged his weapon by mistake,
> And plugged about an ounce of lead
> Piff-bang into his Grace's head –
> Who naturally fell down dead.

The rhymes make a ghastly accident sound neat and clean. The regularity of the rhymes lends an inappropriate, and therefore funny, smoothness to the event. Perhaps the disparity between the harmonies of rhyme and calamitous events is why comic poetry so often depends on rhyming.

Para-rhymes

A *para-rhyme* or, as it is often called, a *half-rhyme*, is not, strictly speaking, a rhyme at all. In rhyme, the final vowels and consonants chime; in para-rhyme the opening and closing consonants are in accord but not the vowels. So 'head'/'hard' and 'boat'/'bait' are para-rhymes. Hence, some call it a *consonantal rhyme*. The effect of para-rhyme is to deny the ear the full satisfaction of a rhyme.

Wilfred Owen is usually credited with inventing para-rhyme. Perhaps because he struggled with conventional rhyme (in 'Greater Love' he tries to rhyme 'lure' with 'pure') he resorted to the dissonance within harmony of para-rhyme. It fits his subject – the dehumanizing effects of war. This is the opening of 'Insensibility' (probably written 1918):

> Happy are men who yet before they are killed
> Can let their veins run cold

'Happy' is ironic. The poet angrily denounces those who deliberately lose their sensitivity – those who allow their blood to be 'cold' before they are 'killed'. Later in the poem there is a para-rhyme at a distance of seven lines on 'brothers'/'bothers'. Bringing those words together enacts Owen's point: brothers are those who are dear to us, but, in the extremes of war, 'no one bothers'.

Summary

Rhyme schemes give stanzas shape. Rhymes resolve and harmonize. They can single out the theme words of a poem. The easy harmonies of rhyme can produce a comic effect. Para-rhymes arouse and frustrate the desire for the harmonious close that rhyme usually creates.

17.4 Rhythm

Rhythm in poetry is both complex and simple. Those who have studied how English verse approximates to a regular pattern have sometimes written lengthy books about the variety and workings of rhythms. It is still an area in which critics are far from satisfied that our descriptive language is helpful and so, as in many other areas of Language study, new terms and methods of analysis are being invented.

Pronunciation

Rhythm is essentially a simple matter. It arises out of the way we pronounce words. Take this sentence; for example:

Because you said lunchtime was busy, I waited until the afternoon before 'phoning you.

We know how to say this sentence because we understand where the stresses or accents fall. 'Until', for example, has a heavier emphasis on the second, but both syllables of 'lunchtime' are stressed. If you read the sentence by giving more stress to the usually less emphasized syllables, you'll find it doesn't sound like English.

Beat

The point about rhythm is that these 'natural' emphases can be organized to create patterns of sounds. All language works like this. Prose is also rhythmical. What makes poetry distinctive is that the patterns of emphasis are continued deliberately. When they are continued with some degree of regularity, a *beat* is created.

There is a physical pleasure in the thrumming rhythm of a beat. (We like rhythm in the other arts, particularly in music.) We should also recall that language is material – we detect it through our senses. The beat of verse reminds us that language is an element in our physical world. We hear that physical world particularly in William Langland, William Dunbar, John Dryden and Robert Browning. This is from Browning's 'Childe Roland to the Dark Tower Came' (1855):

> What made these holes and rents
> In the dock's harsh swarth leaves, bruised as to baulk
> All hope of greenness?
>
> (69–71)

The rhythm struggles through this damaged undergrowth of harsh consonants.

A beat can also be smooth and flowing. Again, there is pleasure in this. We are conducted through a line by the fluid patterning of vowels and consonants. Fluency is a quality found in the poetry of Edmund Spenser, Ben Jonson, Andrew Marvell, Alexander Pope and Alfred Lord Tennyson. This is the moment from the close of Tennyson's 'Morte d'Arthur' (1842), when the boat, bearing Arthur's body, floats away on the lake:

> till the hull
> Look'd one black dot against the verge of dawn,
> And on the mere the wailing died away.

The sharp detailing of the 'one black dot' gives way to the dying wail of the sounds across the still waters.

Metre

Metre is the name for the regular, or nearly regular, sound patternings of verse. There is a largely still accepted technical language about the different kinds of metre found in English, and while labelling is not a high-grade intellectual activity, it is useful to have some terms when discussing the effect of rhythms.

In English, metre has very often been a matter of accenting or stressing words, or parts of words, in a line composed of a fixed number of syllables. Because some syllables are accented and some not, a notation has been arrived at to denote a stressed syllable – ´ – and an unstressed syllable – ˘ –.

The rhythm of a line is determined by the number of stresses. So a *dimeter* has two, a *trimeter* three, a *tetrameter* four, a *pentameter* five and a *hexameter* six. Sometimes the term '*foot*' is introduced to distinguish the units of verse in which the stressed syllable occurs. So a dimeter is also described as a *two-foot line* and so on.

The exact character of a metre is shaped by the patterned arrangement of stressed and unstressed syllables. It is still customary to use the Classical names for these.

The *iambic foot* moves from an unstressed to a stressed syllable. The *trochaic foot* works in reverse, from a stressed to an unstressed syllable. If there are two unstressed syllables before the stressed one, the rhythm is *anapaestic*, and if the stress comes before two unstressed syllables, it is *dactylic*. The full description of a metre combines the number of stresses (or feet) with the patterning of stressed and unstressed syllables. So, to take the most famous example, Shakespeare writes his verse in iambic pentameters – a five-stress line with the stress falling on the even syllables, second, fourth, sixth and so on.

Metres create different effects. Iambic metres (the most common in English) are suitable for the expression of thought and recollection. The movement from an unstressed to a stressed syllable suggests the clarification of thought. The poet moves by steps, always from the hesitancy or uncertainty of an unstressed syllable to the decision and certainty of a stressed one. We can hear William Wordsworth thinking his way through these lines from 'Tintern Abbey' (1798):

> With mănў rĕcŏgnĭtĭŏns dĭm ănd fáint.
> Ănd sŏmewhat óf ă săd pĕrplĕxĭtў,
> The pĭctŭrĕ óf thĕ mĭnd rĕvĭvĕs ăgáin.
>   (60–2)

The iambic rhythm in the last line enacts the revival of which the poet speaks, in part because the disyllabic 'revives' and 'again' work through their 'natural' accents to complete a process of recognition that was 'dim and faint' but has now achieved a clear picture of the matter.

Trochaic metres often sound firm and settled. William Blake's 'The Tyger' (1794) bursts on us with assertive power: 'Týgĕr, Týgĕr, bŭrnĭng bright'.

The longer metres can sound very different from each other. The anapaest builds up tension by hurrying the reader through unstressed syllable to the stress. An example is Algernon Swinburne's 'The Forsaken Garden' (1876): 'Ĭn ă coign of the cliff bĕtwĕen lowland ănd highlănd'. The rhythm singles out the important features in the desolate landscape.

Dactylic metres, with their falling away from a stress, can sound sad and regretful. Browning's 'The Lost Leader' (1845) opens 'Just fŏr ă hándfŭl ŏf silvĕr he left ŭs'. That is the poetry of lost hopes. The metre dies away from the firm opening as the hopes of those who were led die away.

Variation

English metres are very rarely entirely regular. The ear likes variation, and the mind and heart recognize that there are times when the pulse of the poem requires a departure from the pattern of stresses. Furthermore, not every stress is of equal weight. A word is not just material; its meaning is going to shape the extent to which it is important in a line, and that will be reflected in the weight of its stress. Another factor is performance: a reader is free to choose how to emphasize some of the stresses according to the relative importance he or she thinks they have.

Listen to the opening lines of the Sir Thomas Wyatt poem referred to in Chapter 16, section 16.6:

> They flee from me that sometime did me seek
> With naked foot stalking in my chamber.

This foot is iambic. Apart from the interesting uncertainty as to how to stress 'sometime', the first line is regular. The second, however, departs from the established pattern. Should we stress the first or both syllables of 'naked'? If we stress both there is a cluster of stresses early in the line, because 'foot' is certainly stressed. And not only 'foot'. The first syllable of the next word 'stalking' is stressed (probably the most emphatic in the line). This concentration of stresses points to the emotional centrality of the image of hunting. The poem turns on who is hunting whom.

The contribution of rhythm

Rhythm does at least four things:

- It singles out words that are crucial to the meaning of a poem. The verb 'I am' might not be central in many sentences, but the opening rhythm of John Clare's poem (1865) makes it prominent: 'I am, yet what I am none cares or knows'. The rhythm is loosely iambic, but not at the start. Both words of 'I am' are stressed, and the isolation achieved through the rhythm makes us see that self-identity (and the struggle to hang on to it) is the central theme of the poem.

- Rhythm can create urgency. This is particularly the case in poems in a regular and insistent metre. We can hear the power of 'The Tyger' (1794) in Blake's almost mesmeric rhythms.
- The rhythm of a poem can convey far more than mere statements about the emotional significance of what is being said. Listen to how the opening rhythms of Thomas Hardy's 'The Voice' (1912–13) create the aching longing of the bereaved poet:

> Woman much missed, how you call to me, call to me,
> Saying that now you are not as you were.

The ache of bereavement is acted out in the way the stresses fall on the object of his loss – the 'woman much missed' – and then on the plaintive and hauntingly repeated 'call'.

- When all the material aspects of language work together – rhythm, sound, texture – the language can sound impressively final. Donne opens 'The Expiration' (1633), a poem on the parting of lovers, in a regretful manner:

> So, so, break off this last lamenting kiss,
> Which sucks two souls, and vapours both away

It was a convention that the parting of lovers was a kind of death, and here the lingering rhythm, the sighing 's' sounds (as well as the alliterations on 'l' and 'w') and the gesture implied by 'away' all combine to mark the separation with a lamenting finality (see also Chapter 53, section 53.2).

Writing about rhythm

Writing about rhythm might involve technical terms, but chiefly it involves saying something about the *impact* it has.

There are five ways in which people talk about the effects of rhythm. They are not technical, and care is needed to avoid vagueness.

- As indicated already, terms concerning physical movement are often appropriate. Quick rhythms might be 'light', 'tripping', 'jerky' or 'agile'; and slow ones 'heavy', 'stumbling', 'ponderous', 'tired', 'awkward' and 'laboured'.
- Sometimes physical gestures provide an appropriate language. A line, or whole poem, might be described as 'expansive', 'inviting', 'dramatic', 'defiant', 'insulting' or 'sweeping'.
- Occasionally, formal language is required. Neat lines might be described as 'deft', 'dextrous', 'well-shaped' and 'incisive'; and smooth ones as 'polished' or 'easy'.
- The language of music is often useful. The pace or tempo of a line might be 'lively' and 'brisk', or 'stately' and 'measured'. The terms 'crescendo' and 'diminuendo' are useful for climaxes and fades.

- The most supple language is one concerned with tone. Words, to repeat the point, express thoughts and feelings, and the rhythm of a passage can express these. So lines might be 'grave', 'earnest', 'serious' and 'dark'; or 'light', 'carefree', 'buoyant' and 'euphoric'.

Learning to hear

We have to learn to hear. There are several ways to do this. We can listen to poetry being read. This usually brings out the rhythmical movement of the verse. We can also read the poetry to ourselves. If we don't hear the rhythms, we should try poetry that has a very obvious rhythm (comic poetry, for example) and work from there. Finally, we can talk to others. We often learn to hear by being told to listen to an effect.

Summary

English poetry creates rhythm largely through stressing syllables. Besides the technical terms, it is important to think about the effects of the rhythms. This involves using a more flexible language. As it is not always easy to hear rhythm, practice is important.

17.5 Sounds

Poetry uses some of the features of language in heightened ways. This includes the sounds of words. Much of the time, the sounds of words don't matter. If we are reading instructions for assembling, say, a kitchen table, it would seem very odd if the words invited us to perform them aloud. But with some parts of some poems, the capacity to be sounded is an important characteristic.

Cadence

Cadence is the movement and (usually) the change in the pitch of the voice towards a close. The close may be the end of a line, a clause or a sentence. Cadences can be steady, falling or rising. As with 'pitch' the term is drawn from music, though in literary discussion it is used more impressionistically. Cadence is a 'natural' part of speech. Our voices rise at the end of a question and often fall when we deliver bad news. This means that cadence is a matter of tone and also, therefore, of meaning. Poets who depend on the establishment of moods are likely to create a variety of cadences. Take, for example, Matthew Arnold's 'Dover Beach' (1851). The poet reviews the scene:

> The sea is calm to-night.
> The tide is full, the moon lies fair
> Upon the straits

The cadences are those prompted by observation – steady, measured, emotionally cool. Then in the sixth line, he invites his beloved to view the scene:

> Come to the window, sweet is the night-air!

The voice rises; perhaps on 'window', almost certainly on 'night-air'. But when he dwells on the thoughts prompted by the 'grating roar' of the tide, there is a melancholy note. The waves

> Begin, and cease, and then again begin,
> With tremulous cadence slow, and bring
> The eternal note of sadness in.

The poem tells us what kind of cadence we should hear. It is 'tremulous' (trembling, quivering) and expresses the 'eternal note of sadness'. The cadence falls with the final word 'in'.

Alliteration

Alliteration is the repetition of consonants. For example, the second line of Gerard Manley Hopkins' 'Spring' (1877) alliterates on 'w', 'l' and 'sh': 'When weeds, in wheels, shoot long and lovely and lush'. The effect is created by the regularity of the alliteration. The upsurge of life in Spring is present in the pulse established in 'long and lovely and lush'. When alliteration is irregular, readers might get the feeling that the poet's preoccupation with his or her subject occasionally punctuates the line in the form of the repeated consonants. In the opening of Ted Hughes' 'Pike' (1960), the 'p' sound is irregular and insistent:

> Pike, three inches long, perfect
> Pike in all parts

Is there something threatening about the irregularity – the unpredictability – of the repeated consonant?

Assonance

Assonance is the repetition of a vowel sound. What was said about alliteration usually applies to assonance. Two things should be added. First, assonance (like rhyme) can depend on whether a vowel sound is long or short. Take the case of 'a': there is assonance on the short vowel 'can' and 'had' and the long vowel 'day' and 'sail'. Second, assonance often works on a small scale. In just two 'a' sounds, Herbert, in the first line of 'Prayer' (1633), achieves an elevated and spiritual air: 'Prayer, the Church's banquet, angel's age'.

Texture

Texture is hardly a technical word, but it is very useful when talking about the combined physical effects of lines, caesuras, rhythms, cadences and sounds.

A crucial factor is the density of the sounds. When alliteration is combined with strong rhythms, the texture of the verse is often rough and abrasive. When alliteration (or assonance) is light, the textures are often thin and even airy.

The texture of poems is strongly shaped by the arrangement of syllables. A series of monosyllabic words can be stark and even aggressive in their evocation of bleakness, as in R. S. Thomas's 'Evans' (1958):

> the drip
> Of rain like blood from the one tree.
> (11–12)

Polysyllabic words, particularly in short lines, can display the poet's dexterity elegantly. This is an eight-syllable line from a Charles Wesley hymn in which one word supplies six of them: 'Incomprehensibly made man' (1744).

The combination of monosyllabic and polysyllabic words in a poem creates emotionally significant changes in tone as well as texture. Shakespeare has many monosyllabic lines, so the introduction of a disyllabic word, particularly when it is about the beloved, indicates a deeper emotional engagement. There are a series of sonnets about the rival poet. This, number 86 (1609), is the last:

> Was it the proud full sail of his great verse,
> Bound for the prize of (all too precious) you

The verse swells with feeling in that word 'precious'.

Talking about texture

When talking about texture, we should try to do justice to physical and tonal properties. Listen to this passage from Robert Browning's 'A Grammarian's Funeral' (1855):

> Image the whole, then execute the parts –
> Fancy the fabric
> Quite, ere you build, ere steel strike fire from quartz,
> Ere mortar dab brick!
>
> (69–72)

Browning helps us to feel the palpability and solidity of building materials and the determination of the speaker. The urgent imperatives and the awkward, odd angles of the vowels convey the strenuous struggle with materials. *Ellipsis* – the omission of words – creates a closely meshed texture. The last line would have been less effective had it read: 'Ere you use mortar to dab the brick'.

Timbre

In music, *timbre* means the particular sound world of a specific voice or instrument. We know what an oboe sounds like, but we might still talk of the high, hard, bright sound of a particular performer. In the same way, we know what consonants and vowels sound like, but in the work of a poet, his or her tone, attitude and subject matter might create a very particular timbre. Wordsworth's timbre is often that of a thinking and feeling man, who has been deeply touched by experience, so the verse sounds meditated on and thought through. Listen to the timbre of these lines from 'Tintern Abbey' (1798):

> sensations sweet,
> Felt in the blood, and felt along the heart,
> And passing even into my purer mind
> With tranquil restoration
>
> (28–31)

The repeated 'felt' has the timbre of one who dwells on his experience, and in the measured close on 'tranquil restoration' we can hear the achieved calm of his reflections.

Movement, music, enactment

These three terms are used when talking about sounds and meanings. *Movement* is the word by word passage, which establishes meanings and feelings.

The word '*music*' is sometimes used, rather impressionistically, to talk about the movement of a line, passage or whole poem. Because all literature exists in time, it all involves movement. The movement is described as 'musical' because it is a movement of sound and sense created by the sequence of pitch, pace and verbal patternings such as alliteration or assonance. But, as has often been insisted in this section, words have meanings and their use can evoke feelings. Consequently, words concerned with thought and feeling are used when the music of verse is discussed. W. B. Yeats' 'In Memory of Major Robert Gregory' (1919) contains this passage about Gregory, a painter of the Irish landscape:

> For all things the delighted eye now sees
> Were loved by him: the old storm-broken trees
> That cast their shadows upon road and bridge;
> The tower set by the stream's edge;
> The ford where drinking cattle make a stir
> Nightly
>
> (49–54)

Readers have heard a commanding and majestic music in Yeats' voice. Listen to the effect of 'old', 'broken' and 'road'. The pace is easy and yet momentous. There is also an intimacy: we share Gregory's vision because we now see what he brought to our attention.

Enactment is a useful word for the way in which the material elements of language become the means by which the meanings of a poem are conveyed. They are acted out. This is a feature of poetry that has long been recognized. This is Alexander Pope in *An Essay on Criticism* (1711):

> 'Tis not enough no harshness gives offence,
> The sound must seem an echo to the sense
>
> (364–5)

Pope is very careful. The 'echo' is part of the 'sound', so, by analogy, the sound of verse is part of its sense. In one sense, this is obviously true, because words are sounded. We value poetry in which what we hear is appropriate or fitting to what is being said. Sometimes, we say that the poet has matched the sounds with the sense. This is clumsy. The sounds are inseparable from the sense. What we should say is that the poet has so arranged the words that they perform what they are speaking about. Sometimes, the performing is imitative. Shakespeare's sonnet 60 (1609) begins:

> Like as the waves make towards the pebbled shore,
> So do our minutes hasten to their end,
> Each changing place with that which goes before

'Each changing' is virtually onomatopoeic. It enacts the hard sound of the pebbles knocking against each other as they are thrown up the beach by the incoming tide.

Summary

We need to listen to how the sounds of words contribute to the meanings of poems. Sometimes the term 'music' is useful when talking about the movement of verse. We value poetry in which the sounds – cadence, alliteration, assonance, texture – work together to enact the meaning.

⬛ ⌄ 18   The Work of Poets

18.1   Practical criticism

Poetry is usually examined in two ways. One is practical criticism – the close exam-ination of how the words of a poem work to create meaning and express feeling. (This is sometimes called *critical appreciation* or *analysis*.) Most of what has been written in Chapters 14 to 17 has covered this sort of thinking, but here are some points of advice.

- Read the poem several times, so you can follow it through from beginning to end.
- Base your discussion on the sequence of the poem. Look through it stanza by stanza and line by line. Remember: you should write in detail about the whole poem.
- If you are making a point about the poem as a whole – its style, imagery or subject matter – it is wise to refer to passages from various parts of the poem.
- Remember that it is the language of the poem you are thinking about, so when you make a point, try to say how the words themselves create and enact the meanings. This will probably involve you in thinking about how the imagery establishes meaning and feeling, and how the connotations of words enrich the poem's meaning.
- Pay particular attention to how the poem opens. Openings usually bring the reader into the world of the poem by establishing the tone and introducing the subject matter – the experience, place or person.
- Similarly, pay close attention to the ending. The ends of poems can take the reader back to the start, complete an argument, reveal what the poet thinks, conclude a story, surprise the reader with an unexpected point, or resolve the feelings the poem has expressed.
- Technical terms are useful. (Examiners often look out for their appropriate use.)
- Don't be afraid of saying what you you think or feel, and don't be afraid of stating what you are unsure about. When in doubt, the best thing is to give two interpretations or views of the poem.
- Finally, listen for the tone of voice. Poems about gloomy subjects need not always be gloomy poems. You have to listen to the poet's voice to catch the tone and attitude.

Summary

When thinking about an individual poem, attention must be paid to the details of the language – meanings, imagery, sounds and rhythms. The aim of practical criticism is to understand what each element contributes to the poem.

18.2 Questions about whole books: what kinds of poems?

The second kind of question requires you to write about the work of a poet as a whole. In examinations, this means either a selection as in the case of the Odes and narrative poems of Keats, or a book such as Blake's *Songs of Innocence* (1789) and *Songs of Experience* (1794). In this section, we shall look at the kinds of things that are often found in a single poet's work, and we shall illustrate these from the work of Philip Larkin. The poems discussed are from *The Less Deceived* (1955), *The Whitsun Weddings* (1964) and *High Windows* (1974).

Questions about the kind of poems a poet writes cover subject matter, style and tone. For example, some poets choose deliberately to write about history, myth or an imagined past. John Milton wrote about the origin of all things in *Paradise Lost* (1667), John Keats re-worked Classical myths in '*Endymion*' (1818) and '*Hyperion*' (1820), and Edmund Spenser invented a world of magic in *The Faerie Queene* (1590). The subject matter has a bearing on style. Epic poetry, such as *Paradise Lost*, is written in a lofty and high-sounding manner. It is worth asking how the poet presents him- or herself, and for whom he or she is speaking.

The world about us

Larkin is quotidian; in virtually every case he writes about the world he sees about him. In *The Whitsun Weddings* his subject matter includes young mothers taking their children to the recreation ground ('Afternoons'), department stores ('The Large Cool Store'), and advertisements ('Send no Money'; 'Essential Beauty'). As a result, some of the subjects already need explaining. There is, for example, no longer a 'Whitsun' holiday. Even when Larkin writes of the past, it is a past he can get at by way of literature or public memory. As he makes clear, the bleak story of the misused girl in 'Deceptions' (*The Less Deceived*) comes from Henry Mayhew, the nineteenth-century journalist, who wrote about the lives of the London poor.

Summary

When we ask what kind of poems a poet writes, we need to think about subject matter, the place of the poet within the poems, and the style of the writing.

18.3   What forms?

There are many poetic forms available to a writer. Milton chose the Epic; *Paradise Lost* is in twelve books, and the style is elevated. As indicated above (see Chapter 14), poets tell stories and, consequently, frame stanza forms that enable them to narrate. Stanza forms vary from the quatrains of ballads to the longer stanzas used by Spenser and Keats. Blank verse has attracted poets who reflect and meditate, and the heroic couplet is ideally suited to pithy, concentrated thinking.

With the form go the decisions poets make about rhythm, rhyme and matters of sound – textures and cadences. These characterize poets. John Dryden's muscularity and William Wordsworth's sonorous gravity are enacted in the sounds and rhythms that characterize their verse.

Lyric and traditional forms

Larkin, like many twentieth-century poets, largely writes lyric poetry. His poems are rarely more than seventy lines long ('The Whitsun Weddings' is an exception at eighty). Most of them are personal (most are written in the first person) and reflective. They deal with common experiences. Given the way they move from experience to reflection on that experience, they might be called meditative lyrics. In all three of his 'mature' volumes, there are 'big' poems; for example, 'Church Going' and 'At Grass' in *The Less Decieved*, 'Here' and 'Dockery and Son' in *The Whitsun Weddings*, and 'To the Sea', 'The Building' and 'Show Saturday' in *High Windows*. There are also very short poems (often just quatrains) which are punchy, comic, epigrammatic and, in some cases, surprisingly evocative. Larkin sometimes called them 'squibs'.

Larkin and some of his contemporaries – Kingsley Amis and Donald Davie – reacted against the rhapsodic, bardic manner of Dylan Thomas. Their reaction took the form of lucid diction, rational syntax and the traditional disciplines of verse – regular stanzas, discernible rhythms and the presence of rhyme. 'Dockery and Son' is a poem of six eight-line stanzas. The form is the same as in Thomas Hardy's 'After a Journey' (1914). This must have been a conscious choice, because both poems are about returns (Hardy to where he first met his beloved, and Larkin to his old college) and both use the imagery of ghostly haunting – Hardy says he comes 'to view a voiceless ghost', and Larkin says he is a 'Death-suited visitant'. Larkin is concerned to work within the convention of rhyme schemes, but (a typical feature of his work) he varies it carefully from stanza to stanza. The first is ABABCDCD and the second ABABCDDC, which is also the rhyme scheme of the Hardy poem. Sometimes, as in 'Dockery and Son', he uses para-rhyme and sometimes he runs on sentences across stanzas. This gives the impression of the naturalness of organic form while adhering to the discipline of mechanical form. As in the poetry of another poet whom Larkin admired, Edward Thomas, the art of the poems – their design and organization – are 'concealed' by the 'naturalness' of the sentence structure and pressure exerted by the strong speaking voice.

Summary

The genres a poet adopts and his or her attitudes to the traditional disciplines of verse – stanza and rhyme scheme – often reveal his or her attitudes and character.

18.4   What words?

This is the question about diction or lexis. Poets are distinguished by the parts of speech they frequently choose. Generally speaking, poets use many more nouns and adjectives than verbs. Sometimes, as in Milton and Keats, the proportion of nouns and adjectives to verbs is very high. Some poets, however, have almost as many verbs as nouns; examples of these include Ben Jonson and John Donne. Another consideration is the matter of register – the ranking of words in terms of their seriousness and significance. To take one example, we might talk of the 'dead' of the First World War, but often we use the higher-register term 'the fallen'. There is more nobility and dignity (and therefore significance) in the latter term. Other ways of distinguishing language is on a scale between the highly elaborate and artificial and, at the other end, the colloquial and conversational – what is sometimes called *demotic language*.

Empirical language

Larkin's language is often called *empirical*. It is concerned with the immediacy of experience, the things (and the qualities of things) that we encounter in the everyday world. It is consequently a language of nouns and adjectives. A feature of a Larkin poem is the lists isolating the features that give a place or person recognizable identities. There are lists in the long poems such as 'Here', and shorter ones such 'The Importance of Elsewhere' (*The Whitsun Weddings*). 'Show Saturday', Larkin's longest poem, consists of long lists of the activities and exhibits at an agricultural show. Sometimes, as in 'Here', Larkin compounds the adjectives (see Chapter 16, section 16.4). A striking feature is the negative prefix. Larkin can make the reader pause and see things afresh by way of usages such as 'the unmolesting meadows' in 'At Grass' (see Chapter 16, section 16.6). And Larkin has a good ear. Often there are lines made memorable by the cadences and clusters of sounds. 'Water' (*The Whitsun Weddings*) begins with a sort of jokey clumsiness, but closes with a sublime picture of light passing through a glass of water:

> Where any-angled light
> Would congregate endlessly.

The slight awkwardness of the diverse vowel sounds in 'any-angled light' enacts the refracting light passing through the water, and the steady cadence of the last line, culminating on 'endlessly', suggests the wonder of a perpetual state.

Summary

The character of a poet's output is to be found in the grammar of the poems, the register of the language and the sounds of the words.

18.5 What imagery?

In thinking about a poet's imagery, it is useful to ask to which sense the poet appeals. Most imagery is visual, but occasionally touch, taste and smell are appealed to. Questions can also be asked about whether a poet's language is largely descriptive (the plain style of statement and assertion) or figurative, and if figurative, whether the poet inclines to simile or metaphor. Any use of symbolism is also a matter of tradition, that is, of culture and history. There are periods in the history of cultures when certain beliefs (together with their symbols) are dominant, and when certain figures of speech are fashionable.

Everyday images

Larkin is a poet who draws his imagery from the natural world and from familiar, everyday objects: the landscape thawing in 'Faith Healing' and the doors warped tight shut in 'Dockery and Son' (*The Whitsun Weddings*). Sometimes his images are those lists of familiar things: the people in 'Here' and the sights that characterize England in 'Going, Going' (*High Windows*).

Larkin tends to opt for the humbler, more familiar and less 'poetic' simile than for the artful compressions of the metaphor. This is in keeping with his preference for the kind of rational syntax associated with statement. The simile is used interestingly in the complex image at the close of 'The Whitsun Weddings', in which slowing down in the train is 'like' a flight of arrows that somewhere becomes rain.

Opting for similes was a deliberate turning away from the symbolism that was popular in the 1930s and 1940s. Yet, as several readers have noticed, in *High Windows*, symbols appear. In 'Show Saturday' the plethora of detail gives way to an attempt to turn the annual agricultural fair into a symbol of replenishing energy for the people and their way of life. Also, in the later verse, there are more images drawn from the elements or nature. Look at 'Forget What Did' and 'The Trees'. Yet natural imagery was present in earlier verse; the first poem of *The Whitsun Weddings* closes with an image of facing the sun that might have been drawn from the philosopher Plato.

Summary

The work of a poet is characterized by the choice of imagery and the particular forms of figurative language.

18.6   What tone?

In and through the tone of a piece of writing, the reader can 'hear' what an author (or persona) thinks or feels. Tone is elusive. We have to pick it up (often tangentially) in a number of ways. The basics of tone must be sought in the relationship established in the poem between poet and reader. To whom is the poet speaking, and what kind of link is there with the reader? We might detect it in the diction. We might ask what particular nuances a word or phrase has, or why the poet has chosen this particular wording. We can hear tone in the rhythm and sounds of a poem. Timbre and cadences disclose the stance or pose, and therefore the tone, of the poet.

Two voices

Critics have noted two voices in Larkin. Sometimes the tone is that of an 'ordinary bloke'. The kind of voice we hear in 'Self's the Man' (*The Whitsun Weddings*). This voice rarely moves beyond commonplace responses, and has little specialist knowledge or aesthetic insight. It has been called 'philistine'. In the early stanzas of 'Church Going', the persona almost grumbles that he doesn't know whether the roof of the church is cleaned or restored.

The other voice is the 'aesthete' – the perceptive, alert, observant and thoughtful poet. This voice emerges at the end of 'Church Going'. After the ordinary bloke's shrug that he has no idea what the building is worth (very much an ordinary reaction), the sensitive voice takes over to articulate thoughts about how church robes our deepest human impulses as 'destinies'.

Larkin's tone is often described as pessimistic. This is not quite accurate. Certainly, he is concerned with the fading of hope and the failure of ideals, but this makes him a poet of disappointment. The pessimist expects the worst; the poignancy of the disappointed is that they hoped for something better and are conscious, as in 'As Bad as a Mile', of what they have lost.

Summary

Tone must be listened for. It is usually found in the relationship between poet and reader, the choice of diction and the rhythms and sounds of the poem.

18.7   What personas?

To write a poem is to create a voice, and to create a voice is a big step towards creating a self or persona. In one sense, every time a poet writes in the first person, a persona is being created. Yet if we say that every self – every first person – is a persona, there is no way of distinguishing between poets who create a character and those who are writing about what they feel as individuals. There is a difference between a voice in a Browning dramatic monologue and Wordsworth writing about his childhood.

Versions of the self

In most of Larkin's poems, the self is a version of the poet. Nothing is to be gained by pretending that the persona in 'Dockery and Son' is not the poet, nor that when the persona affirms the annual ritual of the agricultural show in 'Show Saturday' he is not expressing his own views. It may be that the persona is adjusted poem by poem, or that in some poems it hardly matters *whose* voice we are hearing. This is not a matter of biography, although biography can confirm impressions produced by the poem. In fact, Larkin did call in at Oxford (the setting for 'Dockery and Son') when he was returning from a funeral – hence the self-description of 'death-suited visitant'.

Some poems are without a distinctive persona. In 'At Grass' the poet is a sensitive observer of salient details, but not a strong personality. Sometimes he chooses to speak on behalf of us all. Some readers have found this awkward. They can accept that he speaks for himself, but why include us? 'Dockery and Son' starts with individual experience but moves into the plural and the general at the end. Readers might say that life is *not* boredom followed by fear.

In one or two poems, however, there is a persona who is *not* the poet. The smugly fashionable and self-congratulatory academic in 'Naturally the Foundation Will Bear Your Expenses' (*The Whitsun Weddings*) epitomizes all that Larkin most hates – a sneering dismissal of our nation's traditions. We can hear Larkin's disapproval in the light, chattering timbre of the poem.

Summary

A first-person presence in a poem raises the issue of who is speaking. In one sense, all voices in poems are personas, but this should not prevent the reader from asking how the voice in the poem is, or might be, related to the poet.

18.8   What attitudes?

When we ask questions about how a writer views things, we are asking not just for an account of the writer's ideas, but also something about basic attitudes. We might ask where the writer starts from, or what he or she takes for granted. An author such as John Donne assumes the existence of God, so his struggles are not those of belief but rather of response. By contrast, Alfred, Lord Tennyson, particularly in 'In Memoriam' (1850), adopts the attitude of the doubter and the earnest inquirer. Attitudes are usually accompanied by a bearing or a stance. Poets might face up to experience or seek to evade its more unpleasant aspects.

The outsider

There is something of the outsider in Larkin. He is very often the uninvolved spectator, the one who is unmarried but enjoys watching the wedding parties through the window of his railway carriage. This detachment has led to the accusation of snobbery. In 'Here' he transfers the term 'cut-price' from the goods in shops to the people who buy them. Perhaps it is inevitable that a poet who sums up scenes and people by selecting what he regards as the characterizing details is going to be accused of simplification and prejudice.

A pose adopted in some of the later poems (and frequently in his letters) is that of the curmudgeon – the aggressively grumbling observer who regrets change. In 'Homage to a Government' (*High Windows*) this takes a decidedly political stance. Larkin's politics within his poems is interesting. While never becoming a conventional establishment figure, he resists change and places his trust in received traditions – even if he doesn't altogether like them. He resists the contemporary world in 'Going, Going'. Britain, full of 'crooks and tarts' (a phrase supplied by his companion, Monica Jones), is bent on destructive consumerism. Yet regret, as in his requiem for pre-First World War England, 'MCMXIV' (*The Whitsun Weddings*), is sometimes much gentler.

Summary

The attitude of a poet is more basic than his or her ideas. Attitude is a matter of how a poet approaches experience; it is found in the bearing or stance of the poet.

18.9   What subjects?

The last two sections are concerned with what in examinations are usually called 'themes' – what a poet writes about and how the poet thinks about those things. Poets write because they are drawn to certain aspects of life. George Herbert's output is almost exclusively about his relationship with God. Sometimes, a more pervasive theme can be felt in and through the number of things a poet writes about. Wordsworth is often described as a nature poet, but what runs through his interest in lakes and mountains is an abiding concern with the human mind – the ways in which we apprehend and make sense of our experiences. Sometimes a poet's range is narrow, but this is not necessarily a criticism. Edward Thomas writes about little other than the English countryside, but what we value is the blend of eye and ear, and the rhythms of the brooding mind that touch on an elusive world of significances.

England

Larkin writes of England. It is an England of shabby provincial towns (the England of 'Mr Bleaney' – *The Whitsun Weddings*) and of the land encroached upon by sprawling development (the England seen from the railway in 'The Whitsun Weddings'). He is a poet of the 'rites of passage' in which he does not participate; he watches weddings from a train, observes the holidaymakers in 'To the Sea', the crowds in 'Show Saturday', and a memorial service in 'The Explosion'. He knows what we aspire to and finds in the arrangement of homes ('Home is so Sad' – *The Whitsun Weddings*) and the allure of advertisements ('Essential Beauty') our expressions of an ideal life.

Summary

What a poet writes about can be narrow or wide. We value what the poet makes of his of her subject matter.

18.10   What thought?

What a poet thinks is present in his or her picture of human life. Poets need not offer creeds or philosophies to make their views evident. Edward Thomas writes about arriving at a country railway station, seeing old buildings and hearing birds sing or the rain fall, but through these there is a melancholy sense of nature and humankind being 'on their own' in a big world.

Poignancy and climax

A good deal of Larkin's work is poignant. His is a world without God, in which our best hopes come to nothing; they shut like doors ('Dockery and Son') or fall wide of their mark ('As Bad as a Mile'). And yet the poems often confront us with the possibility of something else: of love surviving us (An 'Arundel Tomb') and life renewing itself ('The Trees' – *High Windows*). And he can be very funny. Humour is a way of thinking about things, and in his rueful comments on 'love' in 'Wild Oats' (*The Whitsun Weddings*) there is a bracing honesty as well as comedy.

Finally, the poems work towards a 'big finish'. A Larkin poem starts in a flat, almost offhand manner, but the close, made memorable by a striking image, is like the last movement of a romantic symphony – aspiring and original. The end of 'Church Going' is very different from the casual observations about what is found in a church. It is reflective but passionately so in its generalizing assertions. In a high and serious tone he thinks about how our 'compulsions' are shaped into 'destinies'.

Summary

A poet's thinking is evident in what he or she makes of his or her subject matter. Usually, though not necessarily directly, what a poet believes emerges in the selection of detail, the statements and the imagery of a poem.

■ ⩔ **Part Four**   Genre

▮ ✓ 19 Classification

19.1 Butterflies, birds and books

We like to classify. Whether we are studying butterflies or birds, we make distinctions by giving names. We don't name in the way that we use 'Charlotte' or 'Jennifer' as names, but by using names as categories. Charlotte and Jennifer are distinguished from other women by their names (proper nouns), but to call both 'women' is to put them into a category. In the case of butterflies we call one, say, a Cabbage White and another a Red Admiral, and one bird is a Finch and another a Thrush. The word for this is *taxonomy*. Taxonomy covers the laws or principles of classification.

When someone asks why we call some birds Finches, we point to features that they share. We talk about colour, shapes of wings, feeding and breeding habits and so on. Sharing those particular features is what makes a bird a member of this group rather than that one.

Classifying books

People have always classified books. Aristotle classified works in his *Poetics* (c. 335 BC), and, to return to J. K. Rowling: how should we classify the Harry Potter books? Examiners depend on classification when they ask, say, whether *Hamlet* is or is not a tragedy.

The problem of classifying books

The classification of books is not always easy, and some will add that it is not always helpful.

For a start, there has never been complete agreement as to what literary classes there are. For example, is Shakespeare's *Measure for Measure* (1604) a comedy, a dark comedy or a problem play? Nor is there an agreement as to what it is that makes a work one kind rather than another. If tragedies involve the death of a significant character, does this make Shakespeare's *The Winter's Tale* (1609) a Tragedy? A further complication is that we use some literary terms in different ways. For example, the term 'satire' can refer either to a kind of work – a moral examination of human conduct such as in Samuel Johnson's *London: A Satire* of

1738 (see Chapter 24, section 24.1) – or an attitude of moral criticism within a work, such as the affected lovers in Sheridan's *The Rivals* (1775).

Genre

When we answer the question 'What sort of book is this?' we are placing that book in a *genre*.

'Genre' means a literary form – a class, kind, species or a type of work.

The word is French in origin and was originally related to the word 'gender', the root meaning of which is to beget or generate.

Not an exact science

Literary classification is not exact, particularly so in English. It has not been a custom in the English tradition to write according to a set of rules. It was different in France, where rules were numerous, precise and strictly adhered to. Failure to stick to them was an offence against literature. Sometimes, the rules were *very* precise. In tragic verse drama, for example, the meaning of each line was required to be self-contained, so Victor Hugo's verse play *Hernani* (1830) was booed off the stage by an audience in Paris, because in one of the speeches there was a run-on line. Strict adherence to rules was not confined to drama. In 1913 there was a riot at the first performance of Stravinsky's ballet *The Rite of Spring*, because the ballet steps were not in accordance with the ideas of the Paris audience.

The traditional French approach seems ridiculously inflexible. But it does not follow that just because one culture decided to be strict, genre is an arbitrary matter of whim.

We need to do two things:

- To understand what we are doing when we place works in a genre; and
- To form an idea of genre that does not make it depend on unbreakable rules.

Not prescriptive

We usually assume that works in the same category share at least one essential characteristic. This form of classification operates in the sciences. For example, we say that since a spider has eight legs it cannot be an insect, because to be classified as an insect it must have six legs. The word 'must' is decisive; to think in this way is to be prescriptive – we set down beforehand what will or will not belong to a category. If we applied this way of thinking to literature, we would say that works in category X *must* have feature Y.

But, as has been indicated already, this model of classification does not suit literature. For example, tragedy is sometimes defined as the fall of a great man from prosperity to wretchedness, yet Arthur Miller's *Death of a Salesman* (1949), a play with an unremarkable central figure, is commonly called a tragedy. If genre were a matter of finding one determining characteristic, there would be no 'border disputes' in literary debate. Examiners could not set the type of question that starts: 'To what extent…'. But they do. We must conclude that not all works in a genre have one determining characteristic. We need, therefore, a model of classification different from that of the sciences.

Threads and families

The philosopher Ludwig Wittgenstein spoke of things in the same category as being like a piece of thread. The thread is made up of several fibres, not one of which is present throughout the thread's entire length. Yet no one would say that it was not a single piece of thread.

He also spoke of categories as displaying 'family resemblances'. What he meant was that some things in a category share characteristics that they don't have in common with all the other objects in the same category.

Literary categories work much more on the model of the thread or the family resemblance. We should therefore hesitate before we spend a lot of time looking for the one characteristic that, say, all tragedies must have. Talking about books is different from talking about butterflies and birds. We also have to remember that there are some works that we can't assign to a genre. 'The Waste Land' (1922) is an obvious example.

Summary

We need an understanding of genre that does not require each member of a class to share a single defining feature.

19.2   Conventions

Talk about genre is inseparable from talk about conventions.

> A convention is a particular form of literary presentation whereby authors signal to readers that they, the readers, should understand a character or action in a specific way.

All forms of art depend on conventions, and to understand any art we have to know how its conventions work. If there were no conventions, art could not be understood.

The conventions of films

Take the case of films: a thriller is likely to contain a chase; a cowboy film might end with a shoot-out in the deserted main street of a frontier town; and horror films of the Dracula type usually end with the defeat (though not the final one) of the Prince of Darkness. Failure to recognize the genre might result in a failure to understand the function of its conventions. If you don't get the point that the film is a thriller, you might think the chase is a road safety film warning us against reckless driving! We don't, of course; but this shows how deeply rooted is our understanding of conventions.

Each genre is sustained by a number of conventions, so, for example, a James Bond film usually includes a spectacular opening sequence, meetings with M and Q, and early encounters with the villain and a beautiful girl. These conventions establish the genre. They please us, because we expect them. We wait for the hero to say: 'The name is Bond – James Bond'. The more acquainted we are with the conventions, the greater our pleasure.

The durability of conventions

Conventions are durable. They can last for centuries. Take, for example, the 'boy meets girl' story in which there is initial hostility. Shakespeare uses that convention in the opening of *Much Ado About Nothing* (1598), and in 1813 Jane Austen used it in *Pride and Prejudice*. In both cases, the convention works by the reader recognizing that though there is hostility, the characters are suited to each other. In 2005, the BBC broadcast updated Shakespeare under the title *Shakespeare Retold*. The choice of *Much Ado About Nothing* to open the season showed that the transformation of hostility into love was still an appealing convention.

Varieties of convention

As with the term 'genre', 'convention' has a wide application. All sorts of different elements in literature are spoken of as conventions. For example, there are formal conventions such as sonnets having fourteen lines, dramatic conventions such as the stage representing several places, and plot conventions such as the gathering at the end of a detective story when the murderer is revealed. Of course, authors renew conventions. Mark Haddon plays a delightful variation on the convention that novel chapters are numbered consecutively by making the narrator of *The Curious Incident of the Dog in the Night-time* (2003), a fifteen-year-old boy suffering from Asperger's syndrome, use prime numbers instead, simply because they fascinate him.

Public agreements

The word 'convention' has a long history, though only a short one in literary discussion. However, its non-literary meaning throws light on its literary use. A convention is a group of people who come together to make an agreement or any publicly recognized agreement embodied in a generally accepted practice or procedure.

Conventions are therefore, agreements, and they are public. We all agree that a convention has a particular meaning. Conventions have been spoken of as codes or contracts, because understanding them is like knowing how a code works or consenting to the terms of a contract.

Accepting conventions

But readers won't agree to just *anything*. There must be something about a convention that makes us accept it as standing for an idea or action. A convention, we must remember, is always a convention of *something*. Samuel Taylor Coleridge said that when we go to the theatre we willingly suspend (leave hanging in the air) belief and disbelief. But his words apply to conventions such as fairies being tiny creatures who can fly. What we can't abandon is our idea of what people are like, and the moralities that govern their behaviour. Conventions need to be related to our sense of what life is like. This sense of 'what life is like' is wide. Some conventions are close to our lives, while others are more formalized and distant. Take the case of dialogue. It is usually presented as being written in sentences, and sometimes it is elegant and witty, but we don't in fact talk in sentences, and little that we say is witty. But dialogue in novels is sufficiently like conversation to enable us to accept it (see Chapter 2, section 2.4). Dragons and witches are more exclusively literary, and we only accept them in certain books. The fact that we do accept them in some books such as Edmund Spenser's *The Faerie Queene* (1590) probably means that we accept them as a conventional way of writing about the testing struggle against evil.

Conventions are not immune from change. For example, it is interesting to see how productions of *Measure for Measure* (1604) have handled the close. In the last scene, the Duke, who has kept hidden from Isabella the fact that her brother is alive, proposes marriage. Convention tells us that marriage is a common way of closing a comedy, but recently players, judging that Isabella has been unfairly manipulated by the Duke, question whether she would marry him. Hence, there have been performances in which she leaves the stage dramatically.

Conventions and interpretation

There is a principle of interpretation that states

> **Because we cannot understand a work unless we understand its conventions, conventions are central to interpretation.**

If we get the conventions wrong, we are also likely to get the work wrong. In *Validity in Interpretation* (1967), E. D. Hirsch says that some of his students could not understand John Donne's poem 'A Valediction: Forbidding Mourning' (1633), because they did not know the convention that parting in seventeenth-century love poems was often spoken of as a death. Seeing the word 'mourning', the students assumed the poem was actually about death (see Chapter 53, section 53.2).

The way into any work is through its conventions. We have, for example, to accept that characters in disguise are not recognized. Plots work according to conventions. It is a convention in Charles Dickens' writing that a character who makes a dramatic appearance early on in a novel is central to the plot's development and resolution. *Great Expectations* (1860) starts with young Pip menaced by an escaped convict. Once the convict is captured, the soldier's torches are 'flung hissing into the water, and went out, as if it were all over with him' (Chapter 5). According to the conventions of narrative irony, we know this means that, as far as the plot is concerned, things are *not* all over with him.

Conventions and judgement

We sometimes think that a work in a particular genre must observe the rules of that genre by adhering to the appropriate conventions. This is not a popular interpretive practice now, but it is surprising how often we judge a book by the consistency of its conventions.

Conventions set up expectations, and if these are not fulfilled we are inclined to judge the work as a failure. To return to Arthur Miller's *Death of a Salesman*. It is difficult not to use the term 'tragedy' of this play, yet if it is to be regarded as a tragedy, can Willy Loman be called a hero? Is he too foolish, too lost in his illusions and too lacking in self-knowledge to have the stature we look for in a tragic figure?

Summary

Genres rest on conventions – agreements between author and reader that certain incidents are to be understood in a particular way. Conventions are durable; they appear in works written centuries apart. Conventions are public agreements; they depend on our accepting them. We use conventions to interpret and, sometimes, to judge a book.

▶ 20 Tragedy

20.1 The place of Tragedy

Tragedy has an important place in English literary discussion. It is the custom for A-level examiners to set one of Shakespeare's tragedies, the implication being that each student must study at least one tragedy. The centrality of Tragedy is an indication of the way our literary culture has been formed. There must be a strong element of trying to justify the subject against the Classics: Greece had its tragedies, so also must English Literature.

A rare and broad genre

The mention of the Classics – the literature of Greece and Rome – leads to another point: historically, Tragedy is rare. It appears in Greece from the fifth century BC (Aeschylus, Sophocles and Euripedes are the chief playwrights) and then in Christopher Marlowe, Thomas Kyd and William Shakespeare in late-sixteenth-century London. There was another phase of tragic writing in the nineteenth century, Johan von Goethe and Henrik Ibsen being, albeit very different, examples.

Tragedy is a good example of a term consisting of a number of 'family resemblances'. We use the word in a non-literary way to mean an accident, a failure, a death, or even a missed goal. In literature the word has been used more precisely, but, nevertheless, the term is still broad. What follows, therefore, are some of the characteristics found in some of the plays we usually call tragedies.

Summary

Tragedy has a place of honour in literature. Although it is discussed frequently, it is a rare thing. It is a term with a broad usage.

20.2 Philosophical issues

In *The Republic* (c. 375 BC), Plato's discussion of knowledge, morality and the life of the state, poets are banned, because they show that the good man can be hurt and, possibly, because tragedies show that the gods send evil as well as good. The focus of tragedy is also disturbing. We are asked to look away from comforting generalities such as the ennobling nature of suffering to the sheer irreducibility of individual experience – the concrete, excessive and often undeserved anguish, both mental and physical, of one person.

Aristotle

Aristotle's *Poetics* (335 BC) is still the most influential work on Tragedy. In keeping with his other intellectual interests, Aristotle concentrates on problems of definition and literary form. This is a translation of his definition of Tragedy:

> A tragedy, then, is the imitation of an action that is serious, has magnitude, and is complete in itself; in language with pleasurable accessories, each kind brought in separately in the various parts of the work; in a dramatic, not a narrative form; with incidents arousing pity and fear, wherewith to accomplish its catharsis of such emotions.

Three immediate comments are required.

- Tragedy is action of a particular kind. 'Serious' means it is about those experiences that demand deep reflection.
- Because the subject is serious, the action arouses pity and fear in the audience. (Aristotle thinks of Tragedy as a theatrical genre.)
- The experience of viewing Tragedy has a 'cleansing' effect on the audience. Their emotions are aroused, then calmed and settled. As John Milton says at the close of his play in the style of a Greek tragedy, *Samson Agonistes* (1671), those viewing it depart with 'calm of mind all passion spent'. Whether we do feel this, and if we do, what is the significance of the experience, are matters that people still debate.

Aristotle said that Tragedy has six elements: spectacle, character, plot, diction, melody and thought. The most important of these are plot, character and thought, and of these three, plot is the most significant. One of his arguments for the centrality of plot was that two very important dramatic effects are functions of the plot. These are, to use their Greek names, *anagnorisis* and *peripeteia* (see also Chapter 4, section 4.5).

Anagnorisis

Anagnorisis is the crisis of a plot, the moment when the central figure sees what before has been hidden. The term is usually translated as 'discovery' or 'recognition'. Plots are about knowledge. The plot works to dispel ignorance, but in Tragedy knowing the truth is devastating. Aristotle's example is the moment in *Oedipus the King* (c. 430 BC), when a messenger, bringing what is thought to be glad news, in fact discloses the terrible news of Oedipus's identity. Oedipus has killed his father and married his mother.

Peripeteia

Peripeteia is usually translated as 'change' or 'reversal'. Reversal is very often the consequence of anagnorisis. Discovery changes ignorance to knowledge, and so changes the mood of the play. Hope gives way to despair, and the plot goes into reverse. At least two things are reversed: the fortunes of the hero and the direction of the plot. Since, in Aristotle's view, character and plot are interdependent, reversal affects both. When Romeo kills Tybalt, his fortunes decline and what might have been a comic plot becomes a tragic one.

It is difficult to avoid Aristotle when discussing Tragedy. But we must be careful. He was not setting down a set of rules. His aim was to describe what he found in the plays of his time. Later, in the sixteenth and seventeenth centuries (and particularly in France), his remarks were turned into prescriptions. In particular, the remark about the action of Tragedy being complete in itself has become the basis for the idea of the three unities – unity of time, unity of place and unity of action. Unity of time was interpreted to mean that the action should be complete within twenty-four hours, and unity of action required that there be no sub-plot. No one is obliged to accept such rules, and, historically, Aristotle only spoke of unity of action.

Summary

Tragedy makes an audience ask questions about the nature of human life. Because of this, it has attracted philosophical comment. Aristotle stressed the way it engaged the audience and the manner in which tragic plots moved. He stressed the moment of recognition, which often leads to a reversal of the plot and the fortunes of the central character.

20.3   Tragedy and judgement

Those who watch plays and read books do so because they enjoy the way art is shaped and how the artist uses language. People who enjoy art also have beliefs about politics, religion or morality. To have a belief is to hold something to be true. People live by their beliefs. They argue political points, they attend public worship and they choose to act in very particular ways.

Art and belief

What is the relationship between art and belief? In many cases, the answer is: not much. For example, it is hard to see that the enjoyment of *A Midsummer Night's Dream* (1594) depends on our political or religious beliefs.

But Tragedy is a different matter. It is worth asking:

> **Is Tragedy the one genre that is inseparable from the beliefs of those who watch it?**

Tragedy deals with the big questions: human identity, freedom and determinism, public and private moral codes, and the existence and nature of God. At the end of a tragedy, the audience is asked implicitly what they have made of the central figure. How are we, for example, to judge Hamlet? Is he a model of dedication, or one who has sacrificed people in pursuit of revenge? Such questioning recognizes that the play deals with matters of belief.

Summary

Tragedies demand that we recognize the issues as being deeply significant *and* come to some sort of judgement about them.

20.4　The tragic sense of life

The central character in a tragedy often embodies qualities that are significant in human life. Hamlet tries to do justice to thinking, and Othello struggles with those feelings of jealousy that accompany love.

Most tragedies end with the death of the central character. We might be inclined to ask: what is the sum total of such a life, and how should we think of someone who has wrestled with huge problems and now is no more?

In other words:

> **Tragedy makes us engage with the problems of human mortality.**

The Spanish writer Miguel De Unamuno wrote an impassioned book called *The Tragic Sense of Life* (1921). He is concerned with the importance of people – we are ends not means – and with our limitations and frailty. We carry around with us the knowledge of our mortality. It is this that makes our sense of life tragic – we have dreams of immense possibilities but we know our lives will close in death.

Tragedy tries to come to terms with mortality in two ways.

- It shows unflinchingly what it is to live a mortal life. Hamlet is haunted by death. He wears mourning clothes for his father, is eager to the point of rashness to meet the Ghost, and in soliloquy he broods on 'The undiscovered country from whose bourn/No traveller returns' (3.1. 81–2).
- Tragedy suggests that our mortality can be lived with. Tragic art shows us that, in spite of its inevitable close, human life is wonderful. We see what is noble about human life focused with radiant clarity on one who undergoes misunderstanding and suffering. At the end of *Julius Caesar* (1599), Antony praises Brutus by saying: 'This was a man' (5.5. 73–4). This is a testimony to human greatness seen in and through the tragic experience.

Tragedy and Christianity

There is a much discussed statement by the critic I. A. Richards that Christianity is incompatible with Tragedy, because Christianity believes in an afterlife. We must be careful here. Did Shakespeare's audience find the belief that flights of angels will sing Hamlet to his rest (5.2. 313) incompatible with the play's tragic action? And what of the life of Christ as we see it in the Gospels? Might not his life be said to be tragic? His disciples misunderstand him, the authorities plot against him and there is the (tragic?) ambiguity of Judas Iscariot, who, had he not been chosen as a disciple, would never have been a betrayer. Perhaps, tragedy remains a human experience, whether or not there is, in Hamlet's words, an 'undiscovered' country to which we travel.

Summary

Tragedy is a way of coming to terms with our mortality. We know that things end in death, but there is a pressure to see human struggles as noble. Critics have debated whether Tragedy is compatible with a Christian understanding of life.

20.5   Hero

Characters apart

The central tragic figure is usually referred to as the hero. The hero is an incomparably outstanding individual. Other characters cast light on him and he on them. There is a mutual process of definition in *Othello* (1604); his magnanimity reveals the banal littleness of Iago, and the trust of Desdemona shows how Othello has fallen into corrupting suspicion.

The tragic figure is often, but not always, a man: the central figures of John Webster's two most celebrated plays – *The White Devil* (1612) and *The Duchess of Malfi* (1623) – are very formidable women.

Tragic figures are lofty and elevated. There are a number of ways in which they rise above the common ranks of mankind.

Energy

Tragic figures are distinguished by drive and ambition; they are disturbingly single-minded. Listen to Hamlet's zealous commitment to revenge:

> Haste, haste me to know it, that I with wings as swift
> As meditation or the thoughts of love
> May sweep to my revenge.
>
> (1.5. 29–31)

He fuses intellectual energy with the passions of love – both immediate and intense – in an image of the falcon dropping out of the sky upon its victim. We are often so awed by the energy of tragic figures that we tend, at least in some moments, to approve of whatever ambition they have conceived.

Will

The tragic figure shows determination in action and fortitude in the face of the inevitable. This is a matter of will. The tragic figure pursues his or her ambition with resolution. The word 'resolute' echoes through Christopher Marlowe's *Doctor Faustus* (1591). Valdes promises fame and power through magic: 'If learned Faustus will be resolute' (sc. 1. 132). Faustus replies: 'as resolute as I am in this/As thou art to live' (sc 1. 133–4). When he is inclined to give up magic, 'resolute' is the word he clings to: 'no, Faustus, be resolute' (sc. 5. 6).

Authority

The tragic hero has a natural authority. *Othello* opens in a turmoil of emotions; in particular, the anger of Brabantio, Desdemona's father. There is confusion when an attempt is made to arrest Othello – shouts and drawn swords. Othello calms them: 'Keep up your bright swords, for the dew will rust 'em' (1.2. 60). Brabantio is still angry, but there is no fighting. Later, Othello faces a potentially hostile Senate and wins them over by his authoritative manner.

Seriousness

Hamlet is characteristically tragic in his degree of seriousness. He thinks hard; there is an intellectual excitement about his language. He seizes on an idea, pauses, repeats it and comments on it (see Chapter 8, section 8.2).

Nobility

Tragic figures have outstanding moral qualities. In *Julius Caesar*, Brutus is consistently called noble, even by his enemies. His nobility is found in the purity of his motives. He has nothing against Caesar, but because he believes Caesar is a threat to the republican tradition of Rome he joins the conspiracy.

Imagination

Macbeth has the imagination of a poet. Who but a poet could put mental agony in these terms: 'O full of scorpions is my mind' (3.2. 37)?

Courage

Tragic figures need the courage to pursue their own ends. Webster's Duchess of Malfi is a woman of considerable courage. She knows how manically hostile her brothers are to her marrying again, but she makes the decision and picks her husband. The language of her proposal is plain and forthright:

> I do here put off all vain ceremony,
> And only do appear to you, a young widow
> That claims you for her husband
>
> (1.2. 372–4)

Grandeur

Grandeur is not an easy quality to define exactly, but what the use of the word gets at is the superiority of the tragic figure over the other characters. In their personal qualities – their integrity, sincerity, commitment, devotion – they out-shine others. Webster's Duchess rises above her torturers in the darkness of a prison. They are attempting to drive her mad, but she asserts: 'I am Duchess of Malfi still' (4.3. 139). In that simple statement she shows herself to be superior to all those who have power over her.

Summary

The tragic hero is an outstanding figure who surpasses all others. He or she has apparently inexhaustible energy, an unshakeable will, a natural authority, a committed seriousness, a rare nobility, a towering imagination, courage and grandeur.

20.6 Fall

The inner fall

The outstanding figure falls. The fall can be of various kinds: moral disintegration as in *Othello* (1604); mental derangement as in *Death of a Salesman* (1949), and the diminution of human life in *Doctor Faustus* (1591). In these examples, the tragedy is chiefly inward. The mind or soul falls from reason and grace into wildness and triviality. Perhaps this is why sixteenth- and seventeenth-century playwrights dwelt in such disturbing detail on madness. Lear in the storm (and possibly Hamlet in his rantings at Ophelia) epitomize the depths to which a noble figure can fall. Ophelia speaks for the audience when she says 'O what a noble mind is here o'erthrown!' (3.1. 153).

The public fall

The danger of concentrating on the psychology (the inwardness) of Tragedy is that we miss an ancient and awesome aspect:

The tragic fall is public.

The tragic figure is a person of high status – a king, a prince, a duchess – and the decline is social. They fall down the social scale. The original title of Marlowe's *Edward II* (1594) was *The Troublesome reign and lamentable death of Edward the Second, King of England: with the tragical fall of proud Mortimer: and also the life and death of Piers Gaveston, the Great Earl of Cornwall, and mighty favourite of King Edward the Second, as it was publicly acted by the right honourable the Earl of Pembroke his servants, written by Chris. Marlowe Gent.* Three deaths, the second of which – 'proud Mortimer' – is described as a 'tragical fall'.

The words 'publicly acted' bring out something very important about tragedy.

Tragedy is external. Audience and other characters view the appalling decline of a once lofty figure.

Tragedy belongs to the stage because it is witnessed; the mighty fall, and we recoil in horror. We must learn to hear the horror a Gentleman witnesses in the lunatic ravings of King Lear:

> A sight most pitiful in the meanest wretch,
> Past speaking of in a king!
>
> (4.5. 200–1)

This public and external understanding of Tragedy appears with the conciseness of a definition in Chaucer's The Prologue of The Monk's Tale (c. 1390):

> Tragedie is to seyn a certeyn storie,
> As olde bookes maken us memorie,
> Of hym that stood in greet prosperitee,
> And is yfallen out of heigh degree
> Into myserie, and endeth wrecchedly.
>
> (84–8)

Tragedy is a spectacle; we behold with appropriate awe, pity and fear the decline of the hero's fortunes: Oedipus, the king who has saved his city, blinds himself and is cast out. We see Lear as the autocratic king at the start, and by the third act he is a naked madman. The sight of Lear in the storm requires us to use an extreme vocabulary.

Tragedy is strange and terrible.

We cannot always reason why these things happen. Part of what it is to be strange and terrible is that the action defies understanding. All we can do is to view the frightening spectacle. Tragedy is the art form that does this. It presents us with what baffles and terrifies.

Terrifying falls make simple plots.

The rise and fall of a hero structures a play through the trajectory of the plot and the imagery.

Marlowe's *Doctor Faustus* has a clear (even crude) plot line – Faustus rises and falls. Faustus is told that Lucifer, Prince of Devils, was thrown from Heaven for 'aspiring pride and insolence' (sc. 3. 70). And pride is the downfall of Faustus.

At the close of the play, the Chorus spells out the moral of what the audience has seen with an intimidating warning: 'Faustus is gone: regard his hellish fall' (See Chapter 30, section 30.4).

Summary

The fall of the tragic hero is internal and psychological in that he or she suffers pain and anguish, and external and public in that a once great and powerful figure falls to the bottom of society. The tragic fall has a strange and terrible aspect. It is often unfathomable. The fall makes for a simple plot line and graphic imagery.

20.7   Suffering

Kinds of suffering

To fall is to suffer. The tragic figure suffers in body and mind. Because we live in a culture that values inner experience – what we feel about something often determines our judgement – we are inclined to regard mental torment as more significant than the pains of the body. Had we lived in a society that was accustomed to war or famine, we might think otherwise. We can perhaps understand the frisson of the Duchess of Malfi being handed a dead man's hand, because Webster presents the immediate impact of what is lurid and bizarre (see Chapter 7, section 7.4). Shakespeare may have contributed to our assumption that mental pain exceeds that of the body. The physical agony of Lear in a storm – 'O, ho, 'tis foul!' (3.2. 24) – is said by Lear to be less than his mental torment:

> This tempest in my mind
> Doth from my senses take all feeling else
> Save what beats there: filial ingratitude.
> (3.4. 13–14)

The storm is terrible, but Lear sees with a rare clarity that the ingratitude of his daughters is so intense that his mental agony goes beyond physical pain.

Suffering, isolation and exclusion

Suffering is inseparable from isolation. It is the lot of tragic figures that they are shut off from others. This is the gap between the heroic figure and the non-heroic. When Macbeth hears that he is the Thane of Cawdor, he withdraws into a wondering soliloquy. 'Look how our partner's rapt' (1.3. 141) says Banquo. 'Rapt' means carried away; in Macbeth's case, transported by his imagination. Intensity of thought or unbounded ambition makes the hero stand apart.

But it is also the lot of the hero to be excluded. Lear walks out into the storm, but, symbolically, Regan says: 'Shut up your doors' (2.2 476). This is a moment when a good production can bring out the significance of this atrocity. Our place is to be with others, and we build dwellings, where, in safety and warmth, we can enjoy the bonds that tie us each to each.

Exclusion, therefore, is a violation of human belonging. Isolation torments the mind. It is not clear in *Hamlet* (1600) whether the Prince is mad or merely pretending, but in an important sense it does not matter which is the case. Hamlet is alone in the Court in that, with the exception of Horatio, he can trust no one. Madness is an image of having nothing in common with others. With proverbial snappiness, he sums up his state: 'bounded in a nutshell' (2.2. 255).

The fall of kings

Though the tragic figure is isolated, his fall can bring down the nation. The King is the central figure of the nation, so his fall is like a tear in the fabric of the state (see Chapter 7, section 7.4). The bodies littering the stage at the close of a tragedy (four in *Hamlet*) is a consequences of the fall of the mighty. Rosencrantz may be toadying, but he echoes the popular view that the state hinges on its monarch:

> The cease of majesty
> Dies not alone, but like a gulf doth draw
> What's near it with it.
>
> (3.3. 15–17)

The image is of many people being sucked down a whirlpool ('gulf') by the death of the king.

Moral outrage

We are outraged by excessive suffering. Tragedy brings home the inequality of life. Lear says he is 'a man/More sinned against than sinning' (3.2. 59–60).

It is often an experience of watching Tragedy that suffering seems unjustly excessive.

Audiences don't disagree with Edgar when, at the close of *King Lear* (1605), he says 'The oldest hath borne most' (5.3. 300).

Yet we must be careful. How can we know, except in trivial cases, who has suffered the most? There is no finely calibrated scale of suffering, so we cannot measure the extent of someone's suffering. Is Othello's suffering greater than Desdemona's, or Hamlet's more than Ophelia's? And what of the 'larger' questions? What kind of a world is this in which characters can suffer so? Is there any point to suffering? Can suffering be redemptive? As soon as these questions are asked, we are back to an issue raised in section 20.3: discussion of tragedy is inseparable from matters of belief.

Summary

Suffering in Tragedy is inner and outer. The tragic figure is often isolated and excluded. Suffering seems intensified in the fall of kings. Audiences often experience a moral outrage at what seems excessive suffering.

20.8 Faults

Laws, limits and being wrong

Suffering arouses our pity and sense of justice. We feel for the tragic figure. One of the purposes of the soliloquy is to allow us to be inward with the central character. As a result, we often feel much closer to tragic characters than to comic ones. Comedy requires a cooler perspective; Tragedy involves the spectator. And yet no matter what we feel we should never forget that

The tragic figure is wrong.

Tragedy recognizes laws – moral, natural, political, religious – and because there are laws, there are limits. Some things are not permitted. The Chorus in *Doctor Faustus* closes the play by dwelling on the fates of those who 'practise more than heavenly power permits'. Laws are real. Those who think that all our notions of the world are mere linguistic constructions must find it very difficult to write Tragedy.

Choosing wrong

Tragedy starts when someone of outstanding qualities chooses to do what is wrong.

In doing wrong, the tragic figure deliberately defies the laws of life.

Mary Shelley's *Frankenstein* (1818) is about a brave, imaginative and gifted man who commits a primal wrong. He does what only God should do – creates life, and the innocent deaths that follow are his responsibility.

Flaws, hubris, insolence and bravado

A traditional way of talking about the errors of the tragic figures is 'the flaw'. In some cases, the flaw is a matter of excess – the figure is too ambitious or too jealous – and in others it is a moral blemish in an otherwise noble life. Macbeth is too ambitious, and Brutus, for all his admirable selflessness, is overbearingly confident in his own judgement.

But do such failings make a figure tragic? What is often cited as a flaw – the 'fatal flaw' as it is sometimes described – is a fault that can be found in most of us. And most of us are not tragic.

Tragedy cannot just be a matter of doing wrong. If it were, there could be no distinction between a tragic and a criminal action. Macbeth employs three murderers to eliminate Banquo. They are not, unlike Black Will and Shakebag in the anonymous *Arden of Feversham* (1592), professional killers. They speak in verse with a decidedly pictorial flair – 'The west yet glimmers with some streaks of day' (3.3. 5) – so are very probably courtiers who have not flourished and are prepared to act on Macbeth's assurance that Banquo has held them 'So under fortune' (3.1. 79). But they are presented as criminal rather than tragic. They do not display a certain quality:

Tragic figures often exhibit what is called hubris.

Victor Frankenstein shows hubris. No matter how much suffering he has caused, he remains proud and even boastful of his ghastly act of creation.

Hubris was not a word Shakespeare used, but he clearly saw its qualities in the actions of tragic figures. 'Hubris' means pride. Another definition is over-weening or excessive confidence. The word is Greek in origin; it means wanton insolence.

'Insolence' is a word Shakespeare does use. It now means little more than being rude; naughty children, for example, are insolent to teachers. In the past, however, the word was stronger. The first definition of 'insolent' in *The Shorter Oxford English Dictionary* is: 'Proud, disdainful, arrogant, overbearing; offensively contemptuous of the rights of others.'

This definition is a good starting point for considering the distinctive manner of the tragic figure's wrongdoing. Consider Hamlet's description of himself to Ophelia: 'I am very proud, revengeful, ambitious...' (3.1. 125). Hamlet revels in his own sense of tragic insolence; he swaggers with contemptuous pride. Shakespeare uses the word 'insolence' to mean overbearing pride, when Hamlet complains of 'the insolence of office' (3.1. 74) – the arrogance of those in power.

A word that Shakespeare might have used is 'bravado'. This had come into the language in 1599. It is similar to 'insolence'. *The Shorter Oxford English Dictionary* gives this as its first definition: 'Boastful or threatening behaviour; ostentatious display of courage or boldness.' Shakespeare does not use 'bravado', but in some places 'bravery' has a similar meaning. When in *Julius Caesar* (1599) the battle lines are drawn, Antony says of the army of Brutus and Cassius that they could 'come down/With fearful bravery' (5.1. 9–10). 'Bravery' here means an ostentatious show of defiance. The sense of 'bravery' as a display or show of aggressive defiance is present in *Hamlet*, when the Prince says of the vehemence of Laertes' grief at Ophelia's graveside that 'the bravery of his grief did put me/Into a towering passion' (5.2. 80–1).

If we think about the meanings of 'hubris', 'insolence', 'bravado' and 'bravery' we can suggest that three qualities are often found in the tragic figure.

Being one's own judge

It is a principle of natural law that no one should be his or her own judge. It is neither our responsibility nor our privilege to judge ourselves. Yet the tragic figure chooses to do this.

Implicity (and sometimes explicity), the tragic figure passes a positive judgement on what he or she has done.

In arrogance an authority that belongs to others is assumed and a judgement passed that favours what the tragic figure has done. When Othello weeps over the wife he is about to murder, he says of his tears:

> This sorrow's heavenly,
> It strikes where it doth love.
>
> (5.2. 21–2)

We might judge his tears to be good and, indeed, better than the thing he is about to do, but that is *our* privilege; it is not Othello's.

Disdaining others

To judge ourselves is to place ourselves above others.

The tragic hero may well be a superior figure, but that does not mean that it is right to be disdainful of others.

Hamlet is disdainful of Rosencrantz and Guildenstern when he sends them dismissively to their deaths with this grim epitaph: 'they did make love to this employment' (5.2. 58).

Wilful display

The tragic hero wants to display to others the insolent pride that compels him to act with overbearing arrogance.

Shakespeare sees that the show of hubris is essentially theatrical.

The tragic figure calls attention deliberately to what he or she has done, and with a wilful desire acts out his or her own downfall. They display themselves like actors on a stage. They relish their own wickedness. This can be magnificent. There is grandeur in the way a tragic figure makes the fall a matter of public display. Yet the audience shudders at the spectacle. Othello has a speech before he dies in which he talks of his service to the state of Venice. He ends with a story of how he once killed an enemy of the Venetian state:

> And say besides that in Aleppo once,
> Where a malignant and a turbaned Turk
> Beat a Venetian and traduced the state,
> I took by the throat the circumcised dog
> And smote him thus.
>
> (5.2. 361–5)

Othello presents himself as the great warrior who defends Venice against its enemies. This is bravado: the strut and swagger of the proud man who exults as he acts out the moment when he killed one who 'traduced' – slandered – the state. But in acting out this scene, Othello stabs himself – 'thus' – thereby showing himself to be the state's arrogant slanderer.

Summary

Tragedy recognizes moral limits. The tragic figure is always wrong. A figure is tragic not just because he or she is evil but because there is a display of hubris – excessive pride. Other words for tragic qualities are insolence and bravado. Tragic figures choose to judge themselves. They are disdainful of others and relish displaying their bravado. Tragedy, as Shakespeare saw, is essentially theatrical.

20.9   Waste, knowledge and catharsis

Tragedy makes us feel ambivalent. We are pulled in several directions by the complex of qualities displayed in the tragic figure.

> **Tragedy makes us face waste, loss, the destruction of what is good, the corruption of innocence and the feeling that we are little people in a vast universe.**

But we also feel that it wakes us up from a half-life of routine and unquestioned assumptions.

> **Tragedy makes us think; we ask questions and we try to come to an understanding of the mysteries of being alive. Above all, it might give us self-knowledge.**

The generality of that word 'we' masks the fact that we are talking about two sets of people: we who watch Tragedy; and the tragic figures who strut and fret their hour upon the stage.

Catharsis

If we turn back to Aristotle's definition of Tragedy (see section 20.2), we find the puzzling word 'catharsis'. This means purification or, more medically, purgation. The idea is that feelings have been aroused and then allayed, leaving us calm and composed. In one sense, it is difficult to disagree with this. It is the testimony of audiences across the centuries that watching Tragedy can be a strangely uplifting experience. The audience feels release and relief. Rather than casting us down, Tragedy raises the spirits. We catch something of this in the way we want to endorse Horatio's final words to the dead Hamlet:

> Good night, sweet prince,
> And flights of angels sing thee to thy rest
>
> (5.2. 312–13)

This is not a description of catharsis but it might occasion a lightening of the spirit. As the hosts ('flights') of angels lead the sweet prince into paradise, we feel the harmony of song at the close of the great imaginative outpouring that is *Hamlet*.

But what of the characters whom we view? The word 'catharsis' could apply to the characters. It could mean that the tempest of emotions that stormed through Hamlet or Lear has finally been stilled. There must be something in this, because, as noted above, tragedy is about knowledge and self-understanding. Before the duel, Hamlet, with composure, echoes the words of 'St. Matthew' 10.29: 'There's a special providence in the fall of a sparrow' (5.2. 166). His words have a non-chalant confidence. As God imbues even the deaths of tiny creatures with significance, we may face our ends purged of fear.

But there is the case of King Lear. It is difficult to see that Lear himself learns. He is told to 'see better' (1.1. 158) at the beginning of the play, but it is doubtful whether he ever does. When mad, he sees through the sham surface of public life but he is too old to act on his searing insights, even supposing that he remembers what he said in his distraction.

Communal catharsis

Because Tragedy is a vast thing, it should not be treated solely in terms of individuals. There is a communal aspect to the purging. It may be that when Tragedy becomes communal – dealing with the nation as a whole – it is in touch with the religious roots it had in the ancient world, when the performance of plays was part of religious festivals.

The religious dimension of Tragedy may be present at the close of Hamlet when the prince discovers that Claudius and Laertes have been plotting against him. His response has a liturgical edge. It is as if he is taking part in a hallowed ritual:

> O, villainy! Ho! Let the door be locked.
> Treachery! Seek it out.
>
> (5.2. 265–6)

Hamlet has spent the play, as revengers must, waiting for an opportunity to punish those who have done evil. Now he has them in one room. He orders that the doors be locked, so that in a kind of sacrificial rite he can cleanse Denmark.

Summary

It is the experience of those who watch Tragedy that, in spite of its terrors, it is an uplifting experience. Aristotle's word for this is 'catharsis'. It may even be that some characters experience catharsis. In some plays, catharsis has a communal aspect. The evil that has stained a society is driven out in a ritual that has religious connotations.

▤ ⊻ 21   Comedy

21.1   Comic features

Our idea of Comedy is largely drawn from television, either from stand-up comics or sitcoms. Because both of these make us laugh, we expect Comedy to do the same. But to make laughter the defining feature of Comedy causes problems. We are assuming that Comedy is to be defined by the *effect* it has on the audience. Now although some literary concerns touch on matters of response, it is not a very reliable way of thinking about genre. For example, audiences might laugh one night but not another. Response, therefore, cannot be the *only* criterion for deciding what a genre is like.

Comic variety

Comedies are varied. In Shakespeare, plays as different as *The Taming of the Shrew* (1595) and *Measure for Measure* (1604) are counted as comedies. They differ in their themes: the latter play clearly wrestles with big issues – justice, law, mercy, forgiveness – which are absent in the former. Contrasts between authors are even more marked: Ben Jonson's *Volpone* (1607) presents a very dark picture of human folly, but Oscar Wilde's *The Importance of Being Earnest* (1895) is deliberately frivolous.

Comedy is not confined to plays. Henry Fielding, author of *Joseph Andrews* (1742) and *Tom Jones* (1749), started as a playwright but moved to the novel to escape political interference. His novels, with their dialogue and sharply presented action, still owe much to the stage. Jane Austen is clearly comic, even in a novel as sober, brooding and morally demanding as *Mansfield Park* (1814). In the twentieth century, the novels of Evelyn Waugh, which again can be dark and serious, are regarded as comic. Interestingly, although Comedy can be thematically dense, it has traditionally attracted little philosophical comment.

Contemporary settings

Both Jane Austen and Waugh wrote about contemporary society. Jonson did the same: *The Alchemist* (1612) and *Volpone* (1607) are of their time, whereas his tragedy, *Sejanus* (1605), is set in ancient Rome. Perhaps the weighty issues of

Tragedy are more easily seen from a distance, whereas Comedy delights in writing about habits, manners, morals, attitudes and fashions.

Summary

Comedy is a varied genre. It includes novels as well as plays. It often has contemporary settings.

21.2   Characters and plots

A big cast

An interest in contemporary attitudes and manners requires a large cast. Tragedy normally has one big role – the tragic hero – and two or three important ones. In Comedy, there may be, as in *Twelfth Night* (1599), up to ten leading characters. Frequently, characters in Comedy are what we call stock figures – figures who represent a common (and often funny) type. Stock figures are not developed in detail; they usually only have the features that distinguish them as a type. Because they are not complex, they fit easily into a complex plot (see Chapter 10, section 10.3).

Complex plots

A big cast makes for a complex plot.

> **Tragic plots are simple; comic ones complex.**

The experience of watching Comedy is that a lot goes on. In *Much Ado About Nothing* (1598), there are at least nine separate plot elements. The lives of characters intersect, and the intersections produce complications.

Plot functions

Complex plots shape comedies in a number of ways. One is that, when the plot is primary, characters are created to make it work.

> **Some comic characters are functions or agents of the plot.**
> **Something needs to be done, so a character must be created**
> **or adapted to do it.**

In *Twelfth Night*, Shakespeare changed his mind about who should watch Malvolio find the letter, which Maria has written to deceive him. When planning this trick, she says: 'let the fool make a third' (2.3. 167), but Shakespeare decides that the fool – Feste – should wander off to Orsino's court, so an entirely new character – Fabian – appears. This change has the advantage of reserving

Feste, who has been insulted by Malvolio, for the more spiteful tricks played in the second half of the play (see Chapter 10, section 10.4).

A very sophisticated version of characters being shaped by the demands of the plot is a character's consciousness of being in a play. An element in the rapport between character and audience is the recognition on the part of the character that he or she is there to entertain. Important to that entertainment is the knowledge that the character is doing what the audience wants. When, in *Much Ado About Nothing*, Benedick overhears his friends talking about how Beatrice loves him, he speaks to the audience with engaging openness about what he is going to do. When he says 'Love me! Why, it must be requited' (2.3. 212), there is the implicit pleasure of doing what he knows the audience wants him to do.

Summary

Comedy requires a big cast and a complex plot. Comic characters are often of the stock type and sometimes they function according to the demands of the plot. Some characters communicate to the audience that they know they are in a play and know, too, what the audience wants of them.

21.3   Play

A ludic art

Characters in a play often tease one another. Maria, Feste, Sir Toby and Sir Andrew tease Malvolio. They convince him that Olivia loves him and then per-suade Olivia that he is mad.

> **Comedy, to use a word derived from the Latin for play, is *ludic*.**

Comic play is of different kinds: characters play with words; they play with each other by misleading, and the playwright plays with the audience. Play is present in the mood of comedy; there is a carefree, holiday feel about much comic action. Love is like a holiday. In *As You Like It* (1599), Rosalind merrily says to Orlando: 'Come, woo me, woo me, for now I am in a holiday humour' (4.1. 64). Scholars have pointed out that Shakespeare's comedies have links with the games and rituals of folk festivals. Sir Toby in *Twelfth Night* (Twelfth Night marks the end of the Christmas season) resembles the Lord of Misrule, whose task it was to merrily disrupt the order of society. As ordinary life is not all play

> **Comedies work by placing ordinary characters in extraordinary situations.**

As was pointed out in Chapter 11, section 11.2, disguise is something that only happens in fiction.

Summary

Comedies often present characters who play. They play games with or against each other, often in pursuit of love. Comic situations are often unrealistic, though the characters are not.

21.4   Comic plotting

Comic conventions

What happens in a comic plot is highly dependent on a complex of conventions. Of course, this is true of all art, but

> **Comedy is distinctive in that the substance of the play often consists of the conventions that constitute it.**

As You Like It might be said to be about disguise, and disguise is the chief convention of the Rosalind/Orlando plot. So

> **Comedy is about its own processes.**

Enjoying conventions

Part of the pleasure of watching Comedy is recognizing the type of action and the conventions that sustain it. Is the plot about the young tricking the old, the lover proving himself worthy of the beloved, or the villain frustrating the desires of the major characters? And are the characters familiar? Is there a heroine who ventures for love, or an old man in pursuit of a young bride?

Conventions and endings

Dependence on conventions makes Comedy predictable. Furthermore, we know that the end will be a happy one. But there are at least two things we don't know.

- The first is the variations that might be played on familiar conventions. *The Merchant of Venice* (1596) clearly follows comic conventions, but includes a figure that exceeds them. In some parts of the play, Shylock is a standard comic figure – the angry father who is outraged by his daughter's elopement – but his pursuit of justice, a pursuit that will involve the death of Antonio, takes him beyond normal comic conventions. Furthermore, Shylock has a depth of character rarely seen in Comedy. He has a turbulent inner life that makes him writhe with resentment against those who have mistreated him.
- The second thing we don't know is *exactly* how the expected happy end will be achieved. The more complex the plot, the more unlikely a happy ending seems.

There are so many misunderstandings and tricks in *Twelfth Night* that a happy outcome seems very remote, until Orsino visits Olivia. This action brings the two households together, so all the necessary recognitions can occur.

Summary

Comedy is so bound up with its conventions that sometimes they become the chief business of the play. Comedies can be about their own processes. In some plays a character creates considerable interest because he or she exceeds the demands of the conventions. The ends of comedies arouse interest, because although we know that they will end happily, we don't know how.

21.5   Beginning comic plots

Openings

Comic plots often start with the arrival of strangers In *Pride and Prejudice* (1813), Mr Bingley rents a house. Soon afterwards, the Militia (a mobile unit of soldiers) arrives. There are now plenty of young men to allure, offend and puzzle the Bennet girls.

Another popular start is the desire to escape. The plot of *Huckleberry Finn* (1884), stems from Huck running away from his father, and Jim, the slave, escaping.

Opposition to love is perhaps the most important plot element in comedy. Lovers have met, fallen in love and wish to consummate their desires. We want the young to succeed. But there is a problem: the old object.

Bars

In comedy

> **Something prevents the characters from achieving what they desire.**

Several words describe whatever it is that hinders or obstructs. Shakespeare uses three in a single sentence in *Much Ado About Nothing*, when Don John, with an envy approaching obsession, spits out his desire to prevent Hero and Claudio's marriage: 'Any bar, any cross, any impediment will be medicinable to me' (2.2. 4). 'Bar', 'cross', 'impediment' have roughly the same meaning: a 'bar' is a barrier (it bars the way), a 'cross' thwarts and an 'impediment' is anything that prevents the fulfilment of wishes. Behind them all is the image of hindered movement and ways barred. 'Impediment' literally means that the feet are prevented from moving. In the first scene of *A Midsummer Night's Dream* (1594), the lovers, Hermia and Lysander, having been told by Egeus, Hermia's father, that they cannot marry, deliver their carefully shaped laments in the manner rhetoricians called *stichomythia*: dialogue consisting of single lines that work by antithesis and repeated verbal patterns. She begins each sentence with a heart-felt 'O' and he echoes this with 'Or':

HERMIA   O cross! Too high to be enthralled to low.
LYSANDER   Or else misgrafted in respect of years.

$$(1.1. 136–7)$$

Their theme is that lovers are crossed by inequalities in class or age.

Love forbidden and social inequalities are common bars. Other bars include a lover who is too shy to speak (*As You Like It* and Oliver Goldsmith's *She Stoops to Conquer*); the revival of an ancient law that condemns a lover to death (*Measure for Measure*); a character who is disguised so cannot attract the beloved (*Twelfth Night*); an arbitrary parental rule about the order in which daughters are to marry (*The Taming of the Shrew*); and (also in *The Taming of the Shrew*) a girl who is so difficult, no man will consider marrying her. Of course, a bar is not confined to comic plots. The long-standing feud between the Montagues and the Capulets is a bar to the love of Romeo and Juliet, a play that might very well have been a comedy had Juliet's final plan worked.

Occasionally, an author plays with the conventions of the bar. In *The Importance of Being Earnest*, Oscar Wilde parodies the bar in the form of two girls who discover they are both engaged to the same man, who in fact does not exist.

The tensions of comedy

Bars create tensions: Polixenes threatens the Shepherd's daughter; Petruchio deprives Kate, the shrew, of sleep, and in many comedies there are the customary aches, longings and confusions of the young in love. Such tensions show us something:

> **The emotions aroused might be ones of enmity, but not hatred.**

Enmity is the feeling one has for an enemy. One can feel hostile towards an enemy, but hatred is a more extreme state, usually involving malice, detestation and abhorrence. Hatred is not easy to overcome, but enmity, particularly if it has arisen through misunderstanding, can cease. Comedy deals with strong feelings, but they are not usually ones that can be destructive, either of the enemy or of the self. The audience must see that hostile feelings can be overcome. Yet there are characters who might be said to be driven by hatred. Shylock in *The Merchant of Venice* can be played that way.

> **In Comedy, the feelings must be strong enough to cause distress and confusion, but (usually) not so powerful that characters cannot overcome them.**

Fathers cannot prevent their daughters from following their hearts, so when the Duke tells Egeus that Hermia may marry Lysander, he says nothing.

Plotting and scheming

Before a comic plot reaches its happy close, there is a period of plotting and scheming. In many comedies, the main business of the play is what the characters do to achieve their ends. Once they meet a bar, the characters formulate schemes to get round whatever is stopping them.

> **The life of Comedy usually consists of a plan or series of plans that the disadvantaged characters (often young lovers) implement to circumvent a bar.**

A common ploy is disguise; particularly cross-dressing. Characters also gain advantage by overhearing or overlooking those with whom they are competing. A daring plot is the bed-trick; when a man wishes to seduce a reluctant woman, a substitute, who is willing to sleep with the man, takes her place.

Comedy is a female genre. Many of the above schemes are implemented by women, so, for example, Rosalind dresses as a boy (*As You Like It*) and in *Measure for Measure*, Mariana willingly participates in the bed-trick.

Language of scheming

There are a number of words in Shakespeare for the tricks characters invent to get round a bar. The two most common are 'device' and 'practice'; less common are 'deceit' and 'trick'. When, in *The Merchant of Venice*, Portia ceases to be passive, she says to her waiting gentlewoman, Nerissa:

> But come, I'll tell thee all my whole device
> When I am in my coach
>
> (3.4. 82–3)

Hitherto, Portia has been the object of the 'casket' plot. With the word 'device', she becomes the enterprising woman, who delights in scheming.

Deception

Where there are devices, there is deception.

> **Comic plots are created by devices, and devices deceive.**

Deception is not a device but rather the way that a device works. Nor is deception an end. The end for which characters deceive is the removal of a bar.

What in literature is the moral status of deception? The answer varies according to the author. In Shakespeare, deception is not considered immoral. Audiences watching Portia save Antonio and trick Bassanio are not invited to shake their heads critically. Jane Austen, however, consistently disapproves of deception, particularly deception in love. When, in *Mansfield Park*, Fanny Price discovers that she has been tricked into accepting the gift of a necklace, she says that the scheme employed against her was 'unfair' (Chapter 41).

Summary

Comic plots open in a number of ways. One is the arrival of strangers. The most common (particularly in Shakespeare) is the thwarting of love. Young lovers encounter a bar and invent imaginative schemes to circumvent it. Scheming works by deception.

21.6 Bewilderment

Interweaving schemes

The middle sections of Comedy (usually far longer than beginnings and endings) are concerned with the working out of devices. Comic plots are made complex by the interweaving of individual schemes. Audiences enjoy plot complexity – and it is *their* pleasure. The audience can see what is happening, but the characters cannot.

Comic plots create bewilderment and confusion.

In *A Midsummer Night's Dream*, the lovers are disorientated. Under the influence of the fairies, emotions change; a beloved becomes one who is hated. Moreover, so rapid and fierce are the changes that the characters' behaviour is disturbingly manic.

In novels, bewilderment is often created by misinformation, ignorance of another's intentions and lack of self-knowledge. In *Pride and Prejudice*, Mr Wickham misinforms Elizabeth about his past; Elizabeth is unaware of Mr Darcy's feelings for her, and when she reads Darcy's letter, which gives an account of his dealings with Wickham, she declares significantly: 'Till this moment, I never knew myself' (Chapter 36). The importance in *Pride and Prejudice* of distorted understanding shows that in the novel, bars are often mental. It is a character's inability to understand that prevents him or her from achieving happiness. Elizabeth and Darcy are proud and prejudiced; it is only when they have overcome these inner impediments that love can flourish.

Exclusion

A particular form of bewilderment is exclusion. In comic plots there is often a period when a character is shut out of normal society. In *Twelfth Night*, Malvolio is treated as though he were mad and locked up in a prison. In other comedies, a journey leads to exclusion. In *The Taming of the Shrew*, Kate travels to Petruchio's house, where she is excluded from normal life. Exclusion is treated lightly in *The Importance of Being Earnest*. The young men, having disappointed the women because neither is called Ernest, stand in the garden.

Summary

In the middle sections of comedies, characters experience the confusing consequences of interweaving schemes. They often have to overcome inner impediments such as being deceived, being ignorant of others' intentions, and lacking self-knowledge. Enlightenment often involves a period of exclusion, sometimes in the form of a journey to a new place.

21.7   Comic resolution

Beyond bewilderment

As in tragedy,

> The moment of recognition is the turning point that brings about plot resolution.

The bewilderment of the middle part gives way to the clarity of the close. Characters come to know who they are, and who the other characters are. Confusion gives way to enlightenment, and exclusion leads to reintegration with the society from which the characters have been alienated. After the disorientation of a night in the wood to which they have travelled, lovers wake up to the discovery of true love: 'And I have found Demetrius like a jewel' (*A Midsummer Night's Dream*, 4.1. 190). Oscar Wilde, cleverly playing with the conventions of Comedy, makes several of his characters travel into the countryside, where they are first bewildered and then enlightened by finding out who they really are.

Explanation and wonder

Comedies end happily. Comic closure often blends explanation and wonder. Shakespeare's *The Tempest* (1610) is a play about a journey that ends in a shipwreck. The characters are scattered about an island, where they suffer various forms of bewilderment. A father mourns his son, the son falls in love but is enslaved by his beloved's father, and two courtiers plot against their ruler. Before the final scene, most are driven mad by fear and guilt. Then they are restored, and meet the one who has caused their bewilderment. He, Prospero, shows them the young lovers. This moment of theatrical spectacle produces wonder: 'A most high miracle' (5.1. 180).

There is also a need for explanation. Characters need to know what has happened, so the play closes with Prospero inviting them into his 'poor cell' to hear 'the story of my life' (5.1. 305, 308).

Deliverance

Sometimes, Comedy closes with deliverance. There are threats and constraints in the comic world, but they can be overcome. In *Measure for Measure*, Angelo, who has shown himself unworthy of the trust the Duke has placed in him, stands condemned by the same law under which he condemned Claudio to death. Angelo has lived by the law, and the law now sentences him to death. Although Isabella believes that the execution of her brother, Claudio, has been carried out, she pleads for Angelo's life. But then a prisoner is brought on to the stage. It is Claudio. Claudio has been delivered in two senses: delivered from prison, and from death. His deliverance makes possible Angelo's deliverance.

Deliverance occurs in novels: Darcy's arrangement of Lydia's wedding in *Pride and Prejudice* delivers the Bennet family from the shame of her elope-ment, and Mark Twain is clearly joking about comic conventions when he makes the final action of *Huckleberry Finn* the deliverance of Jim from his prison.

Finding the lost

Similar to deliverance is the motif of finding the lost. Finding the lost is central to *The Winter's Tale*. The Oracle, which Leontes declares to be false, specifically says that 'the King shall live without an heir if that which is lost be not found' (3.2. 134–5). Once Perdita is found (and found to be a princess rather than a shepherd's daughter), the play can end happily with the promise of the next generation in the marriage of Perdita and Florizel.

A form of finding the lost is the rediscovery of a character's friends or family. Dickens, whose novels are in the comic genre, often closes his plots with the revelation that those characters who have helped the hero through his difficul-ties are in fact his relatives, or friends of his relatives. Mr Brownlow, who res-cued Oliver Twist, turns out to be a friend of Oliver's father. Mr Brownlow adopts Oliver as his own son, so Oliver, having lost both his parents, finds a new family. *The Importance of Being Earnest* ends with Jack Worthing discovering that he has a family and that he is in fact called Ernest.

The importance of society

Ends reveal that comedies are concerned with society. The pain of exclusion is replaced by the joy of reintegration. This reintegration restores an already exist-ing society and makes it new. *Pride and Prejudice* ends with a picture of Elizabeth as the mistress of Pemberley. Throughout the novel, Darcy, the mas-ter of Pemberley, has been unmarried. With his marriage, Pemberley has a future. To show that this is renewal as well as continuity, Jane Austen tells the reader that this grand house has in the Gardiners new visitors, who, in spite of their less elevated class, are morally worthy of a house noted for its code of charity and public responsibility.

Marriage

Marriage is the fitting close to a comic plot.

> **The plot movement of comedy ends with the promise of the next generation, which is present in marriage.**

In the *Book of Common Prayer* (1662), the marriage service, which most authors would have been familiar with, gives the first reason for which marriage was ordained as the bringing up of children. The promise of bed at the close of *A Midsummer Night's Dream* – 'Lovers, to bed; 'tis almost fairy time' (5.1. 357) – is not only an anticipation of sexual delight but also a recognition that the purpose of sex is the conception of children. The fairies, who come to bless the house, know this:

> To the best bride-bed will we,
> Which by us shall blessed be,
> And the issue there create
> Ever shall be fortunate.

> (5.2. 33–6)

We get the end of comedies wrong if we think of marriage as a convenient way of shutting a story down. What marriage does is to open up the future with the prospect of a birth. The fairies will bless the bed, and the child conceived there will enjoy the blessings of good fortune.

Marriage, then, is something to be celebrated. *A Midsummer Night's Dream* ends with the burlesque of an entertainment in the Mechanical's play, and the dancing and singing of the fairies, which, in a performance, might make a contrast with the Mechanicals through its dignity and elegant seriousness. Benjamin Britten gets the contrast right in his operatic version: the play is a merry parody of other composer's styles, while the lilting fairies' song is arguably the most beautiful music Britten wrote.

Summary

Recognition brings about plot resolution. The ends of comedies are filled with wonder, and wonder prompts the need for explanation. Characters are delivered from their difficulties, the lost are found, and families are reunited. Those who have been alienated from society are restored, and in marriage there is a promise of birth and the hope of renewal.

▣ ⱱ 22   Epic

22.1   Origins

The Classical world of Greece and Rome regarded Epic as the most important literary genre, but the English, in spite of several attempts to base literature on Classical models, have not made the Epic central. In fact, as far as the literary syllabus goes, there really is only John Milton's *Paradise Lost* (1667). (Those who read Anglo-Saxon will want to add the tenth-century *Beowulf*.) To say that only one Epic has entered the canon of literature taught in schools and universities does not rule out the possibility that in the future others will appear. Derek Walcott's *Omeros* (1990) is a reworking of Homeric ideas in a twentieth-century and West Indian setting. It has an epic solemnity – the product, in part, of its employment of some of the syntactical constructions of elevated verse (see the discussion of delayed verbs in Chapter 16, section 16.3). In addition, and like many epics, it deals with a wide range of characters and subject matter. It may yet establish itself in the canon.

The Epic is distinguished by the grandeur of subject matter, scope and style. Something of what it is for a work to be epic can be caught in the way we use 'epic' as an adjective. For example, a football match between two equally matched sides competing for the highest honour is sometimes called an 'epic contest'.

Subject matter

Epics are often concerned with origins: the founding of a city or a nation. Epics imply that a civilization has such and such a character because of the way in which it came into being. Beginnings can still evoke wonder. Often movements of reform in any organization are attempts to go back to how it is imagined things were at the start. The beginning, like water flowing from a spring, is pure. And the great future will be a return to the past – there will once more be an age of gold, and paradise will be restored.

In the beginning

In Milton the origin is universal: *Paradise Lost* deals with the origin of everything. In the debate in Hell on how to conduct eternal warfare against God, Beelzebub, a fallen angel, says:

> There is a place
> (If ancient and prophetic fame in heaven

> Err not) another world, the happy seat
> Of some new race called Man
>
> (Bk 2. 345–8)

That alluring phrase 'another world', which slips so easily off the tongue, is to us not just one more world, as it might be to the minds of angels, but *this* world, *our* world.

Summary

English Epic is rare. The subject matter and style of Epic are grand and elevated. Epics often deal with the origins of a nation. Milton's subject is the origin of all things.

22.2   Epic design

Epic plots

Although the scope of Epic is immense, the plots are rarely complex. Epics are close to the plot movements of sagas – a series of episodes in the lives of a hero and his/her descendents. The overarching structure can be loose, as in the wandering adventures of Odysseus/Ulysses returning from the Trojan War. James Joyce adopted the plot elements of Homer's *The Odyssey* (eighth century BC) to give shape to the wanderings of Leopold Bloom around Dublin in *Ulysses* (1922). The result is that epics often read like a series of set pieces – actions that are almost plots in their own right. Odysseus, for example, has adventures with the seductive Circe, steers between the whirlpool Scylla and the rock Charybdis, and manages to hear the alluring Sirens without yielding to their fatal songs. (All echoed in passages in *Ulysses*.)

Epics in miniature

In *Paradise Lost*, there are small-scale stories that might, had the poet so wished, have become plots of a whole work. There is a beautiful passage in Book 1 concerning the fall of Mulciber. Mulciber is the architect, first, of 'many a towered structure high' (733) in heaven, and then of 'Pandemonium, the high capital/Of Satan' (756–7). Milton says that he was also known in ancient Greece. His story is an epic in miniature:

> how he fell
> From heaven, they fabled, thrown by angry Jove
> Sheer o'er the crystal battlements; from morn
> To noon he fell, from noon to dewy eve,
> A summer's day
>
> (740–4)

What a potential story lies in these few lines! The architect of heavenly mansions and the palace of Hell, who fell a whole day – a summer's day. The cadence, gently and gradually, enacts his fall. Thus his story chimes in with the fallen angels and the fate of humankind. Furthermore, it enacts the fall of genius from building towers in paradise to the infernal seat of government.

Summary

Epics are often episodic in design. In Milton there are miniature epics that echo the themes of his overall design.

22.3   Epic action

Deeds

Epic actions are appropriately elevated. They are usually described as 'deeds' and are said to be high or lofty. In *Paradise Lost*, even Satan performs epic deeds. He resolves to visit the new-made world of earth, and journeys into the immensities that separate Hell from the rest of Creation. He meets Chaos and Night. Chaos urges him on:

> and Satan stayed to reply,
> But glad that now his sea should find a shore,
> With fresh alacrity and force renewed
> Springs upward like a pyramid of fire
> Into the wild expanse, and through the shock
> Of fighting elements, on all sides round
> Environed wins his way
>
> (Bk 2. 1010–16)

Milton's language elevates the action. There is something heroic about Satan's deeds. His renewed force enables him to spring upwards – the image of epic aspiration – with the power of fire. The terrain is daunting – a 'wild expanse' of 'fighting elements' – and yet, with emphatic alliteration, Milton tells us that he 'wins his way'.

Summary

Epic action is lofty and is often described as a 'deed'. We admire the aspiration and energy of epic action even when it is performed by evil characters.

22.4 War

Victory

The sublimity that writers have found in war derives from the epic tradition. *The Iliad* (eighth century BC) is a poem of battles and its central characters are heroic warriors. Beowulf fights monsters. In *Paradise Lost*, there is war in Heaven. Raphael tells Adam of the first encounter between Satan and Saint Michael. At one stroke from Michael, Satan recoils:

> whereat Michael bid sound
> The archangel trumpet; through the vast of heaven
> It sounded, and the faithful armies rung
> Hosanna to the highest
>
> (Bk 6. 202–5)

Defeat

And there is defeat. The Son of God leads the final assault:

> and as a herd
> Of goats or timorous flock together thronged
> Drove them before him thunderstruck
>
> (Bk 6. 856–8)

A defeated army is reduced to a flock of animals. The verb 'driven' is applicable to both; the victors drive the vanquished, and sheep and goats can be driven in terror.

Summary

Epic presents military victory and defeat in appropriately elevated terms.

22.5 The grandeur of Epic

Because Epic is conceived on a grand scale, it deals with many areas of life. Most, for example, contain journeys and battles. Odysseus's and Aeneas's journeys, and *The Iliad* and *The Aeneid* (29–19 BC) feature individual combats and large-scale battles.

History

Epics sometimes have a strong sense of history and the diversity of human cultures. Leo Tolstoy's *War and Peace* is a kind of Epic in that it deals, if not with the founding, then at least the remaking of Russia in and through the Napoleonic wars. At the end, there is a long, philosophical section on the nature of History. In Book 11 of *Paradise Lost*, Adam is taken to the highest peak in paradise, from where he sees the kingdoms of the world, which, in his temptations, were offered to Christ. China, Persia, Russia, Byzantium, Abyssinia, the Congo, Rome and Mexico are viewed (388–411).

And, in a series of visions, Adam is shown what is to come. Old Testament history unfolds before him: the murder of Cain by Abel, wars, decadence and the great flood. These are presented not only as the foundation events of a nation but of the whole world.

Epic range

Milton's epic is encyclopaedic; it includes pastoral and tragic elements. He undertook intense scholarly study for twenty years before he began the work. Religion, Literature, History and Geography, as we have seen, all find a place. There is also Science. In Book 1, Milton writes of the shield that hangs from Satan's

> shoulders like the moon, whose orb
> Through optic glass the Tuscan artist views
> At evening from the top of Fesole,
> Or in Valdarno, to descry new lands,
> Rivers or mountains in her spotty globe.
>
> (287–91)

The 'Tuscan artist' is Galileo. Milton, who probably visited him, places him with geographical exactitude among the hills above the Arno River valley, where Galileo was in exile. Perhaps the Tuscan hills and river valley are an earthly correspondent to the 'Rivers and mountains' that Galileo saw on the moon. The language is strictly accurate. Telescopes were called optic glasses, and scientists were known as artists.

The gods

The Epic interweaves the human world with the gods. In Homer and Virgil there are debates (sometimes quarrels) among the deities that take sides in the human struggles they view. Dryden's translation (1700) of the first book of *The Iliad* turns the quarrel in the household of the gods into something approaching what we now call a 'domestic'.

Heroes visit the underworld. In Book 6 of *The Aeneid*, Aeneas descends to hell, where he meets those who perished in the Trojan War. Joyce's *Ulysses* includes a passage on the dead in the form of a visit to Glasnevin cemetery.

Imagining Hell

The first scene in *Paradise Lost* is in 'the deep tract of hell' (Bk 1. 28), where, 'In adamantine chains and penal fire' (48), Satan and 'his horrid crew/Lay vanquished' (51–2). Milton's creation of Hell shows his creative intelligence. He encounters the problem of how to describe the negation of all that we know in language that has been formed to talk about the world we know. This is one of the passages:

> A dungeon horrible, on all sides round
> As one great furnace flamed, yet from those flames
> No light, but rather darkness visible
> Served only to discover sights of woe
>
> (Bk 1. 61–6)

Milton shows us 'sights of woe', but these are discovered by the flames that are no ordinary flames. Rather, they are 'darkness visible'. That phrase combines what we know – whatever is 'visible' – with what, by its very nature, cannot be seen – 'darkness'.

Humanity

In Classical epics, the characters are related to the gods, or have dealings with them. In tragedy, the hero can seem god-like, but the deeds of the Epic hero, such as Aeneas's descent into Hell, raise him even higher. There are, of course, no gods in Milton, but with epic daring Milton attempts to convey debates in Heaven and Hell and the dialogue between Adam and Michael.

Perhaps it is the Classical inheritance that has influenced readers into thinking that God and Satan are the central figures of *Paradise Lost*. But this is not, as the opening makes clear, the true subject of Milton's work. Adam and Eve are the chief characters; they ate the fruit of the forbidden tree and thus brought death into the world (1. 1–3). In *Paradise Regained* (1671) Christ is the central figure, so in that sense the work is closer to Classical epics in having a divine central figure.

Summary

The epic is characterized by its vast intellectual and imaginative range. It deals with History and the future, and explores many aspects of learning, including Science. Imaginatively, it presents the gods, Hell and humanity.

22.6   Epic style

The opening

There are two conventions for the opening of epics: the Muse is called upon for inspiration (often called the Invocation), and the subject of the work is announced. *Paradise Lost* opens with Milton's Christian alternative to the

Muse; he calls upon the Holy Spirit – the heavenly muse – for aid, and then announces what poem is about:

> what in me is dark
> Illumine, what is low raise and support;
> That to the height of this great argument
> I may assert eternal providence,
> And justify the ways of God to men.
>
> (Bk 1. 22–6)

Milton's writing here is dense and complex. He sees his state as being parallel to the world before the creation of light – 'what in me is dark/Illumine' – and in 'raise' there is the suggestion that he needs the power of Christ's resurrection. He builds to his momentous theme by calling it 'this great argument', and the cadence (and the movement of his thought) climaxes on 'justify'.

The starting point

It is a convention of Epic style that the action starts half-way through the events that are the Epic's subject. Epic therefore requires retrospective passages, in which earlier events are recounted. It may be that the convention of beginning half-way through assists in creating the appropriate sense of immensity. The reader is plunged, perhaps to his or her puzzlement, into the middle of great doings. If we are slightly dazed, this may be a fitting way to approach the theme. *The Iliad* begins with the Greek troops already besieging Troy. *Paradise Lost* begins with the fallen angels, newly ejected from Heaven. The confusions of Hell admit us into the world of evil, misery and deprivation, which are the consequences of the fall that is to come upon mankind.

The elevated style: diction and syntax

Epic style is elevated. Milton's style is often described as 'high', 'lofty' or 'grand'. He achieves this in a number of ways, two of which are Latinate diction and complex syntax.

Latinate diction consists of words, the origins of which are found in Latin. Latinate words tend to be long (they are often polysyllabic) and of a high register. Words in a high register are usually formal, public and stately. High-register language, to use the phrase that Edward Elgar borrowed from Shakespeare, expresses 'pomp and circumstance' (*Othello*, 3.3. 359, 1604). No version of English can be entirely Latinate or, the other major source, Anglo-Saxon, in origin. Much that Milton writes uses Anglo-Saxon words, but when he wants to make an idea sonorous he introduces words of a Latin origin. This is his passage about the tree of life in the Garden of Eden:

> And all amid them stood the tree of life,
> High, eminent, blooming ambrosial fruit
>
> (Bk 4. 218–19)

The first line is not Latinate and nor, in the second, are 'high' and 'blooming', but 'eminent' and 'ambrosial' are, and it is they that give the line its resonance. Should you be in doubt, a good dictionary will give the origin of a word. And remember that French is Latin-based, so a word deriving from French or Old French may be Latin in origin.

Syntax is the order of words in a sentence. Sentences become complex when they have a number of clauses. A *clause* is a unit of speech that contains a verb. *Paradise Lost* begins with five lines in which, through the suspensive syntax, we see the subject matter growing in weight and significance until the full meaning is achieved triumphantly in the appeal to the Holy Spirit for inspiration: 'Sing heavenly Muse' (see Chapter 16, section 16.3).

Epic simile

The epic simile is a comparison extended over a number of lines. Such detail and length gives Epic poems an imaginative amplitude; on page after page, pictures open up before the reader. Epic similes can be very effective when the appropriateness of the simile emerges as the comparison unfolds. In Book 1, the fallen angels rising from the burning lake are compared to the plague of locusts brought upon Egypt by Amram's son – Moses:

> As when the potent rod
> Of Amram's son in Egypt's evil day
> Waved round the coast, up called a pitchy cloud
> Of locusts, warping on the eastern wind,
> That o'er the realm of impious Pharoah hung
> Like night, and darkened all the land of Nile:
> So numberless were those bad angels seen
> Hovering on wing under the cope of hell
>   (Bk 1. 338–45)

The image is appropriate: the thick clouds of locusts were a plague upon Egypt, and the devils will plague humankind. Both the visual and the allegorical meanings meet in 'warping'. In the air the locust clouds are sinisterly curved, and 'warping' – corrupting human souls – is what the devils will do.

Classical allusions

Milton was deeply aware of the tradition of Epic writing. An edition of the poem with notes shows how Milton is dependent on Cicero, Ovid, Pliny and Virgil. In Book 2 he refers to how 'Ulysses on the larbord shunned/Charybdis' (1019–20), a passage in Homer's *The Odyssey*. The numerous Classical references are very significant in a poem which has the Bible and Christian doctrine as its chief sources. Milton was dedicated to writing a Christian epic, so Classical references indicate that, Christian or not, an epic must acknowledge its traditions in Classical writing.

Messengers

A feature of epic is messengers who relate what the gods have said. The messengers are sometimes referred to as *epic apparatus*. In the First Book of *The Aeneid*, Mercury, the messenger of the gods, is sent by Jupiter to ensure that Aeneas will be welcomed by the Carthaginians. Milton is fortunate that in the Christian tradition there is a parallel. Angels are messengers, so Milton uses Raphael to tell Adam about the creation of the world (Book 7) and the movement of the stars (Book 8).

Lists

Lists allow a poet to present the immensity of the Epic world. Homer, for example, lists the ships and armies that have sailed from Greece to lay siege to Troy. Milton lists the countries seen from the highest point in *Paradise Lost* (see section 22.5).

Summary

Epics are sustained by a number of conventions. There is an opening invocation that announces the theme. The action starts in the middle of the narrative. The style is elevated; Latin diction, complex syntax, epic similes, classical allusions, messengers and lists are important features.

22.7   Mock-epics

Parody

Works that rest on a distinctive set of conventions are open to parody. When a work is distinguished by what Matthew Arnold called 'high seriousness', parody can take the form of treating trivial topics as if they were lofty. The result is mock-epic. It is a sophisticated form only fully appreciated by the well-read, who can recognize the inappropriate use of Epic style.

The Rape of the Lock

The one English mock-epic that has established itself on syllabuses is Alexander Pope's *The Rape of the Lock* (1712). With the deftness, lightness and musical subtlety of his best verse, Pope relates a tale with all the elevated language and conventional 'machinery' of an epic, but his subject is a quarrel between two families, occasioned by the surreptitious theft of a young lady's lock of hair. The theft was real, and Pope, unsuccessfully, wrote the poem to pacify the quarrellers.

One of the pleasures in reading *The Rape of the Lock* is seeing how Pope uses epic conventions for his lighter purposes. He begins Canto I (a canto is a subdivision of an epic) in the epic manner with an invocation:

> What dire offence from amorous causes springs,
> What mighty contests rise from trivial things,
> I sing

As in the case of *Paradise Lost* (1667), the syntax is suspensive. We wait for the main verb, and when it comes – 'sing' – we see that it is the same verb that Milton used.

Canto II opens with yet another Epic convention – the journey. Satan travelled from Hell to the earth; Belinda, the young lady from whom the lock is taken, sails up the Thames. In Canto III there is a battle, a standard epic feature, as in the war in Heaven in *Paradise Lost*, but in Pope's mock-epic it is a card game. The epic feature of the list is deployed to introduce the cards:

> Behold, four Kings in majesty revered,
> With hoary whiskers and a forky beard;
> And four fair Queens, whose hand sustains a flower,
> Th' expressive emblem of their softer power
>
> (37–40)

The kings are presented with the kind of regal authority required to lead forces in war, and the queens, like ancient armies, bear emblems.

Summary

The pleasure of a mock-epic lies in the ingenious way in which poets find trivial equivalents for conventional epic features.

▾ 23 Lyric

23.1 Music and poetry

Defining lyric

Traditionally, Lyric, along with Tragedy, Comedy, Epic and Satire, was regarded as one of the genres. But while four of those are still treated as genres (though, see the remarks on Satire in Chapter 24), we no longer think of Lyric in that way. If we use the word 'lyric' at all, it is either when we talk of the words to songs, or of poems that might be set to music.

Originally, it was used of verse that was neither dramatic nor narrative. Although we still talk of verse-drama and narrative verse, Lyric is no longer strictly defined in those terms. In fact, we don't find it necessary to define Lyric strictly. We use it of any poem that is short and voices emotion. This is R. L. Brett's definition: 'any short poem which expresses feeling' (*Introduction to English Studies*, 1965). That definition covers most of the poems, with some interesting exceptions, written today.

Ease and fluency

We value the ease and fluency of lyric poetry. These are characteristics that poetry shares with music. Setting poetry to music is an ancient practice. In Greece, poetry was recited to the accompaniment of a lyre, and it is supposed that *Beowulf* (tenth century), the Anglo-Saxon Epic, was recited to the accompaniment of a harp, perhaps struck regularly in the middle or at the end of a line. In the twentieth century, W. B. Yeats, a poet self-consciously committed to the traditions of Irish culture, tried accompanying his verse on an Irish harp. It was not an experiment he repeated. In the 1960s, there was a fashion for reading poetry to the accompaniment of jazz.

The communal lyric and musical settings

There is a communal version of Lyric. Swinburne's Choruses from his verse-drama *Atalanta in Calydon* (1865) have a joyful energy, particularly at the opening:

> When the hounds of spring are on winter's traces
> The mother of months in meadow or plain

> Fills the shadows and windy places
> With lisp of leaves and ripple of rain

Through the pulsing rhythm and patterned alliterations, the lines share with us the common feeling that life is reawakening.

The most well-known choric poem is the hymn. There are some poets whose best-known output are hymns, Isaac Watts, Wesley and John Keble being the most notable, but for John Donne, John Milton and Christopher Smart the hymn was a form they occasionally turned to (see Chapter 13, section 13.2). The hymns of Donne, Milton and Smart, unlike those of Watts and Wesley, were not specifically written to be sung, but they have been set to music. One of the most notable is Pelham Humfrey's setting of Donne's 'A Hymn to God the Father' with its nervous hurrying over those grave, largely monosyllabic words in the second stanza about the corruption of others:

> Wilt thou forgive that sin which I have won
> Others to sin?

Musical settings of lyric verse can reveal important aspects of the words. A musical setting is like a reading in that it can bring out tone and pace. We are used to songs having repeatable tunes, but composers often vary the melody, key, rhythm and pace to bring out the pulse of thought and feeling in the poem. It is worth listening to musical settings of poems you are familiar with. Ralph Vaughan Williams and Benjamin Britten set William Blake to music, and Thomas Hardy found a most understanding composer in Gerald Finzi. The work of A. E. Housman has been set to music by a number of composers, including George Butterworth and Arthur Somervell. Perhaps poets such as Housman, who are not overtly and strenuously rhythmical, are more amenable to music. The works of Gerard Manley Hopkins have been set by Michael Tippett, but his language is so inherently 'musical' that it resists setting. Two very interesting settings of poems are Samuel Barber's *Dover Beach* (1931) and Michael Tippett's *Byzantium* (1989). Barber's setting for string quartet and voice brings out the anguish of Arnold's words, particularly in the way the music and voice are interestingly out of phase with one other. Tippett opens with a sumptuous fanfare, as befits a Byzantine emperor, and Yeats' difficult second verse about the image that floats before him does indeed float in the soprano's high, lyrical line.

The language of music and the language of poetry

Talk about music can coincide with talk about poetry. Literary study, for example, has borrowed the term 'cadence' from music (see Chapter 17, section 17.5). Musical ideas have been used to structure poetry. Recurring motifs – short lines of melody repeated in a work – have their literary equivalents in the words and phrases a poet significantly re-uses in a single work. We have borrowed (and simplified) the term 'counterpoint' from music for those occasions when the rhythm of a poem changes.

T. S. Eliot's *Four Quartets* (1944) depend on repetitions and echoes, both within a short section and across the poem as a whole. His syntax is also musical in that it is concerned with the sound of thinking rather than the finished product of the concisely stated idea.

Summary

We value lyric poetry for its musical qualities – ease and fluency. Lyric can be communal as well as personal. Musical settings of poetry can bring out aspects of the verse. We borrow terms from music when talking about Lyric.

23.2 Lyric and feeling

Modulation

The changes of pace and tone in lyric poetry enable poets to voice the modulations of thought and feeling. In music, this is done through a number of means – switching keys, counterpoint, swelling of volume, providing appropriate accompaniments, for example. In poetry, the pace, rhythms and emotional tone have to do this.

One moment that might be described as 'musical' is the sudden and full expression of a feeling that has hitherto been held back. This is sometimes called *lyrical release*. Ivor Gurney (also a composer) wrote 'Song' (1917) while serving in the First World War. It is a kind of love poem addressed to the valley of the river Severn:

> Only the wanderer
>   Knows England's graces,
> Or can anew see clear
>   Familiar faces.
>
> And who loves joy as he
>   That dwells in shadows?
> Do not forget me quite
>   O Severn meadows.

The poem is musing and reticent until the last two lines, when the outburst (strictly speaking an *apostrophe* – a direct address to someone or something that is absent) reveals what has been most deeply concerning him. He achieves this within the regularity of the stanza form. The lyrical release in 'Song' shows the emotional flexibility of lyric poetry.

Four subjects are regularly treated in lyric verse: love, celebration, the passing of time, and the natural world.

Love

Love comes in different forms – love that is yearned for, love that is unrequited, and love that is celebrated. Hardy's love poems are made particularly poignant because he longs for someone he can no longer have – his lately dead wife. The aching repetitions of 'The Voice' (written 1912–13) enact his longing: 'Woman much missed, how you call to me, call to me'. The poet hears the woman calling, but the poem's yearning is felt in our realization that both in his life as well as the poem, it is he who is longing for her.

Unrequited love can take the form of regret, as in Feste's song from *Twelfth Night* (1599) in which the lover is 'Slain by a fair cruel maid' ('Come away, come away, death'). Quite different is the physical joy of achieved love. Donne celebrates love achieved with all the pride of male possession in his exultant and exuberant 'The Sun Rising' (1633) (see also Chapter 53, sections 53.1 and 53.2).

Celebration

Lyrical outburst makes celebration a fit subject for poetry. It is not clear exactly what occasion is being celebrated in Christina Rossetti's 'A Birthday' (written 1857). For example, we don't know who the love of her life is, and nor do we know whether the birthday is literal or emblematic. But those issues hardly matter; what is important is the release in song of joyful feelings:

> My heart is like a singing bird
> > Whose nest is in a watered shoot:
> My heart is like an apple-tree
> > Whose boughs are bent with thick-set fruit

The song implicitly asks to be compared with the rush of water in the 'shoot', and 'bent' suggests fullness of growth rather than a heavy burden. The anaphoric verse (repeated words at the opening of the lines) helps to create the sense of a musical as well as an emotional celebration.

The passing of time

The passing of time is often seen in terms of the change of the seasons. Robert Herrick meditates on the brief life of daffodils in 'To Daffodils' (1648), seeing in their fragile and all too ephemeral beauty an analogy with human life. The second verse opens:

> We have short time to stay, as you,
> > We have as short a spring

Herrick trusts his readers to bring to the word 'spring' all the traditional connotations of fresness, vitality and youth.

The natural world

Lyric poetry sometimes treats the natural world as it is in itself. John Clare concentrates on birds' nests and tree stumps without clouding the picture with his own musings. Later, Edward Thomas was able to achieve this in poems such as

'Tall Nettles' and 'Bob's Lane' (written 1916). Other poets value nature precisely because of the feelings it arouses. William Wordsworth is often spoken of as a nature poet, but it would be more accurate to call him a poet who explores the human mind by way of the stimulation nature gives him.

Summary

Lyric poetry is suited to the expression of feeling. Lyrical release and the modulations of feeling are important features. Lyric has treated various aspects of love, the urge to celebrate, the passing of time, and the world of nature.

▪ ☑ 24 Satire

24.1 A moral art

Satire is the moral criticism of individuals and institutions by exposing them to mockery. The reader is invited to clarify his or her moral vision by laughing at absurdities and follies. Fools are made to look small, grotesque and absurd. But Satire can also be more serious; it takes on vice, corruption and the evil will.

Classical Satire

In the Classical world, there were poems styled satires, which were critical assessments of individuals or a society as a whole. Sometimes, as in Horace (65–8 BC), the tone was light. Other writers engaged in more serious criticism. The most severe (and sometimes violent) in manner was Juvenal (second century AD) – where the tone is bitter, and there is an element of disgust in his denunciations. Perhaps, also, he finds the outrageous stimulating. His Rome is peopled by hypocrites and imposters, all bent on gratifying desire and gaining wealth and status. Juvenal assumes the persona of one who looks on as the dishonest flaunt their wealth.

His Satire 3 is about leaving Rome for a saner life in a quieter place. Satire 5 is about spongers and ungracious hospitality. In order to eat, the poor Trebius suffers the indignities of bad wine and food to amuse the rich host, who keeps the good bread and wine for himself. In Satire 10, a gloomy diatribe against human presumption and self-deception, the poet broods on the vanity – the emptiness – of human aspirations.

Satire 'Englished'

Classical Satire has a life in English as model and version: it has been 'Englished'. In Ben Jonson's 'To Penshurst' (1616), the poet expects us to bear Juvenal's fifth Satire in mind, so that we might see, by contrast, that this host is generous in sharing the same food and wine with his guests:

> Where the same beer, and bread, and self-same wine,
> That is his lordship's, shall be also mine.
>
> (63–4)

The trim rhymes and the neat balance of the second line show the harmony of the Penshurst household and, perhaps, the mutual sharing of host and poet.

John Dryden published his translation of Satire 10 in 1692. Samuel Johnson made versions of the third (London) in 1738 and of the tenth (The Vanity of Human Wishes) in 1749. Strictly speaking, Johnson's poems are not translations but Imitations – free and imaginative appropriations of another work in which modern rather than ancient examples are used. Johnson himself defined Imitation in his 'Life of Pope': 'a kind of middle composition between translation and original design, which pleases when the thoughts are unexpectedly applicable and the parallels lucky'.

In Satire 10, Juvenal uses Hannibal to show how brief is military glory. In his poem, Johnson presents 'the lucky parallel' of 'Swedish Charles' (191–222), whose military hopes were defeated by a Russian winter.

Original Satire

In Dryden's *Macflecknoe* (1682), Thomas Shadwell's poetry is judged according to reason and intelligence. Pope extended this idea in *The Dunciad* (1728) – a fierce and funny denunciation of dullness. Satire was also written in prose. In *A Modest Proposal* (1729), Jonathan Swift's manner is apparently so reasonable that the incautious reader is seduced into approving of infanticide.

There are also twentieth-century works that might be called satires. Joseph Heller's *Catch-22* (1955) is about the follies of war and, perhaps even more pointed in the twenty-first century, the irrationalities of administrative language. Evelyn Waugh's *The Loved One* (1948) has the American funeral business as its target.

As an adjective

The above works can properly be said to be satires. But today the most consistent use of the term is as an adjective. We speak of an attitude, tone, mode or manner as *satiric*. An author can adopt a satiric outlook in one area of a work and for a specific purpose. This has always been the case. Malvolio might be said to be satirized for his self-seeking ambition and his adoption of some Puritan habits. In *Northanger Abbey* (1818), Jane Austen satirizes the carelessly extravagant talk of Isabella Thorpe and the equally extravagant implausibilities of Gothic fiction.

Summary

Satire is a moral art that ridicules folly and wickedness. In Classical literature there were poems called satires. These provided a model for English verse, and some poets translated them into English or produced Imitations – free translations with contemporary examples. There is a tradition of Satire in English. The word can also be used to describe passages and attitudes in works that are not satires as such.

24.2 The features of Satire

The art of censure

The aim, motive and purpose of Satire is to expose immorality. Johnson gave this definition in his *Dictionary* (1755): 'A poem in which wickedness or folly is censured.' Johnson continues to say that 'it is distinguished, by the generality of the reflections, from a lampoon, which is aimed against a particular person'. By 'general', Johnson means that it is addressed to all.

A didactic art

Satire thrives when there is a commonly held set of moral views to which the author can appeal. The reader must share (or know that he or she ought to share) the values against which conduct is judged. It follows that Satire teaches. To use a more technical term, it is *didactic* (derived from a Greek word meaning 'to teach'). Johnson's grammar adopts a didactic manner in the passage on the young scholar from '*The Vanity of Human Wishes*', who, in a firm imperative, is told to 'Hear Lydiat's life, and Galileo's end' (164).

Urban and social writing

Satire is suited to city life. Johnson's substitution of London for Rome in his Imitation of Juvenal's third Satire is appropriate. In both, the protagonist flees the city for a quieter life. Johnson's protagonist (he gives him the classical name of Thales) abandons a city 'where all are slaves to gold' (178).

Politics

In that moral emphasis on the corruption of materialism, we might see another aspect of Satire. Because it appeals to values the writer thinks are in danger of being abandoned, the art tends to be morally, and often politically, conservative. The lower case 'c' is important. The word 'conservative' means a determination to uphold and preserve, not, as it tends to do today, an endorsement of free-market economics.

Change and chance

Because Satire is concerned with the changes and chances of public life, its outlook is related to Tragedy's preoccupation with the rise and fall of great figures. In addition to 'Swedish Charles', Johnson presents Cardinal Wolsey as someone who stood with 'Law in his voice, and fortune in his hand', but who was to 'sink beneath misfortune's blow' ('The Vanity of Human Wishes', 100, 127). We need to be reminded that, in this poem, vanity means the fragility, even the emptiness, of all human success. Johnson's view is tinged with a Christian understanding of the ephemeral nature of all worldly power. In the Bible, the book of '*Ecclesiastes*' opens with these sobering words: 'Vanity of vanities, saith the Preacher, vanity of vanities; all is vanity.'

The sceptical outlook

In keeping with the morally conservative and religiously informed understanding of human life, Satire is often cautious and sceptical. Satire retells stories of great action to emphasize how fleeting heroic success is. Johnson writes in 'The Vanity of Human Wishes' of the confident Xerxes, King of Persia, who 'came to seize a certain prey' (227) but, defeated by the Greeks, had to escape in a single boat.

Irony

Given that Satire deals with the gulf between aspiration and actuality, the instrument of warning is irony. Irony depends on our seeing disparities. It is ironic that Charles, who was once victorious, is now defeated:

> Condemn'd a needy supplicant to wait,
> While ladies interpose, and slaves debate.
> (213–14)

This is not merry or playful irony, but a sobering realization of human limitation. To wait is the role of a servant, and so low has Charles sunk that he waits on the deliberations of slaves.

Satire and art

Satire can delight us by the dexterity of its wit; it combines the sting of rebuke with the pleasure of art. This is the close of the passage on Archbishop Laud from Johnson's 'The Vanity of Human Wishes':

> Around his tomb let Art and Genius weep,
> But hear his death, ye blockheads, hear and sleep.
> (173–4)

This is a pleasingly grotesque image of the conventional carved figures on a funeral monument. 'Art and Genius' weep, but the 'blockheads' who sent Laud to the 'block' (the word occurs in the previous line) sleep on.

The heroic couplet

In Dryden and Johnson, the balances in tone and fluctuations in mood are kept in place by the heroic couplet. Its dramatic, pithy and concise form makes it amply suited to the biting and uncomfortable character of Satire. With verbal dexterity, Johnson sums up the rise and fall of those who are 'burning to be great':

> Delussive Fortune hears th' incessant call,
> They mount, they shine, evaporate and fall.
> ('The Vanity of Human Wishes', 75–6)

The image of fireworks ('burning to be great') enforces with sharp exactitude the fate of those who have fallen. There is also an appropriately falling cadence of the rhyme of 'call' and 'fall'.

The heroic couplet is formal and impersonal, so suits an art that is public. An author doesn't speak in his or her own name, but in the name of everyone and on behalf of everyone (see also Chapter 17, section 17.2).

Conclusions

The didactic purpose of Satire is often present in the close of works. Johnson counsels acceptance of Divine providence:

> Implore his aid, in his decisions rest,
> Secure whate'er he gives, he gives the best.
> ('The Vanity of Human Wishes', 355–6)

'Secure' is a weighty word for Johnson. It means free from fear. The world is uncertain, but peace of mind comes from accepting that whatever happens is within the providence of God.

Summary

Satire appeals to a commonly held morality, and so it can teach. Because it appeals to commonly held values it is often successful when dealing with urban life. Its outlook is often conservative. It views the uncertainty of public life – the rise and fall of the great – with cautious scepticism. Its artistic medium is irony and its expression (in the seventeenth and eighteenth centuries) the snappy and formal Heroic Couplet.

▪ ⚡ 25 Romance

25.1 The world of Romance

Romance is a loose genre with a long history. It emerged in twelfth-century France, and was called Romance because it was written in one of the Romance languages. Later, there were Romances in English and German, and prose became a common medium. Originally, the subject matter was closely related to a knightly or chivalric culture; knights faced dangers to serve a beloved lady. The court of King Arthur (commonly called 'The Matter of Britain', as opposed to the 'Matter' of France and Rome) was the setting of many of the tales. The most distinguished author was French: Chretien de Troyes' prose Romance *Lancelot* (twelfth century) follows the life of the hero, which includes the high adventure of his rescue of Arthur's queen, Guinevere. Arthur – the first and most charismatic British hero – was very popular in continental Europe. The first visual representation of him is an eleventh-century mosaic in the cathedral of the southern Italian port of Otranto.

Distant worlds

Romances are usually about a great adventure that takes place in a heightened and attractively distant world, where the laws of everyday life, including the laws of nature, can occasionally be set aside. The time is often remote, characters sometimes meet the fairies or talking animals, and the settings are castles, pastoral landscapes and mysteriously magical forests.

Romance plots

The plots are often episodic, very much a case of 'and then and then...'. The central characters are often touchingly human. They don't have the near-divine status of Epic heroes.

The anonymous *Sir Gawain and the Green Knight* (fourteenth century) follows many of the Romance conventions: a hero who is vulnerable to temptation, a perilous journey and a final test, which turns out to be other than what the young knight expected. Chaucer's 'The Franklin's Tale' (c. 1390) may also be regarded as Romance. In a later period, Edmund Spenser's *The Faerie Queene* (1590 and 1596) is usually treated as the standard form of the English Romance or Epic Romance. The looseness of their plots and the 'magical' nature of the action often leads to Shakespeare's last plays (for example, *The Winter's Tale*, 1609 and *Cymbeline*, 1610) being called romances.

Summary

Romances are set in a distant, chivalric world in which the laws of nature can be suspended. The hero is often more ordinary than those in Epic or Tragedy.

25.2   The phases of Romance

In *Anatomy of Criticism* (1957) the Canadian critic, Northrop Frye, distinguished six phases of Romance. Not every work that can be called Romance has all six, so what follows should not be treated as a prescription.

Birth

The first phase is the birth and, sometimes, the preservation of the hero from danger. These events blend the ordinary with elements of luck or providence. Birth and danger are often associated with water. In the Bible, Moses is hidden in the bullrushes. In *The Winter's Tale*, Shakespeare follows another folklore motif: the child who is exposed in a wild place, where he or she is found and cared for.

Youth

According to Frye, the youth of the hero is often passed in an idyllic pastoral landscape. The hero's innocence is preserved; friendships are chaste rather than erotic. This golden age is hinted at in *The Winter's Tale*, when Polixenes, recalling his boyhood with Leontes, says they were

> Two lads that thought there was no more behind
> But such a day tomorrow as today,
> And to be boy eternal.
>
> (1.2. 64–6)

Shakespeare captures that Arcadian (see Chapter 27, section 27.2) sense of time as an uninterrupted continuum of pleasure.

The quest

The quest marks out Romance as a distinct genre. As noted above, the plots of Romance are digressive. What distinguishes the Romance plot is that in addition to a series of testing incidents there is one major task, which is announced at the start and forms the grand closure of the work.

The quest usually involves a dangerous journey with many setbacks, a battle and then public acknowledgement of the hero. Spenser's Redcross Knight (*Faerie Queene*, Book One) suffers imprisonment before he kills the dragon and is given public approval by being betrothed to Una, who stands for Truth. The battle with the dragon is the quintessence of Romance. Significantly in Spenser, it takes three days: the period of Christ's death and Resurrection.

The hero usually encounters another kind of enemy. In addition to the dragon, there is a deceiver. In Spenser, the Redcross Knight is led astray by two deceivers: Archimago, who stands for hypocrisy and who separates the Knight from Truth; and Duessa, a fatal beauty who embodies falsehood and unfaithfulness.

Temptation

The hero has to maintain his integrity by resisting temptation. In the second book of *The Faerie Queene*, Sir Guyon, who represents Temperance, first resists Mammon (worldly wealth) and then the alluringly presented delights of the Bower of Bliss. This sensualist's paradise – music, the sound of waters, the singing of birds and a white-breasted woman in 'silver thin' silk – is then laid waste by Guyon.

Withdrawal

The hero withdraws to contemplate. Towards the end of Shakespeare's *The Tempest* (1610) the central figure, Prospero, becomes increasingly someone who reflects on his own conduct and that of his enemies.

Fulfilment

Having contemplated, the hero is content to retell his story. Prospero invites the other characters into his cell to hear 'the story of my life' (5.1. 308). Frye calls one aspect of this phase 'cuddle fiction' – the world of 'comfortable beds or chairs around fireplaces'. This domestic close is in keeping with the 'ordinary' nature of the hero. There is a welcome rest in the warmth and safety of the home now that the quest is over.

Summary

Northrop Frye distinguished six phases of Romance. The hero has to overcome the dangers surrounding his birth and enjoys a world of Arcadian innocence in his youth. The central event of Romance is the quest, an aspect of which is resisting temptation. The hero withdraws before settling down to a life of fulfilment.

25.3 The persistence of Romance

Talk about Romance can all too easily have a slightly musty air, the whiff of a world no one takes very seriously any more.

But Romance is flexible and the most durable of genres. Many of the features associated with Romance can be found in science fiction. Here, we find other worlds and other kinds of creatures. The plots often turn on adventure and exploration, the characters are often brave yet touchingly human, and it is easy to imagine that some of the settings are realizations in different terms of enchanted lands. And science fiction exists on the screen. Just think of the phrase 'to boldly go where no one has gone before' and you can see that in the quest of the *Starship Enterprise* the genre of Romance is re-enacted in the terms of science fiction. *Buffy the Vampire Slayer* might be described as Gothic Romance. Each episode can be read in terms of some of Fyre' s categories.

Summary

Romance is a durable genre, as seen in science fiction.

25.4 Twentieth-century Romance

Two contemporary successes can be described as Romance or Epic Romance. The first is Harry Potter. If you know the books, look through the summary of Northrop Frye's phases of Romance. Much of the first book is concerned with the finding of the child, who will become the hero. Trial and temptation is a frequent motif. Very frequently the stories close with the cosy chat with Professor Dumbledore; until, that is, the sixth book.

Tolkien's romance

The second is J. R. R. Tolkien's epic romance, *The Lord of the Rings* (1954–5). This is a world of quests, of magical places and a lot of engagingly ordinary heroes. It is governed by a central quest and at the close the reader is left with the redoubtable Sam Gamgee at home in the Shire. One of its most remarkable achievements is making available once more the mythology of the North. Middle-earth is not drawn from the Classics; its roots are in Norse sagas and Anglo-Saxon epics.

Another of Tolkien's achievements is that this world of varied creatures – dwarves, elves, hobbits, orcs – was composed by someone who had fought in the First World War. For Tolkien, the First World War with its devastated land and endless slaughter did not invalidate literature that created 'other' realms and celebrated heroic virtues – courage, devotion, fortitude and loyalty. The style of the books is not (presumably deliberately) even. There are passages that are plain and purposeful, the aim being to move the narrative on; but Tolkien heightens the writing with a lofty and, appropriately in Romance, archaic vocabulary. At one point in *The Two Towers* (the second book in the trilogy) one of the groups of travellers draw near to Isengard. The forbidding landscape – 'No trees grew there' – might owe something to Tolkien's memories of no man's land. Desolation gives way to the sight of Isengard, home of the most powerful of the wizards, and the language is correspondingly lofty, with phrases such as the one about the 'mighty works the Men of Westernesse had wrought there of old'. The elevated and archaic 'wrought' rather than, say, the plainer 'made', is a rhetorical device that gives the impression that this is an ancient, oral literature, written to be proclaimed by a bard with a strong sense of the rhythmical unfolding of sentences.

Summary

Harry Potter has many features of Romance; Tolkien deliberately uses the plot, conventions and style of Romance.

■ ⋎ 26 Gothic

26.1 Gothic's historical context

Genre and history

Gothic has a specific historical origin in the last three decades of the eighteenth century. It is important to remember this when we are tempted to think that the various genres have always been there and are, consequently, permanent aspects of the world of Literature. Genres are not immune from history; there are social and cultural pressures that help to bring them into existence and assist them to change.

In the case of Gothic, there may have been political reasons for its decrease in popularity in the 1790s. Marilyn Butler (*Romantics, Rebels and Reactionaries*, 1981) suggests that it may have been politically unwise, once the nation was at war with France, to suggest, as Gothic frequently does, that those who wield power are corrupt.

Gothic landmarks

Horace Walpole's *Castle of Otranto* (1765) is one of the earliest. It is a tale of strange events (it begins with a character being crushed by a suit of armour) set in southern Italy. Ann Radcliffe is the most representative Gothic novelist. She wrote a number of novels full of mysteries and pleasing terrors. Her most famous works are: *Romance of the Forest* (1791), *The Mysteries of Udolpho* (1794) and *The Italian* (1797). These, too, have continental settings, as does Matthew Lewis's *The Monk* (1796). Charles Maturin's *Melmoth the Wanderer* (1820) has scenes set on a remote island. The one Gothic novel to have achieved canonical status, at least at the present time, is Mary Shelley's *Frankenstein* (1818). Gothic did not die out. In the twentieth century, Mervyn Peake's *Titus Groan* (1946) may also be spoken of as Gothic, as can a number of Angela Carter's novels and her reworking of fairy tales.

Summary

Genre is not a permanent feature of literature; it has a history. Gothic appeared in the late eighteenth century, and its demise might be associated with the political pressures of the late eighteenth century.

26.2 Gothic influence

Atmosphere

Gothic has influenced the writing of novels, largely by inspiring writers to create eerie atmospheres and settings. As in the case of Satire, the word 'Gothic' has a life as an adjective as well as a noun. The Thornfield scenes of *Jane Eyre* (1847) deploy Gothic features – the rambling house, the threatened woman, the dark secret – as does Wilkie Collins' *The Woman in White* (1860) with its scenes of women effectively imprisoned in a big house by unscrupulous men.

Cinema

Gothic has another life in the cinema. *Frankenstein* (1818) and *Dracula* (1897) are the twin sources of twentieth- and twenty-first-century horror. This is no doubt a result of the skill (greatly assisted by technology) with which cinema can induce fear in its audiences, and the pleasures audiences derive from Gothic's easily recognizable conventions – strange castles, deep forests, monsters, cleavages and fangs.

There are probably two other features that have commended Gothic to the cinema: one concerning plot and the other character. The plots have an archetypal charisma – the creation of life and the strange world between life and death. The central characters have the ability to exist outside the works in which they originally appeared. Many people have heard of Frankenstein's monster and Count Dracula who have never read the books in which their authors created them. Because they exist in the imagination beyond texts, new stories can be written about them. Hence 'son of' Frankenstein and 'brides of' Dracula.

Summary

Gothic has influenced the presentation of atmosphere and enjoys a vigorous life in the cinema.

26.3 Mock Gothic

Gothic might have been forgotten had it not been for its influence on later fiction. Most readers encounter it by way of *Northanger Abbey* (1818), Jane Austen's witty parody. *Northanger Abbey* is self-consciously literary; issues about the nature of fiction are cleverly raised through the satiric presentation of Catherine Morland's Gothic imaginings. It is about learning to read – read fiction and the text of life. Catherine must learn that the events of the world are not to be understood in terms of *The Mysteries of Udolpho*.

Summary

Gothic has a life in works that parody its conventions.

26.4   Gothic conventions and features

Horror and terror

Gothic literature was written in what we now call the Romantic period. Two features of Romantic literature are its concentration on subjective states – what a writer *feels* – and an extension of the areas of literature to the obscure reaches of the mind. In Gothic, this resulted in an exploration of whatever is fearful and terrifying. Gothic often features dungeons and crypts, but what chiefly matters about these are the *feelings* they induce. Hence words such as 'apprehension', 'dread', 'fear', 'horror', 'loathing' and 'terror' are frequent. A reflection on such feelings occurs in a famous passage in *The Mysteries of Udolpho* in which the heroine, Emily, approaches 'the black veil'. This veil

> excited a faint degree of terror. But a terror of this nature, as it occupies and expands the mind, and elevates it to high expectation, is purely sublime, and leads us, by a kind of fascination, to seek even the object, from which we appear to shrink.
>
> (vol. 2, ch. 6)

Mrs Radcliffe shows what might be the basis of our interest in terror. It repels and yet, more powerfully, it allures. The terror we feel is purely sublime, and sublimity, which leads to the expansion and elevation of the mind, entices us to seek the object from which we appear to recoil. It could be a comment on the entire genre.

Locations

Readers of Gothic often remember individual settings. Many of them are continental. (An important influence was contemporary travel writing.) Just as Gothic explores the inner recesses of the mind – the places where nightmares dwell – so it explores wild and remote worlds. In Gothic fiction there are deep valleys, high mountain peaks and wild forlorn wastes which awe and intimidate us by their vastness. Hence the Arctic waters in *Frankenstein*, and the scene in the glacier, when the Monster confronts his maker. These landscapes evoke the sublime – the feeling of overwhelming awe and fear in the presence of natural immensities. Gothic interiors are often dark and labyrinthine – cloisters, vast abbeys, long corridors, castle halls, panelled bedrooms and secret passages.

The historical location of many of the works is Medieval or Renaissance. The English often have prejudices about the past and about Roman Catholicism, so they eagerly lap up tales of superstition, manipulation and the abuse of authority.

Atmosphere

Gothic is read chiefly for its evocation of atmosphere. Those immense landscapes and darkened rooms arouse fear, horror and terror. Night scenes are common. Another is the arrival of the heroine at a sinister castle, as in Emily's arrival at Udolpho (vol. 2, ch. 5):

> though it was now lighted up by the setting sun, the gothic greatness of its features, and its mouldering walls of dark grey stone, rendered it a gloomy and sublime object.

Mrs Radcliffe's diction follows convention in the time of day – 'the setting sun' – the colours and tones – 'dark grey' – and the language of subjective response – 'gloomy and sublime'. 'Gloomy' is perhaps the most-used adjective in the creation of Gothic atmosphere.

The frisson of the supernatural is present in ghosts and spectres; they create atmosphere and arouse fear, but, unlike ghost stories, they are rarely the main business of a Gothic novel.

Gothic language

In Gothic language, atmosphere and emotion are pushed to the extreme. Chapter 8 of *Melmoth the Wanderer* opens: 'I am not superstitious, but as I entered the church, I felt a chill of body and soul inexpressible.' It is 'inexpressible' that makes it characteristically Gothic. In Gothic, light is not merely 'dim' but 'gloomy', silence is 'deep', and characters 'muse' rather than 'think'.

Gothic language is literary in that it draws on earlier writing. There was a tradition of 'twilight writing' in the eighteenth century that had its roots in Milton's 'Il Penseroso' (1645), and its most memorable expression is in Thomas Gray's 'Elegy' (1751), in which, in fading light, the poet contemplates the obscure people buried in a country churchyard. William Collins' 'Ode to Fear' (1747), itself dependent in its diction on Edmund Spenser, gave Gothic writers a vocabulary of what is monstrous and 'madly wild' (see Chapter 25). Edmund Burke's *A Philosophical Inquiry* (1757) provided writers with a language for the Sublime.

Summary

Gothic dwells on what is subjective and extreme, on what appals and allures. Events are set either in wild and remote places (often continental) or in frightening, enclosed spaces. The atmosphere is often gloomy and the language is both excessive and literary.

26.5   Gothic themes

Social and political Gothic

Gothic is a surprisingly ambitious genre. It opens up questions about the family and society. In *Frankenstein*, the monster watches a family through a hole in the wall of the woodshed. Socially and politically, it is an interesting episode, for while the narrative stimulates a radical sympathy for the marginalized monster, the picture of a stable and loving family is conservative.

Creation

Gothic also touches on the metaphysical questions about nature, and good and evil. Frankenstein is not an overtly religious book but it can be read as a parable, which rewrites the story of Creation. In taking it upon himself to make a human being, Frankenstein usurps the position of the Creator, but then, unlike the Creator, he hates his creature. Frankenstein's failure is one of responsibility for the creature he has brought into the world.

Violence

The violence of Frankenstein against what he has made is disturbingly evident in the destruction of the female Monster. Violence, both threatened and actual, features in other Gothic works. No doubt Gothic licensed writers to explore things that could not find their way into other fiction. Gothic violence has a strong sexual element. In Matthew Gregory Lewis's *The Monk* there is a horrible scene of sexual violation. *The Monk*, as near as the Gothic got to pornography, is, significantly, the only novel the oafish John Thorpe in *Northanger Abbey* has read.

Women

Gothic has become popular in recent years, largely because it makes women central. It is possible to read Gothic as a parabolic exploration of the constricted and even threatened life of women. A frequent image is the lonely maiden threatened by sexual violence. Another is the incarcerated victim. This is one of Catherine's imaginings in *Northanger Abbey*. This image persists in later fiction. There are striking scenes in which a woman is alone at night. In Wilkie Collins' *No Name* (1862) the heroine contemplates suicide in the dead of night. The tradition is still alive in the scene in which Tess baptizes her baby.

Summary

Gothic is an ambitious genre that explores society and the family, the religious issue of Creation and responsibility, the human capacity for violence and the place of women in a male-dominated world.

26.6   Gothic plots

Digressive plots

Most readers are disappointed in Gothic plots. They ramble. The precision and classical symmetry of *Northanger Abbey* is an implicit criticism of Mrs Radcliffe's digressive plots.

Characters

Gothic characters are restricted in range and hardly memorable. Gothic characterization is carefully built on a set of clear contrasts. Conventionally, the central figure is a threatened heroine, whom, the reader hopes, will be rescued by the largely absent hero. The hero's binary opposite is the very much present villainous contriver. He is usually aristocratic and often lives in a sinister castle.

Summary

Plot and characterization in Gothic is simple: the plots are digressive and characters often function as binary opposites.

■ ⌄ 27   Pastoral

27.1   Pastoral: English and classical

Shepherds

Pastoral is about country life. In origin, the word means 'concerned with shepherds', and the carefree life of shepherds is, traditionally, Pastoral's major subject. It is not a genre that aims at creating realistic images. Shepherds live in a beautiful landscape, where they compose music and poetry and court shepherdesses, who, by convention, are often called nymphs. Pastoral poems are sometimes described as bucolics.

A genre and a mode

Pastoral is a durable genre which has shown itself capable of transformation. Because it is adaptable, it is, like Gothic, both a genre and a mode. Writers can slip into the Pastoral mode or manner in works that are not otherwise Pastoral.

Miguel de Cervantes' *Don Quixote* (1605) has a number of passages in which the setting and characters are drawn from the Pastoral. Hardy's novels are ambitious undertakings, tackling social, moral and philosophical issues, but when he writes of the countryside, the Pastoral tradition is often deployed and adapted.

The eclogue, the georgic, the idyll

Pastoral is ancient. Theocritus (born 305 BC) wrote in Greek, and Virgil (born 70 BC) in Latin. English Literature has inherited two poetic forms from the Classical writers: the eclogue and the georgic. The eclogue, originated by Theocritus, is a dialogue poem about country life. Virgil, who also wrote eclogues, perfected the georgic – a poem about the labours of the countryside such as ploughing or bee-keeping.

There was a strong tendency to idealize in Classical Pastoral. A word often used in relation to the idealizing element in Pastoral is 'idyllic'. This is an adjective derived from the poetic form, the idyll. Idyll originally meant a short poem, often dealing with the country. Related, no doubt, to the idealizing impulse of Pastoral, it came to mean a life of untroubled and simple pleasure.

Arcadia

In the imaginative geography of poetry, Pastoral became located in Arcadia. Arcadia, an area in southern Greece, became associated with the carefree life of love and pastoral farming. Virgil set his eclogues there, and Sir Philip Sidney wrote a prose Romance called *Arcadia* (1590). One of the later themes of literature and painting was the sad realization that there is death even in Arcadia.

Summary

Pastoral idealizes country life. English literature has inherited Pastoral from the Classical poets, in particular the forms of the eclogue, the georgic and the idyll. The idea of Arcadia – the ideal landscape – has influenced the English imagination.

27.2   Pastoral conventions

The passionate shepherd

Christopher Marlowe's 'The Passionate Shepherd to his Love' (published 1599) is a good introduction to the conventions of Pastoral.

> Come live with me and be my Love,
> And we will all the pleasures prove
> That valleys, groves, hills and fields,
> Woods, or steepy mountains yields.
>
> And we will sit upon the rocks
> Seeing the shepherds feed their flocks,
> By shallow rivers, to whose falls
> Melodious birds sing madrigals.
>
> And I will make thee beds of roses
> And a thousand fragrant posies,
> A cap of flowers, and a kirtle
> Embroidered all with leaves of myrtle;
>
> A gown made of the finest wool,
> Which from our pretty lambs we pull;
> Fair lined slippers for the cold,
> With buckles of the purest gold;
>
> A belt of straw and ivy buds
> With coral clasps and amber studs:
> And if these pleasures may thee move,
> Come live with me and be my Love.

The shepherd swains shall dance and sing
For thy delight each May morning:
If these delights thy mind may move,
Then live with me and be my Love.

Setting

Marlowe's landscape is gentle and welcoming. There is no thought that the steep mountains might be difficult to climb. It seems that the rocks exist solely to provide a seat for viewing the shepherds tending their flocks. The land is productive, but productive of luxuries. Sheep are not kept to produce wool for everyday clothes but for gowns.

Season

Although there is a mention of the cold, the impression is that this is a perpetual world of early summer. The shepherds will dance each May morning.

Art

The shepherd is a poet, and other shepherds dance and sing. Even nature joins in: the birds accompany the flowing rivers with madrigals. 'Sing' in pastoral verse can mean to write poetry as well as perform songs. There is also a special diction: a shepherd is a 'swain'.

Love

The shepherd/lover invites his beloved to a life of delights. Most of the poem is taken up with a list, minutely and gracefully detailed, of all the gifts he will bestow on her. The life of Love is one of pleasure and, by implication, pleasure that will not end.

Security

There is nothing in Pastoral to endanger or distress. There are no poor harvests and no invading armies. There is a tradition in Roman literature of contrasting the sophistications of the town with the crude simplicities of the country, but the praise and preference for the countryside in Pastoral counteracts that tradition. In sixteenth- and seventeenth-century literature (particularly in and around the Civil War), there was a poetry of Retirement, which praised rural quiet as preferable to the corruptions and uncertainties of Court life. In his 'An Horation Ode upon Cromwell's Return from Ireland' (1650), Andrew Marvell draws on this tradition by picturing Cromwell retiring to his garden after his military successes.

Summary

Pastoral poems are set in idyllic landscapes. The weather is warm and sunny. Shepherds are artists, who sing of love. Pastoral is a secure world. The sub-genre of the Retirement poem indicates how preferable it is to the Court.

27.3   Political Pastoral

Big estates

In the eighteenth century, Pastoral became overtly political when it celebrated the grand estates and their landowners. For example, John Langhorne's poem *Studley Park* (1766) pictures happy labourers:

> Hail, charming fields, of happy swains the care!
> Hail, happy swains possess'd of fields so fair!

'Possess'd' is a curious word. Presumably, the swains do not own the fields they till, so it must mean occupying rather than owning. Perhaps the point is that they are so happy, it is as if they owned the land. The productivity of the land is central to the praise of the estate. Having spoken of the teeming earth and commerce in the towns, Langhorne presents a very conventional pastoral image of flocks and piping shepherds ('reed' means pipe):

> On verdant hills, see! Flocks innumerous feed,
> Or thoughtful listen to the lively reed.

But the context implies that the sheep are also productive. Eighteenth-century Pastoral introduced economics into the genre.

Pastoral and economics

It is not, therefore, surprising that there was an interest in the georgic with its detailed celebration of the methods of rural labour. James Grainger wrote *The Sugar-Cane* (1764) and John Dyer wrote *The Fleece* (1757) about the rearing of sheep.

Summary

In the eighteenth century, Pastoral was political in its celebration of big estates. The georgic was similarly used to praise the productivity of the people and the land.

27.4 Anti-pastoral

Undermining a genre

Anti-pastoral is a 'counter-genre' – a genre created in opposition to another. Anti-pastoral subverts both popular conceptions about the ease of country life and the genre that presented rural existence as one of sweet content. Book 1 of George Crabbe's *The Village* (1783) forcefully undoes the illusions that Pastoral has induced. His aim is to present 'the real picture of the poor' (5). The times are gone, he says, when 'The rustic poet praised his native plains' (10) and shepherds no longer 'Their country's beauty or their nymph's rehearse'. Crabbe insists that a literary tradition, that of the Mantua-born Virgil, has clouded our vision of the actualities of rural poverty:

> From Truth and Nature shall we widely stray,
> Where Virgil, not where Fancy, leads the way.
> (19–20)

The opening to *The Village* is Crabbe's poetic testament. What he does, particularly in *The Borough* (1810) with its poems about almshouses and prisons, is look in abrasive detail at what he saw about him.

Pastoral parody

Pastoral, because it is so evidently an artificial genre, has long produced its critical opposite. Sir Walter Raleigh wrote a witty reply to Marlowe, called 'The Nymph's Reply to the Shepherd' (1600). The opening lines strike a playfully critical note with their questioning subjunctive:

> If all the world and love were young
> And truth in every shepherd's tongue

The truth is that love does not stay young, that the year ages, and that poets are not always reliable. If Raleigh's poem is a kind of anti-Pastoral, it shows that it can be still in the Pastoral spirit, for Pastoral is a game of the imagination in which we build, often knowingly, a make-believe world.

Summary

In Anti-pastoral the conventions of Pastoral are subverted either by an abrasive presentation of details of the actual lives of country dwellers or an impish game in which the conventions of Pastoral are playfully overturned.

27.5   Twentieth-century Pastoral

Pastoral did not die with the advance of urban life. Indeed, at the beginning of the twentieth century there was a 'back to the land' movement in which folk songs were collected, traditional rustic crafts revived and houses designed with distinctly cottagey features (see Chapter 54, section 54.6). Thomas Hardy was popular and influenced a new generation of Pastoral writers. The Pastoral note was sounded in the music of Ralph Vaughan Williams, George Butterworth and Gerald Finzi. In his last symphony, the ninth (1958), Vaughan Williams re-creates the feel of the Stonehenge scene in Hardy's *Tess of the d'Urbervilles* (1891).

The strong Pastoral influence in the literature of the First World War shows the hold it has on the imagination. Edmund Blunden ended his *Undertones of War* (1928), a prose account of the Western Front, with a reference to himself as a shepherd in a soldier's coat. His first volume published after the First World War was called *The Wagoner* (1920) and the second *The Shepherd* (1922).

Pastoral changes and grows. To take one example: there are many facets to the poetry of Ted Hughes, one of which is Pastoral. His *Season Songs* (1976) and *Moortown* (1979) are broadly Pastoral in that they are celebratory of the natural rhythms of the earth and our engagement with it. Ted Hughes has this distinction among poets: not many have been, as he was, a farmer.

Summary

The twentieth century has continued the Pastoral tradition in its architecture, music and literature.

Part Five   Context

▓ ⌄ **28** The Past

28.1 A foreign country

The pastness of the past

Without a sense of context, literature can be puzzling. L. P. Hartley gets at this problem at the beginning of his novel *The Go-Between* (1953): 'The past is a foreign country: they do things differently there.' That insight is the basis of the contextual or historical study of literature.

> We cannot assume that in the past people thought in *exactly* the same way as we now think.

Philip Larkin's poem 'An Arundel Tomb' (1964) touches on the differences between past and present. The stone effigies of the Earl and Countess (in Chichester cathedral) have survived into a world very different from the one they dominated. The feudal system that gave them power has gone, and people no longer understand the Latin inscription around the base of their monument. Their identities have been eroded, so they are 'helpless' in 'an unarmorial age' – an unchivalric age with no knowledge of heraldry.

The statues are like literature from the past. Both appear foreign. But the poem indicates that the world of the Earl and Countess is not entirely lost to us. There is writing. It may be in Latin, but some people will be able to read it. We can come to terms with a world different from our own through the study of words. The task of contextual criticism is

> To work at the words we have, so that they bring back to us the world of the writer who wrote them.

Scholarship

Historical criticism is often done for us. Scholars have studied texts and have worked out how words were used in the past. This knowledge is usually conveyed to us in notes, either at the back of the book or at the bottom of the page in the form of footnotes.

The principle that historical criticism works with is:

> The past is present in words.

In order to understand what was written in the past, we have to look at how past generations used words.

Language doesn't stand still; it changes constantly. Moreover, different bits of it change at different rates. The forms and functions of words – grammar – and the way they are organized into sentences – syntax – change very slowly. But meanings – semantics – can change both slowly and rapidly. Prepositions – in, on, up, down – change hardly at all, whereas nouns and adjectives can quickly take on new meanings. For example, not long ago the word 'result' meant the outcome of any sporting contest. Now it means a win.

Help from dictionaries

To understand the literature of the past, the reader needs to know what words meant when writers used them. Take the word 'silly'. In common speech it now means foolish, stupid or thoughtless, as in 'a silly mistake'. *The Shorter Oxford English Dictionary* gives this current meaning – 'foolish, empty-headed' – as coming into use in 1576. This means it was available to Shakespeare. But so, also, were several other meanings. C. T. Onions, in his *A Shakespeare Glossary* (1922) gives, in addition to 'simple-minded', seven distinctive uses in Shakespeare's works: 1. deserving of pity; 2. helpless or defenceless; 3. feeble or frail; 4. scanty or meagre; 5. unsophisticated; 6. plain, simple and homely; 7. petty thievery. When, therefore, Richard speaks of 'silly beggars' in the stocks – *Richard II* (5. 25) (1595) – he uses the word in the first sense. The beggars deserve pity, not derision. When we see what a word means, our understanding of the play might begin to deepen. Although Richard is in a pitiful state, he can still pity others.

Background

Historical criticism tries to establish what is often called the 'background' of a work or works. Other words for 'background' are: 'culture', 'milieu', 'setting', 'world' and 'zeitgeist' (spirit of the age). And, of course, the term 'context' is used this way. What the terms try to get at is the idea that people live in and interact within an enveloping network of thoughts, feelings and artistic ideas.

A modern example might help. At the time of writing there is a suspicion of what we call 'stereotyping' – putting people into categories. We think this is a kind of prejudice – we lump people together rather than treating them as individuals. So we think it is wrong to think of someone as, say, female, middle-aged, middle-class and from Yorkshire. The feeling that this is wrong is so widespread that when we talk to people we automatically rely on them regarding 'stereotyping' as a bad thing. This way of thinking now comes 'naturally' to us, it is an element of the context in which we conduct our lives. In fact, like all things we count as 'background', it has a history. 'Stereotyping' only emerged in the 1980s.

And, of course, there are lots of other attitudes and assumptions that form the background of our thinking and feeling. We are concerned about rights, about equal opportunities and the extension of choice in many areas of life. We think increasingly that people can be understood in genetic terms. We deplore environmental pollution. We like shopping, rhythmical music and think it is important to look slim, trim and healthy. And because we want to talk to each other frequently, we value e-mail and the mobile phone. (You may like to add to the list.)

Summary

Words can form a link with the past. If we can understand the particular meanings of words, we can begin to understand the past. These words form what we call 'background' – the network of ideas, assumptions and attitudes that form an outlook, a world of thought.

28. 2   Many pasts

Many histories

The backgrounds of writers also have a history. In fact, any cultural context consists of many histories. Each thought has a history. Even the most original ones have some links with the past. It seems odd to us that feelings have histories, but they do. Critics talk occasionally about 'structures of feelings', by which they mean the way in which people express and understand themselves. These ways of expression change.

Examples from the twenty-first century will help. Each idea familiar to us today has a history. Some of these histories are quite recent. Take two words: 'allergy' and 'democracy'. The idea that we are 'allergic' to certain foods grew up after the Second World War. Democracy has a longer history, and the growth of the idea was slow. The word 'democracy' entered our language in 1574, but 'democrat' was not used till 1790.

Thus:

> The 'background' of a writer is a web of assumptions, attitudes, beliefs, common references, ideologies, interests, judgements, knowledge, outlooks, prejudices, structures of feeling, theories, understandings and values. Each of these has its own history.

Knowing backgrounds

We have to understand backgrounds, because they mark the works we study. Ian MacEwan wrote *Enduring Love* (1997) when stalking was in the news. The stamp or mark of the past can be found in a number of ways. Because the material a writer uses is words, one of the biggest influences is the books writers read; and of the books Western writers read, none has been more influential than the Bible.

Summary

When we try to understand the past, we have to come to terms with the idea that the words in which we express thoughts and feelings have histories. The background of any work consists of the interweaving of beliefs, attitudes, assumptions and values.

▪ ⋁ 29 Religion and the Bible

29.1 A cultural heritage

Shakespeare and the Bible

Many writers take it for granted that their readers will know something of the Bible. The Bible is part of a Western cultural heritage; it is something most of us know about and it can, therefore, be used as a shared reference point. Shakespeare's plays are full of references to the Bible. They have an almost casual quality, probably expressive of the ease with which he could draw on an apt image from the teeming world of biblical iconography.

In *Measure for Measure* (1604), Isabella, pleading for her brother's life, says that if Angelo were to think of how God saved rather than judged sinful mankind

> mercy then will breathe within your lips
> Like man new made.
>
> (2.2. 79–80)

Shakespeare blends at least three closely related biblical passages in this line and a half of blank verse. When God creates Adam, He breathes into his nostrils, so Adam becomes 'a living soul' (Genesis 2:7). St. Paul teaches that when anyone is 'in Christ, he is a new creature' (2 Corinthians 5:17) and in 'Ephesians' there is talk of putting on 'the new man, which after God is created in righteousness' (4:24).

Biblical imagery in recent authors

Authors still use the Bible as a source of ideas and imagery, and readers are still expected to pick up the references. In *The World's Wife* (1999), Carol Ann Duffy expects readers to know who King Herod, Pontius Pilate and Lazarus are. Duffy's perspective is what the wives (real or imagined) would think of events traditionally presented in terms of men. But her point would be entirely lost if readers did not know who these biblical characters are.

Students

Students today have difficulties because the Bible is no longer a common cultural possession. School does not help much, particularly when religious education lessons tend to be about comparative religion or morality. Fortunately, many editions of literary works have notes that explain references. It is always wise to read these. In addition, you can ask teachers; it is their job to know about these things.

And you can always read the Bible yourself. As it is a very big book of considerable variety, selection is needed. Begin with the first book; Genesis – a repository of stories of the beginning of Creation and the sagas of the founding of Israel. A look at Psalms gives an insight into Hebrew poetry, and Job is a book that wrestles with the tragic theme of undeserved suffering. In the New Testament, the Gospels of St Mark and St John give very different perspectives on Jesus Christ, the founder of Christianity. The last book, Revelation, is the source of Christian iconography for the end of Creation. Revelation had an enormous influence on the Christian imagination. The great east window at York Minster (the work of John Thornton of Coventry, 1405) devotes more space to Revelation than any other part of the biblical record.

Summary

In order to understand the range of references in many literary works (including contemporary writing), we have to be acquainted with the Bible.

29.2   Bible stories

Rewriting the Bible

Writers have rewritten Bible stories. Milton rewrote the story of the Fall in *Paradise Lost* (1667). His 'version' of Genesis brings out that this is 'our' story, the story of humankind as it confronts temptation, yields and loses its innocence. Although Satan has intrigued the critics, it is Adam and Eve who are the central figures. They are the images of what we once were, and may through grace once more become. The passage in Book IV, when Satan first sees them is one of the most elevated pictures of humanity ever created in literature:

> Two of far nobler shape erect and tall,
> Godlike erect, with native honour clad
> In naked majesty seemed lords of all,
> And worthy seemed, for in their looks divine
> The image of their glorious maker shone
>
> (288–92)

Milton brings out what it is to be naked without being ashamed or vulnerable. To be naked is to be majestic, because it is to be dressed in our 'native honour' – our natural clothing. When Adam and Eve have fallen, our links with them are made movingly clear. In the final book (XII), Eve is 'our mother' (624), and as the pair leave paradise, they are spoken of as 'Our lingering parents' (638).

The Bible as judgement

Writers sometimes use the Bible to invite judgement. It is a touchstone of value, so if a character departs from it, that character is judged. Pope brings out the superficiality of Belinda and her world in *The Rape of the Lock* (1712). Sailing down the Thames, Belinda smiles on all:

> Bright as the sun, her eyes the gazers strike,
> And, like the sun, they shine on all alike.
>
> (Canto ıı, 13–14)

Pope expects us to recall the words of Jesus in the Sermon on the Mount that God 'maketh his sun to rise on the evil and on the good' (St Matthew 5:45). God's regard for both the evil and the good is a loving and providential one, but Belinda smiles indiscriminatingly, because, so runs the implication, in her (not unattractive) naivety she cannot tell one from the other.

Pope used the Bible in a similar way in his dark close of *The Dunciad* (1728). The triumph of dullness is expressed as a reversal of both the opening of the Bible and the opening of St John's Gospel. Pope's point is horribly clear. Just as God's Word made the world with its reason and order, so dullness undoes it:

> Light dies before thy uncreating word;
> Thy hand, great Anarch! Lets the curtain fall,
> And universal darkness buries all.

According to Genesis, 'Light' is the first creation of God, so the 'uncreating word' of dullness extinguishes it before, in a great theatrical sweep, the curtain comes down and buries all things in the darkness from which they arose.

Summary

The Bible has supplied writers with patterns for stories and a standard by which to judge characters' actions.

29.3 Biblical variations

Western culture has been influenced by the variety of writing in the Bible: stories, histories, poetry, proverbs, prophecies and laws. These various forms often work through symbols and motifs. Writers have composed imaginative variations on this stock of symbols and images.

Finding the lost

Jesus told three parables (St Luke 15), about a lost coin, a lost sheep and a lost son (usually called the prodigal son). The image of searching for the lost until it is found has become central to our idea of Christian love.

Jane Austen draws on this image in *Pride and Prejudice* (1813). There is a comical (but still persuasively moral) contrast between the clergyman, Mr Collins, who counsels Mr Bennet to abandon his erring daughter, Lydia, and Mr Darcy who searches for the lost girl until he finds her. Then in the spirit of St Nicholas of Bari (the original of Santa Claus), he virtually provides her with a dowry, so that Mr Wickham will agree to marry her.

Blake's re-workings

Blake re-works Biblical stories and images in his *Songs of Innocence* (1789) and *Songs of Experience* (1794). The *Innocence* poems show the lost being found. In 'A Dream' the emmet (an ant) is no sooner lost than a glow-worm guides her home, and as soon as the little boy is lost 'God, ever nigh,/Appear'd like his father in white' ('The Little Boy Lost' and 'The Little Boy Found').

The *Songs of Experience* are troubling variants on Biblical stories; in them the lost are *not* found. In 'A Little Boy Lost' a natural rebelliousness is treated as a sin, and the boy is burnt. In 'A Little Girl Lost', Ona, having lost her fear and finding sexual delight, is rejected by her father. The songs subvert Christian morality, a morality that is shown to distort people by thwarting their natural passions. Strangely, it is a tribute to the imaginative power of the biblical stories that they can be turned to uses never intended by those who have believed in them for generations.

Ironic use of the Bible

If Blake's *Innocence* songs affirm and his *Experience* ones subvert biblical stories and images (see Chapter 15, section 15.1), the ironical use of biblical material sometimes does both. It is clear, for example, that the character Dr Faustus intends an ironic meaning when (sc. 5. 26) he summons the devil Mephastophilis:

> Come, Mephastophilis,
> And bring glad tidings from great Lucifer

Faustus, who is a scholar of the Bible, must know that the word 'tidings' is found in what the Angel says to the shepherds about the birth of Christ: 'I bring you good tidings of great joy' (St Luke 2:10). Faustus, who takes a (childish?) pleasure in misusing Scripture, certainly uses the word 'tidings' ironically. He wants news from the Father of all Lies (an ancient title of the Devil) rather than the God of Truth and Love. It is, however, very likely that Marlowe's audiences would have seen that the irony works against Faustus, a man who does not see that Lucifer cannot bring 'good tidings'.

Summary

The variety of material in the Bible has stimulated authors to use the imagery and motifs in their own works. Sometimes, authors have followed the biblical pattern and sometimes they subvert and treat biblical ideas ironically.

29.4   Parables and journeys

The Bible is, as an old children's hymn says, a book full of stories. Stories of people who fall in love, build, look after their flocks, tend their vines, fight, travel, deceive, stand alone against enemies, go into exile and encounter strange and terrible creatures. The Gospels (Jesus's life seen through the eyes of several disciples) consist largely of pithy stories: Jesus heals, argues with authorities, settles disputes among his followers, is tested by his enemies, clears money changers out of the Temple, is arrested, tried, executed and rises from the grave.

Parables

One of the distinctive features of Jesus's teaching is the parable. These are either single images such as the astonishing growth of the mustard tree from a tiny seed, or quite detailed narratives such as the man attacked on the road to Jericho and helped by the Good Samaritan.

Journeys

From the Bible there has grown the picture of life as a journey. Abraham journeyed, and Jacob, after angering his brother, led a fugitive life. The children of Israel, having crossed the Red Sea, wandered in the desert for forty years. In English, the most memorable rendering of the idea of life as a journey is found in John Bunyan's *The Pilgrim's Progress* (1678). This detailed allegory is concerned with how Christian, having fled from the City of Destruction and losing his burden at the foot of the Cross, encounters trials and comforts until he reaches the Celestial City.

The image of the purposeful journey is present in novels such as Charlotte Brontë's *Jane Eyre* (1847) and Dickens' *David Copperfield* (1849). It is interesting that in English the tradition of the *Bildungsroman*, the novel dealing with growth, takes a distinctly moral interest in the central character (see Chapter 2, section 2.7). Growth might take a number of forms (in some German novels, intellectual growth is important) but the religious background to English literature is evident in the way that self-knowledge and self-control are central. In Elizabeth Gaskell's *North and South* (1855), both the central characters must come to see that their estimations of each other (and therefore of themselves) were mistaken.

Self-discovery

Two other essentially biblical ideas stem from the journey. The first is that the central character must come to see the truth about him- or herself. In D. H. Lawrence's *Sons and Lovers* (1913), Paul Morel is engaged in a sort of 'pilgrim's progress' in search of his art and himself. To find himself he must come to terms with what it is to be a son and what it is to be a lover. *Pride and Prejudice* also has a similar theme – Elizabeth Bennet must come to the point where she says, with the intensity of a religious experience, 'Till this moment, I never knew myself' (ch. 36).

Temptation

The second idea that is derived from the image of life as a journey is the importance of resisting temptation. Elizabeth Bennet is one of those who needs to learn. In terms of the story of Adam and Eve, she has fallen and needs to be rescued from her folly. There are some characters, however, who have already grasped the truth. They do not need to learn, but they can fail. They are characters who can be tempted. Jane Eyre is one such. She loves Mr Rochester, but when she understands that she cannot be his wife, she leaves her own paradise, Thornfield Hall. That word 'paradise' is apt. Jane says she knows that if she had stayed at Thornfield 'There was a heaven' there. Once she has left, Charlotte Brontë echoes Milton's language at the close of *Paradise Lost*. Milton writes 'Some natural tears they dropped' before they 'with wandering steps and slow,/Through Eden took their solitary way.' Jane's loss of paradise contains the same elements: 'I was weeping wildly as I walked along my solitary way' (ch. 27).

Summary

The Bible's chief mode is narrative; it is a book full of stories. The parables of Jesus have given an imaginative picture of life that authors have used as the basis for fiction. A popular theme is the finding of the lost. Other images include life as journey, growth in self-knowledge and resisting temptation.

29.5   Biblical words and images

Many biblical words have a significant place in our language. A word such as 'grace' has many different meanings, and behind them all we can often glimpse the idea that God has freely given a gift.

Shakespeare's words

The significant words in Shakespeare's plays are frequently drawn from biblical and religious sources. In some plays, the religious words are very prominent. It has been observed that the title *Measure for Measure* might refer to the words in the Sermon on the Mount: 'with what measure you mete, it shall be measured to you again' (St Matthew 7:2). Certainly, the plot of that play is concerned with putting the one who dispenses the law in the same position as the one whom the law condemns. The one who measures is measured.

Biblical words occur at crucial moments throughout Shakespeare. In *Measure for Measure* and *The Merchant of Venice* (1596), there are important speeches – Isabella to Angelo in 2.2, and Portia to the court in 4.1 – concerned with 'mercy'. Macbeth's dense meditation on killing Duncan (1.7) is given an eerie twist by its references to the chalice at the Last Supper – Christ's final meal with his disciples that has become the central act of Christian worship. In *The Winter's Tale* (1609), for all its pagan language, the final sight of Hermione 'coming alive' might easily put an audience in mind of the Resurrection. Those are just three examples. Something of the range and depth of biblical language in Shakespeare can be grasped by looking up certain words in a Shakespeare Concordance. Try looking up 'grace', 'heaven', 'mercy' and 'save'. Not all of the references will function religiously, but many will be resonant with the chimes of biblical associations.

Biblical images in English literature

The images of the Bible have also entered our language. Images of the garden, the tree, the apple, the snake and locked gates all appear in the first three chapters of the Bible, and all of them have haunted the imagination of English authors.

Christian interpretation of the Bible has seen patterns in these images. The tree is the one on which the forbidden fruit grew – 'whose mortal taste/Brought death into the world' (*Paradise Lost*, Book I, 2–3). The fruit of the tree brought death into the world, but in Christian iconography the tree is another name for Calvary – the cross upon which Christ died. Calvary was a place of death, but the death of Christ brings life – healing, restoration, salvation. Working on the link between the two trees, the Christian mind pictured the cross of Christ placed in what was once paradise. Bringing in St. Paul's doctrine that Christ is the second Adam (Corinthians 1 15:45–50), the place of the cross was thought of symbolically as the place where Adam died (to fall is to die). Sometimes, in pictures of the Crucifixion the skull of Adam is depicted at the foot of the cross.

This complex of ideas is the subject of the fifth stanza of John Donne's 'Hymn God my God, in my Sickness' (1633):

> We think that Paradise and Calvary,
> Christ's Cross and Adam's tree, stood in one place;

Donne relishes making connections; he thinks of Paradise and Calvary, and then before he completes his statement spells out to himself what those two names mean. Donne writes in a tradition that seizes on polarities and links, opposites and parallels. The tree and the cross are opposites – one brings life, the other death – and they are linked, because what was lost in the first is restored in the second.

The twentieth century and the Bible

T. S. Eliot's 'The Waste Land' (1922), regarded by many as the pivotal poem of the twentieth century, deploys imagery drawn from the Bible. The distinctive achievement of this poem is that it realizes the significances that traditional imagery has always had, but it comes to these significances in a contemporary way. The style of the poem is bitty and oblique, and what emerges through this shifting and unsettling kaleidoscope is a sense of spiritual drought. The people in the poem lead shallow, disturbed, fragmentary lives. They live in a spiritual desert, where there is no refreshment for the soul. This is a thoroughly biblical idea. Christ was tempted in the desert, and the soul is pictured as a deer longing for water (Psalm 42). Also deeply religious is the invitation in the first part to look under a red rock and see fear in a grain of sand. Confronting the arid landscape is a way of coming to terms with our spiritual plight. The poem ends with the promise of rain.

Summary

The imaginative force of many of Shakespeare's words and images comes from their biblical associations. Traditional Christian imagery allows poets to work with polarities and parallels. In the twentieth century, writers sought to use traditional images in contemporary ways.

▪ ☑ 30 Classical Civilization

30.1 The Classics and education

The other great influence on the language of literature is Classical civilization. This is the term we use to refer to the cultures of Ancient Greece and Ancient Rome. 'Culture' is a very broad term. It needs to be. The influence of those civilizations on Britain includes architecture, government and British ideas about history, law, philosophy, politics and sculpture as well as literature.

Schools, universities and the library

Before the twentieth century, Classical literature was handed down in two ways.

- Schools and universities taught Latin and Greek. In the Middle Ages, university education began with a three-year course of grammar, rhetoric and logic. Grammar was Latin grammar, and rhetoric was Latin style. In some cases, a young man (it was possible to go to university at the age of fourteen or fifteen) could do his grammar studies at a local school before he matriculated at university. Thus the grammar school was established. Schools would teach some Classical history and perhaps some mythology, but the main business was language. A common exercise was writing poetry in Latin; indeed, many of our poets must have written verse in Latin before they wrote in English. One of the things they were taught was regular metres. Perhaps this is why nineteenth-century poetry is so metrically fluent.
- The middle and upper classes had libraries at home. Reading for leisure and pleasure included the Classics: Catullus, Homer, Ovid and Virgil. The libraries of England's stately homes are usually stacked with Latin and Greek authors.

Translation

There is a long tradition in English writing of translating the works of Greek and Latin writers. John Dryden and Alexander Pope translated Homer's *The Iliad* and *The Odyssey* (both eighth century BC). Dryden translated Virgil's *The Aeneid* (1697) and some of the tales from Ovid's *Metamorphoses* (1693). Pope's *Iliad* was completed in (1720) and his *Odyssey* appeared in 1726. Many other poets, including Chaucer, Spenser, Marlowe, Swift and Shelley also translated Ovid's

Metamorphoses (2 AD onwards) and *Ars Amatoria* – usually called the *The Art of Love* (c. 1 BC). For Imitations of the Classics, see Chapter 24, section 24.1.

There is a popular prejudice against translation. We are inclined to think it is a lesser art. But original writing and translation have this in common: both must be written in words, and those words must shape meaning. A translation must be written in the words (including the associations, rhythms and forms) of the language into which it is rendered. In that sense, a translation is also an original work. A translation must make sense in the new language and must be judged as a work in that language. Furthermore, a translation can bring out qualities in the original and therefore be a way of understanding and appreciating the original. Once a work is translated into English, it is possible that its insights, attitudes and subject matter will become part of the way that English speakers think and feel.

Summary

Classical writers were read and studied in schools and universities. Private libraries also provided opportunities to read the Classics. There is a tradition of translating Greek and Latin authors. The work of the translator has much in common with the 'original' writer: both have to find words for what they want to say. In translation, the work of one culture enters another, and becomes part of that culture.

30.2 Classical figures

The figures of Classical literature and mythology have impressed themselves on the English imagination. For example, in *Hamlet* (1600) there are three references to Hercules, a mythic hero who performed apparently impossible deeds. In a self-deprecating joke, Hamlet says that his uncle is no more like his father than he is like Hercules (1.2. 153). The second is what might be a reference to the sign of the Globe Theatre – Hercules supporting the world (2.2. 357). The third is a more puzzling passage. Hamlet seems to be comparing Laertes to Hercules, possibly because Hercules, like Laertes, ranted (5.1. 281). It is not a compliment. The significance of these references is twofold. First, Shakespeare shows that it is natural for a character such as Hamlet to talk in this way. Second, Hercules is not presented without ambiguity. It is possible to be wary of Classical figures.

Heroes

Because of his astonishing achievements, Hercules was rewarded by becoming a god. Apotheosis (becoming a god) indicates the very elevated position that heroes had in the Classical world. The hero was far above ordinary men, and not much lower than the gods. People honour the hero because of his impressive individuality. The hero is awesome.

A hero did not need to be a warrior, but he often was. The qualities seen in battle are those appropriate to a hero; a hero is strong, skilful and inspiring to those who follow him. His moral qualities are faithfulness to his cause, determination, courage in the face of danger, and patience in his endurance of suffering.

To us, the hero also has less attractive qualities; he is haughty and disdainful. A word often used is 'proud', meaning both an offensively self-conscious awareness of superiority and the quality of standing above others.

Greek heroes

One of the subtleties of Homer's *The Iliad* is that, although it is a Greek poem, its one unquestionably heroic figure is Hector, the son of Priam, King of Troy. The poem ends with his funeral rites. Hector met his death in single combat with the Greek champion Achilles, but while Achilles, who is virtually invulnerable, wins the combat, Hector far exceeds him in personal qualities. Achilles is moody and unreliable; his motive for fighting is revenge for the death of his lover, Patroclus.

Difficulties with heroes

Achilles is representative. Writers, even when they honour heroism, often have reservations about heroes and the cult of the heroic. In English literature, the heroic was questionable because it departed radically from Christianity. Christianity values humility and compassion; it tries to nurture a sense of common humanity, and teaches the morality of placing others before oneself. In Christ, God became human, rather than, as with Hercules, a man became a god. Moreover, Christianity is sceptical of warrior cultures.

Chivalry

Yet because the heroic is alluring, Christianity tried to blend it with its own very different understanding of humanity. Christ was presented as a hero in Anglo-Saxon literature, and in the Victorian age the code of the gentleman owed a great deal to notions of heroism, in particular, the code of chivalry.

The knight, a man both brave and pious, is an idealized version of the Christian hero. He fights for good and against evil; he stands apart from others because of the degree of his courtesy, charity and compassion for the afflicted. He is humble; his manner being modest and self-effacing. With regard to women he is expected to be a chaste defender of their honour and one who rescues them when they are endangered. He is a St. George figure – a knight who rescues a young woman from a dragon. In some cases his wanderings (that is what it is to be a knight errant) become symbolic of the search for God. It is Sir Gawain who sees the Holy Grail: the cup that Christ used at the Last Supper which becomes a symbol of spiritual fulfilment. Most of Dickens' heroes strive to live according to the chivalric ideal, and Wilkie Collins creates binary opposites in *The Woman in White* (1860): the heroic Walter and the bogus knight, Sir Percival Glyde.

Reservations about the heroic

The English interest in, yet wariness of, the heroic can be seen in Shakespeare. In writing his three Roman plays – *Julius Caesar* (1599), *Antony and Cleopatra* (1606) and *Coriolanus* (1608) – he faced the problem of dealing with societies that honoured the heroic and were not Christian. The limitation is evident in the way they have no object of allegiance apart from the safety and destiny of Rome. Hence the tragedy of the republicans, Brutus and Cassius, in *Julius Caesar*, who resist unsuccessfully the inevitable movement of Rome towards a monarchy. Brutus displays a characteristic found in the other Roman plays: he frames his actions scrupulously according to the heroic code, acting from unselfish motives to maintain his public image of disinterested nobility. In *Antony and Cleopatra*, the heroic code requires Antony to be seen as a great warrior, while in *Coriolanus* it is the society that assumes that to be successful in war means that a man must take on the highest civic office. All three are presented by Shakespeare as falling conspicuously short of the heroic codes they profess, sometimes ridiculously so. For example, Antony makes a number of heroic (perhaps blustering) speeches when he faces defeat, before botching his suicide.

Shakespeare knows that the heroic code is alluring. Macbeth imagines himself as a hero. When he returns from killing Duncan, a killing that Shakespeare indicates to have been a very bloody affair, he makes, in aggressive monosyllables, this boast: 'I have done the deed' (2.2. 15). 'Deed' was the word used of the actions of a hero.

The hero king

Perhaps *Henry v* (1599) is best understood as Shakespeare's exploration of the blend of the heroic code with Christian humility. He braces his troops before Harfleur, and when their spirits have fallen he rouses them before and during the Battle of Agincourt. Yet, when disguised, he says to the honest and sceptical soldiers 'I think the King is but a man, as I am.' He adds that the violet smells the same to him as any man and that, when naked, 'he appears but a man' (4.1. 52–4).

Henry is typical of Shakespeare's heroes – we always see the man in the hero, and the man has failings.

Henry's actions have been questioned. Is his desire to know that the war against France is legal only a pretext for doing what he would do in any case? Does he betray Falstaff? Should he have shown mercy to Bardolph? Can the massacre of the prisoners be justified? For some producers, these are pressing questions. Yet Henry appears to be a humble man. Consistently, he ascribes his success to God. In what he says, he does not present himself as the self-reliant hero.

Summary

The outstanding figures of Classical literature have become part (though a morally questionable part) of English literature. The hero is central to ancient literature. However, although the hero has been influential, the figure does not always fit with Christian ideas of humility. A compromise was found in the knight. Shakespeare may be wary of the heroic in the Roman plays, and even in *Henry v.*

30.3 Classical women

In English literature, women from the Classical world have representative qualities. Ceres is the mother and the Mother Earth, Echo the female unrequited lover, and Eurydice the beloved, for whom a lover would venture even into the Underworld. Lucrece is the defiled woman who yet remains uncorrupted (see Chapter 7, section 7.4).

Helen of Troy

Above all, the classical world has given us the figure of Helen of Troy. In Helen, the two great themes of literature – love and war – are united. Paris, son of Priam, King of Troy, steals Helen from Menelaus, King of Sparta, and under Agamemnon, King of Mycenae, the Greeks sail to Troy and lay siege to the city. Troy is eventually defeated and burnt. And all for Helen.

Helen has long presented a problem for writers. Should they try to capture the wonder of this charismatic beauty, or do they suggest that, were we to meet her, we might wonder what all the fuss was about? Christopher Marlowe's Faustus took the first line: she is 'the face that launched a thousand ships', the one who can make Faustus immortal with a kiss, and is far more lovely than even the most fabulous of mythic beauties (sc. 12, 81–100). Yet Marlowe makes it clear that what Faustus sees is a devil who has assumed the appearance of Helen. Sexual intercourse with a devil (demoniality) is Faustus's final, and perhaps most corrupting, sin. Does Marlowe's presentation hint that, just as Faustus has fantasized Helen, so have we?

W. B. Yeats frequently ponders on Helen. Sometimes, she is the epitome of all beauty and a fitting object of men's strife. In 'No Second Troy' (1910) Yeats acknowledges the 'high', 'solitary' and 'stern' qualities of his beloved, a woman whose beauty is not 'natural in an age like this'. Such beauty is mythic and heroic, but in the modern world without purpose. What could she do, given that there was not 'another Troy' to burn?

The idea that Helen might have seemed a rather ordinary woman is the subject of 'When Helen Lived' (1914). The poet imagines the people of Troy meeting her as they walked its towers and giving her only 'A word and a jest'.

Summary

Many images of women are derived from Classical literature, including the defiled yet uncorrupted Lucrece, and Helen of Troy, in whom the themes of love and war are united.

30.4 Myths

The durability of myths

Classical myths exercise a compelling hold on the imagination. In schools that have abandoned the teaching of Greek and Latin, myths have retained their place in overcrowded timetables. Myths still seem to say: these can be our stories.

But what makes a myth? Myths very often have the following features:

- A striking story with a simple plot line, often based on quests and concerned with the working out of very strong compulsions – making, losing, searching, stealing, loving.
- Characters that are often non-human, and sometimes supernatural. Frequently, humans have dealings with the gods.
- Plots with decisive turning points or climaxes in which the meaning or significance of the story is revealed.
- The revelation is usually concerned with a fundamental and permanent feature of the human condition. Myths confront us with pervasive features of any and every human life, including our relationship with the Divine.
- Because myths are the shared stories of a society, they are an expression of that society's self-understanding and values.

The appeal of myths

Classical myths appear in Chaucer, Shakespeare, Milton, Pope, Wordsworth and Tennyson. In the twentieth century, W. B. Yeats wrote 'Leda and the Swan' (1928), a poem about how Zeus, in pursuit of Leda, took the form of a swan and impregnated her. The child she bore was Helen – Helen of Troy. Yeats turns the story into an exploration of the nature of myth itself: the divine meets the human and in the violent union the whole of the Trojan tragedy is conceived.

Carol Ann Duffy's *The World's Wife* (1999) re-works Classical myths from a feminist standpoint. How did all those high deeds appear from a woman's point of view? For example, she pictures Eurydice glad to be in the Underworld, free from the attentions of the poet, Orpheus. There are plenty of poems on what it is to be an unrequited lover, but a poem from the point of view of the reluctant beloved is rare.

Myths and ideas

Classical myths are sometimes used because they express with imaginative clarity ideas that writers find central to their works. Take the case of Icarus, whose father, Daedalus, made the maze where Minos of Crete kept the strange beast, the Minotaur. To escape Crete, Daedalus made wings for them both, so they could fly to freedom. Once in the air, though, Icarus couldn't resist the lure of flying, so flew very high and too near the sun. The wax holding his wings together melted, and he plunged to his death.

The myth represents the danger of ambitious pride aspiring beyond what is possible. In the Prologue to *Doctor Faustus* (1591), the Chorus uses the image of Icarus to represent the self-destructive ambitions of Faustus:

> His waxen wings did mount above his reach,
> And, melting, heaven conspir'd his overthrow
> (Prologue, 21–2)

There are limits; the wise observe them, but the foolish transgress the boundaries set by God and nature. The folly of Icarus (and of Faustus) is that he mounted 'above his reach'. The image defines the tragic plot. Faustus is the proud man who falls because he tries to rise higher than is permitted.

In 'Musée des Beaux Arts' (1938), W. H. Auden writes about the artistic representation of Icarus. In a picture by Pieter Brueghel, the fall of the aspiring Icarus happens while ordinary life is being conducted in its usual, ordinary way. Everything seems to turn away from the event, and the expensive ship, which must have seen the extraordinary sight of a boy falling out of the sky, sails on.

Extending myths

Writers draw out latent meanings in myths. Prometheus fascinated Romantic writers. There are two strands to the myth. One is that Prometheus made people, by kneading them out of clay. The other is that, in pity for humankind, he stole fire from heaven to warm them. The gods, angry that people now have what once was theirs alone, chain Prometheus to a rock. An eagle eats out his liver. In the night the liver grows again, so with the coming of the day, the eagle returns. Prometheus, then, is the maker and the saviour of mankind who is punished by the jealous gods for his compassion.

Both Mary and Percy Shelley expand and adapt this figure: she wrote *Frankenstein* (1818) and he *Prometheus Unbound* (1820). The full title of Mary Shelley's novel is *Frankenstein, or The Modern Prometheus*. Victor Frankenstein is a Prometheus figure who creates a human being. He declares: 'I became myself capable of bestowing animation upon lifeless matter' (ch. 4) He does what Prometheus did. Later, heeding the pleas of the creature he has made, he sets about making him a companion. He thereby, again like Prometheus, is intent on creating a new race. Unlike Prometheus, however, he recoils from what he has made, destroys his second creation and flees the vengeful creature he has brought into the world.

When the reader first encounters Frankenstein, his story is all but over. The tale of his creation of the monster is delivered to a ship's captain, Robert Walton, who in turn relates it to his sister, Margaret Saville. The story is, in spite of what Frankenstein intends, one of compromised motives, betrayals and irrational hatred. The monster emerges as certainly a more sympathetic and possibly a more noble creature than Frankenstein himself; he is one who has been abandoned by his creator, so takes revenge for his sufferings. Yet at the close, Frankenstein can see nothing wrong in what he has done:

> During these last few days I have been occupied in examining my past conduct, nor do I find it blameable.

> (ch. 24)

But the reader might: life is the gift of God, and Victor seizes that gift and circumvents the natural means of human procreation. He is both hero and villain.

Percy Shelley is not ambiguous about his Prometheus. In his poem, the hero is the champion of man against God. He is, effectively, a rival to Christ for the title of saviour. The poem enacts the belief that human freedom is only possible when we defy the impositions of a divine (or an imagined divine) will. The poem closes with a picture of human liberty, which requires the denial of what most people think of as a given authority: 'To defy Power which seems omnipotent'. Prometheus becomes a model of what humanity can be if only it frees itself from false beliefs.

Summary

Myths are durable. The stories are striking, the turning points significant, and the explorations of the permanent features of humanity are profound. Sometimes the myth is expressive of an idea that the writer wishes to commend. Writers also extend myths, deliberately using them for new purposes.

30.5 Philosophers and poets

Philosophy

Greece taught the Western world about philosophy. The word originally referred to what we would now call science, but with Socrates it came to mean thinking about thinking and human conduct. Socrates took as his starting point the ideas that we all have about, say, organizing society or making moral decisions. Socrates taught people to question what grounds we have for maintaining beliefs and what those beliefs in fact mean. His most celebrated follower was Plato. Plato is the philosopher who has had the most influence on the Western world. Among his many ideas is one about knowledge. How is it that we recognize things as belonging to a category? A poodle is very different from a St. Bernard, but we unhesitatingly call them both dogs. Plato advanced the belief that we know they are dogs because before we were born we saw the eternal forms of any and every kind of thing. Recognizing is a kind of remembrance. In Plato's view, the world is only a shadow of the eternal forms. Only the forms are real. To use a modern example, we are like people in a cinema who see the shadows cast on the screen by people standing in the sight line of the projector. To gain real knowledge, we need to turn away from the shadows and look at the source of light. In Plato's example, philosophy is turning away from the shadows to gaze at the sun.

This view has permeated the way we think about the world. Those distinctions we make (often when talking about books) between appearance and reality owe their interest to the fundamental Platonic insight that what we see is not the same as what is real. Take, for example, this passage from the opening of John Donne's 'The Good Morrow' (1633):

> If ever any beauty I did see,
> Which I desir'd, and got, 'twas but a dream of thee.

Whoever the poet loved before, she was, in comparison with his beloved, only a dream, and his love then was only an anticipation of what he feels now. He might have 'desir'd and got' other women, but neither they nor his love were, in the full sense of the word, real. Plato's influence is very strong. His beloved is the eternal form; others are merely reflections or anticipations – shadows – of her.

Ovid: love and transformation

As mentioned above, the Latin poet Ovid exercised a considerable influence on Western literature. The West learnt two languages from Ovid: the language of love – *Ars Amatoria* – and the language of transformation – *Metamorphoses*. The former, usually translated as *The Art of Love* or *The Art to Love*, is a series of poems about love-making. *Metamorphoses* is a collection of stories, the climaxes of which are changes in form. People are transformed into plants or trees.

The *Ars Amatoria* had a considerable impact on the development of love poetry in the later Middle Ages. The book was popular by the sixteenth century. It was erotic and entertaining. Indeed, Ovid is one of the creators of the idea of the Erotic. Part of its charm derives from it being a mockery of the poem of advice. Scientists and philosophers often used poems as a means of passing on their thinking. Ovid's poem is amusingly didactic: the poet advises his readers, not about scientific method but rather where to find girls and how to win them. Love is an art – one that people can learn. By Marlowe's time the poems were popular enough for him to quote a line from them in Faustus's closing speech. Desperate for time in which to repent, Faustus quotes Ovid's request (sc. 13, 68) that time will go slowly so that he can enjoy at leisure his night of love: 'O Lente, lente currite, noctis equi' (Run slowly, slowly, O horses of the night), he cries. Faustus's situation is fraught with irony. He quotes love poetry when he should be thinking about his soul. Moreover, in the previous scene he has deliberately avoided thinking about his sins by making love to a devil posing as Helen of Troy.

The stories from *Metamorphoses* have haunted the imagination of English writers. In particular, the figure of Orpheus has come to represent both the ardent lover and the poet. As a lover, he braves the Underworld to rescue his beloved, and as a poet he calms the spirits of the dead with his music (music is often a symbol of poetry). The influence of the *Metamorphoses* is not just a thing of the past. Seamus Heaney has written a version of the death of Orpheus, and Ted Hughes won the Whitbread Book of the Year award for his *Tales from Ovid* (1997). Perhaps these tales are popular because we recognize that change is the fundamental feature of nature. We grow up, grow old and in our deaths our bodies return to the elements – ashes to ashes, dust to dust.

Ovid has been said to be have been Shakespeare's favourite poet. Both aspects of Ovid's work appear in one of his earliest plays: *The Taming of the Shrew* (1595). Lucentio arrives in Padua with his servant, Tranio. Lucentio, full of a youthful desire to learn, talks eloquently of philosophy and virtue. Tranio reminds him tactfully that 'Ovid' should not 'be an outcast quite abjured' (1.1. 33). Within forty lines, Ovid comes into his own: Lucentio is in love. In order to be near his beloved he assumes another identity, and in doing so makes an Ovidian joke. He calls himself Cambio, which means change. Having found a way to his beloved (the arts of love include trickery), he tells her what his study is: 'I read that I profess, *The Art to Love*' (4.2. 8). At the close of the play, the theme of metamorphosis returns when assumed identities are discarded: 'Cambio is changed into Lucentio' (5.1. 111).

Summary

English ways of thinking and imagining owe much to Classical philosophy and literature. The idea that there is a gulf between appearance and reality derives from Plato's thinking about knowledge, and the Latin poet Ovid has given the West ideas about love and the importance of change.

30.6 Traditions of writing

The phrase 'traditions of writing' refers to topics writers treated, the forms they chose to write in, the ideas expressed, and the attitudes writers take regarding their subject matter. These traditions are heavily dependent on Classical writing.

Subjects and topics

Classical poets wrote about love, death, change, social life, the city and the country, and battle. We will use the last as an illustration of the way treatment of this topic has influenced writing in English. The resistance of a small force of Greeks at Thermopylae against a huge Persian army fascinates English writers, haunted as they are by stories of the few against the many. W. L. Bowles (1762–1850) translated a two-line epitaph by Simonides about how the Greek army, reduced on orders of the commander to 300 Spartans, defended the pass until death. The epitaph takes the haunting form of an apostrophe – an address to a person who is dead or absent. In Simonides, it is the dead who boldly address the living:

> Go tell the Spartans, thou that passest by,
> That here, obedient to their laws, we lie.

Such heroism gives the dead the authority to order (the mood is imperative) the living. Yet it is not bombastic. Its themes are quiet duty, tough pride and confidence in the cause. These are given dignity by the simple rhyme.

Form and genre

Most of the genres English writers have used derive from the Classics. Greece and Rome have given us the epic, the elegy, the ode, the epitaph (as in the case of Simonides) and the epigram. They have also inspired English writers to compose georgics and pastorals (see Chapter 27, sections 27.2 and 27.4).

Ideas and outlooks

Certain ways of feeling and thinking have their origins in the Classics. These might be described as themes, though they are more general and more deeply embedded in our attitudes and understanding than themes usually are. We have a strong sense of the passing of time, of the pressure (and even obligation) of revenge, and of the uncertainty of worldly success. For example, the fascination of revenge that lies behind many of the plays of the sixteenth and seventeenth centuries was given expression in the works of the Greek dramatists such as *Electra* (probably written between 418 and 410 BC) by Sophocles. There is a Classical dimension to our most powerful revenge play – *Hamlet* (1600). Though he has vowed revenge, Hamlet has not acted so feels reproved when the chief player of a strolling theatrical company delivers a speech about the revengeful Pyrrhus killing Priam, King of Troy (2.2. 452–606).

Attitudes

It is also likely, given the authority the Classics had, that their example was a validation for English writers tackling the subjects for which Classical writers have been celebrated. The expression of grief, an expression that controls rather than conceals what the poet is feeling, becomes an admired stance – a way of encountering, or facing up to, experience. English poets learned to think and feel this way from the Latin poet, Catullus. Catullus's poem on the death of his brother is one of both greeting and farewell. This attitude is echoed in Alfred, Lord Tennyson's *In Memoriam* (1850), a poem about the death of his friend, Arthur Hallam. In Poem 57 he says to his lost friend 'And "Ave, Ave, Ave," said/"Adieu, adieu" for evermore'. 'Ave' (hail) is directly from Catullus – 'ave atque vale'. Tennyson's 'adieu' is his rendering of the poignant 'vale', meaning farewell. In both, the formalities of meeting and parting become the means for the controlled expression of a farewell that is final.

The Classics at work

The influence of the Classics might best be seen in a single example. Ben Jonson wrote this moving poem on the death of his daughter, Mary (published 1616):

> On My First Daughter
> Here lies, to each her parents' ruth,
> Mary, the daughter of their youth;
> Yet, all heaven's gifts being heaven's due,
> It makes the father less to rue.
> At six months' end she parted hence
> With safety of her innocence;
> Whose soul heaven's Queen (whose name she bears),
> In comfort of her mother's tears,
> Hath placed amongst her virgin train;
> Where, while that severed doth remain,
> This grave partakes the fleshly birth;
> Which cover lightly, gentle earth.

The four characteristic influences outlined above – subject, form, idea and attitude – are present here.

As a poem of loss, Jonson's work stands in a long tradition, strongly represented in Classical writers, of meditating on the brevity of life. It is in the form of an epitaph but also has something of the pithy terseness of the epigram. In the final couplet, the idea of the earth protecting the child is strongly shaped by an epigram of the Latin poet, Martial. In Poem 34 of the fifth book of his *Epigrams* (written from 86 AD onwards), Martial wrote about the death of Erotion, a slave girl who (the poet plays with the idea) died just six days before she was six. Martial beseeches the earth to lie lightly upon her body, and in 'cover lightly, gentle earth' Jonson consciously does the same. (This Martial epigram has appealed to several poets; both Robert Louis Stevenson and the contemporary poet Peter Porter have translated it.) Finally, the blending of tenderness (towards both the child and the dumb earth) with grief is distinctly Classical. The strict form of short lines and rhyming couplets both holds back and releases the feelings of regretful loss.

Symbols

The Classics have given literature symbolic objects. Marvell, for example, employs a Classically-based symbolic shorthand. He begins 'The Garden' (c. 1650) with an image of people pursuing worldly success:

> How vainly men themselves amaze
> To win the palm, the oak, or bays

The second line neatly encapsulates the sum total of worldly achievement. The palm was given to successful soldiers; the oak was the token of a valued contribution to public life, and bay leaves (laurels) was the sign that one's poetry was esteemed. Marvell, with cool, knowing detachment, commends solitude by remarking on the trouble people give themselves in pursuing worldly ends.

A conflict

English writers were often aware that the two most potent influences on them – the Bible and the Classics – were not fully in accord. The Christian outlook owed much to the Classics, yet, when writers strove to be explicitly Christian, they were sometimes aware of sharp differences. The heroic tradition raises the problem of reconciling the two. But what writers could do was to blend Classical form and Christian content. This is what Milton did in *Samson Agonistes* (1671). *Samson Agonistes* is the biblical story of Samson, written in the form of a Greek tragedy. The poem follows the conventions of Greek tragedy, so all the action, including Samson bringing down the Temple of the Philistine god, Dagon, is reported rather than acted. In his death, Samson prefigures Christ as both saved their people. Perhaps the tension between the inappropriate form of Greek tragedy, which celebrates the self-inflicted agony of the proud man, and Christian humility gives the work its interest.

Summary

Classical literature has given English writers the authority to tackle the subjects, forms, ideas and attitudes found in Greek and Latin writers. Classical literature has provided a system of symbols and emblems. At times there is a strain, though an interesting one, between Classical and biblical traditions.

▌▾ 31 Books and Ideas

31.1 Referring to other authors

Critics now use the term *intertextuality* to denote the various relations between books. Readers who glance at the notes T. S. Eliot supplied for 'The Waste Land' (1922) can see intertextuality at work. Eliot quotes (he called it stealing) St Augustine, Baudelaire and Dante, Goldsmith, Kyd, Marvell, Shakespeare and Spenser. 'The Waste Land' can still seem a shockingly strange poem, and the shock in part derives from this mesh of quotations. The foreign ones sound like what happens when we turn the dials of a radio and pick up continental stations.

Eliot might have quoted with brazen wilfulness, but it was not a practice that he invented. Authors know they work with words, and they know too that their subject matter has already been treated by other authors. It is, therefore, natural that they should indicate this by referring to other authors' literature. Quite often the context of literature is other literature. We can ask of these intertextual links: what do these references add to the book I am reading?

Quotation

Quotation shows that an author recognizes his or her place in a tradition of writing. In Shakespeare's *As You Like It* (1599), the shepherdess, Phoebe, falls in love with Rosalind, who is disguised as a man. Once Rosalind has gone, Phoebe puts her feelings into words by quoting Christopher Marlowe:

> Dead shepherd, now I find thy saw of might:
> 'Who ever loved that loved not at first sight?'
>   (3.5. 82–3)

As it was a convention to write elegies (Marlowe died in 1593) in the form of a Pastoral (see Chapter 27), it is not surprising that Phoebe should address Marlowe as a shepherd. Moreover, Marlowe had written 'The Passionate Shepherd to his Love' (see Chapter 27, section 27.2). The quotation is from *Hero and Leander* (1598). Shakespeare is deepening the audience's sense that the Forest of Arden is a special place – an essentially (and densely) literary world, where games can be played, poetry quoted and where, at the close, the god of marriage appears to celebrate the nuptials.

Allusion

Allusion is a hint at or pointer to another literary work. Some allusions are very surprising. Macbeth is Shakespeare's most concentrated exploration of human evil, and it is to Macbeth that William Wordsworth alludes in the first book of *The Prelude* (1805). As a boy of nine, Wordsworth set snares for birds. But sometimes he stole birds that others had snared:

> And when the deed was done
> I heard among the solitary hills
> Low breathings coming after me
> (328–30)

This is a passage that tells of the terrors of childhood, of a guilt made actual in the 'low breathings' heard on a dark night. Perhaps because the guilt and the fear are overwhelming to the child, Wordsworth alludes to Macbeth's words on his return from killing Duncan: 'I have done the deed' (2.2. 15). Macbeth's hands are covered in blood. Is Wordsworth suggesting that he also has blood on his hands? Furthermore, one of the central words of Macbeth – 'fear' – is prominent in *The Prelude*. One of Wordsworth's most famous statements of his childhood is

> Fair seed-time had my soul, and I grew up
> Fostered alike by beauty and by fear
> (Book One, 305–6)

By 'fear' Wordsworth probably meant the terrors of nightmare referred to above and the experience of sublimity – the feeling of awe in the presence of anything strange, powerful and intimidating (see Chapter 26, section 26.4). Again, that sublimity is not alien to the world of *Macbeth* (1606) with its moving woods, ghosts and dark nights.

Summary

Literature can work intertextually by establishing links between works. This is often done through quotation and allusion. In both cases, we should ask what the effect is of summoning up one work while reading another.

31.2 Nature

In addition to the influences of Christian and Classical culture, there are other world views present in English literature. These 'big ideas' dominate the way successive writers approach subjects and inform the way readers respond. Four ideas will be looked at: nature, fortune, freedom and order. First, however, we need to say something about how the study of words works.

Words and meanings

As established in Chapter 28, section 28.2, literature emerges from a background of ideas and attitudes. When an idea similar to one in a literary work is found in contemporary writing (say, a book about the authority of kings) we are tempted to think that this is a key to the literary work. But we should be cautious. We cannot assume that the meaning of a word in one place is going to be *exactly* the same as its meaning in another. There is an established understanding about how meaning is created:

> When an author uses a word, that word means whatever the usage makes it mean.

Usage is meaning. A word may potentially mean a number of things, but usage – its place and function in speech or writing – is what gives it the *particular* meaning it has. This goes for all writing. A word in a literary work and the same word in contemporary writing will mean what they mean because of the particular ways in which they are used. Contemporary meanings can help us to see what *potential* a word has, and they can alert us to the meanings a word might have, but the usage – how the word is handled in its context – is what creates meaning.

Nature

'Nature' is one of the most important words of the Western world. It derives from Greek and Roman culture. Interestingly, while the Hebrew people had stories of the creation of all things, they had no word corresponding to our 'nature'. (For the many meanings of the word, see the fifty pages on 'Nature' in C. S. Lewis's *Studies in Words*, 1960.)

To us, nature is the living world and, sometimes, the energy that pulses through it. We sometimes personify the living process as 'Mother Nature', thereby regarding it as being wise and benevolent. 'Nature' is also the character of something; it is any behaviour that reveals what someone or something is like. The word can mean whatever is right. Affections within a family and the duties members recognize are said, with approval, to be natural. But there is also a minimalist usage that speaks of nature, particularly human nature, as the bare, unimproved and unenlightened stuff with which we are born. Thus, a person who has no sense is called a 'natural', and an illegitimate child was once said to be 'natural'. Another minimal view contrasts nature with grace. Nature on its own – base nature as it is sometimes called – lacks spiritual illumination, but the grace that raises it is what God gives and what God only can give. Nature, therefore, is below grace, though nature can be elevated by grace. Another contrast is between nature and civilization. Nature can mean bare, unimproved humankind.

Controversy over nature: *King Lear* (1605)

The word 'nature' appears thirty-seven times, and 'natural' twice in *King Lear*. The words are used in emotionally significant speeches and at plot turning points.

Furthermore, the idea of 'nature' is implicity present in the many images drawn from the natural world – 'the frog, the toad, the tadpole, the wall-newt' (3.4. 121).

'Nature' and 'natural' appear in many contemporary texts (for example, in sermons and political philosophies), but exactly what meanings do the words have in *King Lear*? Take the case of what the Earl of Gloucester says to his illegitimate son, Edmund, when he believes (falsely, in fact) that his legitimate son has been plotting against him. Gloucester praises Edmund by calling him a 'loyal and natural boy' (2.1. 83). Meanings abound here. Edmund is certainly 'natural' because he is illegitimate, but the use of 'loyal' indicates that Gloucester is thinking that Edmund, unlike his treacherous brother, has a right, fitting and proper affection for his father. But the audience knows that Edmund is deceiving his father, so is aware of the irony that Edmund is 'natural' in the sense of being without spiritual illumination. He is base – his nature is untouched by grace or any civilizing influence that has taught him duty. When, in the second scene, Edmund proclaims 'Nature' as his goddess, he seems to be meaning an amoral desire to thrive at others' expense.

Other meanings

The meaning of 'nature' in *King Lear* is not confined to Edmund's view of it as being morally indifferent. Lear talks of nature as a ruling presence. When his daughter, Goneril, thwarts him (she will not allow him to have a large retinue of knights as attendants) he curses her with a terrible and assured solemnity:

> Hear, nature; hear, dear goddess, hear:
> Suspend thy purpose if thou didst intend
> To make this creature fruitful.
> Into her womb convey sterility.
>
> (1.4. 254–7)

Does Lear regard nature as a goddess or a servant? He asks her to hear, but then orders her to act contrary to what is the evident purpose of the natural order. In a grotesque parody of the procreative act, he asks that, rather than the life-giving seed, sterility will be conveyed into her womb. Lear is confident that nature endorses his view. Behind that must stand the idea of nature as the foundation of society, the strong support of order in human society, and the authorization of what is good. The meaning, in short, is opposite to the way that Edmund uses it.

Nature in *King Lear* is a complex word. We might regard its several meanings as a warning against the presumption that the meaning of a significant word can be fully known *prior* to reading the text.

Summary

The meaning of a word in a text is a function of how that word is used. In the case of the word 'nature', there are several possible meanings. This diversity of meaning is explored in Shakespeare's *King Lear*.

31.3 Order

An orderly world

The assumption that the world in which we live is orderly is an ancient one. It can be found in Greek and Hebrew thought. The belief is also, as far as observation is concerned, well-founded. We live in a world of both large- and small-scale observable sequences. The sun rises and sets, and (in most cases) leaves appear on plants before flowers. Even before Isaac Newton explained the workings of the physical world (1687), the world appeared regular to anyone who looked at it. Newton asked why the apples fall as they do, but everyone knew that things fall down rather than go up. Things do not happen at random. Order in nature is often related to order in society. One way in which a prevailing order in society is validated is by appealing to its foundation in the natural world. Sometimes, writers and thinkers have enjoyed seeing order in nature and order in society as mirroring each other. Consequently, the one who disturbs social order is often presented as someone who is an enemy of nature or God.

The language of order

There is a rich language of order in English literature. A. O. Lovejoy produced a study of this very persistent idea called *The Great Chain of Being* (1936). The language of things hanging together is found in different periods of literature. In Chaucer's 'The Franklin's Tale' (c. 1390), Dorigen, a faithful wife whose husband is at sea, is distressed by the sight of dangerous rocks. She pours out her anguish as she looks down from the top of the cliff:

> 'Eterne God, that thurgh thy purveiaunce
> Ledest the world by certein governaunce'
> (135–6)

'Purveiaunce' means both foresight and providence. In his wisdom, God sees what will happen and orders it to bring good. The world is under his 'certein governaunce'; that is, his guidance of it is sure. Dorigen's question is therefore desperate: what place can these rocks have in the scheme of a good God, who wisely guides his Creation?

Order in Shakespeare

The idea of an ordered and harmonious world is central to Shakespeare's plays. In a speech from *Troilus and Cressida* (1602), Ulysses uses the word 'degree' to indicate the place that each object and person has in the universal frame of things. Order is both natural and social. The notion of everything having its own place in the universal order was one with which Shakespeare's audience would have been familiar. Critics have found similar passages in the *The Book of Homilies* of 1547 (official sermons written to promote sound doctrine), in Sir Thomas

Elyot's *Book of the Governor* (1531), and in that representative book on Anglican doctrine, Richard Hooker's *Laws of Ecclesiastical Polity* (1594). Ulysses' point is that everything in the universe observes degree:

> The heavens themselves, the planets, and this centre
> Observe degree, priority and place.
>
> (1.3. 84–5)

The idea that there were minds, or intelligences, in the stars was still available to Shakespeare, so the passage can be read as an image of the planets, including 'this centre' the earth, as spheres that courteously observe (a word used in etiquette) an eternally fixed order of precedence. Remove degree, and everything is sick:

> O when degree is shaked,
> Which is the ladder to all high designs,
> The enterprise is sick.
>
> (1.3. 101–3)

The image of the ladder makes clear the hierarchical idea of degree. Each object and person has a place, so to speak, on a ladder. Wherever we are, we can look up or down.

The imagery of order

Another image of order is the music of the spheres. With the movement of the various spheres that constitute the universe and control the rotations of planets and stars, a heavenly music was created. Shakespeare introduces the image into a love scene between Jessica and Lorenzo in *The Merchant of Venice* (1596). Lorenzo explains to Jessica that, in its movement, each star sings like an angel:

> There's not the smallest orb which thou behold'st
> But in his motion like an angel sings
>
> (5.1. 60–1)

The rhythm of the words climaxing on 'sings' suggests that the lines are delivered as a love song, which expresses the consoling idea that in the mighty system of the universe even the 'smallest orb' has a voice.

A very fully worked-out doctrine of the order of the world is found in Alexander Pope's *Essay on Man* (1733), a long poem of over 1300 lines, divided into four epistles. The tone is philosophical and didactic. The poet instructs and uplifts. The closing lines of the first epistle are concerned with the idea that the order of nature is so complete and right that, were we to see it whole, we would see that it is good:

> All discord, harmony not understood;
> All partial evil, universal good:
> And, spite of pride, in erring reason's spite,
> One truth is clear, Whatever is, is right.

The lines are balanced, and on each side of the caesura there are polarities – discord and harmony, evil and good. But the polarities are apparent rather than real. The truth – insisted upon in the threefold repetition of the word 'is' – stands beyond contrasts. There is only one truth, and that is that what is, is right; the order of the world is moral as well as physical.

Discord

Pope's polarities enforce a point that was evident in some of the passages quoted above. We become more conscious of order when it is threatened. The rocks in 'The Franklin's Tale' are a sign of disorder. In theological terms they present the problem of evil: how can there be suffering in a world made by a good God? 'Discord' is opposite to 'harmony'. Ulysses' speech in *Troilus and Cressida* includes this statement:

> Take but degree away, untune that string,
> And hark what discord follows.
>
> (1.3. 108–9)

The tension between order and disorder was an urgent matter for Tennyson. In 'Locksley Hall Sixty Years After' (1886) he twice patterns the polar words – 'Chaos' for disorder and 'Cosmos' for order: 'Chaos, Cosmos, Cosmos, Chaos' (103, 129). This *chiasmus* (a figure of speech in which the second half of a statement reverses the first) can be read as a disorder always enclosing order, or a process of order replacing disorder before disorder returns.

Political order

It is a characteristic of modern literary criticism to stress the political aspects of ideas. Order, in this view, is fundamentally order in society. It is concerned with the exercise of authority and power, with whatever those ruling do to bolster their regimes.

Several of the passages quoted above have a political dimension. Ulysses' speech is about order in the universe, but the reason he makes it is to quell disorder in the ranks of the Greek army. He claims that Troy would have fallen except that

> The speciality of rule hath been neglected,
> And look how many Grecian tents do stand
> Hollow upon this plain, so many hollow factions.
>
> (1.3. 77–9)

'Speciality' means a legally binding contract or obligation, so 'The speciality of rule' is the duty a subject owes to a ruler. This contract has broken down, so, playing on two meanings of 'hollow, Ulysses says that hollow (false) factions have made soldiers leave, so that the tents are 'hollow' – empty. Consistently throughout his very long speech, Ulysses speaks of division in the Greek camp: 'This chaos, when degree is suffocate,/Follows the choking' (1.3. 124–5).

A frequent image in seventeenth-century drama was that of corruption spreading from the Court to the whole of society. The image of the poisoned fountain is present in the opening scene of Webster's *The Duchess of Malfi* (1623):

> a Prince's court
> Is like a common fountain, whence should flow
> Pure silver-drops in general. But if't chance
> Some curs'd example poison't near the head,
> Death and diseases through the whole land spread.
> (1.1. 11–15)

Water flows everywhere ('in general'), so if the court gives a corrupt 'example' of behaviour, then the whole country (that is, the whole of society) will be poisoned.

King Lear is preoccupied with threats to civil order. The plot traces a series of disintegrations. Lear's family is divided, the consequence of which is a split in the nation and then, as a result of the initial family split, war between Britain and France. These social divisions are matched by Lear's madness and the storm – the madness of nature. The cause of disorder is Lear's failure to carry the burden of kingship. Kings should not abdicate. Because Lear does, all order – both social and natural order – breaks down.

Characters and disorder

Because the breakdown of order is a common theme, certain kinds of character recur in literature. In sixteenth- and seventeenth-century literature it was the Machiavel – the unscrupulous manipulator – or the Malcontent – the one who, because he resents his failure to rise, is willing to destroy order in society through deceit and murder. Bosola in *The Duchess of Malfi* is an example.

Summary

Order, which is grounded in nature, is often expressed in the image of music. In some literature, order is felt to be in danger from encroaching chaos. Order was seen in political terms and certain figures – the Machiavel and the Malcontent – were identified as agents of disorder.

31.4 Fortune

Ups and downs

Not everything in the world works in an orderly fashion. We wonder why things happen to some people and not to others. We still ask: why do some people have all the luck? Good or bad luck seems arbitrary. Even when we have reckoned with the social circumstances into which we are born, or natural features (looks, health and strength), the ups and downs of individual lives remain a mystery.

The wheel of fortune

In the late Middle Ages and the early modern period (sixteenth and seventeenth centuries) the image that helped people to make sense of the sometimes apparently random events of life was the wheel of fortune.

Fortune was female; she wore a blindfold and she operated a wheel. The wheel controlled individual fortunes. We might start at the top and then, as the wheel turned, our fortunes would decline until we ended at the bottom. From there we might rise to former prosperity. (The idea is still with us; there was a song called 'The only way is up'.)

There is no reason in Fortune's choices. She is discussed in characteristically pedantic detail, by Fluellen in *Henry V* (1599):

> Fortune is painted blind, with a muffler afore her eyes, to signify to you that Fortune is blind. And she is painted also with a wheel, to signify to you – which is the moral of it – that she is turning and inconstant and mutability and variation.

> (3.6. 29–32)

Fluellen's insistence on 'painted' is correct; there were painted models of Fortune, representing the blind goddess turning her wheel at will. She causes change ('mutability'). Fluellen gives this little lecture on Fortune, because Pistol, lamenting the misfortune of his friend Bardolph, blames Fortune. Fluellen explains that it is not a matter of blame; it is simply the way in which she works. (Bardolph's plight, as it happens, is not a matter of fortune; he has been caught stealing and is condemned to die for his crime.)

Fortune and Tragedy

The image of Fortune contributes to our idea of Tragedy. The tragic hero/victim is one who starts at the top of the wheel and, often by forces beyond his/her control, ends at the bottom. It is the simplest and one of the oldest understandings of Tragedy – the fall from prosperity to adversity (see Chapter 20, section 20.6).

Stage action sometimes clearly presents the fall of the tragic figure in contrasting tableaux. Lear is a despotic king in the first scene and a naked old man sharing a hovel with a mad beggar in Act 3. Kings fall. Richard II rules as if he were Fortune herself – England being subject to his despotic whims – but he dies by an assassin's knife in prison. Presented most graphically is the commanding figure of Julius Caesar, with imperial aplomb, rejecting the suit of Metellus Cimber and then, within five lines, lying dead at the foot of Pompey's statue (3.1. 73–7).

Joking about fortune

Characters joke about fortune. Because Fortune is female and fickle, she is commonly called a strumpet (prostitute). Lear calls her 'that arrant whore' (2.5. 51), and in *Hamlet* (1600) there is a bawdy conversation between the Prince,

Rosencrantz and Guildenstern about how the latter two live neither on the 'button' of her cap (at the very top) nor on the 'soles' of her feet (the very bottom) but 'in the middle of her favours'. This leads to a pun on 'privates' (people without an office or job, and the sex organs). Hamlet adds that she is 'a strumpet'. It is one of those dialogues that reminds us that the play is about young men.

Talking about Fortune

In his most searching moments, Shakespeare exposes our dependence upon the essentially simple idea of Fortune's wheel. In *King Lear* (1605), Kent, suffering the misfortune of being put in the stocks, robustly asks Fortune to 'turn thy wheel' (2.2. 164). Edmund, at the end of his life, acknowledges that his opponent 'hast this fortune on me' (5.3. 156) and, shortly afterwards, on hearing of the fate of his father, he employs the image with a sure sense of dramatic appropriateness: 'The wheel has come full circle' (5.3. 165).

But in one searing scene, the image is subverted. Edgar has survived the storm in which, playing a mad beggar, he has seen the mad king. He confidently (and perhaps smugly) cheers himself up with the reflection (he is a character who tries to think about what is happening) that since he has reached the bottom, he can only rise:

> To be worst,
> The low'st and most dejected thing of fortune,
> Stands still in esperance, lives not in fear.
> The lamentable change is from the best;
> The worst returns to laughter.
>
> (4.1. 2–6)

The superlative – best, worst – is, by definition, a limit. Nothing can be worse than the worst. But then his father enters – blinded and led by an Old Man. Edgar realizes that we cannot reason about experience merely on grammatical grounds; there is no circumstance in which one can say: 'this is the worst': 'Who is't can say "I am at the worst" ?/I am worse than e'er I was' (4.1. 25–6). Perhaps there is no superlative, just an endless series of comparatives – worse and worse and worse…. If we can never say: 'this is the worst', then we have no use for the image of the wheel of fortune.

Summary

The apparently random events in life were understood in the Medieval and early modern periods as being the work of Fortune. Fortune was imagined as a blindfolded female figure who, by turning her wheel, precipitated individuals into better or worse circumstances. The image lies behind the idea of the tragic fall. In Shakespeare, characters appeal to, joke about and meditate on fortune.

31.5 Freedom

Choice and determinism

In *Twelfth Night* (1599), Malvolio reflects that 'all is fortune' (2.5. 22). One might note that if he really were a Puritan, rather than someone adopting a Puritan manner, he would say that all was Providence – God's ordering of the world. But, in any case, authors (as well as Puritans) have insisted that our lives are *not* entirely subject to fortune. We can choose.

We need to be clear about the terms. *Determinism* is the belief that we have no freedom of choice. All our actions are the results of a chain of causes, which operate without exception and are beyond our control. Against determinism is *freedom* – the view that we are the authors of our own actions. The issue of determinism or freedom intrigues people. It is probably the one question of philosophy with which the general public is consistently concerned, and it has a central place in literature.

The will

Sometimes the individual will is the subject of a work. In *The Spire* (1964), William Golding presents a central character, who exerts his will over those close to him so that the cathedral of which he is Dean can have a magnificent spire. In one of the crucial scenes, Jocelin uses words such as 'dare' and 'faith' to persuade Roger Mason, the man in charge of the building, that, in spite of signs of collapse, they must carry on building. The novel calls into question the danger of the selfish will, but for that will to be effective (and, as Golding shows, to do considerable moral damage), it must be free.

Freedom bestows dignity. Could we really be engaged by the painful struggles of tragic figures – of Hamlet or Juliet – unless we believed that they were free to do the terrible things they contemplated?

The stars

The view that we are controlled by forces beyond us is found in *King Lear*. Reflecting on the difference between Cordelia and her two evil sisters, Goneril and Regan, Kent says:

> It is the stars,
> The stars above us govern our conditions,
> Else one self mate and make could not beget
> Such different issues.
>
> (4.3. 33–6)

The cadence falls regretfully from the first to the second mention of the stars. There is a sad resignation (not typical of Kent) that comes with the acceptance that forces beyond our control shape our destinies.

John Webster uses the image of tennis balls for the way the stars control us. In an enclosed tennis court, the balls bounce, apparently at random, off the walls:

> We are merely the stars' tennis-balls, struck and banded
> Which way please them
>
> (*The Duchess of Malfi*, 5.4. 53–4)

These remarks are painfully wrung from Bosola on the discovery that he has killed the wrong man. The stars have so struck him that he has struck the wrong man.

Natural history

Deterministic interpretations of human behaviour, in part influenced by Charles Darwin, were taken very seriously in the nineteenth century. Natural history, as Gillian Beer has shown in *Darwin's Plots* (1983), provided novelists with images and analogues for understanding human life.

Sometimes, novelists treat the lives of central characters in terms of the birth, flourishing and decay of the individual member of a species. Thomas Hardy views his characters in these terms. Tess grows, suffers a setback, flourishes again, is blighted, and struggles against decline until she finally succumbs. Hardy resorts to the images of natural growth. After the death of her illegitimate child, Tess spends the winter mouths at home, but with the coming of spring 'some spirit within her rose automatically as the sap in the twigs' (ch. 15, *Tess of the d'Urbervilles*, 1891). In the following chapter, Hardy sees Tess and all living things as being subject to the force that runs though nature:

> The irresistible, universal, automatic tendency to find sweet pleasure some-where, which pervades all life, from the meanest to the highest, had at length mastered Tess.

Tess is presented in terms that belong to natural history.

Fatalists

Because Hardy is so influenced by the science of his day, he is sometimes regarded as a determinist or fatalist. Certainly, his characters do have the most awful luck. Also inescapable is the voice he occasionally adopts of the gloomy sage reflecting on destiny. But Hardy is not an easy author to classify. In *Tess of the d'Urbervilles*, for example, there are dramatic turning points – her violation by Alec, her confession to Angel, the murder of Alec. Is this some superintending Fate, the action, to recall the language of the book's close, of 'the President of the Immortals', who is sporting with Tess? Or is it significant that while the reader knows that those events have taken place, they are never presented directly? Is Hardy deliberately omitting them to avoid the iron certainty that a deterministic causal chain is at work? In one of the events – her violation (ch. 11) – Hardy resorts not to assertions about fate or destiny, but to a series of (genuinely?) puzzled questions:

> Why it was that upon this beautiful feminine tissue, sensitive as gossamer, and practically blank as snow as yet, there should have been traced such a

coarse pattern as it was doomed to receive; why so often the coarse appropriates the finer thus, the wrong man the woman, the wrong woman the man, many thousand years of analytical philosophy have failed to explain to our sense of order.

The narrator is emphatic: no satisfactory explanation has ever been given as to why these things happen. Even in his darkest moments, Hardy might be suggesting that literature, unlike science, is not about explanations but about giving as fully as it can the experiences of life that make us seek explanations.

Summary

People have long been fascinated by the question as to whether we are free to act or our lives are determined by forces we cannot control. The assumption that we are free makes the will an important subject in literature. Knowing that characters are free to do what they choose bestows on them the dignity of being responsible agents. Science has often provided the images for a deterministic view of life, whether it be the stars or the natural processes of the living world.

▣ ✔ 32   The Arts

32.1   Literature, the arts and context

A point about study

When we think about literature in relation to the other Arts, we are doing something slightly different from considering how literature draws on a background of the Bible, Classical culture and ideas about the world. In those cases, language provides a direct link between the context and literature. 'Nature', for example, is a word, so scholars can explore how the words authors use to talk about it are linked to the words that contemporary authors use to think about the same, or very similar, issues.

But in the case of the Arts, there is no direct language link. Instead, we have to look for how literature and the other Arts express the attitudes and feelings of the age in which they were composed. A consideration of the Arts does not 'explain' an aspect of literature; rather it might bring out something in literature that it shares with the culture from which it arose. We must be careful how we put this idea. There was not one thing called 'culture' and another thing called 'literature'. Instead, we should think of literature and the other Arts as sharing certain outlooks and values – outlooks and values that exist, and only exist, in those works of art. And, of course, they exist in those works of art in a variety of ways. Works of art from one period do not express exactly the same thing. Yet works that emerge from the same cultural context have things in common. We might describe this by saying that they have a similar 'accent'. Hearing that accent in works that emerge from the same context can help us to appreciate what that particular culture was like. Moreover, a look at the Arts – at painting, architecture and music – can enable us to see more clearly what is going on in the plays, novels or poems of the same period.

Summary

There is no direct language link between literature and the other Arts, but a study of them can help us to appreciate the context in which literature is written, and bring out certain features of a literary work.

32.2 Painting

Painting and writing

There is a long-established link between art and literature. The seventeenth-century emblem books used symbolic images to accompany poems. Novels, particularly in the nineteenth century, were illustrated, and Dickens, in his working notes for novels, described his visual settings as pictures. Furthermore, there have been writers who were also artists. Edward Lear, who invented the limerick, illustrated his comic poems and painted atmospheric watercolours of Italian scenes. Dante Gabriel Rossetti, one of the founders of the Pre-Raphaelites (a group of painters who aspired to recapture the light-filled world of late Medieval art) was also a poet. Something of Pre-Raphaelitism emerges in his 'The Blessed Damozel' (1850). In the nineteenth stanza, he imagines ladies sitting in a grove:

> Circlewise sit they, with bound locks
>   And foreheads garlanded;
> Into the fine cloth white like flame
>   Weaving the golden thread

The ritualistic arrangement in a circle, the garlands, the fine cloth and the golden thread are aspects of a dream world, which, nevertheless, is created in sharply pictured details. His sister, Christina Rossetti, with her crisply delineated images, her feel for narrative and her ritualized settings (see the second stanza of 'A Birthday') is consistently Pre-Raphaelite.

The Pre-Raphaelites are examples of how literature influenced art. They took as their subject matter the poems of John Keats, and were not the only Victorian painters to be influenced by literature. One of the chief modes of painting was narrative. Painters pictured crises, turning points, moments of moral dilemma and significant departures and arrivals. The viewer has to piece together the story from the signs given in the picture. Viewing art in such cases becomes very close to literary interpretation.

Writers, painters and landscape

Some literary works and paintings share a similar interest in their subject matter. A good example of this convergence of interest is landscape painting. Poetic and painterly interest in the landscape grew up in the eighteenth century. Alexander Pope wrote 'Windsor-Forest' (1713), and William Cowper found poetic material in the ancient 'Yardley Oak' (1792).

Cowper's poem is an example of an emphasis in landscape writing that became more evident towards the end of the century – the presentation of wild, uncultivated landscapes. The epitome of this interest is William Wordsworth, who in *The Prelude* (1805) wrote of the mountains in his native Lake District and the Alps. His literary interest was reflected in the work of Richard Wilson, who painted the lakes and mountains of Wales. Wales is also the setting for the last book of *The Prelude*, in which the poet climbs Snowdon. Later than Wilson,

John Constable painted the landscapes of Essex, Suffolk and Hampshire; the Norwich School (John Sell Cotman, John Crome) painted Norfolk – its old mills, gates and heaths – and J. M. W. Turner, an impressionist (and much more) long before Monet painted wild scenery in both Great Britain and on the Continent.

Vistas

Both writers and painters enjoyed vistas: rolling landscapes stretching out into a sunfilled or misty distance. Wordsworth often locates an incident in a landscape that folds round to form a sort of huge arena. When, for example, he writes about himself skating, the scene is enclosed by a succession of cliffs. It is tempting to see in these awesome and consoling vistas a visible manifestation of the all-pervading spirit of nature, about which Wordsworth writes so often. In the first book of *The Prelude*, Wordsworth writes of how, as a child, he played in the open air. He bathed in a mill-race, ran across fields

> or, when crag and hill,
> The woods, and distant Skiddaw's lofty height,
> Were bronzed with a deep radiance, stood alone
> Beneath the sky, as if I had been born
> On Indian plains
>
> (298–302)

The heights of Skiddaw, coloured by the radiance of the sun, form a vast backdrop to the image of the small child at play. In his adult imagination, Wordsworth, perhaps stirred by the evocative memories of sun-bronzed Skiddaw, sees his former self as a native on the wide plains of America.

Details

Both painters and poets also pay attention to the details of landscape and thereby bring out its textures. John Constable and J. M. W. Turner captured the effects of light on water, and the Norwich School of painters brought out the pleasing effects of moss, tufts of grass and bramble. In the first book of *The Prelude*, Wordsworth records how he climbed crags:

> when I have hung
> Above the raven's nest, by knots of grass
> And half-inch fissures in the slippery rock
> But ill-sustained
>
> (341–4)

He is 'ill-sustained' for it seems that the only thing that holds him in place is the wind. Pinned against the crag, he sees tiny details – the knots of grass and the crevices in the face of the rock. The scene has something of the preoccupation with detail found in watercolour paintings.

Ways of seeing

We need to be taught to see that some things are worth looking at, and that there are ways in which things can be seen. At one time, the wild landscapes discussed above were not considered to be of interest. People had to be led into seeing that there is an attraction in whatever is gnarled, rugged, rough and untamed. Again, it was events in the eighteenth century that developed visual taste. For example, the rather English enjoyment of ruins was something that only became widespread in the latter decades of the eighteenth century.

Enjoying ruins was part of a wider interest in Picturesque Landscape. 'Picturesque' should be understood literally; people came to see that woods, hills, fields and rivers could be looked at as if they were in a picture. There were travel books that advised people what to look for in a landscape. The most famous author of such books was William Gilpin. In 1786, he published one on the Lake District. He would recommend his readers to find a particular spot from where they could enjoy the 'prospect' – a scene that pleased because it had picturesque qualities.

A picturesque scene was appreciated through understanding how the elements in it combined to produce a pleasing sight. The capacity of a landscape to be seen in these terms was called its 'capability'. The word was also used of landscape gardening – the art of making a landscape (usually that in a private estate) more attractive. The most famous landscape gardener was called 'Capability' Brown. Viewers of a landscape learnt to appreciate the way things in the foreground – trees, bushes – might form a sort of frame (as in a picture frame) through which the middle ground and background could be viewed. Features on the edge of vision such as a wood, a house or a fence could also give definition to the scene. The background, as in Wordsworth, was often heightened and given dignity and repose by hills and mountains.

Talk of landscape

The Tilneys (Henry and Eleanor) in Jane Austen's *Northanger Abbey* (1818) are well-read in the literature of picturesque landscape. On a walk with Catherine (the heroine) to Beechen Cliff (ch. 14), a place from which the prospect of Bath can be enjoyed, they talk about the capabilities of the landscape for drawing:

> They were viewing the country with eyes of persons accustomed to drawing, and decided on its capability of being formed into pictures, with all the eagerness of real taste.

Jane Austen is aware of how ways of viewing are acquired. It is because the Tilneys draw and have learnt the language of the picturesque (both were part of middle-class culture) that they can see the capabilities in the landscape. Catherine confesses that she would like to draw, and 'a lecture on picturesque landscape immediately followed' from Henry:

> He talked of foregrounds, distances, and second distances – side-screens and perspectives – lights and shades; – and Catherine was so hopeful a scholar

that when they gained the top of Beechen Cliff, she voluntarily rejected the whole city of Bath as unworthy to make part of a landscape.

That passage shows us a great deal: Catherine learns quickly and applies what she has learnt in her, perhaps over-eager, judgement. It also shows that the language of the picturesque was complex, and that acquiring it enabled one to see the world in new terms. There is also a possible analogy between reading a landscape and the readings one must make of people and the morality of their actions. Indeed, 'learning to see' is one of the main themes of Jane Austen.

Art and literary presentation

Some of the ways in which art presents its subject matter have links with literature. In Chapter 17 of *Adam Bede* (1859), George Eliot says that if we examine our words we will see that 'it is a very hard thing to say the exact truth'. She then writes about the delight she takes in Dutch painting:

> It is for this rare, precious quality of truthfulness that I delight in many Dutch paintings, which lofty-minded people despise. I find a source of delicious sympathy in these faithful pictures of a monotonous homely existence…

George Eliot is using Dutch painting as a guide and an implicit standard of judgement for her own writing. She, like the painters, aims at truthfulness, and this truthfulness requires a careful attention to what is familiar and even, as far as art is concerned, unpromising – 'monotonous homely existence'. She goes on to give instances of Dutch subject matter – 'an old woman bending over her flower-plot' and 'that village wedding, kept between four brown walls'. 'Brown' is exactly right; it is the colour that predominates in Dutch painting and it brings out the unspectacular ordinariness of daily life that George Eliot takes as her material.

Twentieth-century art

The theories and techniques of twentieth-century art have had an influence on literature. Kurt Schwitters invented collage – the blending in one picture of scraps of paper to form a composition. There is a nostalgic air about Schwitters' art – the bus and theatre tickets suggest happy, and possibly emotionally significant, times remembered. There is, in some sections, a similar feeling in T. S. Eliot's 'The Waste Land' (1922) – a collage of quotations, voices, memories and incomplete narratives. After the sonorous opening section, there is a memory of life in a spa. In a sudden shower of rain that ushers in the summer, the people walk into the Hoftgarten, where they drink coffee and talk. Were this a Schwitters collage, there would be the bill for the coffee somewhere in the composition. This memory passes into another. Marie remembers her childhood at the archduke's and of how, accompanied by an unspecified 'he', she goes out at night to sledge in the snow. From the conventional sentiment of feeling free in the mountains, the voice returns soberly to her life in which she now reads for much of the night and goes south in the winter.

The art movement that dominated the first decades of the twentieth century was Cubism – the presentation of solid forms as if they were cuboid. Isaac Rosenberg, painter and poet, served in the First World War and brought the angularity of cubism to his subject matter. This is the opening of 'Marching' (1916):

> My eyes catch ruddy necks
> Sturdily pressed back –
> All a red brick moving glint.

Rosenberg presents the marching soldiers from the perspective of one who is part of the group. In front are the ruddy necks pressed back so that they, in the incisive and unexpected image, glint like a red brick (wall?). The reduction of people to rectangular shapes is similar to the cubist reduction of physical objects to a series of planes.

Surrealism

Surrealism was chiefly an art movement, with Salvador Dali, Max Ernst and René Magritte as its leading painters. It explored dreams and fantasies, and exulted in the free, essentially irrational, juxtapositions of unrelated objects. The movement had political aspects (revolution through the destabilizing of the familiar) and depended heavily on Sigmund Freud's theories of the unconscious and dreams. The First World War was probably another influence. Its bizarre sights – dismembered horses stuck in trees and graveyards blown up (a subject that, according to Edmund Blunden in *Undertones of War*, 1928, fascinated the soldiers) – were the stuff of surrealism. Wilfred Owen's 'The Show' (1917) – a battle-field seen from above – might properly be described as surreal (see Chapter 14, section 14.3). Although some French authors attempted surrealistic writing, the link between art and literature is not significant in Surrealism. The term, how-ever, is useful when discussing writing that presents arrestingly odd images. As an adjective, the term can be applied to writing dating to before the 1920s. Look, for example, at this passage from Chapter 52 of Thomas Hardy's *Tess of the d'Urbervilles* (1891). Tess's family, having lost their home, unload their belongings in a churchyard:

> Tess gazed desperately at the pile of furniture. The cold sunlight of this spring evening peered invidiously upon the crocks and kettles, upon the bunches of dried herbs shivering in the breeze, upon the brass handles of the dresser, upon the wicker cradle they had all been rocked in, and upon the well-rubbed clock face, all of which gave out the reproachful gleam of indoor art-icles abandoned to the vicissitudes of a roofless exposure for which they were never made.

Domestic goods in a churchyard looks like the subject of a René Magritte painting – the surreal juxtaposition of the belongings of the living and the resting places of the dead. The objects 'gleam' reproachfully, as if they are uncomfortably aware of being out of place.

Pictures in literature

Genteel ladies in Jane Austen's age were expected to draw. The Tilney brother and sister, as noted above, looked at landscape with eyes of those who composed pictures. Elinor in *Sense and Sensibility* (1811) draws, as does Emma Woodhouse. One of the achievements of *Emma* (1816) is that of using the features of everyday life to establish plot significances. Jane Austen finds the universal in the parochial. Emma offers to draw her newly adopted friend, Harriet, and the responses aroused in two men are indicative of their attitudes towards and interest in Emma. The effusive Mr Elton, whom the reader sees has hopes of Emma, can see nothing in it to criticize, but Mr Knightley, family friend, relative by marriage and wealthy landowner, can see faults in the drawing, as he can see faults in Emma's conduct (ch. 6).

Jane Eyre's paintings may be revelations of her inner world. In Chapter 13 of *Jane Eyre* she shows Mr Rochester three watercolours. The first is a shipwreck with a cormorant – 'dark and large' – sitting on an almost completely submerged mast with a bracelet in its beak, which has been torn from a corpse 'glanced through the green water'. The second is of a hill, a vast sky and rising into it a form of a woman, her forehead 'crowned with a star'. The final one is also of a figure and a landscape: a colossal black-turbaned head and an iceberg. There follows a brief, inconclusive conversation about the state of mind Jane was in when she painted them. The images are akin to John Martin's pictures of apocalypse and tumult. Some prints of Martin's work hang in the Parsonage at Haworth, where the Brontës were brought up.

It might also be observed that the form of Auden's 'Musée des Beaux Arts', discussed in Chapter 30, section 30.4, provides a poetic equivalent of the principle of the golden section. This is a mathematical theory about constructing pleasing compositions. Roughly speaking, it says that a figure placed just over a third of the way from the canvas edge looks correct and attracts the viewer's attention. The golden section can be expressed as a fraction: 8 over 21. Auden's poem is 21 lines long, and the last section on Brueghel's *Icarus* consists of 8 lines.

Summary

Painting is linked to literature in a number of ways. Both can show an interest in landscape – in both vistas and tiny details – and there is sometimes a sharing of artistic ideas and techniques. In the twentieth century, this sharing was evident in the way writers made use of collage, cubism and surrealistic effects. Sometimes, painting forms the subject matter of books. The art and literature of a period often reflect common interests.

32.3   Architecture

Invisible buildings

Wordsworth's poem of 1798, 'Tintern Abbey' (the original title is far longer), is interesting in that the Abbey does not appear in the poem. Such neglect of buildings is not unusual in literature. When Larkin in 'Church Going' (1955) says that somebody must know whether the roof of the church has been cleaned or restored but that he doesn't, he is voicing the situation of many of us – our education does not usually include a knowledge of architecture.

There are, of course, exceptions. William Makepeace Thackeray designed his own house, and Thomas Hardy practised architecture for a number of years. Contemporary architectural theory may have influenced Hardy. There was a vogue for mixing different styles in a single building, called Eclecticism. In his novels, Hardy also mixes styles: the local historian, the connoisseur of art and literature, the gloomy philosopher, the Gothic sensationalist, the keen observer of the natural world, and the ballad maker who tells dramatic local tales of misfortune.

Making architecture central

Yet there are books that take seriously the fact that we live in buildings. Emily Brontë's *Wuthering Heights* (1847) takes its title from a building – an old farmhouse placed high up on a Yorkshire hillside – which is the home of the heroine, a home that, emotionally, she can never leave.

Emily Brontë brings out the potential that buildings have in fiction. Very early on, for instance, when Lockwood, the primary narrator, visits Wuthering Heights, the reader is invited to see a link between the house and the occupant – Heathcliff. In the first paragraph, Lockwood says of Heathcliff that 'his black eyes withdraw so suspiciously under their brows', and later in the chapter he says of the house that 'the narrow windows are deeply set in the wall'. This physical resemblance prepares us for other ways in which character and building are mirrored. Both are remote, wild, associated with violent weather, and have a history of tempestuous passions.

Emily Brontë exploits the physical features of houses. She knows the significances of thresholds, doors and windows, and she is very careful in her location of characters within rooms. Moreover, a reading of this most carefully designed novel allows the reader to see which events took place in which rooms. This is evident near the start, when Lockwood is put into a room that had been Catherine's and which, when she was a child, she shared with Heathcliff. It is the same room from which, much later, her daughter, also called Catherine, escapes to see her dying father. When Lockwood is in the room (Chapter 3), there is a strange visitation – a child at the window. The child cannot get in, because the window has been soldered closed. Heathcliff, aroused by Lockwood's cries, thinks that this visitant is the long-dead Catherine. It is only much later, after the younger Catherine's escape, that the reader might deduce that the window has been soldered closed to prevent further escapes. So preventing the daughter getting out also prevents the mother getting in.

The incident about the window brings out the politics of space. Emily Brontë's chief architectural interest is space. She recognizes how we use it to exert authority over others. After Catherine has married and moved to the Grange, Heathcliff returns. Edgar becomes uneasy about his visits, so on one occasion he orders Nelly, the nurse, to fetch some men to eject Heathcliff. Catherine reacts by locking the door and defiantly throwing the key, a symbol of authority, into the fire (Chapter 11).

Classical and Gothic

Architectural style is a matter of what buildings look like and the ideas we have about their significance. The issue of an appropriate style was important to architects and architectural theorists in the late eighteenth and nineteenth centuries. Some favoured Classical architecture and others valued Gothic. Classical architecture makes symmetrical use of columns, and its openings – doors and windows – have straight heads. Gothic, by contrast, has pointed doors and windows, and is often irregular in its planning. Classical architecture was often thought of as severe, public, respectable and orderly, whereas Gothic was fanciful, romantic and, given its literary associations, imaginative. A famous example of the debate about the respective virtues of the style occurred in 1857, when George Gilbert Scott submitted Gothic plans for the Foreign Office building in Whitehall. A parliamentary debate, known as 'the battle of the styles', followed. The Classicists eventually won, and in 1861 Scott designed a building in the Classical/Renaissance manner.

Dickens and architectural debate

Three years before 'the battle of the styles', Dickens used the terms of the dispute to support the central point of *Hard Times* (1854). This novel is a moral tract against education that neglects the imagination. In the third chapter, Dickens makes use of the contemporary interest in architectural style to characterize the two sides of this starkly polarized novel. On one side stands Mr Gradgrind, the MP who supervises the model school in which facts are taught and the imagination scorned. He embodies the theory of Utilitarianism – the belief that moral decisions can be made by calculating the amount of happiness that an action will bring about. In Chapter 3, he goes home to Stone Lodge:

> A great square house, with a heavy portico darkening the principal windows, as its master's heavy brows overshadowed his eyes. A calculated, cast up, balanced, and proved house. Six windows on this side of the door, six on that side; a total of twelve in this wing, a total of twelve in the other wing; four and twenty carried over to the back wings.

As with Heathcliff and Wuthering Heights, Mr Gradgrind's house is a reflection of its owner. Furthermore, its remorseless symmetry expresses Mr Gradgrind's belief that life can be reduced to numbers. Dickens mischievously introduces arithmetic!

By contrast, and within two pages, we see the 'wooden pavilion' in which the horse-riding establishment has been set up. Horse-riding is the epitome of life lived according to the imagination. Dickens' choice of architectural style is significant. Beneath a flag, there sits the owner:

> Sleary himself, a stout modern statue with a money-box at its elbow, in an ecclesiastical niche of early Gothic architecture, took the money.

Gothic here is the architecture of whim and fancy and perhaps also, given the reference to the church ('ecclesiastical'), a deeper sort of seriousness than that offered by Gradgrind's Utilitarianism. Dickens is careful to avoid the accusation of being impractical; Sleary sits in his exotic Gothic niche to collect money.

Summary

Although architecture is not a prominent feature in much literature, some writers understand how we use space and how it expresses authority and power. In nineteenth-century literature, the contemporary debate between the followers of the Classical and Gothic styles is evident in the way in which architecture is used to characterize attitudes and values.

32.4 Music

The feelings of an age

Those who listen to music can recognize the period in which it was written. This is, in part, a technical matter, because some ways of writing are popular in particular periods. But techniques are not separable from the feel of the music – its emotional and formal life. Eighteenth-century music is often elegant, crisp and disciplined, while nineteenth-century music, by contrast, often exemplifies organic form, with strong emotions shaping the musical line.

Romanticism and music

The change from the precisions of mid-eighteenth century music to exploratory forms begins to occur in the period which, in literary study, we call Romantic – 1780 to 1830. The music of Joseph Haydn (1732–1809) is more experimental in its later phase. The strange exploratory sounds in his representation of chaos at the beginning of *The Creation* (1798) have a decidedly experimental quality. The composer in which musical development is most evident, though, is Ludvig van Beethoven (1770–1827). In his music we can hear the changes that overcame European thinking and feeling in this period. His music, particularly his late string quartets, is like what Wordsworth said of Newton's statue – a mind 'for ever/Voyaging through strange seas of Thought, alone' (*The Prelude*, 1850 version, Bk. 3, 63–4).

At least three features of Romantic art are evident in Beethoven's music: experimentation; thematic and narrative subjects; and the expression of feeling. As discussed above, Beethoven exemplifies organic form – the way the form of a work is moulded by the ideas and feelings it expresses. His experiments in symphonic and string quartet form can be understood as being like the exploratory conversation poems of Samuel Taylor Coleridge, such as 'Frost at Midnight' (1798), in which the direction of the poem is shaped by the musings of the poet.

Beethoven wrote music that was deliberately thematic and sometimes even narrative. This was the period of Coleridge and Wordsworth's *Lyrical Ballads* (1798). Beethoven's third symphony – the *Eroica* (1804) – expresses the magnetism of heroism, and in the sixth symphony – the *Pastoral* (1808) – there is a programme in which the composer walks into the countryside, enjoys a stream and peasant merry-making. After a fierce storm, the symphony ends with a hymn of thanksgiving. To underline the point made above about Coleridge and Wordsworth: it was in narrative that Romantic art was most itself. Lord Byron, for example, is a zestful and astonishingly fluent teller of tales.

In Beethoven's music, the listener always hears the restless emotions of the composer. The changes in key, pace and timbre express a turbulent heart. This is the world of the Romantics. Blake explores contrasting moods in his *Songs of Innocence and Experience* (1794), and there are swift changes of feeling – and great depth of feeling, too – in the novels of Jane Austen, a very different author. Another aspect of the Romantic interest in the expression of feeling was the predominance of the Lyric in literature and the song in music. No assessment of Romanticism is complete without a recognition of Franz Schubert (1797–1828), the composer of over 400 songs.

Opera and ballet

One of the closest associations between music and literature is opera. Many operas take as their story works that have a secure position in literature. Opera emerged in the early seventeenth century and became an established genre in the eighteenth. Many of the most famous operas date from the nineteenth and twentieth centuries. In the nineteenth century there was the work of Hector Berlioz, Georges Bizet, Richard Wagner and Giuseppe Verdi; in the twentieth century, Benjamin Britten, Leoš Janáček, Giacomo Puccini and Richard Strauss. The interplay between opera and literature, particularly in the nineteenth century, is an important aspect of culture. Shakespeare's plays have provided many of the plots. Berlioz wrote a version of *Much Ado About Nothing* called *Beatrice and Benedick* (1862); Verdi wrote operas based on *Macbeth* (1847) and *Othello* (1886), and Britten wrote *A Midsummer Night's Dream* (1960).

Opera can be seen as an interpretation of literature. We can ask what aspects of literature does opera bring out? Shakespeare might be said to be operatic in that he writes plays about communities in which there are outstanding figures.

The former factor makes a Chorus (the voice of the people) possible, and the latter, leading roles for sopranos and tenors. We tend to think of Shakespeare as being about outstanding individuals; perhaps we should remember, as opera does, that he is also about societies. *Hamlet* (1600) is about Denmark and *Macbeth* (1606) about Scotland.

Sometimes it is interesting to ask whether a story would make a good opera. Dickens works very well on television, yet Lionel Bart's musical *Oliver!* (1960) is the only famous attempt to add music to his tales. Emily Brontë's *Wuthering Heights* (1847) rarely works on television or on film (the famous film with Lawrence Olivier has to alter the story so that Nelly Dean is hardly present), but the small number of characters, the sense of community and the impassioned (indeed operatic) speeches make it suitable for opera. Bernard Herrmann composed one in 1951.

Ballet, of course, is not a linguistic art, yet there are parallels in subject matter between dance and literature. Like contemporary literature, Romantic ballets such as Jean-Madeleine Schneitzhoeffer's *La Sylphide* (1832) and Adolphe Adam's *Giselle* (1841) are concerned with folk life rather than the splendours of the Court. The ballets are set in remote places and involve supernatural presences.

Music and culture

Occasionally, music expresses a contemporary cultural interest that can also be found in literature. In *The Great Gatsby* (1925), a novel often said to be set in 'the jazz age', there is a joke about the band that plays 'Vladimir Tostoff's Jazz History of the World'. Perhaps more significantly, there are mood scenes such as the image of Gatsby by the water's edge and the parties (Chapter 3), evoked by the narrator, Nick, in memorably lyrical prose that, in the near regularity of its rhythms, borders on verse:

> There was music from my neighbour's house through the summer nights. In his blue gardens men and girls came and went like moths among the whisperings and the champagne and the stars.

The word 'blue' (proclaimed by a recent art exhibition to be the colour of the twentieth century) enacts the mood of romantic langour and unappeased heartache. The scene invites the reader to think of a bluesy number (a slow track by Sidney Bechet?) to accompany the ephemeral flittings and whisperings.

In T. S. Eliot's 'The Waste Land' (1922) there is, in the second section, 'that Shakespeherian Rag' ('elegant' and 'intelligent'), rag being a jaunty piece of music usually written, in the jazz idiom, for piano. In the third section there is a fragment of a popular (and originally obscene) song about Mrs Porter and her daughter. The embarrassingly overt rhymes are a feature of popular song that has found a place among the many voices of Eliot's collage. Critics have also pointed out that Igor Stravinsky's *The Rite of Spring*, a ballet based on an ancient sacrificial rite to mark the coming of spring, anticipates Eliot. First performed in 1913, it shares an interest in the vegetation cults and the myths of dying and rising gods, the imagery of which pervades 'The Waste Land'. Eliot knew Stravinsky's work. Both ballet and poem share a contemporary interest in the origins of primitive art and religion.

Summary

Music has links with literature in that both express the moods, feelings and interests of a culture. The music and literature of the Romantic period share a common outlook: both value experiment and emotional expression. Opera and ballet share qualities found in literature. Sometimes the feel and the intellectual interests of a culture can be heard in both music and literature.

■ ⌄ **33** Society

33.1 Class

English literature has usually been aware of the distinctions of class. It has worked with these distinctions to produce plots of aspiration (the poor girl who establishes herself in cultured society), plot impediments (class is a barrier to certain marriages), and humour (social pretensions can be pleasingly mocked).

Marriage and class

One of the most popular themes in novels is social inequality, and moral and intellectual equality. Jane Austen's heroines are usually poorer than the men they marry, but in moral penetration and intellectual acuity they equal or exceed their spouses. One of the pleasures of Austen's novels is seeing how her heroines overcome opposition (often from snobbish relatives) to secure the men who have chosen them. In Jane Austen the disparity is usually one of money rather than class. The Bennet girls in *Pride and Prejudice* (1813) are not affluent but they are daughters of a gentleman. Socially speaking, the most interesting match is that of Fanny Price. Her mother, in social and financial terms, made an unwise marriage, whereas her aunt married a rich baronet. The social divide is thus only a generation old, yet Sir Thomas, when he accepts Fanny into his house as a child, is most concerned that the distinctions between his own children and the poor relative should be maintained.

Later, Dickens is still aware of the difficulties of marriage across the social divide. One way of enabling a marriage is to make the gentleman suffer a misfortune that renders him less attractive. Thus, in *Our Mutual Friend* (1865), Eugene Wrayburn, seriously injured in a frenzied attack, is able to marry Lizzie Hexam, a girl who in the first chapter rows a boat on the Thames, while her father, as a living, fishes a dead body out of the water.

Early-twentieth-century literature was still intrigued by the problems of class and marriage. In *Pygmalion* (1912), George Bernard Shaw brought out the linguistic aspect of class in his play about Professor Higgins tutoring a flower seller so that she can pass herself off as a lady (many people know the story from the musical *My Fair Lady*). D. H. Lawrence's *Sons and Lovers* (1913) takes as its subject not wide social division as in the case of Dickens, but different cultures within a broadly similar social band. Miners were relatively well paid, so the disparity between Walter and the more refined Gertrude is not chiefly financial. What distinguishes Gertrude from her husband is her Nonconformist background. The respectable poor, as they were sometimes called, were high-minded in their religion and morality, and usually well educated.

Money

Class is, in part, a matter of money. One of the subjects of nineteenth-century literature is the uneasy relationship between 'old' and 'new' money. 'Old' money is inherited wealth. It is usually derived from land (the owners often have a big country estate), whereas 'new' money is usually only a generation old and comes from trade or industry. Those who have 'old' money might see those with 'new' money as unwelcome interlopers. There is therefore a pressure on 'new' wealth to make itself respectable by acquiring an estate.

This is the situation in *Pride and Prejudice*. The first disjunction in the plot is the news that Netherfield, a large house, has been taken by Mr Bingley. Mr Bingley, we learn, is the son of a northern manufacturer. His father is dead and he is thinking about buying an estate. The situation, therefore, is a familiar one in literature: 'new' money is seeking the respectability of land. Mr Bingley therefore finds Jane Bennet a suitable girl to woo, because although she is not wealthy she comes from a good family who have wealth based on the land. It is also understandable (though plainly ironic) that his sisters should adopt the airs of old wealth status, despising the Bennets' (very sensible) relatives, who are in trade. Mr Bingley's friend, Mr Darcy, has 'old' money – an enormous family estate in Derbyshire. One of Jane Austen's themes is the way 'old' accommodates itself to 'new'. Mr Darcy has not only befriended Bingley but also behaves impeccably when he meets the Gardiners, the relatives in trade.

Because one of her concerns is that England must adapt through a mutual recognition of the virtues of people of both 'old' and 'new' money, Jane Austen is usually critical of the snobbery of the land-based Establishment. Yet there are moments in English fiction when the reader is asked to see that the reservations he or she might have about a character are not unrelated to the character's possession of 'new' money. When, in Chapter 5 of *Tess of the d'Urbervilles* (1891), Tess goes to claim kin of the d'Urbervilles, everything she sees is suspiciously new: 'a crimson brick lodge', a house 'almost new' and 'acres of glass houses'. In fact, 'Everything looked money'. And that is all it is. Tess is a real d'Urberville, a descendant of a once-powerful family of Norman origin, but the owner of the new house is not a d'Urberville at all. His father was 'Mr Simon Stoke', who 'had made his money as an honest merchant (some said money-lender) in the North'. The narrator goes on to recount that he found the name d'Urberville in a book on 'extinct, half-extinct, obscured, and ruined families' and 'annexed' the name 'for himself and his heirs eternally'. The reader feels that this 'new' wealth is alien. The heir, Alec, has few genteel qualities.

Summary

Class is important in marriage, where there is often the issue of social inequality. Class depends on cultural outlook as well as money. When literature deals with money, there is often the distinction between 'old' and 'new' money.

33.2   Love, marriage and families

Betrothal

In Shakespeare's day, the betrothal was an important stage in wooing and marriage. A betrothal was a witnessed agreement that a pair will marry. The betrothal involved the ritual act of the girl's father joining the hands of the contracting couple. Betrothals were binding. If either the man or the woman married another, the marriage was declared invalid. In some cases, it was the custom for the couple to live together. Sometimes, as probably in Shakespeare's own case, a marriage ceremony was only conducted when the woman became pregnant. If we are unaware of the conventions of betrothal, we miss the significance of some stage actions. For example, in *The Winter's Tale* (1609), Polixenes, King of Bohemia, disguises himself so that he can watch how his son, Florizel, woos a country girl, Perdita. Polixenes waits until Florizel asks the Old Shepherd (Perdita's father) to perform the betrothal:

> But come on,
> Contract us fore these witnesses.
> The Old Shepherd replies:
> Come, your hand;
> And daughter, yours.
>
> (4.4 387–9)

'Contract', 'witnesses', 'your hand' – this is the language of betrothal, so Polixenes must stop the proceedings before they are committed to each other. Significantly, when, having been questioned by his still-disguised father, Florizel insists on the betrothal, Polixenes, revealing who he is, uses the language of divorce:

FLORIZEL: Mark our contract.
POLIXENES: Mark your divorce, young sir.
                            (4.4. 417–18)

Correspondence

Two hundred years ago, courtship and engagement had rules different from those of Shakespeare's day. There was certainly no question of cohabitation before the marriage ceremony. Engagements were nevertheless of considerable importance, and privileges were allowed an engaged couple that were forbidden to the unengaged.

Chief among such privileges was correspondence. In Jane Austen's *Sense and Sensibility* (1811), Elinor assumes that because her younger sister, Marianne, writes to Willoughby, that the couple must be engaged, although no announcement of an engagement has been made. *Sense and Sensibility* is a severe novel. One of the things it shows is the folly of Marianne in accepting a situation without the protection that engagement confers. In *Northanger Abbey* (1818) it is a sign of Mr and Mrs Morland's liberality that they allow a correspondence between their daughter, Catherine, and Henry Tilney, no doubt because, although his father has not yet agreed to the engagement, they in fact have.

Living together

The relatively recent practice of living together either as a prelude to marriage or in the absence of the legal sanction of matrimony no doubt has its own social conventions (as has everything we do), but it has yet to produce interesting plot situations. The most that can be said is that what in a novel about marriage would be important – disputes between the couple – merely becomes an opportunity to separate. Thus, in Ian McEwan's *Enduring Love* (1997), when the couple suffer the strain of Joe being stalked, Clarissa leaves. Their eventual reconciliation comes at the end and is not presented in great detail.

Family life

Family life provides many plot opportunities for novelists. In George Eliot's *The Mill on the Floss* (1860), there is the recognition that families, in the language of sociology, are 'extended'. Maggie Tulliver grows up not only with her parents and brother but also with the aunts who comment and criticize. Such families are more likely in places and times in which the population is settled. The society of St. Oggs is enclosed and cut off.

Quite often, novelists find family life of interest if they can present a tension between the generations. Thus *Wuthering Heights* (1847), *Great Expectations* (1860) and *Tess of the d'Urbervilles* (1891) use friction, of various types, between parents and children as a way of making, in novelistic terms, something of the family. A familiar plot is the differences opened up between the generations by education.

Summary

A knowledge of the social conventions that ordered English marriage helps us to see the significance of some events in literature. At one time, betrothal was a legally binding contract, and at a later period, correspondence was only permitted to those who were engaged. The nature of family life – the place of relatives and its continuance through marriage – are important features in some English fiction.

33.3 Town and country

Urban life

Although the traditions of literature are rural (see Chapter 27), in the last 200 years writers have had to come to terms with urban and suburban life.

Charles Dickens is celebrated for his presentation of London. The Thames, its bridges, the dome of St. Paul's, Smithfield Market, the Court of Chancery, Bleeding Heart Yard, the Marshalsea and Newgate have all been rendered in abrasive detail. And London could not have been invented. George Eliot invented Middlemarch, but a capital city – New York, Paris, Vienna – is not a place that an author could invent (see Chapter 50, section 50.3).

However, authors have to re-present capital cities, and readers, when they try to come to terms with an imaginative re-creation of a real place, require historical understanding and critical judgement. The understanding and re-presentation of London is the chief concern of both Peter Ackroyd's fiction and his non-fiction. *The Clerkenwell Tales* (2003) concludes with a chapter called 'The Author's Tale', in which he provides a set of notes on the places he has so carefully delineated in the preceding chapters. One of the locations of Dickens' *Our Mutual Friend* (1865) is the dust heaps, which form the basis of Harmon's wealth. This wealth is first mentioned in the second chapter by Mortimer Lightwood:

> '...he grew rich as a Dust Contractor, and lived in a hollow in a hilly country entirely composed of Dust. On his own small estate the growling old vagabond threw up his own mountain range, like an old volcano, and its geological formation was Dust. Coal-dust, vegetable-dust, bone-dust, crockery dust, rough dust and sifted dust – all manner of Dust.'

The reader first encounters the dust-heaps in Chapter 4, when Mr Wilfer goes home:

> Between Battle Bridge and that part of Holloway district in which he dwelt, was a tract of suburban Sahara, where tiles and bricks were burnt, bones were boiled, carpets were beat, rubbish was shot, dogs were fought, and dust was heaped by contractors.

As a matter of history there were such heaps in the 1850s in an area north of St. Pancras. But what Dickens makes of them – what they stand for in the writing – is something Dickens does, and which the imagination of the reader has to perceive. Dust takes on a symbolic role – it stands for the frailty of human life and the grubby basis of wealth. Dickens' dust heaps are not the only case in literature in which the rubbish of urban life becomes significant. The second chapter of *The Great Gatsby* (1925) opens with Fitzgerald's vision of the valley of ashes – a real urban wasteland, where rubbish is shot and grey people – the failures of society – live out grey, shadowy lives.

Coming to terms with urban life is something we associate with the novel, but in the nineteenth century poets also tackled the problem of bringing the reality of urban life into verse. In Poem 7 of *In Memoriam* (1850), Tennyson pictures himself standing outside the house of his dead friend in 'the long unlovely street'. Negating the conventional word of praise – 'lovely' – is Tennyson's way of getting at the unpoetic drabness of London. The poem closes with another poetic reversal. Dawn comes, but not a conventionally poetic one of hope and new life: 'On the bald street breaks the blank day.' The unexpected word 'bald' gives us the raw emptiness of an urban dawn. There is nothing here to adorn or beautify life; it is not only bereft of visual pleasure but, by implication, unnaturally bereft.

Economics

The life of towns and cities is the life of buying and selling. Perhaps the first writer to recognize the literary potential in the world of trade was Ben Jonson. His plays might not all be set in London (*Volpone* is set in Venice, for example) but all have the feel of London's lively and competitive commercial life. Jonson seems to have a cheerfully ambivalent view of trade and commerce. It encourages cheating, and yet the wit and enterprise of those who deceive is admirable. What he recognizes is that trading is accompanied (and perhaps gives rise to) another form of exchange – the lie – and it is this that makes for his robust and almost diagrammatically simple plots.

Later, William Blake recognizes in 'London' (1794) that economics is the life of the city:

> I wander thro' each charter'd street,
> Near where the charter'd Thames does flow

'Charter'd' means given a charter for trade. Not only the streets but also the river is given over to commercial activity. Perhaps the unnaturalness of this is present in the delay until the end of the line of a word we would expect to find in a poem about rivers – 'flow'. Does the river really feel as if it's flowing?

Outcasts

Blake saw that cities make outcasts. The third stanza of 'London' lists the victims:

> How the Chimney-sweeper's cry
> Every black'ning Church appalls;
> And the hapless Soldier's sigh
> Runs in blood down Palace walls.

'London' deals with the sights and sounds of distress caused by urban life. We hear the rhymed 'cry' of the sweep and the 'sigh' of the soldier. Each is a victim, an outcast. The sweep – a mere child – is misused and exploited, and the soldier, presumably injured in the service of his nation and now discharged, sighs by the walls of the monarch for whom he fought.

Blake was not the only poet who saw the distress of the urban poor. In Book 7 of *The Prelude* (1805), William Wordsworth, both excited and appalled by the teeming life of London, sees

> A travelling cripple, by the trunk cut short,
> And stumping with his arms.
>
> (219–20)

And

> a blind beggar, who, with upright face,
> Stood propped against a wall
>
> (612–13)

Behind these uncomfortably acute observations, there is a clear understanding of how cities attract the maimed and the blind but have no other role for them than begging. The beggars are ambiguous figures; they are abjectly dependent on others, and yet they have an arresting dignity. The cripple has stumped to his place, and the blind man has an 'upright face', which suggests dignity.

Revolution and war

The soldier in Blake fixes the poem to a specific set of events. When literature engages with urban reality, it is usually with the economics and the social life of cities, but occasionally, as here, there is an actual set of historical events implicitly present in the poem. Britain was at war with France from 1793 to 1814 and then, until Napoleon's defeat at the Battle of Waterloo, for part of 1815. (The war followed an event that has long fascinated the English imagination – the French Revolution.) There was fighting at sea, in Spain and in the West Indies. There was, for Britain, a large standing army, and public evidence of the military life was visible in the camps of the Militia (as in *Pride and Prejudice*) and the barracks that were built in the capital and in provincial towns. The discharged soldier (the one no longer able to fight) also turns up in Wordsworth. In Book 4 of *The Prelude*, the poet meets another of those solitaries that haunt the pages of his poetry. The man

> told in simple words a soldier's tale:
> That in the tropic islands he had served,
> Whence he had landed scarcely ten days past –
> That on his landing he had been dismissed,
> And now was travelling to his native home.
>
> (445–9)

The soldier, like the beggars in London, has a dignity that awes Wordsworth. The tale is simple and, we may surmise, not untypical of a serving man. The simplicity of the narration (without comment) shows that although he has been dismissed he is without resentment. In Wordsworth, the marginalized have a repose and become objects of an almost religious contemplation.

Summary

Writers, poets, as well as novelists, had to find ways of creating the realities of urban life. Historical study helps here, though the reader still needs to exercise judgement about how contemporary material is handled. Writers see that city life marginalizes the weak. Literature can show the effects of social change on urban and national life.

33.4 Technology

Agricultural change

Technological change was a feature of nineteenth-century rural life. There is a scene in Thomas Hardy's *The Mayor of Casterbridge* (1886) in which the old agricultural world meets a new one. In a long struggle – a struggle over love and money – Farfrae, the newcomer, outwits Henchard, the local. In Chapter 24 a stir is caused when Farfrae introduces new agricultural technology. Heralded by reflections on the ceiling – 'circling irradiations' – a new piece of machinery arrives in the corn market:

> It was the new-fashioned agricultural implement called a horse-drill, till then unknown, in its modern shape, in this of the country, where the venerable seed-lip was still used for sowing, as in the days of the Heptarchy.

Hardy's point is to show that the advance of technology divides people and alters their ancient working traditions. Needless to say, the traditionalist Henchard mocks it, while Farfrae, who has ordered it, welcomes change. Hardy's prose polarizes the old and the new. The 'seed-lip' was the basket from which the sower broadcast seed, so it has, in addition to an English venerability, associations with the sower, who, in the Bible, goes forth to sow. The Heptarchy was the ancient Anglo-Saxon division of England. Traditions established over a thousand years before were about to be superseded.

Industry

Technological change is usually associated with industry. In the 1840s and 1850s there was a sub-genre of fiction dealing with the conflicts of industry – the industrial novel. What is fundamental to these novels is the acknowledgement that the technology of industrial processes alters the way of life of all those associated with it. In *Hard Times* (1854) industry marks everything. This, from the opening of Chapter 5, is Coketown:

> It was a town of red brick, or of brick that would have been red if the smoke and ashes had allowed it; but as matters stood it was a town of unnatural red and black like the painted face of a savage. It was a town of machinery and tall chimneys, out of which interminable serpents of smoke trailed themselves

for ever and ever, and never got uncoiled. It had a black canal in it, and a river that ran purple with ill-smelling dye, and vast piles of buildings full of windows where there was a rattling and a trembling all day long, and where the piston of the steam-engine worked monotonously up and down like the head of an elephant in melancholy madness.

Industry has invaded and transformed the landscape. What little that is left of nature is discoloured; we shudder at the thought of the black canal and the purple river. The air is full of unnatural sounds – machinery rattles and trembles. It is characteristic of Dickens that he does not tell us what is being made in the factories. Instead, he gives us a strong sense of the all-pervading presence of industrial processes – the piston works monotonously up and down.

The idea that technology has taken over our lives appears in twentieth-century literature as both an occasion for humour and for regret. Towards the end of *Death of a Salesman* (1949), Willy Loman is left in an office with a tape-recorder (then a novelty). He switches it on but cannot work out how to switch it off. The babbling voice reminds us of the past events that return unbidden to Willy, and in his attempt to control the machine there is both comedy and pathos.

Transport

Since the mid-1800s, authors have written about new forms of transport. When Dickens writes of the past he presents, as he does in Pip's journey to London in *Great Expectations*, the world of the stagecoach. But when he writes of the contemporary world, as in *Dombey and Son* (1848), he shows the railway being engineered through north London and manages a climax in which a train kills a character.

The train found its way into poetry. Hardy wrote a number of poems that bring out the melancholy of railway stations and travelling in confined carriages – the farewells, the uncertain future, the loneliness. Many of these impressions and feelings come together in 'Midnight on the Great Western' (1919). A boy, alone with a ticket stuck in his hat-band, sits in a third-class carriage as a Great Western train plunges through the midnight darkness. In the third stanza the poet questions:

> What past can be yours, O journeying boy?
>   Towards a world unknown,
> Who calmly, as if incurious quite
> On all at stake, can undertake
>   This plunge alone?

Hardy wonders about the past of this boy, who plunges into the future of a world unknown. The railway is becoming metaphoric. This journey, we sense, is the journey of life, a journey which we have to make alone but which we don't usually embark on with the strange passivity of the journeying boy.

The impressions of a train journey are captured, perhaps surprisingly, by Dante Gabriel Rossetti in 'A Trip to Paris and Belgium' (1886). The poem opens with glimpses of the landscape as it is seen from a railway carriage:

> A constant keeping-past of shaken trees,
> And a bewildered glitter of loose road;

> Banks of bright growth, with single blades atop
> Against white sky: and wires – a constant chain –
> That seem to draw the clouds along with them

What Rossetti captures (with delight?) is the momentary sight of roads, banks and wires. Although we associate Rossetti with dreamy visions of sad maidens (as in 'The Blessed Damozel' – see Chapter 32, section 32.2), it may be that the fresh quality of those lines is due to the painter's eye. This is a kind of impressionism; what he is aware of are flashes of light, movement in the trees and strange continuities such as the wires. He also describes what it is like to see these things; the phrase 'bewildered glitter' captures the momentary and arresting glimpse of the stones in a road caught for a second as the train speeds by.

Timetables

There is a famous scene in silent films in which the villain ties the heroine to the railway line. This could only be done when there were timetables. One of the effects of technology is that time is regulated, and human activities can be scheduled. This makes certain sorts of fiction possible: the detective story and the thriller. Those who enjoy Sherlock Holmes will recall that the crime is often solved by consulting timetables, and Holmes and Dr Watson often make train journeys. Holmes claims to run the first scientific detective agency. His activities would be impossible if there were no machines, no transport, no clocks and no timetables.

Summary

Authors engage with subjects such as industrial towns or transport by showing how such things affected people's lives. They can also use them symbolically. Technological innovations make possible certain sorts of books; the detective story, for example, requires there to be timetabled transport.

Part Six   Interpretation

■ ▽ 34   Discovering Meanings

34.1   Internal and external interpretation

There are four fundamental points about interpretation.

- Interpretation is reading for meaning.
- In reading for meaning, we look for what is significant, for what matters, and what the writing adds up to.
- Interpretation is something we do every time we read.
- A work can be interpreted in a number of ways, and what we find will depend on the viewpoint we have taken.

The last point is particularly important. Students are often asked to show that a book can be interpreted in a number of ways. We can, for example, look at the genre, the historical context of the work or, say, how it presents women or the working of the mind. In what follows we shall look at some of the ways in which we interpret books, and some of the problems that arise in interpretation.

Two ways of looking

There are two kinds of interpretation:

- Internal interpretation.
- External interpretation.

'Internal' (or *intrinsic*) interpretation is concerned with the text as it stands. It relates to matters such as form and the making of meaning.

'External' (or *extrinsic*) interpretation brings knowledge or ideas to a text. We might ask about the history of the period in which the work was written, or consider it in terms of ideas about people and society.

Theories

Both A-level and university courses recognize the popularity of literary theory. Some of these theories are internal and others external. For example, Structuralism, to put it simply, deals with how works are designed, so it is an internal theory. By contrast, Feminism, which looks at the literary representation of women, is an external form of interpretation.

Summary

To read is to interpret, and there are a number of ways of doing this. Interpretation can be internal or external. Internal interpretation concerns the book as it is in itself, while external interpretation reads a book in terms of ideas and methods that are outside it.

34.2   Words on the page

Questions and answers

If we ask X type questions, we get, and can only get, X type answers. Historical questions, for example, can only produce historical answers. This applies to interpretation:

> **An interpretation is like travelling down a road; we can only get to where the road leads.**

With this point in mind, consider the following question:

Do the different ways in which we interpret books have anything in common?

There would be three consequences if we answered 'No':

- We could never relate one interpretation to another. To use the example of the road: if we go east, we are not going to find places to the north.
- We could never decide whether one interpretation was more helpful than another. We could only list what the viewpoints have shown us.
- Interpretation would be circular. We would always come back to the point from which we started.

But in practice, interpretation doesn't work like this. We can travel in two directions and then compare what we've found. We can ask, say, historical *and* psychological questions. One interpretation does not exclude another. To ask psychological questions does not mean that the work is *merely* psychological. A book can be looked at from many different interpretive standpoints.

And interpretation is not *exactly* like travelling down a road. The difference is that travelling different roads takes the traveller through different parts of the country, whereas an interpretation of a literary work takes us through the same country.

> **However we interpret a work, we are looking at the same work.**

And what does it mean to look at the same work? The answer can only be:

> **We look at the words of which the work is made.**

Whether we are interpreting *Hamlet* (1600) in terms of genre or psychology, it is the *same* play we are looking at because we are looking at the same words. It follows that what different ways of interpretation have in common is *words*.

Summary

Interpretations must have things in common, because if they did not, we could never relate them or prefer one to another. What all interpretations have in common is that they are looking at words.

34.3   Close reading

Close reading is what it says it is: looking closely – attentively and thoughtfully – at the words of a book. Words are all we have to look at. If they were different, it would be a different book. Sometimes we think we know what a book is about, but a close study of its words can reveal new things. Interpretation, unlike computer programming, is not something that has been settled beforehand.

Whenever critics write about books, they are practising close reading.

And this applies no matter what kind of interpretation is being pursued. Literary interpretation of any kind means coming to terms with words.

What words actually say

As words are the *only* way to meaning, we must look at what they *actually* say. For example, we sometimes carelessly say that in *Twelfth Night* (1599), Malvolio is a Puritan. That is not quite what the text says. Maria's words are: 'sometimes he is a kind of puritan' (2.3. 130). The crucial words are 'sometimes' and 'a kind of'. Moreover, that is only Maria's view.

Making links

When we read, we link passages. In the case of names, for example, we bring to the bit we are reading what we know of a character. Alec d'Urberville has wronged Tess, so each time he appears, the wrong he has done her shapes our response.

Contrasts

When we link up areas of a text, differences emerge. Some of these differences are sharp enough to constitute contrasts. Irony depends on being aware of the contrast between present and past actions.

How it is said

Literature is not just something that is said; it is something that is said in a particular way.

How something is said shapes *what* is said.

This means, for example, that genre and figures of speech matter. Andrew Marvell's poem 'To His Coy Mistress' (published 1683) is in the '*carpe diem*' (seize the time) genre – an invitation to love while there is yet time. But the figures of speech reveal that the poem is also concerned with time. We read of 'time's winged chariot hurrying near' and contemplate with fascination and repulsion the scene in the grave, where 'none, I think, do there embrace'.

Significance

Close reading raises the issue of significance (see section 34.1). Books are not lots of bits. They add up to something; usually something that matters. We arrive at what we think is significant by a process of selection. When we single out certain parts as being more important than others we are recognizing their significance.

Judgement

Deciding what is significant is always a matter of judgement. Sometimes authors help us by writing scenes that advertise their own significance. Thomas Hardy, for example, opens *Jude the Obscure* (1895) with a scene in which the young Jude, who is working in the fields, sees, in the distance, the sight of Christminster – the university city. The graphic immediacy of this scene leads us to judge that it is a significant moment.

Debate

Because deciding what is significant involves making a judgement, interpretation can always be debated. It is up to a reader to draw attention to a part of a book that other readers might have overlooked. Literary debate is a matter of saying: don't you think this part is important?

Summary

All interpretation is a matter of looking (usually closely) at the words, seeing how the words of one passage link with those of another, recognizing how words are used, judging what is significant, and being prepared to debate.

■ ⌄ 35 Internal Interpretation: Narratology, Grammar and Genre

Looking at books on their own terms is not something new to us. Earlier, we considered at least three ways of interpretation that treat books as things that can be understood on their own terms.

35.1 Narratology

Narratology is the name given to the study and theory of story-telling. Narratologists are concerned with the nuts and bolts of narration. The issues were looked at in Chapter 3. Narratologists' interests may be summarized in the following ways:

- The story is basic to our lives. When we talk about what we have done, we usually tell stories. Our understanding of life is story-shaped.
- Stories work because we desire to know. Expectation is aroused, and we seek resolution and satisfaction. Stories are not stories unless we read or hear them.
- Tales might be told in the first or third person. First-person narrators might be central figures or observers. Third-person narrators might also be distinctive personalities who intrude into the narrative by giving their opinions and judgements, or might be more neutral figures – the undramatized or covert narrators who are voices or mediums for the events. Very occasionally, a narrator is either uncertain or, the reader might decide, unreliable (see Chapter 3, section 7).
- Henry James formulated the distinction between *telling* and *showing*. Narratologists call telling *diegesis* and showing *mimesis* (originally, this meant imitation). Telling is through summaries and the direct imparting of information, while showing is through dialogue, accounts of action and the presentation of settings. Nearly all stories are both told and shown.
- *What* is told or shown shapes a narration. Narrators might stick to what anyone might observe – action and speech, or choose to have access to the minds – to the unspoken thoughts, of their characters. Narratives can be complex. Sometimes a character is the focus of the story, because events are seen from that character's point of view. But this process (usually called focalization) does not mean that the point of view of the character is the same as the book itself (or the narrator or author). William Golding's *The*

Spire (1964) is focalized through Jocelin, but his viewpoint is not the one that the novel as a whole endorses.

- A story, to be a story, must be a set of events in a time sequence. But in telling a story, the order of events can be rearranged. The distinction between story and plot is that the former is chronological and the latter formal – the order in which events appear in the book. Narratives can look back (*analepsis*) or forward (*prolepsis*). Narratives can introduce events that occurred before the narrative time of the book. A narrator can indicate that two events happened simultaneously, though they appear at different points in the narrative.
- Speech can be handled in different ways. Sometimes it is set out like drama. We hear the separate voices, but are not told who is saying what. Sometimes, authors 'tag' the dialogue by telling the reader who says what. There are other forms of speech. In indirect speech (often a feature of first-person narration), the reader hears the substance of what was said, though not the actual words. Indirect speech can blend what has been said with the response of the narrator.
- Narratologists draw attention to the circumstances or contexts in which a story takes place. The term 'frame' is often used for the way in which a story is told or, to use the popular term, embedded. The frame of Chaucer's *The Canterbury Tales* (c. 1390) is the pilgrimage to the shrine of St. Thomas, during which the pilgrims agree to tell tales. The frame is evident in the lively snatches of dialogue between the tales, and in some cases, the 'Prologues' of the *Tales*. In later fiction, there is often a distinction between the primary narrator – one who introduces the situation – and the secondary narrator, who usually tells the tale. Thus the primary narration encloses the secondary one, as in Joseph Conrad's *Heart of Darkness* (1902) in which, while waiting in a ship for the tide to turn at the mouth of the Thames, the anonymous primary narrator relates the tale that Marlow, the secondary narrator, tells about a journey into the dark heart of man.

Summary

Narratology recognizes the importance of stories and seeks to understand how they are put together. This involves looking at who tells the tale, and how much is imparted to the reader. Narration involves telling and showing, modes that involve readers in different ways. Narratologists consider how time is handled and speech is presented. Sometimes a narrative is framed in a larger narrative.

35.2   Grammar

Grammar matters

Grammar might be said to be the primary way in which we interpret literature. This is because grammar is the fundamental feature of all language. We can only sort out what words mean (*semantics*) when we have mastered the rules of grammar. The sections on grammar (Chapter 16, sections 16.2 to 16.5) were in the Poetry part of this book, but of course all literature – novels, plays – depends on grammar. The following aspects of grammar can help in the study of literature:

- Word classes (nouns, verbs and so on) provide writers with a range of possible meanings and, consequently, effects. For example, as discussed in Chapter 16, section 16.2, the character of literature is shaped by whether nouns are abstract (duty, honour) or common (chairs, tables). Abstract nouns put us in touch with ideas and qualities, whereas common nouns make us concentrate on the physical world. To repeat the point: this is achieved through grammar.
- English syntax is fluid. There are a number word orders in which an idea can be expressed. Syntax shapes meaning in quite specific ways. When an author builds up a sentence with a number of clauses (sub-sections of sentences containing verbs), it is usually because what is being said requires careful definition and qualification. These complex sentences are found in authors such as George Eliot and Henry James, whose thoughts and feelings require a series of refining clauses. Clause by clause, the density and richness of thought and feeling is laid bare.

Summary

Grammar is the fundamental means by which meaning is established. Interpreting literature involves looking at how word classes create particular meanings, and how syntax brings out thoughts and feelings.

35.3   Genre

Part Four of this book is devoted to Genre – the various types and styles of literature that authors have adopted and adapted. Genre helps interpretation in the following ways:

- Knowing about genre and conventions might help us to avoid making mistakes about meaning. A knowledge of genre often helps us to clear up problems we have about the plausibility of events.
- Because writers in English have experimented with genre, we need to be aware of how authors introduce unexpected elements or combine genres (a process called *hybridization*). This might be how we should understand Shakespeare's problem plays and romances.
- Genre controls the words authors use. Tragedy, for example, is grave and elevated, so we expect to find words that are weighty and high-sounding. This is the kind of language we find in Marlowe – lofty, rhapsodic and uplifting. In Comedy, however, language is more demotic – close to the words of colloquial usage.

- We can use genre not only as a means of interpretation but also as a way of judging a work. This is a difficult business, particularly if we accept the idea, outlined above, that we need not be bound by rules. Nevertheless, one way of deciding how we value a work is to judge the extent to which it fulfils the requirements, and consequently the expectations, of its genre.
- Although genre is a form of internal interpretation, there is an important external element. The growth and popularity of genres depends on history. There was a time when, for example, there were no such genres as Romance or Gothic. Some of the issues raised in Part Five – Context – are relevant to a discussion of genre.

Summary

Genre can be a useful guide as to how a work should be interpreted. If we identify what kind of a work it is, we are often in a good position to know what to make of its elements. But we should be wary: Writers in English experiment with genre. Genre usually uses particular levels of diction. We sometimes use genre as a way of judging how good we think a work is.

▪ ⌄ **36** Internal Interpretation: Formalism

36.1 Treating books as art

We now come to three schools or theories of internal interpretation that treat the text as something that has been made – as a construct, as art. Whatever is made has a form, and because literature has a form it can be given a formal interpretation. (Some critics insist that anything that has been made – recipes, television news, text messages – can be given a formal interpretation.) We can study how it is written (viewpoint, style), how it is sequenced (movement, pattern) and how it is put together (design, structure).

When we think about the form of art, we are treating art as something that exists in its own right and has its own 'laws' or 'rules'. This is different from a biographical or social study. A sonnet, for example, might have been written by a young courtier in the Elizabethan Court, and so could be studied as an element of Court culture, but what makes it a *sonnet* and not another kind of poem is its particular form.

Of course, there is no such *thing* in a work as its form, if by form we mean something that can be entirely isolated. The word 'form' refers not to an object or a thing but is rather a way of talking about its shape, design and movement.

Talking in this way is not easy. One of the problems of finding a suitable language is that literature moves in *time*, whereas some of the words we use are to do with *space*. 'Design', for example, is used of objects in space rather than in time. Perhaps because it is not easy talking about form, a highly technical vocabulary has grown up around it.

Summary

Literature is art. It has been formed. A formal approach to interpretation attempts to talk about literature in terms of the art that has made it and given it shape.

36.2 Formalist critics

Aristotle

The formal interpretation of literature has a long history. In the West it began with Aristotle (*Poetics*, c.335 BC). His ideas about plots are discussed in Chapter 4, Section 4.5, so here just three points will be made about his approach:

- Aristotle gave an account of the impact of plays. His starting point is the engagement and response of the audience.
- Because the audience is engaged with the plights of the characters, Aristotle's discussion of form is also a discussion of the themes of the plays. The moment of recognition (*anagnorisis*) is a moment of insight into the significance of what has been going on, and is therefore inseparable from the themes of the play.
- Aristotle was concerned with literature as such, and not just specific plays. He was saying something about the nature of literary art, so what he said was intended to be relevant to the discussion of *any* play.

Summary

Aristotle had a formalist approach to literature. He drew on his knowledge of contemporary plays, was concerned to understand the reactions of the audiences, did not separate form from content, and attempted to work out ways of understanding literature, or at least plays, in general.

36.3 The Russian Formalists

When people nowadays talk about formal approaches to literature, they usually mean the twentieth-century schools of interpretation. One of the first was Russian Formalism.

Making strange

The Russian Formalists were interested in the *literariness of literature*. For example, they said that literature 'made strange'. The phrase comes from Viktor Shklovsky ('Art as Technique', 1917). His point is that we are so accustomed to the world about us that we hardly see it. Literature tries to open our eyes again, but in order to make us see it has, so to speak, to warp or distort our normal and tired ways of seeing. Shklovsky said that our habitual ways of encountering the world were 'automized'. To see it afresh, literary works adjusted pace (usually slowing down), concentrated on details and used arresting imagery (the carefully placed simile or metaphor). 'Making strange' is sometimes called *defamiliarization*.

By stretching language to make us see the automized world afresh, we see (possibly for the first time) the rich possibilities of language. In Philip Larkin's 'To the Sea', the poet returns to the seaside. Perhaps it is because he is 'strange to it' that he can, through minute observation and sharply delineated images, make new what for many is (or was?) an all-too-familiar scene.

Folk stories

The Formalists were interested in folk literature. Vladimir Propp (*The Morphology of the Folktale*, 1928) identified certain 'elements' that constituted the forms of traditional stories. There is a hero, a villain, a beautiful girl, a disruption, a quest, deception, temptation, a battle, a rescue or victory, the punishment of the villain, and the recognition and return home of the hero. Altogether, Propp identified thirty-one such features. (These are listed in the very useful *Beginning Theory* (2002) by Peter Barry.) Propp points to features that are common to many stories: the hero or heroine, the one who helps and the one who hinders, and the desired object or person the hero or heroine seeks to attain. Jane Austen's *Northanger Abbey* (1818) has something of this pattern: Catherine needs to grow in self-understanding and judgement, and in this she is helped by Eleanor and Henry Tilney, and hindered by Isabella and John Thorpe.

Propp's thesis is an ambitious one. He seeks to lay bare what we might call the grammar of story-telling – the rules and conventions of all narratives. Literature, in his thinking, is like a branch of natural history; the job of the critic is to give a complete account of the features that constitute it.

The limits of Formalism

If there is anything in this claim, then it might be that the features are more evident in simple, traditional literature. Propp was interested in action and event rather than character, so his ideas are a help in understanding works that are close to folk literature. For example, John Bunyan's *The Pilgrim's Progress* (1678) is more amenable to a Formalist reading than, say, a George Eliot novel. When novelists seek to understand the bewildering complexity of human motivation, the firm plot features that Propp identified are less important.

Summary

The Russian Formalists were concerned with what was 'literary' about literature. They identified its capacity to 'make strange' what is familiar. Through verbal ingenuity, authors wiped away the film of familiarity from our eyes. They were also interested in identifying the elements that are basic to all plots. Formalism is better at interpreting simple plots than complex writing.

36.4 Structuralism

Origins: anthropology and linguistics

Structuralism emerged in the study of anthropology and linguistics. Like other 'internal' theories, Structuralism sees no need to look outside the text in order to gain insight into what it says.

Shapes, forms and structures

Structuralists believe that literature can be understood by seeing its individual shapes and forms in terms of larger structures. They are therefore interested in genres, conventions, grammar and the cultural presuppositions we have about food, clothes, family, entertainment and moral values. In all of these, Structuralism claims, we can see basic patterns. These patterns, it is argued, are present in all members of a class of activities. There are, for example, certain patterns that are evident in any sets of clothes or ways of cooking. And as in the case of clothes and cookery, so with literature. Literature is built up on a set of patterns – contrasts, doubles and repeated motifs.

Problems with Structuralism

Structuralism is problematic for two reasons:

- It stretches the notion of structure. We can talk safely about the structure of a sentence – the relationship between subject, verb and object – but can we apply that idea reasonably to a long novel such *Middlemarch* (1871)?
- Structuralism takes on so much that, perhaps inevitably, it talks in generalities. What is left of the meaning of the word 'structure' when it is applied to both a simple sentence and an 800-page novel?

Summary

Structuralism, a theory derived from anthropology and linguistics, looks for patterns in literature. In making assertions about literature, we have to stretch the concept of structure.

36.5 Deconstruction

French philosophy

Structuralism gave place to Deconstruction. The philosopher, Jacques Derrida, captured the imaginations of many people with his heady teaching about the nature of language. He saw language as floating free from any contact with 'things'. If language is not rooted in the world of common experience, what gives it an identity is a series of differences. We cannot say to what a word refers, but we can say it is different from another word. Given the instability of language – just a complex set of differences – what characterizes a book is not its coherence but rather its disunity. Language therefore deconstructs rather than constructs meaning. In any work, there are so many tensions between the differences that a consistent reading – understanding – becomes impossible.

The death of the author

The coherence of a book is further undermined by the idea, promulgated in 1968 by Roland Barthes ('The Death of the Author'), of the death of the author. As language is detached from reality, it must exist as an autonomous area in which meanings are generated and undermined. It follows, therefore, that there is no author to direct or control the language. All that exists are the words. The idea is a deliberately excessive one. No one would deny that, say, Charles Dickens wrote novels. What Barthes is getting at is the idea that the author can't help us very much to come to terms with his or her books. Deconstruction looks at the words on the page and finds them unstable and indeterminate. There can be no full and final meaning.

Problems with Deconstruction

There are two difficulties with Deconstruction:

- It is vulnerable to the accusation that the proponents are cutting off the branch on which they are sitting. If meaning is as unstable as they assert, how can we understand the proposition that meaning is unstable?
- Because the theory is concerned with language as a whole, it is not concerned specifically with the particular language uses associated with literature.

Summary

The theories of Deconstruction insist that there is no stability in meaning, only differences between individual words. Additionally, there is the idea that the text is free-floating and therefore we do not need the idea of the author when we are trying to understand it. There are philosophical difficulties: if the meaning is unstable, we cannot understand this sentence.

36.6   Postmodernism

Free play

Deconstructionism influenced Postmodernism. The Postmodernists argued that, because meaning is unstable, there can be no universally valid rational grounds for our beliefs. Beliefs (of any kind) might have their own rational order, but they are ungrounded. There are no overarching rational principles. If there are no general rational principles, we can pick and choose. Thinking becomes the free play of ideas.

Moreover, the Postmodernists did this knowingly and ironically. In 1980s architecture, for example, there was an eclectic mixing of styles in one building – Classical porticos and Gothic windows. As there was no single correct style, architects had fun.

The abolition of reality

Both Deconstructionists and Postmodernists occasionally asserted that, because language has no relationship with what is not language, there is no place for notions of reality or the judgement that something is true. (Postmodernists put words in inverted commas – 'reality', 'true'.) All we have, in their view, is the continuous play of meanings, and, since meanings frequently clash with each other, all that can be said is that within a work meanings are created and destroyed.

Postmodern problems

It is hardly surprising that they have been disputed. One professor of philosophy said that Derrida isn't even *interestingly* wrong. There are two difficulties:

- The first is practical. What do holders of these views think when they are not being Deconstructionists? Do they deconstruct traffic lights, for example, and decide that red really means green?
- Can we *morally* jettison the idea of a real world about which statements might be true or false? Is someone else's pain merely the play of random meanings?

Summary

Postmodernism dispensed with the idea that there are rational grounds for holding one set of beliefs rather than another. As there are no grounds for meaning, intellectual activity becomes the free play of ideas and styles. They also rejected the concept of reality. There are moral objections to this idea.

◼ ⏷ 37 Theorists and Literary Features

37.1 Patterns and repetitions

While it is true that most of us have some idea about how language works and how it is related (if at all) to what is not language, we still have to ask how a general theory about language can help us when we are struggling to make sense of a novel or poem. An answer might come by way of the idea that all literary works are organized. They are, so to speak, held together, and because they are held together they are shaped. Structuralism, Deconstruction and Postmodernism might help us to think about the various ways in which they are shaped.

Patterning in literature

Ordered repetition is a feature of works of art. In music, tunes are repeated, and in architecture windows are regularly spaced. Patterns are also present in literature. Lyrical poems sometimes have a refrain at the end of each stanza, and in the villanelle there is a pleasingly complex pattern of alternating lines. But patterning is not separable from meaning.

Repetition and meaning

Repetition underlines meaning. Philip Larkin ends 'The Trees' (1974) – a poem about trees coming into leaf each spring – with the word 'afresh' repeated three times. 'Afresh' captures the wonder that, each year, nature apparently renews itself.

Repetition and making strange

There is something mesmeric about repetition. In a short poem, a repeated word, phrase or line can bring home to us that it is a *poem* we are reading. We know we are in the presence of art. Perhaps the repetitions of art make us see things more clearly. The familiar is made strange.

William Blake's *Songs of Innocence* (1789) often rely on repetition. We are lulled into this specially created world by the smooth sounds of repeated lines. In 'The

Lamb', a poem of twenty lines, the phrase 'Little Lamb' occurs six times, and there is one more use of 'Little' and two more of 'Lamb'. Furthermore, these repetitions are not random; they are patterned. 'Little Lamb' appears in the opening line and the closing two lines. We are made to see that the world of the Little Lamb remains, at the close, safe and unchanged.

Summary

Literature is organized. There is pleasure in patterning, and repetition can enforce meaning and make strange; that is, we become aware that what we are reading is art.

37.2   Leitmotifs

Defining movement, articulating themes

A leitmotif (sometimes just called a *motif*) is a repeated image, idea or incident, the occurrence of which within a work helps to define the movement of the plot and articulate a theme. Leitmotifs therefore occur in long works such as plays and novels. For example, George Eliot's *The Mill on the Floss* (1860) is built on a number of leitmotifs. One of these is Maggie Tulliver's wild hair. The motif indicates something about her nature. As she grows, it becomes increasingly difficult for her to conform. She is a capable and intellectually sharp girl in a world that has no role for her. In the very powerful scene (Chapter 7) in which she cuts her hair, the reader sees her movingly desperate attempts to please her elders by submitting to convention.

Looking forwards and backwards

Parts of a book depend on what has happened and what might happen. Books make us look to the past (analepsis) or the future (prolepsis) by placing elements – action, dialogue, scenes, images – in a set of relationships that echo or anticipate (see Chapter 4, section 4.5). This is often how irony is generated.

Macbeth (1606) has a very strong plot trajectory, which obliges the audience to look forward to the future and back to the past. The Witches' greeting of Macbeth is proleptic in that we look to see if he will become Thane of Cawdor and then the king. When he has achieved these by his bloody subjection of Scotland, the motif of blood in Lady Macbeth's sleepwalking recalls us to the past.

Genre depends on looking both backwards and forwards. We can only see Tragedy as the rise and fall of an outstanding figure if the work encourages us to cast our minds back over what has happened and forward to coming events.

Summary

Leitmotifs allow the reader to grasp the theme of a work. They also make readers think about what has happened, and to anticipate what might happen. Genre depends on the way a work encourages readers to look both backwards and forwards.

37.3   Binary opposites

Pairs

Structuralists argue that literary works are based on sets of polarities. Sometimes, these are binary opposites – two things linked by their differences. Obvious examples of binary opposites are night and day or male and female. It is not difficult to think of more: hot and cold, happy and sad, high and low, living and dead and so on.

> **Literary critics who have been influenced by Structuralist theories see works as existing through the paired tensions of a series of binary opposites.**

Structuralists like to apply their thinking to prose fiction, but usually the sheer bulk of a novel prevents us from seeing polarities clearly. It is therefore in the short poem that binary opposites are often most evident. Take the case of Thomas Hardy's poem about the Wessex boy who dies in the Boer War, 'Drummer Hodge' (1899):

> They throw in Drummer Hodge, to rest
> Uncoffined – just as found:
> His landmark is a kopje-crest
> That breaks the veldt around;
> And foreign costellations west
> Each night above his mound.
>
> Young Hodge the Drummer never knew –
> Fresh from his Wessex home –
> The meaning of the broad Karoo,
> The Bush, the dusty loam,
> And why uprose to nightly view
> Strange stars amid the gloam.
>
> Yet portion of that unknown plain
> Will Hodge for ever be;
> His homely Northern breast and brain
> Grow to some Southern tree,
> And strange-eyed constellations reign
> His stars eternally.

A Structuralist reading would concentrate on the binary opposites: the sky and the earth, the northern and the southern hemispheres, the brevity of life and the eternity of the stars, the living and the dead, and home and a foreign land. If the pairings are pushed further, the flat plain and the tall tree might be included. A further pairing might be the strangeness of the landscape being the place of which Hodge will for ever be a part.

But at this point, Structuralist readings stop. There are a number of things in this poem that engage us, but a Structuralist reading is of no help in thinking them through. What, for example, is to be made of the tone of the opening? Is the nonchalant tone of 'uncoffined' appropriate because Hodge is a simple rural lad, or does it show a lack of concern in those who 'throw (him) in'? Binary terms are so general that they rarely reveal very much about the individual character of a literary work.

Summary

Some literary works, particularly short poems, can be studied in terms of how they are held together by binary opposites. These may help us see the shape of the poem, but there are issues they leave unexplored.

37.4 Parallels and polarities

Making sense of elements

Repeated motifs, echoes, anticipations and binary opposites are elements in the design of a work. What is their effect?

Here critical fashion comes into play. Do they balance and give shape, or do they indicate unresolved tensions? Structuralists tended to think the former, whilst Deconstructionists see them as promoting the latter. Of course, this is not an issue that can be decided before reading a work. If it could, there would be no point in asking the question.

Deciding on features

The first thing readers need to do is to agree about a work's features; then it might be possible to assess the effect. In 'Drummer Hodge', for example, each stanza starts with the Drummer and closes with the stars. Does this give the poem a feeling of satisfying completeness, or does it produce a tension between the littleness of life and the vastness of the universe? Again, in order to answer these questions, other aspects of the poem – tone, imagery, verbal textures, thought – will need to be brought into play.

Summary

Structuralist critics see works in terms of parallels and polarities. Some critics see these as giving works cohesion, whilst others see polarities as indicating disunity. The first step is agreeing on what elements are in fact present in the work.

37.5   Silences

Because the Deconstructionists were keen to identify elements in a text that made for discontinuity, they were strong on seeing those things that are at odds with what look to be the chief interests of the text.

It is sometimes important to think about what is not (but might have been) said in a literary work.

Literature is about witholding as well as stating.

Silences in a text can be quite loud. To take a famous example: Hardy does not give Tess anything to say at moments of crisis in *Tess of the d'Urbervilles* (1891). This is a textual silence: a moment when the reader expects something but is baulked by silence or an authorial commentary, which is a kind of silence.

The term 'silence' can cover action as well as speech, because if it is not present, then the author (or the text) is silent about it. So, in the case of Tess, it is not clear what is the nature of her undoing (see Chapter 31, section 31.5), and nor, for example, are many details available to the reader about how exactly she kills Alec. Her execution is also, with the exception of the black flag, a silence.

Interpreting silences

Sometimes a silence shows us that an author (and possibly a culture) took no interest in the area of life that is not mentioned. John Carey noted that, in John Donne's 'Good Friday, 1613, Riding Westwards' the poet made a journey through what we now regard as one of the most beautiful parts of the English countryside, yet there is not a single mention of the landscape (*John Donne: Life, Mind and Art*, 1981). Donne is silent about what had no interest for him or his culture.

Summary

It is sometimes important to notice what an author does *not* say. Silences may indicate that either the author or the author's culture has little interest in what the text is silent about.

37.6   Disturbances

A disturbance is anything that disrupts the flow of the text. It might be a shift in subject matter or tone, or the introduction of an idea alien to the passage in which it appears. Sometimes a silence can be a disturbance, because the reader has been led to expect something that does not appear.

Making sense of mental states

In the first book of *The Prelude* (1805), Wordsworth meditates on how nature, 'when she would frame/A favoured being' will, in his infancy, 'open out the clouds'. It also delights her, he insists, to use 'Severer interventions', adding 'and so she dealt with me' (393–71).

He then recounts a tale of one such severe intervention. He begins the story (371–426) in this way:

> One evening – surely I was led by her –
> I went alone into a shepherd's boat,
> A skiff that to a willow-tree was tied
> Within a rocky cave, its usual home.

The parenthetical comment – 'surely I was led by her' – states his conviction that nature is prompting him. It is her wish that he finds the shepherd's boat, which fits almost snugly into its cave. Later, however, he says that the boat was 'Discovered by unexpected chance'. The text is beginning to be disturbed. He takes the boat and rows out on to the lake. He enjoys the physical effort of rowing and starts to speak of the boat as his own – 'I dipped my oars into the silent lake' and 'my boat/Went heaving through the water like a swan'.

But then comes the severe intervention. As he rows away from the cave, a 'huge cliff … Upreared its head' and 'Strode after me.' He returns the boat, walks home 'with grave/And serious thought' and 'for many days' his mind was troubled: 'In my thoughts/There was a darkness'.

But what is the cause of this mental darkness? It was Laurence Lerner ('What did Wordsworth mean by Nature', *Critical Quarterly*, 17/4, 1975) who shrewdly observed that nature seems to be punishing Wordsworth for stealing private property. Alternatively, nature might be severe because the boy is troubled by the issue of private property rather than attending to the sublimity the scene – the lake, the sky, the peak. It is not easy deciding what the nature or the effect of a disturbance is.

Summary

A disturbance in a text raises the issue of what the author is in fact interested in. Is the author at cross purposes with him or herself, or is the disturbance a way of getting at a complex idea?

37.7   Contradictions

Paradox

What is to be made of apparent contradictions in books? Some (earlier) critics regarded contradiction, particularly in poetry, as being both characteristic and welcome features of literature. One such critic was Cleanth Brooks, who insisted that paradox was the language of poetry (*The Well Wrought Urn*, 1947). He used the term rather freely to include any surprise in a text. For example, his point about Wordsworth's sonnet 'Composed Upon Westminster Bridge, Sept. 3, 1803' is that it is paradoxical that such a breathtaking sight should appear in a city. To Brooks, contradiction yielded unexpected sense. They are apparent conceptual contradictions that reveal a new truth.

Books at odds with themselves

The Deconstructionists, by contrast, suggest that books, in spite of the desires of authors and readers to make them coherent, rest on contradictions. In fact, they often revel in the ways in which books appear to be at cross purposes with themselves. *Jane Eyre* (1847) is a novel that resists Calvinism – the doctrine that God predestines people for salvation or damnation. The fearful Mr Brocklehurst, governor of Lowood School, embodies the Calvinistic severity against which Jane revolts. But does she? Surely the events of the novel show that she *is* a favoured being, who thrives by what looks pretty much like a predestinating providence. Those who thwart Jane – Mrs Reed, John Reed – come to fearful ends. Mr Brocklehurst is removed from the governance of Lowood School, and Mr Rochester, because he concealed his mad wife from Jane, is punished by blindness. Is *Jane Eyre* a Calvinist novel which undermines Calvinism?

Summary

The Deconstructionists think that a text contains contradictions. This is a more sweeping idea than thinking that it rests on paradox. Some works seem to undermine themselves with contradictory features.

37.8   Unity and diversity

Unified works

It was once popular in literary criticism to demonstrate that any odd or marginal element in a book (usually a play or a novel) is, contrary to appearance, an important or even central feature. Another version of this impulse was to state that books that appeared to be disjointed are in fact unified, that all the elements hang together.

The Deconstructionists take the opposite view. Meaning is contradicted in books, and so books themselves are a collection of diverse elements.

Diversity reconsidered

Books do not have to obey literary laws. The French, who in the past have demanded that books be written according to strict requirements, found Shakespeare difficult because he switched from verse to prose, from place to place and from tragedy to comedy. But the French had a point. There is diversity in a Shakespeare play, and sometimes we are puzzled about how some things fit in – and indeed, if they do.

But perhaps we should not expect all elements in a book to fit neatly together: some passages might be entertaining in themselves irrespective of their place in the larger design of the work. This idea makes sense of those scenes in drama that interest us while not seeming to contribute to the rest of the play. Perhaps our ideas about literature have been influenced so strongly by neo-classical ideas of symmetry, balance and order that we do not appreciate works that are exploratory and digressive. If we accept that there are different ways of designing a work, then we might come to appreciate the mysterious world of Edmund Spenser's *The Faerie Queene* (1590) and the visionary canvas, packed with lively incidents, of William Langland's *Piers Plowman* (three versions written between 1362 and 1385).

Summary

We do not have to think of all works as constituting a unity. Works can contain a diversity of elements and still make sense. In fact, we might find diverse works more lively and engaging.

37.9 Playing with language

Language games

Although it is Postmodernism, a fashion of the 1980s, that has popularized the notion of culture as a kind of play, writers have long recognized the playful element in culture. The Medieval historian, Johan Huizinga, wrote *Homo Ludens* (man the player) (1944), and the philosopher, Ludwig Wittgenstein, who was interested in the diversity of language, wrote in his *Philosophical Investigations* (1952) of each kind of discourse as a 'language game'.

Linguistic play

Writers have often revelled in the exploration of language. Allusions, etymological speculation and puns indicate the pleasure found in linguistic play. James Joyce is a twentieth-century example.

The sixteenth and seventeenth centuries were rich periods for revelling in words. In John Donne's 'A Fever' (1633), the poet is anxious about the fever that afflicts his beloved. In his imagination, her fever is like the fire that, at the end of the world, will consume everything. This is the fourth stanza:

> Oh wrangling schools, that search what fire
>   Shall burn the world, had none the wit
> Unto this knowledge to aspire,
>   That this her fever might be it.

The 'wrangling schools' are groups of scholars who debate what kind of fire will burn the world at the end of time. With a scholarly relish and academic exactitude the poet deftly punches home the (to him) obvious answer: 'this her fever might be it'. The scholars didn't reach this conclusion, because they didn't have the brains ('wit') to 'aspire' to the knowledge that he has. Donne plays with 'aspire'. It means to have a fixed desire to rise upwards. Now a fever is hot like fire, and as fire rises, so ought scholars' minds. Donne insinuates that his does. 'Aspire' also means breathing, so he might be making a parallel between minds panting for knowledge and the laboured breathing of his fevered beloved.

Summary

Modern theories about literature draw attention to an ancient enjoyment – literature as play. Writers play with the multiple meanings of the words they use.

▪ ▼ **38** Debating Interpretations

38.1   The value of internal interpretation

Ordinary reading

Three points may be made in favour of internal interpretation:

- Internal interpretation accords with what most of us do: we read what is before us in the terms in which it presents itself.
- Many examination questions require candidates to read the words on the page. Examiners assume that, with perception and thought, candidates will be able to make sense of a previously unseen passage.
- If language is as important as we claim it is, it must be the case that it communicates with us as it stands.

Problems with internal interpretation

There are three problems:

- Formalist and Structuralist ideas are general and can therefore be vague. For example, several features of a text can count as structure.
- Internal interpretations can identify features in a work, but are not much use when we try to *think* about those features.
- If, as some theories maintain, meaning is unstable, there would be little point in reading at all.

Summary

Concentrating on the words on the page is what we all do in reading. If words were not accessible as they stand, we would not value literature, and nor would examiners set previously unseen passages. But internal interpretation has problems: its terminology is often general, it can only take us so far, and some of its theories make reading pointless.

38.2   Is internal interpretation sufficient?

Do books stand alone?

There is a case that words do not stand alone.

> **When we think about the words of a text, they are not the only words we are thinking about.**

The connotations of a word in a text depend on its usages outside the text, and we can only understand a sentence because we have read other sentences. Reading has given us the necessary grammatical competence.

Back to history

Words have connotations because they have been used for a long time. The connotations of a word might be understood as the history of its use. Language was not invented yesterday. The historical study of literature is also the *historical interpretation* of literature. History is present in a text in the following ways:

- When words have changed their meanings, past meanings are present in a text.
- Contemporary ideas, attitudes and even (occasionally) events are present in the words of a text. We need to know what these are in order to see what is happening in the book we are studying.
- Writers draw on other books – in particular, the Bible and the Classics – so an acquaintance with those works is often necessary if we are to understand a book fully.
- Ideas have a history. They adjust and change, and their changes are written in language. If we look at books from various periods we see that even our big ideas – ideas about the mind, about love and about society – have undergone changes.

Historical interpretation requires us to look at external factors.

Summary

The words of a text do not stand alone. They belong to the vocabulary and rules of language. They also belong to history. Historical study is also historical interpretation. Historical interpretation works on the assumption that words have a history, that they reflect contemporary ideas, that they are dependent on other texts, and that ideas themselves have a history.

◼ ⌄ **39** External Interpretation: Social

39.1 Beliefs

What matters to us

Concentrating on a text leads us outside it. Books engage our beliefs. We do not leave our beliefs behind when we read. What we find significant in a book usually links up with our beliefs, with what we think matters. Interpretation will therefore touch on beliefs external to the text.

We can say this about schools of interpretation:

Theories arise because critics think certain areas of life are important.

Those concerned about the importance of the living world value writers who appreciate the countryside, wildlife and the moral issues of our responsibility for the created order. Thus there has arisen what is called *Eco-criticism*. Eco-criticism values writers such as John Clare and Edward Thomas. Ecology is external to literature, and critics who are concerned about the state of the planet bring this interest to interpretation.

Because we think that certain ideas are important, we read books in the light of them. Furthermore, we use some of the terms associated with these ideas in the discussion of literature.

When we *knowingly* read books in the light of ideas, we are practising a form of external interpretation.

Ideology

There is a link between the ideas we bring to the interpretation of a book, and books themselves. In both we put together pictures of the world. In the word commonly used, we 'construct' a world. To use the example given above, ecology gives us a picture of the world; it is a picture of what the world is like and how we ought to behave in relation to it.

A literary work is also a picture of the world, a picture that tells us what matters. In literary works, we see what authors value. They may value relationships within families, within communities, with those they love, with the world about them, and with God. It is as if an author is creating a world and saying to us: look at this because it is important.

The popular word for this is *ideology*. Ideology is a very broad term but it might be summed up as meaning any idea that shapes the way we try to understand the world about us. An ideology can be a set of beliefs, an attitude, an outlook or an assumption. It can come in the form of a set of stories (historical or mythical), images, symbols, systems of doctrine and laws. Sometimes we acknowledge consciously that the ideas matter, and sometimes we just take them for granted. Either way, they shape what we say. In that sense external interpretation is ideological. It is concerned with the presence in literature of those things that we think matter in our understanding of the world.

Summary

When we interpret a book we often go outside it to appeal to what we find interesting and valuable. Our beliefs are like pictures of what is important. These ways of thinking are sometimes described as ideologies. External interpretation is often ideological in that it appeals to our beliefs about what is important.

39.2 Marxist interpretation

History and society

The basis of historical interpretation is that books are shaped and moulded by the manners, morals, attitudes and thoughts of the people among whom the author lives. Readers might not be particularly aware of this at the time, but with the passage of time, a book is seen to be very much a part of the world in which it was written. *Nineteen Eighty Four* (1949), for example, is very much a post-Second World War novel.

We often go beyond morals and manners in our interpretations and focus on social and material factors – the organization of society and the distribution of wealth. Society and economics are seen as the context, condition and chief causal feature of literature. Society and economics shape (and in some critics' minds, determine) what is written.

Karl Marx

A number of critics apply the thought of Karl Marx (1818–83) to the interpretation of literature. Marx was a sophisticated German intellectual who lived in England for most of his adult life (he is buried in Highgate Cemetery, London). His interests included economic history, philosophy and sociology.

A theory of history

Marxism has two central ideas. One is a theory of history, which owes a lot to G. W. F. Hegel, a German philosopher who said that through the interaction of two contrary states – the thesis and the antithesis – a new state or condition – the synthesis – emerges. Marx saw this dialectic at work in history. There was an inevitable, though turbulent, progress from Medieval serfdom, through capitalism and on to a Communist state in which all things are held in common, and the state, being superfluous, withers away.

The economic basis of society

The second basic idea of Marxism is that everything we say, do, make and think is the superstructure of a base that is economic. Economics – how wealth is created, goods manufactured and who owns the means of production – is the sole determining factor as to what a society is like. As with the theory of history, this understanding of society is conceived of in terms of scientific laws. Marxism is a causal thesis: what we see going on in society can be explained completely as the product of its economic base.

Marx and literature

If we ask how Marx helps us to interpret a book, the answer is likely to be: hardly at all. The historical thesis barely touches literature. The second makes interpretation unnecessary, because the Marxist knows the answer to everything: whatever the question is, the answer is going to be the economic basis of society. To be true to the principles of Marxism, the theory about the economic basis of everything must explain every detail of a text.

Using Marx

But why should we take any notice of Marxism? The answer can only be that some of the ideas are useful. But they can only be useful if Marxism is tempered to allow some independence to literature. This is what 'soft' Marxism allows. Whatever the economic pressures, the author can treat the elements of a book independently of those pressures. Even if the elements of a book are, so to speak, given by the economic base, the author can still arrange them with some degree of freedom.

Now, if this is the case, then the reader is also free to use some of the emphases of Marxism in the interpretation of literature. This means that someone who is not a Marxist (and most people aren't) can think about the things Marx regarded as important (to him it was a matter of belief) and use them in the interpretation of books.

Summary

Though the ideas of Karl Marx do not seem to offer much help to the interpreter, Marxism can direct the reader to certain social and economic features of a text. Critics can think about these without being committed to Marxist theories.

39.3 Money

Old and new wealth

It is often useful to ask of a book: how is money presented? We have seen in Chapter 33, section 33.1 the important distinction between old (inherited) and new (manufacture and trade) money. In Marxist terms, old and new wealth represent two phases of the economic process. Old wealth has grown out of the feudal system, is based on land and retains some feudal characteristics. The landowner knows those who work on the estate, because they live in estate cottages. His authority is exercised through magistrate's courts and the appointment of clergy to serve in the local church. In technical terms, the landowner is the patron of the living. The social system of old money is hierarchical yet intimate. Many of these features can be found in Jane Austen's presentation of Mr Knightley in *Emma* (1816). He has, for example, a very high regard for one of his young tenant farmers, Robert Martin.

New money is a characteristic of capitalism. This is a system in which money itself becomes the basis of industry. A man invests his capital in the means of production, and workers sell their labour to him in exchange for wages. This often means that the crafts they once practised are no longer of use to them. Moreover, the work reduces them to functions – hands, as they were called in the nineteenth century – in a system that can become anonymous. Both owner and workers are vulnerable to economic change. If demand falls away, production will decrease and workers will be put on short time or lose their jobs.

Workers formed Unions or Combinations in order to protect themselves. These are of considerable interest to historians influenced by Marx, because they are indications of the inevitable hostility between capital and labour. Marx thought that the capitalist system was contradictory, and the contradictions would eventually result in a revolution in which workers would seize the means of production.

Nineteenth-century novelists who wrote about industry were unaware of of the teaching of Marx, but they did recognize the tensions between management and workers. However, their 'solution' is moral rather than political or economic. Both Dickens in *Hard Times* (1854) and Elizabeth Gaskell in *North and South* (1855) look to a recognition of our common humanity as a way of overcoming social hostilities.

Marriage and money

In Jane Austen, the importance of money in marriage is (perhaps uncomfortably) evident. Marriage is an economic institution (though it is not only that). Mrs Bennet is a figure of fun in *Pride and Prejudice* (1813), yet she recognizes that, since the family is not wealthy, her daughters will have to make financially advantageous matches.

In Jane Austen, a good marriage – one in which financial security accompanies equality of thought and feeling in the contracting parties – is usually presented as a 'reward'. This, of course, is hardly a view that a Marxist (or any economist) would take. It looks more like an inheritance from fables in which, through the agency of magic, those who have struggled are compensated by good fortune. Something of this use of wealth is evident in Charlotte Brontë's *Jane Eyre* (1847). Jane has no moral choice other than to leave Mr Rochester, but after distressing wanderings she is taken in by people who turn out to be relatives. Furthermore, it is discovered that she is in fact an heiress to a considerable fortune.

Summary

We can use some Marxist ideas in understanding how money is presented. The novelists who wrote about industrial problems understood how manufacturing created unrest between owners and workers. Money is an important factor in marriage. Some literary uses of money cannot be understood in Marxist terms.

39.4   Work

Silence about work

Work is a central part of life, and it is an activity that Marxists regard as important. But what about its place in literature?

Jane Eyre has a job: she is a teacher and governess. Yet we don't see her working very much. For example, she becomes a pupil teacher at Lowood and later the sole teacher in a rural school, yet we don't learn much about what, or indeed how, she teaches.

There is often a silence about work in English literature.

This is possibly because the English do not consciously have, at least in their literature, an economic understanding of life. Our vocabulary gives value to personal and intellectual matters rather than economic ones. In *Little Dorrit* (1857) Charles Dickens creates a character called Daniel Doyce, who is an inventor, but we never learn what he has invented.

Not all novelists are quite as silent as Dickens. Thomas Hardy deals with the realities of work in *Tess of the d'Urbervilles* (1891). He is interested in how the rural economy works. His understanding is in accord with the emphases of Marxism. In Chapter 47, a threshing machine – 'a timber-framed construction, with straps and wheels appertaining' – is harnessed to an engine – 'black with a sustained hiss'. Technology is transforming farming and the lives of those who, in Hardy's words, 'had come to serve' the machine. He presents this transformation by showing how the division of labour becomes spatial. The women serve the machine by feeding it with the sheaves of hay. The man who operates the engine – 'a tall motionless being ... sooty and grimy' – stands at a 'little way off'. The capitalist farmer oversees the work but does not himself join in the production line. The scene is capitalism pretty much as Marx might have described it. Furthermore, Hardy's language shows how the workers on the machine – all of them women – are kept in subjection. The machine is 'a red tyrant' (agricultural machinery was almost invariably painted red) which 'kept up a despotic demand upon the endurance of their muscles and nerves.'

Summary

Work is an important aspect of our lives, but it is oddly missing from literature. An interesting exception is Hardy, who shows how money determines the patterns of work and the relationships between owner and labourer.

39.5   Trade

Exchange

Money is whatever can be used in exchange. In 1776, Adam Smith published his study of what is now called economics – *The Wealth of Nations*. His fourth chapter deals with the origins of money. This is how he concludes his opening paragraph: 'Every man thus lives by exchanging, or becomes in some measure a merchant, and the society itself grows to be what is properly a commercial society.'

Money is the most convenient means by which wealth can be put to work, and putting wealth to work usually involves exchange. If I need to buy bread, the most convenient form of exchange is money.

It is helpful to quote Adam Smith, because it reminds us that Marx is not the only writer who has put his stamp on our thinking about how wealth works. In fact, our present understanding of wealth owes far more to Smith, a Scottish philosopher, than it does to Marx.

Exchange in literature

Exchange – another word for trade – has an interesting place in literature. Like work, it is not particularly prominent as far as details go, but it is a powerful element in the plotting of some works and it provides a metaphor for some areas of human activity.

Nineteenth-century fiction is a rich source for exploration into the workings of exchange. Some critics have seen the dust-heaps in Dickens' *Our Mutual Friend* (1865) as being symbolic of the power of wealth (see Chapter 33, section 33.3). They dominate the London skyline and, in metaphorical terms, dominate the novel, as in a novel preoccupied with money, they are an example of the power of how, through exchange, wealth is created. Dust – refuse – was collected and then sorted by both men and women into various categories: pots, pans, crockery, bones, rags and metal. These were sold: pots and pans went into road-making, bones were used for glue or soap, rags could be used in paper-making, and metal could be melted down. Everything was used: vegetable matter was used in making fertilizer, and ashes were sold to brick manufacturers. It was very profitable. Trade in dust was an entire economy, and in the novel it is an image of how economies work. As such it is interestingly ambiguous. How should we respond? Should we recoil from a society that has dirt and filth (it has been claimed that dust-heaps contained human excreta) as its base, or should we admire the enterprise that can turn what has apparently no value into wealth?

Merchants

Shakespeare's *The Merchant of Venice* (1596) displays an acute understanding of the working of the Venetian economy. Venice, built on hundreds of tiny islands, has no room to grow crops, so food and goods have to be imported. A merchant, therefore, is essential to the life of the city. In the opening scene, Antonio is sad, and his friends automatically assume that he is anxious about the fate of his ships. In one speech, Salerio says he can well imagine Antonio's anxieties, for, if the boats were his, he would imagine how striking 'dangerous rocks' would

> scatter all her spices on the stream,
> Enrobe the roaring waters with my silks
> (1.1. 33–4)

That eerie, even slightly surreal image of goods lacing the surface of the seas presents the economic life of a state that has to trade for the things it cannot produce, and what the state has to offer in return for spices and silks is money.

Venice's dependence on trade makes Shylock a pivotal figure in the Venetian economy. Because merchants do not always have the necessary means to put a fleet of ships to sea, they need to borrow money, and because borrowing money at interest is forbidden to Christians, recourse has to be made to Jewish money-lenders. But Jews are a despised and mistreated group in Venice (Shylock says this to the Christians, and no one contests the view), so he is in a strange position – a despised figure who is yet central to the economy. Shylock's attempt to 'kill' Antonio might be understood as a failed business enterprise, and at the end one of his punishments is economic. On his death, Shylock's wealth goes to his daughter (now a Christian).

Communication as exchange

A form of exchange that is prominent in English drama is the exchange of information. Characters might be said to trade in knowledge. One way of creating plots is to introduce an element of unreliability into exchanges. When human communication is destabilized by an unreliable exchange, the disruption becomes the means by which the plot moves.

Ben Jonson makes corrupt communications central to his work; in, for example, *Volpone* (1607). Volpone, significantly a citizen of Venice, lets it be known that he is near to death, so that those who claim to be his friends will please him in the hope that, on his death, he will make them his heirs. But Volpone is in fact healthy and vigorous, and relishes duping his visitors. Dependent upon this fundamental deception are particular deceptions, one for each of those who would inherit his wealth. The play opens with each of them visiting Volpone with a gift and being told by Mosca, Volpone's scheming servant, that each has hopes of inheritance.

A Marxist reading would see Jonson as exposing the essentially corrupt nature of capitalism. The fundamental deception would correspond to the capitalist system, which deprives individual workers of their just rewards, and the various corrupt communications that are based on the fundamental deception would be particular transactions in which the one with capital benefits at the expense of the ones who work for him. It is a characteristic of Marxist criticism that, in determining the meaning of a work, the critic gives an essentially allegorical reading.

Summary

Trade or exchange features in literature in a number of ways. We sometimes see how an object is traded. We can also see how societies that exist by trade depend on money and the agreements people make. Trade can be metaphoric of other forms of exchange, such as information.

39.6 Material goods

Marx and material objects

Marxism gives a special place in its thought to material objects. In philosophical terms, the material precedes the notional. Notions (ideas) are dependent on the material world that gives rise to them. Hence a Marxist will find significance in the objects that occur in literature.

It would no doubt be of interest to a Marxist that Ben Jonson's plays are full of physical objects. This can be discovered in performance. Whereas few props are required when playing Shakespeare, Ben Jonson's plays are full of things. *Bartholomew Fair* (1614), in particular, requires all sorts of physical goods. (It is far quieter being a stage manager for a Shakespeare play than one by Ben Jonson.)

Characters and material goods

Some years ago, Arnold Kettle drew attention to how characters were sometimes treated as physical objects. When Tess goes to 'claim kin' at the house of another family called d'Urberville, her mother dresses her up as if she were an attractive gift. Later, her mother almost admits that she had hoped that the owner would seduce and then marry Tess. In other words, her mother did treat her as a material good, which, so to speak, Alec would sexually appropriate and complete the transaction with a marriage contract.

Commodities

Adam Smith used the word 'commodity' of any object that could be bought or sold. The word has been extended to describe the process whereby anything desirable is treated as a material good. This is called *commodification*. By dressing her up, Tess's mother commodifies her daughter. Tess becomes an item of goods and so also, we might argue, does physical beauty. In Tess, beauty is commodified; it becomes something that can be possessed (in Alec's case, sexually) and owned.

Another thing that is commodified in nineteenth-century literature is education. In *Great Expectations* (1860), Pip wants education so that he can attract Estella. When he is told that he has 'great expectations', Pip assumes that this great good fortune, which includes the kind of education a gentleman would have had, is a free gift, a kind of reward bestowed by a fairy godmother (Miss Havisham) upon a male version of Cinderella. (Pip does not exactly sit among the cinders, but he does work in the coals and ashes of the blacksmith's shop.)

But Pip's education is not a free commodity; it has been worked for by a convict, who has been transported to Australia for his crimes. He returns to admire what he has done for Pip. In the passages in which he gloats over the gentleman that he has turned Pip into, the reader can see that Pip himself has been commodified. He has been turned into a material good that might fetch a high price in the market of fashionable society.

Summary

In novels and plays, material goods are sometimes given a significant place. The process of commodification turns people, qualities (such as beauty) and social accomplishments (such as education) into goods that confer status on those that have them.

39.7 Social class

Chaucer and class

Class – the stratification of society into different levels of wealth and esteem – is a very prominent feature of English literature. Geoffrey Chaucer's Canterbury pilgrims represent several different layers of Late Medieval society. The Franklin is a country gentleman, the Monk a powerful prelate, the Merchant a man of European importance, the Doctor a successful professional man, and the Parson a poor servant of the Church.

Chaucer's humour sometimes depends on class. The Maunciple (a lawyer's Steward) is a repetition of the old joke about the servant being cleverer than the master:

> Now is that naf of God a ful fair grace
> That swich a lewed mannes wit shal pace
> The wisdom of an heep of lerned men?
> ('Prologue', 573–5)

The image of 'an heep of lerned men' – all their arms and legs sticking out at ungainly angles – focuses the confusion of the learned lawyers compared to the astute and efficient Maunciple. But, of course, it would not be funny were the Maunciple not a servant.

What makes class

Of course, to the Marxist, class is a matter of wealth. Society is stratified on the basis of who owns the means of production. But wealth is not the only thing that constitutes class. When, in *Great Expectations*, Pip visits Miss Havisham, he is made aware of his class not through money but via language and dress. Estella mocks him for calling 'knaves' (playing cards) 'jacks' and for having thick leather on the soles of his shoes. These social indicators are not just a matter of money. Class is a complex matter. In L. P. Hartley's *The Go-Between* (1953), Leo learns that gentlemen eat their porridge standing up.

Class and space

In Dickens' *Our Mutual Friend*, there is a spatial enactment of social stratifica- tion. The Veneerings are introduced in the second chapter. In the tradition of English comedy, Dickens has given them a name that reflects their social stand- ing. All is a veneer in their nouveau riche world: 'their plate was new, their car- riage was new, their harness was new, their horses were new, their pictures were new'. They are entertaining new friends, when a message is delivered to one of the guests, a lawyer called Mortimer Lightwood. As the other guests are ascend- ing the staircase, Mortimer asks to see the messenger. He is the fifteen-year-old son of Gaffer Hexam, a man who earns a living by recovering dead bodies from the Thames. Space enacts social stratification. The guests go up the stairs, the boy remains below. Soon the boy will be outside the 'bran-new house', while the guests remain within, and had it not been for Mortimer's request to see the mes- senger, the classes would not have met.

Class and education

Space is not the only social signifier. Mortimer asks who wrote the note. The boy answers that he did. When Mortimer asks if any steps were taken to resuscitate the body, the boy answers:

> 'You wouldn't ask, sir, if you knew his state. Pharoah's multitudes that were drowned in the Red Sea, ain't more beyond restoring to life.'

> (ch. 3)

The language slips between biblical reference and the demotic talk of the work- ing poor – 'ain't more beyond'. Mortimer comments that the boy (we are yet to learn his name – another sign of class division) knows about the Red Sea and receives the reply that he 'Read of it with teacher at the school.' Class, Dickens shows, is related to education.

As in *Great Expectations*, Dickens shows that language is an important social signifier. Dickens knew, long before the linguists spoke of language and social class, that our social status is in part established by the way in which we speak. And, of course, how we speak is related, again in part, to the kind of education we have received.

Yet another class factor arises out of the events in Chapter three. Mortimer is accompanied by a friend, Eugene Wrayburn. Thus Eugene meets the boy's sister, the beautiful Lizzie Hexam. He falls in love with her. Eugene is an interesting character, because, for much of the narrative, we don't know whether he is a hero or a villain. Is he honourable in his pursuit of Lizzie or is he merely, like Steerforth in *David Copperfield* (1850), a seducer? (In passing, it might be observed that seduction had an economic aspect. Men would spend money to win sexual favours. Virginity had a price.)

And if he is honourable, there is a social barrier. Can a professional man (he is also a lawyer) of good social standing marry a girl of her class? Dickens' solution – disabling Eugene – is discussed in Chapter 33, section 33.1.

Class and culture

English fiction often insists on the importance of culture. What is emphasized is a way of life – the habits, outlooks, interests and pastimes of a family or social group. In *Pride and Prejudice* (1813), Darcy admits that he had strong reservations about marrying Elizabeth, but these are not, strictly speaking, class matters. As Elizabeth says to Lady Catherine: 'He is a gentleman; I am a gentleman's daughter' (ch. 56). What Darcy finds difficult is the *manners* of the Bennet family – their lack of decorum, lack of restraint, silliness and vulgarity. In Elizabeth Gaskell's *North and South*, which might be described as *Pride and Prejudice* forty years on, the heroine, Margaret Hale, has acquired social standing from her father – being, at one time, a clergyman – and the hero, John Thornton, is a man who has acquired 'new money' from his factory. But what really divides them is, as the title indicates, a cultural matter: their emotional responses and their values are the products of two very different worlds – the North and the South.

The importance of culture shows that, in English fiction, class is not presented *consistently* as the *fundamental* feature of human society. George Eliot saw human society in organic terms; it has grown up like a plant, and, like any other living thing, it had adapted and developed according to the circumstances in which it grew. She recognizes that what holds it together as a living thing is religion. George Eliot had abandoned orthodox Christianity, yet she acknowledged the cohesive power of religious practice. In *Adam Bede* (1859), George Eliot shows the women entering the church for a funeral, leaving the men to talk outside for a time. Inside the church, she tells us that the service was for Adam 'the best channel he could have found for his mingled regret, yearning and resignation'. After the service, the people 'all streamed out through the old archway into the green churchyard, and began their neighbourly talk, their simple civilities, and their invitations to tea' (ch. 18). George Eliot may be more 'sociological' than religious, but the judgements she passes in and through her observations clearly display her belief that religion is the sustaining force of an organic society.

Summary

Class is a long-standing subject in English literature. It is a source of humour. Authors recognize the economic aspects of class, and they recognize how it is evident in dress, language, education and culture. In some cases, authors recognize other factors as being socially fundamental: an example is religion.

39.8   Power

Money and class create power. Influence in commerce, industry, the law and religion often accompanies those who are wealthy.

The powerless

Marxists have directed us to the powerless. It is often said that history favours the victorious. We hear *their* version of things. Similarly, in literature, it is those with power who are usually central to books. This is in part a matter of scope: the powerful can do more than the powerless. It is a sign of his rising in the world, and because there is more opportunity for the author, that Dickens makes Pip go to London to receive the benefits of his 'great expectations'.

Kings, power and the powerless

It is true that Shakespeare presents his kings as being vulnerable and human, but, nevertheless, it is their power that usually drives the plot. Part of the tragic pathos of *Richard II* is that the king is a man who has power and then loses all, apart from the power of poetry.

But there are plays in which the powerless figure as people who are beginning to secure a hold on positions of authority. In *Coriolanus* (1608), the powerless are the plebeians, the lower order of Roman society who had little direct control over the affairs of state and, correspondingly, little control over their own destinies. Shakespeare sees that once a hitherto powerless group has gained some power, they are not content, but desire more. It is a custom of Rome that the one who was elected as consul (the chief political position) seeks the approval of the people by showing them his wounds and telling them about the deeds he has done for Rome. The Third Citizen sees through this ritual:

> We have power in ourselves to do it, but it is a power that we have no power to do.

(2.3. 4–5)

It is like a riddle: when is power not power? Answer, when it is part of the ritual of confirming the consul, as the Citizen goes on to say, 'if he tell us his noble deeds, we must also tell him our noble acceptance of them'. Coriolanus is reluctant, and the crowd becomes hostile and demands the full ritual of recognition. Encouraged by the Tribunes, they reject Coriolanus, and once they have power they do not stop, but demand his death. In the exercise of their power they discover what Sicinius asks rhetorically: 'What is the city but the people?' (3.1. 199).

Summary

Writers see the connection between wealth and power. The powerful also offer more scope. Hence the interest in kings. The powerless are sometimes shown as people who desire power and, when successful, seek more.

▣ ⌄ **40** External Interpretation: Feminism

40.1 The status of women in life and literature

Feminist interpretation has at least two things in common with Marxist interpretation:

- Women are often powerless. Until the passing of the Married Woman's Property Act in 1882, married women had, legally speaking, no property. Jane Eyre was wealthy when she married Mr Rochester, but by law all her wealth would have passed to him.
- As with the poor, both writers and readers have neglected the presence of women.

The second aspect is one of the most important contributions of feminism.

> **Feminist interpretation prompts us to consider the literary presentation of women.**

This involves discerning the assumptions about women with which the author (and society at large) works. Furthermore, the presentation of women is something that both men and women do in their work, therefore both male and female authors need to be studied.

Two points need to be made about the effects of feminist interpretation:

- Feminism has had the effect of making more texts available. Only relatively recently has Christina Rossetti appeared on literary syllabuses.
- There is an important distinction between sex and gender. Sex is biological; while gender is cultural and social. Literature is usually concerned with gender. Gender is socially constructed, consisting of learned patterns of behaviour, attitudes and assumptions. (The distinction also applies to men.)

Two further comments are necessary about sex and gender:

- Authors can think their own way through the issues of gender rather than merely 'reflecting' the views of their time. Were this not so, Mary Wollstonecraft would not have written her plea for female emancipation, *A Vindication of the Rights of Woman* (1792).
- Authors in the same historical period can differ from each other in their presentation of women. Though they were friends, Charles Dickens and Wilkie Collins differ radically. No female character in Dickens is as independent,

resourceful and enterprising as Collins' Marian Halcombe in *The Woman in White* (1860).

Summary

In the past, women had little social or economic power. The rise of feminist interpretation has meant that more books by women are now studied. The distinction between sex and gender is helpful to the reader. Prevailing ideas of gender do not mean that writers cannot think for themselves, nor that writers in the same period all write about women in the same way.

40.2 Doubles

Moral pairings

Women are often presented in moral and temperamental pairs. For example, in the early parts of William Langland's *Piers Plowman* (three versions between 1362 and 1385) two allegorical female figures – Holy Church (Passus 1) and Mede (Passus 2) – form a moral polarity: Holy Church is gracious and truthful, whereas Mede is worldly and deceptive. One might say, as with other aspects of literature, that Langland has created a representative double, which will strongly influence later literature (see Chapter 52, section 52.3).

Temperamental pairings

In *Much Ado About Nothing* (1598) the pairing is temperamental. Hero and Beatrice are cousins; the former is quiet, reserved, patient and tractable, whereas the latter is sociable, open, active and independent. It is a pattern repeated in Wilkie Collins' *The Woman in White*: Laura has Hero's characteristics, and Marian is a Victorian Beatrice. The difference between Shakespeare and Collins shows the influence of the times in which the two were written. It is clear (at least to us) that Beatrice is the more attractive of the two girls, whereas in the case of the Victorian novel, the reader is expected to endorse the hero's aim of pursuing Laura.

Doubles and female authors

Female novelists also create contrasting pairs. *Jane Eyre* (1847) is sustained by a number of pairings. At Thornfield, Jane, plain and unostentatious, is a contrast to the elegant and beautiful the Honourable Blanche Ingram, and in Morton, she is a contrast to a local heiress, Rosamund Oliver.

In Christina Rossetti's parabolic poem *Goblin Market* (1862), there is a temperamental and moral contrast between the two sisters, who encounter the goblins: Laura yields to the temptation of eating fairy food, but Lizzie remains firm and eventually rescues her sister.

Summary

A popular form of the literary presentation of women is the double. Two women are sharply contrasted in terms of their temperaments and moral behaviour.

40.3   Images of women

Defined roles

One of the impulses behind the revival of interest in female issues was the growing awareness in the 1960s that women were habitually presented in advertising, films, books and songs in terms of certain confining images. The feminists saw that these 'social constructions' had no authority other than custom.

The female *Bildungsroman*

A *Bildungsroman* is a novel in which the central figure grows through childhood and adolescence to achieve, usually by way of a struggle, a firm sense of identity (see Chapter 2, section 2.7). Among English novels, D. H. Lawrence's *Sons and Lovers* (1913) and James Joyce's *A Portrait of the Artist as a Young Man* (1916) have the recognizable features – relationships with family, emotional turmoils and an awareness of vocation.

Nineteenth-century novels by women can be read as narratives about achieving female identity. Women have their own particular struggles. One of them is with beauty; the beauty which people expect and admire in a woman. But what of the woman who is not considered beautiful? A comparison with a male *Bildungsroman* will help here. It is not an issue in *Great Expectations* (1860) as to what Pip looks like, but it is an issue in fiction about women, particularly popular fiction. We still, for example, expect beauty in film actresses.

As we have seen in section 40.2, Charlotte Brontë's *Jane Eyre* concerns, in part, the heroine's struggles against the conventional image of female beauty. Another young woman who struggles with her lack of (conventional) female beauty is Maggie Tulliver in George Eliot's *The Mill on the Floss* (1860). The dark, wild-haired Maggie is a contrast to her conventionally pretty cousin, Lucy: 'the neatest little rose-bud mouth ... her little round neck ... her little straight nose ... her little clear eyebrows, rather darker than her curls, to match her hazel eyes' (Chapter 7). Giving prominence to the woman who is not beautiful might be seen as an important assertion about a female identity that is not dictated by prevailing (and largely male?) tastes.

Summary

Literature presents and questions received images of women. The female *Bildungsroman* (the novel of growth) shows women coming to terms with conventional female images, particularly where beauty is concerned.

40.4   Names

Name and identity

Alfred, Lord Tennyson's 'The Lady of Shalott' (1830), an Arthurian story, can be interpreted as an allegory of the place of women in the contemporary world. The Lady is confined (we are not told why) in a tower on the island of Shalott. A curse, she has heard, will come upon her if she looks directly out of the window. Instead of a direct acquaintance with the world, she weaves, from an image in a mirror, a tapestry of the world outside. Hers is a world of shadows. When a knight rides into view, she abandons her work and leaves the tower, takes a boat, sings and dies as it reaches many-towered Camelot.

But before she enters the boat, she establishes her identity:

> And round about the prow she wrote
> *The Lady of Shalott.*

The act of writing establishes her identity. Perhaps the poem can be read as being about the importance of female writing, of giving voice to female experience.

Uncertainty about names

In the struggle for identity, there may be uncertainty about names. There is a scene early in *Wuthering Heights* (1847) in which Lockwood, the primary narrator, finds names scratched on the paint of a ledge: 'Catherine Earnshaw, here and there varied to Catherine Heathcliff, and then again to Catherine Linton' (Chapter 3) As the novel unfolds, the reader sees that the first is the name Catherine was born with and the last the name she assumes when she marries. The middle name might be said to represent who she thinks she is – the soul mate (sister or wife?) of Heathcliff. That there are three names is expressive of the uncertainty of her identity and the emotional struggle she has in trying to establish it. Her daughter, also called Catherine, legally has all three names. She is born Catherine Linton and when she marries she becomes Catherine Heathcliff. The novel closes with the prospect of her marriage to Hareton, whereupon she will become Catherine Earnshaw. The names pair mother and daughter. If it is true, as Q. D. Leavis argues (*Lectures in America*, 1969), that the daughter matures beyond the demanding wilfulness of her mother, does this make, as Feminists might argue, the younger Catherine a conventional mid-Victorian lady?

Summary

Names bestow identities. Characters assert their identities through their names. To write one's name is an establishment of identity. Characters' confusions are sometimes expressed in doubts about their names.

40.5   Virgins

Virgin or mistress?

The story of Jane Eyre is of one who, by leaving the man she loves, chooses to remain a virgin. Jane, therefore, is doubled with Celine Varens, Rochester's French mistress and mother of Adele, whom Jane teaches. Celine stayed with Rochester until she took another lover. But Jane wishes to be a wife, not a kept woman. The novel closes with the fulfilment of her wish; one might even say *vow*. She marries him and becomes a mother.

A cult

The cult of virginity was a feature of the Jacobean Court (early seventeenth century), so perhaps the stress on Miranda's virginity in *The Tempest* (1610) owes something to contemporary notions of purity. Prospero, her father, hopes that Ferdinand will court her, but is constantly warning the pair about the dangers of passion. The Masque he orders for their betrothal is about the allaying of lust through the defeat of Cupid, the son of Venus.

Maiden no more

Loss of virginity outside marriage has been, traditionally, one of the themes of literature. The Medieval world was fascinated by the figure of Cressida or Cressid. Hers is the story of how, during the Trojan War, she yields to Troilus but, having been forced to join the Greek camp because of the defection of her father, she takes a new lover, Diomed. This is the tale told by Chaucer (*Troilus and Criseyde*, c. 1385) and later reworked by Shakespeare (*Troilus and Cressida*, 1601). Interestingly, both versions focus on the sufferings of Troilus. The Scottish poet, Robert Henryson, extended the tale in *The Testament of Cressid* (late fifteenth century), in which he imagines how, after Diomed abandons her, she is passed around the Greek camp, becomes a common prostitute and eventually a leper.

Henryson looks severe (is the poem a sermon on the folly of yielding to passion?), yet it could be argued that he arouses the reader's sympathy for Cressid when, while she is lying by the side of the road, Troilus rides by and fails to see who she is. It is perhaps the most significant scene of *non-recognition* in literature.

It is worth thinking about how Thomas Hardy treats this theme in *Tess of the d'Urbervilles* (1891). He recognizes that loss of virginity is socially significant by calling the first Phase *Maiden* and the second *Maiden No More*. Yet he also provides a sub-title for the novel – *A Pure Woman*. Hardy is being quietly yet firmly subversive. What makes Tess remarkable is something to do with her emotional spontaneity and her sympathy with the living world. It has nothing to do with virginity. Hardy said that complaints about the sub-title made him wish he had never included it. Yet it is a sure guide as to how to interpret the novel.

Brides

The image of the virgin in the form of the white-clothed bride haunts the nineteenth century. Emily Dickinson, who rarely left her house except for church, dressed in white as if she were the bride ready to meet the groom. In *Great Expectations*, Miss Havisham, jilted at the altar, lives in her huge house, dressed in her bridal gown with her decaying wedding cake, the home of innumerable blotchy spiders, still in the centre of the dining table.

Summary

The virgin is a central image in literature. Sometimes she is doubled with her opposite – the mistress. The loss of virginity, other than in marriage, is usually momentous. The image of the bride is a version of the virgin figure. Some authors have subverted the traditional image of the virgin.

40.6   Mothers

Mothers are a clear case of biology and gender. That women give birth is a fact of nature; what we think of mothers is a matter of attitude, opinion and belief. That means, of course, that it is also a matter of literary presentation.

Marginalized mothers

To put the matter simply:

Mothers are not as central as we might expect.

There are mothers in literature, but the sustained exploration of what it is to be a mother is not one of the options that literature in English has commonly taken. This is strange when there are very important mother figures in mythology. Ceres or Demeter is the goddess of natural generation and the mother of Persephone.

Narrative opportunities

Perhaps mothers present insufficient narrative opportunities. Furthermore, the perils of childbirth in past eras gave plausibility to the literary decision to exclude them. Orphans are attractive. The disturbance in what we take to be normal family life is the basis of many of the plots woven around a heroine. From Cinderella to Dorothea Brooke, literature makes motherless girls central. Heroes also lack mothers: Pip and Huckleberry Finn are motherless. And the orphan is not just a nineteenth-century literary phenomenon; think of the plot opportunities that J. K. Rowling would have missed if Harry Potter's parents were alive.

Absent mothers

Sometimes, mothers are never referred to. There are no references to the mothers of Katherina and Bianca in *The Taming of the Shrew* (1595), and neither the mothers of Beatrice nor Hero are mentioned in *Much Ado About Nothing*. And even when mothers are mentioned, many of Shakespeare's plots concern the relationships between fathers and daughters, as in *As You Like It* (1599), *King Lear* (1605) and *The Tempest* (1610). With the exception of Volumnia in *Coriolanus* (1608), mothers are rarely central in Shakespeare. It is the role of Juliet and not Lady Capulet that gives the most opportunities to an actress. Admittedly, Shakespeare had to cope with boy actors playing women's roles, yet he found boys to play Lady Macbeth and Cleopatra.

Jane Austen and the later nineteenth century

Jane Austen is Shakespearian in the way in which her mothers are absent or marginal. It is only Mrs Dashwood in *Sense and Sensibility* (1811) who is around when many of the significant events in her daughters' lives occur. Some mothers are either inadequate (Mrs Price in *Mansfield Park* (1814)) or silly (Mrs Bennet in *Pride and Prejudice* (1813)). Perhaps we judge them by what we expect a mother to be. If that is so, then the image of mothers exists in its most influential form *outside* literature.

If we look at later nineteenth-century literature, the picture is not significantly different. One of the social features of the Victorian period was the honour given to mothers. The photographer Margaret Cameron did many studies of the mother and child, and popular poetry, particularly the type written for public recitation, is full of praise for the goodness, kindness and courage of mothers. Yet they are interestingly marginal in the contemporary fiction and poetry that is now deemed to be worth reading. Where are the mothers in Charlotte Brontë? Is there any mother in Dickens who might be said to be a central figure? Critics point out that mothers do not play a major part in the novels of George Eliot. Elizabeth Barrett Browning's long poem *Aurora Leigh* (1857) has a passage in the first Book in praise of mothers, but these words are wrung from Aurora, because she is motherless.

Mother substitutes

Where there are no mothers, there are mother substitutes. Jane Eyre is an orphan, but Bessie, one of the maids in Mrs Reed's house, fulfils some of a mother's roles. In *Wuthering Heights*, there are plenty of orphans, who are nurtured by Nelly, the housekeeper. In *Pride and Prejudice*, Elizabeth Bennet has parents, but when it comes to advice, she has an alternative set in the Gardiners. But some women who might have substituted for mothers fail in the role. For example, the description of Mrs Joe in *Great Expectations* with her 'square inpregnable bib in front that was stuck full of pins and needles' (Chapter 2) shows that she doesn't cuddle her orphaned brother.

Beyond the last page

In narrative terms, marriage effects closure. Certainly, we must believe that the young women whom readers have grown to like and approve of will be good mothers. Mary Garth in *Middlemarch* (1871) is an example, but her motherhood will be in that world beyond the pages of the novel. Again, we cannot doubt that Jane Eyre will be a good mother, but the reference to her first child matters in the novel chiefly (only?) because the once blind Mr Rochester can see his son's eyes.

Icons of motherhood

Victorian novelists give us 'icons' of motherhood. There are scenes in which we see mothers with their children. In the penultimate chapter of *David Copperfield* (1850), David and Agnes form the image of the Victorian family: 'Agnes and I were sitting by the fire … and three of our children were playing in the room.' The scene is an icon of ideal motherhood, yet its significance is in excess of the role Agnes plays.

Motherhood and judgement

Motherhood is sometimes present as an implicit standard by which the events and characters of a work should be interpreted and judged. Such a case is Mary Shelley's *Frankenstein* (1818). The narrative invites the reader to see that Victor Frankenstein has done wrong in creating the Creature. From a feminist viewpoint, the error is that he chooses to create without the agency of woman. In a sense, the Creature has a father – his creator, Victor Frankenstein – but in no sense can he be said to have a mother. The lack of a mother accounts, in part, for the Creature's disturbing unnaturalness.

Madonnas

The nineteenth century was preoccupied with the image of the Madonna – the Blessed Virgin Mary, the Mother of God. She embodied two ideals: virgin *and* mother. The Madonna was seen as one half of a binary opposite; the mother of Redemption as opposed to Eve, the mother of fallen humankind. By imaginative extension, she is also the opposite of the Magdalen, the fallen woman.

George Eliot's *Romola* (1863) plays on two Madonna images. Chapter 43 is called 'The Unseen Madonna'. This is a picture of the Virgin, carried through the streets during a famine (*Romola* is set in fifteenth-century Florence). The people greet the picture with fervour. The Virgin is traditionally presented as a mother who loves and pities. The next chapter is called 'The Visible Madonna'. This visible embodiment of love and pity is the heroine, Romola, who announces that corn is coming and sits in the straw with the suffering mothers and children. When she rises to go with a promise to return with food, they respond:

> 'Bless you, Madonna! Bless you!' said the faint chorus, in much the same tone as that in which they had a few minutes before praised and thanked the unseen Madonna.

George Eliot's use of this image depends on her belief that religion is a symbolic expression of the highest and the best in human life. She trusts her readers to respond to the image of the Madonna as the ideal woman (see also Chapter 2, section 2.8).

Twentieth-century mothers

That mothers are central to life (and to branches of learning such as psychology) and yet not usually central to literature calls for thoughtful research. Even in the twentieth century, with the impetus of Sigmund Freud, the mother is not commonly a central figure. Mrs Morel in Lawrence's *Sons and Lovers* is clearly a very important figure, though the narrative requires her death about half way through to show that her influence persists.

Woman as mother is the subject of Margaret Atwood's allegorical *The Handmaid's Tale* (1985). The sole thing that matters about a woman is her capacity to conceive. This is presented as a restriction of female freedom. *The Handmaid's Tale* does not see motherhood as something that might be of central interest in fiction. Motherhood is a matter of subjection.

It may be that, had she lived, Sylvia Plath would have written a poetry of motherhood. In 'Morning Song' (1965) she writes of the birth and first days of her child, dwelling on the way she listens to the child's breathing and stumbles about heavily in a Victorian nightgown. Expecting a baby is the theme of Fay Weldon's *Puffball* (1980), but birth, like marriage in Victorian fiction, brings closure. In Carol Ann Duffy's *The World's Wife* (1999), although the protagonist of each poem is a woman, there is little on motherhood ('Queen Herod' and 'Demeter' are exceptions), perhaps because what she offers, in several poems, is a female version of a story originally written by a man. Yet since we all have mothers, men, it might be argued, can be expected to write about mothers as well as women. It looks as if making motherhood central is something that authors have yet to learn.

Summary

Motherhood is a central feature of our lives, but literature is quiet about it. Interest is taken in orphans, so mothers are written out of books. Mothers are presented as moral icons and as a means of judging behaviour, but they do not seem to supply sufficient interest to make them consistently central in English writing.

40.7 Women in love

Courtship

As most of the novels on examination syllabuses are from the nineteenth century and after, they reflect the social code of the time, that men are expected to woo and court. Men show their interest in a woman by offering themselves as dancing partners, making themselves pleasant through conversation and, when they judge the signs are favourable, proposing marriage. Courtship is a matter of reading the signs of a complex code. Emma Woodhouse misreads the signs from Mr Elton, so he, presuming that she is encouraging him, provides a riddle for Emma and Harriet, the subject of which, once decoded, is 'courtship'. Ordinary topics of conversation can be given an amorous edge, as when Henry Tilney in *Northanger Abbey* (1818) states that he regards dancing as an emblem of matrimony (Chapter 10).

Later in the nineteenth century, authors used female blushing as sign of amorous awakening and sexual interest. When Adam, near the end of *Adam Bede* (1859), visits Dinah, George Eliot makes her blush: 'The door opened, and Dinah stood before him, colouring deeply...' (Chapter 52).

The above examples are all from the nineteenth century.

Active heroines

Earlier, however, women are presented as being more active in matters of love. Shakespeare presents his women as bold, tactful and enterprising. They declare their love openly (Olivia in *Twelfth Night*, 1599), adopt disguises to pursue a beloved (Rosalind in *As You Like It*, 1599), tell their admirer to kill (Beatrice in *Much Ado About Nothing*, 1598) and, while concealing their identities, sleep with their beloved (Mariana in *Measure for Measure*, 1604).

Consent or refusal

But in literature that privileges men with the freedom to initiate courtship, there is still the freedom of refusal. This makes the proposal a prominent feature of nineteenth-century literature. In *Pride and Prejudice*, Elizabeth Bennet receives three proposals, two from the same man. But for the issue of female freedom, it is the first, and highly comical one, that is of particular interest.

Mr Collins has no doubt heard that women refuse when first asked, but he doesn't treat this as an indication of their *right* of refusal. To him refusal is part of the code of acceptance: 'it is usual with young ladies to reject the addresses of the man whom they secretly mean to accept' (Chapter 19).

Marriage

In Jane Austen there is no question that marriage is not desirable. In spite of the rather odd marriages we sometimes see in the novels (the Bennets, for example), the reader effortlessly endorses the close that marriage provides. Since marriage is a state to be desired, a young woman is right to be careful in her choice and firm in her refusal of unsuitable offers.

But later in the nineteenth century, there are indications that marriage might not be so valued. In Thomas Hardy's *Jude the Obscure* (1895), Sue Bridehead, soon to be married to a teacher, writes to Jude (Chapter 25) about her shock on reading the marriage service:

> It seems to me very humiliating that a giver-away should be required at all. According to the ceremony as there printed, my bridegroom chooses me of his own will and pleasure, but I don't choose him. Somebody *gives* me to him, like a she-ass, or a she-goat, or any other domestic animal.

This is a case when feminist interpretation needs the language of Marxist (or at least socioeconomic) readings. The bride, Sue discovers, has been commodified.

Summary

Women could be active wooers in Shakespeare, but later they were the objects of male courtship. Courtship was conducted according to a code that gave significance to signs such as linguistic play and female blushing. Proposals are important because they are moments of female power. Marriage is usually seen as desirable, though some female characters questioned its language.

40.8   Goddesses

Saints

In French or Italian churches, images of female saints are often in the majority. The Reformation (the break between the Church of England and the Church of Rome) in the sixteenth century resulted in fewer devotional poems about female saints. But the Roman Catholic Richard Crawshaw wrote a memorable poem, 'The Weeper', on the tears of St. Mary Magdalene, and a poem called 'The

Flaming Heart' on St. Teresa (both 1652). Feminist criticism might want to comment on the fact that in the long title to the St. Teresa poem, she is described as having 'Masculine courage of performance'. Does religion tend to talk of female piety in male terms?

Diana

The influence of the Classical world is so great that literature about female deities – both entire works and images – is an important feature of English literature. Take the figure of Diana, goddess of the moon, of chastity and of hunting. Because of her association with chastity, she was regarded as a patroness of women and her presiding over hunting also meant she was thought of as a goddess of woodlands and untamed nature. Also known as Artemis, Cynthia and Luna, she is, so to speak, the presiding deity of *A Midsummer Night's Dream* (1594) (see Chapter 45, section 45.3). One of Ben Jonson's finest lyrics – 'Hymn to Cynthia' – praises her as 'Queen and huntress, chaste and fair' (1601), seated in the 'silver chair' of the moon.

A story that haunted the English literary imagination is that of Actaeon, the hunter, who, because he saw the naked Diana bathing, was turned into a stag and torn to pieces by his own hounds. The story touches on a number of sensitivities – privacy, nakedness, illicit gazing, taboos and the punishment for infringing them. A feminist might also see it as encapsulating the male desire to look and the female struggle against being reduced to an object. In Ovid's version of the tale (2 AD onwards), Diana and her attendant nymphs are outraged at being seen naked by a man, although he stresses that Actaeon discovers Diana by accident.

The story, however, has been read as being about the self-destructive nature of male desire. Actaeon behaves according to his nature. In the opening scene of *Twelfth Night*, Orsino employs the image of Actaeon to express how, on seeing Olivia, he has been pursued by his desires:

> That instant was I turned into a hart,
> And my desires, like fell and cruel hounds,
> E'er since pursue me.

(20–2)

The image of Actaeon is a useful reminder that gender interpretations can vary according to the perspective of the reader.

The mythic dimension

It is sometimes possible to glimpse in a female character the presence of a mythic or goddess figure. In *The Winter's Tale* (1609), many remarks, both hers and those of other characters, suggest that Perdita might be seen as an earth goddess or the mythical embodiment of the Spring. In the opening speech of the sheep-shearing scene (4.4. 1–5), Florizel, her beloved, says she is 'no shepherdess, but Flora/Peering in April's front'. Flora was the goddess of flowers and the Spring.

Far more elusive – both as a presence in the poems and in terms of interpretation – is Lucy in Wordsworth's 'Lucy Poems' (1798). This girl, who 'dwelt upon th' untrodden ways/Beside the springs of Dove', is never directly met with and seems to be fulfilled in her death, when she is 'Roll'd round in earth's diurnal course/With rocks and stones and trees!' ('A slumber did my spirit seal'.) The picture of the girl as part of the daily cycle of the earth might make a reader feel that this is where she belongs, and the feeling of safety in Mother Earth might prompt the thought that she is like a spirit of the earth.

Summary

Women appear in culture as saints and goddesses. A central figure is Diana, who, in the Actaeon story, raises the issue of male desire and female beauty. Sometimes, the force of a female character depends on our seeing a mythical figure in the woman.

40.9   Female aspirations

Women at work

Female aspiration – what women want to achieve – was a pressing issue in times such as the nineteenth and early twentieth centuries, when social and economic opportunities were widening.

We need to be more exact. Women have always worked, but those who did came from the labouring classes. Hetty Sorrel, whom Adam Bede loves, works in the dairy at the Hall Farm. What is more socially significant is when daughters of middle-class families seek employment. Options were virtually confined to education, either as a governess such as Lucy Snowe in *Villette* (1853), or a teacher, as Tess aspires to be in *Tess of the D'Urbervilles*. Later, there were other options; the fashionably aloof Jordan Baker in *The Great Gatsby* (1925) is a professional golfer.

A double trajectory

Jane Eyre deals imaginatively with the issue of what a woman can achieve. The novel consists of a double trajectory, each plot movement comprising a distinctively female aspiration. Jane passionately longs for love; she desires a husband and a child. This love/domesticity plot suffers a disjunction with the discovery that Mr Rochester has a wife.

Jane's work provides the basis for the second plot. Jane comes from a respectable family but is obliged to work. She begins as a teacher at Lowood, the school to which she was sent as a border by Mrs Reed. She then goes to Thornfield as a governess. After she has left Thornfield she becomes a village schoolteacher. This professional plot is given expression by Jane's increasing control over her own physical space. At Lowood she shares a room with another teacher, so the initial delight of Thornfield, given in a detailed account of its contents, is that she has a room of her own. It was this element of physical space that Virginia Woolf singled out as the significant feature of a woman's life in her discourse on female liberty, *A Room of One's Own* (1929).

When she comes into money, Jane acquires her own house. So there is something of a contradiction, or a potential one, at work in the plot's trajectories. One goes in the direction of female subordination – a wife under the authority of her husband – and the other towards independence, expressed in terms of control of one's own surroundings. This mid-century novel sets out a dilemma that has continued to mark the lives of women.

Summary

What women aspire to do became a central theme at times when opportunities for women were widening. The possibility of work makes possible a conflict with the traditional role of woman as wife and mother.

40.10   The afflictions of women

Patriarchy

Feminism often insists that women are dominated by men through physical force, the control of discourse and notions such as masculine leadership. The name for this complex system of domination is patriarchy – the rule of men. Feminist critics value books that recognize and resist patriarchy. A feature of feminism is that it sees itself as engaging consciously in an ideological struggle. Sometimes, it explicitly argues that its aim is the promotion of women's interests so, quite consciously, it is not a value-free form of study.

Resisting patriarchy

Although it is not by a woman and, in historical terms, is very unlikely to have been written to promote women's causes, Chaucer's 'The Wife of Bath's Tale' (c. 1390) can be read as showing the way in which women resist patriarchy.

This traditional folk story mediated through the sophistications of Medieval courtly culture, concerns a knight of King Arthur's Court who rapes a young woman. Though brief, the text clearly indicates its unfeeling brutality: 'maugre her heed,/By verray force' (30–1). ('Maugre her heed' means: in spite of all that she could do.)

This violence is the high point of male power. What follows is a series of events that shows women resisting patriarchy. Rape is a capital offence, but 'the queen and othere ladyes mo' plead with the king, who allows them to decide the knight's fate. The positions are reversed; rather than a man using force against a woman, women have the power of life and death. In the first long speech in the poem, the queen gives the knight hope: his life will be spared if he can discover 'What thyng is it that wommen moost desiren' (48).

The knight now does what knights do: he goes on a quest, not to fight dragons, but to discover what women most desire. The turning point of the tale comes when an old woman – 'A fouler wight ther may no man devyse' (142) – promises to give him the answer if he promises to do whatever she asks. He agrees. Chaucer is a very adept story-teller, so though the knight is given the answer, the reader doesn't hear it till the knight faces an entirely female court. A reader who has attended closely to the way in which the queen is in control of the knight's life might have already seen that the answer is: 'Wommen desiren to have sovereyne-tee' (181). At this point, the old woman, who is a member of this court of love, insists that the knight keeps his word. She then requests that he marries her. The knight has begun the tale by breaking his code of honour; now he is obliged to keep his promise. The point is neatly made: a promise is a promise whether one is powerful or weak, male or female.

It might be significant that in 'The Wife of Bath's Tale' we know nothing of the raped girl. Perhaps a serious reading might suggest that her invisibility indicates that, in spite of the playful way the women control the knight, the tale is too accepting of the realities of male behaviour. Perhaps, in other hands, the story of the wronged girl might have imagined her as another Lucrece, the wronged woman who has haunted Western imagination (see Chapter 7, section 7.4 and section 40.5 in the present chapter).

Summary

Women are shown consistently in literature as being afflicted. Feminists identify one of the causes of this affliction as patriarchy – the rule of men. It is interesting to ask to what extent patriarchy is resisted in literature.

40.11   Images of woman

The ideal woman

Women can be afflicted by becoming the objects of male imagining. Tess is afflicted in two ways. Alec violates her. But she also suffers (and suffers greatly) because of the imaginings of her husband, Angel Clare. When, on her marriage night, Angel hears her story, he can no longer see her as the girl he imagined her to be. In his words: 'the woman I have been loving is not you' (ch. 35). Tess, like Hero in *Much Ado About Nothing*, is a victim of male idealization. Angel has pictured her as pure, unspoilt and fresh, and he cannot cope with his discovery.

This may be because, as Hardy makes clear, he still loves her. Furthermore, there is his most daring point: Angel Clare is not wrong in seeing her as 'a Fresh and virginal daughter of nature' (ch. 18). In his presentation of Tess, Hardy sometimes works with double irony. In a conventional sense, Tess is not a virginal daughter of nature, but in Hardy's sense she is (see section 40.5). The lie he tells his mother – 'She is spotless!' (ch. 39) – is the truth.

Heart and head

Women are thought to be over-emotional. Men are thought of as calm and rational, and women as emotionally unstable. (It will be interesting to see if this alters now that examination statistics show that girls do better than boys academically.)

Perhaps this dichotomy between rational men and emotional women is present in Ian McEwan's *Enduring Love* (1997). The narrator, Joe, is a scientist who works out what it is that is wrong with the man who is obsessed with him. Clarissa, with whom Joe lives, is a lecturer in English with a special interest in Keats.

The shrew

The shrew was once a popular image of the difficult woman – the belligerent female who has the aggression of a man and the emotional instability of a woman. The shrew will erupt into anger, and men are often the objects of her farcically presented violence.

One of the current challenges in theatrical presentation is what to do with Shakespeare's *The Taming of the Shrew*. The women's movement does not seem to have altered the number of productions, but it might have focused some questions. How is the opening scene to be staged? Should the production endorse Tranio's judgement that 'the wench is stark mad' (1.1. 69), or should we sympathize with Katherina's question to her father: 'is it your will/To make a stale of me amongst these mates?' (1.1. 57–8)? ('Mates' means both husbands and creatures beneath contempt, and 'stale' is rich in meaning. Is she being treated as a decoy for Bianca, an object of derision or a common prostitute?) How should Katherina deliver her final speech about the duties women owe to their husbands? Can it be played straight, or should Katherina speak with a knowing irony that indicates she does not believe a word she is saying?

Madness

Tranio's judgement that Katherina is 'stark mad' indicates how readily the language of madness has been used of women. The term 'hysterical' originally meant a disease of the womb, so, by definition, hysteria was a female affliction. In Shakespeare's day, the disease took the form of choking, hence Lear's words, when he fears he will be overcome by his anger: 'how this mother swells towards my heart;/Hysterica passio! down, thou climbing sorrow!' (2.4. 56–7).

The tradition of the mad woman runs through literature. In drama, it makes possible the 'mad scene', an opportunity for the dramatist to use language that is deranged but which yet makes some sort of (very uncomfortable) sense. The tradition is not confined to plays. Composers of opera, particularly Italian ones such as Gaetano Donizetti and Giuseppe Verdi, were adept in the musical extremities required for the mad scene. In Shakespeare, Ophelia in her madness sings snatches of bawdy songs; and, when sleep-walking, Lady Macbeth reveals something of the bloody horror of Duncan's death.

Summary

Women are afflicted when they become the objects of men's over-idealizing imaginations. Certain images have dominated the presentation of women. Women are thought of as emotional rather than rational, subject to uncontrolled rage, hysteria and madness.

40.12 Language

In the theoretical debate about the status of women, there is an appropriate interest in the nature of language that women use.

Female language?

Is there an essentially female language? The idea might seem attractive, but the answers given usually confirm the idea that women are more emotional than men. When women are presented as using men's language, the same issue emerges: is there a language – a cold, reasoning language, perhaps – that is essentially male? Behind this rests an issue that feminism debates but cannot agree on. Is there something distinctive about female *nature*? Is there a female essence? The idea has its attractions, but there is a fear that, if an answer is given, women might be confined to roles that are thought to be consistent with their natures.

Novelists, unlike theorists and philosophers, are not required to answer these questions. But they notice the problem. There is an extraordinary scene in Hardy's *Far from the Madding Crowd* (1874), when Bathsheba is driving back to Weatherbury with Farmer Boldwood, whose devotion to her is undimished (Chapter 51). He broaches the topic of whether, given that her husband has been presumed dead for a year, she will ever marry again. Bathsheba, however, is not convinced that he is dead: 'From the first I have had a strange unaccountable feeling that he could not have perished'. We might ask whether Hardy intends us to see this language as *essentially* female – emotionally strong and dependent on intuition.

Boldwood turns to an earlier episode when he carried the fainting Bathsheba into the King's Arms in Casterbridge, adding, 'I have always this dreary pleasure in thinking over those past times with you.' The same kind of question might be asked of Boldwood: is there something *essentially* masculine about this sweeping statement that he 'always' dwells with melancholy pleasure upon the past?

He then (in a masculine manner?) asks her to be exact about her present feelings for him. His question is posed in terms of alternatives: 'Do you like me, or do you respect me?' Her answer is one of the most remarkable moments in Hardy:

> 'I don't know – at least, I cannot tell you. It is difficult for a woman to define her feelings in language which is chiefly made by men to express theirs.'

It is difficult to know what weight to place on the word 'made'. Is Hardy suggesting that language is not by its nature gender-specific, but can become so through usage? Again, what importance does 'define' have? Is this the old idea that women are not by nature rational? Does Bathsheba therefore find defining feelings difficult because she is a woman? Alternatively, the implication might be that men are being obtuse in their desire to have a clear answer in terms of alternatives that they have proposed. Why should a woman's feelings (or anyone's feelings) be expressed in polar terms?

Silencing women

It is odd that Hardy can be so sensitive about the difficulties women have with language and yet can, in at least one case, deny a voice to one of his female characters. In several of the crises in *Tess of the d'Urbervilles*, Hardy does not allow his heroine to speak. For example, when Tess tells Angel the story of her misfortune, her narrative is unheard. It happens in the space between two Phases of the novel. Is it because he is so protective of her (and the book seems to be a case of the author in love with the central character) that he wants to speak on her behalf? Perhaps we feel there is something wrong in putting a character through such trials while denying her the dignity of her own speech.

Summary

Literature raises the difficult issue of whether there is something distinctive about female and male language. Sometimes, authors do not allow their female characters to speak for themselves in moments of crisis.

■ ⎙ 41 External Interpretation: Psychological

41.1 The soul

Traditional ideas

'Psychology' means words about the soul, and the idea of the 'soul' – of a self that thinks and feels – has a long literary history. For example, in 'The Ecstasy' (1633), John Donne explores the ancient idea of the soul leaving the body. That is the meaning of the word 'ecstasy'. Although ideas about the mind/soul are older than the ones associated with twentieth-century ideas of psychoanalysis, the starting point of the psychological interpretation of literature is the work of Sigmund Freud and Carl Jung. As in the cases of Marxism and Feminism, these thinkers have enabled us to bring important areas of books into discussion.

Freud

Psychoanalysis derives from Sigmund Freud (1856–1939). He was interested in the importance of sexuality in our lives, the origins of which, he maintained, are to be found in childhood. He also maintained that our mental disturbances are often associated with our forgetting traumatic experiences. He called this forgetting 'repression'. Repressed memories are locked in the unconscious. There, unknown to us, they live their own troubled lives, sometimes presenting themselves to the conscious mind as something altogether more elevated than they in fact are. Freud called this 'sublimation'. Freud regarded people as being masters of self-deception. (Students of literature will see the attractions of this theory when talking about characters, whose motives are mysteriously unclear.) Psychoanalysis is a method of unearthing repressed memories, usually by way of word association or giving the patient the courage to recall what he or she would rather forget.

Freud and Greece

Freud was devoted to Greek civilization. He spent what he earned on visits to Greece and even kept a diary in Greek. He frequently went to Greek language and myth for the terms he used to explain how he thought the mind works. He gave Greek names to three mental functions: the basic energies and impulses he called the 'id'; the self that consciously wills and desires he called the 'ego'; and the higher faculty that controlled both he named the 'super-ego'. That picture tells us a lot about Freud's gloomy and conflictual picture of human life: we struggle constantly against the turbulent pressures of the unconscious (the 'id') and our waking desires (the 'ego'). Freud claimed that even what we regard as the best things in life – art, religion, friendship – are the outworkings of aggressive and murky presences that lurk in the unconscious. Civilization for Freud is possible only because we repress unconscious impulses.

Jung

Freud's disciple, Carl Gustav Jung (1875–1961), was also committed to the importance of the unconscious, though he saw it as something wider and deeper than did Freud. Jung was an inventive thinker. He wrote a long book on psychological types, which has given us the terms 'introvert' and 'extrovert'. He made two claims about the unconscious. The first was that it is innate; we are all born with some of its contents. The contents of the unconscious take the form of images, which Jung called 'archetypes' (another term that has entered our language). These archetypes are figures such as the young girl, the wise woman and the young adventurer, and places such as mountains, valleys, lakes, seas, caves and deserts. Jung, perhaps understandably, had a good deal of time for religion and literature. He saw both of them as dealing at a profound level with the natural material of the unconscious. He was also more hopeful about the possibility of mental wholeness than was Freud: we can achieve integration when we understand the language our souls speak. Hence, for him, the importance of symbols as the focus of particular mental energies.

The familiarity of psychiatry

Because we have absorbed some of the terms of psychoanalysis into our common language, the psychological approach to literature is the one with which we are most familiar. The terms once used by a psychiatrist talking to a patient, usually depicted as being stretched out at ease on a couch, are now part of our everyday conversation. And not the words alone; we very often work with paradigms – mental models – drawn from Freud and Jung. Thus when, for example, we see a man who gets very agitated about what he says he is against, the Freudian paradigm of sublimation makes us think that he is in fact strongly drawn to the very thing to which he appears so hostile. And we do this when we think about books. For example, we understand the hostility between Beatrice and Benedick (*Much Ado About Nothing*, 1598) as masking an unadmitted attraction. And if we call their behaviour a 'defence mechanism', we are employing a term first used in psychiatry.

Psychological interpretation and other forms of criticism

Because psychology has so penetrated our lives, it is not surprising that it is used by critics, of various interpretive schools. For example, the idea of the mind repressing material it would rather forget is used by Marxists to talk of the way in which the poor are often written out of literature (where are the *very* poor in Dickens?). The poor are oppressed and repressed. Similarly, Feminist critics point to how women are either excluded, marginalized or silenced. In both cases, a psychological 'mechanism' is being deployed to understand the way that authors deal with material they would rather not confront.

Literature and psychoanalysis

Literature cannot be psychoanalysed in the way that people can. In psycho-analysis, a patient, through questioning, provides a body of ideas (we might even call it a 'literature'), which is analysed and then applied to the patient in the hope that it will heal the troubled mind. But in literature there is no patient, just the body of ideas. The most we can do is to use some psychoanalytic terms in literary discussion.

Summary

Talk about the soul is a traditional feature of Western civilization. The language of psychology has so entered everyday conversation, that psychological interpretation is familiar to us. We are aware of notions such as repression, sublimation and archetype. Freud reintroduced Greek mythology into our understanding of people. We cannot psychoanalyse literature the way we psychoanalyse people.

41.2   Dreams

Interpreting dreams

Freud's *The Interpretation of Dreams* (1900) was not the first attempt to ponder the elusive stories of our unconscious minds. In the first book in the Bible, 'Genesis', Joseph is both a dreamer and an interpreter of dreams who asked pointedly: 'Do not interpretations belong to God?' (40: 8).

Dream literature

There is a long-established genre of dream literature. At the beginning of John Bunyan's *The Pilgrim's Progress* (1678), the writer comes to a certain place, lies down to rest and dreams a dream. Bunyan, who was steeped in Bible stories, imagines his dream world with the clarity of the dreams Joseph has in 'Genesis'. Possibly because of that, we soon forget that what we are reading *is* in fact a dream. Bunyan's world, for example, has a consistent everyday distinctness in which, unlike dreams, meanings are plain (see Chapter 45, section 45.1).

Dream-like literature

Some literature, while not actually about dreaming, has a dream-like feel to it. Some of T. S. Eliot's poems have the shifting and fragmented quality of dreams: 'The Waste Land' (1922), for example, consists of disjointed images that float before the reader and are then replaced by other, equally transitory, images. 'The Love Song of J. Alfred Prufrock' (1917) has the weird vividness and disconnectedness of dreaming. Prufrock's mind shifts between a journey through streets, a somewhat embarrassing conversation with a sophisticated woman, and apparently unconnected scenes on the shore and at the bottom of the sea.

Dreams in literature

Dreams can contribute to narrative movement. In *Richard III* (1592), the Duke of Clarence, imprisoned in the Tower, has a fearful dream about escaping by boat across the Channel with his brother, Richard. Richard stumbles and knocks Clarence overboard:

> Methoughts I saw a thousand fearful wrecks,
> Ten thousand men that fishes gnaw'd upon,
> Wedges of gold, great ouches, heaps of pearl,
> Inestimable stones, unvalued jewels,
> All scatter'd on the bottom of the sea.
>
> (1.4. 24–8)

This has the disturbing intensity of dreams: the profusion of the so-precisely registered jewels – wedges of gold ouches (brooches), pearls – seems excessive and even surreal. The dream is also proleptic. Clarence is having a premonition; he was to meet his death through his brother Richard, and it was by drowning, though in a butt of Malmsey wine rather than at sea.

Convincing dreams?

Dreams in literature are sometimes problematic, in part because the easier it is to see their meaning, the less they resemble dreams. In *Wuthering Heights* (1847), Cathy tells Nelly that in her life she has dreamed dreams that have stayed with her and changed her ideas (Chapter 9). Although Nelly is reluctant to hear it, Cathy tells her one about being in heaven but

> 'heaven did not seem to be my home; and I broke my heart with weeping to come back to earth; and the angels were so angry that they flung me out into the middle of the heath on top of Wuthering Heights; where I woke sobbing for joy.'

Though this is a passage of great power, its meaning is plain – Wuthering Heights is where she belongs. It is the home in which she shared her childhood (including, in a non-sexual manner, her bed) with Heathcliff. In her soul she can be parted from neither.

But is the meaning *too* plain? The philosopher Ludwig Wittgenstein said that the trouble with Freud's interpretation of dreams is that once a dream has been dismantled, it completely loses its original sense (see *Culture and Value*, 1980). This might be said of any thoroughgoing interpretation. What we end up with is a meaning, but what we have lost are the oddities and charms of dreams – their brightness and wonder. This shows us something about any kind of interpretation: we need to keep hold of what the book actually feels like, and not reduce it to a set of clearly defined meanings.

It also suggests that dreams in literature are always more convincing if they are elusive. Take the case of Stephen Blackpool's dream in Dickens' *Hard Times* (1854). Stephen dreams (Chapter 13) that he stands in a church with someone who is dear to him, though it is not Rachel, the woman he would like to marry but cannot because he is already married. A light comes from one of the commandments on the commandment board (a board set up in church inscribed with the Ten Commandments) and then he finds himself alone with the clergyman. Immediately, he faces a huge crowd:

there was not a pitying or friendly eye among the millions that were fastened upon his face. He stood on a raised stage, under his own loom; and, looking up at the shape the loom took, and hearing the burial service distinctly read, he knew that he was there to suffer death.

Some of the meanings are clear. The light from the commandment board must come from the prohibition on adultery, and the transformation of his loom (his means of work) into the gallows indicates that industry will bring about his death. Yet what convinces us is its blurred and shifting quality, including the identity of the woman and the unexplained transition from church to loom to gallows.

Summary

People have always wondered what their dreams mean. Some works use dreams to admit readers to a special world, while in other works the atmosphere is dream-like. Dreams are a problem for interpretation. Sometimes, the meaning is so plain that the dream does not seem sufficiently dream-like.

41.3   Imagery and archetypes

Imagery and the mind

The life of literature is a life of images and symbols. We turn what we see into images, and we put in concrete form things that are invisible – ideas, doctrines, virtues and so on. One of the things psychological criticism does is to allow us to see imagery in terms of the mind. It does this through a psychological paradigm: something that is ostensibly about one thing can be seen as being about something else. This paradigm rests on the idea that the unconscious speaks through the conscious and, using the language of the familiar, says something about the unfamiliar. An image of something in the world can be understood as being an image of the mind.

If we go back to the passage in Chapter 40, section 40.4, on 'The Lady of Shalott' we see that in addition to interpreting it as a poem about the isolation of women, it can be read as being about the life of the mind. The Lady lives in isolation from the world, seeing everything in a mirror. The mirror is a traditional image of the mind. The Lady's mind is passive, it merely reflects. But when the knight appears in the mirror, she seeks a more direct and active engagement with the world.

Archetypes

'Arche' is the Greek word for beginning, and 'type' means an image or figure. So, an archetype is an image from the beginning, an image that is fundamental to the mind. (Jung did not invent the word, but he did give it a psychological usage.) For Jung, the unconscious is peopled with these images: we did not put them there; we were born with them. They form, in his language, part of the collective unconscious, a reservoir of images that are present in all our minds.

Here we encounter a problem often met with in psychological thinking. Do we believe this? Some find it a very beautiful idea, but that is not quite the same as saying that it is true. Fortunately, we can use the idea without committing ourselves. The term is still useful, even if we are agnostic about the existence of a collective unconscious.

Archetypal images are often based on familiar features of the world – people and places (see section 41.1). Motor cars and washing machines might be treated as symbols, but only young girls, old men, caves and lakes can be archetypes. But not every man, woman, bird, beast or sea is an archetype. They can only be so if they have power and resonance.

Archetypes in romantic literature

The force of Samuel Taylor Coleridge's 'The Rime of the Ancyent Marinere' (1798) can be interpreted in terms of archetypes. The mariner (Coleridge deliberately adopted archaic spelling for his title) is an archetypal wanderer figure. In his guilty restlessness he has been likened to Cain, to the Wandering Jew or the Flying Dutchman. The mariner has killed an albatross, a great bird that was his guide and companion. The killing of the bird is an archetypal crime, one so fundamental that the whole of life is affected by it. The seas he wanders might stand for the mind that his crime has violated. Seas with their surface (the conscious mind) and their depths (the unconscious mind) are apt symbols of the self or soul. At one point, the boat is pursued by a spirit beneath the waves. As this spirit loves the bird the mariner killed, it may stand for the way that conscience both pursues and helps a wounded soul.

Archetypal configurations

Archetypal configurations occur when a set of events form a significant pattern that expresses a deeply-held longing or need. The archetypal pattern of Coleridge's poem is one of crime and absolution or, to put it into religious terms, sin and atonement. The mariner gratuitously (without reason) kills the albatross, suffers and then, as he blesses the sea monsters, is released from his burden. In the poem, the release is literal – the bird falls like lead into the sea.

The mind as main subject

The mind is the main subject in many of William Blake's poems. The disturbing narratives of the *Songs of Experience* (1794) explore the dark workings of thwarted minds. 'The Poison Tree' is about the perverse glee of nurturing hatred (see Chapter 15, section 15.1). In 'A Little Girl Lost' a father reacts with cold dismay at the sexual awakening of his daughter. In the words of twentieth-century psychology, it may be that the father is hostile because he has repressed his own desires. What he denies himself he resents in others.

Freud and symbols

Finally, a note is required about the images that Freud and his followers identified as having psychological significance. Given that Freud believed that sexual desire was the fundamental element in human life, it is hardly surprising that Freud gave a sexual interpretation to familiar objects. Candlesticks and pens, for example, were phallic, and jewel cases and woods symbols of female genitalia. But Freud could also be cautious. He once remarked that sometimes a cigar is just a cigar.

Summary

In psychological interpretation, images can be read in terms of the mind. Jung's idea of archetypes is helpful in talking about the power of images. Romantic literature can be read in terms of archetypes. Some authors create a mythology that captures the workings of the mind.

41.4 Character and trauma

Problems with Freud

Freud once said of his own psychological observations that the poets knew it already. He meant that what he observed was not new, though his explanations were. Our difficulty today is that few people are prepared to accept his explanations. There now appears to be no scientific grounding for Freud's theories.

Observation and explanation

What, then, are we left with? The answer is: the observations. Literature is about showing, about exploring, about bringing home to readers what certain experiences are like. If an author brings out clearly and sharply what it is like to have a particular experience, what could a psychological explanation of that experience add?

The force of this question is even stronger when we recognize that much (probably most) literature doesn't offer explanations at all. Indeed, sometimes, authors are particularly interested in states of mind that are inexplicable. Shakespeare assumes that the sudden jealous rage of Leontes in *The Winter's Tale* (1609) is beyond all reason. Nothing in the play depends on the possibility that a cause might be found.

Significant behaviour

But psychology might still be helpful, because it might allow us to see that some of the things that have been observed down the centuries by poets and playwrights are significant features of human behaviour. When it comes to the behaviour of characters, psychology can be a useful pointer to areas of a text that we might overlook had we not been brought up in a culture in which psychology has a place.

Unusual attractions

Take, for example, unusual attractions. One of the things we sometimes say, both in and out of books, about friendships and marriages is: I don't know what they see in each other. In Jane Austen's *Emma* (1816), for example, most of the attractions make sense to us. The book opens with the marriage of Miss Taylor and Mr Weston. Everyone regards this as a happy and entirely suitable match. It takes a long time for Emma to see whom she must marry, but, again, the reader applauds her choice. But what of the romance that is only revealed at the end, that of Frank Churchill and Jane Fairfax? It is not that either of them is unattractive. Frank has dash, and Jane might be regarded as the most remarkable woman in the novel. But that does not explain why they are drawn to each other. Jane Austen offers no reason. She is aware that human behaviour can be inscrutable. People as different as Jane and Frank *do* fall in love. It is not the business of literature to tell us why.

Split personalities

Even when an author focuses sharply on what we think of as psychological features, the force of the book need not depend on there being an explanation for the conduct of the characters. Take R. L. Stevenson's *Strange Case of Dr Jekyll and Mr Hyde* (1886). Early on, there is a chilling scene in which Hyde tramples on a child. There is no theory, either explicit or implicit, as to why he does this.

There are causes, but these are more in the nature of actions that are necessary to get the plot going. They are not explanations. Stevenson shows that the human mind harbours dark and destructive passions; but he does not explain why.

Books and Freudian understanding

Yet there are books that stick closely to Freudian paradigms. Dickens is a writer who knows what, later, Freud tried to explain in scientific terms. *Hard Times* (1854) shows the distorting effects of an education entirely based on facts and calculation. Dickens' point (one that the book loudly insists upon) is that it is harmful to neglect the imagination. Louisa, daughter of Mr Gradgrind, who owns the school where nothing is taught but facts, is forced into a disastrous marriage and becomes the object of a seducer's ploys.

But, not surprisingly, the books that most frequently work according to Freudian paradigms are of the twentieth century. L. P. Hartley was born in 1895, so he grew up in a culture that was increasingly influenced by Freud. In his *Bildungsroman The Go-Between* (1953), Leo, the protagonist, is a boy who feels very strongly the promise of the new century, a promise symbolized for him by his diary, decorated with the signs of the Zodiac. The Freudian perspective is present in two ways. Leo does not know the basic details of human sexuality, but he is beginning to see its magnetism at work in others. In particular, his relationship with Marian (in the symbolism of the novel, the Virgin) is uncertain. She is a kind of mother to him in that she takes an interest in him, yet the writing suggests that she exercises another fascination, one that he hardly understands. This is represented in the heat of the summer.

The second Freudian element is that the plot presents the effects of trauma and, particularly at the beginning and the end, the healing of a past hurt by a kind of psychoanalytic process. There is no psychiatrist in the novel, but the older Leo (the novel is a retrospective first-person narration) comes to terms with what he has repressed for fifty years.

The novel starts with the mature Leo finding the diary he wrote in 1900. This scene is to be understood as a sort of allegory of psychoanalysis. Leo cannot give the diary a context in his early life, but he does recall that at school he could open the lock when someone else had set the combination. So by a sort of self-induced hypnosis he lets his fingers work until he hears a click. The sides of the lock draw apart and something is loosened in his mind. The secret of the diary flashes upon him. He remembers. He recalls how he was the go-between – the carrier of secret love letters – between Marian and a local farmer, Ted. All this while Marian was expected to marry a young aristocrat, Hugh Trimingham.

Having remembered all the scenes that led up to his traumatic breakdown, he returns to the scene of his terrible encounter with adult passion. He meets Marian, now an old lady who has a very rosy picture of her illicit love affair. She observes that Leo is dry and emotionally crippled. It is the final confirmation of the Freudian paradigm that repression distorts our mental life.

Alternatives to Freud

Psychological ideas exert a very strong hold on the way we interpret the actions of people both in and out of books. But we need to remember that authors are not obliged to think in psychoanalytic terms. Some books don't work that way. Repressed trauma helps us to understand Arthur Miller's *Death of a Salesman* (1949) and Pat Barker's *Regeneration* (1991) but not *Jane Eyre* (1947). Certainly, Jane undergoes what *we* would call a trauma. She is locked in the Red Room, and there she suffers a blackout. But there is no point in the novel when the reader is invited to understand Jane in terms of this event. Literature does not have to conform to certain early-twentieth-century psychological ideas.

Summary

Literature deals with observation but it does not usually find a place for explanation. There are, however, twentieth-century authors who follow Freud's understanding of the mind. We must always remember that the mind can be presented in non-Freudian ways.

41.5   Myths and mothers

Freud is much criticized today. Many degrees in Psychology never even mention him. His critics say that he worked with pretty conventional ideas about how people, and in particular women, behave. He was, for example, very ready to regard women as hysterical, and therefore was sometimes reluctant to accept their accounts of events. Although he claimed to be a scientist, it is in art and literature that he has had the most influence.

The renewal of mythology: Oedipus

Freud was a kind of poet who found in Greek mythology a set of images and myths for our minds and behaviour. The story of Oedipus was of special importance to him. Oedipus is the man who kills his father and marries his mother. He does not know he is doing these things, and that lends Freud's reading support. Freud sees in Oedipus a picture of the unconscious desires of every male child: because he wants his mother and resents his father, he unknowingly wants to replace his father by sharing the bed of his mother. Interestingly, the plot of Sophocles' play resembles the psychoanalytic process. Oedipus gets at the truth through a careful investigation of the early events of his life.

The work that seems to require a Freudian reading is Shakespeare's *Hamlet* (1600). Freud himself commented on the play, and Ernest Jones, Freud's disciple and biographer, wrote a book called *Hamlet and Oedipus* (1949). Those who know *Hamlet* will see the attraction of Freud's theory. To those who are puzzled as to why Hamlet delays killing his uncle, Claudius, Freudians say that

Hamlet is prevented from carrying out the deed because he wants to do what Claudius has actually done – kill Hamlet's father and marry his mother. Yet there are difficulties with such an interpretation. Claudius might now be the one that shares Hamlet's mother's bed, but he is not Hamlet's father. Perhaps a Freudian would say that a substitute father (and Claudius does call Hamlet his son) is the same as a real one? The real problem with treating Hamlet's delay in this manner is that it makes the audience so knowing that they can only pity or patronize Hamlet. They certainly could not become involved in his plight because all the time they would know exactly what was wrong with him.

Perhaps a better way of dealing with Hamlet is to say that Freud saw the importance of the relationship between mother and son, and that Shakespeare presented that relationship with disturbing power. The play is not an explanation but rather an exploration of the turbulent feelings that are aroused in mothers and sons.

Summary

Freud renewed mythology, particularly that of Greece and Rome. The Oedipus story has been used (with some success) in understanding *Hamlet*.

▪ ☒ 42 External Interpretation: Ideas

42.1 Other theories

In looking at external theories of interpretation – Marxist, Feminist, Psychological – we have been dealing with how ideas help us look at literature. We have already noted Eco-criticism (see Chapter 39, section 39.1) as a set of ideas that help us to come to terms with certain aspects of literature. There are others.

Religion

There is a school of critics interested in the relationship between religion and literature. This is hardly surprising, as the books that are interpreted most frequently are sacred scriptures. Critics interested in religion find religious patterns in non-sacred texts. Books are seen as being about the need for forgiveness, the presence of saving and atoning acts, the status of mystical experience, the idea of life as a journey, and the way our ideas of the end of the world are evident in the way we end books. An author such as William Golding needs to be read in terms of the Christian doctrine that we are all fallen creatures inclined to selfish destructiveness.

Lesbian and gay interpretation

The aim of this school of criticism is to alert readers to the presence in the text of homosexual attraction. Some novels such as Radclyffe Hall's *The Well of Loneliness* (1928) and Jeanette Winterson's *Oranges Are Not the Only Fruit* (1985) are about same-sex attraction. There are also works that might be given a homosexual reading. For example, should Antonio in *The Merchant of Venice* (1596) and Antonio in *Twelfth Night* (1599) be played as showing homosexual love? Perhaps Antonio in *The Merchant of Venice* even wants Shylock to kill him, so Bassanio can see how much his friend loves him? Both Antonios are left out of the symmetrical pairings with which both plays close.

Another approach of gay criticism is to draw attention to the homosexual character of works by authors who were undoubtedly homosexuals. In *The First World War and Modern Memory* (1975), Paul Fussell points to the way Wilfred Owen dwells on the horrors of war by way of writing about soldiers' bodies.

Postcolonial interpretation

Postcolonial criticism has at least two interests. One is authors whose countries were once part of the British Empire. In some respects such writing is like 'The Condition of England' novel. The attempt is to see their countries as they are, and this involves recognizing their former political situations and, at the same, refusing to endorse the judgements that their sometime masters imposed on them (see Chapter 2, section 2.8).

A second interest is to show how these sometime dependent countries impinged on the English novel. For example, there is a discussion in *Northanger Abbey* (1818) about Indian muslin (Chapter 3). Such a moment poses interesting challenges to the reader. To what extent should we bring to the reading of the novel *our* knowledge of Britain as an economic and imperial power? A further issue is the extent to which characters are aware of the colonial dimension. The Orient was a place of wonders. In the architecture and design of the time there were drawings of Indian temples (most notably the works of Thomas and William Daniell), and by 1808 Humphry Repton was proposing to use Hindu motifs in the Brighton Pavilion.

Summary

Interpretation through ideas has led critics to approach literature from a number of intellectual standpoints.

▪ ▽ **43** Issues in Interpretation

43.1 Several approaches

Individual books may be interpreted in several ways (see Chapter 34, section 34.3); an example is Christina Rossetti's *Goblin Market* (1862):

- It can be read as a tale of illicit sex. The tale recalls Jeanie, who fell sick and died 'for joys brides hope to have' (314), and the goblin assault on Lizzie reads like attempted sexual violation.
- The poem is about buying and selling. We should not forget the 'market' in the title. A reading of the poem in terms of the deceitful corruptions of commerce is certainly possible.
- It might be about disease, addiction, or what we now call anorexia. The language of Laura's 'cure' contains the word 'antidote'.
- The language of religion is important in the close. Lizzie uses eucharistic language ('Eat me, drink me' – 471) when she invites Laura to eat the juices from the goblin fruit.
- The final lines of the poem are a song in praise of sisterly devotion and then a significant silence, although they are by then wives and mothers, no husbands are mentioned.
- The tale is true to folklore. Folk tales insist that it is dangerous (and often fatal) to eat fairy fruit.

But interpretation is not just a case of taking a number of different approaches. Interpretation requires judgement. We need to judge how appropriate and effective particular approaches are to individual books. We also need to be perceptive, to see things anew. If we only ever followed particular lines, we would only see what that line allowed us to see. As a model of how interpretation requires both specific approaches and the ability to see things anew, the story told by the philosopher, John Wisdom, is helpful (*Paradox and Discovery*, 1965):

> Mr Flood of Dublin Zoo was very successful at breeding lions in captivity. When Mr Flood was asked what was the key to his success, he answered that a lionkeeper needs to know his lions. When pressed to say what he meant by knowing lions, he replied that each lion is different.

So, in literature, we bring to a book all those ways of interpretation that have helped us to see how books work. But we also need to see that each book works in its own distinctive way, so we must remain open to the individuality of each work.

Summary

Interpretation requires us to take a number of approaches and to see that each book works in its own distinctive way.

43.2 Evaluation

Evaluative criticism – judging the success of a work – is not popular at the moment. Relativistic language (used by Deconstructionists and Postmodernists) does not give grounds for judging one piece of work as being better than another.

A difficult challenge

Perhaps we find evaluation difficult because it rarely works in step-by-step arguments from commonly accepted principles. For a start, if the argument is one about value, the principle will already contain statements of value (conclusions are contained in their premises), and those who do not believe in evaluation will object at the first stage.

The fact of evaluation

A better way is to start from the fact that we do, in fact, make judgements about the value of literary works. We might not quite understand what we are doing, but this doesn't alter the fact that we *are* judging. The truth is that we make choices. We decide that one work deserves more attention than another. If we want to put this point another way, we might say that books compete for our attention. Judgements are difficult to escape. The statement that there are no value judgements is itself a value judgement.

Recognizing value

Perhaps, then, we make judgements when we see what is good in a work. Some people are better at this than others, but it is also true that we can learn to make judgements. The best way to learn about judging is to judge. There are no steps, no complex set of reasons: we see what is good and we point to it. Once we have made a judgement we might want to identify what it is we find to be good. One way of learning is to listen to others. Sometimes they say things such as: 'This is good, isn't?'

Valued features

- We are sometimes impressed by the *power* of a work. The rhythms of verse or prose, the originality of imagery, the pressure of feelings and the insistence of thought can make us value a work. When we respond to the sheer power of Shakespeare, we judge. Think of his dramatizing of Hamlet's plight and the poetic intensity of Macbeth's language.

- Some works arouse our *interest*. We are puzzled, intrigued or enticed by a book. The fact that in *Twelfth Night* (1599) Orsino is drawn to Viola when she is disguised as a man raises all sorts of interesting questions about what the mind can know and half-know. We begin to value works that involve us in such thinking.
- And there is *pleasure*. There are several kinds of pleasure. Here are two: the delicate ways in which the rhythms and cadences change in a poem; and the intelligent understanding novelists such as George Eliot or Henry James have of their characters' complex inner lives.
- Very close to pleasure is the feeling that something has been *well done*. When an image enacts a writer's meaning we may marvel at the achievement. George Herbert's invitation to eat in 'Love' (1633) is very simple, yet it fully expresses the invitation to participate in Holy Communion. We might also recognize the elegance of a Jane Austen dialogue, or the unlaboured ease, fluency and poetic rightness of the passages in which Huckleberry Finn talks of the river.
- Finally, literature sometimes appeals to us because we think that what it shows us is *true*. We sometimes say of a work: yes, love or jealousy or ambition is like that. We might think that the emotional strivings of Tennyson's 'In Memoriam' (1850) show us what grief is like. In *King Lear* (1605) we might see how the play reveals that great suffering and profound intellectual issues have their origin in the tensions of family life. If we really thought that literature revealed nothing to us about the lives we lead, we would neither value it nor read it. A feature of value judgements is that we don't always use the terms 'good' or 'bad'. We merely comment that, say, a character's motives are fully presented or that a conclusion is very short.

Summary

We make evaluative judgements. When we make a judgement we might point to qualities such as a work's power, interest, pleasure, the feeling that it is well done and our belief that what it says is true.

43.3   Intention

Those who claim that the author has 'died', regard intention as irrelevant. This was not a new idea when Barthes made the point in 1968 (see Chapter 36, section 5). In 1946, Monroe Beardsley and W. K. Wimsatt published an essay called 'The Intentional Fallacy', in which they argued that we cannot use whatever was in the mind of the author as a guide to interpretation.

As Sherlock Holmes said to Dr Watson, 'These are deep waters'. Intention is a finely nuanced idea. Those who wish to see just how difficult the issue is might look at Elizabeth Anscombe's *Intention* (1957). To help students of literature, three things can be said:

- If an intention is a disposition in the mind prior to action, it is not much help to a student of literature. How could we possibly get at it? But intentions are present in actions. We sometimes ask of a particular action: did you mean to do that? In that sense, intention is relevant. To put words down on the page is an intentional act. It is impossible to practise textual criticism – the business of sorting out what an author originally wrote – without the idea of intention.
- But though literature is inseparable from intention, the idea of intention does not help us much. A book means what it means (or might mean), because the words mean what they do. The author put them there but, at least in some cases, cannot control all the meanings that might emerge from a text. An author can control how a book starts, develops and finishes, but there is no way in which he or she can intend all the connotations of a particular word.
- An author cannot entirely control what a reader will take away from a book. Authors can lead, guide, prompt, suggest and indicate what they think is important, but readers still enjoy autonomy and can make their own judgements. A classic example of this is D. H. Lawrence's *Sons and Lovers* (1913). It is clear that Lawrence intended us to feel for Paul and to be critical of Miriam, but many readers see her as being misused (by the author) and regard the hero as being proudly self-obsessed.

Summary

It is difficult to dispense with the idea of intention. Intention is the meaning in an action, so putting words down on a page is an intentional act. But an author is unable to control two things: all the meanings that a book will generate, and what a reader makes of the book.

43.4   Is all reading interpretation?

Starting with questions

A possible root meaning of the word interpretation is 'to spread abroad'. If meanings are not fully determined, readers have to look about over the text to find them. Interpretation therefore starts when we feel that the text is left open. We ask questions that the text before us does not fully answer.

Not needing interpretation

In practice, not everything is open to interpretation. If some things were not firmly in place, we would not be able to see what *does* need interpreting. Some meanings are clearly determined. In the first chapter of F. Scott Fitzgerald's *The Great Gatsby* (1925), the narrator, Nick Carraway, talks about travelling East to make a living:

> Father agreed to finance me for a year, and after various delays I came East, permanently, I thought, in the spring of twenty-two.

Several things about this passage don't need to be interpreted. We are not, for example, invited to question who 'Father' is or whether the journey from home is to the East. Nor do we question that the date was 1922. None of these things require interpretation.

Distinguishing between determined and open meanings

The things we don't interpret might be described as the 'what' and 'when' questions. These give us clear answers. To the question, 'When did Nick go East?', we answer, 'in the spring of 1922' – and that's that.

If, however, we turn to the 'why' of the text, then interpretation comes into play. The 'whys' of a text are of two kinds. There are questions about the internal workings of the text – about, say, why a character acts in a particular way. The second question is about why the author has chosen to arrange things in a particular way. When we ask *why* Nick went East, we have to go back to what he said earlier: 'so I decided to go East and learn the bond business'. We might also think that the First World War has made Nick restless. This prompts a further question: Is there a link between war and economics, and if so, what kind of link?

Already, the questioning has moved from the characters to the author. *The Great Gatsby* is about post-First World War America. Is Fitzgerald pondering the impact of the war on America? And there are other questions that might be asked. As has been said, we don't question that the year is 1922, but we might ask *why* Fitzgerald has specifically chosen that year. It may be something to do with Fitzgerald's interest in T. S. Eliot's 'The Waste Land', a poem that, like Fitzgerald's novel, broods over the emptiness of people's lives. Did Fitzgerald indicate a link with Eliot by setting Nick's departure for the East in the same year that 'The Waste Land' was published – 1922?

Six things can be learnt from this discussion.

- It is not always easy to distinguish between what does and what does not need interpreting. Readers must learn how far, and in what ways, to question a text. There are no absolute rules about how to do this, but those who read pick up a sense of when a text requires interpretation. But we can all be surprised. Sometimes a feature of a book we thought was a firm fixture can strike us as needing further probing. This often happens when new styles of interpretation come into fashion.
- Interpretation is never a matter of giving final answers. It is always a matter of 'may' or 'might'. The business of interpretation never stops. But areas require interpretation only because much remains firm. Not everything in a reading needs to be interpreted.

- Sometimes people demand a final statement of meaning. This is to misunderstand the nature of interpretation. Interpretation only comes into play when we can't get a fixed and final answer to our questions. Therefore, whatever interpretation is offered, it is always a proposal, a suggestion, a possible way of coming to terms with the book.
- But we should always try to achieve as complete an understanding of a work as we can. At one time it was fashionable to talk about the free play of meaning. But meaning is never free. The notion of meaning is that, by saying something, some others things are excluded. If I live in London, this means I don't live in York. Certainly, words are very rich in their meanings, and sometimes (as in the poetry of W. B. Yeats) the meanings of a text seem to multiply before us, but this is very different from saying that a text can mean anything.
- Sometimes the close reading of a text invites us to interpret it. When language is dense, as in the imagery of certain poets, the reader is provoked by the text into pondering the meaning.
- Personal involvement is always present in interpretation. What we find significant in a book is going to be related to what we find significant outside the book. To say that a work is significant is to say that it deals with something that matters – matters to us and to others.

Summary

We have to distinguish between what in a text is firm, and what is open to interpretation. In any book, the 'what' and 'when' of a text don't usually require interpretation, but the 'whys' of a text usually do. Interpretation is only needed when something is doubtful, so there can be no final answers. Nevertheless, interpretations should be as full as we can make them.

Part Seven Themes

◪ 44   The Scope of Literature

44.1   A fair field full of folk

Dream poems

William Langland's *The Vision of Piers Plowman* (three versions between 1362 and 1385) is a Late Medieval dream-vision poem. In this genre, the writer falls asleep and dreams of strange and wonderful events that are steeped in moral and spiritual significance. The attractions of the genre are twofold: the strange world of dreams, and the creation of a fictional self, who is their subject. In *Piers Plowman*, the dreamer is uneducated and slow.

Dream-poems are often allegorical. In *Piers Plowman* there are robust passages featuring the Seven Deadly Sins, and the whole poem, although tantalizingly elusive, looks like an allegory of the search for the good life, the search for God.

The opening presents the dreamer going to the Malvern Hills, an interest-ingly exact setting for a poem of wonders. There he lies down by the side of a brook and dreams:

> Thanne gan I meten a merveillous swevene –
> That I was in a wildernesse, wiste I nevere where.
> Ac as I biheeld into the eest an heigh to the sonne,
> I seigh a tour on a toft trieliche ymaked,
> A deep dale bynethe, a dongeon therinne,
> With depe diches and derke and dredfulle of sighte.
> A fair feeld ful of folk fond I ther bitwene –
> Of alle manere of men, the meene and the riche,
> Werchynge and wandrynge as the world asketh.
>
> (Prologue, ll. 11–19)

The rough meaning of part of the poem is: I had a marvellous dream. I was in an unknown wilderness, where I saw in the east a tall tower on a hill, and beneath a fearful valley with a dark dungeon. Between was a field full of people of all social degrees, working and going about their business as they are required to do.

Our world

Piers Plowman is an allegorical poem about human life. We live in a 'a fair feeld ful of folk', conducting our lives between a tower that points to the sun and a dark valley, a valley not unlike the one that John Bunyan, following Psalm 23, was to write about – the valley of the shadow of death.

In the second section of the poem (called Passus 1) the dreamer is told by a 'lovely lady', who represents the Holy Church, that the tower is truth and the dungeon is the dwelling of Wrong, the father of falsehood. Humanity lives between truth and falsehood.

The field of literature

This is our world, the world in which the drama of salvation is played out. If we pursue the allegorical reading further, we might see something that Langland almost certainly didn't envisage, and yet is true to the thrust of the poem. The 'fair feeld ful of folk' is a picture of literature. What happens between truth and falsehood gives literature its subject matter. Literature is about humanity struggling between the light of understanding and the darkness of ignorance and wilful error. We can use other terms: literature deals with the fine gradations between what is real, authentic, good, wise (the list can easily be added to) and whatever is deceptive, illusory, intimidating, evil and foolish. And, as Langland imagines the folk 'werchynge and wandrynge', so in books we find the multitudinous doings of mankind. And the field itself – the realm of nature – is a significant feature of literature.

Summary

Literature can be understood as an allegory of a vast field in which, against the background of the natural world, people move between the darkness of evil and the goodness of truth.

44.2   Workings and wanderings

Literature is concerned with the workings and wanderings of folk in the world's fair field.

Themes

Literature makes something and says something. We can't discuss novels, drama and poetry without touching on what they *say*. We can think of any work as form and content: its shapes and patterns and the picture of life that emerges in and through these forms. When we think about what the contents add up to we are talking about themes. Whenever we say we are interested in, or engaged by, or concerned about, what a book is saying, we are talking about its themes.

Recognizing themes is collaborative: the material is there in the book, but the reader draws it out and designates it as subject matter. Themes emerge when the reader recognizes and responds to a work's enriched language, the links between incidents, the features placed near the end or the beginning of a work, the thoughts of characters, and repeated words or images. But the reader does not make up the theme. If the reader did, there would be no point in one reader talking to another, because they would have nothing in common.

Traditional themes

Themes are usually 'traditional' in that they are issues about which earlier writers have written. What matters in an individual work, or in the works of a particular author, are the emphases – the highlighting, underlining, foregrounding – that give an individual nuance or flavour to the subjects. One of the things that makes literature alive is that there is something new to be said about the old subjects – love is not an exhausted theme.

Summary

When we think about what a book adds up to, we are recognizing its themes. Books foreground themes, and readers draw out what they find. Themes are traditional, but writers find new things to say about old subjects.

■ ⅄ **45** The Living World

45.1 Night

Literature locates people in the living world. They respond to what is around them and struggle to understand the world, others and themselves.

Light out of darkness

The cycle of the day from light into darkness and back to light is an unavoidable feature of life. The English imagination has been moulded firmly by the Bible. The majestic opening of Genesis (King James' version) is about darkness giving way to light:

> In the beginning God created the heaven and the earth. And the earth was without form, and void; and darkness was upon the face of the deep. And the Spirit of God moved upon the face of the waters. And God said, Let there be light: and there was light. And God saw the light, that it was good: and God divided the light from the darkness. And God called the light Day, and the darkness he called Night.

Light is the first creation of God, but night is a continuation of the darkness that once covered the face of the deep. Many of our feelings about light and darkness are touched by the solemn, liturgical tones of Genesis. Night is ancient and dreadful; its frightening uncertainties still speak to us of the chaos that reigned before light brought order (remember Langland's dark valley). It is fitting that the last scene of *Doctor Faustus* (1591), in which he waits for the Devil to claim him, takes place, to the chiming of a clock, at midnight. He has created his own spiritual chaos, and it now overtakes him. A night storm is the background for the meeting of the conspiritors in *Julius Caesar* (1599). The storm anticipates the political chaos they will bring upon Rome.

Writing about the night

Perhaps because it disturbs and threatens, writing about the night *as the night* is more prominent in English than writing about the day. Sometimes day and night are contrasted. Richard II in self-mockery, compares himself to Bolingbroke, his cousin who will succeed him: 'From Richard's night to Bolingbroke's fair day'

(*Richard II* (1595), 3.2. 214). – Most of the time, however, day is the setting or context for action rather than a distinctive subject in itself.

Chaos and night

The word 'chaos' echoes through our literature. Its association with the primeval darkness from which Creation arose, makes it stand for a universal disorder that might still break in on our ordered world. There is a suggestion of a more than personal distress in Othello's words about Desdemona:

> Perdition catch my soul
> But I do love thee, and when I love thee not,
> Chaos is come again.
>
> (3.3. 92–4)

Because 'perdition' means damnation; the word has all the associations of the pains of hell. 'Chaos' therefore means something more than an emotional turmoil. It will be as if the world has been plunged again into the night before the Creation. Significantly, Shakespeare chooses to begin and end the play at night.

Primeval chaos is one of Milton's themes. *Paradise Lost* (1667) draws out the latent connotations of chaos and night. In the first book, the fallen angels who have been cast out of heaven because of their rebellion, rise from the darkness to the sound of

> Sonorous metal blowing martial sounds:
> At which the universal host upsent
> A shout that tore hell's concave, and beyond
> Frighted the reign of Chaos and old Night.
>
> (540–3)

'Chaos and old Night' are personifications of the universal darkness from which Creation arose. Later, in Book 2, when Satan leaves for the newly created earth, he passes through the gate of Hell, beyond which is:

> A dark
> Illimitable ocean without bound,
> Without dimension, where length, breadth, height,
> And time and place are lost; where eldest Night
> And Chaos, ancestors of Nature, hold
> Eternal anarchy
>
> (892–6)

The experience of night can be like that, the dizzying feeling that the conditions that give shape to life – length, breadth and so on – are absent.

A few lines later, Milton hints that chaos and night are the stuff out of which Creation came. Beyond Hell's gate, there is a wild abyss, where the elements are in perpetual warfare

> Unless the almighty maker them ordain
> His dark materials to create more worlds
>
> (915–16)

The very matter from which Creation comes is 'his dark materials', a phrase borrowed by Philip Pullman. In the turbulent vacancy in which Hell lies, Satan sees Chaos in his 'dark pavilion spread/Wide on the wasteful deep' and his consort, 'sable-vested Night' (959–63). Night, though formless and invisible, is compared to Rumour, Chance, Tumult, Confusion and Discord (965–7).

Night, sleep and darkness

In literature, night is associated with sleep, and sleep with death. The Elizabethan poet, Samuel Daniel, starts his sonnet on sleep (in *Delia*, 1592) with the lines:

> Care-charmer sleep, son of the sable night,
> Brother to death, in silent darkness born

There is something magical about sleep; it casts spells (charms), and perhaps the picture of night dressed in black (sable) hints that sleep's father is a magician. Sleep and death, are awesome; they emerge from 'silent darkness'.

Irrational fears

In the night, our sense of what is normal is so weakened that we may become subject to irrational fears. What in daylight is a manageable problem becomes a terror at night. In *Tess of the d'Urbervilles* (1891), the failing health of Tess's illegitimate child overcomes her (Chapter 14):

> The clock struck the solemn hour of one, that hour when fancy stalks outside reason, and malignant possibilities stand rock-firm as facts. She thought of the child consigned to the nethermost corner of hell, as its double doom for lack of baptism and lack of legitimacy; saw the arch-fiend tossing it with his three-pronged fork...

Hardy arouses sympathy for Tess by showing her subject to fears we might all experience. Her very thought, through personification, becomes an uncontrollable threat: fancy stalks outside reason and beyond our control.

Night and crisis

In the nineteenth-century novel, many crucial events happen at night. It is at night when Mary Shelley's Frankenstein looks up from his terrible work of making a female monster and sees 'by the light of the moon, the daemon at the casement' (*Frankenstein* (1818), ch. 20) The 'daemon' is his first creation, the monster he has made and rejected. Night is a fittingly symbolic setting both for the maker's fear and his vicious treatment of the monster. The novel poses the question: who really is the monster?

Perhaps because in mythology the night is often female, there are a number of scenes in nineteenth-century novels when women face the dangers and fears of the night. In Charlotte Brontë's *Jane Eyre* (1847), there is an incident at night in which a creature with a savage face and red eyes enters Jane's room before her wedding to Mr Rochester (Chapter 5). According to Jane, she

> took my veil from its place; she held it up, gazed at it long, and then she threw it over her head and turned to the mirror.

The visitor (an echo perhaps of the night-hag of the Bible) turns out to be Mr Rochester's first wife. In this novel of doubles, both women want to be treated as Mrs Rochester. We immediately sympathize with Jane and, in retrospect, feel for the mad creature, who has been banished to the attic. Two wronged women meet in the darkness of the night: Jane is in the darkness of deception and the wife in the night of madness.

The night and love

Traditionally, night is also the time for adventure and love. In Lord Byron's beautifully poised lyric of sensual satiety, 'So, we'll go no more a roving' (1817), we hear the poet declining any further nocturnal roistering. The poem ends:

> Though the night was made for loving,
>   And the day returns too soon,
> Yet we'll go no more a-roving
>   By the light of the moon.

Night and the moon are the appropriate accompaniments of love.

Lovers do not welcome the day's return, for it means there can be no more loving. Hence John Donne's jesting and arrogant opening of 'The Sun Rising' (1633):

> Busy old fool, unruly sun,
> Why dost thou thus,
> Through windows, and through curtains call on us?
> Must to thy motions lovers' seasons run?

This is poetry with the quality of drama. We can imagine the haughty and dismissive gesture as he waves the sun, treated like an irritatingly fussy servant, out of his room.

Resisting the return of light has become standard ploy in the literature of love. Juliet, wanting to prolong her first night of love in *Romeo and Juliet* (1594), says of the singing bird: 'It was the nightingale, and not the lark' (3.5. 2). The nightingale, a bird of night, is here preferred to the poetically celebrated lark, the bird that in Shakespeare's sonnet 29 'at break of day arising ... sings hymns at heaven's gate' (1609). Juliet's preference, therefore, counters the literary convention that welcomes the dawn.

The night poem

There is an English genre (or sub-genre) called the night poem. Our mortal state can be more threateningly real at night, so religious musings and the struggle for calm, philosophical acceptance are appropriate responses. The poem that set the terms for much subsequent writing was John Milton's musing and melancholy 'Il Penseroso' (1645). This world of half-light and the dark is dominated by Philomel (the nightingale) and Cynthia (the moon). The climax is an atmospheric passage about the ideal of a secluded life devoted to religious meditation:

> But let my due feet never fail,
> To walk the studious cloister's pale,
> And love the high embowed roof,
> With antique pillar's massy proof,
> And storied windows richly dight,
> Casting a dim religious light.
>
> (155–60)

In the eighteenth century, Edward Young wrote his long, meditative poem 'Night Thoughts' (1742), and Robert Blair wrote 'The Grave' (1743), a poem that contains the characteristic line: 'Where nought but Silence reigns, and Night, dark night' (13). In Samuel Taylor Coleridge's 'Frost at Midnight' (1798), the poet muses while his child sleeps.

Thomas Gray's 'Elegy Written in a Country Churchyard' (1751), the most famous of these night poems, shows the poet alone in the darkness: 'And leaves the world to darkness, and to me.' This ambiguous opening – is there a feeling of gratification that the curfew bell, rung at the close of the day, has bequeathed him the darkness? – leads to a series of meditations on the lives of the poor. The poem is gentle, yet the thought is such as to question long-held beliefs. Generations of poets, going back to Classical writers, have seen the poor enjoying an ideal freedom from the cares that afflict the rich and famous, but Gray muses on a new idea – people remain poor because they have not had the opportunities to flourish: 'Their lot forbad' (65).

The tradition of the night poem continued in literature. Edward Thomas, who died in action in the First World War, wrote a number of night poems, in which, in the eighteenth-century manner, he explores the vulnerability of the poor. In 'The Owl' (written 1915), he comes to an inn at nightfall and is refreshed with 'Food, fire, and rest'. Yet, although he is tired, he cannot sleep because of 'An owl's cry, a most melancholy cry', which, with a hint at the pain of the bird's singing, is 'Shaken out long and clear upon the hill'. With a passing reference to Shakespeare's song about Winter from *Love's Labours Lost* (1594), he says it is 'No merry note' but one telling him what he escaped that night and others did not. The poem closes with a generous yet unsentimental picture of

> all who lay under the stars,
> Soldiers and poor, unable to rejoice.

Is it too much to claim that by including that word 'rejoice', Thomas is extending the scope of the night poem to include both the plight of outcasts and the thankfulness of the ones who are safe?

The mistakes of a night

The literature of the night is very often troubled, serious and meditative – but not consistently so. The night can make comedy possible. *The Mistakes of a Night* is the sub-title of Oliver Goldsmith's comedy *She Stoops to Conquer* (1773). The play is in the tradition of English comedy in which the plot, and therefore its humour, is built on mistakes. Though the mistakes are not based chiefly on the fact of darkness, the sub-title reminds us that, in literature, darkness is often the condition of confusion. The play the Mechanicals perform in *A Midsummer Night's Dream* (1594) is also about the mistakes of a night, though the mistakes extend to the bathos of their language.

Black night

It is difficult for us to appreciate just how dark nights were when there was no artificial lighting. The Elizabethans (including Shakespeare) spoke of the black night, as in Fulke Greville's sonnet that begins 'In night, when colours all to black are cast' (1633). The night was so dark, that it was impossible to see what was in front of one. In Chaucer's 'The Miller's Tale' (c.1390), Absolon asks Alison to come to the window (though Nicholas takes her place). Absolon says 'I noot nat where thou art' (616). He can only be a few feet away, yet in the darkness, Chaucer's hearers will know, he can see nothing. There is a section in Jane Austen's *Sense and Sensibility* (1811), when Sir John Middleton fails to arrange a large gathering to welcome the Dashwoods, because 'it was moonlight and everybody was full of engagements' (Chapter 7).

Summary

In the Creation story from Genesis, dark precedes light. In much literature about the night, the hint of the chaos out of which all things arose is ever present. Writing about night touches on sleep, death, irrational fears and love. Night is the setting for crises. The tone of night poetry is meditative and serious. There are, however, works in which the comic potential of night is exploited.

45.2   Sunrise and sunset

Dawn

Perhaps the most significant moment of the day as far as literature is concerned is the dawn. As a visual spectacle, the dawn is a challenge to a writer's evocative powers. The unobtrusive beauty of Shakespeare's 'Dapples the drowsy east with spots of grey' (*Much Ado About Nothing* (1598), 5.3. 27) depends on the delicate use of the verb 'dapple' and the noun 'spots'. 'Dapple' is a term from painting, so we imagine dawn, with the deft strokes of a painter, dappling the east with tiny spots.

Typically, Shakespeare shifts into personification – 'drowsy'. Perhaps we should imagine Aurora, the goddess of the dawn, being painted by the strengthening light.

New dawn, new hope

The dawn frequently stands for new beginnings and the renewal of hope. George Eliot depends on the reader supplying these associations, when, in Chapter 80 of *Middlemarch* (1871), she presents Dorothea facing the tasks of the new day after a night of despair. As light penetrates the room, she opens the curtains:

> On the road there was a man with a bundle on his back and a woman carrying her baby; in the field she could see figures moving – perhaps the shepherd with his dog. Far off in the bending sky was the pearly light; and she felt the largeness of the world and the manifold wakings of men to labour and endurance. She was a part of that involuntary, palpitating life, and could neither look out on it from her luxurious shelter as a mere spectator, nor hide her eyes in selfish complaining.

The reader picks up the symbolic resonances of the new day in the way the 'pearly light' reveals 'the largeness of the world'. One of the large aspects of the day is the moral compulsion to live the life of duty. In the light of dawn, these figures represent the 'labour and endurance' that Dorothea must embrace.

Dawn and dedication

In Book 4 of *The Prelude*, William Wordsworth recounts the moment when he knew that his vocation was to be a poet. Having spent the night dancing, the young Wordsworth walks home:

> Magnificent
> The morning rose, in memorable pomp,
> Glorious as e'er I had beheld – in front,
> The sea lay laughing at a distance; near
> The solid mountains shone, bright as the clouds,
> Grain-tinctured, drenched in empyrean light;
> And in the meadows and the lower grounds
> Was all the sweetness of a common dawn –
> Dews, vapours, and the melody of birds,
> And labourers going forth to till the fields.
> (323–32, 1850 version)

Wordsworth evokes what he calls 'a common dawn' with its attendant imagery of dews, vapours and birds, but he also finds something distinctly Wordsworthian in the play of opposites – the 'solid mountains' shine as if they were clouds. He then records the vows made:

> I made no vows, but vows
> Were then made for me; bond unknown to me

Was given, that I should be, else sinning greatly,
A dedicated spirit.

(334–7)

The dawn is the start of his new life. Perhaps there is a link between the sunrise, which is unbidden, and the vows which were made *for* the poet, rather than the poet making them. This sense of the poet as an *object* of another's agency (the Muse?) is strengthened by the religious vocabulary: 'vows', 'sinning', 'dedicated spirit'. It might be that George Eliot had this passage of Wordsworth in mind: figures go forth to labour, and there is one who has a special task.

Aubade

The aubade is a morning song. (The word comes from the French for dawn song.) In John Donne's 'The Good Morrow' (1633), the poet bids good day to his beloved, and her presence makes the day good. It is a poem of celebration and wonder (the poem opens 'I wonder…') in which the marvel of their mutual love is suffused with suggestions of a new day in time and in the history of their lives.

Philip Larkin called one of his late poems 'Aubade' (1977). The title is deliberately unnerving, for although it is a morning song (the poet looks through the curtains at another day) it is very sombre confrontation with mortality. One more day is one day nearer the last day. When the sky lightens, there is a characteristically imaginative encapsulation of its colour and tone – the sky is 'white as clay'. White is opaque, so the connotations of solidity in the word 'clay' are appropriate. Given the pervasive concern with mortality, we may think of the clay out of which we are made (clay is a poetic word for mortal flesh) and, possibly, even to the clay in which are mortal remains will rest.

Sunrise in a strange world

Larkin was not the first twentieth-century poet to write about the dawn in ways that are oblique to the manner in which the subject has traditionally been treated. The occasion of Isaac Rosenberg's 'Break of Day in the Trenches' (probably 1916) is almost certainly the military ritual of the morning stand-to. Awake and alert (the stand-to was instigated in case the enemy launched an early morning attack), he watches the dawn:

> The darkness crumbles away –
> It is the same old druid Time as ever.

There is a considerable shift in tone. The phrase 'the same old' is colloquial. There are eight lines in A. A. Milne's *Gold Braid* (1917) built round the repetition of 'same old': 'Same old trenches, same old view'. But 'druid Time' is neither from conversation nor popular song. It is an original and multifaceted image of the elemental powers of sunrise. Do we see great standing stones as at Stonehenge, or imagine a druidical ceremony to welcome the dawn?

Interestingly, in the music of the early decades of the twentieth century there is a link between the sunrise and the ancient world. Maurice Ravel's ballet *Daphnis and Chloe* (1912) has a momentous sunrise scene, and the same year saw the completion of Igor Stravinsky's ballet about a fertility ritual, *The Rite of Spring*. This starts with a kind of dawn music, expressive of the awakening of the earth.

Sunset

Because the British Isles are situated quite far north, the evening, particularly in the summer months, is long. The light fades gradually and gently, and the colours are slowly muted. In literature, the evening is interestingly ambiguous – it stands for rest and relief, for anonymity and a certain melancholic bleakness in the face of night.

The evening and rest

Philip Larkin's 'At Grass' (1955), a poem about retired racehorses, is a quiet pastoral of ease and freedom. The light is such that the eye can hardly distinguish the horses from the 'cold shade', until a tail moves. Near the close of the poem, a sentence begins 'Dusk brims the shadows', and after the reflection that galloping must now be a joy, the poem ends with the coming of the night as the groom and the groom's boy 'With bridles in the evening come'. In a poet so burdened by his knowledge of mortality, it is interesting that 'At Grass' closes with the coming of night but no accompanying thought of the big sleep of death.

The anonymity of evening

In Chapter 13 of Thomas Hardy's *Tess of the d'Urbervilles*, Tess, pregnant and unmarried, ventures out of her house to wander in the woods. Hardy presents Tess as being so attuned to the natural world that she can judge

> to a hair's breadth that moment of evening when the light and the darkness are so evenly balanced that the constraint of day and the suspense of night neutralize each other, leaving absolute mental liberty.

As often with Hardy, there is an unexpected word, which in tone and register is deliberately out of keeping with the rest of the passage – 'neutralize'. He explains carefully what he means by it – the equality of light and darkness frees the mind from constraint and suspense. And again, as is often the case with Hardy (a poet as well as a novelist), the unexpected word is of considerable significance. The mental liberty that is born of the neutralizing of day and night is precisely what Tess needs. Hardy closes the chapter by indicating Tess's mental state:

> She looked upon herself as a figure of Guilt intruding into the haunts of Innocence. But all the while she was making a distinction where there was no difference. Feeling herself in antagonism she was quite in accord. She had

been made to break an accepted social law, but no law known to the environment in which she fancied herself such an anomaly.

Tess, the passage implies, needs to learn the lesson of the evening's neutrality. Perhaps then she will see that bearing a child makes her 'quite in accord' with her environment.

The coming of night

Hardy's 'The Darkling Thrush' (1900) has the poet, on the last day of the nineteenth century, leaning on a gate as the winter evening draws in. The first stanza is bleak:

> And Winter's dregs made desolate
> The weakening eye of day.

The long, falling cadence with alliterations of 'w' and 'd' enact feelings close to despair. Yet in the third stanza there is an unexpected voice:

> At once a voice arose among
> The bleak twigs overhead
> In a full-hearted evensong
> Of joy illimited

Hardy may not have been religious but he was, as he said, 'churchy', so 'evensong' must be read as evoking the associations of evening prayer with its language of peace and hope. The poem closes on an uncertain note. How are the closing lines about the 'good-night air' the thrush sings to be taken?

> Some blessed Hope, whereof he knew
> And I was unaware.

Who really knows? Who can the reader trust?

Summary

Sunrise and sunset have a number of significant meanings in literature. Dawn is a sign of hope, a time for dedication, an occasion for song and a moment when we are in touch with the primitive world. Sunset signifies rest; its anonymity allows the mind freedom and it heralds the uncertainties of night.

45.3 The moon and the sun

In Philip Larkin's final volume of poetry – *High Windows* (1974) – poems about the moon and the sun are placed next to each other.

The moon

'Sad Steps' is a poem that, in echoing a sonnet by Sir Philip Sidney ('With how sad steps, O moon, thou climb'st the skies!'(1591)), stands, albeit critically, in the tradition of the moon as an appropriate companion to the melancholic. It starts in that casual and slightly coarse manner occasionally found in late Larkin: finding his way back to bed 'after a piss', the poet sees the moon. Almost through embarrassment that he can't appreciate it in the high old manner of poetry, he says 'No' to conventional poetic expressions such as 'Lozenge of love!'. For him, its uncomfortable 'hardness' and 'brightness' is a reminder that youth won't come again.

The sun

'Solar' (the Latin for sun) is the next poem. The tone here is very different; it is quiet and, one might also say, reverent in its wonder. Unusually for Larkin, the poet does not intrude into the poem as an observing 'I' but allows the object – the 'petalled head of flames' – to stand sublimely alone, 'continuously exploding' and giving for ever.

Larkin's wonder recaptures an older way of writing about the sun – and the other elemental forces. To wonder at the sun as the source of life and light is expressed with an assured innocence in Blake's 'The Little Black Boy' (1794). The boy's mother speaks with simplicity and conviction:

> 'Look on the rising sun: there God does live,
> And gives his light, and gives his heat away'

Larkin's vision of the sun is strangely close to that of the black boy's mother: it is a gracious giver, whose giving has nothing to do with exchange or reciprocation.

The problem for contemporary writers

How can contemporary writers find ways in which to write about objects that have an abiding presence in our literature? 'Sad Steps' opts for irony and bathos (thinking of Sir Philip Sidney when coming back from a piss), but in spite of ironic subversion being an easy attitude for twentieth-century writers, in 'Solar', Larkin chooses to wonder. Wonder is harder, so perhaps this is why he, unusually, deploys words for their symbolic resonances: the lion face, stalkless flower, head of flames and gold.

The sun and the moon in the Bible and the Classical tradition

The Hebrew writers were sophisticated; they knew that the names of the sun and moon were also, in the languages of surrounding peoples, the names of gods, so in the opening of 'Genesis' they modestly distinguished them as 'the greater' and 'the lesser light'. Like everything else, the sun and moon were created objects, the handiwork of the Divine Maker:

> And God made two great lights; the greater light to rule the day, and the lesser light to rule the night: he made the stars also.

The language of the translators (1611) gives dignity to the sun and moon while respecting the original Hebrew insistence that they are mere created things. We might also note that the adventitious rhyme on 'light' and 'night' sustains the understanding, expressed elsewhere in the opening chapter of 'Genesis', that ours is a harmonious world.

In Classical literature, the sun and moon were respectively a god and a goddess. The sun was a lordly and sometimes overbearing presence. John Keats' *Hyperion* and *The Fall of Hyperion* (both 1819) are about dynastic struggles within the world of the gods, a world in which the old order of Hyperion is threatened by Apollo. Apollo becomes, though not in Keats' unfinished poem, the god of the sun, music and poetry.

The sun and kingship

It is therefore fitting that the sun is an image of kingship. When, in *Richard II*, the king needs to bolster his waning authority, he resorts to the image of the rising sun, chasing away the darkness and its evil associates: 'When the searching eye of heaven … darts his light … Then murders, treasons and detested sins' will 'Stand bare and naked' (3.2. 33–42). The image of the sun is flexible; it can shine alone in the sky or be concealed behind the clouds. The eclipse of Richard's rule is expressed in the image of 'the blushing discontented sun' perceiving that 'clouds are bent/To dim his glory' (3.3. 62–5). The image comes at a crucial time; from this point onwards, the sun of Richard's power is setting. The setting is actually performed by Richard in the same scene. Asked to descend from the castle walls, he compares himself to Phaethon, who, in Greek mythology, drove the chariot of the sun god, Apollo, across the skies, until he lost control of the chariot and plunged to earth. In keeping with Shakespeare's understanding of the tragic figure, Richard draws attention to himself as the one who is acting out his political downfall by descending from the castle walls to the base (lower) court:

> Down, down I come like glist'ring Phaethon,
> Wanting the manage of unruly jades.
> In the base court? Base court, where kings grow base,
> (3.3. 177–9)

'Wanting' means lacking, and the 'unruly jades' are the uncontrollable horses that pull the chariot. Shakespeare must have known that, historically, Richard's personal badge was the sun.

The power of the sun

English literature sometimes works by re-creating the mythic power of the sun. In Chapter 14 of *Tess of the d'Urbervilles*, Hardy writes in a consciously elevated manner in order to do justice to its god-like force:

> The sun, on account of the mist, had a curious sentient, personal look, demanding the masculine pronoun for its adequate expression. His present aspect, explained the old-time heliolatries in a moment. One could feel that a saner religion had never prevailed under the sky. The luminary was a golden-haired, beaming, mild-eyed, God-like creature, gazing down in the vigour and intentness of youth upon an earth that was brimming with interest for him.

Hardy's imagination turns him, momentarily, into an anthropologist, explaining the naturalness of worshiping the sun. And, adopting the manner of the man learned in the Classics, he presents the sun in his youth. Hardy's golden-haired luminary is Apollo rather than Hyperion.

The mythology of the moon

In Classical mythology, the moon has many names – Cynthia, Diana, Hecate, Luna and Phoebe. She presides over the night as queen, and in her cold aloofness she symbolizes chastity. Yet she is also concerned with fertility, controlling the waters and a woman's monthly cycle. She is associated with madness: the moon is Luna, and the mad are lunatics (see Chapter 40, section 40.8).

The moon watches over the action of Shakespeare's *A Midsummer Night's Dream* (1594). The word 'moon' appears twenty-five times, far more than in any other of Shakespeare's plays. In the opening scene, Theseus, longing for his wedding day, laments 'how slow/This old moon wanes' (1.1. 3–4). Hippolyta, his wife to be, replies that soon they will see the new moon 'like to a silver bow/New bent in heaven' (1.1. 9–10). Hippolyta's promise is one of fertility; the female silver bow draws the male arrow, and a child is released.

Characters frame their actions with reference to the moon. Hermia and Lysander plan to elope when 'Phoebe doth behold/Her silver visage in the wat'ry glass' (1.1. 209–10), and the Mechanicals consult an almanac to see if the moon will be shining on the night of their performance (3.1). Before the play is performed, Theseus, discussing the lovers' story of their distraction in the woods, says:

> The lunatic, the lover and the poet
> Are of imagination all compact
> (5.1. 7–8)

The themes of the play – madness, love and the poetry of dreaming – are related to the moon.

The Moon and the imagination

'The Romantic poets saw the moon as an emblem of the imagination. Just as the moon only gives off light by reflecting light from the sun, so the poet receives and transforms the light of inspiration. In Keats' 'Ode to a Nightingale' (1819), a poem about the transforming power of the poetic imagination, the poet says he is already with the nightingale and in the company of 'the Queen-Moon' (36).

Consequences

English is not a gendered language, but because of Western Classical inheritance English writers have gendered the sun and the moon. To Hardy the sun is male, and the moon in *A Midsummer Night's Dream* is female. In Lewis Carroll's comic poem 'The Walrus and the Carpenter' (from *Through the Looking-Glass*, 1871) there is a comment by the moon on the rudeness of the sun, who shines in the middle of the night:

> 'It's very rude of him,' she said,
> 'To come and spoil the fun!'

Perhaps there is a comic echo here of those scenes in Homer's *The Iliad* in which the gods engage in domestic squabbles.

The stars

Writers have regarded the stars as guides, and in some cases guides to distant worlds. Both these meanings are present in the poem Alfred, Lord Tennyson asked to be placed at the end of his collected works – 'Crossing the Bar' (1889). Tennyson lived on the Isle of Wight, so had to cross the water by ferry. The poem opens with the poet being launched into the night waters:

> Sunset and evening star,
> And one clear call to me!

Tennyson does not say that the sunset and the star call to him, but since it is not said who or what calls, the reader is free to make a connection between them. The poet is summoned, and, in the tradition of all seafarers, is guided by the star.

Summary

The sun is magnificent, powerful and kingly; the moon, by way of Classical literature, is associated with chastity, hunting and madness. It is also linked with melancholy and the imagination. The sun and moon are two of the few things in English that are gendered. The stars are presented as guides.

M 46   The Four Seasons

46.1   Writing about the seasons

The character of the seasons

Like our long evenings, the seasons are a function of our northerly location. The cycle of the seasons is like the cycle of the day. The writer has to convey what each is like. How are the freshness of the morning and the glad return of spring to be conveyed? And morning is like the spring in that both are hopeful beginnings. Days and seasons parallel each other, and their features come to have figurative significances. Youth, for example, is like the morning and the spring.

The labours of the months

There is a long and living tradition of evoking the particular characteristics of each season. Nor is this tradition confined to literature. In the art found in Medieval churches – sculpture around doorways and mosaics on pavements – there is a sequence called the Labours of the Months, in which a typical activity such as killing the pig in December is represented. An English example is the font in Burnham Deepdale church in Norfolk. Sometimes in poetry there is a poem for each month, as in Edmund Spenser's *The Shepherd's Calendar* (1579) and John Clare's poem of the same title (1827). As the titles suggest, these poems are dependent on the conventions of pastoral poetry (see Chapter 27).

James Thomson's *The Seasons* (1730), as the title implies, was divided into four sections. (Joseph Haydn used Thomson's work as the text for his oratorio *The Seasons*, first performed in 1801.) Robert Bloomfield used the same four-poem structure for *The Farmer's Boy* (1800), and Ted Hughes' *Season Songs* (1976) is organized into four sections with individual poems representing aspects of each season. Hughes includes a poem called 'Hay' in the summer section, and one called 'Christmas Carol' in winter.

Summary

Writers establish the symbolic meanings of each season. There is also a long tradition of writing about the labours associated with each month.

46.2 Seasonal myths

Popular pictures

Writers depend on seasonal myths: widely accepted images of the features of each, and their associated moods. The word 'image' reminds us that a seasonal myth is not confined to literature. John Constable tended to paint pictures set in the late summer and early autumn, as in 'The Cornfield' (1826). There are also musical compositions, as in the famous *Four Seasons* (1725) by Vivaldi.

In literature, the seasons are used as emblems of human growth, as in William Wordworth's 'Fair seed-time had my soul' (*The Prelude*, Book 1, 305). His soul was sown and started to flourish as the seeds do in spring. Sometimes, many of the characteristics of a season are clustered in a single work. This happens in Shakespeare's winter song in *Love's Labours Lost* (1594) in which sharply delineated (and still recognizable) scenes create our idea of winter: icicles hanging by the wall, milk frozen in the pail, howling winds and the birds brooding in the snow.

As with any tradition of writing, there is the 'challenge' of making it new. This is what John Keats does in 'To Autumn' (1820), when he makes the textures enact the cloying overripeness of the season. This is the dense, almost clotted, opening:

> Season of mists and mellow fruitfulness,
>   Close bosom-friend of the maturing sun;
> Conspiring with him how to load and bless
>   With fruit the vines that round the thatch-eaves run

The frequency of alliteration, the run of monosyllables and the echoing of 'fruitfulness' in 'fruit' make the lines 'thick' and 'heavy'. The weight and number of the words and their sluggish rhythms enact what it is for autumn to be both fruitful and burdened. There is hardly anything really new in 'To Autumn', yet we know that the seasonal myth of autumn as both fulfilment and the start of decline has been re-made.

Summary

Literature works with 'seasonal myths' – the popular images of the appearances and characters of the seasons. The challenge is to re-create these for each generation.

▮ⱽ **47** The Earth

47.1 Learning to look at landscape

Landscape histories

The landscape has a history: a geological one in the formation of hills and valleys, and a human one in the laying-out of fields and the planting of trees. But landscape also has a history of appreciation, of how people have come to enjoy its shapes, forms and what has been called its moods. The appreciation of landscape requires a vocabulary.

The sublime

The sublime is the experience of finding something awesome, overwhelming and threatening. Edmund Burke, who wrote *A Philosophical Inquiry into the Origin of Our Ideas of the Sublime and Beautiful* (1757), stressed that our experience of the sublime has its roots in pain and danger:

> Whatever is fitted in any sort to excite the ideas of pain,
> and danger, that is to say, whatever is in any sort terrible,
> or is conversant with terrible objects, or operates in a manner
> analogous to terror, is a source of the *sublime*.
>
> (Section VII)

Burke uses very strong words such as 'terrible' (twice) and 'terror'. The sublime, he suggests, is what we recognize and feel when we catch our breath in the presence of whatever is intimidating and threatening.

Recognizing the sublime

People had to be taught to recognize this quality in a landscape. They had to learn to see a mesmerizing attractiveness in whatever was huge, rough and wild. Wordsworth conveys his sense of the sublime in a passage from the sixth book of *The Prelude* (1805), when he descends from the Alps down a narrow and deep river valley:

> The immeasurable height
> Of woods decaying, never to be decayed,
> The stationary blasts of waterfalls,

And everywhere along the hollow rent
Winds thwarting winds, belwildered and forlorn,
The torrents shooting from the clear blue sky,
The rocks that muttered close upon our ears –
Black drizzling crags that spake by the wayside
As if a voice were in them – the sick sight
And giddy prospect of the raving stream,
The unfettered clouds and region of the heavens,
Tumult and peace, the darkness and the light,
Were all like workings of one mind.

(556–68)

This is a landscape (and a language) of terror and fear. It is a strange world where things decay and yet never decay, in which the winds are in perpetual strife, and in which torrents shoot from a clear sky. The landscape is personified: rocks mutter, crags speak and streams rave. But we do not know what the voices say. There are also polarities: height and depth, land and sky, tumult and peace, darkness and light. These voices and polarities enact with giddying turbulence Wordsworth's experience of the sublime – the strange, the terrible, the wild.

Summary

We learn to see qualities in a landscape; an example is the sublime – the feeling of awe and terror induced by what is huge, rough and wild.

47.2   Water

Tales of the sea

Water, one of the four elements, is present in the genre of sea stories, either as adventures, as in R. L. Stevenson's *Treasure Island* (1882) and Meade Faulkner's *Moonfleet* (1898), or as symbolic exploration as in Herman Melville's *Moby Dick* (1851).

Human endurance

Joseph Conrad worked within the genre to turn tales of the sea into explorations of human endurance in an indifferent world. In *Typhoon* (1903), a story that sticks close to the genre of a yarn about the sea, the central figure, Captain MacWhirr, guides his boat through winds and waves. It is an encounter with the sublime: 'The inky edge of the cloud-disc frowned upon the ship under the patch of glittering sky' (Chapter 5). What brings MacWhirr and his crew through is the practical intelligence that comes from experience. At the heart of the storm, MacWhirr's admirably gruff heroism displays the human spirit's endurance of a tempestuous and hostile world. Chapter 5 closes with MacWhirr, a man who says little, attending to the normalities of life, while the storm raves:

> Captain MacWhirr was trying to do up the top button of his oilskin coat with unwonted haste. The hurricane, with its power to madden the seas, to sink ships, to uproot trees, to overturn strong walls and dash the very birds of the air to the ground, had found this taciturn man in its path, and, doing its utmost, had managed to wring out a few words. Before the renewed wrath of winds swooped on his ship, Captain MacWhirr was moved to declare, in a tone of vexation, as it were: 'I wouldn't like to lose her.' He was spared that annoyance.

'Annoyance' captures his heroic, matter-of-fact defiance.

The elemental and the primitive

The poet who celebrates the elemental turbulence of the sea is Algernon Swinburne. Perhaps he is a victim of his verbal dexterity – his pulsating rhythms, the variety of stanza forms and the ease with which he rhymes – so that it is often difficult to work out *exactly* what he is saying about the sea. He is not really a poet of ideas. Yet to make this a complaint might be to look for the wrong thing. Swinburne's power lies in his ability to evoke the moment when we see the beauty and the raw energy of nature. This is the third stanza of 'Off Shore' (1880):

> Then only, far under
>   In the depths of her hold,
> Some gleam of its wonder
>   Man's eye may behold,
> Its wild-weed forests of crimson and russet and olive and gold.

The sheer length of the last line – the sense of this and this and this – enacts the delight of seeing into the depths of nature in all its marvellous, colourful variety.

The sea as metaphor

In both Conrad and Swinburne the journey across the sea can stand for the paths of our earthly lives. The metaphor is common in Victorian literature and the other arts. It gives rise to another – the shipwreck as the symbol of hope dashed. Also in Victorian literature, the journey by sea has the meaning of a new start. The journey to the colonies might be to the beginning of a better life. The subject, if not the style, of Gerard Manley Hopkins' 'The Wreck of the Deutschland' (written 1875–6) is decidedly Victorian.

The sea also separates. Matthew Arnold's haunting poem on the essential loneliness of people 'To Marguerite – Continued' (1849) works with an image of people, who, though they exist as islands, feel they were once part of 'a single continent', but some god has ordered their severance. The poem closes:

> And bade betwixt their shores to be
> The unplumbed, salt, estranging sea.

It is worth thinking about what the word 'salt', singled out by the abrupt caesura, contributes to the tone of sharp regret.

In other Arnold poems the sea is glimsped as something remote and wonderful. It seems to offer peace. *Sohrab and Rustum* (written 1852–3), a poem of fierce hostilities, closes with solemn repose. The River Oxus winds circuitously across the plain

>   till at last
> The longed-for dash of waves is heard, and wide
> His luminous home of waters open, bright
> And tranquil.

Arnold is depending on the river flowing into the sea as an image of the soul finding peace in its eternal home. It is a 'home' that is 'longed-for' and 'tranquil'. This image is used by John Donne in his grave 'A Hymn to God the Father' (1633), in which he fears he will 'perish on the shore', and it has a visionary intensity in Wordsworth's 'Immortality Ode':

>   in a season of calm weather,
>   Though inland far we be,
>   Our souls have sight of that immortal sea
>   Which brought us hither,
>   Can in a moment travel thither,
>   And see the children sport upon the shore,
>   And hear the mighty waters rolling evermore.
>   (164–70)

The rapid movement of the earlier lines gives way to the simple majesty of the closing couplet with its juxtaposition of the everyday detail of the playing children with the sublimity of the rolling waters.

Summary

The sea is a rich area of meaning. In sea stories, human endurance is tested, and sometimes there is a glimpse of what is elemental and primitive. The sea has metaphoric functions: the journey of life, human isolation and our goal beyond this world.

47.3   People and woods

We have links with the living world about us. There is growth, flourishing and decay, and so natural things can be used as emblems and analogues of human growth. One of the intellectual debates of the past posed the question whether our world could best be understood mechanically (on the model of Newton's Mechanics) or organically, as being like a living thing. Moreover, since Darwin, we know that we are, in terms of our very make-up, part of the great web of life.

The organic world

Authors treat the organic world in at least five ways:

- It is interesting in itself, with its own colourings, textures and life-cycles.
- It is a distinctive world with its own atmospheres and narrative possibilities.
- It is an object of meditation about the life of nature and the place of people within it.
- It supplies the imagination with symbols and emblems.
- Contrary to a lot of thinking, we see that the living world is real and not merely a 'social construction'.

It needs to be said that the above points are not 'rules', and that one usage does not exclude another. A landscape can be real and yet work figuratively. For example, in Chapter 16 of *The Scarlet Letter* (1850), Nathaniel Hawthorne understands the forests that surround Boston in terms of natural growth: a 'luxuriant heap of moss' is what remains of a 'once gigantic pine'. But when Hawthorne writes of branches choking up the current of a stream and leaving 'eddies and black depths', we feel that this stands for something dark in nature, and possibly human nature.

Woods

In accordance with the conventions of Romance, the woods in Edmund Spenser's writing are symbolic. In the First Book of *The Faerie Queene* (1590), the Redcross Knight (Holiness) and Una (Truth) enter the forest, initially to escape from a storm. They are soon puzzled: 'So many paths, so many turnings seen' (89). On one level, Spenser's wood is delightfully real. There are beautiful passages about the different trees – pine, cedar, elm and poplar – but the reader also sees it as an emblem of our tangled world.

The dark wood with its confusing paths is frequently found in literature. Dante Alighieri opens his *Inferno* (begun 1308) lost in a gloomy wood, a symbol of the way in which each of us can lose our way in life. In a very different tone is Robert Frost's 'The Road Not Taken' (1916) and 'Stopping by Woods on a Snowy Evening' (1923). In the first, the poet meditates on two roads that diverge in a wood and how taking the less-travelled one has made all the difference. In the second, he stops in a wood as the snow falls and thinks about ownership and promises. In England, a friend of Robert Frost, Edward Thomas, used the image of entering a wood in 'Lights Out' (1916) to represent sleep and what sleep represents – death. Perhaps what fascinates him is that a path is one of the most ancient marks we have made on the landscape. It indicates desired destinations, demarcates territory and delineates space. In 'The Path' (1915), for example, he writes about a bank above a road and how its path creates a special world apart that looks as if it led on to 'some legendary/Or fancied place'.

Improvement

The emblematic possibilities of woods and trees is also exploited by Jane Austen in *Mansfield Park* (1814). The rich and quite silly Mr Rushworth is afflicted by the desire to improve his estate. 'Improvement' meant redesigning the country-side – creating lakes, smoothing the lines of woods and romanticizing the view by building grottoes or temples. It was very fashionable among landowners in the late eighteenth and early nineteenth centuries. As part of his 'improvement', Rushworth wants to cut down an avenue of oak trees. The central conscious-ness of the novel, Fanny Price, is saddened; she recalls lines from Cowper:

> Does it not remind you of Cowper? 'Ye fallen avenues, once more I mourn your fate unmerited.'

> (ch. 6)

It is for the reader to see the significances. The avenue is the work of both nature and humanity. It might remind us of the power of the living world and the trad-ition of estate management that has planted and nurtured the trees. Also, because the trees are oaks, the avenue might represent England and the protect-ing wooden walls of the navy. David Garrick had summed up the patriotic and moral force of oak in his song 'Hearts of Oak' (1758), the chorus of which runs:

> Hearts of Oak are our ships, Hearts of Oak are our men.

Should we, Jane Austen's writing implicitly asks, do away with such a morally significant inheritance on the casual whim of fashion? Oliver Goldsmith's *The Deserted Village* (1770) is an earlier exploration of the effects of an irresponsible landlord on his villages.

Woodlanders – a way of life

In Thomas Hardy's *The Woodlanders* (1887), the wood is a world with its own traditions of living and working. In the book's opening pargraph, the traveller, a frequent figure in Hardy's fiction, sees 'extensive woodlands, interspersed with apple-orchards'. The woodlanders' way of life is made concrete in Chapter 28, when Grace, the girl who might have married Giles, meets him returning from cider-making. He is marked by his labour:

> his sleeves and leggings dyed with fruit-stains, his hands clammy with the sweet juice of apples, his hat sprinkled with pips, and everywhere about him that atmosphere of cider

Does the reader feel that the stains of fruit are in any way negative?

Summary

Writers interest themselves in the details of the natural world, enjoy it as a world apart, consider it an object of meditation, and find symbolic meanings in it. Paths, the 'improvement' of landscape and the life of woodland dwellers have all been the subjects of literature.

47.4   Trees and plants

Trees in literature

There is an ominous tree in Geoffrey Chaucer's 'The Pardoner's Tale' (c. 1390). The riotous youths, seeking to kill Death, meet a mysterious old man, a man who would like to die. They ask him where Death might be found, and he guides them:

> Turne up this crooked wey,
> For in that grove I lafte hym, by my fey,
> Under a tree.
>
> (761–3)

This is a strange landscape – a crooked way that leads to a tree, beneath which is Death. The language hovers between the magic of a mysterious forest (as we later find in Spenser) and the hint that the tree might stand for the tree of the knowledge of good and evil in the Garden of Eden story – the source of misery and of our knowledge of death (see Genesis 3). The old man speaks riddlingly, but the young men do find death.

Writers have learned to see trees and plants as bearing many meanings. In 'Yardley Oak' (1791), William Cowper allows the ancient tree to touch off in him a series of thoughts. Such is the oak's age, that he feels the impulse to 'kneel, and worship'. As well as prompting meditation about decay, the oak is concrete and individual. The tree's wonder is strongly present in the detailed images of its gnarled and twisted shell; its root, for example, is 'A quarry of stout spurs, and knotted fangs'.

Close attention to the particularities of trees, bushes and hedges is a feature of John Clare's poetry. He is responsive to the tangle of bramble and thorn, to hollow trees wasted to shells, and the wild and beautiful neglect of open fields. In 'Langley Bush' (1821) his look lingers on the 'mouldering trunk', which is 'nearly rotten through'. Sometimes (and perhaps most successfully) he refrains from general reflections, concentrating on the knotty angularities of roots or the veined ivy that overhangs wild, crooked brooks.

Making an individual plant or tree the subject of a poem was a feature of Romantic poetry. It raised problems. Some contemporary reactions to Wordsworth expressed disquiet: should everyday objects be the focus of strong feelings and deep thoughts? In 'Daffodils' (1807), Wordsworth wrote of his delight in seeing them 'dancing in the breeze'. He then admits that he 'little thought/What wealth to me the show had brought'. The wealth is that later, in moments of 'vacancy' or 'pensive' thought, the daffodils 'flash upon that inward eye/Which is the bliss of solitude'. Anna Seward found this hard to take:

> Surely if his worst foe had chosen to caricature this egotistic manufacturer of metaphysic importance upon trivial themes, he could not have done it more effectually.
>
> (In *Wordsworth: The 1807 Poems*, ed. A. R. Jones, 1990.)

Do daffodils deserve to be made so important? To those who think that subject matter should match style, such ecstatic feelings are misplaced. Romanticism questioned two conventions. The first is that poetry, an elevated art, should only deal with lofty and important topics. The second is that poetic diction should be appropriate to the subject. That is to say, a trivial subject, as Anna Seward thought a daffodil to be, did not deserve the ecstatic diction of 'vacancy', 'pensive' and 'bliss'.

Summary

Trees and plants can be treated symbolically and as concrete objects. Some readers feel that natural things should not be treated in elevated terms.

47.5   The garden

The garden is a multivalent and ancient image. It is natural *and* the product of human organization. Part of its fascination is that, in the living world, it is the furthest we can get from wild, untamed nature. In English literature it has at least five emblematic functions.

Retreat and repose

In the sixteenth and seventeenth centuries, there was a fashion for the poem of retirement or solitude. By retirement, poets meant withdrawal from the public sphere to the quiet life of country peace, a peace often represented by a garden. Andrew Marvell's elusive 'The Garden' (c.1650) opens by saying that we distract ourselves in seeking the emblems of worldly honour – 'the palm, or oak, or bays' – instead of the 'garlands of repose' woven by flowers and trees (see Chapter 30, section 30.6). In the second stanza Marvell addresses, joyfully and perhaps intimately, 'Fair quiet', which he has vainly sought in the 'busy companies of men'. The close of the second stanza is even more reclusive in its snug contentment:

> Society is all but rude
> To this delicious solitude.

The short line and the rhyming couplet (significantly closing on 'solitude') give Marvell's verse an ordered and epigrammatic quality, yet the word 'delicious' is surprisingly sensuous in its relish of the pleasures of retirement.

The shrubbery was a specific garden feature designed to nurture the pleasures of solitude. This semi-private space, usually enclosed by a hedge, offered quiet and security. In William Cowper's 'The Shrubbery Written in a Time of Affliction' (1773), the poet knows that the enclosure should be a retreat from inner as well as outer turmoil, but so 'fix'd' within is his 'unalterable care' that he finds 'the same sadness (of his soul) ev'ry where'.

Nature and art

A garden is both nature and art. It is natural in that it is concerned with growth, but art in its design and order. Marvell recognizes the designed nature of a garden in the last stanza of his poem:

> How well the skilful gardener drew
> Of flowers and herbs this dial new.

Flowers and herbs are natural, but here they are drawn (as in a picture) in the shape of a sundial by the 'skilful' (artistic) gardener.

The co-operation of people with nature is one of the subjects of Alexander Pope's *Epistle to the Earl of Burlington* (1731). When discussing the correct use of riches, he praises those who, in matters of gardening (this included the shaping of landscapes as well as planting formal gardens), allow sense to follow nature. When building or improving the landscape, he advises that 'Nature never be forgot' (50) and that we should 'Consult the genius of the place in all' (57).

An emblem of the state

The garden is an emblem of the well-ordered state. Just as a garden is trimmed and tended, so should the state be ordered by a sensitive and tactful ruler. In Shakespeare's *Richard II* (1595), two gardeners (speaking elegant blank verse) lament that they keep the garden in good order, 'When our sea-walled garden, the whole land,/Is full of weeds (3.4. 44–5) and 'Swarming with caterpillars' (3.4. 48). 'Caterpillars' is very pointed; earlier in the play (2.3. 165), the word was used of those who corrupt the state by feeding themselves with its wealth and privileges.

The abandoned garden

The image of the abandoned garden haunts later literature, particularly that of the nineteenth century. It stands for neglect, the failure of purpose and lost ideals. Swinburne brings his characteristic energy to the subject in 'A Forsaken Garden' (1876), picturing the garden on the very margin of the land – crumbling cliffs above the sea. The poem is not regretful, for nothing remains to cause regret: 'The thorn remains when the rose is taken' (21) and 'Love deep as the sea as a rose must wither' (51).

The image of the abandoned garden with all its poignant associations of loss lies behind one of the most popular of children's stories – Frances Hodgson Burnett's *The Secret Garden* (1911). The force of this parable of regeneration depends on the reader seeing in the walled and secret garden an emblem of a lost hope, which is recovered as Colin recovers his health.

Eden

Behind many images of the garden, there is the archetypal garden of the Western imagination – the story of how humankind lost the Garden of Eden, and of our sick yearning for our lost paradise. In this memorably simple story, Adam and Eve eat the fruit of the Tree of the Knowledge of Good and Evil and discover that they are naked. They are banished from paradise, and an angel with a fiery sword guards the gate against their return (Genesis 2–3).

John Milton closes *Paradise Lost* (1667) with a scene in which Adam and Eve are ejected from their (and our) paradisical home:

> They looking back, all the eastern side beheld
> Of Paradise, so late their happy seat,
> Waved over by that flaming brand, the gate
> With dreadful faces thronged and fiery arms.
>
> (641–4)

There is no return. Adam and Eve have tasted the fruit of the forbidden tree and so can only do what is so frequently done in literature: look back with regret on what they have lost. All losses – the loss of hope, of innocence, of ideals and beliefs – have been understood in terms of losing that 'happy seat'.

Poetry of the Romantic period often traces the pattern of a return. Blake's 'The Little Girl Lost' and 'The Little Girl Found' explore the imagery of the Eden story. Significantly, the first poem ends with the girl naked:

> While the lioness
> Loos'd her slender dress,
> And naked they convey'd
> To caves the sleeping maid.

Blake renews or re-pristinates language so that in this and other poems the word 'naked' becomes an image of original innocence. Most dictionaries define 'naked' in negative terms – unclothed, uncovered, destitute of clothes – but Una is 'loos'd' – freed from an alien and confining condition (see Chapter 14, section 14.4). She returns to the pure and primal world shared by Adam and Eve in their innocence before the Fall. At the close of the last stanza of 'The Little Girl Found', there is the hint that the girl and her parents now enjoy the primal state of innocence:

> To this day they dwell
> In a lonely dell;
> Nor fear the wolvish howl
> Nor the lion's growl.

Paradise is sometimes pictured as a restoration of peace between animals and humans. In this poem the wolves howl and lions growl, but they do not arouse fear. Animals and people share one peaceable kingdom.

In literature, exclusion from paradise is not always seen as an unambiguous catastrophe. Some things – overcoming fear, self-sacrificing love – would be impossible inside paradise. This insight enriches the close of *Paradise Lost*. In the passage quoted above, Milton continues:

> Some natural tears they dropped, but wiped them soon;
> The world was all before them, where to choose
> Their place of rest.
>
> (Book 12, 645–7)

The swelling movement of the line gives to 'world' a fullness of meaning; it encompasses achievement, endeavour, honour, trust and care. There is a dignity in being able to choose, and 'rest' might be found beyond the gates of Eden. Something of the same vision of Eden being a loss that nevertheless makes possible the realization of certain values is present in Edwin Muir's 'One Foot in Eden' (1956), in which the poet asks 'What had Eden ever to say/Of hope and faith and pity and love' (24–5). In a perfect world, there could be no hope, because goodness of every kind would be assured.

That the loss of Eden has a happy end is an ancient Christian insight. 'O happy fault' the liturgy proclaims, because had there never been sin, there could never have been a saviour. This insight is found in a fifteenth-century carol 'Adam lay y-bounden', which ends with the joyful realization that, had the apple not been taken, we would never have been able to honour Mary as the Queen of Heaven:

> Ne hadde the appel take been,
>   The appel take been,
> Ne hadde never our Lady
>   A been heavene-queen.

Perhaps the fundamental literary insight is that, to have literature at all, the world must be a fallen one.

This may be the fundamental point of William Golding's fiction. The world he presents is incomplete and fractured. In *The Spire* (1964), the egotistical will that drives Jocelin, the Dean, to build a spire, no matter what it will cost, is a realization of what it is to be fallen. The cost of Jocelin's folly, as the novel calls it, is an affair, a ruined marriage, a ritual killing, death in childbirth and the degeneration of a gifted man into drunkenness. Yet the skill of the builder, the sheer achievement of the spire in its unprecedented technical mastery, is something that could only have happened in a fallen world, where the will of the fanatic is irresistible.

Summary

The garden represents a place of retirement and repose in a busily oppressive world. It is both nature and art. It was used as an emblem of the state. The abandoned garden is an image of lost hope. Behind many garden images stands the story of Eden. We feel alienated from our home – the garden – and yet there are things we could not achieve were we safely within paradise.

48.1   Landscape and literature

History in the landscape

Since the 1950s we have learnt to see that landscape has a human history – that it is, in part, a human creation. We have set out the fields, planted woods, quarried stone, created ponds, dug ditches, raised banks and made paths and roads. The seminal work of landscape history was *The Making of the English Landscape* by W. G. Hoskins (1955).

Fields

The appearance of the landscape owes much to cultivation. In the second stanza of A. E. Housman's 'Bredon Hill' (1896), the young man recalls the days of love on the hillside:

> Here of a Sunday morning
>   My love and I would lie,
> And see the coloured counties,
>   And hear the lark so high
>   About us in the sky.

Housman's 'coloured counties' are, at least in part, coloured because of the different crops growing in separate fields. The fields, bordered by hedges, draw the eye to the various colours. Fields are very English. In Kent and Devon, for example, their high hedges are pre-Roman. Elizabeth Barrett Browning's long dramatic monologue, *Aurora Leigh* (1857), has the heroine, born in Italy, coming to England for the first time and seeing its fields as being indicative of the character of the nation:

> The ground seemed cut up from the fellowship
> Of verdure, field from field, as man from man.
>
> (260–1)

Elizabeth Barrett Browning knew Italy, so was aware that in many of its regions the fields are large and hedges rare. To Aurora, the English fields isolate and alienate; they are an emblem of man cut off from man. The colloquial meaning of 'cut up' – hurt, disappointed, distressed – was available to her. *The Oxford Dictionary of Slang* gives 1844 as the first instance of such a usage. As a footnote on hedges, the poets of the First World War noted with a regretful irony that the coils of barbed wire, when rusted, looked like autumnal hedges.

Landscape gardening

In Chapter 47, section 3 there was a brief mention of the art of landscape gardening. This was popular in the latter part of the eighteenth century and the early part of the nineteenth. A landscape architect would look at the grounds, usually of country estates, and, by recognizing its 'capabilities', sought to 'improve' it. Improvement usually meant smoothing the lines of woods, creating lakes, bringing the grass up to the house, cutting through woods to open up vistas and building little hills and terraces, so the owners could enjoy the 'prospects'. Landscape gardening had its own vocabulary. Sometimes, the gardeners saw a landscape as a sentence, which needed punctuating with features such as a Greek temple, an obelisk or triumphal arch. The two most famous gardeners were Lancelot 'Capability' Brown and Humphry Repton. Later, fashion turned against the wholesale redesigning of landscapes. Writers objected to the clearing of woods with the loss of different species and the tangles and tuftiness of natural growth. The spokesmen for this more cautious approach to landscape were Richard Payne Knight and Uvedale Price. There was a political aspect to this debate: the Tories had reservations about the neat and wholesale transformations that Brown and Repton made for Whig magnates. Doubts about wholesale redesigning are present in *Mansfield Park* (1814). Rushworth, who has a friend who employs Humphry Repton, is caught up by fashion (albeit by then a rather dated one) and is heedless about the history of the landscape. Jane Austen's point is a moral one, that improvement of any kind – be it landscape or human nature – is not something that can easily be achieved (see Chapter 47, section 47.3).

Enclosure

One of the subjects of literature, particularly in the nineteenth century, is our misuse of the natural world. Sometimes poets use the analogy of Eden – the beauties of the past and the life it made possible have been wilfully lost.

One of these losses came about by way of enclosure. Enclosure meant the selling off of common land. Once private landowners had acquired land, they divided it up into individual fields and planted hedges. Enclosure is another aspect of the changing English landscape. In the Midland counties (for example, Leicestershire and Northamptonshire), most fields are not much over 200 years old. Before enclosure, the land was open, marked by clumps of trees, bushes and ponds, and in most directions, the eye could reach the horizon without interruption. Rather than Housman's 'coloured counties', wherever the eye turned (and panoramas were consequently circular) the land stretched away until it met the overarching sky. We are fortunate to have one very good poet who grew up and loved the unenclosed landscape – John Clare (1793–1864). Clare was a peasant, brought up on the edges of the Fens in north Northamptonshire. He writes virtually without conventional punctuation and with his own spellings. He is a poet of many moods, one of which is loss. In 'Swordy Well' (written in the 1820s) he laments 'grubbed up trees, banks, and bushes'. In a poem of the early 1820s called 'The Mores' or 'Enclosure', he recalls how once

> In unchekt shadows of green, brown, and grey
> Unbounded freedom ruled the wandering scene
> Nor fence of ownership crept in between
> To hide the prospect of the following eye
> Its only bondage was the circling sky
> One mighty flat undwarfed by bush and tree
> Spread its faint shadow of immensity.

In an unenclosed landscape, the unimpeded eye sees a vast land – 'One mighty flat' – and there is the sublimity of horizontal rather than perpendicular space. In 'Remembrances' (written in the early 1830s) he hauntingly laments a lost landscape, blaming enclosure for the destruction of little places with names such as 'old Sneap Green, Puddock's Nook, and Hilly Snow' (44). Enclosure has invaded these tiny and much-loved spots:

> Inclosure like a Buonaparte let not a thing remain
> It levelled every bush and tree and levelled every hill
> And hung the moles for traitors – though the brook is running still
> It runs a naked stream cold and chill.

> (67–79)

'Inclosure' is like Napoleon Buonaparte – an invader and destroyer. The last line suggests a landscape robbed of its magical and even sacred qualities – 'naked', 'cold' and 'chill'. Enclosure for Clare was a metaphor for anything that intrudes, robs and constrains. It stood for all that threatened him, including, perhaps, conventional spelling and punctuation.

Nature despoiled

Later in the century, G. M. Hopkins wrote knotty, thickly-textured poems about the way we have encroached on the natural world. 'God's Grandeur' (1877) compresses three visions of the world into the confines of a sonnet: the world is charged, like electricity, with 'the grandeur of God'; it is spoilt by humans yet retains deep down 'the dearest freshness'. The human spoilation is achieved through internal rhymes, a marvellously unexpected word and a disturbing appeal to the sense of smell:

> And all is seared with trade; bleared, smeared with toil;
> And wears man's smudge and shares man's smell.

The density of Hopkins' textures makes pollution very close – we are close enough to touch it and smell it. 'Smudge' is a surprise. It stands for the messiness human beings have created and, possibly, for the mess we, in our fallen state, have become.

What writers assume

When writing about landscape – its features and the way we have spoilt it – poets sometimes expect readers to know what certain natural features are like, so they can themselves supply details that are absent from the text. When T. S. Eliot says in the last section of *Little Gidding* (1942) 'History is now and England', he trusts the reader to make the line imaginatively more ample by supplying shared images of the English landscape. This trusting is often evident in English verse: we must know what a daffodil looks like to appreciate William Wordsworth's poem.

Summary

Landscape change is, in part, our work. Writers present fields and hedges, and think about the consequences of landscape gardening and enclosure. They recoil from the spoilation of nature. Writers trust readers to imagine the details they have not supplied.

48.2   Figures in the landscape

People pictured

There is a passage in Chapter 42 of *Tess of the d'Urbervilles* (1891) in which Thomas Hardy presents Tess with the sharpness of a painter:

> Thus Tess walks on; a figure which is part of the landscape; a fieldwoman pure and simple, in winter guise; a grey serge cape, a red woollen cravat, a stuff skirt covered by a whitey-brown rough wrapper, buff-leather gloves.

The writing works like a picture. It is in the present tense, and in so far as tense is appropriate to the discussion of pictures, they are in the present tense, because we see them all at once. Tess is presented pictorially in colours – grey, red, whitey-brown – and clothes – cape, cravat, skirt. Hardy is external; he chooses to know nothing of her thoughts and feelings (see Chapter 3, section 3.6).

Sometimes, in Hardy, the feelings of characters are reflected in the landscape. The blissful feelings of falling in love are reflected in Chapter 20 of *Tess of the d'Urbervilles*, where Tess and Angel, like an unfallen Eve and Adam, meet early in the morning to walk in the water meadows.

Pathetic fallacy, personification and mental landscape

Pathetic fallacy is ascribing human feelings to objects, which could not in nature have them. John Ruskin, who coined the term, thought it a blemish, but there is no need to agree with him. Writers have often spoken of trees, plants, clouds, rivers and mountains as having feelings. The following is from Lord Tennyson's 'Ulysses' (1842):

> The long day wanes: the slow moon climbs; the deep
> Moans round with many voices.
>
> (54–5)

Tennyson's image of the fading light of the evening, enacted in appropriately falling cadences, depends on a standard use of language to establish atmosphere before he ascribes feeling to 'the deep' (the sea).

Personification is 'larger' than pathetic fallacy, because it involves talking of something that is not a person *as* a person. Personification established in a single word can be evocative. This is from the second stanza of Tennyson's 'Mariana' (1830):

> After the flitting of the bat,
> When thickest dark did trance the sky.

The economy of 'trance' transforms the scene into one of eerie mesmerism.

Mental landscapes, unlike pathetic fallacy and personification, do not rest on grammatical manoeuvres. In mental landscape, the reader is implicitly invited to see that the landscape is an expression of the mind of the figure who moves through it. In Tennyson's 'Locksley Hall' (1842), the protagonist, disappointed in love, turns from his shallow beloved to the landscape: 'O the dreary, dreary moorland! O the barren, barren shore!' Dreary and barren indicates his bereft and rejected state.

Summary

Pathetic fallacy, personification and mental landscape indicate the link between the self and landscape. The first ascribes feelings to that which cannot have them; the second, often in a single word, treats the non-human as human, while the third asks the reader to see a link between mind and external scene.

48.3   Animals

Attitudes to animals

Animals have a number of functions in literature:

- They are 'assistants' and 'guides', as in William Blake's 'A Dream' (1789).
- There are imaginary beasts in the tradition of Medieval dragons and serpents. Coleridge's slithery sea-monsters in 'The Rime of the Ancyent Marinere' (1798) owe much to the tradition of sea serpents.

- They are emblems of human qualities, such as Blake's 'The Lamb' (1789) and the 'The Tyger' (1794). Furthermore, in Blake, they form the poles of his imaginative world: the lamb stands for tenderness, patience, mercy and forbearance, while the tiger is elemental energy, force and creativity. In 'The Tyger', Blake asks the question about how the two poles relate: 'Did he who made the Lamb make thee?'
- Birds stand for inspiration, the outpouring of song, and their flight is an emblem of wonder and the aspirations of the soul.
- In Aesop's *Fables* (sixth century BC) animals were emblems of human emotions and responses. The same is true of the fables of La Fontaine (published 1668–94). The fable was once popular in England. John Dryden's (1700) and John Gay's (1727) fables were much read. The tradition has faded, though George Orwell's *Animal Farm* (1945) shows that there is still life in it.

Anthropomorphism

Anthropomorphism is seeing non-human things in human terms. In children's literature, animals talk, are dressed as humans and have jobs. Such practices are often derided, yet anthropomorphism is just an extreme version of what we do all the time – imagine the lives of animals. When we do so, it is hard (perhaps impossible) to exclude human concerns and values. Hence we see animals in terms of things that are basic to our lives: home and motherhood. John Clare writes about nests and animals with their young. He closes 'Birds Nests' (written 1820s) with a comment on a nest:

> an hermitage
> For secresy and shelter rightly made
> And beautiful it is to walk beside
> The lanes and hedges where their homes abide.

He is not unafraid of the quite human word 'home' and the biblically nuanced 'abide'. With those connotations, we can read a human interest in his line about 'secresy' and 'shelter'. Clare writes poems about specific birds' nests – woodpigeon, raven, yellowhammer, peewit (lapwing) and nightingale – and a poem about seeing a mouse scurry out of her nest 'With all her young ones hanging at her teats' (written 1830s).

A world apart

Some writers strive to convey the otherness of animals – their non-human separateness. In Ted Hughes, animals are wild; they are centres of energy that are not human. In his early poems, his approach was to bring out the difference between people and animals. In a poem such as 'Thrushes' (1955) he celebrates the instinctual energy that neither ponders nor is, in its action, hampered by self-awareness. It is that decidedly non-human life that Hughes tries to enter.

Hughes' creatures do not exist in the pages of natural history. He is not a naturalist. What he says about thrushes is not something that can be picked up by looking through binoculars. Perhaps he is best described as a mythologist, who expresses a strong sense of the alien otherness of animals: think of the restless beast pacing its cage in 'The Jaguar' (1957). In 1970 he published *Crow*, virtually a whole mythology from the perspective of a jauntily confident outsider, who, nevertheless, is at the heart of things.

Summary

Writers are interested in animals' habitats and the rearing of their young. Animals can also be presented as being quite apart from people.

49.1 The work of God

The word 'nature'

Unlike say, Hebrew, we have a word that denotes the realm of natural things – the word 'nature'. Our understanding of nature determines what we see and how we interpret the significance of what we think and do. And our understanding changes (see Chapter 31, section 31.2).

Created by God

For most writers in the past, nature was the handiwork of God. God was glimpsed, first, in the very existence of things: there is something when there might have been nothing. Second, the sheer ingenuity and beauty of nature pointed to a designer.

Both existence and design arouse awe and wonder. In the exultant language of Gerard Manley Hopkins, there is a breathless amazement at the world's existence and teeming multiplicity. In the fifth stanza of 'The Wreck of the Deutschland' (written 1875–6) he sees God the Creator behind all things – 'under the world's splendour and wonder'; and in 'Pied Beauty' (1877) it is the character of things that arouses the joy of faith: 'Fresh-firecoal chestnut-falls; finches' wings'. He celebrates the presence of God in nature in the urgent rhythms of his verse. In his sonnet 'The Windhover' (1877), the pell-mell rush of the verse expresses wonder:

> Brute beauty and valour and act, oh, air, pride, plume, here
> Buckle!

He puts the first half of the line together with conjunctions, but then heart and mind, so taken up by the movement of the bird, omit the connecting word, fixing instead on each individual feature.

Hopkins has a distinct philosophy. He learnt from the Medieval philosopher, Duns Scotus, the idea that each object has an irreducible and defining form. He called this 'inscape'. The energy that holds this form in being, he called 'instress'. His sonnet 'As kingfishers catch fire' (written 1881 or 1882) is almost 'doctrinal' in its clarity. He starts, as so often, with a dazzling panorama of distinctive things – kingfishers, dragonflies, stones tumbled into wells – and declares emphatically, and virtually monosyllabically, the principle that each thing is itself in action and being:

> Each mortal thing does one thing and the same;
> Deals out that being indoor each one dwells.

Act and being are one because the act is a dealing out – an outward expression – of each thing's essence. Perhaps the awkwardness of rhythm indicates the struggle to express an idea so fundamental that most words feel inadequate.

Design

The argument from the design of the world or, to use its philosophical name, the *teleological argument*, dominated much eighteenth- and nineteenth-century literature. It is a causal formulation of the second idea set out above: the world has a designed look, so there must be a designer. In the seventeenth century, the mathematics of Sir Isaac Newton bolstered the argument by showing that we live in a rational and reliable universe. William Paley, the argument's most famous exponent, said in *Natural Theology* (1802) that, if a watch implies a watchmaker, then an eye implies an eye-maker. Joseph Addison's hymn beginning 'The spacious firmament on high' (1712), ends with an image of all things singing of their divine origin:

> In Reason's ear they all rejoice,
> And utter forth a glorious Voice,
> For ever singing, as they shine,
> 'The Hand that made us is Divine'.

'Reason's ear' is the mind. Addison knows that there is no music of the spheres, but the mind hears the harmony of nature and understands that the mighty frame of things has been designed by God.

If God guides the world, so the argument runs, then he can guide me. This is the doctrine of Providence. In Charlotte Brontë's *Jane Eyre* (1847), the doctrine of Providence is palpably present in the voice that summons her back to see Mr Rochester (Chapter 35). She has already listened to the voice of conscience – the voice of God within – and now she hears a summons on the air. It is often said that she returns to Mr Rochester not knowing that his wife is dead, but if the voice on the wind is the voice of God, then God knows that it is safe for her to return.

Summary

How we look at Nature depends on the ideas we have about the world. One of the most powerful influences in literature has been the belief that nature is the work of God. The idea that the world is designed by God gave us the picture of the world as being reliable and rational. It also underlined the belief that all things are guided by God's Providence.

49.2 Darwin

The story of late-nineteenth-century thought about Nature might be described as Darwinian disenchantment. In his *The Origin of the Species* (1859), Charles Darwin advanced a view of nature in which the surprising gaps, particularly those between species, could be explained. To many, it seemed that God the designer was no longer needed.

Even before Darwin's book was published, we see this happening in Lord Tennyson's 'In Memoriam' (1850). The intellectual and artistic courage of Tennyson is seen in the way he struggles with biology and geology, both of which seemed to erode a belief in Providence. Paley's argument about the watch and the watch-maker seemed vulnerable. In an attempt to find grounds for religious faith, Tennyson says explicitly in Poem 124 that he does not find it in the design of the world:

> I found Him not in world or sun,
> Or eagle's wing, or insect's eye.

The 'insect's eye', with its echoes of Paley's eye/eye-maker argument, does not point to a universal designer.

The fossil record, a branch of science new in Tennyson's time, weakened a belief in Providence. Fossils showed that nature had allowed whole species to pass away. In Poem 56, nature is dismissive:

> From scarped cliff and quarried stone
> She cries, 'A thousand types are gone:
> I care for nothing, all shall go.'

The poem juxtaposes the sites in which fossil hunters worked with the imperious voice of cold nature. What, at least for a time, Darwin made it difficult to believe in was the image of Mother Nature. If she cares 'for nothing', then she is not kind, benevolent and protecting. Thomas Hardy and A. E. Housman accepted this judgement. There is, as a result, a tension in their work between the beauty of nature and their knowledge that 'she' is indifferent. For example, Housman's haunting lament for a lost landscape of former happiness 'Tell me not here' (1922) closes with a bleak picture of Nature's indifference:

> For nature, heartless, witless nature,
>   Will neither care nor know
> What stranger's feet may find the meadow
>   And trespass there and go,
> Nor ask amid the dews of morning
>   If they be mine or no.

Nature has no feeling – 'heartless', and no mind – 'witless'. Housman also withdraws the comfort of gender.

But Darwin's influence was not wholly negative. There are passages in Hardy when we see him handling imaginatively the huge sweep of geological and biological time (another nineteenth-century discovery). In Chapter 19 of *Tess of the d'Urbervilles* (1891), Angel's playing of the harp draws Tess through the summer garden. There is a hint that she is a representative of emerging life along the evolutionary scale. As she moves, earlier forms cling to her:

> She went stealthily as a cat through this profusion of growth, gathering cuckoo-spittle on her skirts, cracking snails that were underfoot, staining her hands with thistle-milk and slug-slime, and rubbing off her naked arms sticky blights which, though snow-white on the apple-tree trunks, made madder stains on her skin...

Words such as 'profusion' and 'growth' derive extra force from an evolutionary picture of the world. And is there in 'cracking', 'staining' and 'rubbing' a sense of the cost of biological adaption?

Perhaps the growth of ecology has enabled us to recover something of the protecting role of nature. The beauty of the world has been surprisingly prominent in twentieth-century verse. Philip Larkin is increasingly buoyed up by the renewal of the earth and the cycle of nature (see 'Trees' and 'Forget What Did' (1974)), and Ted Hughes shows that we can even wonder at Nature's darkest aspects.

Summary

Darwin made it difficult for some writers to see nature as being kindly and protecting. Nevertheless, the scope of evolution opened up the possibility of appreciating the vistas of time. Fascination with nature was important in twentieth-century literature.

▣ ⌄ **50** Buildings

50.1 Houses

In 1966, W. H. Auden published *About the House*, a series of poems about domestic space. There is a poem called 'The Cave of Making', about his study with its typewriter and dictionaries. He writes also of the cellar, the attic, the kitchen and the bedroom. In 'The Geography of the House' he writes of the lavatory – not a topic usually treated in literature, though Alan Bennett's *The History Boys* (2004) has a scene in which the latrines of a Medieval monastery are explained.

The metaphoric range of the word 'houses' is the starting point of U. A. Fanthorpe's collection *Safe as Houses* (1995). She explores the various uses of this popular phrase to think about the war, childhood, growing up, survival, change, security and vulnerability. In 'Last House' she picks up the meaning of 'house' as the people who have paid to see a cinema performance. This poem on the demolition of an old cinema shows that in this house, people learnt to dream: to talk sharply like Humphrey Bogart, to sing in the rain and to make love to Elizabeth Taylor.

Occupying space

We are creatures of space and time, so our actions happen in space and take time to perform. It is interesting to note how novelists present the actions of their characters. We have a language for the relationships of people in spaces – personal space, body language – but neither of these points about human behaviour would make sense if physical space were not a condition of human life. All the ideas we have about space – territorial space, space and authority, communal space, private space, sacred space – require as their condition the fundamental property of physical space.

Take the example of how movement and position is present in Chapter 34 of *Pride and Prejudice* (1813), the passage in which Darcy proposes to Elizabeth. He is restless:

He sat down for a few moments, and then getting up walked about the room.

He is awkward in her presence, and perhaps this awkwardness is to do with social space. He wants to marry this girl, but is uncertain about the social consequences. He then 'came towards her in an agitated manner' and began to make his offer. His physical approach is emblematic of the offer; he wants to offer himself to her but is still troubled. When she refuses him, his response is represented in terms of his position in the room:

> Mr. Darcy, who was leaning against the mantlepiece with his eyes fixed on her face, seemed to catch her words with no less resentment than surprise.

His pose is, up until this point, the nonchalant attitude of an authoritative man. He leans against the mantlepiece as if he owned it. When, however, Elizabeth makes explicit the grounds for her refusal, he is, again, ill at ease: 'he walked with quick steps across the room'. No longer is he behaving like an owner (of a house or her); he is not at home in this space. When he exits, it is 'hastily'.

Space is an intellectually popular topic. Being so fundamental, our divisions and uses of it reveal something of who we are, how we think and what we value. And, as already indicated, it becomes a metaphor for our inner world. This is the theme of Tom Gunn's measured poem 'Thoughts on Unpacking' (1957). The poet and beloved have moved, and he is now trying to arrange the room to create 'a space for us'. But he finds that, along with the 'knick-knacks', they have brought other things – 'Unpacked, unlabelled' – that belong to their past, unresolved lives. These nameless things, he finds, have filled the spaces he has prepared in the new dwelling. Because he needs the help of the other in dealing with this inner baggage, he realizes that love is a kind of arranging of items in space.

Summary

Space is important as the area in which all actions take place and as a metaphor for the inner world.

50.2 Doors and windows

Particular parts of a building can be imbued with significance: they can be the locations of actions and have symbolic resonances.

Doors

Shakespeare makes much of the two entrances situated at the back of the stage. They can function as doors to admit, eject or shut in. After the murder of Duncan, Macduff knocks at the castle gate. The booming sounds that punctuate the high-tension exchanges of Macbeth and Lady Macbeth represent, as Thomas de Quincey argued in his essay 'On the Knocking at the Gate in *Macbeth*' (1823), the invasion of the normal upon a world in which moral laws have been suspended. King Lear leaves the Duke of Gloucester's castle and is shut out by his daughter, Regan. For Hamlet isolates evil by commanding that the doors be shut, see Chapter 7, section 7.4.

Windows

In Philip Larkin's poetry, the position of the poet in the poem is usually clearly defined. The reader knows from what perspective – both physical and human – the events of the poem are viewed. Frequently, the poet in the poem is looking through a window. In the title poem of *The Whitsun Weddings* (1964), the poet watches the wedding parties from the window of a train, and in 'Dockery and Son', his last view of Oxford and his first of Sheffield are through a railway carriage window. 'Toads Revisited' and 'Afternoons' can be understood as scenes viewed from the distance and elevation of a room overlooking a public park. In the elusively symbolic title poem of *High Windows* (1974), looking through a window is the work's main business. The poet stares at the emptiness of the sky, an experience that transforms and subverts conventional ideas of human fulfilment.

Stairs

W. B. Yeats found symbols in his circumstances. When he bought an ancient tower – Thoor Ballylee – he found that the spiral staircase suggested meanings to him about spiritual and intellectual ascent. That is a traditional image, found in the mystical writings of Medieval England and seventeenth-century Spain. And Yeats saw another significance – it was a staircase up which the leading figures of his nation climbed. In the second part of 'Blood and the Moon' (1933) he writes:

> I declare this tower is my symbol; I declare
> This winding, gyring, spiring treadmill of a stair is my
>   ancestral stair;
> That Goldsmith and the Dean, Berkeley and Burke
> have travelled there.

This is the history of his nation. Its authors and political thinkers have, as it were, gone up these stairs, all of them, like Yeats, in search of Irish identity.

Architects

Though buildings, and hence those who design them, are fundamental features of life, the architect is an interestingly neglected figure in English literature. For example, although Peter Ackroyd's *Hawksmoor* (1985) is plotted round the London churches Nicholas Hawksmoor built in the early eighteenth century, it is dark beliefs, including the necessity of human sacrifice, that chiefly engages Ackroyd.

Summary

The individual parts of a house – doors, windows, stairs – have been given literary significance. These features can be the locations for action; they offer perspectives on the world and they can be used symbolically. But literature neglects architects.

50.3 Settlements

Writers recognize that people become attached to places, and so places have an emotional importance. Writers show that places in fiction are associated in characters' minds with their own pasts and people in whom they are interested. In *Sense and Sensibility* (1811), Jane Austen presents Marianne as feeling deeply for the home she has to leave – Norland – and longing for a place she has never visited – Willougby's Combe Magna.

The small community

Where we live shapes how we live.

Thomas Hardy is the writer of the small community. One of the things that characterizes the life of the small town or village is the knowledge each resident has of other residents. In Chapter 28 of *Tess of the d'Urbervilles* (1891), Tess works with the assumption that people in small communities know each other's histories, and it surprises her when they don't. Angel Clare is pressing her to marry him, but she feels unable to accept because of her past. She laments that people don't know her story:

> 'Why don't somebody tell him all about me?' she said. 'It was only forty miles off – why hasn't it reached here? Somebody must know!' Yet nobody seemed to know; nobody told him.

The literary uses of towns and cities

Towns and cities are useful to authors because they can be places where, quite plausibly, characters can run into one other. At the end of *The Great Gatsby* (1925) Nick bumps into Tom. The chance meeting, briefly reported, allows Nick to reflect that Tom and Daisy were careless people.

Cities can be threatening. There is a moment in Chapter 20 of *Great Expectations* (1860), when Pip, in London for the first time, wanders into Smithfield:

> So, I came into Smithfield; and the shameful place, being all asmear with filth and fat and blood and foam, seemed to stick to me.

The intensity of the writing – all those 'ands' – establishes the viscous nature of urban life. London is smeared, and Pip feels that it sticks to him.

Other writers found London overwhelming. It might be said to be the chief subject of Peter Ackroyd's writing – the biographies as well as the novels. *The Clerkenwell Tales* (2003) is plotted with topographical exactitude around certain sites in Clerkenwell. The final chapter, 'The Author's Tale', is a set of notes specifying the novel's locations (see also Chapter 33, section 33.3). William Blake, the subject of one of Ackroyd's 'London' biographies, closes his 'London'

(1794) with a vision akin to the Last Judgement in which victims cry out against their exploitation:

> But most thro' midnight streets I hear
> How the youthful Harlot's curse
> Blasts the new-born Infant's tear,
> And blights with plagues the Marriage hearse.

Some critics have understood these visionary lines by inventing a narrative in which a husband resorts to a prostitute and thereby infects his child. But given the swirling images, that explanation is too logical. The imagery draws on Macbeth's vision of a last judgement:

> And pity, like a new-born babe,
> Striding the blast.
> (*Macbeth* (1606) 1.7, 20–1)

Shakespeare's 'new-born babe' is present in Blake's 'new-born infant'. Shakespeare's babe strides 'the blast', while 'the Harlot's curse/Blasts' Blake's infant. The images flicker, as if picked out in the flashes of a storm. The word that is absent from Blake's poem is 'pity'.

William Wordsworth wrote of the dizzying effect of London in Book 7 of *The Prelude* (1805). He appears to have been both repelled and fascinated by its moving and multitudinous life (see Chapter 33, section 33.3). In Poem 7 of *In Memoriam* (1850), Tennyson presents a bleak picture of a London dawn, and James Thomson presents a vision of despair in *The City of Dreadful Night* (1874). This poem is perhaps rather sluggish in its movement, yet its eerie and haunting intensity creates a picture both of a darkened mind and a vast and oppressive city.

In the twentieth century, the repellent, though exciting, squalor of cities permeates the early works of T. S. Eliot. Prufrock finds the foggy streets with their drains and lonely men in short sleeves more hauntingly real (and certainly preferable) than the rooms where the women come and go. Graham Greene creates his own world ('Greeneland'), which is not unlike Eliot's; it is seedy, run-down, drab and derelict.

Re-making places

Some places cannot be invented. James Joyce's *Dubliners* (1914) must be set in Dublin. Great cities already have a sort of literary status through their reputation and the stories told about them. Sometimes, readers feel that they themselves have to bring to the text what they know about, say, Berlin, Rome or Vienna. Thomas Hardy re-makes by renaming. Dorchester becomes Casterbridge.

Whatever writers do with London, the location, magnitude and importance of the city is something that the literary imagination has to accept. Charles Dickens' London is always London, though he invests it with a strange, and sometimes lurid, intensity. Bleeding Heart Yard, the ash heaps, Newgate Gaol, Smithfield, the warrens of Bill Sikes and the great and dirty Thames itself all have a significant presence. Dickens responds to decay and confusion; one of his favourite words is 'crazy' (see Chapter 33, section 33.3).

London is not the only city that can't be invented. French novelists cannot avoid Paris. Dickens and Mrs Gaskell in, respectively, *Hard Times* (1854) and *North and South* (1855), invented representative northern industrial towns, but in *Mary Barton* (1848), Mrs Gaskell could not replace Manchester. It is sub-titled *A Tale of Manchester Life*. Detective fiction is usually set in real places: Raymond Chandler in Los Angeles, Donna Leon in Venice and Ian Rankin in Edinburgh. Only when the places are small – as in Agatha Christie's Miss Marple stories – are the settings invented.

Summary

Places are significant because of what happens in them and how characters feel about them. The life characters lead is shown to be dependent on the nature of the settlement. The life of small communities is different from that of big cities. Writers invent small places, but major cities can only be re-imagined.

⬛ ⌄ 51 Mortality

51.1   Creatures of time

Responding to death

The knowledge that all life ends in death is present in the primitive horror that lies behind all narratives of murder (Thomas Kyd's *The Spanish Tragedy* (1592) and Shakespeare's *Hamlet* (1600)) and quiet philosophical meditations on what does and does not last (Herbert's poetry, in particular 'Virtue', 1633).

Closely associated with death is the hope of immortality. John Donne's 'Hymn to God my God, in my sickness' (1633), is a preparation for death. He imagines, as many people do, what the change from time to eternity must be like. His picture is that dying is like being summoned to perform music to a lord. The musician prepares in the ante-chamber: 'I tune the instrument here at the door'. Donne would have been familiar with musicians tuning up before playing to their lord. The very familiarity of it is comforting. The change from mortal life to life eternal is like stepping, no doubt nervously, from a small room to a greater. Tuning the instrument is also a clever conceit for preparing the soul to meet its maker. Both instrument and soul will have to be stretched and adjusted before entry.

Summary

Writers are fascinated by murder and they meditate upon the brevity of life. They also search for ways of writing about the hope of life eternal.

51.2   In memoriam

Death, particularly the death of one who is close, has long inclined us to poetry. Classical poetry exerts a strong influence. Lycidas, the name Milton chose for his elegy on the death of Edward King (1638), occurs in the very influential *Eclogues*, Books VII and IX, by the Latin poet Virgil, written from 42 BC onwards. Poems on the dead often exist in the tension between expressing a Christian hope and using Classical forms and images (see also Chapter 30, section 30.6).

Epitaphs

Some poems are epitaphs; that is, inscriptions on tombs. In 1730, Alexander Pope provided an epitaph for Sir Isaac Newton:

> Nature, and Nature's Laws lay hid in Night.
> God said, *Let Newton be!* And All was *Light.*

Pope exploits the intellectual compression of the heroic couplet. In writing about Newton's discovery of 'Nature's Laws' in terms of God's first act of Creation – light – Pope links the 'night' of our ignorance with the 'darkness … upon the face of the deep' in Genesis 1:2 and God's illumination of all things through Newton's enlightening of our minds. And the rhyme deftly sums up the movement from 'Night' to '*Light*'.

At the graveside

Not all poems about the dead are epitaphs, intended to be engraved on the tomb of the one celebrated. W. H. Auden's 'In Memory of W. B. Yeats' and 'In Memory of Sigmund Freud' (both written in 1939) are tributes, summing up the nature of the achievement of, respectively, the dead poet and the dead psychologist.

In American poetry there are poems about graveyards. In *Spoon River Anthology* (1915), Edgar Lee Masters wrote a whole book of dramatic monologues in which the dead in a cemetery tell the tales of their lives. Alan Tate wrote 'Ode to the Confederate Dead' (1932), and that poem must stand behind two of Robert Lowell's most famous poems: 'The Quaker Graveyard in Nantucket' (1950) and 'For the Union Dead' (1965). The emphases in these poems is not so much the common themes of mortality and the achievement of particular lives, as the exploration of cultural heritages. The dead prompt poets to think about what it is to be American, and, more specifically, Americans of the South, as was Tate, or, in Lowell's case, of the North and the Atlantic seaboard.

Summary

There are formal poems of death – epitaphs – and poems about the departed. Some writers celebrate individual qualities, others explore national identity by thinking about the dead.

▪ ⌄ **52** The Human Mind and Society

52.1 The formation of minds

Growth

Romantic sand Post-Romantic literature is often about how the self is nurtured and shaped. William Wordsworth's *The Prelude* (1805) has as its sub-title *The Growth of a Poet's Mind*. He writes of the influence of his surroundings, the importance of his early contact with fields, lakes and mountains, the changes in his outlook, and events that have made him what he is. There are some moments he knows have had a very potent influence upon him and have made him who he is. He calls them 'spots of time'. They are the places and incidents that resonate in the mind and make it grow:

> There are in our existence spots of time,
> Which with distinct preeminence retain
> A renovating virtue.
>
> (Book 11, 257–9)

Wordsworth was uncertain exactly how these spots of time worked on his mind, so found it difficult to choose an adjective to qualify 'virtue'. His first idea was 'fructifying' and the second 'vivifying'. It seems he wanted to say that these moments both prompted growth and healed the mind.

The work of memory: then and now

Thomas Hardy's poems frequently deal with 'then' and 'now'. In 'A Church Romance' (1909) he writes of a couple drawn to each other when the woman looked up at the band of musicians in the west gallery of the church and caught a look from one of the musicians that claimed her as his. The poem closes with what prompts her memory of that significant moment:

> At some old attitude of his or glance
> That gallery-scene would break upon her mind.

Hardy knows how strange memory is. It is as if, at the sight of an unintended gesture, the memory returns involuntarily. 'Breaks' suggests that memory has an independent life.

Hardy said of past experience that he could disinter or excavate an emotion buried, perhaps, for forty years. Something of this is seen in Philip Larkin's 'Love

Songs in Age' (1964), in which an old woman, looking through her songs, relives rather then remembers the feelings of being young and in love.

The effects of psychology

One of the effects of psychology has been to make memory – particularly the uncontrolled return of unpleasant incidents – a central feature of literature (see Chapter 41, section 41.4). Pat Barker's *Regeneration* (1991) accepts the popular psychological paradigm of trauma and memory, and through the character of Rivers shows how victims are helped to come to terms with their ghastly experiences.

Summary

Writers are interested in the processes by which minds are formed. They write of how memory connects 'then' and 'now' and, under the influence of psychology, how its workings are often unpredictable.

52.2 The Passions, the Virtues and the Deadly Sins

Traditional qualities and values

A traditional way of understanding people is through the Passions and the Virtues. These are traditional ideas with their intellectual roots in the Classical world. The Passions are the various emotional states that afflict people and drive them to action. Passions include anger, cruelty, desire, envy, fear, grief, hatred, jealousy, love, revenge and sadness. Among the Virtues are courage, friendliness, liberality, modesty, patience and temperance.

The importance of the Passions and the Virtues is that they indicate to writers important states of mind and values. Sometimes, we can see that a writer is drawn to a subject because the characters display these qualities. Shakespeare dwells on the corrosive power of jealousy in *Othello* (1604). As with many of the Passions, jealousy is a feeling that is never entirely under control. Othello at times seems to be deliberately feeding his jealousy (sometimes he can sound disturbingly controlled) but there are moments (as in Act 4, sc. 1) when he is helplessly subject to it.

Jane Austen has been read as exemplifying the Virtues. Fanny Price, the central figure of *Mansfield Park* (1814), is patient in her sufferings and temperate in the control of her feelings.

In Aristotle, the Virtues were a *mean* – a middle state between excess and deficiency. Thus courage was the mean between recklessness and cowardice. Perhaps this doctrine is present in Christopher Marlowe's fascination with excessive behaviour. His tragic figures fall because they pursue to excess Passions such as, in the case of Faustus, the yearnings for honour, wealth and sexual pleasure.

The Seven Deadly Sins

The Seven Deadly Sins differ from the Passions and the Virtues because of the manner in which they are presented. In William Langland, Edmund Spenser and Marlowe, the Seven Deadly Sins appear as characters. In Langland and Spenser, they are presented in characteristic poses, while in *Doctor Faustus* (1591) they speak for themselves in a pageant presented to cheer Faustus. The order of their appearance is significant. First comes Pride. Pride is the root of all sins because it means putting oneself before others and before God. Pride is also like the next three – Covetousness, Wrath and Envy – because they are sins of the soul. That is to say, they arise out of our wilful inclination to evil. The final three are the sins of the body – Gluttony, Sloth and Lechery. They are all prompted by our physical weaknesses and inclinations.

Summary

Traditional ideas about the Passions and the Virtues have influenced the subject matter of literature. The Seven Deadly Sins often make the sin of Pride central.

52.3   Doubling characters

Theme and design

The idea of doubles – of two characters so alike that we are invited to view them together – is a matter of theme and design. 'Theme' because two characters help to focus the interests of the book, and 'design' because having two characters gives shape to a work. Doubles assume a mythic status in the idea of the doppelganger – a ghostly other self. There is a memorable Schubert setting (1828) of Heinrich Heine's eerie poem 'Der Doppelganger' in which a man sees a strange figure out of his window, whom he comes to realize is his other self.

Much Ado About Nothing (1598) works by the audience seeing that Benedick is Beatrice's double, her alter ego: both are lively, clever, witty and capable of strong feelings and equally strong convictions. In Charles Dickens' *Great Expectations* (1860), Orlick is a darker and more sinister version of Pip. Both are country boys who work at the forge, are attracted to Biddy, have difficulties with Mrs Joe and are associated with Miss Havisham. In Wilfred Owen's 'Strange Meeting' (1918) the dead man the soldier meets in the strange underworld is, like the soldier, a poet who hoped that his poetry would bring consolation to a hurt world.

The idea of the double possibly arises from the feeling of being divided against oneself: we find it difficult to make decisions and are subject to contrary feelings. This is the theme of R. L. Stevenson's *The Strange Case of Dr Jekyll and Mr Hyde* (1886). The point is that Jekyll and Hyde are not two persons but one, and that Hyde is Jekyll's evil doppelganger. We recognize this in the common phrase: a Jekyll and Hyde personality (see Chapter 40, section 40.2).

Summary

The doubling of characters brings out themes and helps to structure works. The sense that the self is divided may lie behind doubles in literature.

52.4   The inner world

Sleep

Sleep can be disturbing. Hamlet's 'To be or not to be' is an extended metaphor on sleep as an image of death. Shakespeare presents Hamlet as one who explores the image in full:

> to die, to sleep.
> To sleep, perchance to dream. Ay, there's the rub;
> For in that sleep of death what dreams may come,
> When we have shuffled off this mortal coil,
> Must give us pause.
>
> (3.1. 65–9)

The thought is unnerving: we know nightmare's horrors, so what can the nightmares of death be like? The experience of sleep's disturbances is the subject of Samuel Taylor Coleridge's 'The Pains of Sleep' (1803). The poem opens with an account of his normally quiet slumbers, and then he records his anguish and agony as a 'fiendish crowd/Of shapes' (116–17) tortured him. One of the tortures is feeling guilty:

> I could not know
> Whether I suffered, or I did:
> For all seemed guilt, remorse or woe,
> My own or others still the same
> Life-stifling fear, soul-afflicting shame.
>
> (28–32)

The insight into the state of a nightmare is deep and honest. One of the strange effects of dreaming is waking with a cloying sense of guilt for crimes one did not commit. Though we know we are innocent, we suffer a 'soul-afflicting shame'.

Emotions

We often think of emotions as being private. In John Ford's *The Broken Heart* (1633) Armostes says:

> Our eyes can never pierce into the thoughts,
> For they are lodged too inward.
>
> (4.1, 19–20)

That 'never' cannot be true. Emotions are also public. It might be true that no one else can appreciate *exactly* what my joy or sadness is like, but others often know that I *am* joyful or sad. They know this because they can see it. Emotions are visible; the best guide we have as to what others are feeling is written in faces, postures and manners of talking. Others know when people are upset, in pain, happy or gloomy. Emotions are present in smiles, grins, winks, leers, nods, glances, stares, blushes, the raising of the eyebrows, going white, averting the face, lowering the head, sniffs, groans, coughs, splutters and snorts.

If emotions were not public, there would be no point in trying to hide our feelings. Hardy is deeply aware of the visibility of emotions. The face tells what the character feels: 'The old lady's face creased into furrows of repugnance' (*Tess of the d'Urbervilles* (1891), ch. 9).

Tears are a familiar sign of feeling. They have different causes – relief, joy, grief, disappointment – and there are many ways of shedding them – tears are gulped, heaved or hoarse. They are caused by strong emotions and sometimes by a combination of feelings. Some writers make emotions very visible. Dickens, in the manner of a playwright, dramatizes the physical expression of feelings. When, in *Great Expectations* (1860), the convict returns to see Pip, there is a moving passage when Pip, after giving him a chilly reception, says, as he hands him a glass: 'I saw with amazement that his eyes were full of tears' (Chapter 39).

Summary

Writers are interested in sleep because it seems close to death and because it takes us into the strange world of dreams. Literature shows that emotions are public.

52.5   The self and the world

Human society

The self becomes a self in association with others. We are social creatures.

> **How we associate and engage is probably literature's most prominent concern.**

The self exists in, and is in some senses made by, the presence of other people. William Langland saw a fair field full of *folk* – not isolated individuals.

Families

Shakespeare can be read as being about families: hostile families, as in *Romeo and Juliet* (1594), divided families as in *King Lear* (1605) and separated families as in *As You Like It* (1599). To belong is to know who one is. Hence, disruption of the family erodes social identity. This is the central theme of Wilkie Collins. In

No Name (1862), two girls discover that, as a result of their parents not being married, they have no name and thus no identity in society.

Hierarchies

Hierarchical society is the subject of early modern drama. Shakespeare's *Julius Caesar* (1599) deals with a nation in transition. After centuries of being a republic, Rome is moving inevitably towards a monarchy. Shakespeare does not make it entirely clear whether Caesar has ambitions to be a king, so it is not clear whether he betrays the republic or is a martyr to the monarchists' cause. (To this day in Rome, people lay flowers on the place where his body was burnt, so they, at least, regard him as the latter.)

Twentieth-century history has made us suspicious of political hierarchies. We have seen too much of what happened in Germany, the USSR and China to be anything but suspicious about political power falling into the hands of those with systematic political theories. Hence Orwell's liberal plea in *Nineteen Eighty-Four* (1949). Orwell's novel is brilliant in its presentation of the world of collective politics. He sees that collectivist theories erode a rational and reasonable view of the world. If the Party tells us that $2 + 2 = 5$, then it does not make 4. What Orwell sees is that realism – the belief that we can know what the world is like – has moral implications. If $2 + 2 = 5$, then we can easily pretend that we can torture whom we like, because we can decide that their cries are not cries of pain. Today, we are coming to see that he was right about another issue: Orwell's characters are subjected, as we increasingly are, to surveillance.

Work

We have seen in Chapter 39 (section 39.4) that the Victorians, while believing in the virtues of hard work, found it difficult to present it in literature. Langland did far better. Oddly enough he, like the Victorians, viewed work in moral terms In Passus 5 of *Piers Plowman* (three versions between 1362 and 1385), he sees that people, by labouring in the fields, contribute to the goodness of life. Philip Larkin's double-edged poems 'Toads' (1955) and 'Toads Revisited' (1964) bemoan the drudgery of work but also, at least in the latter poem, embrace it gladly as being preferable to the horror of having no routine.

Leisure

There is more in literature about leisure than work. Jane Austen's principal characters (with the exception of Mr Knightley in *Emma*, 1816) don't have paid jobs. Their time is taken up with domestic work, pastimes, visiting, reading and games. *Northanger Abbey* (1818) opens with a passage about what Catherine Morland reads, and later there are at least three discussions about Gothic literature. Sometimes, games have thematic significances. In *Mansfield Park* (1814), Jane Austen plays the card game called Speculation. Mary Crawford speculates about a possible future with Edmund, but when he is disinclined to play along with her, 'All that was agreeable of *her* speculation was over' (Chapter 25).

Games can indicate moral values. In Thomas Hughes' *Tom Brown's Schooldays* (1857), games embody the code of a gentleman: self-reliance, courage, respect for others and fair play. In keeping with the Victorian code of manly independence, boxing is an important gentlemanly accomplishment.

Familiar objects

Material objects are essential to our lives. They are, so to speak, part of our natural history. Writers, particularly Romantic and Post-Romantic ones, often dwell on the arousal of feelings by familiar objects. Thomas Hardy was moved by the importance we attach to clothes. He wrote a plangent poem on seeing a gentleman's suit hanging in a pawn shop – 'A Gentleman's Second-Hand Suit', and a slightly Gothic folk-tale – 'The Catching Ballet of the Wedding Clothes' (both 1928) – about the girl who marries a man wearing the fine clothes given by another. Glamorous clothes fascinate: think of the scene in which Gatsby shows Daisy his collection of shirts (Chapter 5).

Summary

The individual only achieves a full identity in relation to others and the world. Hence, writers dwell on the importance of families and authority in society. In literature, leisure is more prominent than work. Writers also concern themselves with the emotional responses we make to familiar objects.

⊻ 53 Love

53.1 The game of love

Holiday

Love, as was argued in Chapter 21, section 21.3, is like a holiday: there is something playful and merrily irresponsible about it, so metaphors of game are appropriate. In *As You Like It* (1599), Rosalind pursues her beloved into the forest and, in disguise, offers to play games of make-believe, in which she will pretend to be the person she actually is. Love is like a game in so far as both are played according to rules. The rules are social – there are things one can and cannot do – and literary – lovers obey the conventions of literature when they plot and scheme. In a spirit of enterprising adventure, Rosalind, told by her cousin to be merry, says:

> From henceforth I will, coz, and devise sports. Let me see, what think you of falling in love?
>
> (1.2, 22–3)

Rosalind's tone is playful. We might imagine the actress momentarily adopting a pose of mock seriousness while she pondered – 'Let me see' – the weighty matter of being merry. In *The Great Gatsby* (1925), Jay Gatsby relives the conventions of the High Renaissance courtly lover, regarding Daisy as the distant (and almost unattainable) beloved to be wondered at, to be sought and to be won through demonstrations of undying and costly devotion. Perhaps the references to sport in the novel – Jordan's golf, Tom's polo ponies, the fixing of the World Series – are deflating versions of the idea that love is a game.

Inventing the rules

It is a rather difficult idea to swallow, but in an important sense love was invented. (Given the misery it can cause, some have regretted the invention!) In the human world, invention is a matter of language. We can only fully grasp most things when we put them into words. This is true of love. If love is a game, the rules must have been drawn up.

Romantic love, the love of longing, adoration, service, high hopes and bitter disappointments, emerged in the literature of France in the late eleventh century. It had a number of sources, one of the most important being the tradition of songs sung by the troubadours of Provence in southern France. Another was the tales of King Arthur (see Chapter 25, section 25.1). Arthurian stories introduced into literature passions so intense that, in the case of Arthur's Queen Guinevere and Sir Lancelot, it became adulterous.

Courtly love

Love was 'courtly' because the setting was usually the Court of a king or an aristocrat, and the lovers were members of a Court – knights and high-born ladies. A common plot arrangement was a lady wooed by a knight of lower status than herself. The relationship paralleled that between a servant and a lord. Indeed, the language was the same: he served and waited on her. Moreover, there was an elaborate code of behaviour that stipulated what conduct was allowed. The knight/lover, full of longing and desire, would go on perilous quests in order to win his lady's favour, though she was often unmoved by his exploits. There were moral complications: as in the case of Guinevere and Lancelot, the woman was often married. (In *The Great Gatsby*, Daisy is married.) What made this literature distinctive was its focus on the inner life of the characters, their pains, joys, hopes and fears. The inner world of pain, longing and disappointment is explored in the fifth book of Chaucer's *Troilus and Criseyde* (c. 1385). Perhaps the emphasis on feeling was a way of finding relief from marriages made for political reasons.

Three points need to be made about 'courtly love':

- The term was coined in the nineteenth century, so it is not a genre with sharply defined rules. It is best used to signify a High Romantic approach to love, conceived in terms of the code of Medieval chivalry and concentrating on the emotional lives of the characters.
- English literature is often characteristically wary of the High Romantic style. 'The Franklin's Tale' (c. 1390) has many of the features of courtly literature (an ardent young man falling in love with a married lady), but Chaucer's tone is sceptical. He is a shade dismissive of the knight, who goes off to Britain: 'For al his luste he sette in swich labour'. The particular tone of 'swich' (such) indicates that the poet is less than impressed by knightly posturings.
- This literature gave to English a set of images and conventions which, when handled with care, still live for us. Spring is the season of love; lovers sing about their feelings, and the impulses of love are often at odds with the institution of marriage. One of the major images was of love as a kind of religion. The beloved was like a saint, and lovers' journeys were like pilgrimages to a shrine. These images are used to rich effect in Romeo's first meeting with Juliet (Act 1, sc. 5).

Summary

Love has long been imagined as a kind of game with elaborate rules. In this sense, love has been invented. One of the most popular literary presentations of love grew up in Late Medieval Europe. Its setting was the Court, where knights sought to win the love of ladies. There was an

> emphasis on the inner feelings of the lover. The language of this 'courtly love' has deeply influenced English literature, although some writers have been wary about the high tone of its pretensions.

53.2   Petrarch

The conventions of 'courtly love' fed into and were transformed and popularized by the Italian poet, Petrarch (1304–74). The language of sixteenth- and seventeenth-century poetry is in the Petrarchan tradition.

Love at first sight and the ideal beloved

Petrarch once went into a church in France and there he saw Laura. It was love at first sight; indeed, Petrarch is one of the inventors of the language of suddenly falling in love.

Laura became his ideal. His praise shaped Late Medieval and Renaissance literature. (It can still be heard in the lyrics of pop music.) Petrarch created a series of conventions about what the beloved looks like, how she behaves and the impact she has upon the lover.

Conventions of the beloved

Laura was blonde, so golden hair, sometimes called 'wires' (*The Shorter Oxford English Dictionary* gives 1589 as the first usage), is a sign of beauty. Perhaps the delight we take in blondes from Jean Harlow to Marilyn Monroe (neither of whom were in fact blonde), goes back to Petrarch's feelings for the alluring Laura. Portia in *The Merchant of Venice* (1596) is first presented as a blonde:

> and her sunny locks
> Hang on her temples like a golden fleece.
> (1.1. 169–70)

Shakespeare is happy to present her in the Petrarchan mode, but he does more. The golden fleece was an image of epic endeavour (Jason's task was to find the golden fleece) and wealth. This is fitting: Portia is rich, and the play is about the power of wealth.

The Petrarchan beloved had glittering eyes, and, like her golden hair, these were often compared to the sun. John Donne says that his beloved's eyes might even dazzle the sun: 'If her eyes have not blinded thine' he says to the irritating sun that has roused him from a night of pleasure ('The Sun Rising', 1633).

Red lips are desirable. They are like cherries. Robert Herrick (*Hesperides*, 1648) develops the image in terms of estates and gardening, and in doing so makes use of the tradition that a woman's body is like a territory that can be explored and exploited:

> Cherry-ripe, ripe, ripe, I cry,
> Full and fair ones; come and buy.

> If so be, you ask me where
> They do grow, I answer: There,
> Where my Julia's lips do smile;
> There's the Land, or Cherry-Isle,
> Whose Plantations fully show
> All the year, where Cherries grow.

Red-lipped Julia is elusive; her cherries (kisses) can be bought, but those who would make purchases must presumably sail to the Isle, where these inviting fruits grow.

In 'Upon His Julia', another of Herrick's poems on his (imaginary) beloved, another point is made about female colouring:

> Lips she has all ruby red,
> Cheeks like cream enclareted.

The verbal dexterity of 'enclareted' introduces the Petrarchan convention that red cheeks contrasting with otherwise white skin is beautiful. 'Enclareted' is inventive; usually, cheeks are said to be like roses or coral.

A further standard contrast is that between lips and teeth. White teeth are like pearls in Herrick's 'On Lucy':

> Sound teeth has Lucy, pure as pearl, and small,
> With mellow lips, and luscious there withall.

White skin was valued not just as a contrast to rose-red lips, but as beautiful in itself. Skin smooth as ivory and white as snow was a frequent object of praise, as was a high, and also smooth, forehead. This is a distinctly Late Medieval aspect of the Petrarchan tradition – scraping back the hair made the forehead prominent. Chaucer's Prioress was praised for the breadth of her forehead.

A further conventional contrast is that between white breasts and red nipples. In 'Upon the Nipples of Julia's Breast', Herrick proposes a set of images, all of which contrast red and white: a red rose peeping through a white one; a cherry placed in a lily; a strawberry in cream; and rubies among pearls. Then he closes with the comparison for which he has been preparing the reader:

> So like to this, nay all the rest,
> Is each neat niplet on her breast.

In *Hesperides*, Herrick is Petrarchan in that what he says is potentially erotic yet the artificial images (they read like subjects for an emblematic painting) distance us from the object of desire.

Petrarchan beauties also walk as if on air, sound like music when they speak, or the music of the spheres when they sing (see Chapter 31, section 31.3). Richard Lovelace's 'Gratiana Dancing and Singing' (1649) opens with this ideal beauty in 'constant motion/Even and glorious, as the sun' and closes with mythic comparisons:

> So did she move; so did she sing
> Like the harmonious spheres that bring
> Unto their rounds the music's aid;
> Which she performed such a way,

As all th' inamoured world will say:
The Graces danced, and Apollo played.

Lovelace's verse is not as highly wrought as Herrick's. Its distinctive quality here is the representation of an awe, which makes comparisons with the Graces and Apollo – the god of music – pleasingly natural and unforced. Music has added to the poem: W. Denis Browne's setting (1912) has an accompaniment that is as stately and elegant as Gratiana's dancing, and perhaps in its ringing tones there is an attempt to represent the music of the spheres.

Petrarchan beloveds, for all the praise they receive, often remain cold and aloof, refusing to return the ardour of their devoted servants. (To serve a lady was an aspect of the Petrarchan tradition also found in Medieval literature.) They remain emotionally and physically distant. If real Court ladies were the objects of love poems (and, of course, this does not have to be the case), then the lover would see them only rarely, and perhaps never speak to them. There is a touching moment of recollected ardour in the Earl of Surrey's poem on being imprisoned in Windsor Castle ('So cruel prison…', 1537), when the poet writes of the green inner courts

where we were wont to hove,
With eyes cast up unto the maiden's tower.

The physical movement – roaming on the green and looking up – make the maidens seem very distant in their high tower.

The word most often associated with an unresponsive beauty is 'cruel'. In *Twelfth Night* (1599), Shakespeare presents Orsino as trying to love Olivia according to the traditions of courtly love as mediated through the conventions of Petrarch. Orsino is not, as students are often told, a man in love with being in love. Rather, he is a man who has probably never felt such a passion before and he is handling it in the only language he knows. So, when he orders Cesario to visit her once more, he says: 'Get thee to yon same sovereign cruelty' (2.4. 79).

The lover

Petrarch supplied lovers with several roles. They could be unrequited and so behave pretty much as does the listless Orsino – indulging in music, seeking to be alone, turning all conversations to the beloved and adopting moody and melancholy poses. Unrequited lovers also wrote verse and either neglected or spruced up their appearances.

The merciless beauty

Literature is concerned with the pains of love as well as its joys. Again, this goes back to Petrarch and the convention of the indifferent mistress, though there is also an earlier model – the merciless beauties of Medieval literature, as in Chaucer's 'Merciles Beaute' (probably 1390s).

From the realm of faery there come elusive and seductive creatures. In John Keats' eerie and haunting 'La Belle Dame Sans Merci' (1820), a beautiful creature first fascinates and then seduces a knight. He is left, lost and forlorn, wandering in a bleak landscape.

Serving a lady

Petrarchan conventions drew on the Medieval idea of the lover as a knight on a quest to serve his lady. John Donne alludes to tasks at the start of one of his songs (1633):

> Go, and catch a falling star,
>   Get with child a mandrake root,
> Tell me, where all past years are,
>   Or who cleft the devil's foot.

The robust, combative manner of those lines suggests that the persona was not like Orsino. There is a merry cynicism in his use of Petrarchan extravagances, which prepares the reader for the idea that no matter what strange discoveries a lover makes he will not find 'a woman, true and fair'.

But sometimes, even in the Petrarchan tradition, journeys end in lovers meeting, but once they have met, there is not much to say. The Petrarchan tradition does not dwell on the lovers together. It does, however, talk of lovers parting. It is like death, as in the opening of John Donne's 'The Legacy' (1633):

> When I died last, and, dear, I die
>   As often as from thee I go.

Sometimes Donne's tone is not as bluntly matter of fact, not quite a case of saying, look I stick to the Petrarchan tradition. Sometimes the rhythms are meltingly sad. 'The Expiration' (1633) opens:

> So, so, break off this last lamenting kiss,
>   Which sucks two souls, and vapours both away.

Each 'so' represents a lamenting kiss, and, in a characteristically technical manner, he explains that the parting breath of the kiss separates soul from body (see also Chapter 17, section 17.4).

Petrarchan conventions at work

The Petrarchan tradition was built on a set of conventions but, as in the case of the traditions of courtly love, it was not merely a matter of following a formula. A work can draw on Petrarch and yet fail to include several of the features set out above. But some poems do contain many of them. In Sonnet 81 from Edmund Spenser's *Amoretti* (1595) the beloved has golden hair, red cheeks, eyes of fire, a fair breast and teeth like pearls.

Whenever conventions are recognizable and popular, they can easily be undermined. Shakespeare's Sonnet 130 (1609) wittily subverts writing that cannot distinguish between Petrarchan conventions and what girls are in fact like. Unconventionally beautiful girls can be loved:

> My mistress' eyes are nothing like the sun,
> Coral is far more red, than her lips red,
> If snow be white, why then her breasts are dun:
> If hairs be wires, black wires grow on her head.
> I have seen roses damasked, red and white;
> But no such roses see I in her cheeks;
> And in some perfume is there more delight
> Than in the breath that from my mistress reeks.
> I love to hear her speak, yet well I know
> That music hath a far more pleasing sound:
> I grant I never saw a goddess go,
> My mistress when she walks treads on the ground:
> And yet by heaven I think my love as rare,
> As any she belied with false compare.
>
> (see Chapter 16, section 16.6.)

Summary

For centuries, the image of the beloved has been formed strongly by the conventions of writing that stem from the Italian poet, Petrarch. The conventions involve the terms of praise appropriate to a beloved, and the joys and pains of the lover. These conventions can also be subverted.

■ ⊻ **54** War

54.1 Sources and influences

Classical literature

Classical works provide an enduring model of the heroic soldier: suffering is nobly borne and there is pride in victory. Classical writing has created an heroic code, which concentrates on an outstanding individual who impresses all by the valour of his deeds. He is spoken of in a special vocabulary – he is staunch, valiant and bold. He is summoned to the conflict, he faces the enemy host without flinching, and in his death he is described as one of the fallen.

Classical war literature continues to attract poets. Christopher Logue has translated Homer's *The Iliad* (for example, *Kings*, (1991) *Cold Calls* (2005)). In the non-Classical tradition, Seamus Heaney has translated the Anglo-Saxon epic *Beowulf* (1999), and David Jones' long poem *In Parenthesis* (1937) plots the actions of a representative soldier – Private Ball – against war literature of the past, particularly the Welsh Romances and the stories of King Arthur.

Traditions of war writing

Although written nearly twenty years after the end of hostilities, David Jones' *In Parenthesis* is about the First World War (1914–18). This was a very literary war, both in terms of the number of recognized authors who wrote about it – Blunden, Brooke, Graves, Gurney, Owen, Rosenberg, Sassoon – and in the way the literature was very conscious of its traditions. Most First World War poetry is lyrical and draws on traditional imagery. Poets included birds, flowers, clouds and the landscape in their pictures of war.

Summary

Classical heroic literature has influenced war writing. Much of the poetry of the First World War is lyric.

54.2   The First World War

The national imagination

The First World War has entered the national imagination. In grammatical terms, it is present in its proper nouns. The names of the Western Front – Passchendaele, Picardy, the Somme – are a code for events with which, as a nation, we are still coming to terms. When in *The History Boys* (2004), Alan Bennett includes a scene in which the students discuss writing about the First World War, he is depending on his audience knowing something about its importance. The First World War is a touchstone of our culture. It defines the kind of nation we have become.

The two poles of First World War writing

First World War literature, particularly its poetry, varies in tone and attitude. Broadly, however, there are two quite distinct responses:

- War is a grave matter requiring serious reflection and, in some cases, unqualified celebration.
- War is treated with irreverent mockery, particularly of those in authority.

This is a familiar pattern: Epic generates mock-epic, and burlesque (the parodic mockery of high literary styles) is the offspring of stirring tales of valiant deeds. It may be that, because we are ambivalent about war, we veer between the heroic and grim comedy. In Shakespeare's two *Henry IV* plays (1596 and 1597), Hotspur and, when necessary, Hal are heroic figures, whereas Falstaff, while pretending to live as a noble soldier, burlesques the high rhetoric of war.

Sometimes, the mocking manner in First World War writing is looked upon as the most representative. In Siegfried Sassoon, for example, burlesque – in the form of cynical, black humour – is often the dominant manner. In the rhythms of popular songs and rhymes, he punctures the pomposity of unfeeling leaders. 'Base Details' and 'The General' (both 1917) are the most famous examples. In jaunty, demotic speech, they represent the 'us' and 'them' culture that grew up in the First World War.

The quality of First World War literature varies, but it is a cultural fact that it exerts a more powerful imaginative hold on us than the literature of the Second World War. Good as the Second World War poets Keith Douglas and Alun Lewis are, they have not the same place in the national consciousness as have Wilfred Owen or Siegfried Sassoon. Because of its cultural centrality, the following sections will draw heavily on the literature of the First World War.

Summary

The First World War is a central feature of British consciousness. Its literature veers between serious reflection and mocking scorn.

54.3   Love and war

Lovers and war

Soldiers are also lovers. In the 'seven ages' of man speech (*As You Like It* (1599), 2.7. 139–66), Shakespeare places the soldier immediately after the lover. The call to arms therefore often involves bidding farewell to a beloved. Homer presents Hector as saying farewell to his wife and children, and in the seventeenth century, Richard Lovelace, one of the Cavalier poets, courteously explains that he now has a new beloved: 'True, a new mistress now I chase' ('To Lucasta, Going to the Wars', 1649). The theme of Byron's 'On This Day I Complete My Thirty-Sixth Year' (1824) is that he is too old to love but not to fight. Bidding farewell to the beloved is an aspect of a traditional form of war writing: the turning from the habits of peace to the ways of war. In his 'An Horatian Ode upon Cromwell's Return from Ireland' (1650), Andrew Marvell opens with an almost ritualized picture of the 'forward youth' turning away from books to the weapons of war:

> 'Tis time to leave the books in dust,
> And oil the unused armour's rust.

For the young, the books are likely to be about love, a love that now must be treated as dead. Think about the connotations of 'dust'.

The love of comrades

There is a passage in Plato's *Symposium* (384 BC), which argues that the selflessness of lovers and beloveds is a quality desirable in an army. Plato imagines that an army composed of 'none but lover and beloved' could best serve their country. The qualities or virtues required of a soldier – loyalty, faithfulness and selfless service – are found in lovers:

> And men like these fighting shoulder to shoulder, few as they are – might conquer – I had almost said – the whole world in arms. For the lover would rather anyone than his beloved should see him leave the ranks or throw his arms away in flight – nay, he would sooner die a thousand deaths.

> (179a)

Such a feeling is not confined to the Classics. There are First World War poems that speak openly of the mutual loyalty of troops in terms of love. In 'Greater Love' (1917), Wilfred Owen sees the self-sacrificial lives of those in arms as a greater love than that of man and woman. The opening lines deliberately play on the conventional language of love poetry in its praise of red lips:

> Red lips are not so red
> As the stained stones kissed by the English dead.

The success of these lines depends on Owen following through the logic of the language of love and boldly giving us the word 'kissed'. Conventionally, the redder the lips, the greater the beauty and desire of the lover, but Owen finds greater love in the sacrificial ardour of those who, in falling, kiss the stones of the earth (see Chapter 53, section 53.2).

Love in the time of war

Leo Tolstoy wrote *War and Peace* (1865–8), but, given the centrality of Natasha and Pierre's love, the novel might have been called 'War and Love'. Peace, in common usage, is opposite to war, but in Tolstoy (and many other books) it is often love and war that form the major themes of a work.

Homer's *The Iliad* (eighth century BC) is a story of love and war. There would have been no Trojan War had not Paris eloped with Helen, the wife of Menelaus, King of Sparta. Many writers have mused on the conjunction in one event of two of the strongest passions: the desire of love and the desire for conquest. It is significant that in Classical mythology, Venus, the goddess of love, goes to bed with Mars, the god of war.

The language of love and war

Sometimes, the language of the one is playfully applied to the other. Love is often seen as war, so there is talk of the other as the 'enemy', who must be won over – attacked and penetrated – or, to use naval language, boarded. In *Twelfth Night* (1599) Sir Toby encourages Sir Andrew to 'accost' Maria. 'Accost' is a naval term, meaning to draw alongside. He later tells him to 'front her, board her, woo her, assail her' (1.3. 45, 53).

Summary

Love is intimately connected with war in the comradeship of soldiers, the parting of lovers, the causes of war and the sharing of a common language.

54.4 War and sport

Sport trains participants in what Fluellen might have had in mind when he talks of 'the true disciplines of the wars' (*Henry v*, (1599) 3.3. 17). Sport requires participants to work together in a team, so that all act as one. War is similar. The platoon or company must become, in Herbert Read's words, 'a body and soul, entire' ('My Company', 1919).

War and sport share a common language. The aim of both is 'victory'. Both a company and a side have a 'captain'. We talk of 'attack', 'defence', 'outflanking', 'wings', and battlegrounds and sports grounds are called 'fields'. This sharing of a common language must have come easily to public schoolboys. It was in the public school that sport was first introduced, and there can be few such schools that do not have an Officer Training Corps. The importance of co-operation, of sticking together and working for each other was, for many boys, a lesson for war learnt on the playing fields. This is the theme of Henry Newbolt's 'Vitai Lampada' (1897). This very well-known poem begins:

> There's a breathless hush in the Close tonight –
> Ten to make and the match to win –
> A bumping pitch and a blinding light,
> An hour to play and the last man in.

The setting is a particular public school: Clifton College, Bristol, where the cricket field is in the Close. The poem shows that we first learn the language of the heroic through sport. Everything is against the last batsman – pitch, light and time – and, we may assume, that because he is 'the last man in' he is not a good batsman. Newbolt then makes it clear what the 'last man' is fighting for on the 'bumping pitch'. It is neither the hope of school colours nor the desire for fame, but simply that he must play his part in the team:

> But his Captain's hand on his shoulder smote –
> 'Play up! play up! and play the game!'

The point of the poem (and this is the kind of poem in which it is right to say that it has a point) is that what the 'last man in' learns on the cricket field is later used on the field of battle. When the square (a defensive formation) has broken, when the Gatling (an automatic gun) is jammed and the Colonel is dead, England seems a long way away, and 'Honour a name', but, nevertheless, a 'schoolboy rallies the ranks' by telling them to play up and play the game. The poem is often sneered at for its strident rhythm and imperialistic sentiments, but Newbolt is unerringly right in one thing. It is the 'schoolboy' in the soldier that rallies the ranks. On the Clifton cricket field, where he learnt the virtues of war – courage, endurance, fortitude – he was the 'last *man*', and on the field of battle he becomes the '*schoolboy*', who hands on the lesson he has learnt.

Summary

Sport teaches the virtues of loyalty and duty, which are essential to the soldier. Both activities share terms such as 'attack' and 'defence'.

54.5 War and religion

An uneasy relationship

War would seem to be the denial of everything religion stands for and yet, as with sport, it has seemed appropriate to many people to talk of religion in the language of war and, in some cases, to use religious terms of warfare. The Bible is full of stories of battles; Christians launched the Crusades; William Booth founded the Salvation Army; and popular hymns include 'Fight the Good Fight' (1863) and 'Onward Christian Soldiers' (1864). But while St Paul writes of 'the whole armour of God' and gives to each piece of that armour a spiritual significance – 'the breastplate of righteousness' and 'the shield of faith' (Ephesians 6:12–18), elsewhere he makes it clear that these are metaphors – 'the weapons of our warfare are not carnal' (2 Corinthians 10:4).

Death and sacrifice

Confronted by death in war, one impulse is to reach for the language of sacrifice. Sacrifice has many uses and connotations; it involves death and, more particularly, it is strongly associated with the shedding of blood. A sacrifice is offered, and the one being sacrificed can be the offerer. There is also the set of thoughts concerning to whom, or on behalf of whom, the sacrifice is made. The sacrifice can be made to God on behalf of those whom one is defending, or, more primitively, it can be offered to the soil, one's nation or even to war itself. When so offered, it is done for others with, perhaps, the idea that it is offered instead of others. The one who is sacrificed is a chosen victim, dying for and instead of the nation.

Religion in First World War literature

The title of Wilfred Owen's 'Greater Love' comes from the words of Jesus Christ. In St. John's Gospel, Jesus is quoted as saying that there is no greater love than that in which a man lays down his life for his friends (15:13). Owen's 'The Parable of the Old Man and the Young' (1918) is a story of sacrifice, based, perhaps rather awkwardly, on the biblical story of Abraham's intended sacrifice of his son, Isaac. The biblical story (Genesis 22) is one that strongly asserts that God does not require human sacrifice. At the climax, as the knife in Abraham's hand hovers, almost in slow motion, above the bound Isaac, God intervenes to offer, instead of Isaac, a ram caught in a thicket. This moment is also the climax of Owen's poem, but the outcome is very different. Abraham is told to offer 'the Ram of Pride' –

> But the old man would not so, but slew his son,
> And half the seed of Europe, one by one.

Owen rewrites the story, making it one about the stubborn sacrifice of the young in the name of 'Pride'.

Ritual

Owen had been a church worker, so, like many of his generation, was familiar with the rituals of the Church. In the sonnet 'Anthem for Doomed Youth' (1917) he asks what kind of ceremony is fitting for those who 'die as cattle'. The poem uses religious language (anthems are written for church choirs) while probing the adequacy of such talk. In the octave (the first eight lines), Owen concentrates on sound, setting the rituals of the funeral service with its bells, prayers and choirs against the noises of battle, while in the sestet (the last six lines) the emphasis is on sight – candles, girls' brows and the drawing down of blinds. The focus is not always steady. Why, for example, does he introduce the bugles calling from sad shires in a section otherwise concerned with the rituals of the Church? Nevertheless, at some points he creates an eerie, almost surreal note in the way battle distorts the sounds of Christian anthems. The only choirs suitable for soldiers are 'The shrill, demented choirs of wailing shells'.

Summary

Religion is linked to war through a shared language. The notion of sacrifice was readily adopted in order to understand death in battle. First World War poets referred to biblical stories and the rituals of the Church.

54.6 War and the countryside

A contrast

Those who go to war experience a sharp contrast in the landscapes of their former and present lives. To Edward Thomas, the difference is a matter of profession. In his poem about an ordinary foot soldier, 'A Private' (1915), there is a glimpse of the man's former life:

> This ploughman dead in battle slept out of doors
> Many a frozen night.

As with many Edward Thomas poems, the language is rich without being explicitly symbolic. 'Slept' can mean the sleep of death, and 'night' has similar connotations. But we know that his very different former life was one that allowed him to sleep safely 'out of doors' on the cold uplands.

Thomas presents countrymen at war. One of W. B. Yeats' versions of death in war is explicitly in the pastoral tradition. 'Shepherd and Goatherd' (1919) is a dialogue poem, set in a rural landscape in the spring of the year, in which an old goatherd talks to a young shepherd (conventionally presented as a poet) about another young shepherd/poet, who has died 'in the first world war beyond the sea'. The pastoral tradition allows Yeats to bring out both the contrasts and the links between the countryside and the war. Quiet country ways and the ravages of war seem to have nothing in common, yet those who go to fight are shepherds. And it was always so; David, who slew Goliath, was a shepherd at Bethlehem (1 Samuel 17:15).

The destruction of a landscape

Edmund Blunden, born in London but brought up in rural Kent, wrote in the second stanza of 'Report on Experience' (in *Poems 1914–30*):

> I have seen a green country, useful to the race,
> Knocked silly with guns and mines, its villages vanished,
> Even the last rat and kestrel banished.

War generates paperwork. One of the jobs of an officer was writing reports on trench life, skirmishes, attacks and discipline. Blunden exploits the significant contrast between the cool language of the title and his anguish at seeing 'a green country ... knocked silly'. The word 'green' sums up, long before we spoke of green politics, the goodness and freshness of the earth. Blunden must be articulating what soldiers saw on the Western Front. Many rural lads, serving in regiments named after rural counties (Gloucestershire, Shropshire and Worcestershire), must have found it puzzling to see farming – their profession – still being practised just behind the lines. And think of the connotations of the name 'no man's land' – the devastated wastes between allied and enemy trenches. All land is someone's land, and it is our duty to tend it and till it. Here was land so alien, so ruined and marked, that it was no one's. The recurrence in Owen of mud expresses the same feeling. War is horrible because it reduces landscape to

> a sad land, weak with sweats of dearth,
> Gray, cratered like the moon with hollow woe,
> And pitted with great pocks and scabs of plague.
> ('The Show' (1917), 3–5)

The images, as is often the case in Owen, change rapidly. In the first three lines the images of a land that is melancholy, diseased (sweats) and subject to famine (dearth) intertwine, suggestive, perhaps, of disordered nature.

Incentive and consolation

The poetry of Ivor Gurney presents the countryside, in his case Gloucestershire, as an incentive for fighting and the consolation of those who see the war through. The sonnet 'Servitude' (1917) puts the point plainly about how he survives the war. It opens:

> If it were not for England, who would bear
> This heavy servitude one moment more?

To be a soldier is, in strictly technical terms, to serve. 'Servitude' also means the condition of being a servant. A further meaning is the attention a knight bestows on his lady in the literature of courtly love. Servitude is taken up in 'Strange Service' (1917). This poem closes with the thought that only England – 'O Mother' – can reward him:

> None but you can know my heart, its tears and sacrifice,
> None, but you, repay.

This is close to the language of love poetry, and, in an important sense, that is what it is. The frank admission that England, his 'mother', knows his heart is followed by the addition of 'but you', which in its touching intimacy, reminds us of the talk not of mother and son but of lovers.

The fullest expression of England as reward and consolation comes in 'Crickley Hill' (1919). The poem recounts a conversation with a fellow soldier during an evening stroll. The poet admits that he is hardly listening until, in the fourth stanza, the other mentions a familiar name – Crickley Hill:

> When on a sudden, 'Crickley' he said. How I started
> At that darling name of home!

Most soldiers, if asked, would say they are fighting for home and the thought of home brings comfort. For Gurney, home is not domestic – the world of Ivor Novello's First World War song 'Keep the Home Fires Burning' – but rural. Boldly he speaks for all in the poem's close:

> We think of you and dream in the first sleep
> Of you and yours –
> Trees, bare rock, flowers
> Daring the blast on Crickley's distant steep.

In the manner of a lover-poet dwelling on his beloved's beauties, he lovingly recalls the trees, rock and flowers. With those on his mind he, like the flowers, will dare 'the blast' of war in the service of his beloved.

Summary

The countryside is present in war literature as a contrast to battle, as a way of recognizing the destructiveness of war and as an incentive and consolation for those fighting.

 Glossary

Abstract and Concrete

Abstract words refer to qualities such as goodness or justice; concrete words refer to things that can be detected by the five senses – for example chairs and tables. In English, abstract and concrete words are usually nouns and adjectives. Abstract words are concerned with ideas, allowing us to see what the issues in a work are; and concrete words, because they bring out the physical force of the material world, root literature in our familiar experience. (See also **Image and Imagery**.)

Allegory

An allegory is a genre in which the chief elements of the story – character, event, setting – correspond directly to an aspect of a moral, religious or political set of beliefs. John Bunyan's *The Pilgrim's Progress* (1678) is an allegory of the Christian life, so the hero is called Christian, and he journeys from the City of Destruction (the fallen state) to the Heavenly City (the state of those who are saved). Allegory can also be a mode; that is to say, one part of a story can be treated allegorically, as in *Mansfield Park* (1814), where Maria'a desire to climb round the locked gate into the Wilderness is an allegory of a moral lapse and, possibly, of the fall of humankind.

Alliteration

The repetition of the same consonant sound. Alliteration is pleasing and memorable: we enjoy patterns of sound, and these patterns impress themselves upon the mind. Alliteration is a chief factor in the creation of poetic texture. It can enforce the meaning of the words, as in Wilfred Owen's 'Exposure' (1916): 'Pale flakes with fingering stealth come feeling for our faces'. Here the texture is light and fluid, and the alliterating words suggest the snow's furtive and chilling movement. It is an important structural principle in Middle English verse, such as William Langland's *Piers Plowman* (three versions between 1362 and 1385): 'And you lovely ladies with youre longe fyngres' (Passus 5, 10).

Allusion

A reference, usually implied or hinted at, to another book, event, person or place. Allusions work when the reader knows what is being alluded to, so there is often the pleasure of being trusted by the author. Allusions can be used in moral criticism. Allusion is an example of what Julia Kristeva called *intertextuality* – the ways in which one text links with another.

Ambiguity

The capacity of a word or group of words to have two or more different meanings. Ambiguity is usually valued because it enriches the meaning of the work. William Blake's 'London' (1794) is about the way urban life confines people and inflicts pain on them. At one point he writes about

> How the chimney-sweeper's cry
> Every blackening church appals

Is 'blackening' active or passive? Does the church blacken or is it being blackened? The ambiguity suggests that, in London, people and institutions can be both the agents and the victims of corruption.

Analepsis and Prolepsis Analepsis is looking back and prolepsis looking forward. Any moment in a narrative that refers back to an earlier part is analeptic, and moments that look forward to future events are proleptic. The two effects usually contribute to the illumination of plots and themes.

Assonance The repetition of vowel sounds in adjoining words. The effects are similar to *alliteration*. Tone is sometimes established by assonance, as in the 'I' sound in these lamenting lines from Donne's 'Song' (1633):

> When thou sigh'st, thou sigh'st not wind,
> But sigh'st my soul away

Audience Those who watch a theatrical performance. By extension, it is also used of those for whom any work is written. By being aware of the resources of the theatre – actors, costume, music, lighting and so on – you can share imaginatively in the experience of those who watch a play.

Ballad A traditional narrative poem that is direct, fast-moving and contains brief but telling details. The subjects are often love, war, adventure and travel. Ballads are usually written in quatrains, rhyming ABCB. The *literary ballad* was a late-eighteenth-century poem written in imitation of the traditional sixteenth-century ones.

Bildungsroman The novel of growth in which a young person encounters the pressures of growing up and the responsibilities of adult life.

Blank Verse Poetry written in unrhymed iambic pentameters. It is suitable for exploring thought and feeling and has become the standard form for serious writing about important subjects. Shakespeare uses it in his plays; Milton wrote *Paradise Lost* (1667) in blank verse, and Wordsworth used it in *The Prelude* (1805).

Bravado The outlandish and extrovert manner in which tragic heroes draw attention to their defiance of moral laws, their sufferings and their falls. The bravado of a tragic figure makes him or her both attractive and reprehensible. We warm to the relish of the figure's whole-hearted embracing of the tragic role, and recoil from the pride and arrogance of his or her wilful display. In Shakesperian drama, the word 'insolence' is close in meaning to bravado.

Burlesque A form of *parody* commonly associated with the theatre in which the style of a theatrical presentation is mocked. The usual form is a low and vulgar version of a serious and noble action. Thus Falstaff in Shakespeare's *Henry IV* plays (1599 and 1597) burlesques the high traditions of military writing.

Cadence The rise, fall or sustaining of pitch in a voice, particularly towards a caesura or the close of a line, clause or sentence. Cadences often enact the emotional life of poetry. When writing about them, it is important to characterize the emotional effects of the cadences.

Caesura The break in a line of poetry, conventionally indicated by ||. Caesuras mark changes in tone, argument and feeling. They can produce comic effects when what follows the break is very different from what preceded it.

Caricature	The deliberate distortion or exaggeration of a character's features or manners in order to ridicule or amuse. Novelists sometimes juxtapose caricatures and fuller characters.
Character and Characterization	A character is a literary figure; characterization is the way a character has been created. Fully presented characters are often described as 'round' as opposed to stock characters, who are 'flat'. When the capacity of a character to change is under discussion, a character may be described as 'open' as opposed to a 'closed' character, who does not change. (See also *Stock characters*.)
Code	The term has two senses. First, the beliefs a character tries to live up to, as in the code of gentlemen. Second, it is a set of conventions authors employ to create meanings and sustain a genre.
Comedy	A story (often a play) in which the aims of characters, often prompted by love and furthered by deceptions and misunderstandings, produce a period of confusion before the characters recognize what has been happening and the action closes happily and harmoniously. The plot is often complex and the action is amusing. In *black comedy*, the audience is invited to laugh at sensitive matters such as disease and death.
Complex	Anything – line, poem, image, plot – consisting of several connected elements. Literature is often praised for the way several things can be held together in one work.
Compression	The economical concentration of meaning. It is often valued in poetry.
Conceit	An elaborate and usually extended image that at first appears to be far-fetched but which, with thought, is seen as appropriate. Conceits are strange but true. They were popular in the Metaphysical poetry of the seventeenth century, and re-surfaced in the poetry of the Martians (poets who viewed life from unusual angles); for example, Craig Raine: 'A Martian Sends a Postcard Home' (1979). When writing about conceits, try to convey the shock, the challenge to thought and the pleasure of discovering that the image is apt.
Consonance	The repetition of consonants in adjoining words in which the vowels are different. The effect is of interest when the words are related in meaning, as in W. H. Auden's 'swiftly' and 'softly' in his poem 'O where are you going' (1931).
Consonants and Vowels	The sounds of individual letters: 'a', 'e', 'i', 'o' and 'u' are vowels; the other letters are consonants. The clustering of vowels and consonants helps to create the textures of language.
Construction	A term used in two ways. First, the design or structure of a work; and, second, the way that ideas, gender and beliefs are put together. Critics, for example, talk about the construction of our ideas about men and women.
Convention	An agreement between author and reader that a device stands for an aspect of life. Each genre is created and sustained by a series of conventions.
Counterpoint	A term borrowed from music to indicate a change in the rhythmical pattern of a line of verse.
Courtly Love	A nineteenth-century term to describe the code and conventions of love in late medieval and early modern literature. Common elements are a knight loving a high-born lady, who is often married. He undertakes quests and dangerous exploits,

but she remains unmoved. He also sings to her, writes poetry and often languishes in despair of ever winning her favour. It is sometimes gently mocked in the works of Chaucer.

Deixis
Language that refers to the context in which it is delivered. Hence, terms such as 'this' and 'that' are deictic.

Denotations and Connotations
The denotations of a word are its standard meanings in everyday speech. Dictionary definitions usually give the denotations of words. Connotations are the associations and undertones of meaning.

Denouement
The untying (usually at the end of a play or novel) of the tangled elements of a plot.

Diction
The selection of words in any literary work. In the past, people spoke of *poetic diction* – a set of words that were thought to be specially appropriate to poetry.

Direct Self-explanation
Dramatic speech in which a character reveals something directly about him- or herself not in soliloquy but so as to inform audience and other characters.

Disjunction
An event that disturbs or ruptures the customary pattern of life and thereby initiates the main business of the plot. Disjunctions therefore usually occur near the beginning of a work. It is often said that there is no plot that does not depend on a disjunction.

Distance
The intellectual and emotional gap between author and work, or between author and reader or reader and work. Distance controls sympathy and understanding and is evident in the tone of a work.

Dramatic Monologue
A poem in which a persona or protagonist reveals his or her feelings about a situation or issue. Sometimes, as in Browning's 'My Last Duchess' (1842) there is an imaginary listener. Browning used the form to explore extreme and disturbed states of mind, as in 'Porphyria's Lover' (1836).

Elegy
A poem written in memory of the dead. The tone is often meditative and regretful.

Ellipsis
Writing which deliberately omits many words. The effect is terse and sometimes blunt.

Empathy/Sympathy
Empathy is the imaginative act whereby we put ourselves in the place of another. Sympathy is the feeling, usually of pity, we have for someone's plight. Literature does not always require us to feel sympathy. Empathy is rarer, but some characters, particularly in drama, invite us to feel as they do.

Enactment
The way all aspects of a work – sounds, rhythms, lines, verbal textures, stanza forms – act out the meaning of the words. Enactment insists that words are not divisible into form and content, and that *how* something is said shapes *what* is said.

End-stopped and Run-on lines
An end-stopped line is coterminus with a grammatical unit. It produces the satisfaction of finding meaning complete at the end of a line. In a run-on or *enjambed* line, the sense is left unfinished, so readers enjoy the pleasure of expectation until the meaning is completed.

Epic
A high genre in which a hero of almost god-like status accomplishes many noble deeds, often by way of a quest or war. Epics often deal with the founding of nations. They usually require the writer to have learning and acquaintance with other epics. The style of writing is elevated.

Epic Simile
An extended simile in which the vehicle (that which compares) is elaborated in detail. The art of the Epic simile is to make the

language of the vehicle appropriate to the tenor (the object being described). The Epic simile is prominent in Milton's *Paradise Lost* (1667).

Epigram	Either a brief, witty statement or a short poem that makes a simple and often humorous point. Any deftly executed line or stanza can be said to be epigrammatic. Examples include the short poems of Walter Savage Landor, Arthur Hugh Clough and W. B. Yeats.
Epiphany	A term coined by James Joyce for a character's moment of illumination at the climax of a short story or novel. An epiphany might be something seen, or the familiar understood for the first time. Epiphanies often form the climaxes of Katherine Mansfield's short stories.
Epistolary Novel	The novel in the form of letters such as Tobias Smollet's *Humphrey Clinker* (1771).
Expectation	The way a text leads reader or audience to think that some particular thing is going to happen. Authors arouse expectation by leading readers to think about how what they know might lead to a further event. Coleridge said Shakespeare was a poet of expectation rather than of surprise.
Exposition	The part of a work (usually the beginning) that conveys to the reader all that is required for the understanding of the plot.
Farce	Rapid and violent stage action in which characters (often stock types) are viewed as mere bodies wildly and comically gesticulating. Manic chases or the beating of servants are standard elements of farcical action. Some plays, such as those by Ben Travers, are called farces. There are also farcical elements in other plays, such as the low-life scenes of Christopher Marlowe's *Doctor Faustus* (1591).
Fictionality	The ways in which fictional works draw attention to themselves as being fictional. For example, Victorian novelists address their readers directly, and in *The French Lieutenant's Woman* (1969), John Fowles discusses his problems as the novelist writing the novel.
Focus and **Focalizing**	The focus of a narrative is the character through whom and, frequently, from whose perspective the tale is told. The process is called focalizing. The focus of a novel need not be the same as the viewpoint of the author. Lockwood and Nelly are the points at which *Wuthering Heights* (1847) is focalized, but it does not follow that this is the viewpoint of Emily Brontë.
Foregrounding	The process of singling out a character or incident for special interest. Usually, foregrounding is the way an author explores what he or she thinks is important in the work. For example, Hamlet's soliloquies show that Shakespeare is especially interested in the thinking of his central character.
Frame	A context within a work for the actions of characters. The Induction provides a frame for *The Taming of the Shrew* (1595).
Free Verse	Verse which observes no regular line length, rhythm or stanza form. It is often characterized by alliterative clusters and local rhythmical patterns. It is sometimes called *vers libre*.
Genre	A literary type or kind. Traditionally, Tragedy, Comedy, Epic, Lyric and Satire are genres. It is also used rather more broadly to indicate novels or poetry.
Gothic	A (usually prose fiction) genre in which the settings are wild and remote, the atmosphere gloomy and eerie, and the action often involves supernatural presences. The genre flourished

in the late eighteenth century. It gave prominence to female figures, who were often threatened by villainous nobles. The plots are digressive.

Heroes and **Heroines**
The central figures of plays and novels. Traditionally, they have admirable characteristics and are superior to the common run of people. In tragedies, the heroes and heroines not only stand above and apart from others but are proudly confident. The *anti-hero* is a central figure who is quite ordinary and may even have qualities that the reader criticizes.

Heroic Couplets
Two lines of rhyming iambic pentameters. Heroic couplets sound assertive and self-confirming, so are appropriate in arguments. They were common in the eighteenth century. They are best appreciated when read slowly.

Image and **Imagery**
Any figurative language – metaphors, personifications, simile, symbols – or descriptive language that appeals to the senses is called imagery. Images make ideas concrete; they create atmosphere and when they recur in a work enforce themes and act as a structural device.

Imitation
A kind of translation in which contemporary examples replace the original images, characters and incidents. The genre flourished in the eighteenth century.

Intrusion and **Narratorial Intrusion**
Intrusion occurs when a narrator enters his or her own narrative in order to make comments on the action and characters.

Inversion
A change in the 'natural' or 'standard' word order of a sentence. Inversion draws attention to the crafted nature of writing. It is found most commonly in poetry.

Irony
Irony occurs when the reader sees a gap between words and the meanings those words in fact have in the work. Irony takes a number of forms. There can be gaps between words and truth, between words and meaning, between intention and outcome, and between the interpretation a character gives of the world and what the world turns out to be like. The term *dramatic irony* is used of narratives (often but not always plays) in which the reader/audience sees an ironic discrepancy in what a character says, an irony that is manifested by later events.

Irony is always against a character. He or she is *impercipient* – that is, unable to see what is really happening. It can have a number of effects: bitter, comic, serious, tragic and so on.

Knowledge
Knowledge gives a character power. Many novels and plays work by establishing disparities in knowledge. When studying works in which there are disparities of knowledge, it is important to remember who knows what.

Low-life
Characters and scenes (often in drama) featuring the poorer and usually less respectable members of society. The action is often vigorous and entertaining. Sometimes, audiences are invited to compare the low-life scenes with the more elevated ones of the main plot.

Lyric
Lyric is one of the traditional genres. It is now a term applied to short poems, which express thoughts and feelings. Traditionally, it is associated with music, so writing that is smooth and fluent is often described as lyrical.

Making Strange
A phrase from the Russian Formalists indicating that literature, by way of editing, concentration, omission and heightening, makes the world we know look new. The term *defamiliarization*

is also used for the way literature makes the familiar world fresh.

Masque
A highly elaborate entertainment involving verse and song, usually performed in lavish costumes and sets that, in the sixteenth and seventeenth centuries, were ingenious and complex. The characters are often gods or allegorical figures. Shakespeare's *The Tempest* (1610) includes a masque to celebrate the betrothal of Miranda and Ferdinand.

Mental Landscape
A landscape that reflects the thoughts and feelings of the characters, who view it or journey through it. Often the language about the landscape can also be used of the mind.

Metaphor
A metaphor is a comparison in which there is an implicit identity. Metaphors thus give us two things together and give them in few words. (See *Tenor* and *Vehicle*.)

Metonymy
Originally, a figure of speech in which the name of a thing stands for another thing that is closely associated with it. For example, Number 10 stands for the Prime Minister. Today, it is used for any way in which literature establishes significant links between two things. Thus in Jane Austen's *Mansfield Park*, the estate of Sotherton is linked with the state of England.

Metre
The regular beats of poetic lines, created by a sequence of stressed and unstressed syllables. Traditionally, the unit of stressed and unstressed syllables is called a *foot*. Traditionally, special terms are used for the different patterns of feet and the length of line. The following are popular metres:

Iambic:	an unstressed syllable followed by a stressed syllable.
Anapaestic:	two unstressed syllables followed by a stressed syllable.
Trochaic:	a stressed syllable followed by an unstressed syllable.
Dactylic:	a stressed syllable followed by two unstressed syllables.

The standard names for the number of feet in a line are as follows:

Monometer:	one foot.
Dimeter:	two feet.
Trimeter:	three feet.
Tetrameter:	four feet.
Pentameter:	five feet.
Hexameter:	six feet.
Heptameter:	seven feet.
Octameter:	eight feet.

The classification of metre is called *scansion*. There is little to be gained from mere labelling; what matters is the effect.

Monosyllabic and **Polysyllabic**
Words such as 'did' and 'good' are monosyllabic (one syllable) and words such 'necessary' or 'volunteer' are polysyllabic (more than one syllable). Monosyllables can sound forceful and tough, and polysyllables, when handled well, are flowing and lyrical. Sometimes readers are struck by the ingenuity of the poet who has fitted a long polysyllabic word into a line without distorting the pronunciation of the word.

Multiple Narration
A story told by more than one narrator. Such narrations give a series of viewpoints and can raise the issue of reliability.

	Wilkie Collins' *The Woman in White* (1860) and *The Moonstone* (1868) are both multiple narrations. Sometimes there is one narrator, who is the source of all the others. This is the *Primary narrator*. It does not follow that the primary narrator is the most important. Lockwood is the primary narrator of *Wuthering Heights* (1847), but the most important narrator is Nelly Dean.
Narrative and **Narration**	A narrative is a story – the events related by the storyteller. Narration is the business of how a tale is told. The study of the various devices, such as the choice of the narrator or how time is handled, is *Narratology*.
Narrator	The narrator tells the story. Narrators can be first-person and can therefore only see events from a single viewpoint, or third-person, in which the novelist has the choice of deciding whether to know what the characters are thinking or whether they are to be viewed externally. First-person narrators can be central figures (hero-narrators) or onlookers (observer narrators). Sometimes, a novelist chooses to know the mind of the central character but not the minds of the others. Some narrators establish themselves as personalities and so intrude comments into their narrations, while others are covert or effaced, mere channels through which the tale is told.
Nuance	A useful word to describe the delicate gradations of the meanings and emotional colourings of words.
Onomatopoeia	The effect of the sounds of words mimicking the sounds of the object they are describing. Individual words such as 'bang' and 'crash' are onomatopoeic. A group of words such as Keats' 'The murmurous haunt of flies on summer eves' from the fifth stanza of 'Ode to a Nightingale' (1819) is an example.
Overtones and **Undertones**	Overtones are the explicit tonal resonances of words, while undertones are hinted implications. Undertones are often more troubling.
Pastoral	A genre in which an idealized countryside is the setting for shepherds (poets) to woo shepherdesses (beloveds). The genre is of Classical origin. *Anti-pastoral* is the deliberate subversion of the conventions that sustain the genre.
Pathetic Fallacy	The giving of human feelings to objects that could not in their nature have them. Pathetic fallacy often indicates the mood of the one who bestows feeling on things.
Pathos	The arousal of feelings of pity and tenderness in a reader or audience by the presentation of a sad event. It is often the helplessness of the reader, audience or other characters that arouses pathos.
Persona	A created voice in a poem, novel or short story. Personas usually speak in the first person and thus provide a consistent viewpoint, attitude and tone in a work. Personas must not be assumed to be the voice of the author.
Personification	Treating a non-human object as if it were a person. The grammatical basis of personification is that we use the same verbal forms of abstractions, things and persons. For example, we say 'Beauty is …'. (See **Mental landscape** and **Pathetic fallacy**.)
Picturesque	A mode of appreciating landscape in which the pictorial qualities of a natural scene are recognized and treated as if they formed an actual picture. Picturesque values were celebrated in late-eighteenth and early-nineteenth-century literature.
Plot and **Story**	Plot is the order of events in a literary work; story is the chronological order in which such events would have happened.

A *sub-plot* is a minor plot, often echoing the concerns of the main plot. (See *Analepsis* and *Prolepsis*.)

Post-colonial

Literature and criticism written in the wake of the contraction of the British Empire. The novels explore the meeting of different cultures and emerging national identities. Post-colonial criticism attempts to show that British experience need not determine the literary possibilities of the English language.

Problem Plays

A late-nineteenth-century term for a group of Shakespeare's plays – *All's Well That Ends Well* (1604), *Measure for Measure* (1604) and *Troilus and Cressida* (1601) – that treat serious and troubling issues through comic conventions. The term can also be applied to plays that tackle important moral questions.

Protagonist

The main figure in a work, often the voice of a narrative poem or dramatic monologue. Originally, it referred to the hero in a Greek play.

Quatrain

A stanza of four lines popular in ballads and lyric poetry.

Realism and **Naturalism**

Historically, realism is any fiction that presents characters in everyday settings, whereas naturalism is a more philosophical kind of literature, in which characters are presented solely as the products of biological inheritance and social circumstances. Emile Zola, in nineteenth-century France, is an example of Naturalism. The following points should be remembered: (i) most literature is not realistic (Shakespeare, for example); (ii) realistic literature is not superior to other kinds of literature; (iii) all literature is made; and realism depends on a judicious selection of surface details; (iv) the adjective 'realistic' is often useful in describing an aspect of a work.

Recognition

A discovery or disclosure, usually made towards the close of a plot, after which the situation of the characters changes and it becomes possible for the plot to be wound up. The Greek word *anagnorisis* is used for the moment in drama when characters make significant discoveries.

Reflexivity

The manner in which a book presents itself as a created object. Reflexivity can alert readers to the fascinating nature of art, and/or distance us because we are reminded that we are encountering art.

Register

Levels of language. Words are imagined as being ranked, so that lofty and high-sounding terms are said to be in *high register* and colloquial language in *low register*.

Reliability

The extent to which a narrator, often a first-person one, can be trusted. The issue does not often arise; when it does, the reader has to weigh carefully what is being recounted.

Relief

The release of tension. Relief can take the form of laughter or a period of serious reflection.

Resolution

A term for the way plots are sorted out, tied up or wound up at the end of a work. Resolution applies to the lives of the characters – the success of their plans, the difficulties they face, those whom they marry – and the formal patterning of the plot, often after a period of confusion. The two are not unrelated.

Retrospective Narration

A form of narrative (usually first-person) in which the narrator looks back over his or her life. It is very useful for showing growth (as in the *Bildungsroman*) and the importance of subjective experience. Retrospective narration can allow narrator and reader to perceive irony. Although the narration must, in a formal sense, be delivered from the point of view of the situation the narrator has achieved at the end, this situation

	need not intrude upon the narrative. First-person narrators such as Huckleberry Finn, who do not see a difference between their past and present selves, are called *naïve narrators*.
Reversal	The point in a plot, when events, so to speak, go into reverse. This often involves a change in characters' fortunes. Often a reversal coincides with a recognition or discovery. Aristotle's name for this is *peripeteia* or *peripety*.
Rhyme	The chiming of the sound of one word with another, achieved by identical final vowels and consonants. Rhymes bring words to the attention of the reader, create a pleasing harmony of sound, assist in achieving the resolution of an idea, and can be used to provoke laughter. *Monosyllabic* rhyme is sometimes called 'masculine' and *disyllabic* rhyme, with the stress on the first of the two syllables, is called 'feminine'. When only the consonants chime, critics talk of *para-rhyme* or *half-rhyme*. Handled well, para-rhyme can produce a sense of distortion or thwarted expectation. *Para-rhyme* is a feature of Wilfred Owen's poetry.
Romance	An ancient and durable genre in which an attractively ordinary hero undertakes a quest. The landscape is often eerie, and magical events occur.
Satire	The art of exposing vice and folly to ridicule. The impulse behind Satire is moral; the aim is often to awaken people to a sounder sense of values. It was once regarded as a genre but is now more often used to describe an effect. A scene within a work can be described as satirical, as when Dickens mocks time-wasting administration in his scene in the Circumlocution office in *Little Dorrit* (1857).
Setting	The location of the action, period or place of a work. Settings sometimes reflect the characters – their moods and plights – and the events – the significance of what is going on. (See also *Mental landscape*.)
Simile	A figure of speech in which one thing is compared explicitly to another, usually by using 'as' or 'like'. Similes are close to ordinary speech, and often provide the reader with the pleasure of following them through to see how the comparison works.
Soliloquy	A speech delivered by a lone or isolated character. In *public soliloquies* a character addresses the audience; in a *private soliloquy*, the audience overhears a character commune with him- or herself. In Shakespeare, soliloquies are usually given to important characters.
Song	Either verses intended to be sung by a character or a lyric poem. In drama, the mood, themes and natures of characters are often established through the kinds of songs they sing.
Sonnet	A poem of fourteen lines. It might be in two parts – an octave (eight lines) followed by a sestet (often called the *Petrarchan sonnet*) or three quatrains and a closing couplet (the *Shakespearian sonnet*). Sonnets can be used for the precise expression of thought and the exploration of emotions.
Stanza	The group of lines that form the structural unit of a poem. The word is Italian; it is equivalent to verse. The rhyme scheme gives definition to a stanza, although occasionally a poet (Thomas Hardy, for example) keeps the same number of lines but alters the rhyme scheme.
	Standard stanza forms include: **terza rima** (three lines rhyming ABA BCB); **quatrain** (four lines); **rime royal** (seven

	lines rhyming ABABBCC); **ottava rima** (eight lines rhyming ABABABCC), and the **Spenserian stanza** (nine lines rhyming ABABBCBCC), with a final line in hexameters rather than pentameters).
Stock Character	A character in a play or novel who is representative of a type. Stock characters have little individuality and are often comic.
Subversion	Any feature of a literary work that undermines or criticizes a character, idea, institution, system of belief or genre.
Surprise	The effect of expectation not being fulfilled. Popular fiction often depends on surprise. Shakespeare uses it only very rarely.
Suspension of Belief	A term introduced by Samuel Taylor Coleridge for the way in which theatre audiences accept conventions such as ghosts or witches by laying aside what they normally believe.
Symbol	An object that stands for, points to and shares in a significant reality over and beyond it. Some symbols are traditional (such as the rose for beauty); others are created by an author such as William Blake's 'The Tyger' (1794). Symbols resonate with associations; it is never possible to say *exactly* how extensive that range is.
Syntax	The order of words in a sentence, and their relationships with one another. Syntax is therefore the means by which the meanings and feelings are voiced. Things to look for include whether the syntax is simple or complex (several clauses), where the object comes in relation to the subject, and where the verb is placed.
Tags, Tagging	In dialogue, the narrator's additions that indicate who is speaking and, sometimes, in what manner the words are delivered. Common examples are 'She said' or 'He commented'.
Tenor and Vehicle	In the discussion of metaphor, the thing being talked about (the subject) is the *tenor* and that to which it is implicitly compared is the *vehicle*.
Texture	The material feel of language. Texture is formed by the sounds of words, clusters of monosyllables and polysyllables, pace and grammar.
Theme	What a literary work is about – its subject, concerns, interests, issues and preoccupations. Sometimes it is important to recognize the role of the reader in bringing out the theme, often by making connections and following through patterns of thought.
Tone	The emotional and intellectual attitude, manner or poise of a piece of writing. As in ordinary conversation we pick up the feel of speech, so in literature we depend on the choice of words and the rhythms and textures of the language to give us the emotional colouring of the writing. Because tone conveys feelings, you should always try to characterize it when writing.
Tragedy	A story (usually in dramatic form) in which an outstanding and socially elevated figure chooses to flout moral laws and, as a consequence, falls from power, suffers excessively, is excluded from the community and dies. The strong element of wilful display in the action and fall of the hero or heroine both awes and repels the audience. The effect of Tragedy is often to purge the audience of their feelings of pity and fear.
Trajectory	The direction and movement of a plot. Recognizing trajectory depends on our seeing the possibilities in the plot situation and how these raise expectations in us.

Unities	The consistency of a work in action, time and place. The unities are not rules, though observing them can create a sense of dramatic urgency. With the exception of *The Tempest* (1610), Shakespeare does not heed them.
View and **Viewpoint**	How an author presents and implicitly invites readers to regard the action of a work. The viewpoint of an author covers the issue of how close to characters the reader is invited to be, the moral light in which they are presented, and possibilities of irony.
Villanelle	A verse form (usually of five stanzas) of three-line stanzas in which the first and third line of the first stanza appear alternately at the close of each following stanza until they form a couplet at the end. The last stanza is usually a quatrain.

# Suggestions for Further Reading

The best ways to start further reading are, first, to ask friends and teachers what they find useful and, second, to look at books on library shelves. A glance at the table of Contents and the Index will give you some idea about how helpful a book might be. These books might get you started.

Texts

The editions listed have introductions and notes:
Arden Shakespeare (Thomson)
Everyman Library (Dent & Dutton)
The New Mermaids (A. & C. Black/W. W. Norton)
The New Penguin Shakespeare
Oxford World Classics (including the *Oxford Shakespeare*)
Penguin English Library
Penguin English Poets

The novel

Wayne C. Booth, *The Rhetoric of Fiction* (University of Chicago Press)
Deirdre David (editor), *The Cambridge Companion to the the Victorian Novel* (Cambridge University Press)
John Peck, *How to Study a Novel* (Palgrave Macmillan)

Drama

Alan Ayckbourn, *The Crafty Art of Playwriting* (Faber and Faber)
J. L. Styan, *Shakespeare's Stagecraft* (Cambridge University Press)
G.J. Watson, *Drama: An Introduction* (Palgrave Macmillan)

Poetry

Charles Barber, *Poetry in English: An Introduction* (Palgrave Macmillan)
John Lennard, *The Poetry Handbook* (Oxford University Press)
Philip Davies Roberts, *How Poetry Works* (Penguin)

Criticism

M. H. Abrams, *A Glossary of Literary Terms* (Thomson)
Chris Baldick, *The Concise Oxford Dictionary of Literary Terms* (Oxford University Press)
Peter Barry, *Beginning Theory* (Manchester University Press)

General Index

A

abstract and concrete 169–71, 501
action 56, 75–6, 104–15
action and themes 94, 103–4, 111
actors, acting 84, 92, 115, 135–6
alexandrine 186
allegory 62, 170, 295, 383, 390, 392, 397, 415, 429, 501
allusion 168, 313, 372, 501
ambiguity 181, 501–2
anagnorisis 47–8, 222, 360; *see also* recognition
analepsis and prolepsis 47, 104, 356, 366, 410, 502
animals 463–5; anthropomorphism 464; attitudes to 463–4; a world apart 464–5
apocalypse and apocalyptic 160
appearance and reality 41–2
appetite 80
architects and architecture 332–4, 472; Burnham Deepdale church 446; Chichester cathedral 287; Classical 333; Clifton College 496; Thomas and William Daniell 419; doors 471; Gothic 333; houses 470; Otranto Cathedral 267; Postmodern architecture 364; Repton, Humphry: Brighton Pavilion 419; Scott, George Gilbert: Foreign Office 333; space, politics of space 333, 470–1; stairs 472; windows 472; York Minster 292
argument 148, 162, 187
art 6–7, 9, 15, 26, 74, 88, 108, 148, 167–8, 223, 265, 280, 359, 365–73
art and belief 223–4, 230
aside 97–8
association 297
atmosphere 133–5, 141
audience 83–4, 86–7, 95–8, 106, 115, 121, 141, 222–3, 228, 238, 243, 273, 315–16, 360, 366, 417, 502
authority figures 21, 110
autobiography 167

B

background 288–90, 314
ballad 155–7, 186, 188, 205, 502
ballad, the literary 156, 502
ballad, the romantic 156, 175
bawdy 90, 102
beginnings 43–4, 104, 107
belief 223–4, 376–7
bergamasque 138
Bible, the 37, 53, 311, 345, 375, 385; finding the lost 293–4; imagery 291, 297; judgement 293; parables and journeys 295; re-workings 292, 294; self-discovery 295–6; Shakespeare 291, 296–7; temptation 296; twentieth century 297–8; variations 293
Bildungsroman 20–2, 295, 415, 502, 509
binary opposites 277, 367–8
blank verse 86–7, 205, 502
Booker Prize 3
brothers and sisters 69–70
bucolic 278
burlesque 114, 246, 493, 502

C

cadence 124, 249, 253, 258, 266, 322, 441, 463, 502
caesura 186–8, 451, 502
Cameron, Margaret 395
caricature 24, 503
carpe diem 354
celebration, communal celebration 138–9, 260
character in drama 116–21, 133–4; characters, flat and round, open and closed 24–5; characters, language about 18–20; characters, the language in 11–15, 116–18; character in the novel 9–25, 57, 150; characters, the plot function of 120–1; characters in poetry 153–4; characters, stock 119–20, 237, 511; characters on themselves and others 117–18
characterization 10, 503
chivalry 267, 301–2, 485–6
choosing 21–2
chorus 86, 88, 94–5, 112, 117, 138, 229
Christianity 224, 264–5, 274, 301, 311, 399–400, 458, 466–7, 476–7, 496–8
cinema 109–10, 273
cities: Berlin 474; Cambridge 170; Edinburgh 475; London 60, 63, 170, 262–4, 343–4, 474–5; Los Angeles 475; New York 63, 342; Paris 342, 475; Rome 262, 264, 479, 483; Venice 342–3, 382–3, 474–5
class 14–15, 338–40, 384–7
classical civilization and literature 158, 221, 247, 262, 278–9, 299–311, 375, 400, 442–5, 479, 492; attitudes 309–10; Daedalus and Icarus 305; Ceres 303; Chivalry 301–2; Echo 303; education 299; Eurydice 303; form and genre 309; Helen of Troy 303–4; heroes 300–2; libraries 306–8; Lucrece 81–2, 303; metamorphoses 299–300, 307–8; myths 110, 146–7, 204, 304–6, 434, 443–5, 495; Orpheus 304, 308; Philosophy 306–8; Plato and Socrates 306–7; Prometheus 305–6; symbols 310–11; themes 308–11; translation 299–300; writing Latin poetry 299

epigram 309–10, 505
epiphany 52–3, 505
essays xxix–xxx
Essex rebellion 85
Etymology 372
examinations and study xxvii–xxxii, 116, 118, 131, 203–11, 215, 217, 221, 374, 398, 404
excess 74–5, 114
expectation 105–7, 128, 356. 505
experience and thought 164
explanation 414–16
exposition 44, 95, 505

F
fabliaux 152
fades 109
faery lands 157–8
family 341, 482
fantasy and magic realism 61–2
farce 114, 129, 505
Feminisim xxvi, 389–406, 409; biology and gender 389, 394; brides 394 courtship 398; Cressida 393–4; Diana 400; double trajectory 401–2; female *Bildungsroman* 391–2; ideal women 397, 403–4; language 405–6; madness 404; madonnas 397; mothers 399–400; marriage 399; Married Women's Property Act 389; mythic women 400–1; pairings 393–4; patriarchy 402–3; proposal, consent and refusal 398–9; saints 399–400; shrews 404; virgins 393–4; work 401
fiction, fictionality 6, 505
fictional and literary worlds 44, 59–70, 157–61
fights 139–40
film 73, 137–8, 217–18, 347; *Four Weddings and a Funeral* 150; James Bond films 218; *Pride and Prejudice* 3; *Star Wars* 73; *To Kill a Mocking Bird* 51
flashback 109
fluency 13, 151
foregrounding 505
Formalism 359–61, 374; Aristotle 360; automized seeing 360; defamiliarization 360–1; folk stories 361; helpers and hinderers 361; 'making strange' 360–1, 365, 506; Russian Formalists 360–1, 506
Fortune 319–21; imagery and language of Fortune 321; joking about Fortune 320; Fortune and Tragedy 320; wheel of Fortune 320
France, French culture 216, 223, 372, 485–6
freedom 322–4; choice and determinism 322; fate 323–4; natural history 323; the stars 322–3; the will 322
French drama 107

G
garden 455–8; abandoned gardens 456; Eden 454, 456–7, 460; emblem of the state 166, 456; nature and art 166, 456; retreat and repose 455
gender and gendered 22–3, 124, 445
general statements 165
genre xxv, 60, 215–83, 354, 357–8, 366, 505; hybridization 357
Georgic 278, 309
ghost stories 53–4
ghosts 140–1, 275

Gothic 272–7, 358, 483, 505; atmosphere 273–5; cinema 273 creation 276; horror 274; influence 276; language 275; locations 274; mock Gothic 273; origins 272; plot and character 277; political aspects 272, 275–6; violence 276; women 276
grammar 169–78, 206, 288, 356–7, 362; adjectives 174–5; adverbs 175; articles 176; conjunctions 177; interjections 177; modifiers 174–6; negatives 178, 206; nouns 169–71, 493; participles 173 prepositions 176–7; pronouns 171; verbs 30, 159, 171–4, 256
Greek drama 86, 107, 110, 137, 150, 221, 309, 407–9, 509
grouping in drama 89, 93–4

H
Headlam, Stewart 85
hearing and overhearing 150
hero and heroine 220, 225–7, 300–3, 347 506
historical interpretation 375, 377
historical scholarship 287–90
history 112–13
human responses 27
hymns 146, 258

I
icons, iconography 297
ideas 312–24
ideology 289, 376–7
Idyll 278
illness 50
image, imagery 111, 147, 156, 160, 166, 180, 182–3, 203, 207, 228–9, 293–8, 323, 361, 368, 377, 382, 397, 411–12, 421, 425, 438–9, 481, 486, 492, 506; image clusters 103
imagination 157, 444–5; *see also* moon and sun
Imagism 182
imitation 263, 300, 506
immediacy 109, 145
inspiration 146–8, 156
Interlude, the 114
interpretation 131, 219–20, 351–425; close reading 353–4; contrast 353; debate 354; evaluation and judgement 421–2; intention 422–3; internal and external 351, 374–5; links 353; significance 354, 421–3
intertextuality 312, 506
inversion 506
irony 40–2, 220, 265, 294, 307, 315, 353, 366, 506; double irony 42; dramatic irony 41

J
journeys 243, 295
judgement in and of literature 50–1, 220, 232–3
juxtaposition 46, 68, 88, 118, 161, 163, 170, 330, 451

K
killing the king 80, 121
kings and queens 89, 92–3; Elizabeth I 85; Charles II 84; James I 85
Knightley, Keira 3
knowledge 10, 26–8, 30–1, 34–6, 40, 43, 47–8, 122–3, 222, 382, 506
disparities in knowledge 40–2, 122, 128

Index of Authors and Works

Hughes, Ted (*contd*)
  from *Season Songs* (*contd*)
    'Hay' 446
    Tales from Ovid 308
    'Thrushes' 464
Hughes, Thomas
  Tom Brown's Schooldays 3, 484
Hugo, Victor
  Hernani 216
Huizinga, Johan
  Homo Ludens 372
Hymns
  'Fight the good fight' 497
  'Onward Christian Soldiers' 497

I
Ibsen, Henrik 133, 221
  A Doll's House 137, 139, 165

J
James, Henry 355, 357, 422
  The Turn of the Screw 32
James, M.R.
  from *Ghost Stories of an Antiquary*
    'The Rose Garden' 54
James, P.D. 53
Johnson, Samuel
  Dictionary 264
  'Life of Pope' 263
  London: A Satire 215–16, 263–4
  The Vanity of Human Wishes 263–6
Jones, David
  In Parenthesis 492
Jones, Ernest
  Hamlet and Oedipus 416
Jones, Monica 210
Jonson, Ben 194, 206, 343
  Bartholomew Fair 113, 383
  Eastwood Ho! 85
  Explorata: or Discoveries 11–12
  Every Man in his Humour 130
  'Hymn to Cynthia' 400
  'On My First Daughter' 310
  Sejanus 236
  The Alchemist 125, 236
  'To Penshurst' 262
  Volpone 75, 77–8, 99, 106, 120, 125–6, 130,
    236, 343, 382–3
  Works 84
Joyce, James 372, 505
  Dubliners 474
  A Portrait of the Artist as a Young Man 391
  Ulysses 248, 251
Jung, Carl Gustav 150, 408, 412
Juvenal
  'Satire 3' 262–3
  'Satire 5' 262
  'Satire 10' 262–3

K
Keats, John 86, 160, 181, 204–6, 326
  Endymion 204
  Hyperion 204, 443
  'In drear-nighted December' 166–7
  Isabella 156
  'La Belle Dame sans Merci' 175, 490
  'Ode on a Grecian Urn' 157–8, 182
  'Ode on Indolence' 187
  'Ode on Melancholy' 187
  'Ode to a Nightingale' 187, 445, 508
  'Ode to Psyche' 187

The Eve of St Agnes 156, 158–9, 186
  The Fall of Hyperion 443
  'To Autumn' 187, 447
Keble, John 258
Kettle, Arnold 383
Kristeva, Julia 501
Kyd, Thomas 221, 312
  The Spanish Tragedy 114, 476

L
La Fontaine
  Fables 464
Landor, Walter Savage 505
Langhorne, John
  Studley Park 281
Langland, William 148, 194, 480
  The Vision of Piers Plowman 372, 390,
    429–30, 432, 482–3, 501
Larkin, Philip 145, 148
  'Aubade' 181, 439
  from *High Windows*
    'Dublinesque' 175
    'Forget What Did' 207, 469
    'Going, Going' 207, 210
    'High Windows' 150, 472
    'Homage to a Government' 210
    'Livings' 150
    'Show Saturday' 205–7, 209
    'Sad Steps' 441–2
    'Solar' 441–2
    'The Building' 205
    'The Explosion' 188, 211
    'The Trees' 207, 211, 365, 469
    'To the Sea' 205, 211, 361
  from *The Less Deceived*
    'At Grass' 205–6, 440
    'Church Going' 164, 205, 208, 211, 332
    'Deceptions' 204
    'Toads' 483
  from *The Whitsun Weddings*
    'Afternoons' 204, 472
    'An Arundel Tomb' 145, 165, 211, 287
    'As Bad as a Mile' 211
    'Dockery and Son' 205, 207, 209, 211, 472
    'Essential Beauty' 204, 211
    'Faith Healing' 207
    'Here' 175, 205–7, 210
    'Home is so Sad' 186–7, 211
    'Love Songs in Age' 478–9
    'MCMXIV' 210
    'Mr Bleaney' 210–11
    'Naturally the Foundation will Bear Your
      Expenses' 209
    'Send no Money' 204
    'Talking in Bed' 188
    'The Importance of Elsewhere' 206
    'The Large Cool Store' 204
    'The Whitsun Weddings' 207, 211, 472
    'Toads Revisited' 160–1, 472, 483
    'Water' 206
    'Wild Oats' 211
Lawrence, D.H.
  Odour of Chrysanthemums 52–3
  Sons and Lovers 9, 21, 69, 295, 338–9, 391,
    397, 423
Lear, Edward 326
Leavis, Q.D.
  Lectures in America 393
Lee, Harper
  To Kill a Mocking Bird 51